The Blue Guides

S0-BHZ-415

Please write in with your comments, suggestions and corrections for the next edition of the Blue Guide. Writers of the most helpful letters will be awarded a free Blue Guide of their choice.

City Guide
Florence

Alta Macadam

A&C Black • London
WW Norton • New York

Eighth edition 2001

Published by A & C Black (Publishers) Limited
37 Soho Square, London W1D 3QZ

A CIP catalogue record of this book is available from the British Library.

ISBN 0–7136–5454–6

Published in the United States of America by
WW Norton and Company, Inc
500 Fifth Avenue, New York, NY 10110

Published simultaneously in Canada by
Penguin Books Canada Limited
10 Alcorn Avenue, Toronto, Ontario M4V 3B2

ISBN 0–393–32202–5   USA

The author and the publishers have done their best to ensure the accuracy of all the information in Blue Guide Florence; however, they can accept no responsibility for any loss,
injury or inconvenience sustained by any traveller as a result of information or advice contained in the guide.

Alta Macadam has been a writer of Blue Guides since 1970. She lives in Florence with her
family the painter Francesco Colacicchi, and their children Giovanni and Lelia. Combined
with work on writing the guides she has also been associated in Florence with the Bargello
Museum, the Alinari photo archive, and Harvard University at the Villa I Tatti in Florence.
As author of the *Blue Guides* to Rome, Venice, Sicily, Florence, Tuscany and Umbria she travels extensively in Italy every year to revise new editions of the books.

Cover picture: detail of the Christ Child from the *Madonna delle Ombre* (Madonna and
Child enthroned with saints and angels), 1450, by Fra Angelico, in the dormitory corridor
in the Convent of San Marco, ©Museo di San Marco/Bridgeman Art Library.
Title page illustration: *Spring* by Pietro Francavilla on Ponte Santa Trinita.

Printed and bound in Great Britain by Butler and Tanner, Frome and London.

Contents

Introduction 9
Acknowledgements 10
How to use the Guide 10
Highlights of Florence 11

Practical Information

Background information

The Guide

Environs of Florence

Maps and plans

Colour street map *at the back of the book*

Introduction

Florence (*Firenze* in Italian) is one of the three most visited cities in Italy. It is famous as the birthplace of the Renaissance when, from the 15th century onwards, there was an extraordinary flowering of the arts and a return to classical ideals. At this time, some of the most important artists who have ever lived were at work in Florence, including Donatello, Masaccio, Brunelleschi, Ghiberti, Botticelli, Raphael, Leon Battista Alberti, Michelangelo and Leonardo da Vinci. Indeed, the last three stand out not only for their artistic achievements but also for their writings and 'universal' talents.

Today some of the greatest works of art and most beautiful buildings in the world are preserved in Florence. The great dome of the cathedral—a supreme masterpiece of the Renaissance, designed by Brunelleschi—dominates the city and can be seen from most of the surrounding hills. Among the other famous works of the Renaissance are Masaccio's frescoes in the Carmine and Lorenzo Ghiberti's east doors of the Baptistery. The Bargello museum contains many of the most important Renaissance sculptures (with Donatello well represented) and the world-renowned Uffizi gallery has the leading collection of paintings in Italy, including famous works by Botticelli. In the huge Pitti palace, the Galleria Palatina has superb portraits by Raphael and Titian. The Galleria dell'Accademia contains Michelangelo's *David*, probably the best-known work of art in Europe, along with his remarkable statues of the *Slaves*. Other important sculptures by him decorate the Medici tombs in the New Sacristy of San Lorenzo.

In the early 14th century, the painter and architect Giotto was at work in Florence and his friend Dante Alighieri, the greatest Italian poet of all time, was born here and took part in the government of the city. The writer Boccaccio also lived and died in Florence.

For nearly three centuries, the control of the city government was entrusted to the Medici family, who were also great and influential patrons of the arts. They were represented in the early 15th century by Cosimo il Vecchio and his brilliant grandson Lorenzo il Magnifico, and in the 16C by Cosimo I who became official ruler of the city and established the Medici dynasty of grand-dukes.

Florence, with a population of around 380,000, remains a relatively small city, a *misura d'uomo*, its human scale appreciated by both residents and visitors alike. All its great monuments and most famous museums are concentrated in a small area, within easy walking distance of one another. The historic centre is remarkably well-preserved and the low hills which surround the town have retained their vineyards, olive groves and handsome villas which provide a prelude to the beautiful Tuscan landscape. No visitor should leave Florence without seeing the city from a raised vantage point, from the top of the Duomo or the Campanile, or from one of the surrounding hills.

Florence has long been admired by visitors and a large Anglo-American community lived here in the 19th century. Nowadays, the best time to visit Florence is in late autumn or even in winter: it can be unpleasantly crowded with bus loads of tourists and school parties in the spring and autumn, and unbearably hot in July and August. However, it is always possible to find delightful, quiet spots within the city, while the immediate environs of Florence remain relatively peaceful.

Acknowledgements

As in past editions, I am extremely grateful to **Marco and Françoise Chiarini**: Marco's article on the Florentine Renaissance in this guide remains a perfect introduction to the city, and Françoise has often provided useful information which has helped me to ensure that the text is accurate. Roberta Berni of the Florence Agenzia per il Turismo (APT) once again provided assistance with the practical information section. For the choice and description of restaurants, I am indebted, as in the past, to **Carlo Colella**. Maurizio Chiessi and Ingrid Kopra also provided a useful contribution to the section on eating out in Florence.

How to use the Guide

The guide is divided into 23 chapters, 22 of them devoted to **walks** within the city, all of which are designed to be followed without the help of public transport (except for chapter 22). The last chapter covers the immediate environs of Florence, which can be reached easily in a day by public transport from the centre of the city.

Each important monument in the city is given a **map reference** in the text (**Map 1; 1**) referring to the colour map at the back of the book. Each page of the atlas is divided into numbered squares. The first figure in the reference denotes the page of the street map, and the second denotes the grid square. References to **ground plans** are given in the text as a bracketed single figure or letter.

Opening times of the museums and monuments correct at the time of going to press are given in the text, using the 24-hour clock (for example, 09.00–13.00, 15.00–19.00). Since opening hours change frequently, telephone numbers have also been provided, and it is advisable to check the latest times on arrival in Florence. Prices, which vary greatly, have also been listed.

The **most important monuments** or **works of art** in Florence have been highlighted in bold throughout the text, and **stars** are used to indicate works of art which are particularly beautiful or interesting. The **highlights** section on p 11 singles out the major monuments of each period and the works of art which should not be missed.

All **churches** are taken as being orientated with the entrance at the west end and the altar at the east end, the south aisle on the right and the north aisle on the left. Although many churches in the city are not, in fact, orientated in this way, it seems the simplest way of providing a standard description of church interiors, beginning at the entrance and following the right side up to the sanctuary and then returning down the left side to the entrance. Opening times of most churches have been given within the text.

An exhaustive section at the beginning of the book lists all the practical information you are likely to need during a visit to Florence. A small selection of **hotels** has been given on pp 23–29, listed according to category (which indicates the price range). They have been keyed in the list with a letter or letters and a plan reference: this refers to the letter or letters shown on the colour street map at the back of the book, with the reference to the atlas page number and grid square, for example (**s; Map 4; 1**). Their addresses and zip codes are provided, as well as their telephone and fax numbers, email addresses and/or web sites. A small selection of **restaurants**, with a short description, is given; they are listed according to price range and their telephone numbers are supplied so that you can check if they are open and, if necessary, book a table.

Numerous references to the **Medici family** appear throughout the text: their dates have not been repeated at every reference, but can easily be found in the family tree on pp 94–95. **Artists' dates** are given in the index of artists, and the most important artists are referred to in the introductory article on the Florentine Renaissance. Unfamiliar art and architecture terms are explained in the **glossary** on p 363.

Abbreviations used in the guide

APT	Agenzia per il turismo di Firenze (Florence Tourist Office)
ATAF	Azienda Trasporti Area Fiorentino (municipal bus company)
C	century
(C)	Museums owned by the Comune of Florence
c	circa
ENIT	Ente Nazionale per il Turismo (Italian State Tourist Board)
fest.	*festa* or festival (i.e. holiday)
Map	map reference to the Atlas at the back of the book
(S)	Museums and monuments owned by the Italian State

Highlights of Florence

Renaissance works

The masterpiece of the Florentine Renaissance and the city's most visible land-mark is the dome of the cathedral designed by Brunelleschi. Other works by him include the portico of the Spedale degli Innocenti, the Pazzi chapel and the Old Sacristy in San Lorenzo, as well as the churches of San Lorenzo and Santo Spirito. Lorenzo Ghiberti's east doors of the Baptistery, with their relief sculptures of Old Testament scenes (some of the restored originals are now in the Museo dell'Opera del Duomo) along with Masaccio's frescoes in the Cappella Brancacci (Santa Maria del Carmine) are two more key works of the early Renaissance. The Chapel of the Cardinal of Portugal in San Miniato displays the skill by which architecture, painting and sculpture were combined at this period. Leon Battista Alberti, the theorist and architect of the Renaissance who was born in Florence, designed the façade of Santa Maria Novella as well as (almost certainly) that of Palazzo Rucellai, and the exquisite little Cappella di San Sepolcro.

Romanesque buildings

The Baptistery is the most important early building in the city, and the classical geometrical design of its exterior is repeated in the beautiful 11C façade of San Miniato. The little church of Santi Apostoli has a lovely early basilican interior, while the imposing Palazzo Vecchio, built in the first years of the 14C, was to influence the architecture of town halls all over Tuscany.

Museums

The Uffizi is one of the great museums of the world and contains the most impor-tant collection of paintings in Italy; it is now particularly famous for its works by Botticelli. The Galleria Palatina, in the huge Pitti palace, contains masterpieces by Raphael, Titian and Rubens. The Bargello has the most important collection of Renaissance sculpture, including numerous works by Donatello. The Galleria dell'Accademia houses the famous statue of *David* by Michelangelo, as well as other works by him.

Small museums

The city also has numerous smaller (and less crowded) museums of exceptional interest: the Museo dell'Opera del Duomo (sculpture); the Casa Buonarroti (works by Michelangelo), the Museo di San Marco (paintings and frescoes by Fra Angelico), the Palazzo Davanzati (a restored medieval palace, at present closed for restoration); the Museo Bardini and the Museo Horne (both private collections formed in the 19C, the former closed for restoration), and the Museo di Orsanmichele (with the original statues from the exterior).

Palaces

Many palaces in Florence have fine facades and handsome courtyards (although the interiors are often inaccessible). These include Palazzo Medici Riccardi, Palazzo Pitti and Palazzo Strozzi, as well as Palazzo Antinori and Palazzo Rucellai. Streets with particularly handsome palaces include Via Tornabuoni and Borgo degli Albizi.

Sculpture

For centuries, it was the custom in Florence to erect sculptures in the main squares (*piazze*) or on the exterior of buildings. Some of these works have now had to be restored, moved and placed under cover, and replaced *in situ* with copies. There are numerous important sculptures (by Donatello, Cellini and Giambologna) in the central Piazza della Signoria and under the Loggia dei Lanzi. The exterior of Orsanmichele is decorated with statues in niches, including three by Lorenzo Ghiberti, and others by Donatello, Nanni di Banco and Verrocchio. The originals are being restored and are displayed in the Museo di Orsanmichele. Piazza Santissima Annunziata also has an equestrian statue by Giambologna.

The best collection of sculpture in Florence is to be found in the Bargello museum. The Museo dell'Opera del Duomo and the Galleria dell'Accademia are also famous for their sculpture. Roman masterpieces which formed part of the Medici collections are kept in the Tribuna and corridors of the Uffizi, and there is some very fine Etruscan and Roman sculpture in the Museo Archeologico. Garden statuary can be seen in the Boboli gardens as well as the Medici villas in the environs (notably Villa di Castello).

Frescoes

Florence has a great number of frescoed chapels and cloisters. Those dating from the 14C include the chapels in Santa Croce (two by Giotto, and others by Agnolo and Taddeo Gaddi, Maso di Banco and Giovanni da Milano), the Strozzi chapel in Santa Maria Novella (Nardi di Cione), the sacristy of San Miniato (Spinello Aretino), and the Spanish Chapel (Andrea di Bonaiuto). Renaissance frescoes include those in the sanctuary of Santa Maria Novella and the Sassetti chapel in Santa Trìnita by Domenico Ghirlandaio, the chapel in Palazzo Medici Riccardi by Benozzo Gozzoli, the convent of San Marco by Fra Angelico, and the Chapel of Filippo Strozzi in Santa Maria Novella by Filippino Lippi. 16C works include the frescoes in the atrium of Santissima Annunziata (Andrea del Sarto, Franciabigio, Rosso Fiorentino, Pontormo), the Capponi chapel in Santa Felicita by Pontormo, and the Cappella di Eleonora in Palazzo Vecchio by Bronzino. The reception rooms in Palazzo Pitti were frescoed in the 17C by Pietro da Cortona.

Many cloisters have frescoed lunettes, and convent refectories are frescoed with scenes of the Last Supper (*cenacolo* in Italian, see below).

Cenacoli
Numerous convents in Florence have refectories with the depiction of the Last Supper (*cenacolo*) in fresco. These include works by Taddeo Gaddi (Santa Croce), Orcagna (Santo Spirito), Domenico Ghirlandaio (Ognissanti and San Marco), Andrea del Castagno (Sant'Apollonia), Perugino (Cenacolo di Fuligno), Andrea del Sarto (San Salvi), Franciabigio (Convento della Calza), Alessandro Allori (Santa Maria Novella), and Sodoma (San Bartolomeo, Monteoliveto).

Cloisters
The beautiful cloisters of Florence provide some of the city's most peaceful spots. They include Brunelleschi's cloister at Santa Croce, and those attached to San Lorenzo and Santa Maria Maddalena dei Pazzi. Other lovely cloisters have frescoed lunettes: Santa Maria Novella (Paolo Uccello), the Badia Fiorentina (early 15C frescoes in the Chiostro degli Aranci), the Chiostro dello Scalzo (Andrea del Sarto and Franciabigio), Santissima Annunziata (Chiostro dei Morti, with the Madonna del Sacco by Andrea del Sarto), Ognissanti (Iacopo Ligozzi and Giovanni da San Giovanni), and San Marco (17C lunettes in the Chiostro di Sant'Antonino).

Environs of Florence
The most interesting place in the environs of Florence is Fiesole. Beautiful country walks can be taken in this district and towards Maiano and Settignano. There are also a number of Medici villas open to the public including the Villa di Castello and Villa della Petraia. For the gardens in the surroundings of Florence see p 52.

Views of the city
The best view of the city is from the Forte di Belvedere, but this is currently closed for restoration. Piazzale Michelangelo provides a famous panoramic view, but San Miniato affords an even better—and more peaceful—vantage point. The city and its surrounding hills can also be appreciated from the tops of the cathedral's dome and campanile. The tall building of Orsanmichele provides a fine view of the city centre. The Corridoio Vasariano affords delightful glimpses of the river and there are also good views from the Boboli gardens, particularly from the Kaffeehaus, the Giardino del Cavaliere and the terrace by the Fontana del Carciofo. Via di Bellosguardo also has splendid views back towards Florence. The roads up to Fiesole all give excellent views of the city, as does the hill of San Francesco above Fiesole.

Gardens

For gardens and parks in and around Florence, see p 52.

Anglo-Americans in Florence

There were numerous Anglo-American residents in Florence in the 19C. Mementoes of their stay and the legacies they left can be seen in the Brownings' Casa Guidi, and the museums founded by Frederick Stibbert and Herbert Percy Horne. The distinguished art historian Bernard Berenson lived at the Villa I Tatti where he created a very fine art collection, library and garden. More recently, one of the best-known English residents was the historian and aesthete Sir Harold Acton who inherited the art collection and lovely garden at Villa La Pietra. Both these villas are now owned by American universities. Many illustrious foreigners are buried in the Cimitero degli Inglesi.

Famous artists who worked in Florence

Giotto frescoed two chapels in Santa Croce as well as designing the Campanile. Paintings by him are preserved in the Uffizi, the Museo Horne and the Museo Diocesano d'Arte Sacra, and there are Crucifixes by him in Santa Maria Novella (being restored), Ognissanti and San Felice. The best sculptures by **Donatello** are to be found in the Bargello, the Museo dell'Opera del Duomo, Palazzo Vecchio, San Lorenzo, Santa Croce, the Baptistery, and the Museo dell'Opera di Santa Croce. Important enamelled terracottas by the **Della Robbia** family can be seen in the Duomo, Museo dell'Opera del Duomo, the Spedale degli Innocenti, the Bargello, and the Pazzi Chapel; there are other characteristic works at the Accademia di Belle Arti, Santa Croce, the Museo Bardini, San Miniato, Santi Apostoli and the Certosa di Galluzzo. There are works by **Paolo Uccello** in the Uffizi, the cloister of Santa Maria Novella, and the Duomo. The most important works of **Botticelli** are in the Uffizi, but there are other works by him in the Galleria dell'Accademia and the church of Ognissanti (where he is buried). **Raphael** and **Titian** are superbly represented in the Uffizi and Pitti palace (Galleria Palatina). Masterpieces by **Michelangelo** are kept in the Galleria dell'Accademia, the Bargello and Casa Buonarroti. The Biblioteca Laurenziana and New Sacristy, both at San Lorenzo, are famous works by him. Two more of his sculptures are kept in the Museo dell'Opera del Duomo and Palazzo Vecchio. His painting known as the *Tondo Doni* is housed in the Uffizi. Frescoes and paintings by the Florentine **Mannerists** are to be found in the atrium of Santissima Annunziata and the Studiolo of Francesco I in Palazzo Vecchio, as well as in the Uffizi and Galleria Palatina at the Pitti. Pontormo is also particularly well-represented in Santa Felicita and San Michele Visdomini, as well as (in the environs) at the Certosa di Galluzzo. The Bargello has numerous Mannerist sculptures.

PRACTICAL INFORMATION

 Planning your trip

When to go

The most pleasant time to visit the city is in May, or October and November when the temperature is often still quite high. Spring can be unexpectedly wet and cold until well after Easter. The most crowded periods of the year are from Easter to June and in September. The winter in Florence can be as cold as an English winter, but the only time the city is comparatively empty of tourists is in January, February and November (the best months to visit the major museums). The changeable climate of Florence is conditioned by its position in a small basin enclosed by hills. It can be extremely hot and oppressive in July and August. In August the city is empty of Florentines, and numerous shops, bars and restaurants close down for the whole month.

Passports

Passports are necessary for all travellers from Britain and North America entering Italy. Visitors from Australia and New Zealand do not require visas, but those from South Africa do. A lost or stolen passport can be replaced by the British or US embassy in Rome (information from the Consulates in Florence, see p 65). You are obliged to carry some means of identity with you at all times when in Italy.

Italian tourist boards

The Italian State Tourist Office (Ente Nazionale Italiano per il Turismo, ENIT) provides detailed information about Italy at www.italiantourism.com or at the following addresses:

Australia c/o Italian Chamber of Commerce and Industry, Level 26, Market St, Sydney; ☎ (0061) 2 92662 1666; ▤ (0061) 2 9262 1677

Canada 1 Place Ville Marie, Suite 1914, Montreal, Quebec; ☎ H3B 2C3; (001) 514 886 7667; ▤ (001) 514 392 1429; e-mail: initaly@ucab.net

Netherlands Stadhoudeskade 2, 1054 ES Amsterdam; ☎ (003) 120 616 8244; ▤ (003) 120 618 8515

UK 1 Princes Street, London W1R 8AY; ☎ 020 7408 1254 or 020 7355 1557; ▤ 020 7493 6695; e-mail: enitland@globalnet.co.uk

USA 630 Fifth Avenue, Suite 1565, New York, NY 101111; ☎ (001) 212 245 5633; ▤ (001) 212 586 9249; e-mail: enitny@italiantourism.com
500 North Michigan Avenue, Suite 2240, Chicago I, IL 60611; ☎ (001) 312 644 0996, ▤ (001) 312 644 3012
12400 Wilshire Blvd, Suite 550, Los Angeles, CA 90025; ☎ (001) 310 820 1898, ▤ (001) 310 820 6357; e-mail: enitala@earthlink.net

Web sites on Florence and Italy

APT (tourist office) of Florence: www.firenze.turismo.toscana.it
Comune (municipality) of Florence: www.comune.firenze.it

Region of Tuscany: www.regione.toscana.it
Italytour.com: www.italytour.com

Tour operators
Among the many UK tour operators which offer package holidays to Florence from the UK are:

City breaks
British Airways, ☎ 0870 242 4243, www.british-airways.com
Citalia's Italy, ☎ 020 8686 5533, www.citalia.co.uk
Crystal International Travel Group, ☎ 020 8241 5040, www.crystalcities.co.uk
Magic of Italy, ☎ 0990 462 442, www.magictravelgroup.co.uk
Simply Travel's Brief Encounters, ☎ 020 8987 6108, www.simply-travel.com
Travelscene, ☎ 020 8424 9648, ▤020 8861 4154, www.travelscene.co.uk

For students and young people
CTS Travel, ☎ 020 7636 0031, www.ctstravel.co.uk

Guided tours by art historians
Andante Travels, ☎ 01980 610 555, www.andantetravels.co.uk
Inscape Fine Art Study Tours, 01993 891 726, ▤ 01993 891 718
Prospect Music and Art Tours, ☎ 020 7486 5704, email: sales@prospecttours.com
Martin Randall Travel Ltd, ☎ 020 8742 1066, email: info@martinrandall.co.uk

Health and insurance
British citizens, as members of the EU, have the right to claim health care in Italy if they have the E111 form issued by the Department of Health and available at main post offices. For additional cover, they may want to take out a private insurance policy; this is certainly advisable for visitors from outside the EU. Keep the receipt (*ricevuta*) and medical report (*cartella clinica*) to present to your insurer if you have to make a claim.

Currency
The monetary unit is the Italian *lira* (pl. *lire*). There are notes of 1000, 2000, 5000, 10,000, 50,000, 100,000 and 500,000 lire. Coins are of 50, 100, 200, 500 and 1000 lire. There are currently three sizes of 50 and 100 lire coins. The Euro will replace the lira as the official monetary unit in 2002 (the fixed exchange rate for one Euro is Lire 1936.270). Until then, both currencies will be in use. Travellers' cheques are the safest way of carrying money while travelling, and most credit cards are now generally accepted in shops, hotels and restaurants, and at some petrol stations. In the centre of town outside banks there are numerous cashpoints called Bancomat (check with your own bank about any charges associated with their use), and also automatic machines which change foreign bank notes.

Disabled travellers
Italy is at last catching up with the rest of Europe in the provision of facilities for the disabled. All new public buildings are now obliged by law to provide access and specially designed facilities for the disabled. In the annual list of hotels in Florence published by the APT, hotels which are able to provide hospitality for the disabled

are indicated. Information on facilities for the disabled on trains and at railway stations can be obtained from Stazione Santa Maria Novella in Florence, ☎ 055 2352275. The disabled are entitled to a *carta blu* which allows a discount on the price of the fare. Trains equipped to carry wheelchairs are listed in the railway timetable published by the FS (Ferrovie dello Stato, the Italian State Railways), which is available at newsstands. The seats at the front of city buses are reserved for disabled passengers. The city bus service provides facilities for wheelchairs on lines 7, 12 and 13, and D, and there is a special bus for the disabled (no. 99): for information and booking ☎ 055 565 0443. There are free parking spaces for disabled drivers. Even though the curbs of many pavements have recently been redesigned to facilitate wheelchair use, many pavements are too narrow, making the historic centre a difficult place to move around in a wheelchair (even though it is an easier city than Rome for the disabled traveller). Museums and galleries should now have toilets for the disabled, and twelve public toilets, also with facilities for the disabled, were opened in Florence in 2000 (see p 69). For more information contact the Province of Florence, ☎ 055 276 0570.

 Getting there

By air

Air services from the UK
Flights between London Stansted and Gatwick and Pisa airport are operated by: *British Airways* (☎ 0990 444000 or 0345 222111; www.british-airways.com) and *Alitalia* (☎ 0870 544 8259; www.alitalia.co.uk).
Ryanair (☎ 0870 156 9569; www.ryanair.com) operates from London Stansted to Pisa and Bologna airports.
Meridiana (☎ 020 7839 2222; www.meridiana.it) flies from Gatwick to the small airport of Florence (Amerigo Vespucci at Peretola). There are also flights from Manchester, Glasgow and Dublin to Pisa.
Other companies with flights to Italy include:
British Midland (☎ 0870 6070 555; www.iflybritishmidland.com)
Buzz (☎ 0870 240 7070; www.buzzaway.com) and
Go (☎ 0845 605 4321; www.go-fly.com)

Air services from the USA
Non-stop services from New York, Boston, Chicago and Los Angeles to Rome are operated by *Alitalia* (☎ 1 800 223 5730; www.alitaliausa.com).
Flights from New York to Rome are also operated by:
Continental (☎ 1 800 231 0856; www.continental.com)
Delta (☎ 1 800 241 4141; www.delta-air.com)
TWA (☎ 1 800 892 4141; www.twa.com)
United Airlines (☎ 1 800 538 2929; www.ual.com) operate between Washington DC, and Rome.
British Airways, *Air France*, *KLM*, *Lufthansa* and *Sabena* offer flights connecting through London, Paris, Frankfurt, Amsterdam and Brussels to Rome or Milan which are often more economical than direct flights.

Airports

The nearest international airport is at **Pisa** (☎ 050 500 707), 85km west of Florence. There is a railway station in the airport (tickets are bought in the air terminal) which has a direct train service (10 a day) to Florence (Santa Maria Novella station) which takes 1 hour (via Pisa central and Empoli). In summer there is also a direct *SITA* coach service between the airport and Florence (which also takes 1 hour). There are also town buses (no. 7; every 15 minutes) from the airport to Pisa central station where there are other train services to Florence. Taxis for the centre of Pisa are also available (or ☎ 050 541600). For return flights from Pisa, there is an air terminal (☎ 055 216 073) at Santa Maria Novella Station in Florence (on platform no. 5, near which the airport trains depart), which is open from 06.00 to 16.30. Luggage can be checked in here for all flights except Ryanair, and boarding cards obtained (not later than 15 minutes before the departure of the airport train).

The small airport of **Florence** (Amerigo Vespucci at Peretola, ☎ 055 315 874 or 055 373498), a few kilometres north of Florence, has some flights from Europe (including London Gatwick operated by *Meridiana*, and Amsterdam, Barcelona, Brussels, Frankfurt, Munich, Paris and Vienna), as well as internal domestic flights. *ATAF/SITA* shuttle bus every 30mins from the arrivals terminus to the SITA bus station next to the railway station of Santa Maria Novella in about 20mins. Tickets (Lire 6000) can be bought on board. Taxis are also usually available (otherwise ☎ 055 4798, 055 4390). For baggage lost and found, ☎ 055 308023. For airline companies, see p 64.

Bologna airport also has direct flights from London. It is at Borgo Panicale, 7km northwest of the city. There is an excellent bus service (Aerobus) every 20 minutes to Bologna station in about 10 minutes (Lire 7000). This runs from the station 05.55–22.30 and from the airport 08.30–23.45. A taxi costs around Lire 26,000. There are trains from Bologna station (on the main Milan–Rome line) which take 60–75 minutes to Florence.

By rail

From Britain

Florence can be reached via *Eurostar* (from Waterloo, London, or Ashford, Kent, to the Gare du Nord, Paris) and the overnight sleeper from Paris Gare de Lyon. For more information, contact *European Rail Ltd* (☎ 020 7387 0444; 🖹 020 7387 0888; www.raileurope.co.uk).

Websites

www.fs-on-line.com (Italian State Railways website)
www.freedomrail.co.uk
www.itwg.com/home.asp
www.railchoice.co.uk (arranges rail travel between London and Italy via Paris, and will also supply tickets for travel within Italy)

For travellers from the USA and Canada

In North America, contact the following *Citalia* offices:
CIT New York: 15 West 44th Street, 10th Floor, New York, NY 10036. (800) CIT-TOUR for tour information, email: tour@cittours.com
CIT Chicago (CIT RAIL): 9501 West Devon Avenue, Suite 1, E Rosemont, IL 60018. (800) CIT-RAIL for information, email: rail@cit-rail.com

CIT Montreal: 1450 City Counselers ST Quebec, Montreal H3A 2E6. (800) 3617799 for the Montreal area, local area dial 514 845 9101

CIT Toronto: 80 Tiverton Crt, Suite 401, Markham, ON L3ROG4. (800) 387 0711 for the Toronto area, local area dial (905) 415 1060

For general information contact your local travel agent or call ☎ 1 800 248 8687; website: www.fs-on-line.com

Railway stations in Florence
Stazione di Santa Maria Novella (**Map 5; 6**) is the main station for all services of the State railways, and it is very close to the centre of the city. It has a restaurant, a left-luggage office, a bank and a tourist information office with hotel booking facilities (see below). Information office: ☎ 1478 88088 (07.00–21.00) or ☎ 110. The station is well served by buses (see below) and taxis, and there is an underground car park.

The slower trains also stop at **Stazione Campo di Marte** (beyond **Map 7; 4**), when coming from the south, and **Stazione Rifredi** (north of **Map 5; 2**), when coming from the north. Some overnight sleeper trains only stop at Stazione Campo di Marte. **Train tickets** can be bought at certain travel agents in Florence, or by telephone 24 hours before departure (with delivery to your address for an extra charge of Lire 4800): ☎ 055 265 4618.

By coach
For details of the coach services available from the UK to Florence, contact **Eurolines**: ☎ 01582 404 511; www.eurolines.com. In Florence, ☎ 055 357 110. Services operate from London's Victoria Coach Station on Mon, Wed, Fri and Sun (usually five days a week in summer). They depart at 09.00 and arrive in Florence, at Piazza Adua, the next afternoon at 15.00 (change bus in Milan). Lire 260,000 one-way; Lire 398,000 return. There is a discount of 10 per cent for those under 26, but even so the fare is high when compared to the cut-price air tickets now available between Italy and Britain.

By car
Florence is approached by a network of motorways, including the A1 from northern Italy. The 'Firenze Nord' exit is the most convenient for travellers coming from the north; the 'Firenze Sud' for those coming from the south. For car parks, see below.

British drivers taking their own cars by any of the routes across France, Belgium, Luxembourg, Switzerland, Germany and Austria need the vehicle registration book, a valid national driving licence (accompanied by a translation, issued free of charge by the ENIT), proof of insurance cover and a nationality plate attached to the car. If you are not the owner of the vehicle, you must have the owner's permission for its use abroad. A Swiss motorway pass needed for that country is obtainable from the RAC, AA or at the Swiss border. Membership of the AA or RAC entitles you to many of the facilities of affiliated societies on the Continent.
- AA ☎ 0990 444 444
- RAC membership and insurance ☎ 0800 550 550

   Additional route information is available from www.autostop.it/

Motorways   In Italy, motorways (*autostrade*) charge tolls according to the rating of the vehicle and the distance covered. There are service areas (open 24

hours) on all motorways and, generally speaking, the FINI cafés and restaurants are usually the best. Most motorways have SOS points every 2km. Unlike in France, motorways are indicated by green signs and normal roads by blue signs. At the entrance to motorways, the two directions are indicated by the name of the most important (not the nearest) town, which can be momentarily confusing. The Autostrada del Sole (A1) which runs down the centre of Italy between Milan, Florence, Rome and Naples is narrower than some of the more recently built motorways and carries very heavy traffic including numerous lorries, especially between Bologna and Florence. Driving on this road is easier on Sundays, when lorries are banned.

Superstrade These dual carriageways do not charge tolls. They do not usually have service stations, SOS points, or emergency lanes. They are also usually indicated by green signs.

Petrol stations Stations are open 24 hours on motorways, on other roads 07.00–12.00 and 15.00–20.00 in summer, 07.30–12.30 and 14.30–19.00 in winter. There are now quite a number of self-service petrol stations open 24 hours and operated by bank notes or credit cards. Unleaded petrol is available all over Italy. Petrol in Italy costs more than in Britain, and a lot more than in North America.

Rules of the road The Continental rule of the road is to drive on the right and overtake on the left. Italian law requires that you carry a valid driving licence when at the wheel. It is obligatory to keep a red triangle sign in the car in case of accident or breakdown. This serves as a warning to other traffic when placed in the road at a distance of 50m from the stationary car. It is now compulsory to wear seatbelts.

Driving in Italy is generally faster (and often more aggressive) than driving in Britain or North America. Road signs are more or less standardised to the international codes, but certain habits differ radically. Unless otherwise indicated, cars entering a road from the right are given precedence, as they are at roundabouts. If a driver flashes his headlights, it means he is proceeding and not that he is giving you precedence. Italian drivers are very lax about changing lanes, often giving little or no warning, and they tend to ignore pedestrian crossings. Beware of motorbikes, mopeds and Vespas, the drivers of which seem to consider that they always have the right of way.

Police (see p 65) The police sometimes set up road blocks to check cars and their drivers. It is important to stop at once if you are waved down by a policeman at the side of the road and you must immediately show your driving licence and the car documents.

Maps The Italian Touring Club publishes several sets of excellent maps: these are constantly updated and are indispensable to anyone travelling by car in Italy. They include the *Grande Carta Stradale d'Italia* on a scale of 1:200.000. This is divided into 15 sheets covering the regions of Italy. These are also published in a handier form as the *Atlante Stradale d'Italia*, an atlas in three volumes, with a comprehensive index; the volume entitled *Centro* covers Florence and Tuscany.

These maps can be purchased from Italian Touring Club offices and at many booksellers: in Britain they are available from Stanfords, 12–14 Long Acre, London WC2E 9LP, ☎ 020 7836 1321.

Tourist offices in Florence

The **main information office** of the *Agenzia per il Turismo di Firenze* (APT), is at 1 (red) Via Cavour (**Map 1;2**), ☎ 055 290 832 or 055 290833, 🖹 055 276 0383, e-mail: infoturismo@provincia.fi.it It is open Monday–Saturday 08.15–19.15; in summer it is also open on Sunday 08.30–13.30, but is closed on Sunday in winter. Up-to-date information is supplied here, as well as a (free) list of hotels, a map, opening times of museums and current exhibitions. The office also supplies free advice to visitors in difficulty or with complaints. There are subsidiary APT information offices at Amerigo Vespucci airport in Florence, in the bus shelter on the right side of the Stazione Santa Maria Novella, and at 29 (red) Borgo Santa Croce (**Map 6;1**). There are also often mobile units in Piazza della Repubblica and at the Oltrarno end of Ponte Vecchio which offer help to tourists.

The headquarters of the APT is at 16 Via Manzoni (**Map 4; 8**), ☎ 055 23320, 🖹 055 234 6286 (written enquiries only; e-mail: apt@firenze.turismo.toscana.it and info@firenze.turismo.toscana.it).

The information office in Fiesole is at 3 Via Portigiani, ☎ 055 598 720.

A **hotel booking office** (ITA), which makes reservations on arrival, is open (daily 09.00–20.30) at the Stazione Santa Maria Novella, and on the motorway approaches to Florence, and at Pisa airport.

Where to stay

Information

Information about hotels and other accommodation in Florence can be obtained abroad from ENIT State tourist offices (see above), and on arrival at the APT information offices at Stazione Santa Maria Novella and 1 Via Cavour. Reservations may be made on arrival at the ITA office at the Stazione Santa Maria Novella.

The APT of Florence produces an annual publication—available free from their offices—that lists all the hotels in Florence and their charges.

Hotels

There are five official categories of hotels in Italy from the luxury 5-star hotels to the most simple 1-star establishments. These categories are bound to disappoint many travellers, however, for they are now based on the services offered (television in each room, private telephone, and *frigobar*, for example) and often do not reflect quality. In Florence, ✩✩✩ and ✩✩✩✩ hotels are not always on a par with hotels with the same designation in other large European cities.

It is essential to **book well in advance** in summer, at Easter and in September and October; you are usually asked to send a deposit or leave a credit card number to confirm the booking. You have the right to claim the deposit back if you cancel the booking at least 72 hours in advance.

Accommodation booking services from the UK are offered by:
Accommodation Line Ltd ☎ 020 7409 1343; ▤ 020 7409 2606
Hotel Connect ☎ 020 8381 2233; ▤ 020 8381 1155; email: hotel.connect @virgin.net
The Italian Connection ☎ 020 7486 6890; ▤ 020 7486 6891; email: italian connection.london@btinternet.com; offers hotels and self-catering apartments.
Room Service ☎ 020 7636 6888; ▤ 020 7636 6002; email: room@netcomuk. co.uk
Once in Florence, bookings can be made through *Florence Promhotels* (72 Viale Volta, ☎ 055 570481, ▤ 055 587189) and *Top Quark/Family Hotels* (5 Via Trieste, ☎ 055 4620080).
If you have complaints go to the APT Tourist Office at 1 (red) Via Cavour, ☎ 055 290 832.

Prices Every hotel has to declare its prices annually. Prices change according to the season and can be considerably less in off-peak periods. In the foyer, there should be a list of all the rooms in the hotel with their rates, and the total charge for a room (excluding breakfast) should be displayed on the back of the room door. For tax purposes, hotels are obliged by law to issue an official receipt (*ricevuta fiscale*) to customers; you should not leave the premises without this document.

In all hotels, service charges are included in the rates, so tipping is not necessary. You should beware of **extra charges** added to the bill. Drinks from the *frigobar* in your room are extremely expensive, so it is always best to buy drinks yourself from a shop outside the hotel. Telephone calls are also more expensive if made from your room; there is usually a pay telephone in the lobby which is the most economical way of telephoning and is more convenient than using the public telephones in the streets. A large supplement is usually charged for breakfast served in your room. You are usually also charged extra for garage parking.

You should be cautious about arranging to hire a car and driver with the hotel porter: everyone involved expects to take a large cut and a day in Florence spent in this way is bound to cost you a great deal and is hardly ever worthwhile.

Breakfast Breakfast (*prima colazione*) can be disappointing and costly. By law it is an optional extra charge, although a lot of hotels try to include it in the price of the room. When booking, always specify if you want breakfast or not. If you are staying in a one- two- or three-star hotel, it is usually a good idea to go round the corner to the nearest *pasticceria* or bar for breakfast. In some of the more expensive hotels, good buffet breakfasts are now provided, but even here the standard of the 'canteen' coffee can be poor: you can always ask for an *espresso* or *cappuccino* instead.

A selection of the 350 or so hotels in Florence has been made below, listed according to category. To find the location of a particular hotel on our colour street map, look up the number for the hotel and the map reference, both of which are given in brackets after each hotel name (e.g. **3; Map 6;1**).

Prices per double room per night
☆☆☆☆☆ 900,000–1,400,000
☆☆☆☆ 550,000–700,000
☆☆☆ 280,000–360,000
☆☆ about 200,000
☆ 100,000–150,000

Hotels in Florence

☆☆☆☆☆ hotels

Excelsior (**1; Map 2; 8**), 3 Piazza Ognissanti, 50123, with restaurant (☎ 055 2715, 🗐 055 210 278, www.Starwood.com). A hotel since 1863, it was taken over by the Sheraton group in 1994. 168 rooms heavily furnished with carpets, wallpaper, and drapes, but some with terraces with good views of Florence and the Arno. The public rooms and restaurant also have gloomy décor.

Grand Hotel Villa Medici (**3; Map 2; 6**), 42 Via il Prato, 50123, with restaurant and swimming pool (☎ 055 238 1331, 🗐 055 238 1336, www.Sinahotels. com). Typical of the 1960s with 103 rooms, with close carpeting, but rather more pleasantly and simply furnished than the other 5-star hotels in the centre. The small swimming pool is in a little garden at the back.

Helvetia e Bristol (**21; Map 1; 3**), 2 Via de' Pescioni, 50123, with restaurant (☎ 055 287 814, 🗐 055 288 353, www.charminghotels.it). Similar to the other 5-star hotels in the centre of Florence, although smaller with only 52 rooms. Heavily furnished with close carpeting, drapes and wallpaper, and marble bathrooms. However, its small luxury-class restaurant, The Bristol, is renowned in Florence.

Grand Hotel (**63; Map 2; 8**), 1 Piazza Ognissanti, 50123 with restaurant (☎ 055 2716, 🗐 055 217 400, www.Starwood.com).

Regency (**16; Map 4; 6**), 3 Piazza d'Azeglio, 50121, with restaurant (☎ 055 245 247, 🗐 055 234 6735, www.regency-hotel.com).

☆☆☆☆ hotels

Berchielli (**16; Map 1; 5**), 14 Lungarno Acciaiuoli and Piazza del Limbo, 50123 (☎ 055 264 061, 🗐 055 218 636, www.berchielli.it). An old-established hotel in the centre of Florence, decorated in Art Nouveau style. The 76 rooms are rather unimaginatively furnished, with wall-to-wall carpeting. Most of the rooms overlook Piaza del Limbo or interior courtyards: those on the Arno have the better views but are noisier. Some rooms on the upper floors overlook a little terrace where breakfast is served in summer. No large groups taken.

Continental (**19; Map 1; 5**), 2 Lungarno Acciaiuoli, 50123 (☎ 055 272 622, 🗐 055 283 139, www.lungarnohotels.com). An old-established hotel in the very centre of Florence, one of three recently bought by the Ferragamo family (the other two are the Gallery Hotel Art and the Lungarno). Despite the cramped lobby, it has pleasant public rooms on the first floor and a delightful roof garden where breakfast is served in summer. Some of the attractive rooms on the fifth and sixth floors have outstanding views over Ponte Vecchio. The five double rooms in the tower are particularly delightful: those on the upper floors also have remarkable views. There are six comfortable single rooms. The rooms without views are quiet and tend to be a little larger. No large groups taken. Efficient management and pleasant staff.

Gallery Hotel Art, 5 Vicolo dell'Oro, 50123 (☎ 055 27263, 🖹 055 268 557, www.lungarnohotels.it). This hotel is almost next door to the Continental and is under the same management. Opened in 1999 in a renovated, rather pokey building without much character, it has ultra-modern decor and exhibitions of modern art in the public rooms. The rooms tend to be small and rather too simply furnished; however, they are all quiet, and one of the penthouse suites on the seventh floor has a superb view. No groups taken.

J & J (23; Map 4; 7), 20 Via di Mezzo, 50121 (☎ 055 234 5005, 🖹 055 240 282, www.jandjhotel.com). A 16C convent which was sensitively converted into a delightful hotel in 1988. It has 20 large rooms which are particularly attractive, spacious and tastefully furnished—although there is no lift. It is tucked away on a very quiet road in a pleasant district with lots of good restaurants, away from the tourists. Family run, with friendly staff.

Lungarno (12; Map 6; 1), 14 Borgo San Jacopo, 50125 (☎ 055 263 121, 🖹 055 240 282, www.lungarnohotels.com). This is the third hotel owned by the Ferragamo family (see above). It is in a modern building near the Ponte Vecchio which was built following the destruction of this area in the Second World War. The public rooms are comfortable and the staff friendly. The rooms have balconies directly on the Arno. Convenient for those with a car as it has its own garage.

Monna Lisa (44; Map 4; 7), 27 Borgo Pinti, 50121 (☎ 055 247 9751, 🖹 055 247 9755, www.monnalisa.it). In a lovely old palace on a quiet street, with attractively furnished and spacious public rooms and a delightful large garden at the back. The 35 rooms (no lift), with small bathrooms, are rather pokey and less well furnished.

Astoria Boscolo Hotel (4: Map 1; 1), 9 Via del Giglio, 50123, with restaurant (☎ 055 239 8095, 🖹 055 214 632, www.boscolo.com).

Croce di Malta (5; Map 3; 7), 7 Via della Scala, 50123 with restaurant (☎ 055 218 351, 🖹 055 287 121, www.crocedimalta.it).

De la ville (6; Map 1; 3), Piazza Antinori, 50123, with restaurant (☎ 055 238 1805, 🖹 055 238 1809, www.hoteldelaville.it).

Grand Hotel Baglioni (7; Map 3; 5), Piazza Unità Italiana, 50123, with restaurant (☎ 055 23580, 🖹 055 235 8895, www.hotelbaglioni.it).

Grand Hotel Majestic (8; Map 3; 5), 1 Via del Melarancio, 50123, with restaurant (☎ 055 264021, 🖹 055 268 428, www.panciolihotels.it).

Grand Hotel Minerva (9; Map 3; 7), 16 Piazza Santa Maria Novella, 50123, with restaurant and swimming pool (☎ 055 27230, 🖹 055 268 281, www.sole.it).

Kraft (10; Map 2; 10), 2 Via Solferino, 50123, with restaurant and swimming pool (☎ 055 284 273, 🖹 055 239 8267, www.firenzealbergo.it/home/hotel kraft).

Londra (11; Map 2; 6), 18 Via Jacopo da Diacceto, 50123, with restaurant (☎ 055 27390, 🖹 055 210 682, www.sole.it/hlondra).

Montebello Splendid (72; Map 2; 6), 60 Via Montebello, 50123, with restaurant (☎ 055 239 8051, 🖹 055 211 867, www.milanflorencehotel.it).

Plaza Hotel Lucchesi (13; Map 7; 3), 38 Lungarno della Zecca Vecchia, 50122, with restaurant (☎ 055 26236, 🖹 055 248 0921, www.plazalucchesi.it).

Savoy (2; Map 1; 3), 7 Piazza della Repubblica, 50123, with restaurant (☎ 055 283 313, 🖹 055 284 840, www.rfhotels.com).

Villa Carlotta (60; Map 5; 8), 3 Via Michele di Lando, 50125, with restaurant (☎ 055 233 6134, 🖹 055 233 6147, www.venere.it/firenze/villacarlotta).

☆☆☆ **hotels**

Annalena (**35; Map 5; 4**), 34 Via Romana, 50125 (☎ 055 229 600, 🖹 055 222 403, www.hotelannalena.it). Opened as a *pensione* in 1919 in an old convent, much frequented by the British. An attractive building with high ceilings and furnished in a pleasant old-fashioned style. The 20 rooms all have bathrooms and are quiet, some on a long terrace which overlooks a pretty garden.

Beacci Tornabuoni (**34; Map 1; 3**), 3 Via Tornabuoni, 50123, with restaurant, (☎ 055 212645, 🖹 055 283594, www.bhotel.it). Set on Florence's smartest street, this is another old-established hotel where many well-known Anglo-Americans have stayed. On the top floor of two adjoining palaces, it has a slightly shabby, old-fashioned atmosphere, but a lovely roof terrace. Some of the 28 rooms are very spacious. Particularly friendly service.

Della Signoria (**20; Map 1; 5**), 1 Via delle Terme, 50123 (☎ 055 214 530, 🖹 055 216 101, www.hoteldellasignoria.com). In a characterless building built after the Second World War near Ponte Vecchio, the 27 rooms are on five floors, and breakfast is served on a terrace. The rooms have wallpaper and close carpeting but large bathrooms. No groups taken.

Hermitage (**40; Map 1; 5**), 1 Vicolo Marzio, 50122 (☎ 055 287 216, 🖹 055 212 208, www.hermitagehotel.com). Efficiently run, with 28 very small rooms on five floors. Its special feature is a delightful roof garden with superb views.

Loggiato dei Serviti (**32; Map 4; 5**), 3 Piazza Santissima Annunziata, 50122 (☎ 055 289 592, 🖹 055 289 595, www.venere.it/firenze/loggiato_serviti). In a lovely palace with vaulted rooms in the most beautiful square in Florence. It has recently been converted with great taste into a small hotel (34 rooms). The simple furnishings and stone floors make it cool and pleasant, and the rooms have lovely views of the city.

Porta Rossa (**28; Map 1; 5**), 19 Via Porta Rossa, 50123 (☎ 055 287 551, 🖹 055 282 179). This is one of the historic hotels of the city which retains its Art Nouveau decorations from the first years of this century. Spacious and old-fashioned, most of the rooms (not all with bathrooms) have high ceilings and are well furnished. Since 1994 no groups have been allowed, so its charming character has been maintained.

River (**68; Map 7; 1**), 18 Lungarno della Zecca Vecchia, 50122 (☎ 055 234 3529; 🖹 055 234 3521, www.hotelriver.com). Due to reopen soon after renovations. On the Arno, a little way outside the heart of Florence, but only about 10 minutes walk from Ponte Vecchio. It has a discreet atmosphere, with 40 pleasant and spacious rooms: those at the back overlook a peaceful courtyard and are much quieter. There is a terrace on the second floor and a good breakfast is provided. Comfortable public rooms and friendly staff. No groups taken.

Torre Guelfa (**56; Map 1; 5**), 8 Borgo Santi Apostoli, 50123 (☎ 055 239 6338, 🖹 9055 239 8577, email: torre.guelfa@flashnet.it). This efficiently run hotel is set in a beautiful old 13C palace which was well renovated in 1994. There are 12 quiet rooms, all with bathrooms, and most with air conditioning. Pleasant single rooms also. A lovely loggia is used for breakfast and there is a delightful living room. A 19C wooden stair leads up to the exceptionally high tower which has breathtaking views.

Ambasciatori (**14; Map 3; 5**), 3 Via Alamanni, 50123 (☎ 055 287 421, 🖹 055 214 456, www.dada.it/ambasciatori).

Ariele (**36; Map 2; 6**), 11 Via Magenta, 50123 (☎ 055 211 509, 🖹 055 268 521).

Balestri (15; Map 6; 4), 7 Piazza Mentana, 50122 (☎ 055 214 743, 🖹 055 239 8042, www.italyhotel.com/firenze/balestri).

Bonciani (17; Map 3; 17), 17 Via Panzani, 50123 (☎ 055 26090, 🖹 055 268 512, www.hotelbonciani.it).

Consigli (39; Map 2; 8), 50 Lungarno Vespucci, 50123 (☎ 055 214 172, 🖹 055 219 367, www.hotelconsigli.com).

Dante (73; Map 7; 1), 2 Via San Cristofano, 50122 (☎ 055 241 772, 🖹 055 234 5819, email: faxadm@venere.it).

Duomo (41; Map 1; 4), 1 Piazza Duomo, 50122 (☎ 055 219 922, 🖹 055 216 410).

La Residenza (42; Map 1; 3), 8 Via Tornabuoni, 50123, with restaurant (☎ 055 218 684, 🖹 055 284 197, www.laresidenza hotel.com).

Liana (27; Map 4; 6), 18 Via Vittorio Alfieri, 50121 (☎ 055 246 6004, 🖹 055 234 4595, www.venere.it/firenze/liana).

Pendini (45; Map 1; 3), 2 Via Strozzi, 50123 (☎ 055 211 170, 🖹 055 281 807, www.tiac.net/users/pendini).

Pitti Palace (59; Map 1; 7), 2 Via Barbadori, 50125 (☎ 055 239 8711, 🖹 055 239 8867, www.vivahotels.com).

Rapallo (29; Map 3; 4), 7 Via Santa Caterina d'Alessandria, 50129, with restaurant (☎ 055 472 412, 🖹 055 470 385, www.dinonet.it/rapallo).

Royal (30; Map 3; 4), 52 Via delle Ruote, 50129 (☎ 055 483 287, 🖹 055 490 976, www.paginegialle.it/royal-05).

Select (66; Map 2; 1), 24 Via Galliano, 50144 (☎ 055 330 342, 🖹 055 351 506, www.selecthotel.it).

Silla (61; Map 7; 3), 5 Via dei Renai, 50125, with restaurant (☎ 055 234 2888, 🖹 055 234 1437, www.tiscalinet.it/hotelsilla).

Villa Azalee (31; Map 2; 4), 44 Viale Fratelli Rosselli, 50123 (☎ 055 214 242, 🖹 055 268 264, email: villaazalee@fi.flashnet.it).

☆☆ **hotels**

Boboli (53; Map 5; 6), 63 Via Romana, 50125 (☎ 055 229 8645, 🖹 055 233 7169). A simple but pleasant hotel, although lacking in character. The 18 rooms, with small bathrooms, are on three floors (no lift), only a few of which are on the back, but those on Via Romana have double glazing. Good views from the rooms on the upper floors.

Bretagna (37; Map 6; 1), 6 Lungarno Corsini, 50123 (☎ 055 289618, 🖹 055289619, http://dbweb.agora.stm.it/market/bretagna). In a very fine position in the centre of Florence, it has a charmingly old-fashioned living room and dining room overlooking the Arno, with echoes of E.M. Forster. The 18 very simple rooms vary a great deal: some are more spacious than others; some are family rooms; some have their own bathrooms and some do not. They all have their own air conditioners, and one has its own tiny terrace. Only one room overlooks the Arno, but all the others are quiet. Takes small groups.

Casci (33; Map 1; 2) 13 Via Cavour, 50129 (☎ 055 211 686, 🖹 055 239 6461, www.hotelcasci.com). There are 25 quiet rooms, simply furnished, only two of which are on the noisy Via Cavour, and all of which have bathrooms. Friendly atmosphere.

La Scaletta (54; Map 6; 3), 13 Via Guicciardini, 50125 (☎ 055 283028, 🖹 055 289562, www.italyhotel.com/firenze/lascaletta). An old-established family-run hotel on the top floor with a delightful roof terrace with views of the Palazzo Pitti and the Boboli gardens. Of the 14 rooms, 12 have bathrooms; all have high ceilings and those on Via Guicciardini have double glazing.

Villani (**65; Map 1; 4**), 11 Via delle Oche, 50122 (☎ 055 239 6451, 🖹 055 215 348, email: evillani@tin.it). A simple hotel on a top floor, very close to the Duomo. The 13 rooms, all with bathrooms, are very quiet and have wonderful views. Arrangement with the restaurant below.

Alessandra (**48; Map 1; 5**), 17 Borgo Santi Apostoli, 50123 (☎ 055 282 156, 🖹 055 210619, www.hotelalessandra.com).

Bellettini (**52; Map 3; 6**), 7 Via dei Conti, 50123, with restaurant (☎ 055 213 561, 🖹 055 283 551, www.firenze.net/hotelbellettini).

Centrale (**38; Map 3; 8**), 3 Via dei Conti, 50123, with restaurant (☎ 055 215 761, 🖹 055 215 216).

Chiazza (**74; Map 7; 7**), 5 Borgo Pinti, 50121 (☎ 055 248 0363, 🖹 055 234 6888).

Delle Nazioni (**26; Map 2; 6**), 15 Via Alamanni, 50123 (☎ 055 283 575, 🖹 055 283 579, email: htlnazioni@iol.it).

Medici (**43; Map 1; 4**), 6 Via dei Medici, 50123 (☎ 055 284 818, 🖹 055 216 202, email: medici@dada.it).

☆ hotels

Azzi (**69; Map 3; 3**), 56 Via Faenza, 50123 (☎ & 🖹 055 213806). In a side street close to the station which has numerous small cheap hotels, and in a building which consists entirely of hotels. Despite this, it has 12 cosy, old-fashioned rooms, most of them on the back and totally quiet, three of them with their own bathrooms. There is one comfortable, spacious single room, and one with three beds overlooking a little garden. Breakfast is served at a communal table in a charming breakfast room, which has a door onto a terrace which is a cool place to sit on summer evenings. The pleasant young owner runs two more hotels on the upper floors of the same building and, if you specify your precise requirements, will take the trouble to give you the most suitable room. Takes small groups. No lift.

Brunetta (**70; Map 4; 7**), 5 Borgo Pinti, 50121 (☎ 055 247 8134 or 055 240 360, 🖹 055 247 8134). A very pleasant, small family-run hotel on the third floor of a building set on a delightful, narrow old road with little traffic in the town centre. The 11 rooms, with cool floors, are spotlessly clean, but none of them have bathrooms (there are three communal bathrooms). Half of the rooms overlook Borgo Pinti and the others are totally quiet looking out over the roofs of Florence. One spacious single room. The hotel closes at midnight. No lift. At present, it doesn't have a licence for breakfast, but there are plenty of bars close by.

Maria Luisa de' Medici (**67; Map 1; 4**), 1 Via del Corso, 50122 (☎ & 🖹 055 280048). An eccentric hotel with a weird atmosphere, crammed full of 17C paintings, sculptures and *objets d'art*, on the top floor of an 18C palace (no lift). Nine very quiet rooms, some of which can accommodate large families, two of which have bathrooms. An ample breakfast is served in your room.

Scoti (**55; Map 1; 5**), 7 Via Tornabuoni, 50123 (☎ & 🖹 055 292 128, email: hotelscoti@hotmail.com). A very friendly family-run hotel with just 7 large rooms, two of them singles (none with their own bathrooms, although there are three bathrooms which are shared) on the second floor, all very quiet (not overlooking Via Tornabuoni). A charming frescoed main room, and old fashioned furniture. Breakfast, available on request, is served in your room.

Fiorentina (**71; Map 3; 1**), 12 Via dei Fossi, 50123 (☎ 055 219 530, 🖹 055 287 105). In a nice palace with a handsome entrance in a smart street. 16 rooms on two floors some with bathrooms. The rooms on the garden and inner courtyard are quieter than those on Via dei Fossi. Spacious breakfast room, friendly staff. Only takes visitors (no groups) from June or July to September, as the rest of the year it is entirely occupied by students from American campuses studying in Florence.

Bandini (**50; Map 6; 3**), 9 Piazza Santo Spirito, 50125 (☎ 055 215 308, 🖹 055 282 761). An old, established hotel in a very fine palace in one of the loveliest squares in Florence. Unfortunately, it has become very run down in the last few years and is not as clean as it might be (partly because there are too many cats). The management can also be unreliable. Its special feature is a lovely loggia over-looking the piazza, and most of the rooms and the breakfast room have fine views. In a labyrinth of corridors and stairs, there are 12 rooms which vary in size; some are unusually large; five have bathrooms. There is a slightly spooky atmosphere presided over by a grey cat and its numerous relations.

Hotels outside the centre of Florence

All of these hotels have gardens, and are convenient if you have a car.

On the south bank of the Arno

☆☆☆☆☆
Grand Hotel Villa Cora (**57; Map 6; 7**), 18 Viale Machiavelli, 50125, with restau-rant and swimming pool (☎ 055 229 8451, 🖹 055 229 086, www.villacora. com).

☆☆☆☆
Park Palace (**62; Map 6; 7**), 5 Piazzale Galileo, 50125, with restaurant and swimming pool (☎ 055 222 431, 🖹 055 220 517, www.parkpalace.com).

Torre di Bellosguardo (**65; Map 5; 5**), 2 Via Roti Michelozzi, 50124 with swim-ming pool (☎ 055 2298145, 🖹 055 229008, email: miam@dada.it). A very ele-gant hotel in a beautiful villa with a garden.

☆☆☆
David (**58; Map 7; 6**), 1 Viale Michelangelo, 50125 (☎ 055 681 1695, 🖹 055 680 602, www.davidhotel.com).

Villa Montartino (south of **Map 6;7**), 151 Via Gherardo Silvani, 50125, with swimming pool (☎ 055 223 520; 🖹 055 223 495). Recently opened in a restored watchtower above the Ema Valley, it is in a lovely position surrounded by its own olive groves and vineyards. Not classified as a hotel since it only has a few bedrooms, but beautifully furnished and very comfortable (on a par with a ☆☆☆☆ star hotel). Meals can be ordered. Self-catering flats are also available. Lovely country walks can be taken near Arcetri.

On the north bank of the Arno

☆☆☆☆
Ville sull'Arno (east of **Map 7; 4**), 1 Lungarno Cristoforo Colombo, 50136, with swimming pool (☎ 055 670 971, 🖹 055 678 244, www.villesullarno.it).

On the northern outskirts of the city

☆☆☆
Villa Le Rondini (north of **Map 4; 1**), 224 Via Bolognese Vecchia, 50139, with restaurant and swimming pool (☎ 055 400 081, 🖹 055 268 212, www.vil-lalerondini.it).

Hotels in Fiesole

Fiesole is a particularly pleasant place to stay (especially in summer) and is within easy reach of Florence. It is convenient if you have a car (see the map on pp 338–39) and there is an excellent city bus service which takes 20–30 minutes. All the following hotels have gardens and are in good positions.

☆☆☆☆
Villa Aurora, 39 Piazza Mino, 50014, with restaurant (☎ 055 59100, ▤ 055 59587, www.logicad.net/aurora).
Villa San Michele, 4 Via Doccia, 50014, with restaurant and swimming pool (☎ 055 567 8200, ▤ 055 567 8250, www.orient-expresshotels.com). A famous, established hotel in a lovely villa in a superb position, with a good restaurant.

☆☆☆
Bencistà, 4 Via Benedetto da Maiano, 50014 (☎ & ▤ 055 59163, email: bencista@uol.it). An old-fashioned hotel with a charming atmosphere, which has been favoured for decades by English visitors, on the hillside below Fiesole.
Villa Bonelli, 1 Via Poeti, 50014, with restaurant (☎ 055 59513, ▤ 055 598942, www.hotelvillabonelli.com).

Hotels in the environs of Florence

Bagno a Ripoli

☆☆☆☆
Villa La Massa, 6 Via La Massa, Candeli, 50012, with restaurant and swimming pool (☎ 055 62611, ▤ 055 633 102, www.villamassa.com).

Sesto Fiorentino

☆☆☆
Villa Villoresi, 2 Via Ciampi, Colonnata, 50019, with restaurant and swimming pool (☎ 055 443212, ▤ 055 442063, www.ila-chateau.com/villores).

Pratolino

☆☆☆☆
Demidoff, 51 Via San Jacopo, Vaglia, 50036, with restaurant and swimming pool (☎ 055 505641, ▤ 055 409780).

There are numerous other hotels in good positions near Florence, in Impruneta, the Mugello, Vallombrosa, Reggello, Artimino and the Chianti district (see *Blue Guide Tuscany*).

Youth and students' hostels

Ostello per la Gioventù, Villa Camerata, 2 Viale Righi (☎ 055 601 451, ▤ 055 610 300). This is the largest youth hostel in Florence and is set in a good position in a park at the bottom of the hill of San Domenico (220 beds). Bus no. 17 from the Stazione Santa Maria Novella (west side, Via Alemanni) via Via Cavour and Piazza San Marco (the service operates 05.30–01.15). Villa Camerata is also the regional headquarters of the Italian Youth Hostels Association. A bed (usually six in one room) costs Lire 25,000 a night (including breakfast; lunch or dinner costs an extra Lire 14,000). Similar rates are available at two other hostels in the centre of Florence:
Santa Monaca, 6 Via Santa Monaca (☎ 055 268 338).
Archi Rossi (☎ 055 290 804), 94 (number in red) Via Faenza.

Youth Residence Firenze 2000, 16 Viale Sanzio (☎ 055 233 5558) costs Lire 55,000 a night, but also has double rooms and a swimming pool.

Casa di Ospitalità per Universitari, Sette Santi, 11 Viale dei Mille, ☎ 055 504 8452; ▤ 055 504 7055 is another student hostel.

The national headquarters of the **Associazione Italiana Alberghi per la Gioventù** is at 44 Via Cavour, Rome (☎ 06 487 1152).

Hostels (case per ferie)

Many hostels run by religious organisations are open to both young and old, and offer cheap if rather spartan accommodation. They often have restricted hours and early curfews, but are generally well run. They are all listed in the annual hotel list supplied by the APT. Among the most pleasant in the historic centre are: **Francescane Missionarie di Maria**, 21 Piazza del Carmine (☎ 055 213 856; ▤ 055 281 835).

Istituto Gould, 49 Via de' Serragli (☎ 055 212576, ▤ 055 280274).

Istituto Oblate dell'Assunzione, 15 Borgo Pinti (☎ 055 2480582; ▤ 055 2346291).

Istituto Pio X – Artigianelli, 106 Via dei Serragli (☎ 055 225044).

Bed and breakfast

This type of accommodation is new to Italy and was first seriously introduced in 2000 in anticipation (largely unfounded) of the arrival of a large number of visitors to Italy for Holy Year. However, it looks as if this may become an alternative form of hospitality, although at present it tends to be as expensive as hotel accommodation. The first TCI guide to *Bed and Breakfast in Italy* came out in 2000, along with some other guides to the more expensive establishments of this kind (*Caffelletto: High quality Bed and Breakfast in Italy*, Le Lettere (ed) and *Dolce Casa: Italian quality Bed and Breakfast*).

Camping

Sites in and around Florence are listed in the annual hotel list supplied by the APT, divided into official categories by stars, from the most expensive 4-star sites, to the simplest and cheapest 1-star sites. Their classification and rates must be displayed at the camp site office. Full details of the sites in Italy are published annually by the Touring Club Italiano in *Campeggi e Villaggi Turistici in Italia*. The Federazione Italiana del Campeggio has a booking service at 11 Via Vittorio Emanuele, Calenzano, 50041 Florence (☎ 055 882391).

Italiani e Stranieri (✩✩), 80 Viale Michelangelo (**Map 7; 6**), ☎ 055 681 1977 (takes 260 tents). This is the main camp site in **Florence**. It occupies a wonderful position overlooking the city and is only a 20–30 minute walk from the centre. Bus 12 from Largo Alinari, just off Piazza Stazione (and Bus 13 for the return to the station): the service operates daily 06.00–01.00.

Villa Camerata (✩), 2 Viale Righi in the park of the Youth Hostel (see above) at the bottom of the hill of San Domenico (55 tents), ☎ 055 600 315.

In **Fiesole**, **Panoramico** (✩✩✩) in Via Peramonda, Borgunto (see p 339) is another site in a good position (95 tents), ☎ 055 599069. Bus 7 from the Stazione Santa Maria Novella to the terminus in Fiesole, and from there bus 47-49 (very infrequent service).

There are also camp sites in the environs, at Impruneta, in the Mugello and at Calenzano.

Food and drink

Food in Florence, as in the rest of Italy, is generally good, but traditional local dishes have become more difficult to find, and Florentine cookery is now similar to that to be found all over the country. Traditional Florentine cuisine is characterised by the abundant use of olive oil (Tuscan olive oil is the best in Italy) and by some elaborate meat dishes which are cooked slowly (usually in a tomato sauce). The court of the Medici in Florence was famous for its banquets at which delicious food was served. When Caterina dei Medici married Henry II of France in the 16C, she took with her to the French court her cooks (as well as her perfume-makers) which had a profound influence on French cuisine. Unfortunately, very few dishes which adorned the tables of the rich during the Renaissance have survived today. A seminal work (still in print) on Italian cookery (*La Scienza in Cucina e l'arte di mangiar bene*) was published in Florence in 1891 by Pellegrino Artusi (1820–1911) who came from Romagna to live in Piazza d'Azeglio in 1852. Some of the best items of traditional Florentine cuisine often served in the more simple Florentine restaurants are listed below.

The menu

Hors d'oeuvres (*antipasti*)
Crostini, small pieces of toast or bread with a type of paté made out of chicken livers, capers and anchovies.

Affettati usually include raw Parma ham, *salame* and *finocchiona* or *sbriciolona* (a delicious salami cured with fennel). In summer raw ham (*prosciutto crudo*) is served with melon or figs.

Pinzimonio, a plate of fresh raw vegetables (artichokes, fennel, celery and carrots) which are dipped in a dressing (usually oil and lemon).

Fettunta or *bruschetta*, served in the autumn, consists of toasted bread with garlic and oil straight from the olive press; if it is topped with hot black cabbage it is called *cavolo con le fette*.

First courses (*primi piatti*)
As in the rest of Italy, numerous pasta dishes are always served.

Ragù or *sugo di carne*, Tuscany is well known for this elaborate meat sauce cooked at length, made with minced meat, sausage, herbs and tomato which is used in pasta dishes.

Penne all'arrabbiata or *penne strascicate*, short pasta in a rich spicy sauce.

Pappardelle alla lepre, large flat noodles made with flour and egg with a rich hare sauce.

Fettuccine, ribbon noodles usually freshly made on the premises, often served with a meat sauce or with *porcini* mushrooms.

Minestrone, a thick vegetable soup with chopped vegetables (and sometimes pasta), the most famous first course produced in Florence. In winter, bread, cabbage and white beans are sometimes added to the soup and it is called *ribollita* or *minestra di pane*.

Panzanella, a cold salad made with bread, raw onions, tomatoes, cucumber, basil, oil and vinegar, often served in the summer.

Pappa al pomodoro, usually served hot or tepid, consists of tomato sauce, basil and bread.

Haricot beans and chick peas are a favourite winter dish; beans (*fagioli*) are cooked with sage and dressed with oil, or in a tomato sauce *all'uccelletto*.

Main courses (*secondi piatti*)

Meat in Florence is often stewed slowly for a long time in red wine and a tomato sauce: there are a number of variations generally known as *umido*, *stufato*, *stracotto* or *spezzatino*.

Bistecca alla fiorentina, a large T-bone steak which can be grilled in one piece and served to two or three people; although famous, this is not always easy to find.

Coniglio (rabbit) is often served in Florence, usually *in umido* or *alla cacciatora*, stewed in tomato sauce. The meat of rabbit and *faraona* (guinea fowl, almost always served roasted) is usually of better quality than chicken.

Arista, a joint of pork ribs cooked in the oven.

Ossobuco, stewed shin of veal.

Braccioline (veal escalopes) are also usually available (either cooked in lemon or wine).

Trippa alla fiorentina, an unusual traditional dish, is tripe cooked in a tomato sauce and served with parmesan cheese.

Fish (*pesce*)

Fish is always the most expensive item on the menu but can be extremely good in specialist fish restaurants. Among the most succulent and expensive are *dentice* (dentex), *orata* (bream) and *triglie* (red mullet) usually cooked simply *arrosto* (roast) or *alla griglia* (grilled).

Fritto di pesce or *fritto misto di mare*, various types of small fried fish, almost always including *calamari* (squid) and *seppie* (cuttlefish), is usually the most inexpensive fish dish on the menu.

Shellfish, often served cooked in white wine with garlic and parsley, includes *cozze* (mussels) and *vongole* (clams). These can also be served as a sauce for spaghetti.

Good fish dishes often to be found in simpler restaurants are *baccalà* (salt cod), usually cooked in tomato sauce, and *seppie in zimino*, cuttlefish cooked with spinach. *Zuppa di pesce* is a rich fish stew made with a wide variety of fish: if cooked with tomato sauce it is called *alla Livornese* (or *Caciucco*) since it is a speciality of Livorno, a port on the Tuscan coast.

Vegetarian dishes (*piatti vegetariani*)

Porcini are large wild mushrooms and an expensive delicacy (only served in season). They are best grilled and are also often used as a sauce for pasta.

Melanzane alla parmigiana, aubergine cooked in the oven with a cheese and tomato sauce, is a good vegetarian main course.

Vegetable *tortini* are similar to omelettes and are good made with *carciofi* (artichokes) or *zucchini* (courgettes).

Insalata (salad) is the most popular vegetable dish; *insalata verde* is green salad (only lettuce), and *insalata mista* usually includes tomato and raw carrot.

Some restaurants in Florence serve excellent lightly fried vegetables, including courgette slices, artichoke hearts, courgette flowers, onions, tomatoes and sage.

In season, artichokes (served in a variety of ways), asparagus, courgettes and *gobbi* (a vegetable related to the artichoke) are usually good.

Fagioli all'uccelletto (see above) is also a vegetable dish.

Raw or cooked fennel (*finocchio*) is another characteristic Florentine vegetable.

Dessert (*dolce*)

Italians usually prefer fresh fruit for dessert and sweets are considered the least important part of the meal. In many simple restaurants and *trattorie* often only fruit is served at the end of the meal. The fruit available varies according to what is in season; strawberries (*fragole*) are good served with fresh lemon juice or red wine (rather than with cream). In summer, water melon (*popone*) is particularly refreshing. Fresh fruit salad (*macedonia*) is often good.

Biscotti di Prato are hard almond biscuits which you dip in a glass of 'Vin Santo' or 'Morellino' wine.

Castagnaccio, a traditional Florentine pudding, is a thin chestnut cake with pine nuts, rosemary and sultanas.

Schiacciata alla fiorentina, a plain cake.

Crostata, a fruit flan.

Zuppa inglese, a rich trifle sometimes offered in smarter restaurants.

Torta della nonna, a good pastry filled with custard and garnished with almonds.

Tiramisù is a rich pudding based on mascarpone cheese, mixed with egg, chocolate, biscuits, and sometimes a liqueur.

Gelato (ice-cream) is also widely available, although is not usually home-made in restaurants.

Cheese (*formaggi*)

Bel Paese, a soft cheese made from cow's milk; it is rarely offered by restaurants.

Gorgonzola, a delicious strong creamy cheese made from whole cow's milk.

Grana, a type of Parmesan cheese produced in northern Italy.

Groviera italiano, Italian gruyère.

Mascarpone, a fresh rich cream cheese, usually used in desserts and not served on its own.

Parmigiano-Reggiano, usually the best quality Parmesan cheese made in the districts of Parma and Reggio Emilia.

Pecorino, a sheep's cheese, is almost always available, and in spring is eaten with fresh raw broad beans.

Wines

The cheapest wine is always the house wine (*vino della casa*), which varies a great deal, but is normally a drinkable *vin ordinaire*. The world-famous Chianti red wine is made from a careful blend of white and black grapes. Only wine produced from grapes grown in a limited area of the Chianti region, between Florence and Siena, can bear the label of the black rooster on a yellow ground in a red circle and be called *Chianti Classico gallo nero*. The other Chianti wines, some of which rival the *Classico*, include *Chianti Colli Aretini*, *Chianti Colli Fiorentini*, *Chianti Colli Senesi*, *Chianti Montalbano* and *Chianti Rufina*. The bright ruby-red Chianti is drunk younger than most French wines, and has between 11.5 and 13 per cent alcoholic content.

Other wines in Tuscany (where the red table wine is usually of better quality than the white) such as *Vino nobile di Montepulciano*, *Vernaccia* (white, from San Gimignano) and *Brunello di Montalcino* (not cheap) are particularly good. Excellent red wine is also produced at Carmignano, near Florence, and around

Lucca. Pitigliano, Montecarlo and the Val d'Arbia are good areas for white wine. Elba used to produce excellent wines (now hard to find), including *Aleatico*, a dessert wine. *Vin Santo* is an amber dessert wine (aged for a minimum of three years and with 17–18 per cent alcoholic content), produced in Tuscany and Umbria, similar in taste to an excellent sherry. It is often served with dry almond biscuits (biscotti di Prato) at the end of a meal. Sulphate-free wine is now unfortunately rarely served in restaurants.

Restaurants

It has become extremely difficult to recommend restaurants (*ristoranti, trattorie*) in Florence since they change hands frequently and the standard often deteriorates once they become well known. In the simplest *trattorie* the food is usually good, and considerably cheaper than in the more famous restaurants, though furnishings and surroundings can be a lot less comfortable. Most restaurants display a menu outside which gives you an idea of the prices; however, many simpler restaurants do not, and here, although the choice is usually limited, the standard of the cuisine is often very high.

Some restaurants still have a cover charge (*coperto*), shown separately on the menu, which is added to the bill, although this practice has officially been discontinued. Prices are almost always inclusive of service, so always check whether or not the service charge has been added to the bill before leaving a tip (if in doubt, ask the waiter). It is customary to leave a few thousand lire on the table to convey appreciation. For tax purposes, restaurants are now obliged by law to issue an official receipt to customers *(ricevuta fiscale)*; you should not leave the premises without this document.

Lunch is normally around 13.00 and is the main meal of the day, while dinner is around 20.00 or 21.00. Very few restaurants in Florence stay open later than 23.00 or 23.30. It is acceptable to order a first course only, or to skip the first course and order only a main course. Many restaurants in Florence close down for part of August (or July), and throughout the year many are shut on Mondays. Restaurants in Florence have been very slow to introduce no smoking areas.

A selection of a few restaurants—divided into six categories according to price per person for dinner (wine excluded)—is given below. Those in the lower categories are almost invariably the best value, particularly those in ££ range, but they can be crowded and are usually much less comfortable than the *trattorie* and restaurants in the higher price ranges.

££££££	over Lire 250,000 a head
£££££	around Lire 100,000—Lire 200,000
££££	around Lire 80,000—Lire 100,000
£££	around Lire 60,000 a head
££	around Lire 30,000–40,000 a head
£	around Lire 25,000 a head

££££££

Enoteca Pinchiorri, 87 Via Ghibellina (**Map 7; 1**), ☎ 055 242 777. One of the most famous and expensive restaurants in Italy which opened in 1974 and has managed to retain its reputation as probably the best luxury restaurant in the country for well over a decade, despite some criticisms about its prices which scare away many Florentine gourmets. It is run by Giorgio Pinchiorri and Annie Feolde, and is closed Sun and Mon. It has an exceptional selection of wines, arguably the best in Italy, and a remarkably creative cuisine. On the ground floor of a palace, it can seat about 80 people in two comfortable rooms, one with a balcony, and, in good weather, on tables in the interior courtyard and in a loggia off it. There is a lunch menu for Lire 150,000, and a set menu in the evening for Lire 250,000, but the minimum you can spend *à la carte* is around 300,000 a head (all prices exclusive of wine). Non-smokers should request a table outside; there is a room reserved for cigar smokers.

£££££

The Bristol, in the Hotel Helvetia e Bristol, 2 Via de' Pescioni (**Map 1; 3**), ☎ 055 287 814. This small restaurant is an elegant place to dine, although the décor is a little kitsch. In a long-established hotel which has been modernised, the service is very professional. International cuisine of high standard.

Harry's Bar, 22 Lungarno Vespucci (**Map 2; 8**), ☎ 055 239 6700. A very elegant cocktail bar renowned for its impeccable service and formal old-fashioned atmosphere. Leo, the barman, produces superb cocktails, and you can also have just a club sandwich. In the restaurant, the food sometimes leaves something to be desired. A few tables are put out in the summer on the Lungarno.

Taverna del Bronzino, Via delle Ruote (**Map 3; 4**), ☎ 055 495 220. One of the finest restaurants in Florence, which has maintained an extremely high standard for many years. Elegant and comfortable with impeccable service, the cuisine is creative and very good, and it is one of the best places to eat fish in the city.

££££

Il Cibreo, 8 Via Andrea del Verrocchio (**Map 7; 2**), ☎ 055 234 1100. This is one of the best-known restaurants in Florence, especially famous in north America, and has been recommended for years in all the restaurant guides to Italy. It is therefore best to book well in advance. It has a rather unusual atmosphere with informal service, and you are not given a menu. It seems, oddly, to be more like an Italian restaurant in North America rather than an Italian restaurant in Italy. It is an expensive place to eat, and lacks an expert wine waiter. You should be aware that on the menu outside service is included, but this is not specified on your bill. It has a simpler one-room *trattoria* next door in Via dei Macci, which has the same chef, but a reduced menu, and costs half (**££**). You can also eat a plate of the same food across the street at the rather more pleasant, if somewhat pretentious, *Caffè del Cibreo*. This has tables outside, but even here the prices are in the £££ category.

Caffè Concerto, 7 Lungarno Colombo (beyond **Map 7; 4**), ☎ 055 677 377. Although not in the historic centre of the city, this is in a particularly attractive building with wood furnishings, and is situated on the Arno. It has a veranda in summer. It is relatively informal and the food is generally creative. A separate section operates as a wine bar which serves light lunches. It has a very good selection of French wines and whiskeys.

Don Chisciotte, 4 Via Ridolfi (**Map 3; 4**), ☎ 475 430. Set in a rather unattractive street, near Piazza dell'Independenza, this is a restaurant which has acquired a good name for reliability and therefore has a devoted clientele and is almost always busy. It is a little bit pretentious and without much style, though the food is good (it specialises in fish), if rather expensive.

Oliviero, 51 Via delle Terme (**Map 1; 5**), ☎ 055 212 421. A comfortable restaurant with great charm and excellent service. Its atmosphere is reminiscent of the 1950s and 1960s and it is entered through a revolving door. It has a well-known chef and is a little cheaper than the other restaurants mentioned in this category.

Orient Express, 9 Borgo Allegri (**Map 7; 1**), ☎ 055 246 9028. This fish restaurant has just opened in a quiet side street off Piazza Santa Croce. Traditional cooking of a very high standard. Well ventilated locale (so particularly attractive for non-smokers).

£££

Acqua al Due, 40 Via Vigna Vecchia (**Map 7; 1**), ☎ 055 284 170. Opened about 20 years ago, this restaurant is one of the very few in the city that stays open until late (01.00). It is frequented by actors and theatre-goers. It has good pasta dishes, and steak is served in an original way.

Beccofino, 1 Piazza degli Scarlatti (Lungarno Guicciardini; **Map 5; 2**), ☎ 055 290 076. Run by a Scottish proprietor (who also runs Baldovino, see p 38), this restaurant serves a modern variety of Tuscan food and has tables outside. Beccofino has an excellent selection of international wines, which can also be ordered just by the glass. There is a reduced menu in the wine bar (££).

Cavallino, 28 Piazza della Signoria (**Map 1; 6**), ☎ 055 215 818. A long-established and reliable restaurant in Piazza della Signoria, the main square of Florence, with tables outside. Its splendid setting is without equal.

Il Cavolo Nero, 22 Via di Ardiglione (**Map 5; 4**), ☎ 055 294 744. Set in a delightful little side street, this is a pleasant restaurant, with creative and well-presented international cuisine. It has the atmosphere of an English or French restaurant rather than a traditional Tuscan restaurant. You can eat outside in summer in an internal courtyard.

Cocco Lezzone, 26 Via del Parioncino (**Map 1; 5**), ☎ 055 287278. This has also had a good name for many years as a typical Florentine *trattoria*, and the food has maintained a high standard. However, it lacks atmosphere and is not a particularly attractive place. On the plus side, the service is extremely fast and you can have a very quick meal here if you choose to.

Domani, 80 Via Romana (**Map 5; 6**), ☎ 055 221 166. An excellent fish restaurant which serves a superb variety of Japanese and Italian cuisine. It is one of the best places to eat in Florence and very good value, despite the fact the setting is rather anonymous and without much character. It is very well attended by the Japanese.

Latini, 6 Via Palchetti (**Map 2; 7**), ☎ 055 210 916. This has been famous for decades as a typical Florentine *trattoria* with long, crowded tables and Tuscan cuisine, and a bustling atmosphere. However, its fame has meant that there are usually long queues of tourists on the street outside, and the food is no better than numerous other restaurants in the same price range.

Mamma Gina, 36 Borgo San Jacopo (**Map 1; 5,7**), ☎ 055 239 6009. A famous Florentine *trattoria*, now rather lacking in character.

Osteria dei Benci, 13 Via dei Benci (**Map 7; 1**), ☎ 055 234 4923. Opened by a law student at Florence university, this is modelled on a typical Florentine *trattoria*, and is frequented by the young. It serves good Tuscan food, specialising in meat (excellent raw ham and Florentine steaks). Very good desserts.

Osteria del Caffè Italiano, 11 Via delle Stinche (**Map 7; 1**), ☎ 055 289 368.

Opened in 1998, this is housed on the ground floor of one of the best preserved medieval palaces in Florence. Its atmosphere recreates that of a typical Florentine *trattoria* and it is run by the same proprietor as the Caffè Italiano in Via della Condotta. Unfortunately, since it has become discovered by tourists, the quality of the food and the service has lowered (and some of the staff have left), and the prices risen. It has a few tables outside in summer in the narrow old Via della Vigna Vecchia, round the corner. It also has a wine bar, where you can just have a snack.

Osteria di Santo Spirito, 16 Piazza Santo Spirito (**Map 6; 3**), ☎ 055 238 2383. This used to be a typical Florentine *osteria* but it has recently been transformed and given a somewhat more trendy atmosphere, similar to a London or Parisienne restaurant. However, the food is good and there are tables outside in one of the loveliest squares in Florence.

Ottorino, 20 Via delle Oche (**Map 1; 4**), ☎ 055 218 747. This has been known for years as a place to eat Tuscan food and it has maintained its standards. Although only a few metres from the Duomo, it is a very large restaurant with little character.

Paoli, 12 Via dei Tavolini (**Map 1; 4,6**), ☎ 055 216 215. At the heart of the historic centre, this is a very old restaurant in a fine vaulted room with mock Renaissance decorations and frescoes. It serves traditional, if rather unimaginative Florentine fare. The tables are rather close together but there is a nice atmosphere, and service and cover price are included, so it is good value. It tends to be frequented mostly by tourists.

La Pentola dell'Oro, 24 Via di Mezzo (**Map 4; 7**), ☎ 055 241 821. A club (membership by previous appointment; annual subscription) run by Giuseppe Alessi, a scholar of Renaissance cuisine who produces excellent traditional Tuscan dishes. This is a place in a category all of its own, with an extraordinarily imaginative menu, and a consistently high standard of cuisine. You eat downstairs in a cool cellar. The restaurant is frequented by Florentines and Italians serious about their food, but it has recently also been 'discovered' by foreign tourists. Genuine local wine. Family run, with Alessi's wife in control in the kitchen, and his son sharing the management.

Perseus, 10 Viale Don Minzoni (**Map 4;1**), ☎ 055 588226. Situated in a noisy street outside the historic centre, this is a fairly new restaurant favoured by the young with a pleasant, lively atmosphere. It serves very good meat and has tables outside in the summer.

Quattro Leoni, Via Toscanella (1 Via Vellutini; **Map 1; 7**), ☎ 055 218 562. This was once a simple, cheap *trattoria*, but it has now been livened up and serves traditional Tuscan cuisine, with good meat. Tables outside.

Trattoria del Carmine, Piazza del Carmine (**Map 5; 2**), ☎ 055 218 601. A typical Florentine *trattoria* which has existed for many years. A pleasant place to eat outside in summer. Good Tuscan food and homemade sweets. Frequented by both Italians and foreigners.

'Il Troia' (Trattoria Sostanza), 29 Via Porcellana (**Map 3; 7**), ☎ 055 212 691. Founded in 1869, this has maintained the character of a genuine Florentine *trattoria* perhaps more than any other restaurant in the city. It has sober furnishings and a marble bar at the entrance. Set in a dark narrow side street, it can sit only about 40 people in one long, narrow room with marble tables (some of which you share). Some elderly locals come here for lunch every day (and their napkins are

kept for them). It has a restrained, distinguished atmosphere, with professional service. It serves traditional Tuscan fare and is particularly famous for its T-bone steaks (*bistecca alla fiorentina*). You are expected to eat a full meal; no credit cards are accepted; the *trattoria* is closed at weekends—rules which suggest that tourists are not as welcome as they might be. It is always advisable to book in the evenings.

Alla Vecchia Bettola, 32 Viale Ariosto (**Map 5; 2**), ☎ 055 224 158. Another typical Florentine *trattoria* on the edge of the Oltrarno, although its setting is not very attractive. The food is usually adequate and you can eat outside.

Vino e Carpaccio, Via Pier Capponi 72a (**Map 4; 4**), ☎ 055 500 0896. Set outside the historic centre, this is an unusual restaurant with a very limited menu. The food is cooked by a Sardinian chef and is good—the fish is particularly fresh. As the name suggests, it also specialises in a great variety of *carpacci*. The desserts are excellent. The restaurant is lined with hundreds of wine bottles, any of which you are invited to chose (you can also try them by the glass). The only criticism is that it is a little bit over priced.

££

Antico Ristoro di' Cambi, 1 Via Sant'Onofrio (**Map 5; 2**), ☎ 055 217 134. This began as a *vinaio* in the heart of the popular district of San Frediano in the Oltrarno and it retains the atmosphere of a traditional Florentine *osteria*, always busy and with a fast turnover. It serves excellent classic Tuscan dishes, including good steak and tripe. Even though large, it can be difficult to find a place and is not somewhere you can linger over your meal; the tables can also be crowded. There are lots of tables outside in the charming little Piazza dei Tiratoio. The clientele is both Italian and foreign.

L'Assassino, 17 Via Senese (**Map 5; 8**), ☎ 055 225 877. A short way outside Porta Romana, this is a popular restaurant with plenty of room and a consistent standard of cuisine. Jewish food is served once a week.

Baldini, 96 Via il Prato (**Map 2; 6**), ☎ 055 287 663. This has been a popular place to eat for many years and the cooking is sound traditional Tuscan fare.

Baldovino, 22 Via San Giuseppe (**Map 7; 1**), ☎ 055 241 773. Run by the same Scottish man as Beccofino (see p 36), this has an international feel since numerous foreigners work here. Traditional Tuscan food and good Neapolitan pizzas (that is, the thicker variety). It also has a wine bar close by where you can just have a snack.

Benvenuto, 16 Via Mosca (**Map 1; 6,8**), ☎ 055 214 833. An established and reliable *trattoria*, with standard Tuscan cuisine.

Borgo Antico, 6 Piazza Santo Spirito (**Map 6; 3**), ☎ 055 210 437. A typical Florentine *trattoria* in one of the most attractive squares in Florence. It has tables outside in summer and is also a pizzeria.

Ciao Bella, 18 Piazza del Tiratoio (**Map 5; 2**), ☎ 055 218 477. A pizzeria owned by a Sicilian, with a German wife. Cheap and friendly but without much character. At night, when it is frequented by the young, only pizza is served; though during the day, other dishes are available.

Diladdarno, 108 Via de' Serragli (**Map 5; 4**), ☎ 055 225 001. Another pleasant traditional Florentine *trattoria*, where you usually share a table. The food is adequate and there is a small internal garden where you can eat outside during the summer.

Le Mossacce, 55 Via Proconsolo (**Map 1; 4**), ☎ 055 294 361. In a central street close to the Bargello museum, this has been open for many years, and serves good quality food of a consistently high standard at very reasonable prices.

Pandemonio, 50 Via del Leone (**Map 5; 2**), ☎ 055 224 002. A little-known restaurant with good food.

Ruggero, 89 Via Senese (**Map 5; 8**), ☎ 055 220542. A typical family-run Florentine *trattoria* of reliable standard, a little way out of the city beyond Porta Romana.

Da Sergio, 8 Piazza San Lorenzo (**Map 1; 2**), ☎ 055 281 941. Family-run *trattoria* behind the market stalls outside the church of San Lorenzo. This has been a good, simple place to eat for many years, although perhaps a little more expensive than other restaurants in this category.

Lo Skipper, 70 Via degli Alfani (**Map 4; 5**), ☎ 055 284 019. An unusual restaurant located at the end of a short arcade and so not visible from the street. It is run by a nautical club which offers free membership for a year. Every month the menu changes and follows a certain theme, such as Greek, Mexican or Italian regional food. Simple, authentic ingredients. No cover or service charge. Very good value.

Al Tranvai, 14 Piazza Tasso (**Map 5; 4**), ☎ 055 225 197. Good cheap food. The atmosphere is friendly and there are some tables outside. At lunch, the clientele is mostly local, while in the evening it comprises the young and foreigners.

£

La Casalinga, 9 Via dei Michelozzi (**Map 6; 3**), ☎ 055 218 624. One of the best simple, cheap places to eat in Florence, just out of Piazza Santo Spirito. It is run by a very friendly family, though it can be quite hectic at lunch-time when it is full of builders, foreign students and tourists.

Mario, 2 Via Rosina (**Map 1; 1**), ☎ 055 218550. Open only at lunchtime and set in a side street close to the central food market of San Lorenzo, this restaurant is always crowded with stall-holders and locals. There are a few tiny wooden tables and stools, but remarkably efficient service and traditional Tuscan food for very reasonable prices. A favourite cheap eating place in Florence, and just the answer if you need a quick, substantial meal.

Da Nerbone, inside the Mercato Centrale di San Lorenzo (**Map 3; 6**), ☎ 055 219 949. A good cheap place to eat inside the busy central food market of Florence where the stall-holders eat as well as discerning Florentines.

Pruto, 9 Piazza Tasso (**Map 5; 4**). Cheap tourist menu for lunch, although the service is slow. The fish is usually good. Tables outside in the summer.

Sabatino, 2 Via Pisana (**Map 5; 4**), ☎ 055 225 955. This became established many years ago in Borgo San Frediano as one of the most typical cheap places to eat in Florence. It has recently moved to just outside Porta San Frediano, but retains the same atmosphere and is run by an extremely friendly family. It is frequented by elderly Florentines who live near by and go there most days for lunch, as well as builders and artisans who work in the area. Well worth a visit.

Salumeria/Vini (trattoria), 27 (red) Via Ghibellina (**Map 7; 1**). This grocery shop serves good meals at lunchtime only, Monday to Friday. It has no name outside but is run by the Bigazzi family. Chickens are roasted in an open fire and traditional Florentine dishes are served to locals who live or work in the area.

Trattoria Girrarosto da Pietro (Fratelli Leonessi), 8 Piazza delle Cure (**Map 4; 2**). This is a very ordinary simple Florentine trattoria frequented by locals and market stall holders in a part of the city far away from any museums or monuments. It is not worth coming here specially, but if you happen to be in the area, it is a sound choice.

Pizzerie

Florence is not a particularly good place to eat pizza: the best place is probably *Santa Lucia*, 102 Via Ponte alle Mosse (**Map 2; 3**), ☎ 055 353 255, but it is in an area a long way for the historic centre. *Dante*, 12 Piazza N. Sauro (**Map 6; 1**), ☎ 055 293 215 and *Il Pizzaiuolo*, 113 Via dei Macci (**Map 7; 2**), ☎ 055 241 171 are both *pizzeria* in the historical centre. *Ciao Bella* and *Baldo Vino* (see above) also serve pizza.

Wine bars (Enoteche)

Pane e Vino, 70 Via San Niccolò (**Map 7; 3**), ☎ 055 247 6956. In a lovely old road close to the Arno, this has a rather unusual atmosphere. It has one of the very best selections of wine in the city and you can also eat well here (£££).

Le Barrique, 40 Via del Leone (**Map 5; 2**), ☎ 055 224 192. An excellent and extensive selection of wines, with food (££).

Fuori Porta, 10 Via Monte alle Croci (**Map 7; 5**), ☎ 055 2342483. This is located outside Porta San Miniato, with outdoor tables in a particularly pleasant and peaceful area of the city. A delightful wine bar with very fine wines which you can also order by the glass, and good simple snacks. It is considered the best wine bar in town by numerous young Florentines (£).

Vinai (£)

These are traditional Florentine wine bars which sell wine by the glass and good simple food. Many of them have closed down in the last few decades, but the few that are left are well worth seeking out, as they have a very special atmosphere and are much loved by the Florentines. The *vinaio* at no. 70 Via Alfani (**Map 4; 5**), and the one in Via della Chiesa (corner of Via delle Caldaie; **Map 6; 3**) both have seating accommodation. Others are no more than 'holes in the wall' but have excellent snacks (as well as a good selection of wines) which you eat standing on the pavement: *Cantina Ristori* (Antico No), 6 Volta di San Piero (**Map 4; 7**); *Donatello*, Via de' Neri (corner of Via de' Benci; **Map 7; 3**); *Fratellini*, 38 Via dei Cimatori (**Map 1; 5**); and the *vinaio* at no. 25 Piazza Castellani (**Map 1; 5**).

£££ Vegetarian restaurants

Il Vegetariano di Ambrosini, 30 Via delle Ruote (**Map 3; 4**), ☎ 055 475 030. This is perhaps the best vegetarian restaurant in Florence, with excellent food.

Il Sedano Allegro, 20 Borgo La Croce (**Map 7; 2**), ☎ 055 234 5505.

Gauguin, 24 Via degli Alfani (**Map 4; 5**), ☎ 055 234 0616.

£££ Non-Italian restaurants

Chinese: *Fior di Loto*, 35 Via dei Servi (**Map 4; 5**), ☎ 055 239 8235; *Il Mandarino*, 17 Via Condotta (**Map 1; 6**), ☎ 055 296 130; *Peking*, 21 Via del Melarancio (**Map 1; 1**), ☎ 055 282 922.

Indian: *India*, 43 Via Gramsci, Fiesole, ☎ 055 599 900.

Japanese: *Domani* (see above).

Jewish: *Ruth*, 2 Via Farini (kosher vegetarian) (££) (**Map 4; 8**), ☎ 055 248 0888.

Mexican: *Café Caracol*, 10 Via Ginori (**Map 3; 6**), ☎ 055 211 427.

Spanish: *Il Barone*, 123 Via Romana (**Map 6; 3**), ☎ 055 220 585.

£ Snack bars

Amon, 28 (red) Via Palazzuolo (**Map 3; 7**), open 12.00–15.00 and 18.00–23.00. Serves excellent Egyptian snacks (though no wine is served and there is no seating).

Hemingway, 9 Piazza Piattellina (**Map 6; 1**), ☎ 055 287781, open 16.30–02.00. Popular with the young, Hemingway serves a variety of snacks and drinks, and is renowned for its chocolate. It is open for brunch on Sundays (11.30–14.00). Rather over-friendly service.

Lobs, 75 Via Faenza (**Map 3; 5,6**), ☎ 055 212 478. Specialises in fish snacks.

Bar Ricchi, Piazza Santo Spirito (**Map 6; 3**). With its tables in the piazza, this is a pleasant place to have a cheap snack.

Mariano, 19 Via Parione (**Map 3; 7**). Very good snacks and a few seats.

Giuliano Centro, 74 Via dei Neri (**Map 7; 1**), ☎ 055 2382723. Another snack bar.

Ramraj, 61 red Via Ghibellina (**Map 7; 2**). A rosticceria serving Indian food (also a take away).

More elegant (and more expensive) snack bars where you can order a light meal include the *Caffè Italiano*, 56 Via della Condotta (**Map 1; 6**), ☎ 055 288 950, and *Boccadama*, 25 Piazza Santa Croce (**Map 7; 1**; recently opened with tables outside). *Procacci* in Via Tornabuoni (**Map 1; 3**), ☎ 055 211 656, is famous for its truffle sandwiches, and also has an unusual selection of cheeses.

Snack bars open late include *Du Monde*, 103 Via San Niccolò (**Map 7; 3**), ☎ 055 234 4953 and *Eskimo*, 12 Via dei Canacci (**Map 2; 4**).

At 25 Via San Gallo is Florence University students' canteen (*mensa*).

Restaurants in the environs of Florence

These are mostly in the £££ category and many have tables outside.

Fiesole and San Domenico: *Pizzeria di San Domenico*, San Domenico (☎ 055 59182).

Maiano: *La Graziella* (☎ 055 599 963), *Le Cave di Maiano* (☎ 055 59133).

Settignano: *Osvaldo* (☎ 055 603972), Ponte a Mensola; *La Capponcina*, 17 Via San Romano (☎ 055 697 037).

Bagno a Ripoli: *L'acquacheta* (£; pizza and fish, open till late; ☎ 055 696 054); *Donnini*, Via di Rimaggio (☎ 055 630 076).

Arcetri: *Omero*, 11 Via Pian de' Giullari (☎ 055 220 053).

Galluzzo: *Da Bibe*, 1 Via delle Bagnese, Ponte all'Asse (☎ 055 204 9085).

Serpiolle: *Strettoio*, 7 Via di Serpiolle (☎ 055 425 0044).

Cercina: *Trianon* and *Ricchi*, ☎ 055 402 024.

Sesto Fiorentino: *Dulcamara Club*, 2 Via Dante da Castiglione (☎ 055 4255 021).

Olmo: La Torre di Buiano (☎ 055 548 836); *Casa del Prosciutto*, 58 Via Bosconi (☎ 055 548 830), *Da Mario alla Querciola*, 428 Via Faentina (☎ 055 540 024).

Pratolino: *Villa Vecchia*, Vaglia (☎ 055 409 476).

Snacks (spuntini)

For a slice of pizza and other hot snacks go to a *rosticceria* or *tavola calda*. Some of these have no seating accommodation and sell food to take away or eat on the spot. They sometimes also sell *calzoni* (a pizza 'roll' usually filled with ham and mozzarella) and *crocchette* (minced meat or potato croquettes), grilled chicken and pasta dishes. The one at 48 Via di Sant'Antonino, off Via dell'Ariento by the San Lorenzo market, is particularly good as it serves the locals and those who work at the market. The bakery (*Forno Sartoni*) at 34 Via dei Cerchi has excellent pizzas and buns.

Friggitorie are small shops which fry snacks (sweet and savoury) on the spot and sell them over the counter to customers on the pavement. Though favoured by Florentines, many have closed down in the last few years. However, one particularly good one that is still open is *Friggitorie No. 34* at 48 Via di Sant'Antonino (next to the *rosticceria*, see above) which sells donuts (*ciambelle* and *bomboloni*), rice fritters (*frittelle di riso*), and *coccoli* (simple fritters made with water, flour, yeast and salt). It also sells pizza and *schiacciato* (flat bread topped with oil and salt). *Friggitoria Rossi*, in Via dell'Albero (between Via del Palazzuolo and Via della Scala), is also worth trying and sells *arrancini di riso* (rice balls fried in breadcrumbs, filled with butter and cheese or meat) and *polpettine di patate* (potato croquettes).

Trippai sell tripe, a Florentine speciality, in sandwiches from barrows on street corners. Good *trippai* include those in: Via dell'Ariento (corner of Via Sant'Antonino), Piazza de' Cimatori (Via Dante Alighieri), Via dei Macci (corner of Borgo la Croce), Via Gioberti, Piazza del Porcellino and outside Porta Romana.

Cafés

Cafés (bars) are open all day. Most customers choose to eat and drink standing up—you pay the cashier first, and show the receipt to the barman in order to get served. In almost all bars, if you sit at a table you are charged considerably more—at least double—and are given waiter service (you should not pay first).

Well-known cafés in the city, all of which have tables (some outside) include: *Rivoire*, Piazza Signoria; *Le Giubbe Rosse* and *Gilli*, both in Piazza della Repubblica; *Giacosa*, Via Tornabuoni; *San Firenze*, Piazza San Firenze; *Il Café*, 9 Piazza Pitti; *Cibreo*, 5 Via Andrea del Verrocchio. A café specialising in tea is *La Via del Tè*, 22 Piazza Ghiberti. In Settignano, *Caffè Desiderio*, 5 Piazza Tommaseo.

Caffelatte, 39 Via degli Alfani (near Via della Pergola), open 08.00–24.00, except Sunday, is a particularly delightful café. It is set in an old dairy with its original furniture and counter, and serves delicious organically grown vegetarian snacks made on the premises. Reasonable extra charge for table service.

Other busy cafés include *Le Colonnine*, Via dei Benci (corner of Corso Tintori), and *Caffetteria Piansa*, 18 Borgo Pinti. The *Chalet Fontana* is a pleasant, comfortable café outside the historic centre on the corner of Via San Leonardo and Viale Galileo, with a garden in the summer.

Cake shops (pasticcerie)

By far the best cake shop in Florence is *Dolci e Dolcezze*, 8 Piazza Beccaria (**Map 7; 2**), but it is certainly not cheap, and has no seating accommodation. Other cafés well known for their cakes, pastries and confectionery, include: *Rivoire*, Piazza della Signoria (famous for its chocolate); *Robiglio*, Via dei Servi and Via Tosinghi; *Giurovich*, Viale Don Minzoni; *Gambrinus*, Via Brunelleschi; *Maioli*, Via Guicciardini; *Patrizio Cosi*, 11 Borgo degli Albizi; and *Scudieri*, Via Cerretani. The *Forno Sartoni*, 34 Via dei Cerchi, sells exceptionally good simple cakes (as well as pizzas), at reasonable prices. The *Pasticceria Alcedo Falli* in Fiesole (29 Via Gramsci) also makes particularly good cakes and pastries.

Ice-cream

Some of the best ice-cream shops in Florence include: *Vivoli*, 7 Via Isola delle Stinche (near Santa Croce); *Badiani*, 20 Viale dei Mille; *Cavini*, 22 Piazza delle Cure; *Perchè no?*, 19 Via dei Tavolini; and *Veneta*, 7 Piazza Beccaria.

Outside the centre of Florence, the following ice-cream shops are particularly good: *La Fattoria di Maiano*, 3 Via Cave di Maiano, and *Villani*, 8 Piazza San Domenico (San Domenico di Fiesole).

Chocolate

Excellent chocolate in numerous different forms is sold at *Rivoire*, Piazza della Signoria. Delicious Dutch chocolate (together with other Dutch specialities) is sold at very reasonable prices at *L'Olandese Volante*, 44 Via San Gallo.

Picnics

Excellent food for picnics can be bought at delicatessens (*pizzicherie*), grocery shops (*alimentari*) and bakeries (*fornai*). Sandwiches (*panini*) are made up on request, and bakeries often sell good individual pizzas, rolls and cakes. In the autumn, many bakeries sell *schiacciata all'uva*, a delicious bready dough topped with fresh black grapes and cooked in the oven. *Pan di Ramerino* is a bun with rosemary and raisins (traditionally made during the Easter season, but now usually available all year round). *Fritelle di San Giuseppe* are fritters made with rice, eggs, milk and lemon rind; *cenci* are simpler fritters.

Some of the most pleasant spots in the city to have a picnic include: Forte di Belvedere (**Map 6; 6**; closed in 2000), the Giardino dell'Orticoltura (**Map 4; 1**), the park of Villa il Ventaglio (beyond **Map 4; 2**; closed Monday), the park of Villa Stibbert (beyond **Map 4; 2**) and the gardens off Viale Machiavelli (**Map 6; 7**). It is no longer possible to picnic in the Boboli gardens. In the environs, particularly beautiful countryside can be found near Fiesole, Maiano, Settignano and Ponte a Mensola.

Getting around

By bus

Although buses provide the best means of transport in Florence now that the city centre has been closed to private traffic, they tend to be crowded and it is usually worthwhile walking instead of waiting for a bus, especially as the centre (within the *Viali* or avenues forming a ring road around Florence) is so small. However, the small electric buses follow four interesting circular routes through the historic centre and are well worth taking once for the ride, especially if you are on your first visit to Florence. The town bus service is run by ATAF, which has an information office under the bus shelter on the east (right) side of the Stazione Santa Maria Novella (**Map 3; 5**) open daily 6.30–20.00. For information, ☎ 800 424 500 or consult the website: www.ataf.net

Tickets

Tickets can be bought at machines at some bus stops, or from tobacconists, newspaper kiosks and some bars. There are various types of ticket which vary in price: a ticket (Lire 1500) for unlimited travel on any bus for 60 minutes (a multiple ticket valid for four rides costs Lire 5800); a ticket valid for 3 hours (Lire 2500); and for 24 hours (Lire 6000). There are also tickets valid for two days (Lire 8000), three days (Lire 11,000) and seven days (Lire 19,000). There is a night ticket valid from 08.30–01.30 which costs Lire 5000. Monthly season tickets are also available, including a student ticket. All tickets have to be stamped once at automatic machines when you board the vehicle. Those found travelling without a valid ticket are liable to a fine of Lire 75,000. At night (from 21.00–06.00) you can purchase a ticket (Lire 3000) from the driver of the bus.

As in other large cities, you should always beware of **pickpockets** on buses, and it is advisable to avoid very crowded buses by waiting for the next one.

Bus routes These tend to change frequently (sometimes due to road works or restoration projects) and you should always check bus numbers at the ATAF information office. Because of one-way streets, return journeys do not always follow the same route as the outward journey. A map of the central bus routes and an up-to-date timetable (*Muoversi a Firenze*) is usually available free from the ATAF information office.

Many buses start or stop at the Stazione Santa Maria Novella, although there are two separate bus terminuses here, for different directions of travel. The one on the west (left) side of the station (Via Alemanni) serves buses which traverse the centre of Florence or the Oltrarno, and the one on the east (right) side of the station (known as the *pensilina*), where the ATAF information office is, serves buses going north away from the centre of the city. There is a separate stop for the electric minibuses A and D in the square in front of the station.

Town bus services

There are plans to replace the present noisy buses in the centre of the city with smaller electric buses. However, at present there are only four lines (A, B, C and D) served by these **small electric (or 'green' diesel) buses** which cross the historic centre of Florence (and some pedestrian zones) on circular routes. Some of them also serve car parks. They run Monday–Saturday every 10 or 15 minutes from 07.00 or 08.00 to 19.00 or 20.00 (line D also runs on Sundays), and their routes are indicated at each bus stop.

A runs from Piazza Stazione in front of the Stazione Santa Maria Novella (**Map 3; 5**) to Via Tornabuoni and then north via Piazza dei Ciompi to Piazza Beccaria car park (**Map 7; 2**).

B runs from Piazzale Vittorio Veneto at the Cascine (**Map 2; 5**) along the Arno as far as the car park of Piazza Piave (**Map 7; 4**).

C connects Piazza San Marco (**Map 4; 5**) with Sant'Ambrogio and Santa Croce and terminates on the other side of the Arno near Ponte Vecchio at the end of Via dei Bardi (**Map 6; 4**).

D runs from Piazza Stazione in front of the Stazione Santa Maria Novella (**Map 3; 5**) across Ponte Vespucci and then traverses the Oltrarno as far as Piazza Ferrucci (**Map 7; 4**).

There are numerous other frequent bus services in the centre of Florence, but the most useful ones are those that go to places of interest outside the historic centre. Some of these are listed below. All services run at frequent intervals (at least every 10 minutes, unless otherwise indicated).

Buses to places of interest outside the historic centre of Florence

4
Piazza Unità Italiana
Fortezza da Basso
Via dello Statuto
Via Vittorio Emanuele (for the **Museo Stibbert**)

6
Via Tornabuoni
Piazza San Marco
Piazza d'Azeglio
San Salvi (for the Cenacolo di Andrea del Sarto)

7 (every 20 minutes; 05.10–01.15)
Stazione Santa Maria Novella (east side)
Piazza Indipendenza
Piazza San Marco
San Domenico
Fiesole

10 (every 20 minutes; 06.00–21.00)
Stazione Santa Maria Novella (Via Valfonda)
Piazza Indipendenza
Piazza San Marco
Ponte a Mensola
Settignano

11
Piazza San Marco
Piazza Indipendenza
Piazza Stazione (Largo Alinari)
Ponte alla Carraia
Via Serragli
Porta Romana
Poggio Imperiale
The **return route** from Porta Romana to Piazza San Marco follows Via Romana, Ponte Santa Trinita, Via Tornabuoni, Piazza Duomo and Via Cavour.

12 and **13** (06.00–01.00)
A circular route from near Stazione Santa Maria Novella to Piazzale Michelangelo (also for San Miniato al Monte): the outward journey is best made on no. 12 and the return on no. 13.

12
Piazza Santa Maria Novella
Via il Prato
Ponte della Vittoria
Viale Raffaello Sanzio
Piazza Tasso
Porta Romana
Viale Machiavelli
Viale Galilei
Piazzale Michelangelo (for **San Miniato al Monte**)
Lungarno Serristori
Lungarno della Zecca Vecchia
Piazza Beccaria
Stazione Campo di Marte
Via Masaccio
Ponte Rosso
Via Nazionale
Piazza Santa Maria Novella

13
Stazione Santa Maria Novella (east side)
Ponte Rosso
Stazione Campo di Marte
Piazza Beccaria
Lungarno della Zecca Vecchia
Lungarno Serristori
Piazzale Michelangelo
Viale Galileo
Viale Machiavelli
Porta Romana
Piazza Tasso
Ponte della Vittoria
Porta al Prato
Stazione Santa Maria Novella

14C
Via de' Martelli (just out of Piazza Duomo)
Stazione Santa Maria Novella (east side)
Viale Morgagni
Careggi (for the **Villa di Careggi**; penultimate stop)

17 (operates 05.30–01.15)
Stazione Santa Maria Novella (west side)
Via Martelli
Via Cavour
Piazza San Marco
Via La Marmora
Viale dei Mille
Salviatino (**Youth Hostel**)

25 (every 20 minutes)
Piazza Stazione (east side)
Piazza Indipendenza
Piazza San Marco
Piazza Libertà
Via Bolognese
(25A continues to **Pratolino**)

28
Stazione Santa Maria Novella (east side)
Via Reginaldo Giuliani
Stazione Rifredi
Via Sestese
Castello (the second 'Castello' stop for
Villa della Petraia, and the last

'Castello' stop for the **Villa di Castello**)
Sesto Fiorentino

31 and 32 (every 20 minutes)
Stazione Santa Maria Novella (east side)
Piazza San Marco
Via della Colonna
Ponte da Verrazzano
Badia a Ripoli
Ponte a Ema
Grassina or Antella

37 (every 20 minutes)
Piazza Santa Maria Novella
Ponte alla Carraia
Porta Romana
Galluzzo
Certosa di Galluzzo

38 (infrequent service, but operates if pre booked, ☎ 800 019 794)
Porta Romana
Largo Fermi
Pian dei Giullari

For **Amerigo Vespucci Florence airport** take the **SITA/Ataf** shuttle bus from the SITA bus station next to the Stazione Santa Maria Novella. Departing every 30 minutes the journey takes about 20 minutes.

On Sundays a **small electric bus** traverses the park of the **Cascine** from Piazza Vittorio Veneto (every 10–15 minutes;10.00–18.00).

Buses accessible to the disabled
Facilities for wheelchairs are usually available on bus nos 7, 12 and 13 and D. **Line 99** is a special service reserved for the disabled which can be booked, ☎ 055 565 0443.

By coach
From Florence a wide network of bus services in Tuscany is operated by Lazzi, 4 Piazza Stazione (☎ 055 351 061), SITA, 15 Via Santa Caterina da Siena (☎ 800 373 760 or 055 214 721), COPIT and CAP, 9 Largo Alinari (☎ 055 214 637). Details of the main services are given on pp 63–64.

By car
The centre of Florence is closed to private cars (except for those belonging to residents) from Monday–Saturday, 08.30–18.30 (and also usually at night in summer), except on holidays. The limited traffic zone (ZTL) includes virtually all the area within the Viali and the Oltrarno. There are expensive **fines** for cars found

within this area without authorisation and they are sometimes towed away. **Access** is allowed to hotels within the limited traffic zone, but cars can only be parked outside hotels for a maximum of one hour (and must display a card supplied by the hotel). Access is also allowed for disabled drivers (and well-signposted parking places are reserved for them in a number of streets). On certain Sundays of the year, the whole of Florence is closed to traffic (10.00–18.30) in an attempt to combat pollution. However, visitors arriving in Florence on those days are sometimes allowed access, for information ☎ 800 831 133.

Parking This has become increasingly difficult and new car parks are still mostly at the planning stage. There are very few large car parks with long-term parking near the centre of the city. The car park at the **Fortezza da Basso** (**Map 3**; **3**) is open 24 hours (Lire 2000 an hour). The large underground car parks beneath **Piazza Stazione** (**Map 3**; **5**) and the **Parterre** (north of Piazza della Libertà; **Map 4**; **1**) are also both open 24 hours (Lire 2000–3000 an hour; special rates at the Parterre car park for the day if you are staying in a hotel). For bicycle hire from these car parks and elsewhere in Florence, see below.There is a large car park along the inside of the walls between Porta Romana and Piazza Tasso (entered from **Piazza della Calza**; **Map 5**; **4**, **6**). This costs Lire 2000 an hour for the first two hours, then Lire 3000 an hour (Lire 18,000 for 24 hours). The car park beneath the **Mercato Centrale** (San Lorenzo; **Map 3**; **6**) is open weekdays 07.00–14.00, Saturdays and days preceding national holidays, 07.00–20.30, and is used by shoppers at the central market—the tariff is prohibitively expensive after the first 1.5 hours. The car park near the market of **Sant'Ambrogio** (**Map 7**; **2**), open 08.00–20.00, is used by shoppers in the morning (cheap rate limited to 1.5 hours), but is a bit cheaper in the afternoons. **Smaller car parks** open 08.00–20.00 except *fest.* have an hourly tariff of Lire 2000–3000: these include **Piazza di Porta Romana** (**Map 5**; **6**), **Piazza Beccaria** (**Map 7**; **2**) and **Lungarno della Zecca Vecchia** (**Map 7**; **4**). The car park at **Amerigo Vespucci airport** of Florence is open 24 hours and costs Lire 1500 an hour (Lire 12,000 for 24 hours).

The car parks are run by *SCAF*, ☎ 055 363 362 and *Firenze Parcheggi*, ☎ 055 499 159 or 055 272 011 (email: info@firenzeparcheggi.it). Students studying in Florence are entitled to half-price monthly rates at the Parterre and Piazza della Calza car parks.

A number of streets and *piazze*, and some of the *Viali* (the avenues forming a ring road around the centre of Florence) also now have parking metres (Lire 1500 or Lire 2000 an hour for a maximum of 2 hours), operational from 08.00 to 20.00. Florence also has a number of **garages** (Via Nazionale, Via Ghibellina, Borgo Ognissanti, and in some hotels).

It is best to leave your car well outside the Viali and use buses to reach the centre of the city. Areas which usually have ample parking space are around the Stadium (Campo di Marte) and at Bellariva along the Arno (upstream, near the headquarters of the RAI). However, even outside the ZTL some streets are reserved for residents (look out for the red and blue 'no parking' signs). In all areas of the city, cars have to be removed once every two weeks when the streets are cleaned overnight (otherwise they are towed away). The cleaning day is usually indicated by temporary signs put up the night before, but it is always best to ask locally about this. It is forbidden to park at all times outside a Passo Carrabile (indicated by a red and blue sign on a private entrance for cars or a private garage).

If your car is towed away, it will probably be taken to 16 Via Circondaria, Rifredi (☎ 055 308 249), where it can be retrieved after the payment of a heavy fine (be sure to keep with you the number of your car licence plate in order to be able to identify your vehicle). The local municipal police (Vigili Urbani, ☎ 055 212 290) who wear blue uniform in winter and light blue during the summer, and helmets similar to London policemen, are usually helpful. Always lock your car when parked, and never leave anything of value inside it. When driving in Florence, pay particular attention to motorbikes, mopeds and Vespas, which seem to consider that they always have the right of way.

Accidents In the event of an accident, the **traffic police** can be called on ☎ 055 577 777. The headquarters of the *Automobile Club d'Italia* (ACI) is at 36 Viale Amendola; for emergency breakdown service, dial 116 (in Florence, ☎ 055 524 861).

Car hire The principal car-hire firms (which include Maggiore, Hertz and Avis) have offices at Pisa and Florence airports as well as in the centre of Florence.

Road conditions For information call: ☎ 06 4212.

By bicycle

The Comune of Florence rents bicycles for the day for Lire 3000 throughout the year (08.15–19.30 except Sundays and holidays) from the car parks at the Fortezza da Basso, the Parterre (Piazza della Libertà), Piazza Vittorio Veneto, Piazza del Cestello, Piazza Torquato Tasso, the Mercato Centrale, Viale Matteotti, Piazza Beccaria, Piazza Piave, Piazza Poggi and the bike stands in Via della Ninna, Piazza Strozzi and Piazza della Stazione. The service is suspended from 1–15 January and 6–27 August. You have to leave a valid document and return the bike before 19.30 to the place from which you hired it. For Lire 25,000 you can have a season ticket for the whole year, and can pick up and leave the bike at any of the above parks. For further information, contact *Firenze Parcheggi* at the Parterre car park (Piazza della Libertà), ☎ 055 500 0453 or 055 500 2994.

There are also private bike-hire firms which have mountain bikes, including *Alinari*, 85 Via Guelfa, ☎ 055 280 500 and *Florence by Bike*, 120 Via San Zanobi, ☎ 055 488 992.

By taxi

Taxis (painted white) are provided with taximeters. The fare includes service, so tipping is not necessary. They are hired from ranks or by telephone: there are no cruising taxis. There are ranks at the Stazione Santa Maria Novella, Piazza Santa Maria Novella, Piazza San Marco, Piazza Santa Trìnita, Piazza del Duomo, Piazza della Signoria, Piazza della Repubblica, Porta Romana, and elsewhere. For Radio taxis ☎ 055 4390, 055 4798, or 055 4242. A supplement is charged for night service and luggage.

Twelve **horse-drawn cabs** survive in the city for the use of tourists (in 1869 there were 518). From Easter to early October they can be hired in Piazza Duomo or Piazza della Signoria, and you should agree the fare before starting the journey.

Language

Although many people speak a little English, some basic Italian is helpful for everyday dealings. If you are able to say a few words and phrases your efforts will be much appreciated. See Food and wine section for relevant vocabulary.

good morning *buon giorno*
good afternoon/good evening *buona sera*
good night *buona notte*
goodbye *arrivederci*
hello/goodbye (informal) *ciao*
see you later *a più tardi*

yes/no *sì/no*
okay *va bene*
please/thank you *per favore/grazie*

today *oggi*
tomorrow *domani*
yesterday *ieri*
now *adesso*
later *più tardi*
in the morning *di mattina*
in the afternoon/evening *di pomeriggio/di sera*
at night *di notte*

Monday *lunedì*
Tuesday *martedì*
Wednesday *mercoledì*
Thursday *giovedì*
Friday *venerdì*
Saturday *sabato*
Sunday *domenica*

spring *primavera*
summer *estate*
autumn *autunno*
winter *inverno*

January *gennaio*
February *febbraio*
March *marzo*

April *aprile*
May *maggio*
June *giugno*
July *luglio*
August *agosto*
September *settembre*
October *ottobre*
November *novembre*
December *dicembre*

what is your name? *come si chiama/come ti chiami?* (informal)
my name is ... *mi chiamo ...*

I would like *vorrei*
do you have ...? *ha ...?/avete ...?* (plural)

where is ...? *dov'è ...?*
what time is it? *che ore sono?*
at what time? *a che ora?*
when? *quando?*

how much is it? *quanto è?*
the bill *il conto*
where are the toilets? *dove sono i gabinetti?*

do you speak English? *parla inglese?*
I don't understand *non capisco*

cold/hot *freddo/caldo*
with/without *con/senza*
open/closed *aperto/chiuso*
cheap/expensive *economico/caro*

left/right/straight on *sinistra/destra/diritto*

Museums, galleries and monuments

Hours of admission to museums, galleries and monuments in Florence are given in individual entries in the Guide. **Opening times** vary and often change without warning; those given should therefore be accepted with reserve. An up-to-date list of opening times is always available at the APT offices, but even this can be inaccurate. To make certain the times are correct, it is worth telephoning first. It is likely that the opening hours for state-owned museums and galleries will be modified over the next few years and more and more museums will introduce longer opening hours. Most of them now open at 08.30 and close at 13.50, but the Uffizi, Galleria Palatina (Palazzo Pitti) and the Galleria dell'Accademia now stay open all day until 18.50 (19.00 on Sunday). These three are closed on Mondays, but some of the other important state museums in Florence are, open on two or three Mondays of the month, and closed on two or three Sundays of the month, so you should check carefully before planning a visit. Ticket offices close half an hour (45 minutes at the Uffizi) before closing time. The Uffizi and the Galleria dell'Accademia are also usually open on Thursday, Friday and Saturday evenings (20.30–23.30) from the end of June to early September.

Sometimes state museums are closed on the main public holidays: 1 January, Easter Day, 25 April, 1 May, 15 August and Christmas Day, but at Easter and Christmas they now usually have special opening times; for up-to-date information, ask at the APT. On other holidays (see below) they open only in the morning (08.30–13.50). The opening hours for holidays (*fest.*, *giorni festivi*) apply also to Sundays.

There is now an excellent **telephone booking service** for the state museums of Florence (☎ 055 294 883) which, for a small extra charge of Lire 2000, allows you to enter at a specific time without having to queue (you collect and pay for the ticket at the museum just before the booked time of entrance).

Entrance charges have been given in the text, since it has become much more expensive to visit museums in Italy in the last few years. Entrance is free if no price is indicated. EU citizens under the age of 18 or over the age of 65 are entitled to free admission to state-owned museums and monuments (marked 'S'), and EU students between the ages of 18 and 26 are entitled to a reduction (usually 50 per cent). There is a cumulative ticket for the museums in Palazzo Pitti, see p 158, and a cumulative ticket (Lire 20,000) for the Galleria dell'Accademia, Cappelle Medicee and Museo del Bargello. State museums are free during Museum Week (see below). A *carnet* can be purchased for Lire 10,000 for the museums owned by the Comune of Florence (marked 'C') which allows a 50 per cent reduction on the entrance fee.

The Comune (Assessorato alla Cultura, 30 Via Ghibellina, ☎ 055 262 5945), with the help of the Amici dei Musei Fiorentini, organises the **special opening** of numerous museums, palaces, churches, oratories, cloisters and gardens normally closed to the public at certain times of the year. This project usually includes evening admission (from about 09.00–23.00) from July to September to a number of museums and palaces. Gardens are often specially opened in October. Information is given in the local press (and at the APT and Comune information offices). Information about state-owned museums (marked 'S' in the text) is available from the Soprintendenza per i Beni Artistici e Storici, 5 Via della Ninna (☎ 055 238 85).

The Associazione Dimore Storiche Italiane and the Fondo per l'Ambiente Italiano (FAI) in conjunction with the Region of Tuscany also sometimes arrange for a number of monuments and courtyards to be opened on certain days of the year, for information ☎ 055 2740 447.

Museum Week (*La Settimana dei Musei Italiani*) has now become established as an annual event (traditionally in late November or early December but for the last few years in March). Entrance to most state-owned museums is free during the week, and some have longer opening hours, while private collections may be specially opened.

For a week, usually in late spring, the numerous important **scientific institutes** in the city are opened to the public and special exhibitions, lectures and tours held (a week known as the *Settimana della Cultura Scientifica*).

There are a number of organisations for safeguarding and restoring monuments in Florence, which arrange visits and lectures throughout the year. The following have an annual membership subscription: Amici dei Musei Fiorentini, 39 Via Alfani; Associazione Dimore Storiche Italiane, 17 Borgo Santi Apostoli (☎ 055 212 452); Fondo per l'Ambiente Italiano (FAI), 18 Borgo San Frediano (☎ 055 214 595); Amici di Palazzo Pitti, Palazzo Pitti (☎ 055 222 320). The regional headquarters of Italia Nostra is at 9 Viale Gramsci.

Churches and church ceremonies

The opening times of churches vary a great deal but the majority are open from 07.00–12.00. In the afternoons many remain closed until 15.00, 16.00 or even 17.00, and close again at about 18.00; some do not reopen at all in the afternoon. A few churches open for services only. The opening times of the major churches in Florence have been given in the text. Closed chapels and crypts are sometimes unlocked on request by the sacristan. Many pictures and frescoes are difficult to see without lights which are often coin operated (100 lire or 500 lire coins). A torch and a pair of binoculars are especially useful to study fresco cycles. Most churches now ask that sightseers do not enter during a service. If you are wearing shorts or have bare shoulders you can be stopped from entering some churches. Churches in Florence are very often not orientated. In the text the terms north and south refer to the liturgical north (left) and south (right), taking the high altar as the east end.

Roman Catholic services On Sunday and, in the principal churches, often on weekdays, Mass is celebrated up to 12.00 and from 18.00 until 19.00 in the evening. Confessions are heard in English on Sunday at the Duomo, San Lorenzo, San Marco, Santa Trìnita, Santa Croce, Orsanmichele, and San Miniato al Monte.

Church festivals On Saints' days, Mass and vespers with music are celebrated in the churches dedicated to the saints concerned. On the feast of the patron Saint of Florence, San Giovanni (24 June), a local holiday and special services are held. On Easter Day the *Scoppio del Carro* is held in and around the Duomo (see below).

Non-Catholic churches and places of worship

Anglican: St Mark's, 16 Via Maggio.
American Episcopalian: St James, 9 Via Bernardo Rucellai.
Lutheran: 11 Lungarno Torrigiani.

Waldensian: 26 Via Micheli.
Greek Orthodox: 76 Viale Mattioli.
Russian Orthodox: 8 Via Leone X.
Jewish Synagogue: 4 Via Farini.

Parks and gardens

The following gardens and parks are all described in the text (with their opening times). Many are of the greatest botanical interest and also contain superb fountains and sculptural masterpieces. The most beautiful garden in Florence is the huge Boboli Garden, open regularly to the public. The botanical gardens are also of great interest. Just outside the centre of Florence are the famous Medici gardens at the Villa di Castello and the Villa La Petraia.

Parks Public parks open daily in Florence include the huge Cascine, Villa il Ventaglio, Villa Fabbricotti, Villa Stibbert and Villa Strozzi. The lovely park of Villa Demidoff at Pratolino outside Florence is open from March to October on certain days of the week in summer only.

There is a rose garden on Via di San Salvatore al Monte (entrance at 2 Viale Poggi) open from May to mid-June, and a particularly beautiful iris garden open in May below Piazzale Michelangelo. In the horticultural gardens, the splendid 19C greenhouse was restored in 2000. There are also shady gardens on either side of Viale Machiavelli.

Private gardens Those in the centre of Florence include Palazzo Corsini sul Prato which is now open on weekdays. Other gardens opened specially on a few days of the year include the Giardino della Gherardesca, Giardino Torrigiani, Giardino Corsi, the Orti Oricellari and the garden of Palazzo Vivarelli Colonna, for information, contact the Comune, ☎ 055 262 5945.

Two famous historic private gardens near Florence are at Villa Gamberaia (Settignano), which is open on weekdays, and Villa Medici (below Fiesole), open on weekdays by appointment.

Three beautiful gardens now owned and carefully maintained by American universities are at Villa I Tatti (Harvard University), shown to visitors only with a letter of presentation and by previous appointment; Villa La Pietra (New York University), which is being replanted, but which will probably be reopened to the public by appointment; and Villa Le Balze (Georgetown University), which can also sometimes be seen by previous appointment.

Other beautiful privately owned gardens on the outskirts of the city—only accessible with special permission—include Villa Capponi (Arcetri) and, near Fiesole, Villa Palmieri. Villa Schifanoia at San Domenico di Fiesole is now used by the Istituto Universitario Europeo. A little further away are the gardens of Villa Corsi Salviati (Sesto Fiorentino) and Villa I Collazzi (Galluzzo).

A number of private gardens in Fiesole are generally opened specially and shown on guided tours by the Comune in spring and autumn by appointment. In the last few years these have included Villa Le Balze, Villa Medici, Villa Riposo dei Vescovi, Villa al Bosco di Fontelucente, Villa di Maiano, Villa Il Roseto, Villa La

Torraccia, Castello di Vincigliata and Castel di Poggio. The Comune of Florence also sometimes organises tours of gardens in October.

The splendid gardens of Tuscany are described in *Blue Guide Tuscany*.

Flower markets Flowers and plants are sold at the daily morning market of Sant'Ambrogio, and every Thursday morning there is a flower and plant market beneath the arcades in Piazza della Repubblica. An annual exhibition of plants is held at the end of April or beginning of May for a few days at the Giardino dell'Orticoltura.

 ## Festivals

Scoppio del Carro Held on **Easter Day**, this is the most famous traditional religious festival in Florence and has taken place for centuries. It is held in and around the Duomo at 11.00. An ungainly, tall wooden carriage known as the *Brindellone* (which dates from 1764; restored after the flood in 1966), covered with fireworks, leaves its huge garage on Il Prato around 09.00 and is drawn by two pairs of white oxen (dressed for the occasion) through the streets of Florence to the main door of the Duomo, accompanied by a procession and band. Inside the cathedral, a 'dove' (nowadays nothing less than a rocket) is lit by the archbishop at the high altar and sent along a wire through the cathedral to ignite the bonfire of fireworks on the carriage (after which it returns to the high altar). The great dramatic explosion, which lasts several minutes, is accompanied by the ringing of the cathedral bells. The origin of this festival appears to go back to the Florentine capture of a war carriage from Fiesole in 1152. Later, richly decorated triumphal carts were constructed to convey the holy symbol of fire through the streets on religious festivals. Formerly, the mechanism of the 'dove' was less sophisticated and was sometimes not successful; if it failed to ignite the carriage it augured a poor harvest.

St John's Day St John (San Giovanni) is the patron saint of Florence. St John's Day is 24 June, a local holiday celebrated with fireworks at Piazzale Michelangelo at 22.00.

Calcio Storico Fiorentino This is a 'football' game in 16C costume (Calcio in costume or *Calcio Storico Fiorentino*); it is held in three heats during the latter part of June (one game always takes place on 24 June) usually in Piazza Santa Croce. The teams represent the four *quartiere* of the city: Santa Croce (*azzurri*; blue); Santa Maria Novella (*rossi*; red); Santo Spirito (*bianchi*; white); and San Giovanni (*verdi*; green). Tickets are sold at Box Office, see p 57, or can be purchased a few days before the game at the Chiosco degli Sportivi near the arcades beside the post office in Via Pellicceria. The more expensive tickets are for numbered places; the team supporters (sometimes rowdy) choose the cheaper seats on the stands at the two short ends of the piazza. There are no seats in the shade.

At about 17.30, there is an exhibition of flag throwing and then a long procession in period costume through the centre of Florence enters the arena accompanied by drummers and led by the gonfalons (standard bearers) of the city. The various historic figures, bands, representatives and players of the four districts (who throw flowers to their supporters) are announced as they enter the arena. Some figures are mounted and a bullock (once the prize for the winning team) traditionally takes part in the ceremony. It takes about 40 minutes for the whole procession to enter the piazza and after *la grida* and the presentation of arms everyone except the players runs out of the arena. The 27 players of each team are presented by name and a cannon shot signals the start of the game. During the game, which is played with few rules and considerable violence, a *caccia* or goal (when the ball is sent into the low net along one of the short sides) is announced by two cannon shots fired from the steps of Santa Croce.

Festa della Rificolona On 7 September, the eve of the Birth of the Virgin, the Festa della Rificolona is celebrated by children carrying colourful paper lanterns through the streets (especially in Piazza Santissima Annunziata). Some children now carry pea-shooters with which they try to destroy the lanterns. The name is a corruption of *fierucolone*, the name the Florentines gave the peasant women from the surrounding countryside who came to Florence carrying lanterns for the ancient traditional festival to honour the Virgin at Santissima Annunziata.

On the weekend preceding 7 September, the **Fierucola del Pane**, a market of organically grown food, and natural products is held in Piazza Santissima Annunziata.

On 25 March, the **festival of the Annunziata**, another fair is held in Piazza Santissima Annunziata when homemade sweet biscuits are sold from the stalls. A **Fierucola del Pane** is also held here on 8 December. The **Festa del Grillo**, on Ascension Day (in May), is a large fair in the Cascine where crickets were traditionally sold in little cages: since 1999 this has no longer been allowed but the fair still takes place and is a lively event for children.

For the **Festa di San Romolo** on 6 July in Fiesole, see p 335.

Shops and markets

Clothes   The smartest fashion shops in Florence are in Via Tornabuoni and Via della Vigna Nuova. There are other elegant clothes shops in Via Calzaioli, Via Strozzi, Via Calimara, Via Roma, Via Guicciardini, Lungarno Acciaioli and Lungarno Corsini. Well-made leather shoes at reasonable prices are sold in numerous shops in the centre of Florence. *Gucci* and *Ferragamo*, both in Via Tornabuoni, are famous for their shoes. Less expensive but good quality shoes are sold at *Cresti* (several branches). Clothes for the young, apart from the excellent outdoor markets (see below), can be found in various shopping streets such as Borgo San Lorenzo and Via del Corso. Italy has notably few department stores: the best known in Florence are *La Rinascente*, Piazza della Repubblica and *Coin*, Via dei Calzaioli. There are several branches of the chain department stores called *Standa*, *Upim* and *Oviesse* in Florence. Silk ties and scarves are sold in many shops and in the markets at reasonable prices. An old-established shop specialising in smart childrens' clothes is *Anichini* at 59 Via del Parione.

Leather Florence is well known for its leather goods (handbags, purses, belts and jackets) which are sold in the open-air markets of San Lorenzo and the Porcellino, and from the stalls in Via dei Gondi and Lungarno Archibusieri. There are also numerous shops specialising in leather (including Grazia Gori, 64 Via Faenza). The large leather 'factories' in the district of Santa Croce cater mostly for tour groups and their guides. *Gucci* and *Ferragamo*, both in Via Tornabuoni, are famous for their fashion handbags.

Stationery Another speciality of Florence is its fine marbled paper, used to decorate stationery such as albums, boxes and picture frames. The best known shop is *Giulio Giannini*, 37 Piazza Pitti. Other shops include *Il Papiro* (several branches, including 24 Piazza Duomo, 13 Via dei Tavolini and 55 Via Cavour), *Il Torchio*, 17 Via dei Bardi. A less well-known shop which has excellent handmade products made on the spot by a family of artisans (also to order) is *Lo Scrittoio*, 126 Via Nazionale. Another artisan, *Carlo Saitta* has his workshop at 28 Via dell'Agnolo. Simple Florentine paper products are also sold in stationers' shops and in the open-air markets. A well-known stationery shop is *Pineider* (13 Piazza della Signoria and 76 Via Tornabuoni).

Jewellery This is another speciality of Florentine craftsmen: the shops on Ponte Vecchio and its immediate vicinity have superb displays. Some of these specialise in pearls, silver, gold or semi-precious stones. Artisans who repair jewellery (or make it to order) have their workshops in the *Casa dell'Orafo* close by.

Ceramics Italian pottery is sold at *Sbigoli*, 4 Via Sant'Egidio. The shop called *Ceramica Artistica Migliori*, 39 Via dei Benci makes good copies of classic Italian majolica. *Andreini*, 63 Bargo degli Albizi also sells majolica. Shops specialising in kitchenware, ceramics and glass include *La Ménagère*, 8 Via dei Ginori, and *Bartolini*, 24 Via dei Servi. Simple traditional pottery at reasonable prices and good kitchenware is sometimes sold in hardware stores, including *Mazzanti* (101 Borgo La Croce). *Richard Ginori* ceramics are sold at 17 Via dei Rondinelli (although much cheaper seconds can be found in Sesto Fiorentino, at the warehouse next to the Doccia porcelain museum).

Fabrics Fabrics can be found at the *Arte della Seta*, 45 Via dei Fossi. Exquisite hand-woven silk is made and sold at the *Antico Setificio Fiorentino*, 4 Via Lorenzo Bartolini (near Porta San Frediano, see p 300). *Lisa Corti Home Textile Emporium*, 58 Via de' Bardi, is a delightful little shop at the foot of Ponte Vecchio which sells lovely and unusual fabrics (including velvet, organza and muslin) for home furnishings as well as clothes and accessories all from exclusive designs by Lisa Corti.

Lace and embroidery These are sold at *Loretta Caponi*, 4 Piazza Antinori, *Cirri* in Via Por Santa Maria and numerous other shops, as well as in the open-air markets.

Hats Hats can be bought from *Borsalino*, 40 Via Porta Rossa, and models for hats at *Bini*, 5 Piazza Santo Spirito. Lovely **straw hats** can still be found on some stalls at San Lorenzo market. Other articles in **straw** (including baskets) are sold at *Martini*, 6 Via Santa Verdiana (near the market of Sant'Ambrogio).

Knives Good places to buy knives are the *Coltelleria Bianda*, 86 Via della Vigna Nuova and the *Antica Coltelleria Fiorentina*, 63 Via dei Neri.

Soap and perfume Very fine soap and perfumes are made at the *Farmacia di Santa Maria Novella*, 16 Via della Scala, as well as at numerous *erboristerie* in the town (including *Palazzo Vecchio, Dott. Di Massimo*, 9 Via Vacchereccia).

Haberdashery A well-known haberdashery store is the *Passamaneria Toscana*, at 12 Piazza San Lorenzo, and Via della Vigna Nuova.

Antique shops There are numerous antique shops in Via Maggio and the small streets leading to Piazza Pitti, as well as in Via dei Fossi, and Borgo San Jacopo.

Bookshops Shops specialising in English books include: *Paperback Exchange*, 31 Via Fiesolana; *BM Bookshop*, 4 Borgo Ognissanti; and *After Dark*, 47 Via Ginori. The bookshop at 41 Borgo degli Albizi called *Il Viaggio* has a wide selection of travel books, guides and maps. The largest bookshops in Florence (which also stock English books) include *Marzocco*, 22 Via de' Martelli; *Seeber*, 70 Via Tornabuoni; *Feltrinelli*, 30 Via de' Cerretani; and *Feltrinelli International*, 12 Via Cavour. Bookshops specialising in **art history** include: *Salimbeni*, 14 Via Palmieri; *'SP 44'*, 44 Via del Tosinghi; and *Art & Libri*, 32 Via dei Fossi.

Artists' materials Shops selling artist's materials include: *Rigacci*, 51 Via dei Servi; *Leoncini*, Via Ricasoli; and *Zecchi*, 19 Via dello Studio.

An old-fashioned shop specialising in **British products**, beloved by nostalgic Florentines, is the *Old England Stores*, 28 Via dei Vecchietti. A great variety of **teas and herbal infusions** are sold at *Peter's Tea House* at 12 Piazza degli Strozzi. **Toys** are sold at the *Cooperativa dei Ragazzi*, 27 Via San Gallo. For **camping equipment**, *Alessandro Sieni*, 71 Via dell'Ariento.

Markets

The main **food market** in Florence is the **Mercato Centrale**, also known as the **Mercato di San Lorenzo**. It is located in a covered market building near the church (Map 3; 6; open Monday–Saturday, 07.00–13.00; also 16.30–19.30 on Saturday except in July and August); **Sant'Ambrogio** is another good produce market near the church of the same name (Map 7; 2; open mornings only), where butchers and grocers have their shops in a market building, and fruit and vegetables are sold from stalls outside. Food supermarkets in the centre of Florence include *Standa* in Via Pietrapiana (also open on Sundays and most holidays).

Open-air general markets The biggest general market in Florence is in the **streets near San Lorenzo** where stalls sell clothing, leatherwork, cheap jewellery and shoes (generally of good quality and cheap in price) throughout the day every day (except Sunday and Monday from mid-November to mid-December, and in January and February). Another similar general market (straw, leather and lace) is the *Porcellino* (or 'Straw Market') open at the same times. There are also stalls in **Via dei Gondi** and **Lungarno Archibusieri** which sell similar goods at the same times as the markets mentioned above. At **Sant'Ambrogio** there is also a general market (new and second-hand clothing, hardware, household linens, shoes) open in the mornings (except Sunday). A very large general market is held every Tuesday morning at **Le Cascine**, where numerous bargains can be found.

The **Mercatino delle Pulci** or flea market (antiques and junk) is open weekdays in Piazza dei Ciompi. On the last Sunday of every month an antique and junk market is held in and around this piazza.

A market (*Fierucola*) of **organic food and hand-made products** is held every third Sunday of the month in Piazza Santo Spirito. On the second Sunday of the month, a market of **artisans' work** is held in Piazza Santo Spirito. **Artigianato e Palazzo** is an annual festival of handmade artisans' wares held for three days in late May or early June in the beautiful garden of Palazzo Corsini sul Prato (entrance at 115 Via della Scala).

 # Entertainment

Listings information

Concerts, theatre performances and exhibitions are organised throughout the year and are advertised in the local press and on posters. They are listed in *Firenze Spettacolo* which is published every month and sold at newsagents—a few pages of the main events are in English. Information can also be found at: www.firenzespettacolo.it

An up-to-date list of exhibitions is printed about every fortnight by the APT, and monthly leaflets called *Informacittà* give news of current events (there is also a website: www.informacitta.net).

Tickets for many concerts and plays are sold at *Box Office*, 39 Via Alemanni (**Map 2; 4,6**), ☎ 055 210 804, and 8 Chiasso de' Soldanieri (**Map 1; 5**), just out of Piazza Santa Trinita, off Via Porta Rossa, ☎ 055 219 402. It is often possible to buy them at the theatre on the evening of the performance.

Theatres

La Pergola, 12 Via della Pergola (**Map 4; 7**), ☎ 055 247 9651, is used for drama and chamber music throughout the year.

Puccini, Piazza Puccini (**Map beyond 2; 1**), ☎ 055 362 067.

Teatro di Rifredi, 303 Via Vittorio Emanuele (**Map beyond 3; 2**), ☎ 055 422 0361.

Teatro Tenda, Lungarno Aldo Moro (**Map beyond 7; 4**).

Teatro Verdi, 101 Via Ghibellina (**Map 7; 1**), ☎ 055 212 320.

The *Teatro Comunale Metastasio* in Prato (☎ 0574 608 501) has a renowned theatre season October–April (tickets also available in Florence) and a music festival October–December.

Films Foreign films shown in Italy are almost always dubbed. **Films in English** are shown every evening (except Monday) at the little *Cinema Astro*, Piazza San Simone. Every Monday, films in their original language are shown at the *Odeon*, Piazza Strozzi. All cinemas offer a substantial discount on Wednesdays. The **Festival dei Popoli** is an extremely interesting Film Festival of documentary films from all over the world. It is held every year for about a week in November–December, usually in the Cinema Alfieri Atelier, 6 Via dell'Ulivo and the Auditorium Regione Toscana, 4 Via Cavour (for information, ☎ 055 294 353). In October/November an important French film festival, **France Cinéma**, is organised by the French Institute.

In summer, films are shown in the open-air at Forte di Belvedere (temporarily closed), Palazzo dei Congressi, the Roman Theatre in Fiesole, at Poggetto and the Palasport at Campo di Marte.

Spazio Uno, 10 Via del Sole, is a cinema club and *Mediateca Regionale Toscana*, 4 Via dei Pucci, has a large film library.

Music *Teatro Comunale* (Map 2; 6,8), 16 Corso Italia, for symphony concerts and opera, and the *Maggio Musicale*, an annual music festival (May–July). The Ridotto of the Teatro Comunale has a smaller auditorium. Other concerts are held in the little *Teatro Goldoni* (Map 5; 4), Via S. Maria. Excellent chamber music concerts given by famous musicians from all over the world are organised by the *Amici della Musica* January–April and October–December at the Pergola Theatre. The *Orchestra Regionale Toscana* hold concerts regularly at the Teatro Verdi, and the *Orchestra da Camera Fiorentina* hold chamber music concerts (usually at Orsanmichele).

Interesting concerts are also held at the *Accademia Bartolomeo Cristofori* (Amici del Fortepiano), 7 Via Camaldoli. The *Scuola di Musica di Fiesole* give concerts at 24 Via delle Fontanelle, San Domenico di Fiesole. Occasional concerts are also given in churches (including San Lorenzo, Santa Croce and San Felice), and in some oratories (including the Oratorio dei Vanchetoni). Concerts are often held in the courtyard of Palazzo Pitti and in the Giardino Botanico Superiore in the Boboli gardens in summer (by members of the *Maggio Musicale orchestra*, for information, ☎ 055 290 838).

Florence has a number of historic organs (recently restored) including those in the churches of Santissima Annunziata, San Niccolò sopr'Arno, the Badia Fiorentina and San Giorgio alla Costa. Organ concerts are often held in winter.

The Estate Fiesolana is an annual festival of music, drama, and films held from the end of June to the end of August in Fiesole.

Exhibitions These are held in the Forte di Belvedere (temporarily closed), Palazzo Pitti (Sala Bianca), Palazzo Medici-Riccardi, Palazzo Vecchio, Palazzo Corsini, the Accademia di Belle Arti (Piazza San Marco), the Museo Marino Marini, the ex Stazione Leopolda (Viale Fratelli Rosselli at Porta al Prato). The material owned by the Biblioteca Laurenziana and the Gabinetto Disegni e Stampe degli Uffizi is mounted in regular exhibitions of great interest.

An antiques fair, the **Mostra Mercato Internazionale dell' Antiquariato**, is held biennially (next in 2001) in the autumn in Palazzo Corsini. Numerous annual exhibitions are held at the Fortezza da Basso, including the **Mostra dell'Artigianato**, an exhibition of artisans' products from all over the world.

On certain Sundays of the year, the whole city is closed to traffic, and on these occasions special events are organised in the streets and *piazze*, for information ☎ 800 831 133.

Sports and leisure

Swimming The three open-air municipal swimming pools owned by the Comune of Florence are open June–September, usually every day 10.00–18.00, for a fee of about Lire 10,000 a day: *Costoli*, Viale Paoli (Campo di Marte), *Bellariva*, 6 Lungarno Aldo Moro, and *Le Pavoniere* at the Cascine (2 Via della Catena). Other open-air pools run by clubs include: *Il Poggetto*, 24 Via Mercati and *Zodiac*, 2 Via Grandi, Tavarnuzze (open at roughly the same times and for the same price as those above) and (slightly more expensive) the *Health Center*

Vivarium, 4 Via Accursio, and *Le Bagnese*, Via Cassioli, Scandicci (open only in the afternoons). Covered pool open all year round at the *Rari Nantes Florentia*, 24 Lungarno Ferrucci.

Tennis   There are tennis courts at *Le Piagge*, 2 Via Lombardia, *Albereta*, Viale dell'Albereta, at the *Assi*, 64 Viale Michelangelo, at the *Affrico*, 20 Viale Manfredo Fanti, and at the Cascine and Campo di Marte.

Skulling and rowing   There is skulling and rowing on the Arno at the Canottieri Comunali, 6 Lungarno Ferrucci (for 2km) and Canottieri Firenze, 8 Lungarno de' Medici (for 1km).

Gyms   There are numerous gyms in the centre of Florence, including the *Palestra Ricciardi*, 75 Borgo Pinti.

Golf   There is an 18-hole golf course at Ugolino, 12km southeast of Florence on the Strada Chiantigiana, beyond Grassina (☎ 055 230 1009). It has reciprocal arrangements with two other Tuscan 18-hole golf courses nearby, Le Pavoniere at Prato (designed by Arnold Palmer), ☎ 0574 620 855, and Poggio dei Medici at Cignano near Scarperia in the Mugello, ☎ 055 843 0436.

Walking   For walking excursions, contact *Club Alpino Italiano* (CAI), 5 Via dello Studio, ☎ 055 2398580.

Information for students

US college campuses   In Florence, these include:
The California State University, 12 Via Giacomo Leopardi, ☎ 055 234 5700
Florida State University, 15 Borgo degli Albizi, ☎ 055 234 0604
Georgetown University, Villa le Balze, 26 Via Vecchia Fiesolana, ☎ 055 59208
Gonzaga University, 3 Piazza Antinori, ☎ 055 215 053
Middlebury College, 12 Via Verdi, ☎ 055 245 790
New York University, Villa la Pietra, 106 Via Bolognese, ☎ 055 50071
Pepperdine University, 41 Viale Milton, ☎ 055 474 120
Sarah Lawrence, 10 Borgo Santa Croce, ☎ 055 240 904
Smith College, 4 Piazza della Signoria, ☎ 055 238 1674
Stanford University, 1 Piazza Santa Maria sopr'Arno, ☎ 055 234 4741
Syracuse University, 15 Piazza Savonarola, ☎ 055 571 376
University of Michigan, and University of Wisconsin, Villa Corsi Salviati, 460 Via Gramsci, Sesto Fiorentino, ☎ 055 444 300.

Post-graduate universities   These include the European University Institute, 5 Via dei Roccettini, Fiesole; the Harvard University Center for Italian Renaissance Studies at Villa I Tatti, 26 Via di Vincigliata, Ponte a Mensola, near Settignano (with a fine arts consulting library open to graduate students), and the Charles S. Singleton Center for Italian Studies at the Johns Hopkins University, Villa Spelman, 13 Via San Leonardo.

The Centro di Cultura per Stranieri (attached to the University of Florence) at the Villa Fabbricotti, 64 Via Vittorio Emanuele, gives courses including Italian language and history of art. The Università Internazionale dell'Arte is at Villa il Ventaglio, 24 Via delle Forbici.

Cultural institutes and libraries See p 65.

Language schools There are numerous language schools in Florence, two of the most famous are the British Institute (see p 292), 2 Piazza Strozzi, ☎ 055 267 781, and the Centro Linguistico Italiano Dante Alighieri, 5 Piazza Repubblica, ☎ 055 210 8708.

Sports facilities and bicycle hire See p 58.

Nightlife For information on concerts, nightlife and late night cafés, consult *Firenze Spettacolo*, a monthly publication sold at newsagents, or *Vista* magazine which has monthly listings in English.

Information There is an information office for foreign students at Florence University: *L'Ufficio per studenti stranieri*, 4 Via La Pira, ☎ 055 275 7229. The APT produces a leaflet entitled: *Studying in Florence: a Guide*.

Reductions for students A special season ticket for foreign students aged under 26 for use on ATAF buses can be purchased at *Student Point*, 9 Viale Gramsci. EU students under the age of 18 are allowed free entrance to state owned museums and galleries, and EU students between the ages of 18 and 26 are allowed a reduction (usually 50 per cent) at these museums. Students are allowed to park their cars for half the monthly rate at certain car parks, see p 47. Cinemas are cheaper on Wednesdays.

Youth hostels and student hostels See pp 29–30.
For the **student canteen** and **cheap eating places** see pp 41–42.
For **bookshops**, see p 56. **Camping equipment** is sold at *Alessandro Sieni*, 71 Via dell'Ariento. For **internet centres**, see p 67, and for **laundrettes**, see p 67.

Telephones and postal services

There are numerous **public telephones** all over the city in kiosks, as well as in some bars and restaurants. These are operated by coins or telephone cards (Lire 5000, 10,000 and 20,000), which can be purchased from tobacconists displaying a blue 'T' sign, bars, kiosks and post offices. Placing a local call costs Lire 200. Numbers that begin with 800, called *numero verde*, are toll-free, but require a deposit of at least Lire 200. **Telephone numbers** in Italy can have from seven to eleven numbers. All now require the area code, whether you are making a local call or a call from outside Florence.

   Directory assistance (in Italian) is available by dialling 12. Most cities in the world can now be dialled direct from Florence. International telephone cards (Lire 10,000–50,000), which offer considerable savings, are now widely available from the same outlets as above. For long-distance calls, the telephone exchange at the Post Office in Via Pellicceria is always open. At *Il Cairo Phone Center*, 90 Via de' Macci, near Sant'Ambrogio (open daily 09.30–21.00) you can make low-cost international phone calls.
Florence area code 055
Dialling UK from Italy (0044) + number

Dialling US from Italy (001) + number
Dialling Florence from UK (0039) 055 + number
Dialling Florence from US (0039) 055 + number

The head **post offices** are in 53 Via Pietrapiana (**Map 7; 1**) and Via Pellicceria (**Map 1; 3**) and they are open 08.15–19.00 (except on the last day of the month when they are open 08.15–12.00); on Saturday they are open 08.15–12.30; and on Sunday the Via Pietrapiana office is open 08.15–12.30, and the Via Pellicceria office is open 08.30–19.00. Branch post offices are usually open Mon–Fri 08.15–13.40 (Saturday 08.15–12.00). A small post office was opened in 2000 in the Uffizi gallery. For information about the Italian postal services, ☎ 160, or 055 27741.

Stamps are sold at tobacconists (displaying a blue 'T' sign) as well as post offices. Stamps for postcards and letters weighing up to 20g cost Lire 800 for Italy and the EU, and Lire 900 for other destinations.

A **priority postal service** (for which special stamps must be purchased) for Italy and abroad, which promises delivery within three days, was introduced in 1999. CAIpost is a guaranteed, but much more expensive, express postal service which gives you a receipt. At post offices there are special boxes for letters abroad.

Visiting Florence with children

Florence is one of the most pleasant cities to visit in Italy for children as it is comparatively small and the main monuments and museums are all within easy reach of one another.

Museums
A visit to the famous museums of the Uffizi, the Palatine gallery in Palazzo Pitti, and the Accademia gallery are probably obligatory, but you should never attempt to see them on the same day, and there is no sense trying to see all the rooms in the Uffizi in one visit. At the Pitti, the **Museo degli Argenti** is a delightful, fairly small museum with some unexpected treasures which appeal to children— exotic objects and jewellery in the shape of animals. At the Uffizi, the **Corridoio Vasariano**—the covered passageway which runs across Ponte Vecchio to the Pitti—fascinates children and it is worth arranging a visit. However, if you decide to visit just one museum in the city to illustrate the Florentine Renaissance, you could make no better choice than the **Bargello**.

In 2000, a delightful **children's museum** was opened in Palazzo Vecchio, which can be visited by families at weekends (prior booking necessary). It is aimed at teenagers, but also has sections for the very young. In parts of the palace not otherwise open to the public, it illustrates certain historical periods of the city, and explains architectural principles and scientific theories which were first experimented with in Florence.

Other visits which should appeal to children include the famous sculptures by Michelangelo in the **Cappelle Medicee**—while here, it is well worthwhile asking to see the drawings by him on the walls of a small room below the chapel, which has an atmosphere all of its own. Nearby, the tiny chapel frescoed by Benozzo Gozzoli in the **Palazzo Medici Riccardi** is one of the most charming sights in the city, while a remarkable idea of monastic life is provided by the cells on the upper floor of the **Museo di San Marco**, frescoed by Fra' Angelico.

Other less well-known museums in the city, particularly interesting for children, include the little **Museo degli Innocenti** in a room once used as the day nursery of an orphanage, and the **Casa Buonarroti**, with two sculptures carved by Michelangelo when he was a boy.

Florence is particularly rich in scientific collections, notably the beautifully arranged **Science Museum** and the **Zoological Museum** at the Specola. The **Anthropological Museum** is the most important collection of its kind in Italy. The delightful **Palazzo Davanzati** gives a vivid idea of life in Florence in the Middle Ages, although it is at present closed for restoration. The **Archaeological Museum** has an Egyptian section, and Etruscan and Roman masterpieces, and the Attic vases (including the François Vase) on the top floor have remarkable illustrations of the Greek myths.

The most eccentric museum in the city is the **Museo Stibbert**, which is well worth a visit. It has an extraordinary miscellany of objects and a unique collection of arms and armour (other displays of arms and armour are to be found in the Bargello and Museo Bardini).

The tiny chapel of **San Martino del Vescovo** has appealing frescoes of everyday life in 15C Florence.

The artistic developments of the Florentine Renaissance can perhaps be best appreciated by a visit to Masaccio's frescoes in the **Cappella Brancacci** at Santa Maria del Carmine, and by climbing to the top of the cupola of the **Dumo** (a particularly exciting experience which should be complemented by a visit to the nearby Museo dell'Opera del Duomo, where the hoists and tackle used in its construction are preserved).

There is a football museum, **Museo del Calcio**, at Coverciano, between Florence and Settignano (see p 348).

Outdoor activities

The ramparts of **Forte di Belvedere** are a lovely place to play and picnic, and provide one of the best views of the city (although they are closed at present). The extensive **Boboli gardens** are a wonderful place to visit with children (local children tend to gather at the lower end towards Porta Romana). Children are also usually at play in Piazza Santa Croce, Piazza d'Azeglio (which has a little playground), the little garden off Borgo Allegri, Piazza Tasso in the Oltrarno, and in the park of the Cascine (good for bicycling or roller skating). Outside Florence, the huge park of the **Villa Demidoff at Pratolino**, open several days a week in summer, is a good place to go for the day with a ball and a picnic. Another place outside the city, where it is fun to spend a day, is **Fiesole**, which has a Roman theatre (and a market in the piazza on Saturdays).

The bustle and colour of the **markets** of San Lorenzo and the Porcellino will certainly captivate children and the **annual festivals** held in Florence (see p 53) are also particularly exciting. If you are in the city over Easter, you should see the **Scoppio del Carro** outside the Duomo, and in September the **Rificolona** is particularly celebrated by children. The traditional football game **Calcio in Costume** (*Calcio Storico Fiorentino*) held on three days in June in Piazza Santa Croce is another exciting spectacle, accompanied by processions and bands. At **Carnival** time, the week in February before Lent, various festivities are organised for children, and the youngest dress up and parade up and down the Lungarni near the Cascine (especially on Sundays preceding Lent and on Shrove Tuesday), or walk through the centre of town throwing confetti. At the **Festa del Grillo** in May at the Cascine a big fair is held. There are splendid fireworks at the **Festa di San Romolo** held on 6 July in Fiesole.

Of course, Italy is famous for its **ice-creams**, which are best from *gelaterie*. The best of all is probably *Vivoli* near Santa Croce.

Days out of Florence

The most attractive and interesting place in the neighbourhood of Florence, and the most frequently visited, is **Fiesole** (see p 335). Not only is the little town interesting in itself (particularly for its Roman theatre and Etruscan remains), but also, from its hill, there is a superb bird's-eye view of Florence. You can also take delightful walks in the vicinity. Other places of interest within easy reach of the city (and all within its Province) are described in the last section of the book, 'The Environs of Florence' (see pp 335–362). A plan of the immediate environs of Florence can be found on p 352.

If you have a little more time at your disposal (and preferably your own transport), and wish to see something of the magnificent countryside around Florence, you should visit the following districts (all described in *Blue Guide Tuscany*).

Vallombrosa (SITA bus in 90 minutes), a summer resort on the wooded slopes of the Pratomagno hills, reached via Pontassieve. It has extensive forests and is the coolest place near Florence in summer. In its famous monastery, founded by St John Gualberto in 1040, Milton may have been a guest.

The upper valley of the Arno, beyond Vallombrosa, is known as the **Casentino** (SITA bus in about 2 hours). It contains several castles, and the little towns of Poppi and Bibbiena, all rich in Florentine history.

The **Chianti** district to the south of Florence, where the famous Tuscan wine is grown, is crossed by a beautiful road known as the 'Chiantigiana' (N 222) which runs to Siena via Greve (SITA bus in 1 hour).

The **Mugello**, north of Florence at the foot of the Apennines, is an attractive cultivated valley, surrounded by wooded hills, reached via Borgo San Lorenzo (SITA bus in 1 hour).

Prato is the most important town near Florence. Although it is now industrialised, there are a number of interesting Renaissance monuments in the old centre, including the church of Santa Maria delle Carceri by Giuliano da Sangallo, and the Duomo with a pulpit by Donatello and Michelozzo, and important frescoes in the choir by Filippo Lippi. (A frequent train service from Florence takes about 20 minutes, or there is a bus service about every 20 minutes, with a journey time of 30 minutes—via the motorway; services run by Lazzi and CAP.)

The new province of Prato includes the Medici **Villa di Poggio a Caiano** and the nearby **Villa di Artimino** surrounded by superb Tuscan countryside, in which there are also some interesting Etruscan tombs. Poggio a Caiano is well served by buses from Florence (COPIT or CAP) from 9 Largo Alinari (at the station end of Via Nazionale) every 30 minutes, with a journey time of about 30 minutes. From Poggio a Caiano, buses run via Comeana to Artimino in 20 minutes, and via Seano to Carmignano (in 20 minutes).

• Country bus services from Florence are run by *SITA* (Via Santa Caterina da Siena 15 (**Map 3; 5**; ☎ 800 373 760 or 055 214 721), *Lazzi* (Piazza Adua; **Map 3; 5**, ☎ 055 351 061), *CAP* and *COPIT* (Largo Alinari, Via Nazionale; **Map 3; 5**, ☎ 055 214 637).

Other famous Tuscan cities, farther afield, and worth visiting include Siena, San Gimignano, Volterra, Pistoia, Lucca, Pisa and Arezzo. *Blue Guide Tuscany* includes descriptions of all of these places. Across the Apennines in Emilia is Bologna, also one of the most important and interesting cities in Italy (described in *Blue Guide Northern Italy*). The best way of reaching these cities is listed below.

Siena Frequent bus services (SITA) terminating in Piazza San Domenico in Siena, taking 75 minutes (via the *superstrada*), or 2 hours (via the old road, N 2). The train service takes 1.5–2 hours, with a change sometimes necessary at Empoli. However, despite passing through pretty country on a secondary line, it is less convenient since the railway station is outside Siena.

San Gimignano Frequent bus services (SITA) via Poggibonsi, takes 1 hour 40 minutes.

Volterra SITA bus services take 2 hours.

Lucca The city is on a direct railway line from Florence via Prato and Pistoia with frequent (but slow) services (to Lucca in 1.5–2 hours; to Pistoia in about 45 minutes). Bus services (Lazzi) to Lucca take 80 minutes; to Pistoia 50 minutes.

Pisa A frequent rail service runs here via Empoli, with trains taking about 1 hour; bus service (Lazzi) takes 1.5 hours.

Arezzo This city is on the main railway line between Florence and Rome; although not all of the fast trains stop here, there is one about every hour and the journey takes 30–40 minutes.

Bologna The main railway line to the north runs through the city and it can be reached by fast train in 60–75 minutes.

Additional information

Airline companies
Airfrance ☎ 1478 84466
Alitalia ☎ 1478 65641 or 1478 65643
Luthansa ☎ 02 8066 3025
Meridiana ☎ 055 32961
Sabena ☎ 055 337 1201

Banking services
Banks are usually open from 08.30–13.30, and 14.30 or 14.45–15.30 or 15.45 every day except Saturday, Sunday and holidays. They close early (about 11.00) on days preceding national holidays. The commission on cashing travellers' cheques can be quite high. Money can also be changed at exchange offices (*cambio*) and at travel agencies (but usually at a less advantageous rate), as well as at

some post offices and main railway stations. Some hotels, restaurants and shops exchange money, but usually at a lower rate.

Chemists
See Pharmacies (p 68).

Consulates
British Consulate, 2 Lungarno Corsini (**Map 6; 1**), ☎ 055 284 133.
American Consulate, 38 Lungarno Vespucci (**Map 2; 8**), ☎ 055 239 8276.
The British, American, Canadian, Australian, Irish and New Zealand embassies are in Rome.

Crime and personal security
For all emergencies, ☎ 113. As in cities all over the world, pick-pocketing is a wide-spread problem in Florence. It is always advisable not to carry valuables in hand-bags and to take extra care on buses. You should be careful when using a credit card to withdraw money from an automatic teller machine. Cash, documents and valu-ables can be left in hotel safes. It is a good idea to make photocopies of all important documents in case of loss. Italian law requires that everyone carries with them a document of identification (with a photograph): it is therefore best to keep your passport with you. Lost or stolen passports will be replaced by the British and American consulates in Florence (see above). They will also help British and American travellers who are in difficulty and will give advice in emergencies.

Police
There are three categories of policemen in Italy:
Vigili Urbani, municipal police who wear blue uniforms in winter and light blue during the summer and have helmets similar to those of London policemen; their headquarters are at 6 Piazzale di Porta al Prato, ☎ 055 328 3333.
Carabinieri, military police who wear a black uniform with a red stripe down the side of the trousers; their headquarters are at 48 Borgo Ognissanti, ☎ 112.
Polizia di Stato, state police who wear dark blue jackets and light blue trousers; the Central Police Station (*Questura*) is at 2 Via Zara (☎ 055 49771).

Crime
Crime should be reported at once; if it is theft, it should be reported to to either the *Polizia di Stato* or the *Carabinieri*. A detailed statement has to be given in order to get an official document confirming loss or damage (*denunzia di smarrimento*), which is essential for insurance claims. Interpreters are usually provided. If you have **legal problems**, contact the APT office at 1 (red) Via Cavour.

Lost property
The central office of the Comune is at 19 Via Circondaria, ☎ 055 328 3942. To report the **loss or theft of a credit card**, call:
Visa ☎ 800 877 232
Mastercard ☎ 800 872 050
American Express ☎ 055 238 2876

Cultural institutes and libraries
British Institute, 2 Piazza Strozzi (Italian language courses), with an excellent library and reading room at 9 Lungarno Guicciardini.

Institut Français, 2 Piazza Ognissanti.
German Institute of Art History, 44 Via Giuseppe Giusti (with the best art history consulting library in Florence, open to graduate students).
Dutch Institute, 5 Viale Torricelli.
Fondazione di Studi di Storia dell'Arte Roberto Longhi, Villa il Tasso, 30 Via Benedetto Fortini.
Accademia della Crusca, Villa Medicea di Castello.
Istituto Nazionale di Studi sul Rinascimento, Palazzo Strozzi.
Società Dantesca Italiana, 1 Via Arte della Lana.

Libraries

Biblioteca Nazionale Centrale, 1 Piazza Cavalleggeri.
Archivio di Stato, Viale Giovine Italia (Piazza Beccaria).
Gabinetto Scientifico e Letterario G.B. Vieusseux, Palazzo Strozzi.
Biblioteca Medicea Laurenziana, Piazza San Lorenzo.
Biblioteca Riccardiana & Moreniana, 10 Via Ginori.
Biblioteca Marucelliana, 43 Via Cavour.
Biblioteca Comunale, 21 Via Sant'Egidio.
The French, German, Dutch and British Institutes also have libraries (see above).
Istituto Geografico Militare, 10 Via Cesare Battisti has a cartographic library.

For universities and language schools, see pp 59–60.

Dress codes

If you are wearing shorts or miniskirts, or have bare shoulders, you might be refused admission to some churches.

Electric current

The electricity supply is 220 watts. Visitors may need round, two-pin Continental plugs for some appliances.

Emergencies

For all emergencies, ☎ 113: the switchboard will coordinate the help you need. First aid services (*Pronto Soccorso*) are available at hospitals, railway stations and airports. The most central hospital is *Santa Maria Nuova*, 1 Piazza Santa Maria Nuova (☎ 055 27581). Large general hospitals on the outskirts of the town are: *Careggi*, Viale Morgagni; *San Giovanni di Dio*, Via Scandicci, Torregalli, and *Santa Maria Annunziata*, Via dell'Antella. Children's hospital: *Meyer*, 14 Via Luca Giordano.
A volunteer service (AVO) helps translate for non Italian patients in hospitals (☎ 055 425 0126).
First-aid and ambulance emergency 24hr service, ☎ 118
Ambulance service (run by volunteers of the Misericordia, Piazza del Duomo) ☎ 055 212 222
Ambulance service (run by volunteers of the Fratellanza Militare) ☎ 055 215 555
Mobile coronary unit ☎ 055 283 394
Fire brigade ☎ 115
Road assistance ☎ 116
For all other emergencies, see 'Crime' above.

Internet centres

Internet Train has eight shops in Florence open 7 days a week: 24 Via Guelfa (**Map 3; 6**), 40 Via dell'Oriuolo (**Map 3; 8**), 30 Borgo San Jacopo (**Map 6; 1**), 36 Via de' Benci (**Map 7; 1**), 9 Via Giacomini (**Map 4; 2**), 1 Via Zannoni (**Map 3; 6**), 11 Via del Parione (**Map 6; 1**), and 15 Via Corridoni (north of **Map 3; 1**). In addition it has a shop in the campsite near Piazzale Michelangelo, and one close to the Camerata Youth Hostel (at 1 Via Nullo).

Laundrettes

Wash & Dry, 105 Via dei Servi, 143 Via Ghibellina, 87 Via dei Serragli, 52 Via della Scala, 29 Via del Sole, 129 Via Nazionale, and 21 Viale Morgagni. All these shops are open 7 days a week 08.00–22.00 (a wash takes 25 minutes, and drying also 25 minutes). For information, ☎ 055 580 480.

Markets

See Shops (p 54).

Newspapers and magazines

Italian newspapers which carry local news of Florence are *La Repubblica* and *La Nazione*. Other national newspapers include *Corriere della Sera* and *La Stampa*. **Free publications** include *Chiavi d'oro*, issued every 2 months in Italian and English, which gives detailed practical information on Florence and lists concerts and exhibitions, usually available at the APT information offices and in hotels. *Turismonotizie* magazine is also issued every two months and distributed at the APT information office and in hotels.

Magazines with information about the city include *Firenze Spettacolo*, which comes out every month and can be purchased at newsagents; this gives detailed information about events in Florence. *Vista* is a magazine in English on Florence and Tuscany.

Foreign newspapers can be purchased at most kiosks and the *New York Herald Tribune*, published in Bologna, carries news on Italy.

Nightlife

Up-to-date listings of discos and bars with live music open till late can be found in *Firenze Spettacolo* (see above).

Opening hours

Shops (for clothes, books and hardware) are generally open from 09.00–13.00 and 16.00–19.30, including Saturday, but are closed on Monday morning for most of the year. Hardware shops are usually closed on Saturday afternoon and open Monday morning. Some shops in the centre of Florence now stay open all day (09.30 or 10.00–19.30). Food shops usually open Monday–Saturday, 07.30 or 08.00–13.00, 17.00–19.30 or 20.00, but are closed on Wednesday afternoon for most of the year. The *Standa* supermarket in Via Pietrapiana (**Map 4; 7,8**) is usually open on Sundays and holidays.

Ladies' hairdressers are open 09.00–13.00, 16.00–19.30, except on Friday and Saturday when they do not close at lunch time. They are closed all day on Sunday and Monday.

From mid-June to mid-September all shops close on Saturday afternoon instead. Government offices usually work weekdays 08.00–13.30 or 14.00.

For banking hours, museum and church openings, see the relevant sections above.

Pensioners

There is free admission to all state-owned galleries and monuments for British citizens over the age of 65 (you should carry your passport for proof of age and nationality). There are no concessions for foreign pensioners on public transport.

Pharmacies

Pharmacies or chemists (*farmacie*) are identified by their street signs, which show a luminous green cross. They are usually open Monday–Friday 09.00– 13.00, 16.00–19.30 or 20.00. Some are open 24 hours a day, including those at the Stazione Santa Maria Novella, at no. 7 Via Calzaioli, and at no. 20 Piazza San Giovanni. A few are open on Saturdays, Sundays (and holidays), and at night: these are listed on the door of every chemist and in the daily newspapers.

Photography

Rules about photography vary in museums, so it is always best to ask first for permission (the use of a flash is often prohibited).

Public holidays

The main holidays in Italy, when offices, shops and schools are closed, are as follows:

1 January	New Year's Day
25 April	Liberation Day
Easter Monday	
1 May	Labour Day
15 August	Assumption
1 November	All Saints' Day
8 December	Immaculate Conception
25 December	Christmas Day
26 December	St Stephen

In addition, the festival of the patron Saint of Florence, St John, is celebrated on **24 June** as a local holiday in the city.

Museums are usually closed on 24 June, Easter Sunday and 15 August, although sometimes some of the state museums remain open on these days. There is usually no public transport on 1 May and the afternoon of Christmas Day. For annual festivals, see above.

Street numbering

In Florence, the numbers of all private residences are written in **blue** or **black**, and those of all shops in **red**, so the same number often occurs in blue or black and in red in the same street.

Tipping

Most prices in hotels and restaurants include a service charge, and so tipping is far less widespread in Italy than it is in North America. Even taxi-drivers rarely expect more than a few thousand lire added to the charge (which officially includes service). In restaurants, prices are almost always inclusive of service. In hotels, porters who show you to your room and help with your luggage, or find you a taxi, usually expect a few thousand lire.

Toilets

There is a notable shortage of public toilets in Italy. All bars (cafés) should have toilets available to the public (generally speaking the larger the bar, the better the facilities). Nearly all museums now have toilets. A number of public toilets, with facilities for the disabled, run by the municipality of Florence were opened or re-opened in 2000. They cost between Lire 500 and Lire 1 500 and most of them are open 09.00–19.00. The most central are in the underpass for the Stazione Santa Maria Novella; at 25 Via della Stufa, near the Mercato Centrale di San Lorenzo; at 29 red Borgo Santa Croce, just off Piazza Santa Croce; and at 3 Via del Pavone (corner of Via dello Sprone), near Piazza Pitti. There are also toilets at Piazzale Michelangelo, Lungarno del Tempio, the market of Sant'Ambrogio, and in the gardens of the Cascine, the Fortezza da Basso, and the Giardino dell' Orticoltura. There are toilets at the underground car parks at Stazione Santa Maria Novella and Parterre (Piazza della Libertà), and at the Fortezza da Basso.

The Florentine Renaissance

by Marco Chiarini, former Director of the Pitti Gallery

The city

When seen from the circle of hills which surrounds the city, Florence gives an impression of completeness, its medieval and Renaissance architecture dominated by Brunelleschi's immense terracotta dome *'erta sopra e cieli, ampla da coprire chon sua ombra tucti e popoli toscani'* (Soaring above in the sky, large enough to cover with its shadow all the Tuscan people), as Leon Battista Alberti described it in his *Trattato della Pittura* with its celebrated dedication to 'Filippo di Ser Brunelleschi'. The city is a perfect whole to which nothing can be added or removed without altering the harmony which has been attained over the last eight centuries. Perhaps in no other city are the intention of man and the design of nature so entwined. Florence was born out of the valley, its monuments enclosed by an amphitheatre of hills. Its architecture has been created by the human mind in imitation of its natural setting, and Brunelleschi cemented this relationship with his great cupola, a poetic masterpiece of engineering.

I advise any visitor, before penetrating the streets and *piazze* of the city, to go 'without the city gates', up into the surrounding hills, in order to appreciate the physical unity which embraces the spirit of Florentine art. Probably the most remarkable of all Florentine views is that from the hillside of Bellosguardo, approached by a winding road from which the natural landscape can be seen blending with that of the city. The view from the top of the hill takes in the façades of the most important buildings in an almost unconscious summary of the beauties of Florence (to paraphrase one of the oldest guides to the city). Thousands of modest roofs covered by simple terracotta tiles are a reminder of the humble but highly skilled craftsmanship which is still an important characteristic of daily life in the city. Above these rise the principal monuments of the city which testify to the presence of exceptional artists, who, from the Romanesque period onwards, made Florence the centre to which the art world looked for inspiration and guidance.

The birth of Florentine art

The most distinctive feature in the evolution of Florentine art—not only in architecture, sculpture and painting, but also in the decorative arts—is the continuity of its figurative language. This logical development results in a clearly defined style of a consistently high standard. It is as if there were no break in time between the works of the anonymous architects of the Baptistery, Santi Apostoli and San Miniato al Monte, and the later buildings of Brunelleschi, Michelozzo and Michelangelo: they all represent an unmistakable, uniquely Florentine style. This style is based on forms of such essential simplicity that it lends itself to endless repetitions and variations, without ever becoming stale, reaffirming the simple perfection of the civilisation of Athens at the time of Pericles and Phidias.

The orientation of the centre of the city, based on the Roman encampment which preceded it, still follows a plan according to the cardinal points: the religious centre with the cathedral and the political centre with the town hall and its piazza at either end of one axis; and on the other axis the two most important conventual houses, the Dominicans in Santa Maria Novella to the northwest, and the Franciscans in Santa Croce to the southeast. In these two different worlds some of the most important developments in the artistic history of the city have taken place over the centuries.

The first buildings in Florence to signal the birth of a characteristic style, with a clarity of design based on classical elegance, are the Baptistery, Santi Apostoli and San Miniato al Monte, built during the 11C and 12C. The octagonal **Baptistery**, surmounted by a dome and lantern, clearly takes its inspiration from the centrally planned Pantheon in Rome. It became the prototype for the centralised churches of the Renaissance which were modelled on Brunelleschi's incomplete project for the church of Santa Maria degli Angeli. The green-and-white marble facing of the Baptistery, a dichromatic type of decoration also found in contemporary Pisan architecture and, slightly later, in Siena, emphasises the geometric design of the structure. This relationship between structure and decoration had a fundamental influence on contemporary architecture as well as later buildings, such as the Duomo and the 15C façade of Santa Maria Novella, designed by Alberti. The rhythmical arrangement of architectural elements which characterises Florentine Romanesque architecture is applied with particular elegance to the distinctive, luminous façade of **San Miniato al Monte**. Here, the beautiful arches show a study of proportion and an understanding of harmonic rhythms which were later important elements in Brunelleschi's artistic language. The same attempt to find a rhythmic proportion, rescinding the gigantic forms which characterised the architecture of the late Roman Empire, can be seen in the interior of Santi Apostoli where the double line of columns, derived from the basilican form, is surmounted by Romanesque arches in a spatial synthesis which was to find its ultimate refinement in the basilicas of Brunelleschi.

In the 13C, Florence expanded both politically and economically, despite the strife between the Guelfs (supporters of the Pope) and the Ghibellines (supporters of the Emperor). Thanks to its flourishing commerce and the shrewdness of its businessmen, the city assumed a central position in the Tuscan economy. The rich merchants, rather than the aristocracy, now began to come to the forefront of the political scene, and it was they who determined the new plan of the city, whose territorial expansion was growing alongside its commerce.

It was at the end of the 13C, possibly because of the Gothic influence spreading throughout Europe from France, that a series of building and decorative enterprises was started in Florence, which had no equal in any other part of Italy. They not only gave a new face and character to the city, but also determined the beginnings of a new figurative language in art which would eventually become common to other Italian cities. At the same time, the city's great religious and civic monuments were begun; building continued in the 14C and, in some cases, such as Santa Maria Novella, was not completed until the 15C.

The religious orders, too, had their moment of particular importance in the civic and cultural history of the city, and the two convents of **Santa Maria Novella** and **Santa Croce** were to become the scene of the great triumphs of Florentine painting. These two 14C buildings offered space for the great families of Florence to build chapels bearing their names and dedicated to their patron saints. Soon, rich citizens were competing with each other to have their chapels decorated by the best artists of the day. In the sombre but elegant architecture of these two churches, the Gothic style is evident, but it is reinterpreted in the Florentine manner. The accent is on perspective and spatial relationships, and on light, which was absent in the great cathedrals of northern Europe. Fresco cycles on the white walls of the side aisles and chapels illustrated some of the important features and stories of Christianity for the common people. For the next two centuries, the technique of fresco was to play a vital part in Florentine art.

Cimabue (fl. 1272–1302) and Giotto returned from Assisi—then one of the most important artistic centres in Italy—where they had decorated the transept and nave of the upper church of San Francesco. Under the influence of the classical tendencies of the Roman artists involved in the same project, they created a new pictorial language which, according to the 16C art historian and painter Vasari, translated painting 'from Greek to Latin'. A memorable event of the time, also related by Vasari, was the people's procession in honour of Cimabue's *Maestà*, painted for the church of Santa Trìnita (now in the Uffizi), around the year 1285. This event signalled the advent of a new spirituality in pictorial forms which had been absent in the Byzantine style that had hitherto dominated Europe. The *Maestà* altarpiece and that painted at about the same time for the Rucellai chapel in Santa Maria Novella by the Sienese master, **Duccio** (1260–1319), mark the birth of the two important schools of Florentine and Sienese painting, which were to contend for predominance in 14C art.

The fourteenth century

The painter who first put the accent on the continuity between classical and medieval art, creating new forms which were clearly a prelude to Humanism and the Renaissance, was **Giotto** (1266/7–1319), Cimabue's great pupil. Dante Alighieri noted this when he wrote his famous lines:

> *Credette Cimabue nella pintura*
> *Tener lo campo, ed ora ha Giotto il grido,*
> *Si che la fama di colui è oscura.*

> (Cimabue thought he held the field
> In painting, and now Giotto is the cry,
> The other's fame obscured.)

Giotto became the protagonist not only of Florentine art but of all Italian art of the 14C. Active as a painter, architect and inspirer of sculptural forms, he embodied the idea of the 'universal' artist which was to culminate in the High Renaissance with Leonardo, Michelangelo and Raphael. It is significant that some of Giotto's most important works, from his early youth to his full maturity, lie outside Florence: his fame was such that he was called on to work in northern Italy (in Padua, his fresco cycle for the Scrovegni chapel is considered the masterpiece of his mature years), in central Italy, at Rimini, and in the south, in Rome (St Peter's) and Naples. This is an unmistakable sign of the diffusion of his pictorial language, which must have touched all the most important centres of the 14C Italian school. His style was a synthesis of the exalted dramatic qualities of Cimabue (as can be seen by comparing Cimabue's *Crucifix* now in the Museo dell'Opera di Santa Croce with that by Giotto in the sacristy of Santa Maria Novella) and the classical influence he had encountered in Assisi, and perhaps directly in Rome.

Giotto sought a return to realism in painting that finds a parallel in the poetry of his friend and admirer, Dante Alighieri. The simplicity of Giotto's style can be seen in the *Maestà*, a work with its origins in the Byzantine tradition, painted for the church of Ognissanti in Florence in the first decade of the 14C (now in the Uffizi). In this work, one of three large paintings to be dedicated to the Madonna in Florence, Giotto affirms a new humanity in the grave but smiling face of the Madonna, and in the upward movement of the figures of the angels and saints which surround her. Here there is the same highly religious but deeply human spirit that pervades the *Divina Commedia*, a spirit absent from the paintings of the same subject by Cimabue and Duccio thirty years earlier. In Giotto's *Maestà*, the regal, Byzantine qualities of Cimabue and Duccio are softened by contact with a sense of human reality, and it was this that became the main characteristic of Florentine art, eventually influencing the whole of Italian art. It is difficult to put into words the spirit which pervades Giotto's frescoes in the Bardi and Peruzzi chapels in the church of Santa Croce, which were rediscovered after centuries of critical oblivion by John Ruskin. In these and in Giotto's other Florentine works can be seen the beginning of a style that was continued by his followers, though in a progressively more diluted form, as the Gothic style gained influence during the late 14C.

Giotto's influence was also felt in architecture and sculpture: the early project for the Campanile of the cathedral was entrusted to him and there is evidence of his style in some of the relief panels which decorate the base, although they were probably executed by Andrea Pisano. Giotto's most able follower was **Arnolfo di Cambio** (c 1245–1302), the architect and sculptor who played a prominent part in the reconstruction of the city under the Republic. The building which was to become the symbol of Florence and its government, the Palazzo dei Priori, today known as **Palazzo Vecchio**, was entrusted to him. This was the residence of the *Priori* elected from the rich and powerful city Guilds, whose rule superseded that of the *Capitano del Popolo* and the *Podestà*, as power gradually shifted from the nobility to the rich merchants and bankers. Begun during the last year of the 13C, the tower was probably completed by 1323, and the rest of the building was enlarged and enriched over the course of the century. As P. Toesca, the Italian art historian, wrote: *Rappresenta il palazzo dei Priori, non meno della Cattedrale, l'essere della città e dell'arte fiorentina: fermezza e agilità, austerità e finezza; e già vi si esalta quel senso di movimento che è anima di tutte le più grandi creazioni fiorentine* (Like the cathedral, Palazzo Vecchio represents the essence of the city and of Florentine art: it has a strength and agility, an austerity and finesse which already demonstrates that sense of movement which enlivens all the greatest Florentine works of art) (*Il Trecento*, 1951).

Two-and-a-half centuries after the building of Palazzo Vecchio, Vasari emphasised its political and social importance when he framed it in a view from the river with the long arcades of his Uffizi building. Its imposing rusticated exterior, lightened by elegant mullioned windows, was also used as a model during the

Renaissance by Brunelleschi and Michelozzo, when they designed the first great houses for the rich and powerful families of the city. Arnolfo, who was an engineer (he built a circle of city walls), as well as a sculptor and architect, also designed other key buildings during this important period; they included the cathedral of Santa Maria del Fiore, built on the site of the older and much smaller Santa Reparata, and probably also Santa Croce, the Franciscan church which, more than any other, sums up the spatial and structural qualities of Florentine architecture in the late 14C and early 15C. Arnolfo had envisaged an elaborate marble façade for Santa Maria del Fiore, populated with statues and reliefs, but, like the interior, it was left incomplete at his death. The surviving drawings of the façade and the sculptures preserved in the Museo dell'Opera del Duomo are testimony to Arnolfo's powerful imagery and clarity of form which place him, as an artist, on a par with Giotto.

Exactly how Arnolfo planned the interior of the cathedral is unknown, since it was continued in a new spirit after his death, and the architectural framework put to different use. However, Santa Croce—which is probably based on Arnolfo's designs—seems to preserve his sense of monumental yet lithe clarity in the wide bays between the pilasters of *pietra forte* and the Gothic arches above them. This church, although fundamentally Gothic in form and influenced by contemporary architecture north of the Alps, is still characteristically Florentine in its use of light, in the width of its nave, and in the prominence given to the supporting structure in relation to the decorative details in the apse and the side chapels.

Other churches besides Santa Croce underwent alteration and enlargement at this time, including the Badia whose bell tower rises next to the tower of the Bargello and competes with the heavier, more imposing campanili of Santa Maria Novella, and Santa Trìnita and San Remigio, both with overtly Gothic interiors. Meanwhile, alongside Arnolfo's façade of the Duomo rose the Campanile which traditionally bears Giotto's name, even though he only built the first storey. It is an imposing structure framed by corner buttresses. The tower rises without diminishing in volume towards the upper storeys (completed in the second half of the 14C) where the structure is lightened by large Gothic windows. Giotto here repeated the Romanesque style of green-and-white marble decoration, adding pink marble, a colour scheme which was copied on the exterior of the Duomo.

The classicism of Giotto and Arnolfo had enormous influence not just in Florence but throughout Italy. Although it was of short duration, it was taken up again in the 15C by Donatello and Masaccio. The various interpretations given to Giotto's art by his immediate followers can be seen in the decoration of Florence's most important churches: Santa Croce and Santa Maria Novella. It is important to try to imagine these interiors as they were then, almost completely covered by frescoes depicting religious subjects, arranged in a way which took into account the organic divisions of the wall space determined by the architectural structure. In the Baroncelli Chapel in Santa Croce, **Taddeo Gaddi** (fl. 1332–63) rendered his narrative more complex (showing the influence of Giotto's work in Padua), by using perspective in the painted niches on the lower part of the walls where the liturgical objects give a strong impression of illusionism. In his scenes from the life of Mary, above, the buildings and landscapes are given more satisfying proportions in relation to the figures, even though they lack the coherent strength of the master's hand. **Maso di Banco** (fl. 1341–46) produced yet another personal interpretation of Giotto's style in his stories from the life of St Sylvester in the Bardi di Vernio chapel in Santa Croce. He gave a remarkable chromatic emphasis to the plastic qualities of Giotto's painting, as can be seen also in his *Deposition* for San Remigio (now in the Uffizi; also attributed to Giottino). The delicate works of **Bernardo Daddi** (c 1312–48), in particular his small religious paintings and polyptychs, show the influence of the Giottesque school. His paintings approached the dazzling colours of the Sienese school and their gracefulness won him great popularity during his lifetime.

In sculpture, **Andrea Pisano** (c 1270–1348/9) followed Giotto's design in the relief panels on the base of the Campanile, but came less under his influence when the Opera del Duomo commissioned him to produce some bronze doors for the Baptistery. The doors, produced between 1330 and 1336, are a masterly piece of metal casting and signal the rebirth of bronze sculpture in which the Florentines were to emulate the art of Ancient Rome. Furthermore, the design of these doors was later to serve as a model for the second pair made by Ghiberti during the first quarter of the 15C, the competition for which marked the change from Gothic to Renaissance art. Andrea, in his work on the Campanile begun by Giotto, opened large Gothic niches for statues in the second storey, which were echoed later in the external tabernacles of Orsanmichele, already under construction nearby. The sculpture of Andrea Pisano, and even more so that of his son Nino (who worked mostly in Pisa), derived its elegance of style from Gothic forms but at the same time made obvious reference to the powerful plastic qualities to be found in the work of Giotto. This is evident particularly in the solidity of the four prophets sculpted for the niches of the Campanile, and also in his bronze reliefs for the Baptistery doors, an open challenge to the more Gothic style developed by the two great sculptors active in Pisa and Siena, Nicola Pisano and his son Giovanni.

Meanwhile, the commercial and political power of Florence continued to flourish and the conquest of Prato, Pistoia and San Miniato firmly established the autonomy and sovereignty of the independent Comune. Notwithstanding the great famines of 1346 and the plague that broke out in 1348—which reduced the populations of Florence and Siena by half—the Florentines did not cease to embellish their city with imposing works of art, including buildings destined for practical use. The church of Orsanmichele, begun in 1337 as a loggia for the storage of grain and only completed in 1404, summarises, especially in its sculptural decoration, more than half a century of Florentine art, and shows the transition from Gothic to Renaissance style. **Andrea Orcagna** (fl. 1344–68), one of the most important figures in Florentine art during the second half of the 14C, built a Gothic tabernacle dedicated to the Madonna for the interior, in the area which was then enclosed for use as a chapel. This represented a definitive break with the clarity and simplicity of Giotto's style, and the adoption of a flowery, decorative language. This taste for affected elegance and decorative richness later developed into the International Gothic style.

It is possible that this radical change in Florentine art owed much to the effects of the plague which caused an accentuation of religious feeling. In what can be seen of the remains of Orcagna's frescoes of the *Triumph of Death* from the left nave of Santa Croce (now detached and exhibited in the Museo dell'Opera di Santa Croce), the characterisation of the figures achieves a dramatic force that is almost expressionistic. Churches were enriched by more and more decoration, inspired not only by the life of Christ and of the saints, but also by allegories exalting the function of religion and of the saints in daily life. Whilst the simpler style of **Giovanni da Milano** (fl. 1350–69), in his frescoes in the Rinuccini chapel in Santa Croce, looked back to Giotto, and **Giovanni del Biondo** (fl. 1356–92) filled churches throughout Florence and its surrounding territories with polyptychs that were easy to understand and bright with colour highlighted with gold, Orcagna and his brothers, **Nardo and Jacopo di Cione** (d. 1365 and fl. c 1365–98 respectively), together with Andrea di Bonaiuto, evolved a more inspired pictorial language, that was solemn and allegorical in its overtly didactic intent.

A large part of Andrea Orcagna's frescoes in Santa Croce were destroyed and those in the choir of Santa Maria Novella were replaced a century later by the frescoes of Ghirlandaio, so his most important surviving work is probably the triptych in the Strozzi Chapel of Santa Maria Novella. The walls of the chapel were painted by his brother, Nardo, with a rather crowded but picturesque representation of *The Last Judgement, Paradiso and Inferno*. The allegorical style of Nardo's work, with its throng of figures, leaves little space for any clarity of concept. This pictorial style was carried still further in the frescoes by **Andrea di Bonaiuto** (1343–77) in the Chapter House of Santa Maria Novella, known as the Cappellone degli Spagnuoli. The general effect is most impressive; the colours are extremely well-preserved and the decoration is complete in every detail. This is one of the few decorative schemes of the 14C to have reached us intact, complete with its altarpiece, a polyptych by Bernardo Daddi. A particularly interesting element present in these frescoes, which depict the work of the Dominicans for the Church, is the inclusion of a representation of the Duomo, then under construction, showing it complete with its three polygonal tribunes and dome, which would suggest that the east end had already been given this plan by Arnolfo.

Agnolo Gaddi (c 1333–96), Taddeo's son, continued in the wake of Orcagna and Bonaiuto. In his cycle dedicated to the *Legend of the Cross* in the choir of Santa Croce, he exhibits a narrative style which is completely removed from that of Giotto, in which bright colours tend to replace formal structure. Landscapes in pictures of this time show the increasing influence of the Gothic style, while the individuality of Giotto disappears. The late-Gothic poetical imagination found in Lorenzo Monaco and Gentile da Fabriano had yet to be developed.

Another artist active in Florence at the end of the 14C was **Spinello Aretino** (fl. 1373–1410). His beautifully preserved frescoes depicting stories of St Benedict in the sacristy of San Miniato al Monte are rich in poetry and pictorial values, and anticipate the delicacy and elegance of Lorenzo Monaco's paintings. The technique of fresco painting—which was to play such an important role in the development of Florentine, and subsequently Italian, art—was explicitly formulated in the *Libro dell'Arte*, a treatise on painting written by **Cennino Cennini** (c 1370–1440), a pupil of Agnolo Gaddi, towards the end of the 14C. Cennini's work inspired other treatises written in the following century, including that by Leon Battista Alberti.

However, it was, above all, around the workshops of the Opera del Duomo that the creative energies of the city were concentrated. The Duomo was to be the largest and most important church of Tuscany, more imposing even than the cathedral of Siena which was then being enlarged according to very ambitious plans—though it was left unfinished. The chief architect in the second half of the Trecento was **Francesco Talenti** (fl. 1325–69), who had already completed the last three storeys of the Campanile, decorating them with double- and triple-mullioned windows which unite the styles of his predecessors with Gothic motifs. In fact, as was always the case in Florentine art (in direct contrast to the Sienese school), the Gothic style was classicised. The exterior decoration of the Duomo recalls the Romanesque style with its different coloured marble facing, and the Gothic element is more apparent in the sculptural decoration of the doors and windows on its two flanks. However, it is at the east end of the cathedral, with its harmonious rhythm of architectural elements and volumes, that the architects' originality is fully revealed. The apsidal structure, with its tribunes, appears almost independent from the nave, and provides a fitting prelude to the cupola which rises abruptly and is only fully visible from this end of the church. The huge dome, already planned by this time, was to defy construction until the time of Brunelleschi.

In the interior of the Duomo, there is the same structural emphasis, the same clarity of conception and spatial amplitude as in Santa Croce, but the nave is higher owing to the use of Gothic vaulting. This Florentine interpretation of Gothic architecture is further emphasised by the massive pilasters crowned by capitals designed by Francesco Talenti. These pilasters were copied by Benci di Cione and Simone Talenti in the Loggia della Signoria, where the three great round arches and horizontal frieze are motifs derived from the two major ecclesiastical buildings of Florence. It seems that no pictorial decoration was envisaged for the solemn and bare interior of the cathedral, as it was for Santa Maria Novella and Santa Croce; instead, all the decoration was concentrated on the exterior. The carvings and statues in the tympanum above each of the doors, and on the pinnacles and buttresses, repeated the decorative spirit of the Campanile (which was further enriched with statues after the turn of the century).

The building generally considered to be next in importance to the cathedral as regards sculptural decoration is Orsanmichele. The developments seen here in Florentine sculpture of the late 14C and 15C were not equalled in painting until the arrival of Masaccio. The individuality of Florentine art seemed to follow the political vicissitudes of the city where power was increasingly concentrated in the hands of a few families who fought for control of the Signoria, always within the limits of the law. The emergence of the Medici as leaders through their financial supremacy and their ability to govern was accompanied by an extraordinary blossoming of brilliant artists who also made their contribution to the field of humanistic studies, already awakening in Florence. Whereas in the 14C, the writings of Dante, Petrarch and Boccaccio predominated amongst a multitude of followers of the *dolce stil novo* (new sweet style), the 15C saw a series of developments which were to make Florence, as in the days of Giotto and Arnolfo, the artistic centre of Italy.

Humanism

Although the Renaissance is usually considered to have begun in 1401—the year of the competition for the second Baptistery doors—it was only very slowly that the new ideas inspired by the Classical world made any headway in Florentine art and literature. These were linked to a new conception of the representation of space for which Brunelleschi was primarily responsible. The times were ripe for this turning point and the first signs of its arrival were to be seen in the cathedral workshop and at Orsanmichele. **Nanni di Banco** (c 1384–1421) demonstrated an evident interest in classical sculpture in the Porta della Mandorla on the left side of the cathedral and in his statues of St Eligius and of the Four Soldier Saints (the *Quattro Santi Coronati*) in two tabernacles at Orsanmichele.

In painting, however, the International Gothic style became established throughout the first quarter of the 15C. This style had made its first appearance in the 14C in the work of the Sienese artist **Simone Martini** (c 1284–1344) and was taken up by Lorenzo Monaco and Masolino, while one of its greatest exponents, **Gentile da Fabriano** (c 1370–1427), was also present in Florence. It was here in 1423 that he painted the *Adoration of the Magi* (now in the Uffizi) for the Strozzi chapel in Santa Trìnita. For this same chapel Fra Angelico later painted his *Deposition* (now in the Museum of San Marco), in full Renaissance style.

However, above all, it was **Brunelleschi** (1377–1446) in architecture and **Donatello** (c 1386–1466) in sculpture who determined the real change in style which was to mark the epoch known, from Vasari onwards, as the Renaissance. By this term is meant the rebirth of the laws of ideal beauty and perfection of the Classical world. Brunelleschi's artistic personality matured slowly, as he became increasingly subject to the influence of Antique models. In his relief panel for the competition for the Baptistery doors (now in the Bargello), his concepts of space and structure are still Gothic, even if they are informed by a new sense of rationality and realism that contrasts to the superficial linear elegance of the late-Gothic style. In the event, the doors were commissioned from Ghiberti who worked on them throughout the first quarter of the 15C, winning the acclaim of the Florentine people. Brunelleschi had to wait patiently to realise the triumph of his engineering genius in the creation of the cathedral dome, the commission for which he managed to obtain only in 1423. He had already proved his originality as an architect with the building of the Ospedale degli Innocenti and the sacristy of San Lorenzo (known as the 'Old Sacristy' to distinguish it from the later one built by Michelangelo). At this time, the Medici began to rebuild San Lorenzo, which was later to become their family mausoleum. Brunelleschi became increasingly involved with Giovanni and later Cosimo de' Medici, who founded the great power and fortune of the family, which, from then on, was to play a central role in the political, cultural and artistic life of the city.

Brunelleschi's style, based on a uniquely personal interpretation of classical forms (columns, capitals, arches, central or basilican plans, all of which he brought back into use), was expressed through harmonious and well-proportioned internal and external spaces. This was emphasised by his use of *pietra serena* to underline the architectural forms, which he alternated with plain white plastered surfaces, apparently inspired by the geometrical quality of Romanesque architecture. However, the most important aspect of Brunelleschi's architecture is his use of perspective; it was he who first used regular mathematical proportions in the elevation of his buildings, achieving an appearance of geometrical perfection. The laws which he studied and systematically applied revolutionised architecture which, like all the visual arts, had been dominated, especially in the late-Gothic period, by an abstract use of form and colour, tending to create a completely transfigured image of reality. Brunelleschi emphasised instead the real, tangible values of representation, indicating to his contemporaries and successors a way forward that was followed for the next five centuries in Western culture.

The Early Renaissance

The impression made by Brunelleschi's buildings (San Lorenzo, Santo Spirito, the Pazzi Chapel and Santa Maria degli Angeli), rising harmoniously out of the medieval fabric of the old city, was tremendous. For the first time, not only architects, but painters and sculptors as well, realised the possibilities that the use of perspective offered in the representation of reality. **Donatello** entered the intellectual circle under the patronage of the Medici with Brunelleschi, with whom he had studied the ruins of ancient Rome. He immediately mastered the idea of perspective and gave it its first interpretation in sculpture, in the statue and bas-relief (*schiacciato*) panel which he made for the tabernacle of the armourers' guild for Orsanmichele. In the statue of the young *St George*, and even more in the *schiacciato* relief representing the *Saint freeing the Princess*, he applied Brunelleschi's principles of a unified point of vision and perspective (which were to be so important in the work of the young Michelangelo). Donatello's style seems rougher and less sophisticated than that of Brunelleschi; in some of his sculptures, he may have drawn inspiration from the intense realism found in certain Etruscan portraits. Indeed, Donatello seemed to breath new life into the aesthetic ideals of classical sculpture: his cherubs are full of life and energy; in his bronzes, he revived a technique of sculpture which had not been employed since Antiquity; and in his use of very low *schiacciato* relief, he brought to the metal or marble surface a completely new pictorial quality, using Brunelleschi's principles of perspective to create an illusion of depth. These were all innovations which must have made a great impact on the younger generation.

The purpose of the sculptures also changed. They were no longer intended simply to decorate public buildings, but began to stand alone as refined products bought by the rich bourgeoisie for their palaces, villas or gardens, buildings which were now being constructed according to the new principles of Brunelleschi.

For their palaces, the great families adopted new Renaissance forms. The first notable example was the palace built by Brunelleschi's pupil, Michelozzo, in Via Larga (now Via Cavour) for Cosimo il Vecchio. Cosimo appointed **Michelozzo** (1396–1472) as architect after having rejected a plan drawn up for him by Brunelleschi as too expensive. It is almost certain, however, that the design was inspired at least in part by Brunelleschi (although on a simplified scale). Cosimo also employed Michelozzo on more modest building projects, and he commissioned from him the convent of San Marco, built in Florence for the use of the Dominicans of Fiesole, the villa of Careggi and the castle of Cafaggiolo.

The third great personality of the Early Florentine Renaissance was **Masaccio** (1401–c 1428), who effected the same revolution in painting as Brunelleschi had done in architecture and Donatello in sculpture, despite his death at the early age of 27. Although younger than his two colleagues, he was yet able to impose great changes on the artistic world through the work he did in collaboration with **Masolino** (1383–c 1440; a painter who still worked in the International Gothic style) in the Brancacci Chapel in the church of the Carmine. The decorations consisted of a cycle of frescoes depicting scenes from the life of St Peter, and the parts painted by Masaccio show a spiritual parallel with the work of Donatello, especially Donatello's *Prophets* made for the Campanile. Masaccio's figures are powerful, sculptural and simple, without the linear and chromatic grace that had distinguished the Gothic style. He uses colour not to please the eye but to construct the form, and this he evidently derived from Giotto's frescoes in Santa Croce (which also provided the young Michelangelo with the model for his earliest drawings). Masaccio's figures express the same profound sentiments as those of Giotto, but within a structure derived from Brunelleschi's use of perspective which offered greater possibilities of concentration and realism. Masaccio remained excluded from the protected circle of the Medici and had to seek work outside Florence during the years which saw their rise to power. He was already dead when Cosimo il Vecchio returned, triumphant, to govern Florence after a year of exile in Padua. The first followers of Masaccio, Donatello and Brunelleschi had already appeared, and it was they who established the new language of the Renaissance with the help of the most powerful family in Florence.

The artists' patrons were still, for the most part, the religious orders, the cathedral workshop, and the *Signoria*. It was for them that the artists produced the works which unmistakably characterise the Florentine Renaissance. **Luca della Robbia** (1399/1400–1482), who was a follower of Donatello and like him collaborated on the decoration of Brunelleschi's buildings, created a new material—enamelled terracotta—which remained the speciality of his family workshop until the 16C. Using transparent glazes over red clay which had been simply coloured with white and blue slip, Luca della Robbia was able to achieve effects which were quite unique and which harmonised perfectly with the grey and white of Brunelleschi's buildings. Luca also created purely decorative forms inspired by motifs taken from classical sculpture, such as the garlands of flowers, fruit and leaves that encircle his reliefs, and the coats of arms of the Guilds (on Orsanmichele) or noble families, all of which became extremely popular. The rather severe dramatic language of Donatello was now overlooked by the younger generation who turned more to his joyful, vigorous works such as the reliefs of the cathedral Cantoria, the Prato pulpit, and the so-called *Atys-Amorino* made for the Doni, and now in the Bargello (the same family was later to commission works from Michelangelo and Raphael). Donatello's affectionate reliefs of the Madonna anticipate the paintings of the young Raphael. They were also to inspire **Antonio** and **Bernardo Rossellino** (Antonio 1427–79; Bernardo 1450–1526), **Desiderio da Settignano** (1428–64), **Mino da Fiesole** (1431–84), **Benedetto da Maiano** (1442–97) and **Agostino di Duccio** (1418–81), each of whom created his own individual interpretation of Donatello's art. At this time, portraiture was also revived, realistically drawn from life or from death masks. Portraits were used in funerary monuments, for which the Renaissance model was Rossellino's tomb of Leonardo Bruni in Santa Croce.

In painting, Masaccio's work had breached the Gothic tradition, imposing the new laws of perspective in drawing and a rigorous, three-dimensional composition. However, some of his followers could not forget the more colourful, lively aspects of the Gothic style, still present in the second decade of the 15C in Lorenzo Monaco's elegant work, packed full of colour and narrative detail. Lorenzo's work brings us to that of **Fra' Angelico** (c 1395–1455), who managed to transform the refined colouring of the Gothic style into a remarkable luminosity, derived from his study of natural light—an innovative quality even when compared with the work of Masaccio. His great *Deposition*, painted for the Strozzi chapel in Santa Trìnita (now in the Museum of San Marco), as well as the altarpieces he painted for several of the religious houses in Florence (especially the Dominican convent where he took his vows), and the frescoes he painted in the convent of San Marco, place Fra Angelico among the most spiritually rich and talented interpreters of Masaccio's style. Another artist who developed Masaccio's ideas in terms of light and colour was **Domenico Veneziano** (1404–61), the master of Piero della Francesca, who later transmitted the Renaissance style throughout central Italy. This is also the place to mention **Filippo Lippi** (c 1406–69), a Carmelite friar of indifferent vocation (he eventually left the Order to marry an ex-novice, and their son, Filippino, became a talented follower of his father). Filippo painted a fresco in the cloister of the Carmine directly inspired by Masaccio but with a sense of humour and a closeness to the realities of everyday life which were quite new. In his mature works, notably his frescoes in Prato cathedral, Lippi was to find a balance between draughtsmanship, colour and the expression of movement which was to have great importance for his most gifted pupil, Botticelli.

In this climate of artistic renewal, the time was ripe for experimentation—even of an extreme kind—as **Paolo Uccello** (1397–1475) demonstrated. He was one of the most relentless investigators of the laws of perspective and illusion in painting. He, too, was connected with the Medici and it was for them that he painted the three paintings of the *Battle of San Romano*, today distributed between the Uffizi, the Louvre and the National Gallery, London. In the biblical fresco cycle he painted for the Chiostro Verde of Santa Maria Novella, he gave a Renaissance interpretation to this medieval decorative practice. As a historical painter (the Battle of San Romano is one of the first paintings to depict an actual event) he was asked by the Signoria to paint a memorial to *Sir John Hawkwood* in the cathedral. Hawkwood was an English mercenary who led the Florentine army into battle against the Sienese. A bronze equestrian statue had been planned for his tomb, but this was never carried out because of the expense. Uccello's fresco, on the left wall of the nave, depicts the bronze horse and rider that should have been there, and its greenish colour imitates the patina of bronze. Uccello also painted the cathedral clock and supplied the cartoon for one of the windows in the drum of the dome.

Andrea del Castagno (c 1420–57), the youngest of Masaccio's followers, played a similar role to that of Uccello. Primarily a fresco painter, he rigorously applied Brunelleschi's rules of perspective in his great fresco of the *Last Supper* in the refectory of the convent of Sant' Apollonia, animating it with nervously drawn, grandiose figures in an 'heroic' style, a style which could not fail to impress the young Michelangelo. Similar monumental figures appear in Andrea's frescoes of 'illustrious men and women' painted in a room of the Carducci villa and now in the Uffizi, and in the equestrian painting of *Niccolò da Tolentino* next to Uccello's John Hawkwood in the cathedral. In all these works, the plastic energy and sculptural feeling of the forms take precedence over the harsh, metallic colour.

After Cosimo il Vecchio's triumphal return in 1434, he increasingly assumed the role of enlightened 'ruler' of the city, even though he maintained the existing governmental structures. His strong personality was evident in all public works and he determined the development of Florentine culture. He surrounded himself with the most talented artists of the day to whom he entrusted important commissions for his family or for the state, and he began to form the rich Medici art collections which were to become renowned. The houses of wealthy

Florentines also became more and more luxurious. They were filled with elaborate furniture, gilded and painted (notably *cassone*, or marriage chests) and even the beds were often decorated with paintings. The walls were hung with pictures, often of very large dimensions, and sometimes in the form of a roundel (for example, the celebrated tondi by Filippo Lippi and Sandro Botticelli), and they were enriched by elaborate carved frames recalling the wreaths of Luca della Robbia, with their flowers and foliage. It seems, indeed, as though there were hardly enough painters available to satisfy the demands of the rich families who competed with the Medici and each other. Some of the most beautiful palaces of the city were built during these years, such as those designed for the Pazzi and the Antinori by **Giuliano da Maiano** (1432–90); the Pitti, which was probably based on plans by Brunelleschi, and Palazzo Rucellai, designed by Leon Battista Alberti (who was also commissioned by Giovanni Rucellai to complete the façade of Santa Maria Novella, and to build the chapel of the Holy Sepulchre in San Pancrazio). The rivalry between families also extended to the various family chapels in the most important churches, built and renovated as a testimony to the increasing prosperity of the bourgeois city. One of the finest funerary chapels of this period is that of the Cardinal of Portugal in San Miniato al Monte, which is an exceptional example of collaboration between artists (Rossellino, Pollaiolo and Baldovinetti).

The arts were codified by **Leon Battista Alberti** (1404–72) who established himself, before Leonardo da Vinci, as a 'universal' artist and theoretician of Renaissance art and whose ideas were to become law for anyone wanting to follow the new Renaissance style. The artist became an increasingly complex figure, and research in the artistic disciplines of architecture, painting and sculpture was on a theoretical and intellectual level unknown to the medieval world. Artists now tended to work in a number of different fields, and, very often, their careers began in the goldsmiths' workshop because of the ever-increasing demand for precious objects. It is not strange, then, that Pollaiolo and Verrocchio not only produced paintings and sculpture for their patrons, but also armour, crests and jewels for display in parades, festivals—and tournaments—such as that held in 1471, in which Giuliano and Lorenzo de' Medici distinguished themselves.

The stability of Cosimo il Vecchio's government (he died in 1464) ensured the city's great prosperity, a prosperity founded on commerce. In Florence at this time, the principal desire seems to have been to brighten life with all that was most beautiful and precious in art and nature. Even the subject matter of works of art changed and artists increasingly drew inspiration from mythological subjects of Antiquity, in the same way as allusions to the classical world abounded in the literature of the time. The *Procession of the Magi*, by **Benozzo Gozzoli** (1420–97) in the chapel of the Medici palace, is almost a manifesto of this new ideal. Here there are portraits of members of the family, richly dressed and surrounded by pages and courtiers, set against an imaginary landscape. There is little emphasis on the mystical aspect of the event, more on the worldly one, the atmosphere being that of a cavalcade for a tournament or some fairytale procession. At this time, Florence reached the height of its political importance, and in 1439 the meeting of the Council of the Eastern and Western Churches took place here, underlining the socio-political function of the city. The house of the Medici had by now become a royal palace, its rooms decorated with works of art by Paolo Uccello, Filippo Lippi, Benozzo Gozzoli, Pollaiolo and Verrocchio.

Cosimo's treasury, with all its marvellous antiques (which he passed on to Lorenzo), had its vault decorated with enamelled terracotta tiles by Luca della Robbia (now in the Victoria & Albert Museum, London).

The 'crisis' of the 1460s

Around 1460, Florentine art reached a turning point: the **Pollaiolo** brothers (Piero 1443–96; Antonio 1433–98) sought, above all, new expressive values and imparted a dynamic force to line and form. They were masters at casting bronze, and imposed a new artistic canon on sculpture. This was based on linear elegance and a swirling spiral movement, adding an expression of force and balance which emulated the art of the ancient world. **Verrocchio** (1435–88) was also at work at this time, and was long favoured by the Medici as a painter and sculptor. He reached a measured perfection and a monumentality even in his small-scale works (for example, his bronze *David* in the Bargello), and marked the advent of a new figurative and aesthetic concept which was to be fully realised by his greatest pupil, Leonardo da Vinci. Verrocchio's highly intellectual and sophisticated style is evident in his creation of the tomb destined for the father and uncle of Lorenzo and Giuliano de' Medici in the Old Sacristy of San Lorenzo: the sumptuous sarcophagus, devoid of figure decoration, is framed by a bronze grille of studied simplicity. The importance of Pollaiolo and Verrocchio can also be measured by the role they assumed outside Florence: two Popes' tombs in St Peter's were commissioned from Pollaiolo, and Verrocchio was responsible for the equestrian statue of *Colleoni* in Venice, a superb sequel to Donatello's *Gattamelata* monument in Padua, directly inspired by the heroic world of Antiquity.

Not even the conspiracy devised by the Pazzi family in 1478 against Lorenzo and his brother Giuliano seemed to interrupt this period of incredible creative activity in the artistic life of Florence. Moreover, despite the murder of Giuliano, Lorenzo emerged from the fray even stronger, the absolute ruler of the city, establishing himself as the greatest political and diplomatic genius of the time, besides being something of a poet. He surrounded himself with men of letters, poets and philosophers, and his 'round table' of Humanists, based at the villa of Careggi, seemed to have brought the culture of Periclean Athens to life in Florence. In the figurative arts, the most obvious reflection of this was in the mythologies painted by **Sandro Botticelli** (1444–1510) which, in their play of line taken from Pollaiolo, carried the rhythmic capacity of drawing to its utmost limit. Botticelli worked mostly for private patrons, and his paintings, even those of religious subjects, reach an almost abstract intellectual level that seems to be in direct antithesis to the world of intensely human images created by Donatello and Masaccio.

Renaissance architecture left little space for the large mural decorations which were such an important feature of 14C Florentine art. The masters of the new style, although interested in the techniques of their predecessors (with the exception of Botticelli who made very limited use of this medium), either had to content themselves with a lesser part in the new architecture or re-use the existing surfaces in older buildings. The latter was often the case, and **Domenico Ghirlandaio** (1449–94) was among the painters who dedicated themselves to fresco painting, reawakening the glories of the 14C. Indeed, he was said to have wanted to cover even the city walls with frescoes. Ghirlandaio typified, in the best possible way, the bourgeois spirit that now increasingly dominated Florentine society, setting his stories from the past against a background of contemporary Florence. He adapted the new style to pre-existing Gothic spaces perfectly, and there is a consistency of style in the narratives painted by him and his assistants spread over the vast areas available. His works include the stories of the life of St Francis in the Sassetti chapel of Santa Trìnita, and lives of the Virgin and St John the Baptist in the Tornabuoni chapel of Santa Maria Novella; the decoration of the Sala dei Gigli in the Palazzo Vecchio; and a series of vividly coloured altar-pieces reminiscent of Flemish painting. Ghirlandaio was an accomplished draughtsman and a painter of supreme technical skill, and his easy and pleasing style made him a popular artist in his day. As a result of his success, he was called to Rome by the Pope to paint part of the cycle of frescoes in the Sistine Chapel.

During these years, Florence increasingly became the meeting place of some of the most fundamental tendencies in Italian art. **Pietro Perugino** (c 1450–1523), the Umbrian artist who taught Raphael, preceded him in leaving some of his greatest works in Florentine churches and private collections. **Filippino Lippi** (1457–1504) and **Piero di Cosimo** (1462–1521), who were also active in Florence then, anticipated to a certain extent the restless aspect of Mannerism.

In the field of architecture, **Giuliano da Sangallo** (1443/45–1516) built the villa at Poggio a Caiano for Lorenzo il Magnifico, and Santa Maria delle Carceri at Prato, two buildings which reiterated the fundamental teachings of Brunelleschi, though with some original developments. Within the city, new buildings sprang up to embody the wealth and ambitions of the richest families: the Gondi palace by Giuliano da Sangallo, the Guadagni palace by Cronaca and, above all, Palazzo Strozzi, also by Cronaca. Although he did not complete it, this palace represents the most ambitious and perfect example of a palatial residence of the Renaissance. In sculpture, however, after the death of Pollaiolo and Verrocchio, Sansovino lacked the capacity for innovation. It required the nascent genius of Michelangelo to show that in this field—and not only in this field—art was to take a new direction.

The genius who, more than anyone else, embodied the Renaissance ideal of the 'universal' artist, **Leonardo da Vinci** (1452–1519), was born near Florence in 1452. A pupil of Verrocchio, he was undoubtedly influenced by him in his early works but, as he matured, developed an entirely personal vision which, together with his writings, made him a celebrated figure not only in art but in every field of knowledge. His tireless research and ingenious engineering, his rare pictorial works, his wanderings throughout Italy, his exile in France, and his unique style which opened new horizons in painting and sculpture (thanks to his anatomical studies), all served to make him an almost mythical figure. Strange, then, that his genius went unremarked by Lorenzo il Magnifico. He was, however, increasingly involved with the political problems then troubling Italy towards the end of his life. Perhaps Leonardo's subtle and introverted spirit had little appeal to a man of Lorenzo's temperament, who was drawn instead to the sort of conceptual clarity derived from Platonism, and to the Classicism evident in the sculptural works he had collected over the years in the garden of San Marco.

The artist who embodied Lorenzo's ideals was the very young **Michelangelo Buonarroti** (1475–1564), a pupil of Ghirlandaio and Bertoldo. Legend has it that he came to the notice of Lorenzo when he sculpted the head of a faun in the garden of San Marco. There is no doubt that the young genius who began his career under the wing of the Medici, represents, more than any other Florentine artist of the time, the aesthetic ideal on which the whole century's art was based; that mythicised vision of the ancient world which represented absolute perfection and the highest embodiment of human genius. Michelangelo soon established himself as the artist who could offer Florence that continuity in art which summarised the possibilities of so many generations, and that universality so sought after by his predecessors. Sculptor, painter and architect, poet and philosopher, the importance of this solitary personality was recognised not only in Florence but throughout Italy and Europe. His prodigious capacity for work allowed him to develop from his early Florentine style, in which he absorbed 15C experiences, towards the creation of an artistic idiom, which—although indebted to Masaccio, Luca Signorelli, Donatello, Verrocchio, Brunelleschi and Sangallo—enabled him to develop a highly individual style, whilst reaching back to the heroic, monumental conception of the art of Imperial Rome.

The early period of this indefatigable artist, which can be defined as 'classical', culminated in his famous sculpture of **David**. At this time, certain 15C motifs, such as the use of the tondo in both painting and sculpture, reappear in his work (for example, his reliefs for the Pitti and Gaddi, and his painting for the Doni, the married couple whose portraits Raphael was painting at about the same time). Next came a more complex phase in Michelangelo's art. Works such as his *St Matthew* and the first *'Prisoner'* for the tomb of Julius II (now in the Louvre) belong to this period, and show clear signs of the artist's disturbed state of mind, reflecting his sensitivity to the difficulties Florence was undergoing in these years. Dividing his time between Florence and Rome, Michelangelo seemed to reflect in his constantly changing projects an instability that became typical of his art and often caused him to leave his work unfinished.

There is no doubt that the break with 15C Humanism—the serene, joyous style that had characterised the works of the Early Renaissance—came with Michelangelo. Although he still used some of the elements which had distinguished those works, he forged a new style that deliberately seemed to disrupt that balance so carefully sought by his predecessors. An obvious example is the construction of the New Sacristy in San Lorenzo, a mausoleum for the Medici family. Here the graceful shapes, reminiscent of Brunelleschi, are reinforced by elements taken from Roman architecture and, above all, by the massive sculptures, conceived as an essential complement to the design. In these figures, as in those of the 'prisoners' for the second project for the tomb of Julius II (now in the Accademia), Michelangelo eschewed the 15C forms which had interested him up until then, in favour of dynamic, articulated forms, turning in on themselves, which were to be the model for all the 'serpentine figures' of Mannerist sculpture in the 16C. In the staircase of the vestibule of the Laurentian Library, the same instability of form is evident, the same desire to break up the centralised perspective which had been Brunelleschi's great innovation. Here the alternating plays of light and points of view are clearly a prelude to the Baroque.

After the demise of the short-lived Florentine Republic (see p 93), Michelangelo expressed his disillusionment and disapproval of the Medici by leaving Florence for good, leaving behind many of his works incomplete. Nevertheless, it was his example which established the birth of a new style known as Mannerism in Florence. This style interpreted that aspect of Michelangelo's art which seemed to break away from the classical forms that had been the concern of Florentine artists since Giotto and Arnolfo.

The High Renaissance

Despite the disturbances which troubled Florence after the death of Lorenzo il Magnifico in 1492, the city still remained the centre of some of the most important developments in Italian art between the end of the 15C and the beginning of the 16C. Apart from Michelangelo, who after 1508 was increasingly occupied with commissions from the Pope in Rome, other important artists worked in Florence and created a mature, grandiose language, complex in form and colour, which was to characterise the High Renaissance. When the young **Raphael** (1483–1520) arrived in the city, it was here that he developed his unique, pure, classical style, and local artists were influenced towards an evolution of form based primarily on drawing, a medium in which the Florentines excelled. **Fra Bartolomeo** (1475–1517)and **Andrea del Sarto** (1486–1530) were the two greatest exponents of this trend. Andrea del Sarto, whom Vasari christened 'the faultless painter', undertook important public works, including altarpieces and frescoes of masterly execution, and created a school of painting which dominated Florentine art in the first half of the 16C. His pupils included **Pontormo** (1494–1556) and **Rosso Fiorentino** (1494–1541), who were important for their original interpretation of Mannerism, a style which became increasingly intellectualised and refined, far removed from the rationalism of the Early Renaissance. In their unique forms and colours, they re-elaborated the teachings of Michelangelo who was still regarded as the supreme master, but in an even more pronounced, stylised, almost abstract language.

This period of Mannerism, at its most original, was soon to come to an end. After the assassination of Duke Alessandro in 1537, a distant cousin, Cosimo de' Medici, took over the government of the city. He brought about rapid changes in its cultural life, since his political ideas prevailed in everything, including the arts. The commissioning of great public works which had characterised the regimes of the Republic and later the Medici *Signoria* now ceased almost entirely. Even the cathedral workshops fell silent and work on the embellishment of the interior proceeded only sporadically. Artistic manifestations were now almost entirely controlled by the absolute ruler who determined their nature. The face of the city was changed by the work of **Giorgio Vasari** (1511/12–74) and of **Bartolomeo Ammannati** (1511–92), the two architects to whom the grand-duke entrusted most of the important works of the period. Vasari constructed the new centre of government, the Uffizi, which, with its arcades (still inspired by Brunelleschi), frames the view of Palazzo Vecchio on one side and the Arno on the other. He also built (in five months) the Corridor, which bears his name, connecting the Uffizi with the grand-ducal residence. Ammannati enlarged the palace, which, after its purchase from the Pitti family, became the home of the reigning families of Florence for the next three centuries. The bridge of Santa Trìnita is also the work of Ammannati.

Cosimo continued the tradition of enlivening the city with statuary, but in a way which gave Florence the aspect which it still has today: that of a great, open-air museum of sculpture. Piazza della Signoria was peopled with works by the most prestigious sculptors of the day: Ammannati made the *Fountain of Neptune*, assisted by some of the most important protagonists of Mannerism in Florence, such as **Giambologna** (1529–1608), **Vincenzo de' Rossi** (1525–87) and **Vincenzo Danti** (1530–76). **Bandinelli** (1493–1560; sculpted the *Hercules and Cacus* which can be seen almost as a challenge to Michelangelo's *David* nearby; **Benvenuto Cellini** (1500–71) made his beautiful bronze *Perseus*, poised on an exquisite marble base decorated with bronze statuettes; Giambologna sculpted the ***Rape of the Sabines***, one of the finest examples of a 'serpentine figure', borrowed from Michelangelo's mature period. The equestrian monuments to Cosimo I (by Giambologna) and Ferdinando I (by Tacca) are an attempt to recreate the climate of Imperial Rome by imitating Roman statues rather than works by Donatello or Verrocchio.

Garden architecture became more complicated during this period, enriched with statuary, fountains and artificial grottoes which gave ample opportunity for Florentine architects and sculptors to express their talent and refinement. Art became, increasingly, the private expression of the Duke, who dictated the fashion and imposed the tastes of his Court on the great families of Florence. Interiors became more and more sumptuous and loaded with decoration. **Bronzino** (1503–72) came to the fore in painting with a very personal form of classicism, seen through the formal refinements of Pontormo's Mannerism. His use of gem-like, enamelled colours give his paintings an almost surreal aspect, and his portraits represent the social standing of the sitters rather than their personalities.

The reworking of all the motifs which had characterised 15C Florentine art seemed to find its conclusion in the historical events taking place in the city from the 16C onwards. Ably governed by Cosimo I and his successors, Florence grew as a centre of cultural elaboration rather than original creativity as it had been for three centuries. Even Mannerism, which in its early phase had influenced the whole of European art with its sophisticated style, began to show an irreversible involution, merely repeating the talented inventions of its early protagonists. Court art reflected more and more the private nature of the artist's product, even in fresco—now chiefly used in the decoration of great houses—once the glory of Florentine art. When the legacy of Michelangelo's direct influence was exhausted, Florentine art was no longer capable of formulating its own original language; the city became a provincial centre reflecting pictorial trends from other, more important centres such as Rome, Bologna and Venice. Florentine art continued to follow forms which had their roots in the past and especially in the 16C.

Even in the so-called Baroque period, architecture, sculpture and painting reflect the ideas of the great Renaissance tradition. In fact, the medieval-Renaissance structure of the city seemed almost to resist the spatial ideas of Baroque art and when this style was adopted—for Santi Michele e Gaetano, San Firenze and San Frediano—it was in a form that was linked to the past. Ancient churches and palace interiors were renovated with Baroque sculpture and painting, for example Santa Maria Maggiore, San Jacopo sopr'Arno and Palazzo Feroni, but in a way far removed from Pietro da Cortona's sumptuous Roman Baroque decoration of the grand-ducal apartment in the Pitti Palace. Artists were primarily engaged on new altarpieces for churches, or on commissions for private collectors. Stylistically, they sought a blend between tradition and a more modern idiom (for example, the frescoes by Giovanni da San Giovanni, Francesco Furini and Cecco Bravo in the so-called Sala di San Giovanni in the Pitti Palace), but their technical skills often concealed a lack of inspiration.

As late as the 19C, when the city was enlarged during its brief period as the capital of Italy, there was the same recourse to ecleticism: all the architectural styles developed by the great artists of the Renaissance were employed—except, a little later, when mock-Gothic became the fashion. However, by this time, we are dealing with the history of taste rather than the history of the art of a city that has given an unequalled contribution to European civilisation.

Historical sketch

In 2,000,000 BC, the site of Florence was as near to the sea as Venice is today. The plain of the Arno was first inhabited in Neolithic times when Italic tribes from the north settled here towards the end of the 10C BC. Although some Etruscan tombs have been found on the plain towards Sesto, there is no evidence of an Etruscan city preceding Florence. The Etruscans preferred to build their stronghold on the hill of Fiesole (5C BC or earlier). The Roman colony of 'Florentia' was founded in 59 BC by Julius Caesar, and the city was built on the Arno where the crossing is narrowest. The river, navigable up to this point, had great importance in the early economic development of the city. The Roman city, which was enlarged in the Augustan era, flourished in the 2C and 3C AD, when it probably had a population of more than 10,000.

By the early 5C, the city was already threatened by Ostrogoth invaders. Despite the Byzantine walls erected in 541–544, the Ostrogoth leader Totila was able to inflict considerable damage on the city in 552. By the end of the 6C, Florence had followed the fate of the rest of central and northern Italy and was firmly held under Lombard dominion. Charlemagne visited the city in 781 and 786, and the Carolingian circle of walls was set up in 869–896. In the 11C, Florence was one of the principal centres of Christianity. The city was favoured by Matilda, Margrave of Tuscany, who saw to the building of a fourth circle of walls in 1078 as a defence against the Emperor Henry IV. Thus the Florentines, who espoused the cause of the Pope, were able to withstand a siege of Imperial troops for ten days. In 1125, the rival town of Fiesole was finally overcome after a fierce battle.

The thirteenth century

The **Comune** of Florence came into being in the first decades of the 12C, with a college of officials, a council of some 100 men, and a *Parlamento* which was called regularly to approve government policy. The *Comune* protected the business interests of Florentine merchants who had begun to prosper through the cloth trade and money-lending. The fifth line of walls, which now included the Oltrarno, was built in 1172–75. In 1207, the consular regime was replaced, and a *Podestà* (chief magistrate) installed who held executive power in the government. The post was traditionally reserved for a foreigner. At this time, the first guilds (*Arti*) were formed to protect the commercial interests of the merchant and banking community. During the course of the 13C, three new bridges were built over the Arno, the Palazzo del Popolo (Bargello) was erected, and the two great mendicant Orders, the Franciscans and Dominicans, came to Florence to found Santa Croce and Santa Maria Novella.

The political life of the 13C was dominated by the long drawn-out struggle between the **Guelfs** and **Ghibellines**. This was sparked off by the feuds arising from the murder of one of the Buondelmonti by the Amidei in 1215. (The Buondelmonti became the Guelf and the Amidei the Ghibelline faction.) The Ghibelline faction, which supported the Emperor, derived its name from Weiblingen, the Castle of the Hohenstaufen, and the Guelfs, who supported the Pope, from the family name (Welfs) of Otto IV. By the middle of the century, Florentine merchants—who travelled as far afield as England and the Near

East—were established in a privileged and independent position in trade and commerce. The florin, first minted in silver c 1235, and soon after in gold, was used as the standard gold coin in Europe. The regime of the Primo Popolo (1250–60), supported by the Guelfs, now included the merchant class. The towers built to stress the status of the great noble families in Florence were reduced in height by order of the government. The city was victorious in battles against Pisa, Pistoia and Siena.

In a renewed war against Siena (and the German army led by Manfred) the Florentines were defeated at Montaperti in 1260. However, the city was spared from destruction at the hand of the Ghibellines through the generosity of their leader, Farinata degli Uberti, a member of one of the oldest noble families of Florence. Count Guido Novello took up residence in the Bargello as *Podestà* of the Ghibelline government. After continuous struggles between the two factions, the regime of the *Secondo Popolo* was set up in 1284 by the *Arti Maggiori* (Greater Guilds). In 1292, Giano della Bella became *Priore* and through his famous *ordinamenti di giustizia* the Florentine nobility were excluded from high political office. The last circle of walls was begun in 1284, and the centre of government was moved from the Bargello to Palazzo della Signoria (begun in 1294), the residence of the *Priori*.

By the beginning of the 14C, Florence was among the five largest cities in Europe with a population of about 100,000. Its prosperity was based largely on the woollen cloth industry which had accounted for her significant economic growth in the 13C.

The fourteenth century

The internal struggles within the Guelf party were renewed in the 14C with unrest between the rival factions known as the *Neri* (Blacks) and *Bianchi* (Whites), which were led by the Cerchi and Donati families respectively. Charles of Valois, called in as a peacemaker by Boniface VIII, favoured the *Neri* and sent 600 *Bianchi* into exile in 1302, among them Dante. In 1342, Walter de Brienne, Duke of Athens, was elected *Signore* for life and given absolute power, but an insurrection led to his expulsion from the city a year later. The Florentine economy suffered a severe crisis in the 1340s with the bankruptcy of the two most powerful banking families: the Bardi and the Peruzzi (the Mozzi bank had already failed in 1311). This was partly due to the inability of Edward III of England to repay his debts during the disastrous Hundred Years War, and also to the Black Death, a catastrophe in which the population was reduced by more than half (and which was to recur seven times between 1350 and 1430). Meanwhile, the uprising of the *Ciompi* (wool-carders) in 1378 under Michele di Lando represented a high point in labour unrest in Florence's chief industry. The demands for recognition and the right to form a guild were met with the creation of three new guilds and direct representation in government for a brief period. However, in 1382, the *popolo grasso*, a relatively small group of wealthy middle-class merchant families, united with the Guelf party and established an oligarchic form of government; from this time on, the guilds lost ground in the political life of the city after nearly a century of pre-eminence.

The regime of the *popolo grasso* succeeded in holding power in Florence for 40 years. Every so often, the heads of rival families were exiled in order to lessen the risk of power being concentrated in the hands of any one man. Benedetto degli

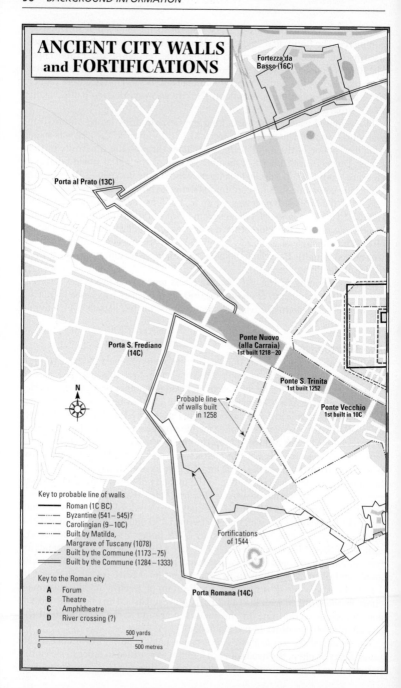

ANCIENT CITY WALLS and FORTIFICATIONS

Fortezza da Basso (16C)

Porta al Prato (13C)

Porta S. Frediano (14C)

Ponte Nuovo (alla Carraia)
1st built 1218–20

Ponte S. Trinita
1st built 1252

Ponte Vecchio
1st built in 10C

Probable line of walls built in 1258

N

Fortifications of 1544

Porta Romana (14C)

Key to probable line of walls
— Roman (1C BC)
—·— Byzantine (541 – 545)?
—··— Carolingian (9–10C)
—···— Built by Matilda, Margrave of Tuscany (1078)
----- Built by the Commune (1173 – 75)
— Built by the Commune (1284 – 1333)

Key to the Roman city
A Forum
B Theatre
C Amphitheatre
D River crossing (?)

0   500 yards
0   500 metres

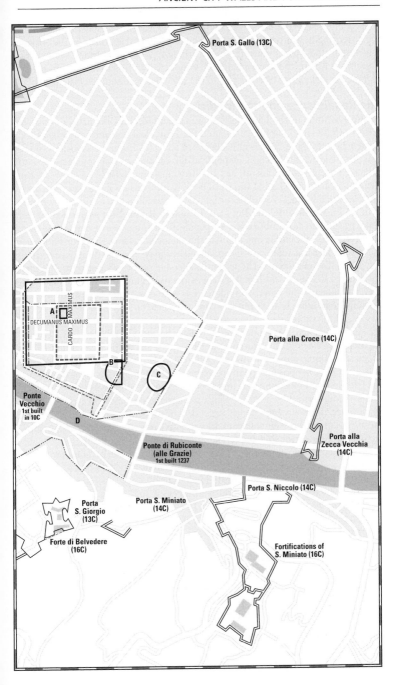

Porta S. Gallo (13C)

Porta alla Croce (14C)

DECUMANUS MAXIMUS

CARDO MAXIMUS

A

B

C

D

Ponte Vecchio
1st built in 10C

Porta alla Zecca Vecchia (14C)

Ponte di Rubiconte (alle Grazie)
1st built 1237

Porta S. Niccolo (14C)

Porta S. Giorgio (13C)

Porta S. Miniato (14C)

Forte di Belvedere (16C)

Fortifications of S. Miniato (16C)

Alberti, one of the wealthiest men in the city, and leader of a moderate faction in the government, was banished in 1387; he was followed into exile by the Strozzi, and finally the Medici. During these turbulent years of warfare against the Visconti in Milan, the government still conducted an ambitious foreign policy. Florence at last gained direct access to the sea when it conquered Pisa in 1406.

The Renaissance and the Medici

At the beginning of the 15C, Florence was the intellectual and artistic centre of Europe. Cultivated Florentines adopted the civic ideal and the city proclaimed herself heir to Rome. In this city *a misura d'uomo* (of human dimension), there was a profound involvement in political life on the part of intellectuals and artists. A new conception of art and learning symbolised the birth of the Renaissance. Chancellors of the republic now included humanist scholars such as Coluccio Salutati, Leonardo Bruni, Poggio Bracciolini and Carlo Marsuppini.

In 1433, **Cosimo de' Medici** (called **Cosimo il Vecchio**) was exiled for ten years by Rinaldo degli Albizi since his popularity was increasing among the merchant faction in the city, in opposition to the oligarchic regime. However, his return just a year later was unanimously acclaimed by the people, and he at once became the first citizen of Florence. His prudent leadership of the city lasted for 30 years. He adhered to the constitutional system of the old regime and managed to dominate the policy of the government abroad as well as at home. He usually avoided holding public office himself, but was careful to keep the support of a wide circle of friends. At the same time, he increased the immense wealth of his family banking business which had been founded by his father, Giovanni de' Bicci. In 1439, Cosimo succeeded in having the Church Council—which led to the brief union of the Greek and Roman churches—transferred to Florence from Ferrara. The city, now at the height of her prestige in Europe, played host to the emperor John Paleologus, the Patriarch of Constantinople, and Pope Eugenius IV along with their huge retinues of courtiers and scholars. Cosimo, perhaps the greatest figure in the history of Florence, symbolised the Renaissance ideal of the 'universal man'; a successful businessman and brilliant politician, he was also a patron of the arts and an intellectual (he founded the first modern libraries in Europe in Florence).

On the death of Cosimo il Vecchio in 1464, Pater Patriae, his son Piero automatically took over his position in the government of the city. Known as Piero il Gottoso ('the gouty') because of his ill-health, his brief rule was characterised by his great interest in the arts, and a number of notable monuments of the Renaissance were commissioned by him. His son, **Lorenzo**, called **Il Magnifico**, was another famous Medici ruler during the Renaissance. His princely 'reign' fostered a revival of learning that led to the foundation of the Platonic Academy at Careggi, which included among its members Lorenzo's friends Marsilio Ficino, Angelo Poliziano and Pico della Mirandola. Lorenzo himself was a humanist scholar and poet of considerable standing. In a famous conspiracy in 1478, the Pazzi, old rivals of the Medici, with the help of Pope Sixtus IV, attempted to assassinate Lorenzo. His brother Giuliano was killed, but Lorenzo escaped, with the result that his position in the government of the city was even more secure. Francesco de' Pazzi and the other conspirators were hung from a window of Palazzo Vecchio. In 1489, Lorenzo succeeded in having his son Giovanni (later Pope Leo X) created a cardinal at the tender age of 13, one of his most significant political achievements. However, he was a less able businessman than his grandfather and was unable to save the Medici bank from failure before he died in 1492 at the age of 44.

The sixteenth century

Lorenzo il Magnifico's eldest son Piero was driven out of the city after his surrender to Charles VIII of France at Sarzana (1494). The Florentines, inspired by the oratory of the Dominican **Girolamo Savonarola** (see p 125), rebelled against the Medici and a Republican government with a Great Council was formed. Savonarola was burnt at the stake as a heretic (1498) but the Republic continued, and in 1502, under Piero Soderini, succeeded in retaking Pisa. After the defeat of Florence by the Spanish army in 1512, Giuliano and Giovanni de' Medici returned to the city with the support of the Pope. However, in 1527 when Rome had been sacked by the troops of Charles V, they were again sent into exile. The new Republican government led by Niccolò Capponi lasted only until 1529, when a peace treaty between the Emperor and Pope provided an opportunity for the reinstatement of the Medici in the government of Florence. The Florentines resisted their return in a last bid for independence but finally succumbed after a famous siege in which even the new fortifications, hastily erected by Michelangelo, were unable to withstand the united armies of Pope and Emperor.

The Medici grand-dukes

The great-grandson of Lorenzo il Magnifico, Alessandro, was married to the Emperor Charles V's daughter Margaret of Parma, and was appointed Duke of Florence in 1530. Alessandro's unpopular rule, in which he was opposed by those who had supported the Republican regime, and by the patricians who saw their power in the government diminished, came to an abrupt end with his murder in 1537 by a cousin, Lorenzaccio. He was succeeded by **Cosimo de' Medici** (1519–74), son of the famous *condottiere* (army leader), Giovanni delle Bande Nere. A last attempt by the Republican exiles (led by the rich aristocrat Filippo Strozzi) to abolish the Medici principate ended in Republican defeat at the battle of Montemurlo. During his long despotic rule, Cosimo I brought the subject cities of Tuscany under Florentine dominion, but his active and in some ways enlightened reign assured the independence of the Tuscan State from both Emperor and Pope. In 1570 Cosimo received the title of Grand-duke of Tuscany from Pope Pius V and the Medici absolutist principate continued for another two centuries. Cosimo I commissioned numerous works of art and architecture to embellish the city and glorify his name, and this patronage was continued by his successors (who also amassed remarkable private collections). The Medici grand-dukes were responsible for the Uffizi collection, which they augmented over the centuries, particularly Ferdinando II and his brother Cardinal Leopoldo. The last of the Medici, Anna Maria Lodovica, settled her inheritance on the people of Florence.

The Lorraine grand-dukes

Two years before the death of Anna Maria de' Medici in 1737, the succession of Francesco of Lorraine, afterwards Francis I of Austria, had been arranged by treaty, and Tuscany became an appendage of the Austrian Imperial house. The reign of **Pietro Leopoldo**, Grand-duke in 1765–90, stands out for his remarkable scientific interests and the agricultural reforms he introduced to Tuscany (it was at this time that many of the handsome *case coloniche*, or farm houses, were

The Medici Family

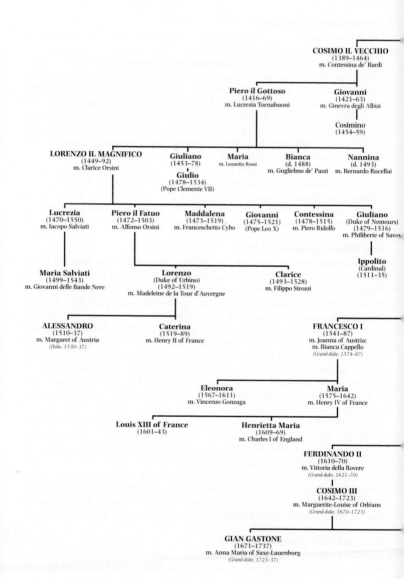

COSIMO IL VECCHIO
(1389–1464)
m. Contessina de' Bardi

Piero il Gottoso
(1416–69)
m. Lucrezia Tornabuoni

Giovanni
(1421–63)
m. Ginevra degli Albizi

Cosimino
(1454–59)

LORENZO IL MAGNIFICO
(1449–92)
m. Clarice Orsini

Giuliano
(1453–78)
Giulio
(1478–1534)
(Pope Clemente VII)

Maria
m. Leonetto Rossi

Bianca
(d. 1488)
m. Guglielmo de' Pazzi

Nannina
(d. 1493)
m. Bernardo Rucellai

Lucrezia
(1470–1550)
m. Iacopo Salviati

Piero il Fatuo
(1472–1503)
m. Alfonso Orsini

Maddalena
(1473–1519)
m. Franceschetto Cybo

Giovanni
(1475–1521)
(Pope Leo X)

Contessina
(1478–1515)
m. Piero Ridolfo

Giuliano
(Duke of Nemours)
(1479–1516)
m. Philiberte of Savoy

Maria Salviati
(1499–1543)
m. Giovanni delle Bande Nere

Lorenzo
(Duke of Urbino)
(1492–1519)
m. Madeleine de la Tour d'Auvergne

Clarice
(1493–1528)
m. Filippo Strozzi

Ippolito
(Cardinal)
(1511–35)

ALESSANDRO
(1510–37)
m. Margaret of Austria
(Duke, 1530–37)

Caterina
(1519–89)
m. Henry II of France

FRANCESCO I
(1541–87)
m. Joanna of Austria;
m. Bianca Cappello
(Grand-duke, 1574–87)

Eleonora
(1567–1611)
m. Vincenzo Gonzaga

Maria
(1575–1642)
m. Henry IV of France

Louis XIII of France
(1601–43)

Henrietta Maria
(1609–69)
m. Charles I of England

FERDINANDO II
(1610–70)
m. Vittoria della Rovere
(Grand-duke, 1621–70)

COSIMO III
(1642–1723)
m. Marguerite-Louise of Orléans
(Grand-duke, 1670–1723)

GIAN GASTONE
(1671–1737)
m. Anna Maria of Saxe-Lauenburg
(Grand-duke, 1723–37)

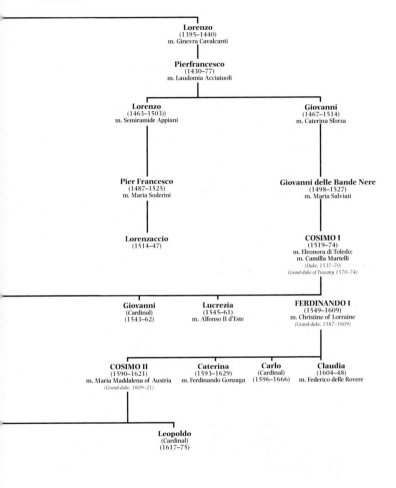

Giovanni di Bicci
(1360–1429)
m. Piccarda Bueri

Lorenzo
(1395–1440)
m. Ginevra Cavalcanti

Pierfrancesco
(1430–77)
m. Laudomia Acciaiuoli

Lorenzo
(1463–1503))
m. Semiramide Appiani

Giovanni
(1467–1514)
m. Caterina Sforza

Pier Francesco
(1487–1525)
m. Maria Soderini

Giovanni delle Bande Nere
(1498–1527)
m. Maria Salviati

Lorenzaccio
(1514–47)

COSIMO I
(1519–74)
m. Eleonora di Toledo;
m. Camilla Martelli
(Duke, 1537–70;
Grand-duke of Tuscany 1570–74)

Giovanni
(Cardinal)
(1543–62)

Lucrezia
(1545–61)
m. Alfonso II d'Este

FERDINANDO I
(1549–1609)
m. Christine of Lorraine
(Grand-duke, 1587–1609)

COSIMO II
(1590–1621)
m. Maria Maddalena of Austria
(Grand-duke, 1609–21)

Caterina
(1593–1629)
m. Ferdinando Gonzaga

Carlo
(Cardinal)
(1596–1666)

Claudia
(1604–48)
m. Federico delle Rovere

Leopoldo
(Cardinal)
(1617–75)

Anna Maria
(1667–1743)
m. William, Elector Palatine

built in the Tuscan countryside). In 1799, the French expelled the Austrians and, after an ephemeral appearance as the Kingdom of Etruria (1801–02), under the Infante Louis of Bourbon, the grand duchy was conferred in 1809 upon Elisa Bonaparte Baciocchi, Napoleon's sister. The Bourbon restoration (1814) brought back the Lorraine family, whose rule, interrupted by the revolution of 1848, ended in 1859. In March 1860, Tuscany became part of united Italy, and from 1861 to 1875 Florence was the capital of the Italian kingdom.

The post-war period up to the present day

All the bridges in Florence except the Ponte Vecchio were blown up by the Germans in the Second World War, despite the efforts to prevent it by Gerhard Wolf, the wartime German consul (later made a freeman by grateful Florentines). The city was then occupied by the Allies in August 1944, after considerable although desultory fighting.

Part of the city centre near Ponte Vecchio had to be rebuilt, and Ponte Santa Trinita was carefully reconstructed in 1957. In the post-war years, Florence spread out on the plain to the north-west to provide housing for an expanding population. In 1989, a huge new urban development (4 million cubic metres, including tower blocks 50m high) on a piece of land owned by the Fiat and Fondiaria companies was temporarily halted, but a subsequent city administration has given it the go-ahead even if on a somewhat reduced scale. This 'urban sprawl', so familiar in other large cities, is seen by many people as a threat to the character of the city and a negation of enlightened town planning. Despite the fact that Florence has an international airport on the coast at Pisa within as easy reach as those of other important cities, the small airport at Peretola on the northern outskirts of Florence has been enlarged to take European flights, to the consternation of many residents.

In 1966, the Arno overflowed its banks and severely damaged buildings and works of art. This was treated as an international disaster, and numerous historical buildings, paintings and sculptures had to be restored, a task which took several decades. It was also necessary to reconstruct hundreds of houses and artisans' workshops.

Since the first recorded flood in 1177, the Arno has overflowed its banks 57 times (small plaques throughout the city show the level the water reached during some of these disasters). Uncontrolled building along the banks of the Arno both upstream and downstream from the city since 1966 have greatly increased the risk of another flood, and the authorities admit that if the whole of the Arno basin is affected by heavy rainfall the river will flood again. Building on its banks was forbidden by the regional government only in 1994, and there is now a 15-year programme of flood prevention awaiting definitive approval and allotment of government funds. Meanwhile, the city's only protection is an alarm system which can give a warning only six hours in advance.

After the 1966 flood, great advances were made in conservation work, and numerous remarkable restoration programmes have been carried out (most recently, on the frescoes of the cupola of the Duomo, in the Cappella di Filippo Strozzi in Santa Maria Novella, and in the Bardi di Vernio Chapel in Santa Croce).

Because of pollution levels in the air, it has been agreed that many statues originally made for exterior locations must remain under cover once restored. Ghiberti's East Doors of the Baptistery were removed in 1990 and replaced *in situ* by casts (the original panels, which are being restored one by one, are exhibited in the Museo dell'Opera del Duomo). The statues from the exterior niches of Orsanmichele are being restored and have been replaced by copies: the originals are now appropriately housed in a museum on the upper floor of the building. In Piazza Signoria, Donatello's statue of *Judith* has been replaced by a copy after the original was restored (now in Palazzo Vecchio), although Cellini's statue of *Perseus* was returned outside to the Loggia dei Lanzi in 2000 after its spectacular restoration. Many statues and sculptures in the Boboli gardens are currently being restored.

Paintings which have been restored in the last few years include Leonardo da Vinci's *Annunciation* in the Uffizi, as well as important works by Giotto, Lorenzo Monaco, Raphael, Andrea del Sarto, Titian, Rubens and Giovanni Fattori, as well as most of the altarpieces in Santo Spirito.

During recent years numerous museums in the city have been expanded, rearranged or re-opened including the Museo dell'Opera del Duomo, Palazzo Vecchio, the Galleria dell'Accademia, the Museo di San Marco, the Museo Horne, the Galleria d'Arte Moderna, the Galleria del Costume, the Museo Stibbert and the Museo Archeologico. A general restoration programme has been under way since 1985 on the three floors of Palazzo Pitti, and suites of rooms used by the Medici and Lorraine grand-dukes, and later by the royal house of Savoy have been restored. The superb ceilings of the main reception rooms in the Galleria Palatina frescoed by Pietro da Cortona have been restored. The Galleria d'Arte Moderna and the Galleria del Costume there were reopened in 1999/2000. The ground floor of the Uffizi gallery has been opened to provide more space for the reception of visitors, and the Contini-Bonacossi collection has been rearranged in a wing of the building. Many more years will be needed before the first floor is opened as an extension of the gallery in rooms occupied by the state archives until 1989. A new exit is also under construction in Via de' Castellani. In 1993, a car bomb placed by the Mafia exploded in Via Lambertesca killing five people and causing much structural damage to the Uffizi. Some 90 paintings had to be restored, and repair work continues in the west corridor.

An excellent booking service has been introduced for the state museums in Florence, which means you no longer have to queue for admission. If you are on your own, it is surprisingly easy to book a visit only a few days in advance even at the most crowded times.

In the last few years a number of churches have been restored, including Santa Croce, Santa Maria Novella, and Santo Spirito.

Many small tabernacles in the streets of the old city have been restored since 1991. These contain painted or sculpted devotional images and are still an integral part of city life, honoured daily with flowers and candles. Their restoration has been financed by private citizens, local parishes, and Florentine companies. Precious Renaissance organs in various churches (including Santissima Annunziata, San Niccolò oltr'Arno, and the Badia Fiorentina) have been restored recently and concerts on them are usually given in the winter months.

Careful restoration work is in progress on the gardens of the Medici villas of La Petraia and Castello, as well as the Boboli gardens, and the private garden of Villa La Pietra.

Serious concerns in the 1980s about the levels of traffic pollution in the city and its effect on the exterior of buildings and external sculpture—to say nothing of its damage to the air we breathe—led to the closure of the historic centre to traffic (except for residents) in 1988. More streets in the Oltrarno were closed to traffic in the 1990s. The whole of Florence is now closed to all traffic on certain Sundays of the year. This is a major step forward, but Florence's geographical position in a shallow basin enclosed by low hills and its sultry climate means that the city is particularly subject to air pollution, and on certain days of the year the city council have to enforce a total ban on cars (except those using 'green' petrol) in a large area of the city in order to protect the health of residents. Even more drastic measures are evidently required to safeguard both inhabitants and visitors from the effects of pollution, and there are plans to introduce more electric buses, and those fuelled by natural gas. The problem of car parking in the city still has to be resolved, and Florence also has to work out a way in which Italy's new high-speed train system can traverse the city.

Since 1995 the mayor has been elected directly by the citizens, following a new electoral system recently introduced throughout the country. There are hopes that a more responsible administration may in time be able to deal with all the many problems besetting the city, including pollution, traffic, urban planning and the reception of mass tourism (over two and a half million people visit Florence every year).

Further reading

Historical works

Renaissance Florence by Gene Brucker (1969). Studies of the Medici family include: *The Government of Florence under the Medici, 1434–94* by Nicolai Rubinstein (1968); *Florence and the Medici* by John Hale (1977); *The Last Medici* by Harold Acton (1932, reprinted 1980); and *The Rise and Fall of the House of Medici* by Christopher Hibbert (1983). *The City of Florence: Historical Vistas and Present Sightings* by R.W.B. Lewis (1995) is a general historical work.

Art historical works

Classic accounts of the Renaissance include: Jacob Burckhardt's *The Civilisation of the Renaissance in Italy* (1860, reprinted 1965) and Walter Pater's *The Renaissance* (1873, reprinted 1967). Bernard Berenson wrote pioneering studies of Florentine art including *The Italian Painters of the Renaissance* (1930, and many subsequent editions). John Pope-Hennessy also wrote numerous monographs on Renaissance artists (including Donatello, Luca della Robbia, Cellini, Fra Angelico and Paolo Uccello) as well as general studies on Florentine sculpture. Other useful studies of the Renaissance include: Charles Avery's *Florentine Renaissance Sculpture* (1970); Michael Levey's *Early Renaissance* (1967) and *High Renaissance* (1975); Howard Hibbard's *Michelangelo* (1978); and Mary Hollingsworth's *Patronage in Renaissance Italy* (1994). *Brunelleschi's Dome* (2000) by Ross King is an interesting study of Brunelleschi's life and the construction of the dome of the cathedral.

Guidebooks

Old guides which are still of great interest include: John Ruskin, *Mornings in Florence* (1873); Susan and Joanna Horner, *Walks in Florence* (1877); Grant Allen, *Historical Guide to Florence* (1897); Augustus Hare, *Florence* (1904); Janet Ross, *Florentine Palaces and Their Stories* (1905); Arnold Bennett, *Florentine Journal* (1910, republished in 1967); E.V. Lucas, *A Wanderer in Florence* (1912); and works by Edward Hutton, *Country Walks about Florence* (1926), *Florence and Northern Tuscany* (c 1926) and *Florence* (new edition in 1966).

Literature

Literature from the 19C and 20C with a Florentine background includes: *Romola* by George Eliot (1863, and numerous subsequent editions); the poetry of Robert and Elizabeth Barrett Browning; short stories by Henry James (*Madonna of the Future*, 1879) and Vernon Lee (*Il Cassone Nuziale*); Anthony Trollope's novel *He Knew he was Right* (1869). John Keats' 'Isabella, or the Pot of Basil' (1820) is based on a story by Boccaccio. Shelley wrote his 'Ode to the West Wind' in Florence in 1819. William Blundall Spence described the activities of art dealers in Florence in *The Lions of Florence* (1852). There are also descriptions of Florence in W.D. Howells' *Indian Summer* (1886) and D.H. Lawrence's *Aaron's Rod* (1933).

Recent books set in Florence include the numerous crime stories by Magdalene Nabb, such as *Death of a Dutchman* and *The Marshall and the Murderer* (1980s), Robert Hellenga's *The Sixteen Pleasures* (1994), Penelope Fitzgerald's *Innocence* (1986), and *Galileo's Daughter* by Dava Sobel (1999), a novel based on translations of the fascinating letters written by daughter to father. A useful general book is *Florence: a Literary Companion* by Francis King (1991).

Memoirs

Memoirs by Florentine residents include: Iris Origo, *Images and Shadows* (1970); Harold Acton, *Memoirs of an Aesthete* (1948); and Nicky Mariano, *Forty Years with Berenson* (1966). *Paradise of Exiles* (1974) and *The Divine Country: The British in Tuscany 1372–1980* (1982), both by Olive Hamilton, describe the foreign residents of Florence.

General

General books include: *Florence, a Travellers' Companion* (1986) by Harold Acton and Edward Chaney; *Florence: Biography of a City* (1993) by Christopher Hibbert; and *Florence: a Portrait* (1996) by Michael Levey.

THE GUIDE

View of Florence with the Duomo, Campanile and Palazzo Vecchio

1 • The Baptistery and the Duomo

The Baptistery

The Baptistery of San Giovanni (**Map1; 4**) is one of the oldest and most revered buildings in the city. Opening times 12.00–18.30; *fest.* 08.30– 13.30. Lire 5000.

> Called by Dante his *bel San Giovanni*, it has always held a special place in the history of Florence. The date of its foundation is uncertain; in the Middle Ages, it was thought to have Roman origins. It is now generally considered to have been built for the first time in the 6C or 7C, or even as early as the 4C–5C, but certainly no later than 897 when it is first mentioned. It was reconsecrated in 1059. A Roman palace of the 1C AD has been discovered beneath its foundations. It is an octagonal building of centralised plan derived from Byzantine models, with an exceptionally large dome.

The **exterior** was entirely encased in white marble from Luni and green marble from Prato in a classical geometrical design in the 11C–13C, at the expense of the *Arte di Calimala* (cloth-importers), the most important Guild of the medieval city. The decoration became a prototype for numerous Tuscan Romanesque religious buildings. At the end of the 13C, the striped angle pilasters were added, and the semicircular apse was probably replaced at this time by the rectangular *scarsella* (although it is possible that this had already been built by the 11C). The cupola was concealed by an unusual white pyramidal roof, probably built in the 13C (when the 12C lantern was placed on top). The larger arch which marks the main east entrance faces the Duomo. The two porphyry columns here were brought back as booty by the Florentines who took part in the Pisan war in the Balearic Islands in 1115.

The bronze doors

The building is famous for its three sets of gilded bronze doors at its three entrances. The earliest doors are by Andrea Pisano (1336) on the south side. They were followed by those on the north and east sides erected a century later by Lorenzo Ghiberti after a competition held by the Arte di Calimala in which his work was preferred to that of many of the greatest artists of his time, including Brunelleschi and Jacopo della Quercia. This competition of 1401 is often taken as a convenient point to mark the beginning of the Florentine Renaissance, and it is significant that the Baptistery should have been the monument chosen for adornment. Two trial reliefs for the competition, entered by Brunelleschi and Ghiberti, are preserved in the Bargello (see p 253).

The ***south door**, by Andrea Pisano, was erected in 1336 at the main entrance facing the Duomo. It was moved to its present position in 1424 to make way for Ghiberti's new doors. It has 28 compartments containing reliefs enclosed in Gothic quatrefoil frames. They illustrate the history of St John the Baptist and the theological and cardinal Virtues. The decorations of the bronze frame were added by Vittorio Ghiberti (1452–64), son of Lorenzo. Over the doorway are bronze figures of the Baptist, the Executioner and Salome, by Vincenzo Danti (1571).

The ***north door** (1403–24), by Lorenzo Ghiberti, is again divided into 28 compartments, and the scenes of the Life of Christ, the Evangelists and the Doctors of the Church, have Gothic frames copied from the earlier Pisano doors. The chronological sequence of the scenes from the Life of Christ begins on the left-hand door on the third panel from the bottom and continues towards the top, running left to right. The two lower registers depict the Evangelists and Doctors. Ghiberti's self-portrait appears in the fifth head from the top of the left door (middle band); he is wearing an elaborate hat. The beautiful decoration of the frame is also by Ghiberti. The bronze statues (1506–11) above the door of St John the Baptist preaching, the Levite and the Pharisee are by Francesco Rustici, from a design by Leonardo da Vinci (mentioned by Vasari).

The ****east door** (1425–52) is the most celebrated work of Lorenzo Ghiberti and it took him most of his life to complete it. Michelangelo is said to have called it the 'Gate of Paradise'. The ten separate panels contain reliefs of scriptural subjects, the design of which probably owes something to Ghiberti's contact with the humanists. The artist was assisted by Michelozzo, Benozzo Gozzoli and others. The pictorial reliefs, no longer restricted to a Gothic frame, depict each episode with great conciseness. They are exquisitely carved, with scenes in low relief extending far into the background. The use of perspective here is of great importance, and typical of the new Renaissance concept of art.

A copy of the door made from casts taken in 1948 was installed here in 1990 and the original panels will all be exhibited inside the Museo dell'Opera del Duomo after their restoration. So far six panels have been restored and can be seen in the museum. The subjects from the top downwards are (left to right): 1. *The Creation and Expulsion from Paradise*; 2. *Cain and Abel*; 3. *Noah's Sacrifice and Drunkenness*; 4. *Abraham and the Angels and the Sacrifice of Isaac*; 5. *Esau and Jacob*; 6. *Joseph Sold and Recognised by his Brothers*; 7. *Moses Receiving the Tablets of Stone*; 8. *The Fall of Jericho*; 9. *Battle with the Philistines*; 10. *Solomon and the Queen of Sheba*.

Surrounding the reliefs are 24 very fine statuettes of prophets and sibyls, and

24 medallions with portraits of Ghiberti himself (the fourth from the top in the middle row on the left) and his principal contemporaries. The splendid bronze door-frame is also by Ghiberti. Above the door the sculptural group of the *Baptism of Christ*, attributed to Andrea Sansovino and Vincenzo Danti, with an angel by Innocenzo Spinazzi (18C) has been removed to the Museo dell'Opera del Duomo and replaced here by casts.

Interior

The harmonious interior (now entered by the north door) is designed in two orders, of which the lower has huge granite columns from a Roman building, with gilded Corinthian capitals, and the upper, above a cornice, a gallery with divided windows. The walls are in panels of white marble divided by bands of black, in the dichromatic style of the exterior. The decoration has survived intact. As the floor shows, the centre of the building was occupied until 1576 by a large octagonal font. The present Gothic font dates from 1371 and the oldest part of the splendid *mosaic pavement (begun 1209) lies near it. The decoration in *opus tessellatum*, which recalls that of San Miniato (see p 311), includes geometrical designs, oriental motifs and the signs of the Zodiac.

Beside the handsome high altar (13C; reconstructed) is an elaborate paschal candlestick delicately carved by Agostino di Iacopo (1320). To the right is the *tomb of the antipope John XXIII (Baldassarre Cossa, who died in Florence in 1419) by Donatello and Michelozzo; it is one of the earliest Renaissance tombs in the city. Apart from the exquisite carving, this monument is especially remarkable for the way it is inserted into a narrow space between two huge Roman columns, in no way disturbing the architectural harmony of the building. The bronze effigy of the pope is generally attributed to Donatello (1424–25). On the left of the apse are two late Roman sarcophagi adapted as tombs (one showing a wild boar hunt and the other, the tomb of Bishop Giovanni da Velletri, 1230, with scenes of Roman life).

The *mosaics in the vault, the only mosaic cycle which exists in Florence, are remarkably well-preserved (and now superbly lit). The earliest (c 1225) are in the *scarsella* above the altar; they are signed by the monk 'Iacopo', a contemporary of St Francis, who was influenced by Roman or Venetian mosaicists. The little vault is decorated with an elaborate wheel with the figures of the prophets which surround the *Agnus Dei*. This is supported by four caryatids kneeling on Corinthian capitals. On either side are the *Virgin and St John the Baptist Enthroned*. On the first arch are half-figures of saints flanking a striking image of the Baptist, and on the intrados of the outer arch a frieze of Saints in niches, and the outer face is decorated with vine tendrils. The same artist is thought to have begun the mosaics on the **main dome**, the centre of which (around the lantern) is gracefully decorated with early Christian symbols surrounded by a band of angels. Lower down is a broad band with full-length figures of angels in pairs and the Baptist between seraphims. On the three sections nearest to the altar is the *Last Judgement* with a huge figure of Christ (8m high), in a central tondo, attributed to Coppo di Marcovaldo. The remaining section of the cupola is divided into four bands: the inner one, beneath the frieze of angels, has *Scenes from Genesis* (beginning over the north entrance door) with the Creation; the second band, the *Story of Joseph* (the design of some of the scenes is now attributed to the Maestro della Maddalena); the third band, the *Story of Christ*; and the lowest band, the

Story of St John the Baptist (some of the early episodes are attributed to Cimabue). All the scenes are divided by mosaic columns of different designs. Work on the mosaics was well advanced by 1271, but probably continued into the 14C. The marble rectangular frames at the base of the dome contain mosaic saints.

The Duomo

The Duomo (**Map 1; 4**), the cathedral dedicated to the Madonna of Florence, Santa Maria del FioreSanta Maria del Fiore, fills Piazza del Duomo making a comprehensive view of the huge building difficult in the confined space. It produces a memorable effect of massive grandeur, especially when seen from its southern flank, lightened by the colour and pattern of its distinctive marble walls (white from Carrara, green from Prato, and red from the Maremma). The famous dome, one of the masterpieces of the Renaissance, rises to the height of the surrounding hills (from which it is nearly always visible), holding sway over the whole city.

- **Opening times** 10.00–17.00; *fest.* 13.30–17.00. The Duomo can only be entered from a door in the main façade: the entrance and exit gates are electronically monitored so that no more than 800 people are inside the building at any one time. The dome (entrance from Porta dei Canonici; see **2** on the plan) can be climbed 08.30–18.20; first Saturday of the month 08.30–15.00; other Saturdays 08.30–17.00; closed *fest.* Lire 10,000. The excavations of Santa Reparata are open 10.00–17.00 every day except *fest.* lire 5000. Every year on 8 September the roof and galleries are opened to the public.

History of the Duomo

The early Christian church dedicated to the Palestinian saint, Reparata, is thought to have been founded in the 6C–7C, or possibly earlier. It was reconstructed several times in the Romanesque period. Considerable remains of this church were found in 1965–74 beneath the present cathedral (see below). The Bishop's seat, formerly at San Lorenzo (see Ch. 10) is thought to have been transferred here in the late 7C. By the 13C, a new and larger cathedral was deemed necessary. In 1294, Arnolfo di Cambio was appointed as architect, and it is not known precisely how far building had progressed by the time of his death in the first decade of the 14C. In 1331, the Arte della Lana (Guild of Wool Merchants) assumed responsibility for the cathedral works and Giotto was appointed *capomaestro* (director of works). He began the campanile in 1334. It was not until 1355 that work was resumed again on the cathedral itself, this time by Francesco Talenti. It seems he followed Arnolfo's original design of a vaulted basilica with a domed octagon flanked by three polygonal tribunes. During the 14C, Alberto Arnoldi, Giovanni d'Ambrogio, Giovanni di Lapo Ghini, Neri di Fioravante, Orcagna and others, all joined Talenti as architects, and the octagonal drum was practically completed by 1417. The construction of the cupola had for long been recognised as a major technical problem. A competition was held and Brunelleschi and Ghiberti were appointed jointly to the task in 1418. Brunelleschi soon took full responsibility for the work and the dome was finished up to the base of the lantern by 1436 when Pope Eugenius IV consecrated the cathedral.

The dome

The majestic **dome or cupola (1420–36), the greatest of all Brunelleschi's works, is a feat of engineering skill. It was the first dome to be projected without the need for a wooden supporting frame to sustain the vault during construction. This was possible partly because the upper section was built in bricks (rather than the heavier sandstone used in the rest of the structure) in consecutive rings in horizontal courses, bonded together in a vertical herring-bone pattern. However, the exact constructional technique used by Brunelleschi has still not been satisfactorily explained. The dome was the largest and highest of its time. Its pointed shape was probably determined by the octagonal drum which already existed over the crossing and from which the eight marble ribs ascend to the lantern. The cupola has two concentric shells, the octagonal vaults of which are evident both on the exterior and interior of the building. This facilitated construction and lessened the weight; the outer shell is thinner than the inner shell. Some of the apparatus invented by Brunelleschi which was used during the building of the dome can be seen in a storeroom on the descent from the dome (see below), and in the Museo dell'Opera (Ch. 2). Since 1980, detailed long-term studies have been carried out by a special commission to establish whether the stability of the cupola is in danger. The weight of the dome had caused cracks in the drum by the mid-17C, and the structure is now being observed using a sophisticated system of monitors.

On the completion of the cupola, Brunelleschi was subjected to another competition as his ability to crown it with a lantern was brought into question. It was begun a few months before the architect's death in 1446, and the work was continued by his friend Michelozzo. Brunelleschi also designed the four small decorative exedrae with niches which he placed around the octagonal drum between the three domed tribunes. In the late 1460s, Verrocchio placed the bronze ball and cross on the summit. The balcony at the base of the cupola, covering the brick work, on the southeast side, was added by Baccio d'Agnolo, on a design by Giuliano da Sangallo and Cronaca in 1507–15. According to Vasari, it was never completed because of Michelangelo's criticism that it reminded him of a crickets' cage.

Exterior

The building of the cathedral was begun on the south side where the decorative pattern of the marble can be seen to full advantage. The 14C sculptures of the *Annunciation* above the Porta del Campanile (1), have been removed to the Museo dell'Opera del Duomo. The Porta dei Canonici (2) has fine sculptured decoration (1395–99) by Lorenzo d'Ambrogio and Piero di Giovanni Tedesco.

On the north side is the most elaborate door, *Porta della Mandorla (3), dating from 1391–1405. The sculptures have been blackened by the polluted air and are difficult to appreciate from this distance but they had an important influence on early Renaissance sculpture. The sculptural decoration on the lower part is by Giovanni d'Ambrogio, Piero di Giovanni Tedesco, Jacopo di Piero Guidi and Niccolò Lamberti. In the gable is an *Assumption of the Virgin* in a mandorla (an almond-shaped frame) by Nanni di Banco (c 1418–20), continued after his death by his workshop. Two heads in profile carved in relief on either side of the gable (very difficult to see) of a prophet and sibyl are considered early works by Donatello. In the lunette is an *Annunciation* in mosaic (1491) by Domenico and Davide Ghirlandaio.

The **façade**, erected to a third of its projected height by 1420, was demolished in

1587–88 (the sculptures are preserved in the Museo dell'Opera del Duomo, see Ch. 2). Ideas for a new façade were first mooted in 1858, and an international competition was held in 1864. The conservative Gothic design by Emilio de Fabris was chosen, and work was begun in 1876 funded by public subscription (with conspicuous contributions from the foreign community resident in Florence, including Frederick Stibbert and Paolo Demidoff). Some of the best-known artists of the day worked on the elaborate decoration, including Raffaello Romanelli, Ulisse Cambi, Vincenzo Consani, Giovanni Duprè, Tito Sarrocchi, and Niccolò Barabino (who made the lunette mosaics). It was unveiled, after De Fabris' death, in 1887. The bronze doors by Augusto Passaglia and Giuseppe Cassioli date from 1899–1903.

Interior

The Gothic interior is somewhat bare and chilly after the warm colour of the exterior, whose splendour it cannot match. The huge grey stone arches of the nave reach the clerestory beneath an elaborate sculptured balcony. The massive pilasters which support the stone vault have unusual composite capitals. The beautiful stained glass windows (restored in 1984–1991) date mostly from 1434–45, and are among the most important works of their kind in Italy. Three dark tribunes with a Gothic coronet of chapels surround the huge dome. The beautiful marble pavement (1526–1660) was designed by Baccio d'Agnolo, Francesco da Sangallo and others.

West wall Mosaic (4) of the *Coronation of the Virgin*, attributed to Gaddo Gaddi. Ghiberti designed the three round stained-glass windows. The 16C frescoes of the angel musicians are by Santi di Tito. The huge clock uses the *hora italica* method of counting the hours—the last hour of the day (XXIIII) ends at sunset or Ave Maria (a system used in Italy until the 18C). Paolo Uccello decorated it and painted the four heads of prophets in 1443. The recomposed tomb (5) of Antonio d'Orso, Bishop of Florence (d. 1321) by Tino da Camaino, includes a fine statue. The painting of *St Catherine of Alexandria* is by the school of Bernardo Daddi.

South aisle In a tondo (6) is the bust of *Brunelleschi* by Buggiano, his adopted son (1446; probably taken from his death mask). This is one of three similar monuments in the Duomo, interesting works commissioned by the Opera del Duomo with commemorative busts in medallions. In the first 'marble' side altar (7; in fact built in wood) is a statue of a *Prophet* (1408) attributed to Nanni di Banco. Below the idealised bust of *Giotto* (8; 1490) by Benedetto da Maiano, in another tondo, is an inscription by Politian. The elaborate Gothic stoup (9; c 1380) is attributed to Urbano da Cortona. The angel and basin are copies; the originals are in the Opera del Duomo (Ch. 2).

Santa Reparata Steps lead down (A) to the excavations of the ancient cathedral of Santa Reparata (see above) uncovered in 1965–74 beneath the present cathedral (for opening times see p 104). At the bottom of the stairs to the left—now disturbed by a bookshop—the simple **tomb-slab (E) of Brunelleschi** can be seen beyond a grille; the slab was found here in 1972. The architect of the cupola was the only Florentine granted the privilege of burial in Santa Maria del Fiore.

The complicated excavations (admission fee), on various levels, include Roman edifices on which the early Christian church was built, a fine mosaic pavement from the earliest church, and remains of the pre-Romanesque and Romanesque reconstructions. Since only a few column bases and parts of the pavement of the

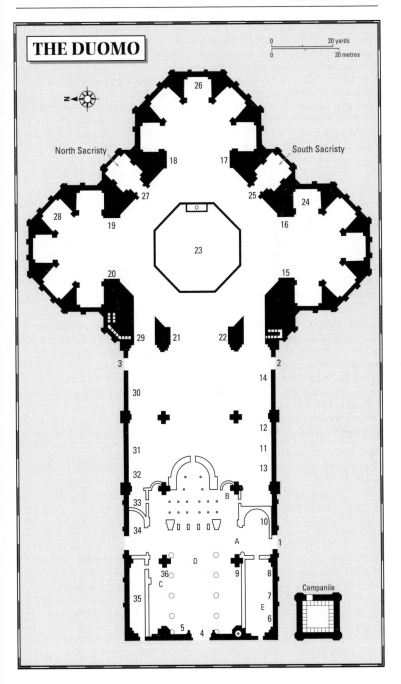

THE DUOMO

0   20 yards
0   20 metres

N

26

North Sacristy

18

17

South Sacristy

27

25

24

28

19

16

23

20

15

29

21

22

3

2

14

30

12

31

11

32

13

B

33

10

34

A

1

D

9

8

36

C

35

7

E

5

6

4

Campanile

first church were discovered, its precise plan is not known; the excavated area corresponds to the plan of the Romanesque church with its five apses. Four of the massive nave pilasters of the present cathedral above intrude into this area. The excavations are explained by a model (**C**).

At the entrance, cases contain finds from the excavations which include: the gilded bronze sword and spurs of Giovanni de' Medici (see below); Roman sculpture and paving tiles; Romanesque architectural fragments; majolica and unglazed pottery from earth fills and tombs dating from the construction of the present cathedral (1296–1375). To the right is the Romanesque crypt of Santa Reparata with 13C tomb slabs in the floor. The fresco fragments include a 14C Pietà between the Madonna and St John the Evangelist (**B**). In the area towards the north aisle is part of the mosaic pavement from the first church with a fragment of Romanesque pavement above it. Plutei of the 8C–9C are displayed near the base of the stairs which led up to the raised choir. Beyond the huge square base of one of the nave pillars of the present cathedral are some fragments of Roman buildings below floor level. A model here (**C**) explains in detail the various levels of excavations. Nearby is part of a pavement, thought to be from the pre-Romanesque period, and several tomb-slabs. From here a walkway leads across the best-preserved part of the early Christian mosaic floor, interrupted here and there by fragments of brick, marble and *pietra serena* from later buildings. Walkways lead back across a wall of the Roman period to the imposing raised tomb (**D**) of Giovanni de' Medici, who was buried here in 1351.

South aisle By the south door (10) is the painting *St Blaise Enthroned* by Rossello di Jacopo Franchi (1408). On the second altar (**11**) is a statue of *Isaiah* (1427), by Ciuffagni, between two painted sepulchral monuments (**12**, **13**) to Fra' Luigi Marsili and Cardinal Pietro Corsini (d. 1405) by Bicci di Lorenzo.

The beautiful stained glass window, with six saints (1394–95), was designed by Agnolo Gaddi. The bust (**14**) of the famous philosopher and friend of Cosimo il Vecchio **Marsilio Ficino** (1433–99), shown holding a volume of Plato, is by Andrea Ferrucci (1521). Beyond the second south door is the entrance (admission only from the outside of the Cathedral) to the steps which ascend the cupola.

East end Only part of the east end of the church is open to visitors as most of it is reserved for private worship. Above the octagon, the great dome soars to a height of 91m. The fresco of the *Last Judgement* by Vasari and Federico Zuccari (1572–79) was restored in 1981–94. The overall design by Vasari was altered on the lower part of the dome by Zuccari. The 15C stained glass in the round windows of the drum is described below. Against the piers of the octagon stand eight 16C statues of *Apostles* by: Giovanni Bandini, *St Philip* (**15**), and *St James the Less* (**16**); Benedetto da Rovezzano, *St John* (**17**); Baccio Bandinelli, *St Peter* (**18**); Andrea Ferrucci, *St Andrew* (**19**); Vincenzo de' Rossi, *St Thomas* (**20**) and *St Matthew* (**22**); Jacopo Sansovino, *St James* (**21**). The marble sanctuary (**23**) was part of a grandiose project begun in 1547 by Baccio Bandinelli who had been appointed head of the Opera del Duomo in 1540 by Cosimo I. It includes bas-reliefs by Bandinelli and Bandini, and encloses the High Altar, also by Bandinelli. The wood Crucifix is by Benedetto da Maiano.

Each of the three apses is divided into five chapels with stained glass windows designed by Lorenzo Ghiberti. In the right and left apse, beneath the windows, are frescoes after Paolo Schiavo (c 1440; heavily restored). Right apse: fifth chapel (**24**) *Madonna del Popolo*, fragment of a Giottesque fresco. Above the entrance to the south sacristy (**25**), large lunette of the *Ascension* in enamelled terracotta by Luca della Robbia. The interesting interior, with a lavabo by Buggiano and Pagno di Lapo, is not open to the public.

Central apse: third chapel (**26**). On the altar, two graceful kneeling angels by Luca della Robbia. Beneath the altar is a *bronze reliquary urn* by Lorenzo Ghiberti with exquisite bas-reliefs.

Over the door into the **north sacristy** (**27**: delle Messe) is another fine relief by Luca della Robbia of the *Resurrection*. This was his earliest important work (1442) in enamelled terracotta. The iconographical composition was copied by later artists. The doors were Luca's only work in bronze (1446–67); he was assisted by Michelozzo and Maso di Bartolomeo. It was in this sacristy that Lorenzo il Magnifico took refuge on the day of the Pazzi conspiracy (see p 92) in 1478; he was saved, but his brother Giuliano was murdered.

The *interior* has fine intarsia cupboards (seen through glass doors) dating from 1436–45. Those on the south wall are by Agnolo di Lazzaro, Bernardo di Tommaso di Ghigo, Francesco di Giovanni di Guccio and Lo Scheggia; those on the north wall by Antonio Manetti. The end wall was continued by Giuliano da Maiano in 1463–65: below are beautiful panels of *St Zenobius Enthroned Between Two Saints* and above, the *Annunciation* flanked by the prophets *Amos* and *Isaiah* (possibly based on a cartoon by Antonio del Pollaiolo). On the entrance wall is a fine marble lavabo by Buggiano (1440) probably on a design by Brunelleschi, and a cupboard by Mino da Fiesole. The carved frieze of putti supporting a garland is by various hands including, probably, Benedetto da Maiano.

Left apse In the pavement (partly hidden by pews) is Toscanelli's huge gnomon (1475) for solar observations (related to a window in the lantern of the cupola). Toscanelli, a famous scientist, mathematician and geographer, discussed his calculations concerning perspective with his friend Brunelleschi. In the second chapel (**28**), there is a dossal of the *Madonna and Child with Four Saints*, and, on the back the *Annunciation* with four more saints. Formerly thought to be by the school of Giotto, this is now attributed to the hand of the master himself (probably with the intervention of his *bottega*).

North aisle (**30**) Domenico di Michelino, *Dante with the Divina Commedia which Illuminates Florence* (1465; showing the drum of the cupola before it was faced with marble); Bicci di Lorenzo, *Saints Cosmas and Damian*. The two stained glass windows were designed by Agnolo Gaddi. On the side altar (**31**), Bernardo Ciuffagni, *King David* (1434; designed for the old façade of the Cathedral). Beyond are the two splendid *equestrian memorials* (**32, 33**; being restored at the time of writing) to two famous condottieri, the Englishman *Sir John Hawkwood* (Giovanni Acuto), who commanded the Florentine army from 1377 until his death in 1394, and *Niccolò da Tolentino* (d. 1434). They are both frescoes executed to look like sculpture: the former by Paolo Uccello (1436) and the latter by Andrea del Castagno (1456). The portrait bust (**34**) of the organist Antonio Squarcialupi is by Benedetto da Maiano (1490; the epigraph is thought to be by Politian). On the last altar (**35**), Donatello (attributed), the *Prophet Joshua* (traditionally thought to be a portrait of the humanist friend of Cosimo il Vecchio, Poggio Bracciolini), originally on the façade of the Duomo. On the nave pillar (**36**) is a painting of *St Zenobius* by Giovanni del Biondo (late 14C).

The climb to the top of the Dome

For opening times see p 104. The entrance is from outside the cathedral through the south door (2). The climb (463 steps) is not as difficult as one might expect, and is highly recommended (except for those who suffer from claustrophobia). It follows a labyrinth of corridors, steps and spiral staircases (used by the builders of the cupola) as far as the lantern at the top of the dome. During the ascent, the structure of the dome (described above) can be examined, and the views of the inside of the cathedral from the two balconies around the drum, and of the city from the small windows and from the lantern, are remarkable.

Beyond the ticket desk steps ascend inside one of the piers, and a window at the end of a short corridor frames a view of the top of Palazzo Vecchio. The steps emerge inside one of the small **exedrae** which Brunelleschi added beneath the drum. Here are displayed some of the original (or reconstructed) devices—including winches and iron supports—used in the construction and mainte-nance of the dome (also labelled in English). From here a spiral staircase contin-ues up, past a landing with a view of Santo Spirito and the hill of Bellosguardo. At the top there is another view of Santo Spirito and, on the extreme left, Palazzo Pitti and the top of Orsanmichele. A corridor emerges on the **balcony which encircles the octagonal drum**, providing a splendid view of the inside of the cathedral, and of the late 16C frescoes by Vasari and Federico Zuccari which cover the dome. When Brunelleschi was commissioned to construct the cupola, the cathedral was already built to this point: from here one can appreciate the huge space (45.5m in diameter) which the architect was required to vault. The seven beautiful *stained glass windows* in the roundels were designed in 1443–45 by Paolo Uccello (*Nativity*); Andrea del Castagno (*Deposition*); Paolo Uccello (*Resurrection*); Donatello (*Coronation of the Virgin*); Ghiberti (*Ascension*, *Prayer in the Garden* and *Presentation in the Temple*).

The balcony is followed for part of its length to another corridor which leads to the base of the **double dome**, the curve of which can be seen clearly. The ascent continues and now becomes more arduous because the steps are used by visitors going up and coming down. It passes between the two shells by means of short corridors and flights of steps, and small windows frame views of the monuments of the city, including Santa Croce, the Bargello and the Badia Fiorentina, Palazzo Vecchio with Forte di Belvedere on the skyline, the top of the Campanile, and the side of Santa Maria Novella. The distinctive herring-bone pattern of the bricks (which vary in size, see above) used at intervals in the construction of the dome is clearly visible here, as well as the transverse arches which strengthened the structure. On the right, a steep flight of steps (one way up) scales the uppermost part of the inner dome. Another short flight of steps continue out onto the **lantern**, beautifully carved in marble. The bronze ball (no admission) can hold about ten people at a time. The mighty marble ribs which decorate the exterior of the dome can be appreciated from here.

The *view* from here (91m) embraces the city; the most conspicuous buildings include (right to left): the campanile, Palazzo Strozzi and the church of the Carmine in the distance; Santo Spirito with its dome and campanile and the huge Palazzo Pitti, and (nearer) the tall Orsanmichele. At the foot of the cathedral is a group of small medieval houses and towers. The Fort di Belvedere can be seen in the distance on its hill behind Palazzo Vecchio, the Uffizi and the Loggia della Signoria. Farther left is the Badia with its tall tower, and the Bargello, the marble façade of Santa

Croce with its campanile, and, across the Arno, San Miniato. Beyond the arcaded façade of the hospital of Santa Maria Nuova rises the green dome of the Synagogue. The straight Via dei Servi leads to Santissima Annunziata, to the right of which are the extensive buildings of the Innocenti with a garden, and nearer at hand the octagonal rotunda of Santa Maria degli Angeli, also by Brunelleschi. In the distance rises the hill of Fiesole. The long façade of Palazzo Medici-Riccardi on Via Cavour can be seen in front of the tall iron roof of the 19C market beside the domed church of San Lorenzo next to its cloister and the Biblioteca Laurenziana. Near the station is Santa Maria Novella with its cloisters and campanile.

Another flight of steps is taken down to scale the inner dome and then, at first, the same route is taken on the descent. A spiral staircase continues down to emerge on the lower balcony round the drum overlooking the interior of the cathedral. A corridor leads off it (with a view from the window of the green market building of San Lorenzo) and then a spiral staircase continues down to an exedra beneath the drum which is used to store casts of statues. The exit is from the Porta della Mandorla.

The Campanile

The Campanile (**Map 1**; **4**; nearly 85m high) was begun by Giotto in 1334 when, as the most distinguished Florentine artist, he was appointed city architect. It was continued by Andrea Pisano (1343), and completed by Francesco Talenti in 1348–59. It is built of the same coloured marbles as the Duomo, in similar patterns, in an extremely well-proportioned design. Between the various storeys are horizontal bands of green, white, and pink inlay. The lowest storey bears two rows of bas-reliefs which have been replaced by copies. The originals, now in the Museo dell'Opera, are described in Ch. 2. The lowest row are contemporary with the building, and some of them are thought to have been designed by Giotto. They were executed by Andrea Pisano and illustrate the *Creation of Man*, and the *Arts* and *Industries*. Five reliefs on the north face were added by Luca della Robbia. The upper register has reliefs by pupils of Andrea Pisano. The niches in the row on the second storey contain casts of the statues of *Prophets* and *Sibyls* (1415–36) by Donatello and others, also removed to the Museo dell'Opera (see Ch. 2). There are two storeys above, each with a pair of beautiful double-arched windows in each side, followed by the highest storey, with large and triple-arched openings, and the cornice. The parapet, low roof and wood mast were all replaced during restoration work in 1981–83.

The **ascent of the bell-tower** by 414 steps is interesting for its succession of views of the Duomo, the Baptistery, and the rest of the city. Opening times 09.00–18.50; summer 09.00–19.30, ☎ 055 230 2885, Lire 10,000.

Although lower than the cupola, the climb is steeper. The third and fourth storeys, with their Gothic windows, overlook the Duomo and the Baptistery. The terracotta pots along the roof of the aisle of the Duomo serve to protect the building from the direct fall of rainwater from the gutters. On the Campanile's highest storey, with its beautiful slender windows, the modern **bells** can be seen hanging above the original ones (the Apostolica bell, displayed on a platform, dates from the beginning of the 15C). Steep steps continue to emerge beside the simple tiled roof above the cornice.

The splendid **panorama of the city** includes (right to left): Piazza della Repubblica (with its conspicuous advertisements), with Palazzo Strozzi behind and the Carmine in the distance. Farther left is Santo Spirito; then Palazzo Pitti with the Boboli gardens stretching as far as the Fort di Belvedere on its hill. Nearer at hand rises the tall Orsanmichele. Farther left is the Loggia della Signoria beside Palazzo Vecchio and the Uffizi, and, at the foot of the Campanile, is a group of medieval houses with red-tiled roofs and towers. The Badia is marked by its tall bell-tower next to the Bargello. Beyond Santa Croce, the Synagogue can be seen just to the right of the cupola. On the other side of the dome, the long, straight Via Ricasoli leads out of the city towards the hills of Fiesole in the distance. On the parallel Via Cavour stands Palazzo Medici-Riccardi. The huge 19C market building is near San Lorenzo with its dome and the large church of Santa Maria Novella can be seen beside the railway station.

2 • Piazza del Duomo and Piazza San Giovanni

The Duomo, Campanile and Baptistery (see Ch. 1) fill these two adjoining *piazze*. The most important building on Piazza del Duomo is the Museo dell'Opera del Duomo which has a superb collection of sculpture from these three buildings. The headquarters of the two charitable institutes of the Bigallo and Misericordia also here, both with a number of interesting works of art, are not regularly open to visitors.

Museo dell'Opera del Duomo

Behind the east end of the Duomo, at no. 9 Piazza del Duomo, is the entrance to the Museo dell'Opera dell Duomo (**Map 1; 4**), with a bust of Cosimo I by Giovanni Bandini (dell'Opera) over the door. This building has been the seat of the Opera del Duomo (responsible for the maintenance of the cathedral) since the beginning of the 15C. First opened in 1891 it was one of the most pleasant museums in the city until it lost much of its character in 2000 after renovations in questionable taste. However, it contains numerous masterpieces of sculpture from the Baptistery, Duomo and Campanile, and successfully illustrates the complicated histories of all these buildings.

• **Opening times** 09.30–18.30; *fest.* 08.00–14.00 (☎ 055 230 2885). Lire 10,000. The rooms are un-numbered but the description below follows a logical itinerary.

Ground floor

Beyond the ticket office are displayed some **Roman fragments** including a very fine sarcophagus with the story of Orestes (2C AD), and part of an Etruscan *cippus* (5C BC) showing musicians and dancers. The room beyond has **Gothic statues by Tino da Camaino** from the Baptistery, including some fine *female heads*, *Christ Blessing* and the *Head of St John the Baptist*. The small room straight ahead, formerly the entrance to the museum, preserves a niche with a marble bust of *Brunelleschi*, attributed to Buggiano or Giovanni Bandini. This is thought to have been commissioned by the Opera del Duomo for its present position. The enamelled terracotta relief lunette of the *Madonna and Child* is by

Andrea della Robbia and the flat enamelled terracotta lunette of *God the Father Between Two Angels* is also attributed to him. Exhibited here are sculptures from the **Porta della Mandorla** of the Cathedral, including a fragment of a frieze from the doorway substituted by a copy in situ in 1869–71, and two statuettes of *Prophets* from the pinnacles of the tympanum attributed to Donatello and Nanni di Banco (or Luca Della Robbia). The *Madonna* and *Annunciatory Angel* attributed to Giovanni d'Ambrogio (or Nanni di Banco) were made for the lunette of the door but were removed in 1489–90 when the mosaic was installed. The interesting hexagonal glazed terracotta relief of the *Creation of Eve* which may have decorated a marriage chest is attributed to Donatello.

In the **courtyard**, recently covered with a glass roof, are displayed six restored ****gilded bronze panels** by Lorenzo Ghiberti removed from the east door of the Baptistery (see p 102; the remaining four will be housed here when restoration work on them has been completed). They are masterpieces of the early Renaissance and it took Ghiberti 22 years to complete them. Each panel describes in continuous narrative various episodes from Old Testament stories.

The *Creation* and the *Story of Adam and Eve* is perhaps the most beautiful of them all, showing the Creation of Adam, the Creation of Eve, the Fall (in a wood full of birds), and the Expulsion from Paradise. The human figures are extraordinarily elegant, and the numerous graceful angels add particular charm to the scenes.

The *Story of Benjamin and Joseph* takes place in front of a lovely circular building in which the Egyptians are emptying sacks of grain. In the left foreground are Joseph's brothers opening their sacks to find, to their despair, Joseph's chalice, and in the background, Joseph is embracing his youngest brother Benjamin. In the right foreground, a camel is being loaded with sacks while Joseph takes leave of his brothers, on their way back to their father. Another scene in low relief at the top of the panel shows Joseph revealing his identity to his brothers.

In the *Story of Jacob and Esau*, Isaac is shown with his eldest son Esau (accompanied by two dogs) asking him to go out and kill a deer and bring him the meat in order that he may receive his blessing. In her bedroom, in the background, Rebekah overhears him. She is then shown instructing her younger son Jacob, and another scene shows Jacob, disguised by the kid on his shoulders, kneeling in front of his blind father to receive his blessing while his mother looks on. Above Esau is shown leaving for the hunt, and God appearing to Rebekah to ask her why she persuaded Jacob to trick his father. In the left foreground is an elegant group of four serving women.

The *Meeting of Solomon and the Queen of Sheba* takes place in a splendid vaulted hall filled with a large crowd of people.

The panel illustrating *Saul* with *David and Goliath* shows the battle between Saul (in his war chariot) leading the men of Israel against the Philistines. At the bottom of the panel, David cuts off Goliath's head with a sword, after the giant has fallen 'upon his face to the earth' having been killed by a stone from David's sling. In the background can be seen a group of singing and dancing women coming out of the city to meet Saul and David with the head of Goliath.

The panel illustrating the story of *Cain and Abel* shows the elderly Adam and Eve sitting in front of their hut with their children Cain and Abel. Below are two distinct scenes with Abel tending his flock of sheep and Cain tilling the ground with the help of two oxen. The brothers are then shown sacrificing a lamb and the fruits of the land to the Lord, who shows his preference for Abel's offering. Then Cain, in anger, is shown killing Abel, and in the last scene the Lord appears to Cain asking him where his brother is and Cain replies, 'I know not; am I my brother's keeper?'

The large statuary group of the *Baptism of Christ*, formerly over the East Door of the Baptistery, by Andrea Sansovino (1502–05) was finished by Vincenzo Danti. The angel was substituted in 1792 by Innocenzo Spinazzi.

Another room displays marble statues in high-relief removed from the **Porta del Campanile** of the Duomo; they include the *Annunciation* in which the angel is by Jacopo di Piero Guidi (c 1380) and the Madonna by a follower of Giovanni di Balduccio (c 1330).

The large hall displays **sculptures from the old façade** (never completed) of the Duomo designed by Arnolfo di Cambio and demolished in 1587. The facsimile displayed here of a drawing of the old façade made shortly before its demolition by Bernardino Poccetti is the most detailed illustration of it to have survived. On the long wall are numerous **sculptures by Arnolfo di Cambio** and his *bottega*. Arnolfo was the architect of the Duomo, but died soon after building had begun. His sculptures include a seated *Madonna and Child* (a somewhat enigmatic work with striking glass eyes), flanked by *St Reparata*, *St Zenobius*, the *Madonna of the Nativity* (shown lying on her side; displayed on the upper part of the wall), and (at the end of the room) *Boniface VIII* (restored). The statuettes from the main door (late 14C) are the work of Piero di Giovanni Tedesco. On the other long wall are the **four seated Evangelists** which were added to the lower part of the façade in the early 15C: Nanni di Banco, *St Luke* 1410–14; Donatello, *St John the Evangelist*; Bernardo Ciuffagni, *St Matthew*; Niccolò di Piero Lamberti, *St Mark*. In the centre of the room is the tomb of Piero Farnese (d. 1363) which incorporates a relief from a Roman sarcophagus of the late 2C AD, and the angel and basin of the 14C stoup (attributed to Urbano da Cortona) from the Duomo.

A few steps lead up to a room which displays paintings formerly in the Duomo including *St Zenobius Enthroned* and *Stories from his Life* by the mid-13C Maestro del Bigallo, and works of the 14C–15C Florentine school. The triptych of the *Martyrdom of St Sebastian* is by Giovanni del Biondo. The processional painting of *St Agatha* has two paintings of the saint, one dating from the 13C and the other from the 14C (attributed to Jacopo del Casentino).

The *marble panels from the choir of the Duomo* by Baccio Bandinelli and Giovanni Bandini (1547) are part of an unfinished project which was to have included some 300 reliefs. Representing prophets, apostles and nude male pagan figures, they are beautifully carved. In the modern chapel is a precious collection of 15C–16C reliquaries, including one of 1501 by Paolo di Giovanni Sogliani. The painting of *St Catherine* is attributed to Bernardo Daddi (1334).

There is a room with architectural fragments from the Duomo, fragments of the 13C font from the Baptistery, and a lunette of *St Zenobius with Two Angels* by the *bottega* of Andrea della Robbia (1496). Beyond these are the stairs which lead up to the first floor.

On the **landing** is displayed the *Pietà* by **Michelangelo**. A very beautiful late work, carved when he was almost eighty years old, it was intended for Michelangelo's own tomb which was to have been in the basilica of Santa Maria Maggiore in Rome. According to Vasari, the head of Nicodemus is a self-portrait. Dissatisfied with his work, the sculptor destroyed the arm and left leg of Christ, and his pupil, Tiberio Calcagni, restored the arm and finished the figure of Mary

Magdalen. The sculpture was brought to Florence by Grand-duke Cosimo III for the crypt of San Lorenzo, and then in 1721 installed in the choir of the Duomo, but moved to a chapel at the east end in 1931. It has been in the museum since 1981.

First floor

The first room is dominated by the two famous *cantorie by **Luca della Robbia** and **Donatello** made in the 1430s, probably as organ-lofts (rather than singing galleries) above the two sacristy doors in the Duomo. The one on the left, by Luca della Robbia, was his first important commission, and is his masterpiece. The original panels are displayed beneath the reconstructed cantoria. As the inscription indicates, the charming sculptured panels illustrate Psalm 150. The children (some of them drawn from Classical models), dancing, singing or playing musical instruments, are exquisitely carved within a beautiful architectural framework. Donatello's cantoria, opposite, provides a striking contrast, with a frieze of running putti against a background of coloured inlay.

Around the walls are the **16 statues removed from the Campanile** (see p 111), but in a very ruinous state. They were made for the niches on the four sides of the bell-tower, and the earliest ones by the Pisano date from after 1337. On the right of the entrance door: Donatello, *Bearded Prophet*, *Abraham and Isaac* (part of the modelling is attributed to Nanni di Bartolo); Nanni di Bartolo (attributed), *Prophet*; Donatello, *Beardless Prophet*. On the wall beneath Donatello's cantoria are four *Prophets*, the first one attributed to Maso di Banco, the next one by the workshop of Andrea Pisano, the third by Andrea and Nino Pisano, and Moses attributed to Maso di Banco. On the next wall: Abdia by Nanni di Bartolo, *Geremiah*, *Habbakuk* (*lo zuccone*: bald-headed; removed some years ago for restoration) both by Donatello, and *St John the Baptist* or *Jonah*, attributed to Donatello. On the wall beneath the Della Robbia cantoria: *Sibyls* and *King Solomon* and *David* by Andrea and Nino Pisano.

On the right, beyond a bas-relief of the *Madonna and Child* attributed to Pagno di Lapo Portigiani, is a room which displays **Donatello's** *St Mary Magdalen*, an expressive wooden statue (formerly in the Baptistery), thought to be a late work. The painted wooden *Crucifix*, which was in the Baptistery up until 1912, is attributed to Giovanni di Balduccio (early 14C). At the other end of the room is the magnificent *altar of silver-gilt, from the Baptistery, a Gothic work by Florentine goldsmiths (including Betto di Geri and Leonardo di Ser Giovanni), begun in 1366 and finished in the 15C, illustrating the history of St John the Baptist. The statuette of the *Baptist* was added by Michelozzo. On the left flank, reliefs of the *Annunciation to St Zacharias* and the *Visitation* by Bernardo Cennini, and the *Birth of the Baptist* by Antonio del Pollaiolo; on the right flank, reliefs of the *Banquet of Herod* by Antonio di Salvi and Francesco di Giovanni, and the *Beheading of the Baptist* by Verrocchio. The altar is surmounted by a silver *Cross* by Betto di Francesco (1457–59), Antonio del Pollaiolo, and probably other artists (Bernardo Cennini?).

In the side case on the wall opposite the entrance are a Farnese chasuble designed by Annibale Carracci and 17C brocade vestments with lovely floral decorations. The *27 needlework panels** with scenes from the *Life of St John the Baptist*, formerly decorated vestments made for the Baptistery. These are exquisite works by the craftsmen of the *Arte di Calimala* (cloth importers' guild) made in 1466–87 to a design by Antonio del Pollaiolo. On the other wall: a mosaic of St

Zenobius by Monte di Giovanni(1505); two ***Byzantine mosaic tablets** illus-trating the twelve Christian festivals of exquisite workmanship, thought to date from the early 14C and the most beautiful portable diptych from Constantinople known of this date; a Venetian 15C reliquary coffer; the reliquary of Santa Reparata by Francesco Vanni (14C, but restored and altered in the 17C); a pro-cessional Cross attributed to Luca della Robbia; a 15C reliquary casket in *pietra dura*; and an antiphonal illuminated by Monte di Giovanni, one of the 58 beauti-ful choirbooks which belong to the cathedral. Above the door is a lunette of *St Mary in the Desert* by Benedetto Buglioni.

On the other side of the Cantoria room are exhibited the original ***bas-reliefs removed from the two lower registers of the Campanile**. The lower row, which date from the early 14C, are charming works by Andrea Pisano (some per-haps designed by Giotto); they illustrate the *Creation of Man*, and the *Arts and Industries*. Starting on the entrance wall: *Creation of Adam*, *Creation of Eve*, *Labours of Adam and Eve*, *Jabal* (the Pastoral life), *Jubal* (Music), *Tubalcain* (the Smith), *Noah*, *Gionitus* (Astronomy), *The Art of Building*, *Medicine*, *Hunting*, *Weaving*, *Phoroneus the Lawgiver*, *Daedalus*, *Navigation*, *Hercules and Cacus*, *Agriculture*, *Theatrica*, *Architecture*, *Phidias* (Sculpture), *Apelles* (Painting). The last five reliefs (on the right wall) were made in 1437–39 by Luca della Robbia to fill the frames on the north face of the Campanile: *Grammar*, *Philosophy*, *Orpheus* (representing Poetry or Rhetoric), *Arithmetic* and *Astrology* (with the figure of Pythagoras). The upper row of smaller reliefs by pupils of Pisano, illustrate the seven *Planets*, the *Virtues* and the *Liberal Arts*. The *Seven Sacraments* (right wall) are attributed to Maso di Banco. The lunette of the *Madonna and Child* formerly over a door of the Campanile is by Andrea Pisano, who also carved the exquisite statuettes of the *Redeemer* and *St Reparata* exhibited here.

A door leads out of this room into a corridor where scaffolding and tools recon-struct a building site thought to be similar to that set up by Brunelleschi when work-ing on the dome of the cathedral. The apparatus which may have been used in the construction of the cupola (or in its maintenance), including pulleys, ropes, tackle, hoists and technical instruments, is displayed here. It was found in a storeroom at the foot of the cupola, together with Brunelleschi's original brick moulds. At the end is a wooden model of the lantern thought to have been made by Brunelleschi as his (winning) entry in the competition of 1436, as well as the architect's death mask. When the shutters are open there is a view of the dome from the window.

Off the next corridor are three rooms relating to the **architecture of the Duomo**: the first has numerous models (never before exhibited) entered for a competition held in 1507 for the execution of a balustrade to cover the brick-work on the upper part of the drum at the base of the dome. These are attributed to the leading artists of the day including Michelangelo, Giuliano da Maiano, Antonio da Sangallo, Andrea Sansovino and Antonio Manetti Ciaccheri. None of them was accepted and the brick work remains bare to this day except for a strip on the southeast side which was begun by Baccio d'Agnolo but never completed. Also here is a model in wood of the dome and tribunes probably made by a con-temporary of Brunelleschi. The next room has large models entered in the com-petition held in 1587 for a new façade (after the unfinished one by Arnolfo di Cambio had been torn down). These are attributed to Giovanni Antonio Dosio, Don Giovanni de' Medici, Giambologna and Bernardo Buontalenti. Although

Grand-duke Ferdinando II chose Dosio's design in 1633, it was never carried out because of objections voiced by the people of Florence. The grand-duke therefore asked the Accademia del Disegno to produce a design which is also preserved here. However, the west front remained without a permanent façade until the 19C: early 19C designs never carried out are exhibited in the next room, together with objects used in the inauguration ceremony. The last room has drawings by Emilio de Fabris who finally built the façade in 1860.

The museum has purchased a former theatre next door (later used as a garage) so there are long-term plans to expand the museum, and move Michelangelo's *Pietà* and the Ghiberti doors there.

From this corner of Piazza del Duomo (by Via del Proconsolo), there is a good view of the cathedral and dome. Next to the museum is the large 17C **Palazzo Strozzi di Mantova**, which may become the seat of the Regional Government of Tuscany. The piazza follows the curve of the east end of the Duomo. The 16C **Palazzo Strozzi-Niccolini** bears a 19C plaque and bust of Donatello since it stands on the site of a house where the sculptor had his studio. At the end of Via dei Servi can be seen Piazza Santissima Annunziata with the equestrian statue of the Grand-duke Ferdinando I. Nos 5 and 3 in Piazza del Duomo are restored medieval houses decorated with coats of arms (some of them put up in 1390), and a pretty top-floor loggia. Opposite a side door of the Duomo, the long straight Via Ricasoli leads towards San Marco.

Across the busy Via de' Martelli (with a view of Palazzo Medici-Riccardi) is Piazza San Giovanni. Beside the Baptistery is the **Pillar of St Zenobius**, erected in the 14C to commemorate an elm which came into leaf here when the body of the bishop saint (d. c 430) was moved from San Lorenzo to Santa Reparata in the 9C. In the piazza, at no. 7 is the ancient little **Casa dell'Opera di San Giovanni**, with a copy in the lunette of a statuette of St John by Michelozzo (the original is now in the Bargello). The medieval courtyard survives.

The west end of the square is occupied by the huge **Palazzo Arcivescovile**, partially reconstructed by Giovanni Antonio Dosio in 1584 (the façade was rebuilt in 1895 when the piazza was enlarged). The palace incorporates the church of **San Salvatore al Vescovo** (admission sometimes on request at Palazzo Arcivescovile). The interior was entirely frescoed in 1737–38. The *quadratura* is by Pietro Anderlini. In the vault, the *Ascension* is by Vincenzo Meucci, who also frescoed the *Resurrection* on the right wall. On the left wall is a *Deposition* by Mauro Soderini. The frescoes in the apse and dome, and the monochrome figures of the *Apostles*, are all by Gian Domenico Ferretti. The little Romanesque façade of the earlier church can be seen behind, in Piazza dell'Olio.

Between the Baptistery and the Campanile is the small Gothic **Loggia del Bigallo** built for the Misericordia (see below) in 1351–58 probably by Alberto Arnoldi, who carved the reliefs and the lunette of the *Madonna and Child* (1361) above the door into the Oratory (facing the Baptistery). The Compagnia del Bigallo, founded in 1245, and involved, like the Misericordia, in charitable works, moved to this seat in 1425 when the two confraternities were merged. Lost and abandoned children were exhibited beneath the loggia for three days before being consigned to foster-mothers. The three 14C statues in tabernacles high up on the façade came from the Bigallo's former headquarters near Orsanmichele.

The Museo del Bigallo

This is the smallest museum in the city (**Map 1; 6**; no. 1 Piazza San Giovanni) but one of the most charming. It is, however, now open only by previous appointment, ☎ 055 230 2885.

It preserves most of the works of art commissioned over the centuries by the Misericordia and the Bigallo from Florentine artists. These include the *Madonna of the Misericordia* by an artist in the circle of Bernardo Daddi, which dates from 1342, a fresco which includes the earliest known view of Florence, with the marble Baptistery prominent in the centre near the incomplete Campanile and façade of the Duomo; a small portable *triptych, dated 1333, which is one of Bernardo Daddi's most important early works; a beautiful *Madonna of Humility* with two angels by Domenico di Michelino (1359–64); a tondo of the *Madonna and Saints* in a beautiful contemporary frame by Jacopo del Sellaio; and a 13C painted Crucifix attributed to the Maestro del Bigallo. There are also works by Desiderio da Settignano, Alberto Arnoldi, Ridolfo del Ghirlandaio and Carlo Portelli.

The Misericordia

Across Via de' Calzaioli (which leads to Piazza della Signoria) is the Misericordia, a charitable institution which gives free help to those in need, and runs an ambulance service. The Order, founded by St Peter Martyr in 1244, moved to this site in 1576 from the Bigallo across the road. In the Middle Ages, the brotherhood was particularly active during the plague years when it gave medical care to the poor and attended to their burial. The lay confraternity continues its remarkable work with about 2000 volunteers who still wear distinctive black capes with hoods. One of them is shown carrying a sick person in the painting outside by Pietro Annigoni (1970).

The main door leads into the busy **Sala di Compagnia** which preserves its old-fashioned cupboards and furniture, and the staff are elegantly dressed. On the end wall is a seated statue of the *Madonna and Child* by Benedetto da Maiano (left by him to the Bigallo; finished by Battista Lorenzi in 1575). The two kneeling statues of angels are by Giovanni della Robbia. On the side wall is a relief of the *Madonna* dating from c 1480 flanked by busts of the *Christ Child* and *Young St John* by the *bottega* of the Della Robbia.

The pretty little **Oratory** (entered to the left of the main door), decorated in the 17C, contains an enamelled terracotta altarpiece by Andrea della Robbia (commissioned by Francesco Sassetti for his chapel in the Badia Fiesolana). The very fine marble statue of *St Sebastian* by Benedetto da Maiano was left unfinished in the sculptor's studio on his death in 1497, and left by him to the Bigallo. It is said to have influenced the early work of Michelangelo.

The rest of the building—which contains numerous interesting works of art, including a room arranged as a small museum on the upper floor—is not normally open to visitors.

There are some interesting, quiet, narrow streets just off this side of Piazza del Duomo which preserve their old paving. The narrow Via del Campanile leads past a tabernacle where, since 1991, a photograph has replaced the fine fresco by the late 15C Florentine school of the *Madonna and Child with Two Saints*, which is now in the Misericordia. In Via della Canonica, a building with wooden *sporti* is used as offices by the Opera del Duomo and in the little piazza here is the

Capitolo dei Canonici of the Duomo in a building which was formerly a church and library, and, since 1680, has been used for meetings of the Cathedral Chapter. The narrow Via della Canonica continues to Via dello Studio, on the corner of which is a low building used as a workshop by the stonemasons of the Opera del Duomo. Outside is a cast of the relief of the stonemasons and carpenters guild on the outside of Orsanmichele.

In Piazza del Duomo is **Palazzo dei Canonici** built by Gaetano Baccani in 1826 with heavy columns. The colossal statues of Arnolfo del Cambio and Brunelleschi are by Luigi Pampaloni (1830).

3 • Piazza del Duomo to Piazza della Signoria

Between the Baptistery and the Campanile, the straight Via de' Calzaioli (**Map 1; 4**) leads due south towards Piazza della Signoria. On the line of a Roman road, this was the main thoroughfare of the medieval city, linking the Duomo to Palazzo Vecchio, and passing the guildhall of Orsanmichele. Although many of the shops on the ground floors of the buildings still have arches, the street was transformed when it was widened in the 1840s.

Piazza della Repubblica

Via degli Speziali diverges right for Piazza della Repubblica (**Map 1; 3**), on the site of the Roman forum, and still in the centre of the city. It was laid out at the end of the 19C after the demolition of many medieval buildings, the Mercato Vecchio, and part of the Ghetto (which was created in 1571 and extended from the north side of the present square to Via de' Pecori). Much criticised at the time, the Piazza remains a disappointing intrusion into the historical centre of the city, with its sombre colonnades and undistinguished buildings.

The Colonna dell'Abbondanza, a granite Roman column, was first set up here in 1428. The statue is a copy of a work by Giovanni Battista Foggini.

The piazza has a few souvenir stalls and several large cafés with tables outside, including the *Giubbe Rosse*, a famous meeting place in the early 1900s of writers and artists (including Eugenio Montale, Italo Svevo, Aldo Palazzeschi, Felice Carena, Elio Vittorini, Libero Andreotti, Alberto Carocci, Alessandro Bonsanti and Giovanni Colacicchi). Beneath the arcades is the central post office and (on Thursdays) a flower and plant market. In the bar of the Cinema Gambrinus is an encaustic allegorical painting by Giovanni Colacicchi (1948). The triumphal arch on the west side of the piazza leads into Via Strozzi (p 244).

Orsanmichele

On the other side of Via de' Calzaioli is the narrow Via del Corso (p 323). Farther on, opposite Via dei Tavolini (with a view of a medieval tower) rises the tall rectangular church of Orsanmichele (**Map 1; 4**), on the site of San Michele *ad hortum* founded in the 9C, and destroyed in 1239. It is thought that a grain market was erected here c 1290 by Arnolfo di Cambio which was burnt down in 1304.

The present building was built as a market by Francesco Talenti, Neri di Fioravante, and Benci di Cione in 1337. The arcades were enclosed by huge three-light windows by Simone Talenti in 1380. These, in turn, were bricked up shortly after they were finished (but their superb Gothic tracery can still be seen). The upper storey, completed in 1404, was intended to be used as a granary, but housed archives after 1569.

The statues on the exterior

The decoration of the exterior was undertaken by the Guilds (or Arti) who commissioned statues of their patron saints for the canopied niches. They competed with each other to command work from the best artists of the age, and the statues are an impressive testimony to the skill of Florentine sculptors over a period of some 200 years.

The Florentine Guilds

The *Arti Maggiori* or Greater Guilds took control of the government of the city at the end of the 13C and the regime of the *secondo popolo* lasted for nearly a century. Merchants in the most important trades, bankers and professional men were members of these guilds: the *Calimala* (the first guild, named from the street where the wholesale cloth-importers had their warehouses), the *Giudici e notai* (judges and notaries), the *Cambio* (bankers), the *Lana* (woollen-cloth merchants and manufacturers), the *Por Santa Maria* (named after the street which led to the workshops of the silk-cloth industry), the *Medici e speziali* (physicians and apothecaries, the guild to which painters belonged), and the *Vaiai e pellicciai* (furriers). The *Arti Minori*, created in the 13C, represented shopkeepers and skilled artisans. Guild members were required to maintain a high standard in their work, and carry out specific duties and respect their obligations to other members. In the early 15C, most of the public works in the city were commissioned by the guilds, and many important buildings were put in their charge (the cathedral itself was the responsibility of the *Arte della Lana* from 1331 onwards). They competed with each other in spending vast sums of money on buildings and their embellishment in order to add to their prestige.

Restoration of the 14 statues and beautiful niches has been underway since 1984. The statues are being restored one by one and replaced by copies (the originals are now kept in the hall above, see p 122). The description of the tabernacles, and the guilds to whom they belonged, begins on the side facing Via de' Calzaioli, at the corner of Via de' Lamberti, and goes round to the right.

1. *Calimala* (wholesale cloth-importers). Tabernacle and **St John the Baptist** (1413–16) by Lorenzo Ghiberti. A copy of the statue is to be made.

2. Beyond the church door, *Tribunale di Mercanzia* (the merchants' court, where guild matters were adjudicated). Bronze group of the **Incredulity of St Thomas** (1473–83) by Verrocchio (replaced by a copy). The tabernacle was commissioned earlier by the Parte Guelfa; it is the work of Donatello, and formerly contained his St Louis of Toulouse, now in the Museo dell'Opera di Santa Croce (see Ch. 15). Above is the round *stemma of the Mercanzia in enamelled terracotta by Luca della Robbia (1463).

3. *Giudici e Notai* (judges and notaries). Tabernacle by Niccolò Lamberti (1403–06), with a bronze statue of *St Luke* (1601) by Giambologna.

4. *Beccai* (butchers). *St Peter* (c 1425) attributed to Bernardo Ciuffagni (replaced by a copy). The fine Della Robbian stemma was made in 1858.

5. *Conciapelli* (tanners). Tabernacle and *St Philip* (c 1410–12) by Nanni di Banco (replaced by a copy).

6. *Maestri di Pietrai e di Legname* (stonemasons and carpenters, the guild to which architects and sculptors belonged). Tabernacle and statues of **Four Soldier Saints* (the *Quattro Santi Coronati* by Nanni di Banco (c 1415; removed). The *relief, by the same artist, illustrates the work of the Guild. Above is their stemma in inlaid terracotta by Luca della Robbia.

7. *Armaiuoli* (or *Corazzai e Spadai*) (armourers). *St George* by Donatello (c 1415–17). The marble statue was removed to the Bargello in 1891 and replaced here by a bronze copy by Oronzio Lelli in 1892. The exquisite bas-relief is also now in the Bargello.

8. *Cambio* (bankers). Tabernacle and bronze statue of *St Matthew (1419–22), by Lorenzo Ghiberti. Beyond the door,

9. *Lanaiuoli* (wool manufacturers and clothiers). Bronze *St Stephen by Lorenzo Ghiberti (1427–28).

10. *Maniscalchi* (farriers). *St Eligius* (c 1417–21), replaced by a copy, and bas-relief of the *Saint in a Smithy* by Nanni di Banco.

St Luke by Giambologna, on the exterior of Orsanmichele

11. *Linaioli e Rigattieri* (linen merchants and used-clothes' dealers). *St Mark (1411–13) by Donatello, replaced by a copy.

12. *Pellicciai* (furriers). *St James the Greater* (replaced by a copy), with a bas-relief of his beheading attributed to Niccolò Lamberti.

13. *Medici e Speziali* (physicians and apothecaries). Gothic tabernacle attributed to Simone Talenti (1399), with a **Madonna and Child* (the *Madonna della Rosa*, removed and to be replaced by a copy) thought to be the work of Pietro di Giovanni Tedesco. Above, *stemma by Luca della Robbia.

14. *Setaiuoli e Orafi* (silkweavers and goldsmiths). *St John the Evangelist*, bronze statue by Baccio da Montelupo (1515).

Interior

The interior (opening times 09.00–12.00, 16.00–18.00) is usually entered from the side opposite Via de' Calzaioli. The dark rectangular hall now serves as a church. It is divided into two aisles by two massive pillars, and two altars are set at one end on a raised platform. The vaults and central and side pilasters are decorated with interesting frescoes of patron saints painted in the late 14C or early 15C by Jacopo del Casentino, Giovanni del Ponte, Niccolò di Pietro Gerini, Ambrogio di Baldese and Smeraldo di Giovanni. In the 15C–16C, more frescoes were added (and some panel paintings) by Giovanni Antonio Sogliani, Il Poppi, Lorenzo di Credi and Mariotto Albertinelli. The fine Gothic stained glass windows include one showing *St Jacob Among the Shepherds* designed by Lorenzo Monaco.

The Gothic *tabernacle by Andrea Orcagna (1349–59) is a masterpiece of the decorative arts, ornamented with marble and coloured glass, as well as with reliefs and statuettes. This is the only important sculptural work by this artist who was also a painter and architect. Around the base are reliefs of the *Life of the Virgin* (including, in front, the *Marriage of the Virgin* and the *Annunciation*). Behind the altar is an elaborate sculptured relief of the *Transition* and *Assumption of the Virgin*. A beautiful frame of carved angels encloses a painting (removed) on the altar of the *Madonna* by Bernardo Daddi. On the other altar is a statue of the *Madonna and Child with St Anne* by Francesco da Sangallo (1522). The fresco in the vault above shows *St Anne* holding a 'model' of Florence (with the Baptistery prominent).

Museo di Orsanmichele

This museum, on the upper floors of Orsanmichele, is entered from Palazzo dell'Arte della Lana by an overhead walkway built by Cosimo I in 1569, when these floors were used as an archive for contracts and wills.

- **Opening times** Daily on request at Orsanmichele at 09.00, 10.00 and 11.00 except the first and last Monday of the month (☎ 055 218 741).

A large Gothic hall with fine brick vaulting exhibits the restored marble and bronze statues from the niches outside. *St Eligius* by Nanni di Banco (c 1417–21). *St Mark* by Donatello (1411–13), still showing Gothic influence. *St James the Greater* attributed to Niccolò di Pietro Lamberti (c 1422), also with Gothic elements. The *Madonna della Rosa* is usually attributed to Pietro di Giovanni Tedesco (c 1400), but is also thought by some scholars to be the work of Niccolò di Pietro Lamberti or Simone Ferrucci. It is in a better state of preservation than the other statues since it was moved in 1628 to the inside of the church (but then replaced in the exterior niche in 1925).

The bronze statue of *St John the Evangelist* by Baccio da Montelupo (1515) has not yet been restored. The *St John the Baptist* by Lorenzo Ghiberti (1413–16) was the first life-size statue of the Renaissance to be cast in bronze. It is the largest statue made for Orsanmichele and is still very Gothic in spirit (it is signed on the cloak). The statue group representing the *Incredulity of St Thomas* is a superb bronze work by Verrocchio (1473–83). The bronze statue of *St Luke* by Giambologna (1583–1601) has not yet been restored.

St Peter (c 1425) is generally attributed to Bernardo Ciuffagni, but some scholars think it could be by Brunelleschi or Donatello. *St Philip* is the work of Nanni di Banco (c 1410–12). The *Four Soldier Saints* (*Quattro Santi Coronati*) (c 1409–1416/17) are the masterpiece of Nanni di Banco, modelled on Roman statues. They have not yet been restored. The statue of *St George* by Donatello (c 1415–17) is in the Bargello. The two bronze statues by Lorenzo Ghiberti of *St Matthew* (1419–22) and *St Stephen* (1427–28) have not yet been restored.

A steep, modern flight of stairs leads up to another Gothic hall with a fine wooden roof. Around the walls are displayed 40 very damaged stone statuettes of saints and prophets dating from the late 14C. These were removed from the Gothic windows and portals on the exterior of the building in the 20C.

The splendid **view of Florence** takes in (on the far right) Santo Spirito, with its dome and campanile (and Bellosguardo on the hill behind), Palazzo Pitti, the Boboli gardens (with the Kaffehaus), Forte di Belvedere on the skyline and Palazzo Vecchio. From the windows at the end can be seen the tower of the Badia Fiorentino, the green dome of the Synagogue, and the cupola of the Duomo (with the hill of Fiesole behind). From the windows on the left there is a view of the Campanile and flank of the Duomo, the white roof of the Baptistery, and the dome of the Cappella dei Principi. From the windows at the top of the stairs can be seen the iron weathervane (with the Agnus Dei) on the Palazzo dell'Arte della Lana and Santo Spirito. The exterior of Palazzo dell'Arte della Lana and Palazzo dell'Arte dei Beccai in Via Orsanmichele are described on p 316.

On the other side of Via de' Calzaioli is the church of San Carlo dei Lombardi (1349–1404) with a severe (much ruined) façade. In the unattractive interior is a *Deposition* by Niccolò di Pietro Gerini. The road ends in Piazza della Signoria (see Ch. 4).

4 • Piazza della Signoria

History of the Piazza

Piazza della Signoria (**Map 1; 6**), dominated by Palazzo Vecchio, the town hall, has been the political centre of the city since the Middle Ages. Here the *Signoria* (the magistrate and priors who ruled the city) would, in moments of crisis from the 13C onwards, call a *parlamento*, or an assembly of Florentine citizens. It was the scene of public ceremonies, but also a gathering place in times of trouble. The history of the square has followed that of Palazzo Vecchio. The area at the foot of the palace was laid out as Piazza del Popolo in 1307. During the 14C, houses were demolished nearby in order to expand the size of the piazza. By 1385, when it was paved, it had nearly reached its present dimensions. In the life of the city today, the piazza is still the focus of public celebrations and political manifestations. It is now a pedestrian precinct (heavy traffic was banned as early as 1385), and is usually crowded with tourists as well as Florentines. Several cafés and restaurants have tables outside.

Controversial 'restoration' work was carried out in 1991 on the 18C paving of the piazza, when the old paving stones were taken up and new ones laid. The destruction of the old pavement has caused permanent damage to the appearance of the square. Excavations were carried out in the 1980s beneath the square: this huge area had been preserved intact by the paving, first laid in the 14C. Remains of Roman baths were found as well as traces of the south wall of the Roman colony founded in 30 BC. Later edifices included an early Christian basilica and medieval buildings.

Loggia della Signoria

Beside the splendid Palazzo Vecchio (described in Ch. 5) is the huge Loggia della Signoria (**Map 1; 6**), also known as the Loggia dell'Orcagna or the Loggia dei Lanzi after the *Lanzichenecchi* (bodyguards) of Cosimo I who were stationed here. Its three beautiful lofty arches, semicircular in form, break free from Gothic shapes and anticipate the Renaissance. The loggia was built in 1376–82 by Benci di Cione and Simone Talenti (probably on a design by Orcagna) to be used by government officials during public ceremonies, and as an ornament to the square. In the spandrels are seven marble statues of *Virtues* (1384–89) against a blue-enamelled ground, designed by Agnolo Gaddi. The head of **Faith** was probably substituted by Donatello, after the original fell to the ground. The columns are decorated with (worn) statuettes and lions' heads and have composite capitals; there are two elaborate corbels on the back wall.

It is only since the end of the 18C that the loggia has been used as an open-air museum of sculpture. Cellini's magnificent bronze **Perseus*, in which Perseus exhibits the Medusa's severed head, was returned here in 2000 after its restoration. It was commissioned by Cosimo I in 1545 and placed under the loggia near Donatello's *Judith* (see below); it is considered Cellini's masterpiece. He provides a graphic description in his *Autobiography* of the great difficulties he encountered while casting it (during which time his studio caught fire and he retired to bed with a fever). He saved the situation at the last moment by seizing all his pewter plates and bowls and throwing them into the melting-pot. The elaborate pedestal (replaced by a copy; the original is in the Bargello, see Ch. 13), using classical motifs, incorporates bronze statuettes and a bas-relief of *Perseus Rescuing Andromeda*.

On either side of the central arch is a pair of lions, formerly in the Villa Medici in Rome and put here in 1789: that on the right is by Flaminio Vacca and the one on the left is a Roman work. Beneath the front arch is Giambologna's last work, the **Rape of the Sabines* made for this position in 1583. It is a three-figure group commissioned by Francesco I. One of the most successful Mannerist sculptures, much praised by his contemporaries, the elaborate serpentine composition is designed to be seen from every side. The pedestal bears a bronze bas-relief.

Under the loggia is *Hercules and the Centaur*, also by Giambologna, with the help of Pietro Francavilla, set up here in 1841. *Ajax with the Body of Patroclus* is a Roman copy of a Greek original of 240 BC which entered the Medici collections in 1570. It was restored in the 17C and 19C, and was first displayed here in 1841. The *Rape of Polyxena* is the work of Pio Fedi (1866). Against the back wall are Roman statues (2C AD) transferred here in 1789 from the Villa Medici in Rome.

Beyond the corner of the piazza with the Uffizi buildings (see Ch. 6) is the main entrance (now closed) to Palazzo Vecchio (see Ch. 5). In front stands a copy of Michelangelo's famous *David*. The huge statue was commissioned by the city of Florence in 1501 and set up here in 1504 as a political symbol representing the victory of Republicanism over tyranny. When it was unveiled, it was heralded as a masterpiece and at once established Michelangelo as the greatest Florentine artist of his age. It was removed to the Accademia in 1873 (see Ch. 9). The colossal statue of *Hercules and Cacus* was sculpted in 1534 by Bandinelli; it is an unhappy imitation of the *David*, all the defects of which were pointed out by Cellini to Cosimo I in the presence of the sculptor. Between them are two bizarre terms by Bandinelli and Vincenzo de' Rossi.

Farther to the left, in front of the palace, is the copy of the statue of *Judith and Holofernes* by Donatello; the original has been exhibited inside Palazzo Vecchio since its restoration (see p 134). It was the first of all the statues to be installed in the piazza, after its confiscation from Palazzo Medici. Beyond a copy of Donatello's *Marzocco*, the heraldic lion of Florence (the original is in the Bargello, see p 252) is the **Neptune Fountain** (1560–75). The colossal flaccid figure of Neptune is known to Florentines as *il Biancone*. It was carved from a block of marble which, despite the efforts of Cellini, was first offered to Bandinelli and on his death to Ammannati. In the more successful elegant bronze groups on the basin, Ammannati was assisted by other sculptors including Giambologna and Andrea Calamech.

The porphyry disc with an inscription in the pavement in front of the fountain marks the spot where Savonarola was burnt at the stake on 23 May 1498.

Girolamo Savonarola

Girolamo Savonarola (1452–98), born in Ferrara, became Prior of the Dominican convent of San Marco in 1491. A learned theologian, admired by the Florentine humanists, he was famous as a preacher, and in his dramatic sermons he denounced 'immoral luxuries' and advocated a return to simple Christian principles. At his instigation, bonfires were lit in the Piazza to destroy works of art and books. An enemy of the Medici, his address to the Great Countil in 1496 did much to establish, albeit for a brief period, Republican values in the government of the city. However, the Borgia pope Alexander VI finally managed to excommunicate him and he was then accused by the Florentine government of attempting to organise a political party. Denounced for heresy and treason, he was executed, together with two of his companions, in the Piazza. Every year, on 23 May, a ceremony is held here in his memory.

On a line with the statues across the front of Palazzo Vecchio is a beautiful bronze equestrian monument to *Cosimo I* by Giambologna (1595). It was commissioned by Ferdinando I, and on the base are scenes of Cosimo's coronation and conquest of Siena. The horse's head is particularly fine.

At the end of the piazza (which opens out towards Piazza San Firenze, see p 258), and opposite the long flank of Palazzo Vecchio (see p 127) is the **Tribunale di Mercanzia** (or Merchants' Court), founded in 1308 and established in this building in 1359. Guild matters were discussed here. Palazzo Uguccioni (no. 7) has an unusual but handsome façade attributed to Mariotto di Zanobi Folfi (1550), perhaps on a design by Michelangelo. The bust of Cosimo I is attributed to Giovanni Bandini.

Above a bank at no. 5 is displayed the **Collezione Della Ragione** (Map 1; 6), a representative collection of 20C Italian art left to the city in 1970 by Alberto della Ragione. Opening times 09.00, 10.30, and 12.00; closed Tues, ☎ 055 283 078; Lire 4000 (C). There are plans to move the collection to the Museo di Firenze com'era in Via dell'Oriuolo (see p 260).

It includes mostly representational works (exhibited on two floors) by Arturo Tosi, Carlo Carrà, Giorgio Morandi, Ottone Rosai, Gino Severini, Mario Sironi,

Felice Casorati, Giorgio de Chirico, Arturo Martini, Virgilio Guidi, Massimo Campigli, Filippo de Pisis, Lucio Fontana, Marino Marini, Carlo Levi, Mario Mafai, Scipione, Giacomo Manzù, Corrado Cagli and Renato Guttuso.

5 • Palazzo Vecchio

Palazzo Vecchio (**Map 1; 6**), also known as Palazzo della Signoria, was the medieval Palazzo del Popolo and is still the town hall of Florence.

It is an imposing fortress-palace built in *pietra forte* on a trapezoidal plan, to a design traditionally attributed to Arnolfo di Cambio (1299–1302). The façade has remained virtually unchanged, with its graceful divided windows and a battlemented gallery. It became the prototype of many other *Palazzi Comunali* in Tuscany. It was the tallest edifice in the city until the 15C; the tower (1310), asymmetrically placed, is 95m high. Many of the rooms on the upper floors are open to the public.

• **Opening times** 09.00–19.00; Thurs and *fest.* 09.00–14.00, ☎ 055 276 8325 (C). Lire 11,000. Reduction for young people aged 12–20, and free for those under 12. A *carnet* can be purchased for Lire 10,000 which allows a 50 per cent reduction on the entrance fees to all museums owned by the Comune. The room numbers given below refer to the plans in the text. In 2000, three 'secret' itineraries (*percorsi segreti*) were opened to the public: these can usually be seen on Monday and Friday, Saturday afternoon and Sunday morning (booking preferable, ☎ 055 276 8224). The delightful children's museum (**Museo dei Ragazzi**) is open to school children during the week but can be visited by families usually on Saturday afternoon and Sunday morning, and sometimes also on other afternoons (booking also preferable, as above). There is a café restaurant on the ground floor.

Palazzo Vecchio

History of Palazzo Vecchio

The palace stands on part of the site of the Roman theatre of Florence built in the 1C AD. The *priori* (the governing magistrates of the city) lived here during their two months' tenure of office in the government of the medieval city. The bell in the tower summoned citizens in times of trouble to *Parlamento* in the square below. In 1433, Cosimo il Vecchio was imprisoned in the Alberghetto in the tower before being exiled. The building became known as Palazzo della Signoria during the Republican governments of the 15C, and alterations were carried out inside by Michelozzo, Giuliano and Benedetto da Maiano and Domenico Ghirlandaio. After the expulsion of the Medici in 1494, a huge hall (later known as the Sala dei Cinquecento) was built by Cronaca to house the new legislative body, the Consiglio Maggiore, which represented the aristocratic character of the new regime. Savonarola, at first a supporter of this government, was imprisoned in the Alberghetto in 1498 before being burnt at the stake in the piazza outside. In 1529, a frieze dedicated to Cristo Re with the monogram of Christ flanked by two symbolic lions was added above the main entrance.

One of the most significant moments in the history of the palace occurred in 1540 when Cosimo I moved here from the private Medici palace in Via Larga (now Via Cavour). Battista del Tasso, Vasari and later Buontalenti were called in to redecorate the building, now called Palazzo Ducale, and to extend it at the back for the early Medici dukes without, however, altering the exterior aspect on Piazza della Signoria. It became known as Palazzo Vecchio only after 1549 when the Medici grand-dukes took up residence in Palazzo Pitti. The Provisional Governments of 1848 and 1859 met here, and from 1865 to 1871 it housed the Chamber of Deputies and the Foreign Ministry when Florence was capital of the Kingdom of Italy. Since 1872, it has been the seat of the municipal government.

The flank of the building on Piazza della Signoria includes the battlemented 14C nucleus of the palace, the unfinished exterior of the Salone dei Cinquecento, with a hipped roof and marble window, and the handsome façade added by Buontalenti in Via de' Gondi. The 16C additions at the back of the building on Via dei Leoni incorporate medieval houses.

The **entrance** for visitors is now from Via della Ninna on the right side of the building: here can be seen parts of the 14C masonry, and extensions of various dates (the three large windows high up, with two smaller ones below, belong to the 15C Salone dei Cinquecento).

Ground floor

Near the 15C weather-vane with the Marzocco lion, which was removed from the top of the tower in 1981 (when it was replaced by a copy), a fragment of the original terracotta pavement in herring-bone style has been revealed. On the right is the ticket office and bookshop. Outside the entrance to the café there is a detached fresco of the *Crucifixion*, an early work by Andrea del Castagno (from Santa Maria Nuova).

To the left is the **cortile**, a courtyard reconstructed by Michelozzo (1453). The elaborate decorations were added in 1565 by Giorgio Vasari on the occasion of the marriage between Francesco, son of Cosimo I, and Joanna of Austria. The columns

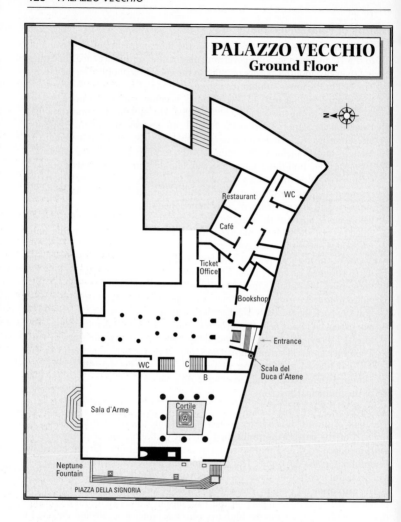

were covered with stucco and the vaults and walls painted with grotesques and views of Austrian cities. The fountain (**A**) designed by Vasari bears a copy of Verrocchio's popular *Putto Holding a Dolphin* (c 1470), a bronze made for a fountain at the Medici villa at Careggi. The original is preserved inside the palace (see below). The statue of *Samson Killing the Philistine* (**B**) is by Pierino da Vinci.

In the large rectangular **Sala d'Arme**, the only room on this floor which survives from the 14C structure, exhibitions are held. The rest of the ground floor is taken up with busy local government offices.

The monumental **grand staircase** (**C**) by Vasari ascends (right) in a theatrical double flight to the first floor (there is also a lift for the disabled).

First floor

The immense *Salone dei Cinquecento (53.5m x 22m, and 18m high) was built by Cronaca in 1495 for the meetings of the Consiglio Maggiore of the Republic (addressed here in 1496 by Savonarola). Leonardo da Vinci was commissioned in 1503 by the government to decorate one of the two long walls with a huge mural representing the Florentine victory at Anghiari over Milan in 1440. He experimented, without success, with a new technique of mural painting and completed only a fragment of the work before leaving Florence for Milan in 1506. It is not known whether this had disappeared or was destroyed (probably by order of Cosimo I) before the present frescoes were carried out under the direction of Vasari. Michelangelo was asked to do a similar composition on the opposite wall, representing the battle of Cascina between Florence and Pisa in 1364, but he only completed the cartoon before being called to Rome by Julius II. The cartoons of both works and the fragment painted by Leonardo were frequently copied and studied by contemporary painters before they were lost (a copy survives in the Sala di Ester, see below).

The room was transformed and heightened by Vasari in 1563–65 when the present decoration (designed with the help of Vincenzo Borghini) was carried out in celebration of Cosimo I. In the centre of the magnificent ceiling is the **Apotheosis of the Duke** surrounded by the stemme of the Guilds. The other panels, by Vasari, Giovanni Stradano, Jacopo Zucchi and Giovanni Battista Naldini, represent **Allegories of the Cities of Tuscany** under Florentine dominion, the **Foundations and Early Growth of Florence**, and the **Victories over Siena** (1554–55) and Pisa (1496–1509). On the walls are huge frescoes by the same artists illustrating three more episodes in the wars with Pisa (entrance wall) and Siena. The decoration was completed by Jacopo Ligozzi, Domenico Passignano, and Cigoli. The narrow triangular section of the ceiling above the raised tribune (known as the Udienza) was filled in with putti and self-portraits of Vasari's assistants who worked on the ceiling.

Michelangelo's *Victory (D), a strongly knit, two-figure group, was intended for a niche in the tomb of Julius II in Rome. It was presented to Cosimo I by Michelangelo's nephew in 1565 and set up here by Vasari as a celebration of the victory of Cosimo I over Siena. The serpentine form of the principal figure was frequently copied by later Mannerist sculptors. On the entrance wall (E) is Giambologna's original plaster model for **Virtue overcoming Vice** (or 'Florence victorious over Pisa') commissioned as a pendant to Michelangelo's *Victory* (the marble is in the Bargello). The other statues, representing the **Labours of Hercules** (F), are Vincenzo de' Rossi's best works.

The raised **Udienza** was begun by Giuliano di Baccio d'Agnolo and completed by Giorgio Vasari. It contains statues of distinguished members of the Medici family, many of them dressed as Romans. In the niche on the left: **Cosimo I** by Baccio Bandinelli and Vincenzo de' Rossi; on the end wall the seated **Leo X** begun by Bandinelli and completed by Giovanni Caccini is flanked by **Giovanni delle Bande Nere** and **Duke Alessandro** both by Bandinelli. In the large niche on the right wall, **Clement VII Crowning the Emperor Charles V**, a less successful work by Bandinelli, also completed by Caccini, and (in the smaller niche) **Francesco I** by Giovanni Caccini.

On the end wall, opposite the Udienza, are antique Roman statues.

Studiolo di Francesco I

An inconspicuous door in the entrance wall, to the right, opens into the charming *Studiolo di Francesco I. This tiny study (with no

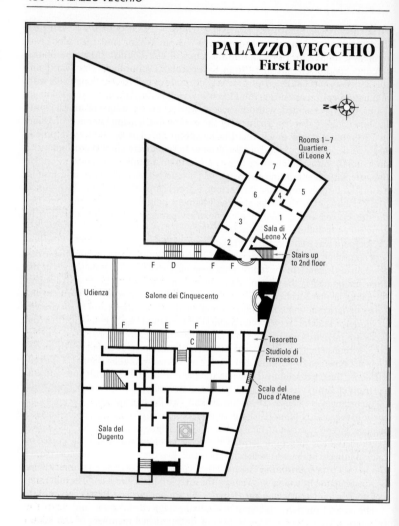

windows) was created by Vasari and his school in 1570–75 on an iconographical scheme devised by Vincenzo Borghini. It is a masterpiece of Florentine Mannerist decoration.

The present entrance from the Salone was opened later and unfortunately it can now only be seen from the doorway. The original entrance from the private rooms of the dukes is used in one of the *percorsi segreti* of the Palace (see below) when the interior of the Studiolo is shown to the public.

The Studiolo is entirely decorated with paintings and bronze statuettes celebrating Francesco's interest in the natural sciences and alchemy. The lower row of paintings conceal cupboards in which he kept his treasures. On the barrel vault, by Il Poppi, are *Allegories of the Four Elements* and portraits by Bronzino of Francesco's parents, *Cosimo I* and *Eleonora di Toledo*. The four walls, symbolising the *Four Elements*, include: left wall (Water): Vincenzo Danti, *Venus* (bronze); Vasari, *Perseus Liberating Andromeda*; Santi di Tito, *Crossing of the Red Sea*; Giovanni Battista Naldini, *Finding of Amber*; Giovanni Stradano, *Circe and the Companions of Ulysses*; Alessandro Allori, *Pearl Fishing*.

On the end wall (Air): Giovanni Bandini, *Juno* (bronze); Maso di San Friano, *Diamond Mine*, *Fall of Icarus*. Right wall (Fire): Giambologna, *Apollo* and Vincenzo de' Rossi, *Vulcan* (both bronzes); Giovanni Maria Butteri, *Glass-blowing Factory*; Alessandro Fei, *Goldsmiths' Workshop*; Giovanni Stradano, *Alchemist's Laboratory*. Entrance wall (Earth): Bartolomeo Ammannati, *Opi* (bronze); Jacopo Zucchi, *Goldmine*.

Quartiere di Leone X The door opposite the Studiolo leads into the well-preserved Quartiere di Leone X (1–7) decorated by Vasari and assistants (including Marco da Faenza and Giovanni Stradano) in 1555–62 for Cosimo I. The subjects for the mural paintings were chosen by Cosimo Bartoli and Vasari to illustrate the political history of the Medici family. Only the first room is regularly open to the public, since the others are used as offices by the mayor of the city. The **Sala de Leone X** (1) illustrates the life of cardinal Giovanni de' Medici, son of Lorenzo il Magnifico, and later Leo X. The paintings on the walls are by Vasari and assistants, and the monochrome works are by Giovanni Stradano. The busts of members of the Medici family are by Alfonso Lombardi and others. The wood ceiling carved by Domenico del Tasso contains paintings by Vasari, Giovanni Stradano and Marco Marchetti da Faenza. The good red-and-white terracotta pavement was made by Santi di Michele Buglioni, and the fireplace designed by Ammannati.

Second floor

Stairs, decorated with pretty grotesques by Marco Marchetti da Faenza, lead up from the Sala di Leone X to the second floor, past an interesting fresco (c 1558) by Giovanni Stradano of the fireworks in Piazza della Signoria celebrating the festival of St John the Baptist.

Quartiere degli Elementi At the top of the stairs (left) is the Quartiere degli Elementi, rooms (12–18) decorated with complicated allegories of the Elements and classical divinities in a programme devised by Cosimo Bartoli linking these rooms with those in the Quartiere di Leone X as a glorification of the Medici. The paintings are by Vasari and assistants (including Cristofano Gherardi). The **Sala degli Elementi** (12), which gave its name to this group of rooms, has paintings on the walls and ceiling illustrating the *Elements*: on the left wall, *Earth*; on the fireplace wall, *Fire*, and on the third wall, *Water*. The panel paintings set into the deeply recessed ceiling illustrate Air. There is a good view of the Forte di Belvedere on the skyline and the top of the tribune above the Uffizi building. The **Sala di Opi** (14) has another fine ceiling carved by Battista di Marco del Tasso, and a beautiful red-and-white terracotta floor (1556) by the *bottega* of Santi di Michele Buglioni. Here are displayed two fine cabinets in tortoiseshell and brass, decorated with mythological scenes and birds, fruit and flowers, both dating from the late 17C. The **Sala di Cerere** (13) has a ceiling painted by Vasari, with the help of Cristofano Gherardi, and a frieze by Marco da Faenza. Off it is the **Scrittoio di**

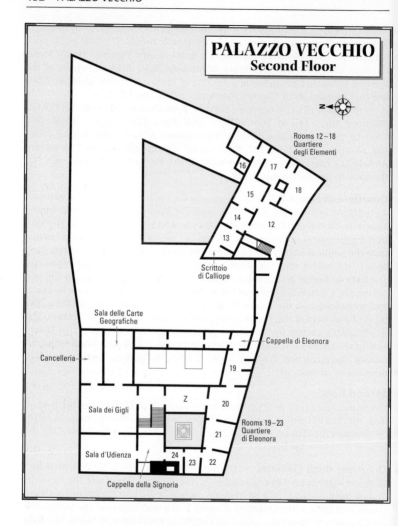

Calliope where Cosimo kept his precious treasures including miniatures, coins and statuettes. It has a charming ceiling painting of *Calliope* by Vasari. The late-16C stained-glass window by Walter of Antwerp is the only one of this date to survive in the palace. In the **Sala di Giove** (15) with more ceiling paintings, is another cabinet decorated with birds and flowers in *pietre dure*. The little **Terrazzo di Giunone** (16) was formerly open on three sides and surrounded by a hanging garden, but it was enclosed in the 19C. This is where Verrocchio's **Putto with a Dolphin* is displayed, the original removed from the courtyard below. Beyond, a little room with *grotteschi* decorations has a view of Santa Croce and the hill of San Miniato. The **Sala di Ercole** (17) has another delightful cabinet in *pietre dure*.

The **Terrazza di Saturno** (**18**) was sadly reduced in size in the last century. The damaged ceiling was painted by Stradano on a design by Vasari. Beyond the delicately carved eaves, the fine view of Florence includes (on the extreme right) the Corridoio Vasariano running from Palazzo Vecchio to the Uffizi, and beneath it can be seen the side of the Loggia dei Lanzi; farther left is the back of the Uffizi building with the lantern of the Tribuna, the Kaffehaus in the trees of the Boboli gardens, Forte di Belvedere on the skyline, and on the extreme left San Miniato and the façade and campanile of Santa Croce.

It is now necessary to return through the Sala degli Elementi to reach the balcony which leads across the end of the Sala dei Cinquecento. The following rooms (**19–23**) form part of the **Quartiere di Eleonora di Toledo**, the apartments of the wife of Cosimo I. The vault in the **camera verde** (**19**) was painted with grotesques by Ridolfo del Ghirlandaio (c 1540). The ***Cappella di Eleonora**, entirely decorated by Bronzino for Cosimo I in 1540–45, is one of his most important and original works. On the vault, divided by festoons, are *St Francis Receiving the Stigmata*, *St Jerome*, *St John the Evangelist at Patmos*, and *St Michael the Archangel*. On the walls are episodes from the *Life of Moses*, which may have a symbolic reference to Cosimo I. The original altarpiece by Bronzino of the *Lamentation* was sent by Cosimo to the Granvelle funerary chapel in Besançon and was replaced here by Bronzino with the present replica. The little **study** has a ceiling painted by Salviati.

The next four rooms were decorated in 1561–62 with ceilings by Battista Botticelli and paintings (illustrating allegories of the female Virtues) by Vasari and Giovanni Stradano. The **Sala delle Sabine** (**20**) has a cabinet which belonged to Don Lorenzo de' Medici, which incorporates a view of the Villa della Petraia, on a design by Giovanni Bilivert. The **Sala di Ester** (**21**) has a pretty frieze of putti intertwined in the letters of the name of Eleonora, and a 15C lavabo from Palazzo di Parte Guelfa. There is also a painting of 1557 which shows the lost fragment of the *Battle of Anghiari* by Leonardo (see above), probably the best copy that has survived. The *Sala di Penelope* (**22**) has a good ceiling with a frieze by Giovanni Stradano, and a Madonna and Child by the school of Botticelli.

In the **Sala di Gualdrada** (**23**) there is a frieze at the top of the wall with charming views of festivals in Florence, and a cabinet in *pietre dure* and mother of pearl with mythological scenes.

A **passage** (**24**) where remains of the old 14C polychrome ceiling and parts of the ancient tower are visible, contains a copy of the death mask of Dante. It leads into the older rooms of the palace. The **Cappella della Signoria** (or dei Priori; 1511–14) was decorated by Ridolfo del Ghirlandaio, including an *Annunciation* with a view of the church of Santissima Annunziata in the background (before the addition of the portico). The altarpiece is by his pupil, Fra Mariano da Pescia.

The **Sala d'Udienza** (**25**) has a superb ***gilded ceiling** by Giuliano da Maiano and assistants. The huge mural paintings illustrate stories from the *Life of the Roman Hero Marco Camillus* and were added c 1545–48 by Salviati; they are one of the major works by this typically Mannerist painter. From the windows can be seen Orsanmichele, the Campanile and the Duomo, and the two towers of the Badia Fiorentina and the Bargello. Above the door from the chapel, designed by Baccio d'Agnolo, is a dedication to Christ (1529). The other ***doorway** crowned by a statue of *Justice* is by Benedetto and Giuliano da Maiano. The intarsia doors, with figures of Dante and Petrarch, are by Giuliano da Maiano and Francione

The **Sala dei Gigli** (26) takes its name from the irises, symbol of the city, which decorate the walls and magnificent *ceiling. The other face of the doorway has a statue of the young *St John the Baptist* and putti by Benedetto and Giuliano da Maiano. The *fresco by Domenico Ghirlandaio shows *St Zenobius Enthroned Between Saints Stephen and Lawrence and Two Lions*, and lunettes with *Six Heroes of Ancient Rome*. Here, since its restoration, is displayed Donatello's bronze statue of *Judith and Holofernes* removed from Piazza della Signoria. One of his last and most sophisticated works (c 1455), it was commissioned by the Medici and used as a fountain (the holes for the water can be seen in the cushion) in the garden of their palace. On their expulsion from the city in 1495, it was expropriated by the government and placed under the Loggia della Signoria with an inscription warning against tyrants. There is a superb view of the cupola and campanile of the Duomo as well as the towers of the Badia Fiorentina and the Bargello.

A window of the old palace serves as a doorway into the **Cancelleria**, built in 1511 (the stone bas-relief of St George attributed to Arnolfo di Cambio used to decorate the Porta San Giorgio). This room was used as an office by Niccolò Machiavelli during his term as government secretary. He is commemorated here with a fine bust (16C) and a painting by Santi di Tito.

Niccolò Machiavelli

Niccolò Machiavelli (1469–1527) is famous as a historian and statesman. In 1498, he became secretary of the Ten and was used by Piero Soderini, the *gonfaloniere* (ruling magistrate) of Florence, for diplomatic missions, during which he wrote detailed reports. He was impressed by Cesare Borgia (Alexander VI's son) when he was sent as an envoy to investigate his activities in the Romagna. After the return of the Medici, he was imprisoned (in 1513) on a charge of conspiracy and even though released he never returned to public life. He wrote numerous historical studies, and in 1520 Giulio de' Medici (later Pope Clement VII) commissioned him to write a history of Florence. His most famous work is *Il Principe*, in which he illustrates the effectiveness of strong government. He is also known as a playwright (his best-known play is *La Mandragola*).

The Guardaroba or **Sala delle Carte Geografiche** (28) was decorated with a fine ceiling and wooden cupboards in 1563–65 by Dionigi di Matteo Nigetti. On the presses are 57 maps illustrating the known world at that time with a remarkable degree of accuracy: this was one of the earliest attempts to produce an atlas. Of great scientific and historical interest, the maps were painted by Fra Egnazio Danti for Cosimo I (1563) and completed by Stefano Bonsignori (1585) for Francesco I. The map on the left of the entrance shows the British Isles. The huge globe in the centre was also designed by Danti for Cosimo I.

Stairs lead down from outside the Sala dei Gigli towards the exit, passing a **mezzanine floor** in which four rooms display the **Collezione Loeser**, left to the city in 1928 by the distinguished American art critic and connoisseur, Charles

Loeser. The first room has an old painted ceiling, and beyond a corridor with three *Madonnas*, the third room displays the masterpiece of the collection, the portrait of *Laura Battiferri*, wife of Bartolomeo Ammannati, one of Bronzino's most sophisticated portraits. Also here is a portrait of *Ludovico Martelli* attributed to Pontormo. In the last room: painted *Crucifix* dating from 1290; marble angel by Tino da Camaino(from the Bishop Orso monument in the Duomo); *Madonna and Child* by Pietro Lorenzetti; *tondo* of the *Madonna and Child with the Young St John* by Alonso Berruguete; and the *Passion of Christ*, a very unusual painting by Piero di Cosimo. The sculptures include two statuettes of angels by Jacopo Sansovino, a head of *Cosimo I* by Vincenzo de' Rossi, a bronze statuette of *Autumn* by Benvenuto Cellini, a small bronze of *Hercules and the Hydra* by Giambologna, and two battle scenes in terracotta by Gianfrancesco Rustici.

The stairs continue down to a vestibule (the coved ceiling of which has painted grotesque decorations) outside the **Sala dei Dugento** (usually closed), where the town council meets. The name is derived from the council of 200 citizens who met here. This was reconstructed in 1472–77 by Benedetto and Giuliano da Maiano who also executed the magnificent wood ceiling (with the help of Domenico Marco, and Giuliano del Tasso).

The 'Percorsi Segreti' To see one of the three 'secret itineraries' of Palazzo Vecchio on a guided tour, one of which is included in the price of the ticket, it is advisable to book in advance (see p 126).

The **first itinerary** follows the staircase known as the **Scala del Duca d'Atene**, built in 1342 by Walter de Brienne—known as the Duke of Athens—who held absolute power in the city for one year before his expulsion by a popular rising. The entrance is through the small rectangular door beside the present visitors' entrance to the palace in Via della Ninna, and in the first little room the original wall of the back of Arnolfo's building can be seen. The secret staircase, partly spiral, built inside the later wall leads up to the first floor into a room which was later part of Cosimo I's private apartment.

From here visitors on the **second itinerary** are taken into the **Studiolo** (see p 129) through its original entrance. From here a small staircase leads up to the **Tesoretto**, the richly decorated, tiny private study of Cosimo I. The stuccoes are by Tommaso Boscoli and Leonardo Ricciarelli and the vault frescoes by Il Poppi or Stradano (1559–62). The original cupboards are preserved which used to house Cosimo's treasures, and the pavement in white and red marble and *pietra serena*.

The **third itinerary** includes a room (marked **Z** on the plan of the second floor) off the Sala delle Sabine on the second floor (**20** on the plan) which contains a sculpted relief showing Palazzo Vecchio and a detached 14C fresco illustrating the expulsion of the Duke of Athens. From the balcony above the Salone dei Cinquecento a staircase leads up to the remarkable *roof of the Salone*, where the complicated system of rafters and beams can be seen which support both the roof and the paintings of the ceiling.

The Museo dei Ragazzi

The Children's Museum (open to school children during the week, but to families on Saturday afternoon and Sunday, and sometimes at other times: booking advisable, see p 126), opened in 2000, is a remarkably successful project which uses parts of the palace not otherwise open to the public to illustrate certain historical periods, or to explain architectural principles or scientific theories to teenage children. It is run by a group of energetic and informed young people. It includes an **architectural laboratory** entered from the Sala delle Carte Geografiche in a room at the top of the palace with very fine views of the Duomo. Here children can experiment with models which explain statics in architecture. Another part of the museum includes a **theatre workshop** where representations of the Medici court of Cosimo I and his wife Eleonora da Toledo are held and children can dress up in costumes of the period. On the ground floor, rooms off the entrance courtyard have models of **scientific experiments** which illustrate Galileo's telescope, and the discovery of the vacuum by Evangelista Torricelli in 1643. Also here, in the Sala di Bia e Garcia, named after the children of Cosimo I, there are games for younger children (aged 3–6).

6 • Galleria degli Uffizi

The massive Palazzo degli Uffizi (**Map 1; 6**) extends from Piazza della Signoria to the Arno. Houses were demolished to create this long, narrow site next to Palazzo Vecchio, and Vasari was commissioned by Cosimo I to erect a building here to serve as government offices (*uffici*, hence uffizi). The unusual U-shaped building with a short façade on the river front was begun in 1560 and completed, according to Vasari's design, after his death in 1574 by Alfonso Parigi the Elder and Bernardo Buontalenti (who also made provision for an art gallery here for Francesco I). Resting on unstable sandy ground, it is a feat of engineering skill. The use of iron to reinforce the building permitted extraordinary technical solutions during its construction, and allowed for the remarkably large number of apertures. A long arcade supports three upper storeys pierced by numerous windows and a loggia in *pietra serena*. In the niches of the pilasters are statues of illustrious Tuscans made in 1842–56 (and restored in 2000) by Emilio Santarelli, Luigi Pampaloni, Odoardo Fantachiotti, Vincenzo Consani, Lorenzo Bartolini, Giovanni Duprè, Pio Fedi, Aristodemo Costoli, Ulisse Cambi and others. The building now houses the famous Galleria degli Uffizi, the most important collection of paintings in Italy and one of the great art collections of the world.

• **Opening times** Daily except Monday 08.30–18.50; *fest.* 08.30–19.00; in summer 08.30–21.00; *fest.* 08.30–20.00. Lire 12,000. ☎ 055 238 8651 (S). There is now an excellent booking service (☎ 055 294 883 Mon–Fri 08.30–18.30; Sat 09.00–12.00) which is highly recommended as it means you avoid the queue, which can be very long. You pick up your ticket at a special ticket office on the ground floor five or ten minutes before the booked time (and pay an extra booking fee of Lire 2000).

The **Corridoio Vasariano** (Lire 50,000 including entrance to the Uffizi and Boboli gardens) and **Collezione Contini Bonacossi** (free) can be visited by appointment only, call ☎ 055 265 4321. There is a **café** with a terrace on the third floor, and a **post office** on the ground floor.

Plan of visit The gallery tends to be extremely crowded with tour groups, but is usually more peaceful in the early morning, over lunch-time and in the late afternoon. Automatic signals on the ground floor provide information about expected waiting time if there is a queue (a maximum of 660 people are allowed into the gallery at any one time). You are strongly recommended not to attempt to see the entire collection in one day; the first rooms (up to Room 15) include the major works of the Florentine Renaissance; the later rooms can be combined in a second visit.

The collection is arranged chronologically by schools. The following description includes only some of the most important paintings and sculptures (and stars, which indicate the most important of all, have been used sparingly). Many of the paintings have superb contemporary frames. The labelling of the works is kept to a minimum and the lighting is very poor in the earlier rooms. Since the gallery is undergoing re-arrangement the works in some of the later rooms (from 41 onwards) may be moved around. Round red labels indicate the date a work was restored. There is a lift for the use of the disabled.

History of the Uffizi Collection

The origins of the collection go back to Cosimo I de'Medici (1519–74). The galleries were enlarged and the collection augmented by his son Francesco I. The Medici dynasty continued to add numerous works of art in the following centuries: Ferdinando I transferred sculptures here from the Villa Medici in Rome; Ferdinando II inherited paintings by Raphael, Titian and Piero della Francesca from Francesco Maria della Rovere of Urbino; and Cardinal Leopoldo began the collection of drawings and self-portraits. The last of the Medici, Anna Maria Lodovica, widow of the Elector Palatine (d. 1743), settled her inheritance on the people of Florence through a family pact (1737). The huge collection was partly broken up during the last century when much of the sculpture went to the Bargello and other material was transferred to the Archaeological Museum. This century many paintings removed from Florentine churches have been housed in the gallery which was partly redesigned for them in the 1950s by Giovanni Michelucci and Paolo Scarpa.

Since the Archivio di Stato was moved from the building in 1989, plans have been under way to expand the gallery in stages. The rooms on the third floor will probably remain more or less as they are, while the *piano nobile* below will be used to exhibit paintings at present in the deposits and in the Corridoio Vasariano. Alterations are expected to take until 2005, when the exhibition space will be more than doubled and about 3000 paintings will be displayed (instead of the present 1000). At the same time, it will be possible to house 1500 visitors simultaneously (over twice the number at present permitted). The modifications to provide an exit from the gallery at the back of the building in Piazza de' Castellani are expected to be completed in 2002. These include a huge projecting roof designed by the Japanese architect Arata Isozaki, already criticised for its gigantic proportions.

In 1993, the gallery was damaged by a bomb placed in a car (by the Mafia) in Via Lambertesca which killed five people and injured 29. There was severe structural damage to the first part of the Corridoio Vasariano and the rooms off the west corridor. About 90 works of art were damaged, but they have been (or are being) carefully restored, except for three paintings (two by Bartolomeo Manfredi and one by Gherardo delle Notti) which were totally destroyed. Rooms 43–45 off the west corridor are still closed for restoration.

Ground floor

The **entrance** is through a room which displays some restored doors. A series of large rooms beyond, once occupied by law courts and then by the state archives, were restored and opened in 1998 to house ticket offices (separate one for pre-booked visits), a bookshop, information centre and cloakrooms. Tickets are shown at the foot of the grand staircase, just beyond which there are lifts, officially reserved for the staff, but which can usually be used on request if you are on your own. From here can be glimpsed a lovely detached fresco of the *Annunciation* by Botticelli. Beyond is a room (often closed) which incorporates remains of the church of San Pier Scheraggio, founded c 1068, and one of the largest churches of its time in Florence. It was altered when the Uffizi was built. Remains have also been found of an 8C Lombard church on this site. Here are displayed detached *frescoes (c 1450) by Andrea del Castagno of illustrious Florentines including Boccaccio, Petrarch and Dante. These splendid monumental figures decorated a loggia of the Villa Pandolfini at Legnaia (and were later housed in the monastery of Sant'Apollonia). In 1983, a large painting (the *Battle of San Martino*, inspired by Paolo Uccello's famous triptych) by Corrado Cagli was also placed here. The apse of the church has traces of damaged frescoes, c 1294–99.

The **staircase**, lined with antique busts and statues, leads up past part of the huge theatre built in the building by Buontalenti for Francesco I in 1586–89. Over the central door is a bust of the grand-duke by Giambologna (or his workshop). On the left the old entrance now serves as the entrance to the **Prints and Drawings Room** (open to scholars with special permission, 09.00–13.00). The collection is one of the finest in the world and is particularly rich in Renaissance and Mannerist works. Exhibitions are held periodically.

Third floor

At the top of the stairs are 10 busts of the *Medici* from Lorenzo il Magnifico to the last grand-duke, including one by Giambologna (Cosimo I) and two by Giovanni Battista Foggini. Tickets are checked in the **vestibule** (A) which contains antique sculpture including a statue of *Augustus* and two dogs—well-preserved Greek works, perhaps of the Pergamenian School.

Beyond is the **east corridor** of the long U-shaped gallery with its vault painted with grotesques in 1581 by Alessandro Allori and Antonio Tempesta. Although the splendid tapestries which used to hang on the walls have been removed for conservation reasons, the corridor is arranged with portraits and antique sculpture (all of them well labelled with diagrams) more or less as it was in the 16C. At the top of the walls is a series of *Portraits of Famous Men* commissioned by the Medici in 1552–89 from Cristofano dell'Altissimo, copies of the works collected by the historian Paolo Giovio who died in 1552. At intervals between them are hung portraits of members of the Medici dynasty in the 15C and 16C, beginning at the short north end of the corridor with a portrait of Giovanni de' Bicci de' Medici by Alessandro Allori. Both series of paintings are continued right round the walls of all three corridors.

The superb collection of **antique sculptures** (mostly Hellenistic works) collected by Cosimo I and augmented by Francesco and Ferdinando, was first

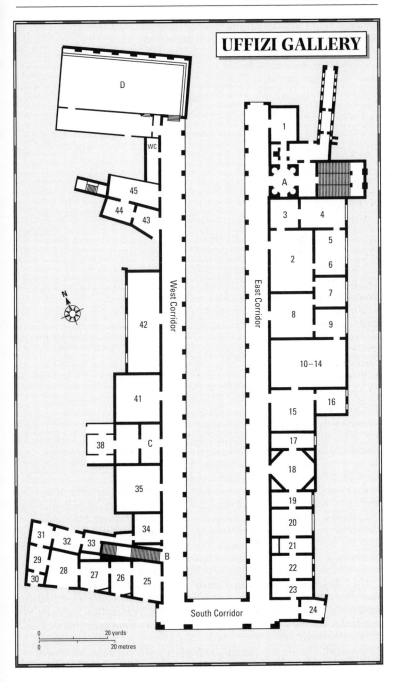

UFFIZI GALLERY

D

WC

45

44   43

West Corridor

East Corridor

N

42

1

A

3   4

5

2   6

7

8   9

10–14

16

41   15

38   C   17

18

35   19

20

34   21

31   32   33   22

B   23

29   28   27   26   25   24

30

South Corridor

0   20 yards
0   20 metres

arranged in this corridor in 1595 (and the first inventory dates from 1597). The statue of *Hercules and a Centaur*, which has been at the end of the corridor since that time, is a Roman copy of a Hellenistic original, but with numerous restorations: the Hercules was restored in 1579 (only the feet are original), and the tail, head and upper part of the torso of the Centaur were remade by Giovanni Battista Caccini in 1589. The busts include one known (erroneously) as *Augustus* and one of *Agrippa* (the heads are original, but the busts are probably by Caccini), considered the founders of Rome; these were given to Lorenzo il Magnifico in Rome by Sixtus IV and bought back to Florence to decorate Palazzo Medici. On the window wall, the statue of the so-called *Mercury* or *Hermes* was formerly in the Cortile del Belvedere in the Vatican and was moved to Florence in 1536 when it was displayed in the Sala delle Nicchie in Palazzo Pitti. The hat, arms and base are all restorations, and it in fact represents a young man or satyr (and is a replica of a work of Praxiteles). The statue of a *Dancing Girl*, formerly called Pomona, is now thought to be an allegory of Autumn (the head is a restoration). Five other similar statues are known and it is possible that one of them could have influenced Botticelli when he painted the figure of Flora in his *Primavera*. By the entrance to the Tribuna is a male statue in Parian and rare black marble known as the *Ares Borghese* (a Roman copy of an Attic original, with restored arms and head).

Room 1 (closed indefinitely) This contains fine *Antique Roman sculptures which clearly influenced Florentine Renaissance sculptors. Opposite the windows overlooking the narrow piazza are doors leading into the numerous galleries of paintings.

Room 2 The collection begins in Room 2, to the left, which provides a fitting introduction to the painting galleries illustrating Tuscan painting of the 13C. Three huge paintings of the *Madonna Enthroned* (known as the *Maestà*) dominate the room. On the right, the *Madonna in Maestà* by **Cimabue** (c 1285), painted for the church of Santa Trìnita, marks a final development of the Byzantine style of painting, where a decorative sense still predominates. On the left is another exquisite version of this subject, the *Rucellai Madonna* by **Duccio di Buoninsegna**, commissioned by the Laudesi confraternity in 1285 for their chapel in Santa Maria Novella. Between the 17C and 18C it was put in the Rucellai chapel (hence the name) in the same church and has been housed in the Uffizi since 1948. It was painted on five planks of poplar wood 4.5m high and c 60–65cm wide. Since the wood was unseasoned, huge cracks formed, but the painting was beautifully restored in 1990 when the splendid blue mantle of the Virgin was discovered beneath a layer of over-painting carried out in the 17C. The frame, with painted roundels, is original. The painting was traditionally attributed to Cimabue, but is now recognised as the work of the younger Sienese artist, Duccio, who is known to have worked in Cimabue's studio.

The *Madonna in Maestà* by **Giotto**, painted some 25 years later for the church of Ognissanti, has a sense of realism which had never been achieved in medieval painting or by his master Cimabue. The figure of the Madonna has acquired a new monumentality and she is set in a more clearly defined space. This is considered one of Giotto's masterpieces whose art heralded a new era in Western painting. He also painted the polyptych which is displayed here of the *Madonna and Four Saints* for the Badia Fiorentina.

Room 3 (left) This room displays 14C Sienese painting which flourished at this period under the influence of Duccio. His greatest follower was **Simone Martini** whose charming *Annunciation* (1333) dominates the room. The Gothic elegance of the Madonna and annunciatory angel set against a rich gold ground make this one of the masterpieces of 14C Tuscan painting, and one of the most memorable paintings in the gallery. It is the only major work by Simone in Florence (painted for the Duomo of Siena, it was moved here by the Tuscan grand-duke in 1799). It is signed by Simone and his brother-in-law Lippo Memmi who may have painted the lateral Saints. The neo-Gothic frame was added in 1900. The small *Madonna and Child* exhibited on the same wall, by Andrea Vanni clearly shows the influence of Simone.

The brothers **Pietro and Ambrogio Lorenzetti**, also important protagonists of the Sienese school, are represented here in a number of fine works: the *Presentation in the Temple* (1342), four *Scenes From the Life of St Nicholas*, and a *Triptych* reassembled when the central panel was left to the Uffizi by Bernard Berenson in 1959, are all by Ambrogio, while the panels of a dossal with the story of the *Blessed Umiltà* and the *Madonna in Glory*, signed and dated 1340, are both by Pietro.

Room 4 Florentine painting of the 14C. *Deposition* (from the church of San Remigio) attributed to Giottino, a painter otherwise little known, and who has affinities with Giotto's most gifted pupils Maso di Banco and Giovanni da Milano, who is represented here with panels of *Saints, Martyrs* and *Virgins*. There are also works here by Bernardo Daddi (including a triptych and a tiny portable altar), as well as Orcagna, and his brothers, Nardo and Jacopo di Cione, all of whom left numerous works in the city. The elegant dossal of *Santa Cecilia*, by an unknown master who takes his name from this work (the Santa Cecilia Master), is another beautiful work.

Rooms 5 and 6 These are in fact one room, and illustrate the International Gothic style. The monk known as **Lorenzo Monaco** is represented by two superb altarpieces: the large *Coronation of the Virgin* (1413) and the *Adoration of the Magi*. His wonderful colouring and graceful, elongated figures make him one of the greatest artists of this period who concentrated on the depiction of the human figure leaving the landscape behind (as can be seen in the *Adoration of the Magi*) an abstraction of rocks and unreal buildings seemingly there to add yet more colour to the work. The central angel (playing the organ) in the Coronation was carefully painted in 1998 to cover a hole when the altarpiece was restored. The other important painter of this period was **Gentile da Fabriano**. He was born in the Marche but moved to Florence in 1420 at the invitation of Palla Strozzi, who commissioned the richly decorated *Adoration of the Magi* (at the other end of the room) in 1423, in which the horses' bridles and the brocaded costumes, as well as the crowns worn by the Kings, are highlighted in gold. This famous work has a charming, fairy-tale quality and numerous delightful details including the animals and the servant bending down to take off one of the king's spurs, and the two graceful serving ladies behind the Madonna examining one of the king's gifts. The predella is also exquisitely painted, with a beautiful scene set in a grove of orange trees showing the *Flight into Egypt*. Gentile also painted the *Mary Magdalen, St Nicholas of Bari, St John* and *St George* in 1425 (formerly part of a polyptych), all of them sumptuously dressed and standing on a decorated pavement.

The window in this room affords a good view of the top of Santa Croce and the hill of San Miniato.

Room 7 Early 15C paintings representing the early Renaissance. The **Battle of San Romano* is an amusing exercise in perspective by **Paolo Uccello**. Together with its companions, now in the Louvre and National Gallery, London, it decorated Lorenzo il Magnifico's bedroom in Palazzo Medici-Riccardi in 1492. It celebrates the battle in which the Florentines were victorious over the Sienese. The most important elements in the painting are the horses and lances. By the window is the famous **diptych* by **Piero della Francesca**, with the portraits of *Federico di Montefeltro* and his duchess, *Battista Sforza*, in profile against a superb detailed landscape in a transparent light stretching into the far distance. On the reverse are their allegorical triumphs in a rarefied atmosphere with another wonderful landscape. These exquisite works, profoundly humanist in spirit, were painted in Urbino c 1465 in celebration of this famous Renaissance prince, always depicted in profile since he lost his right eye in a tournament.

The **Madonna Enthroned with Saints Francis, John the Baptist, Zenobius and Lucy* by **Domenico Veneziano** is one of the few known works by this artist, who was born in Venice but moved to Florence where he lived until his death in 1461. It is painted in beautiful soft colours in a Renaissance setting, and is one of the loveliest altarpieces of this familiar subject in Florence (the figure of St Lucy recalls the style of Piero della Francesca, who was Lorenzo's pupil). The *Madonna and Child with St Anne* was painted by Masolino, but Masaccio is thought to have added the Madonna and Child to his master's painting, which has, however, otherwise been completely repainted. The tiny painting of the *Madonna and Child* (with the Madonna tickling the Child's chin) is an undocumented work attributed to Masaccio. Also here are two works, including the *Coronation of the Virgin* by Fra' Angelico.

Room 8 This contains paintings by **Filippo Lippi** and his son **Filippino**. The best works here by Filippo Lippi are perhaps the **Predella of the Barbadori Altarpiece* (the rest of the altarpiece is now in the Louvre), which has a remarkable sense of space and the **Madonna and Child with Two Angels* (c 1465), with a particularly beautiful Madonna, justly one of his most famous works. There are also two paintings of the *Adoration of the Child*, a crowded *Coronation of the Virgin*, and a *Madonna Enthroned with Saints* by him. Filippino Lippi is represented by a lovely **Adoration of the Child* and two large altarpieces (*Madonna and Saints* painted for the Sala degli Otto in Palazzo Vecchio, and the *Adoration of the Magi*). Another *Madonna and Child with Saints* and an **Annunciation* are by Alesso Baldovinetti.

Room 9 The altarpiece of **Saints Vincent, James and Eustace* by **Antonio del Pollaiolo** is one of his best works. The three saints, full of character, are splendidly dressed with rich costumes and stand on a terrace behind which can be glimpsed an open landscape. It was painted for the Chapel of the Cardinal of Portugal in the church of San Miniato, where it has been replaced by a copy. Antonio is also thought to have painted the famous *Portrait of a Lady in Profile*, a charming girl in Renaissance dress. The portrait of *Galeazzo Maria Sforza* is now usually attributed to his younger brother Piero. The six paintings of *Virtues*, some of which are being restored, are also by the Pollaiolo brothers except for

Fortitude, which is an early work by Botticelli. In the case are ***four exquisite small panels**, two of them by Antonio del Pollaiolo showing the *Labours of Hercules*, and two by Botticelli illustrating *Judith Returning from the Camp of Holofernes* and the *Discovery of the Decapitated Holofernes in his Tent* (c 1470). These last two are among the most exquisite works in the gallery. The very fine portrait of a *Young Man in a Red Hat* is by an unknown artist (usually attributed to Filippino Lippi).

Rooms 10–14 These rooms have been converted into one huge space and the rafters of the stage of the old Medici theatre (see above) exposed. This is now home to **Botticelli**'s masterpieces, which include both religious and mythological subjects. The ***Primavera** is one of his most important and most famous pictures. It was painted probably c 1478 for Lorenzo di Pierfrancesco de' Medici, Lorenzo il Magnifico's younger cousin. An allegory of spring, which was the season which began the year in 15C Florence, it is thought to have been inspired by a work of Politian, although its precise significance is still debated. There is a rhythmical contact between the figures who are placed in a meadow of flowers within a dark orange grove, the Garden of Hesperides of classical myth. To the right, Zephyr chases Flora and transforms her into Spring, who is shown bedecked with flowers. In the centre Venus stands with Cupid above her, and beyond the beautiful group of the Three Graces united in dance, is the figure of Mercury (perhaps an idealised portrait of Lorenzo il Magnifico). The work is richly painted on panels of poplar wood. The varnishes which had been added in various restorations were removed in 1982 and the painting was cleaned to restore its original appearance. The botanical details which were revealed include a variety of spring flowers, most of which can still be seen today growing in Lorenzo di Pierfrancesco's Villa of Castello (see p 359).

Sandro Botticelli

Botticelli (1446–1510) was one of most important and most original painters of the Italian Renaissance, greatly admired in his lifetime. But he fell into oblivion soon after his death and was only 'rediscovered' by the Anglo-American community living in Florence at the end of the 19C and beginning of the 20C. John Ruskin, Walter Pater, Dante Gabriele Rossetti, Herbert Percy Horne and Ezra Pound all wrote about him at this time with great enthusiasm. In 1870, Walter Pater noted, 'the peculiar character of Botticelli is the result of a blending in him of a sympathy for humanity in its uncertain condition, its attractiveness, its investiture at rarer moments in a character of loveliness and energy, with his consciousness of the shadow upon it of the great things from which it shrinks, and that this conveys into his work somewhat more than painting usually attains of the true complexion of humanity.' In 1881, Dante Gabriel Rossetti wrote a poem entitled 'Spring by Sandro Botticelli':

... the Graces circling near,
Neath bower-linked arch of white arms glorified:
And with those feathered feet which hovering glide
O'er Spring's brief bloom, Hermes the harbinger.

The *Birth of Venus* is perhaps the most famous of all Botticelli's works. It was probably also painted for Lorenzo di Pierfrancesco and hung in the Medici villa of Castello. The pagan subject is taken from a poem by Politian and illustrates Zephyr and Chloris blowing Venus ashore while Hora, her fluttering dress decorated with cornflowers and daisies, hurries to cover her nakedness. The elegant figures are painted with a remarkable lightness of touch in a decorative linear design. The classical nude figure of Venus balances on the edge of a beautiful scallop shell as it floats ashore. A strong wind blows through this harmonious Graeco-Roman world.

The splendid religious works by Botticelli in the room include two tondi of the Madonna (the *Madonna of the Magnificat* and the *Madonna of the Pomegranate*), the *Madonna of the Rose Garden* and the *Madonna of the Loggia*. Of the three fine altarpieces painted for Florentine churches, the *Madonna and Saints* from Sant'Ambrogio is the earliest and is particularly lovely, with a beautiful Mary Magdalen. The *Coronation of the Virgin* (from San Marco), which has been restored, has a charming circle of angels in the sky and a delightful predella. The late *Annunciation* shows an extraordinary spiritual bond between the two figures. The relatively small *Adoration of the Magi* has an interesting setting but the Holy Family are relegated to the back of the painting and the interest lies above all in the portraits of the Medici courtiers who are depicted as the Kings and their entourage. Giuliano de' Medici (or possibly Lorenzo il Magnifico), lost in thought, is dressed in black and red on the right and Botticelli himself is shown in a self-portrait (dressed in a yellow cloak) on the extreme right. The standing figure by the horse's head on the left may be Lorenzo il Magnifico next to the poets Politian and Pico della Mirandola, and the kneeling 'Magi' in black represents Cosimo il Vecchio, and the one dressed in red, Piero il Gottoso.

Botticelli's skill as a portrait painter is also shown in the *Portrait of a Man in a Red Hat*, a very fine and well-restored painting of an unknown sitter who is holding a medal of Cosimo il Vecchio.

The subject of the small, elaborate painting entitled *Calumny* (painted after 1487) is taken from the ancient Greek writer Lucian's account of a picture by Apelles described in Alberti's treatise on painting. The *Pallas and the Centaur* was probably intended as a moral or political allegory, the significance of which has been much discussed. Pallas, whose clothes are decorated with Lorenzo's emblem, is shown taming the centaur, and it may be that Pallas represents Florence or Lorenzo il Magnifico, and the centaur—half-man and half-beast—represents disorder and barbarism. Another interpretation is that Pallas symbolises Humility or Prudence, restraining Pride. The tiny painting of *St Augustine in his cell* is one of a number of pictures Botticelli painted of this saint.

The huge triptych of the *Adoration of the Shepherds* was commissioned by the Medici agent in Bruges, Tommaso Portinari from **Hugo van der Goes**. It was shipped back to Florence in 1475 for his family chapel in Sant'Egidio. On the wings are saints and members of the Portinari family. It includes exquisitely painted details such as the still-life in the foreground showing two vases of flowers and a sheaf of wheat, and the charming portraits of the two Portinari boys. The painting had an important influence on contemporary Florentine artists.

Also in this room are three good works by Michelangelo's master **Domenico Ghirlandaio**: two beautiful altarpieces of the *Madonna Enthroned with Saints*, one with a lovely vase of flowers on a carpet, four delightful angels and orange trees behind the balustrade, and a tondo of the *Adoration of the Magi* with a pretty landscape (1487).

Room 15   Here are displayed the early Florentine works of Leonardo da Vinci and the paintings of his master Verrocchio. **Leonardo da Vinci**'s *Adoration of the Magi* (1481) is a huge, crowded composition, remarkable for its figure studies and unusual iconography. The painting was left unfinished when Leonardo left Florence for Milan; it remains in its preparatory stage of chiaroscuro drawn in a red earth pigment. His *Annunciation*, painted in Verrocchio's studio, was restored in 2000. The extent of Verrocchio's intervention is unclear: it is thought that he was probably responsible for the design, for the figure of the Madonna and for the classical sarcophagus. Verrocchio's *Baptism of Christ* was begun c 1470. According to Vasari and Albertini, the angel on the left was painted by the young Leonardo.

The *Crucifix* by Luca Signorelli is one of his most remarkable paintings: Mary Magdalene is shown at the foot of the Cross with a dramatic, strong, dark figure of Christ; while in the background scenes of the Crucifixion are set in a desolate landscape against a light ground. The botanical details are also exquisitely painted. Signorelli's *Trinity with the Madonna and Saints* has been removed for restoration. There are also four works by the Umbrian painter Perugino, *Madonna with Saints Sebastian and John* (the figure of St Sebastian is particularly beautiful), *Pietà*, *Crucifix with Saints* and *Christ in the Garden*. A charming painting of the *Three Archangels* by Francesco Botticini is also sometimes exhibited here.

Room 16   This room is the Sala delle Carte Geografiche and its walls are painted with maps of Tuscany by Stefano Bonsignori. The panelled ceiling is ascribed to Jacopo Zucchi. Some fine Roman sarcophagi are exhibited here, and sometimes important works from rooms in the gallery which are at present closed.

Room 18   The beautiful octagonal *Tribuna*, inspired by classical models, was designed by Buontalenti for Francesco I (1584) to display the most valuable objects in the Medici collection. It has a mother-of-pearl dome and a fine pavement in *pietre dure*. It formerly had only one entrance, from the corridor. Now, unfortunately, you are obliged to visit it from a walkway and so it is impossible to examine the works in the centre of the room. The *octagonal table* is a masterpiece of *pietre dure*, made in the Florence Opificio between 1633 and 1649 (to a design by Bernardino Poccetti and Jacopo Ligozzi). The magnificent **cabinet** in ebony and *pietre dure* belonged to Ferdinando II and dates from c 1650. Since the 17C, the room has contained the most important **classical sculptures** owned by the Medici, the most famous of which is the *Medici Venus*, probably a Greek marble copy (made around the 1C BC) of the Praxitelean *Aphrodite of Cnidos*. The so-called *Arrotino* (Knife-grinder) is now thought to represent a Scythian preparing to flay Marsias, as part of a group of Apollo and Marsias. It is the only surviving replica of an original by the school of Pergamon (3C or 2C BC), and it was purchased by Cosimo I in 1558 on Vasari's advice. It is of extremely high quality (and has had very few restorations). The group of *Wrestlers* is a much restored copy of a bronze original from the school of Pergamon, of which no other replicas are known (though only the two torsos are original). The moment of victory in the contest was signalled when the winner was able to place his knee on his opponent's back. The *Dancing Faun* is a beautifully restored work and the *Apollino* (Young Apollo) is derived from an Apollo by Praxiteles.

The Tribuna

The tribuna was for centuries the central attraction of the Uffizi. During the Grand Tour of Italy in the 18C—when Florence was one of the principal destinations and classical works were much in vogue—the Medici Venus, renowned for her beauty, was perhaps the most famous work of art in Florence. Numerous travellers left records of their admiration, including Goethe in 1740, Edward Gibbon in 1764, and Charles Burney in 1770. Queen Charlotte, wife of George III, commissioned Johan Zoffany to paint a conversation piece of the room in 1772. From this time on, no more replicas were allowed to be made of the statue since there were fears that it would be damaged. It was seized by Napoleon and taken to Paris, but returned here in 1816 (in the interim it was 'replaced' by another statue of Venus, especially commissioned by Napoleon from Canova, and which is now in the Galleria Palatina in Palazzo Pitti). In the early 19C, Hazlitt, Leigh Hunt, Byron and Shelley all left enthusiastic descriptions of the statue. The Venus was one of six important classical statues which had been acquired by Cardinal Ferdinando de' Medici, and which were brought from the Villa Medici in Rome in 1677–80 by Cosimo III to be exhibited here. Although the arrangement of the room has changed over the centuries, the paintings of a *Girl with a Book of Petrarch* by Andrea del Sarto, the *Madonna and Child with the Young St John* by Pontormo, and the *Young St John the Baptist in the Desert by Raphael* (discussed below) have all hung here since 1589.

Around the walls are a remarkable series of distinguished **court portraits**, many of them of the family of Cosimo I commissioned from Bronzino. They include a fresco of *Bianca Cappello* by Alessandro Allori; *Lorenzo il Magnifico* by Vasari and *Cosimo il Vecchio* by Pontormo, both posthumous and idealised portraits; *Madonna and Child with St John* by Pontormo.

The little **Sala dell'Ermafrodito** (**room 17**) is named after the statue of a *Sleeping Hermaphrodite*, a copy of a Greek original of the 2C BC. The room is decorated with small bronzes.

Beyond the door: *Young Girl with a Book* by Bronzino; *Young Man* by Ridolfo del Ghirlandaio; and *Bartolomeo and *Lucrezia Panciatichi, Maria dei Medici* and *Francesco I de' Medici* (the son of Cosimo I, as a boy), all by Bronzino; *Madonna 'del Pozzo'* by Franciabigio (showing the influence of Raphael); *Young St John in the Desert* by Raphael (and his *bottega*); *Madonna and Child* by Giulio Romano; *Don Giovanni de' Medici*, as a very young child by Bronzino; *Angel Musician* (probably a fragment) by Rosso Fiorentino; *Isabella de' Medici* (daughter of Cosimo I), **Portrait of a Man*, an intellectual typical of his time, and **Eleonora di Toledo* (Cosimo I's wife), with their son Giovanni de' Medici, a fine portrait which speaks eloquently of its period, all by Bronzino; **Girl with a Book of Petrarch* by Andrea del Sarto and *Cosimo I*, dressed in armour, by Bronzino.

Rooms 19–23 have ceilings decorated with grotesques and views of Florence carried out in 1588 by Ludovico Buti and in 1665 by Agnolo Gori.

Room 19 Paintings in this room include four portraits by Perugino, among them a **Young Boy* and **Francesco delle Opere*, a Florentine artisan who was the brother of a friend of Perugino's. There are also are two beautiful **tondi** by

Luca Signorelli of the *Madonna and Child*, one with allegorical figures in the background which clearly influenced Michelangeo (the other one is currently being restored). The portrait of *Evangelista Scappi* is by Francesco Francia and the half-length figure of *St Sebastian* by Lorenzo Costa. The *Crucifixion* by Marco Palmezzano shows the influence of Giovanni Bellini. The *Annunciation*, with a lovely landscape beyond the loggia, and the remarkable female nude **Venus* are both interesting works by Lorenzo di Credi. *Perseus Liberating Andromeda*, an unusual mythological scene, is by Piero di Cosimo.

Room 20 Works by German artists. **Durer** painted the **Adoration of the Magi* in 1504 after a visit to Italy. The portrait of the *Artist's Father* is Durer's first known work, painted when he was 19. The two bearded heads of the *Apostles St James* and *St Philip* are also by him. **Lukas Cranach the Elder** is represented by two fine portraits of *Martin Luther*, whose Protestant cause he supported (the smaller one shows him with Filippo Melantone, and the other with his wife Katherina Bore). Cranach also painted the tiny *St George* and the two full-length figures of *Adam and Eve* (showing the influence of Durer). The portrait of *Cranach* (formerly thought to be a self-portrait) was painted by his son, Lukas Cranach the Younger. There is also a fine *Portrait of a Boy* by the Netherlandish painter Joos van Cleve.

Room 21 Works by the Venetian school. Paintings by **Giovanni Bellini** include a **Sacred Allegory*, an exquisite painting of uncertain meaning, infused with an exulted humanist quality, and *Lamentation over the Dead Christ*, an unfinished painting left at the chiaroscuro stage. The other key painter of the Venetian Renaissance, **Giorgione** is represented with the *Judgement of Solomon* and its companion piece the *Infant Moses Brought to Pharoah*, showing the influence of Bellini. They are exhibited on either side of a splendid **Knight in Armour with his Page*, traditionally thought to be a portrait of the Venetian condottiere Gattamelata, by an unknown Venetian painter, but often attributed to Giorgione. The two large figures usually identified as a *Prophet* and *Sibyl* are attributed to Vittore Carpaccio.

Room 22 Fine portraits by Flemish and German artists. The series of five superb male **portraits* by **Hans Memling** exhibited on one wall, are mostly of unidentified sitters, except for the one of *Benedetto di Tommaso Portinari*, Memling's Italian patron. Portraits by **Hans Holbein the Younger** include a *Self-portrait*, and **Sir Richard Southwell* (1536), which was given by Thomas Howard, Duke of Arundel, to Cosimo II in 1620. The supposed portrait of *Thomas Moore* is now thought to be a work by the school of Holbein. The double **Portrait of a Man and his Wife* is by Joos van Cleve the Elder, and the *Adoration of the Magi* by Gerard David.

Room 23 Works by northern Italian artists, including three very fine works by **Mantegna**: a small triptych of the **Adoration of the Magi*, *Circumcision* and *Ascension*, exquisitely painted and preserving its beautiful frame; a remarkable portrait thought to show **Cardinal Carlo de' Medici*; and the tiny *Madonna delle Cave*. The *Leda* (the best-known copy of a lost painting by Leonardo da Vinci) is sometimes attributed to Francesco Melzi. Another Leonardesque work is the small painting of *Narcissus* by Giovanni Antonio Boltraffio. The small portrait of a *Gypsy Girl* is by Boccaccio Boccaccino. On another wall are three good works by the Emilian artist Correggio: a tiny *Madonna in Glory*; the *Rest on the Flight* and *Madonna in Adoration of the Child*.

Room 24 The Collection of Miniatures (15C–18C) is exhibited in this little oval room (only visible through the doorway) designed in 1781 by Zanobi del Rosso and painted by Filippo Lucci.

South corridor The short south corridor has a wonderful **view** of Florence. Across the river, on the extreme left, is San Miniato with its campanile on the skyline and the Forte di Belvedere. In the other direction, beyond the Uffizi building, is Palazzo Vecchio and the cupola of the Duomo. At the far end of the corridor one can see the tiled roof of the Corridoio Vasariano leading away from the Uffizi to Ponte Vecchio. The Arno flows downstream beneath Ponte Santa Trìnita and the bridges beyond. On the south bank the dome and campanile of Santo Spirito are prominent, and further downstream the dome of San Frediano in Cestello is visible.

Some fine pieces of **ancient sculpture** are arranged in the south corridor. At the end of the east corridor: *Doryophoros*, a Roman copy made in 1C AD of an original by Polycleitos. Outside Room 24, *Sleeping Cupid*, a Roman copy in black marble of a Hellenistic original. The four walnut stands here are the only original ones to survive; they were made to display the collection of Roman busts but were later replaced by marble columns. On the window wall looking towards Palazzo Vecchio: Roman statues of *Demeter* (copy of a Hellenistic original); *Leda* (restored by Giovanni Battista Foggini; *Amore and Psyche*; and *Apollo* (a copy of an original by Praxiteles). On the opposite wall (overlooking the Arno), the beautiful *Colossal Head* in Greek marble is probably a late Hellenistic original (one of the few in the whole gallery) of a triton (river god). It was long thought to represent Alexander the Great dying; as the only portrait of the emperor known until 1780, it was considered extremely important, and in the 16C and 17C was one of the most frequently copied in the whole gallery. It was displayed in the pieces of sculpture Sala delle Nicchie in Palazzo Pitti in 1568, and the bust was restored in 1795 (including part of the hair and the nose). The *Seated Nymph* dates from the 2C BC, and *Amore* (or Eros) is a 17C work. The statue of *Pothos* is a Roman copy of an original by Skopas. In the centre of the south corridor is a fragment of a *She-wolf* in porphyry, a Hadrianic copy of a 5C original.

West corridor At the beginning of the west corridor there are two *statues of *Marsyas*, from Hellenistic originals of the 3C BC. The one in red marble was, according to Vasari, restored by Verrocchio, but the upper part of the torso is now thought to be the work of Mino da Fiesole. It is known that it belonged to Lorenzo il Magnifico who kept it by the door from Via dei Ginori into Palazzo Medici. The one opposite which was formerly in the Capranica collection, and entered the Uffizi in 1780, is a Roman copy of a 2C BC original.

Room 25 Opposite the entrance is the famous *Tondo Doni of the Holy Family* by **Michelangelo**, his only finished tempera painting. It was painted for the marriage of Agnolo Doni with Maddalena Strozzi (1504–05), when the artist was 30 years old. Although owing much to Signorelli (see Room 19), it breaks with traditional representations of this familiar subject and signals a new moment in High Renaissance painting, pointing the way to the Sistine chapel frescoes. The splendid contemporary frame is by Domenico del Tasso. The *Portrait of a Lady* ('*la Monaca di Leonardo*') is a beautiful work now thought to be by Ridolfo del Ghirlandaio. Also here are works by Fra' Bartolomeo, Mariotto Albertinelli (*Visitation*) and Francesco Granacci.

Room 26 Here are some masterpieces by **Raphael**. *Leo X with Giulio de'*

Medici and Luigi de' Rossi was painted shortly before Raphael's death, and is one of his most powerful portrait groups; it was to have a great influence on Titian. The first Medici Pope is shown with his two cousins whom he created cardinals: Giulio de' Medici later went on to become Clement VII. The painting was commissioned in Rome from Raphael by Leo X in 1518 so that it could be sent to Florence on the occasion of the wedding of Leo's brother Giuliano, Duke of Nemours, with Philiberte of Savoy, since the Pope was unable to attend. The various shades of red are extremely effective and all three prelates express their self-assurance through their attitudes of proud independence. The portrait of *Julius II* is usually thought to be a replica of a painting of the same subject in the National Gallery of London. The **Madonna del Cardellino* (of the Goldfinch), is one of Raphael's most famous religious works. Painted for the marriage of the artist's friend, Lorenzo Nasi, it was shattered by an earthquake in 1547, but carefully repaired by the owner, although it remains in a very ruined state (it is at present being restored). Raphael's *Self-portrait*, in a lovely frame, is painted with a remarkable freshness of touch. The portrait of a young man (formerly thought to be Francesco Maria della Rovere) is also by Raphael, but other portraits here are now only attributed to him (including the man once thought to represent Perugino). Other very fine portraits by lesser-known artists include *Pietro Carnesecchi* by Domenico Puligo and *Young Man with Gloves* by Franciabigio. The **Madonna of the Harpies* (named after the carvings on the throne) is by Andrea del Sarto.

Room 27 Florentine Mannerism. **Rosso Fiorentino** is particularly well represented with: *Madonna and Saints*, *Portrait of a Man in Black*, *Portrait of a Girl* and *Moses Defending the Children of Jethro* (possibly a fragment). The geometrical forms of the nudes in the foreground display a very original and modern tendency. There are also good works by **Pontormo** including **Portrait of Maria Salviati*, widow of Giovanni delle Bande Nere; *Martyrdom of St Maurice and the Eleven Thousand Martyrs*; and *Supper at Emmaus* (1525), painted for the Certosa del Galluzzo, an uncharacteristic work by this artist (above the head of Christ is a surrealist symbol of God the Father). The portrait of the musician *Francesco dell'Ajolle*, formerly thought to be by Pontormo, is now attributed to Pier Francesco di Jacopo Foschi. The *Holy Family* which belonged to the Panciatichi is by **Agnolo Bronzino**.

Room 28 Contains some of **Titian**'s most remarkable works. The **Venus of Urbino*, was commissioned by Guidobaldo della Rovere, later duke of Urbino, in 1538. It is one of the most beautiful nudes ever painted and has had a profound influence on subsequent European painting. **Flora* is another masterpiece by Titian, a seductive, exquisite portrait of a girl with beautiful hair, holding roses in her hand. The male portrait is known as the **Sick Man*. Other superb portraits by Titian here are *Eleonora Gonzaga*, duchess of Urbino, in a splendid dress, and her husband *Francesco Maria della Rovere*, wearing armour; a *Knight of Malta*, charged with religious fervour; and *Bishop Ludovico Beccadelli*. The *Portrait of Sixtus IV* in profile, although full of character (and in bad condition) shows the intervention of Titian's *bottega*.

The **Death of Adonis* is a very fine work by **Sebastiano del Piombo**. Beyond an autumnal landscape there are views of Palazzo Ducale and the Piazzetta in Venice. Sebastiano also painted the beautiful *Portrait of a Lady* (formerly called *La Fornarina*). Three works by Palma Vecchio are also exhibited here.

Rooms 29 The *Madonna dal collo lungo* (Madonna with the long neck) by Parmigianino (1534–36) is a work of extreme refinement and originality, encapsulating the Mannerist style. Also here are works by Dosso Dossi.

Room 30 Small works of the 16C Emilian school by Garofalo and Ludovico Mazzolino.

Room 31 Works by **Paolo Veronese**, including the *Annunciation*, designed around a perspective device in the centre of the picture. The work is delicately painted in simple colours, in contrast to the rich golden hues of the figure of St Barbara in the *Holy Family with St Barbara*, a work of the artist's maturity. When the curtains are open, the window in this room offers a good view of Palazzo Vecchio, the Duomo and the top of Orsanmichele.

Room 32 *Leda and the Swan* is a good work by Tintoretto, with the fine nude figure of Leda and her pretty serving girl; he also painted the *Portrait of Jacopo Sansovino*. There are also two *Male Portraits* by Paris Bordone and *Two Hunting Dogs* by Jacopo Bassano.

Room 33 16C works by French and Italian artists. The tiny equestrian portrait of *Francis I* of France is by the court painter François Clouet. It was probably brought to Florence in 1589 by Christina of Lorraine, wife of Ferdinando I. The amusing painting of *Two Women in the Bath* is by the late 16C School of Fontainebleau. In the corridor are two *Portraits* by Federico Barocci, (one of them a self-portrait) and *Christ Appearing to St Mary Magdalene* by Lavinia Fontana, one of the few women painters represented in the gallery. On the opposite wall are small works by Agnolo Bronzino, Giorgio Vasari, Alessandro Allori, Il Poppi and Iacopo Zucchi.

Room 34 Lorenzo Lotto and the 16C Lombard school. Lorenzo Lotto is represented with small works including the fine *Head of a Young Boy* and *Holy Family with Saints*. Another remarkable portrait in this room is that of an old man with long grey hair, thought to represent *Teofilo Folengo* (in poor condition), by an unknown 16C painter. Fine portraits by Giovanni Battista Moroni include *Count Pietro Secco Suardi* (1563), a full-length standing portrait and a *Man with a Book*. The portrait of *Raffaello Grassi*, with his hand on a bust, is by the little-known painter from the Veneto called Sebastiano Florigerio. The *Female Nude* is an extraordinary work attributed to Bernardino Licino. Portraits by Giulio Campi include *Galeazzo Campi*, wearing a hat, and *Guitar Player*. The *Transfiguration* is by Giovanni Girolamo Savoldo.

Room 35 Religious works and portraits and a good collection of paintings by **Federico Barocci**. Barocci's paintings include: the *Madonna del Popolo*, a delightful crowded composition, a *Noli me tangere* and portraits such as that of *Francesco Maria II della Rovere*. Also here are works by Gregorio Pagni, Poccetti, Passignano, Alessandro Allori, Lodovico Buti and Santi di Tito.

From the west corridor, a door (**B**) provides access to the Corridoio Vasariano, described below. Beyond are the stairs down to the exit (C).

Room 42 Called the **Niobe Room**, this was designed by Gaspare Maria Paoletti and Zanobi del Rosso in 1771–79; its gilded stucco vault is by Giocondo Albertolli. It was built to house the statues forming a group of *Niobe and her Children*, found in a vineyard near the Lateran in 1583, and transferred to

Florence in 1775 from the Villa Medici in Rome. These are Roman copies of Greek originals of the school of Skopas (early 4C BC); many of the figures are badly restored and others do not belong to the group (the lying figure of Niobe is in different marble). On the end wall, to the right, is Niobe herself with one of her children, and on the opposite wall is a statue of a Pedagogue. The horse, probably part of a group of the Dioscuri, was found offshore near Rome, and the tail and legs are restorations. The *Medici Vase*, also in the centre, is a neo-Attic work acquired by Lorenzo de' Medici. The room was beautifully restored after serious bomb damage in 1993. The view includes the top of the dome and campanile of Santo Spirito on the left, with the trees of Bellosguardo on the skyline.

In the **corridor** outside (on the window wall) is a *Wounded Warrior*, kneeling, recognised in 1992 as a Greek original of the 5C BC (only the shield and arms have been restored). The head is antique but comes from another statue of a barbarian. The 'leather' armour is extremely delicately carved. Next to it is a seated *Apollo* and, opposite, *Ganymede*, both of them Roman copies of Hellenistic originals.

Rooms 41 and 43–45 are still closed for repairs after the bomb damage of 1993, but their contents (which may alter when they reopen) dating from the 17C and 18C are described below.

Room 41 Fine works by **Rubens**. These include the *Triumphal Entry of Ferdinand of Austria into Anversa*; *Henri IV Entering Paris*, *Henri IV at Ivry*, two huge paintings comprising the first part of a cycle depicting the king's history; *Portrait of Isabella Brandt*; and an equestrian portrait of *Philip IV of Spain*. Works by **Van Dyck**, include *Margaret of Lorraine*, equestrian portrait of the *Emperor Charles V*, *Susterman's Mother* and *John of Montfort*. There are also portraits by Jacob Jordaens and Sustermans (Galileo).

Room 43 Contains works by **Caravaggio**: *Sacrifice of Isaac*, *Young Bacchus* and *Medusa Head* (painted on a shield). Also here is a *Port Scene* by Claude Lorrain, and a *Man with a Monkey* and *Bacchic Scene* by Annibale Carracci.

Room 44 Three splendid works by **Rembrandt**: *Self-portrait*, *Portrait of an Old Man* and *Self-portrait as an Old Man*. Also here are Dutch and Flemish works including Jan Steen's *Lunch-party* and a fine landscape by Jacob Ruysdael.

Room 45 18C paintings: *Susannah and the Elders* by Piazzetta; a ceiling painting showing the *Erection of an Imperial Statue* by Giovanni Battista Tiepolo; and Venetian views by Francesco Guardi and Canaletto; two portraits of children by Simeon Chardin. Among the portraits are two beautiful paintings of *Maria Theresa* by Francisco Goya; the *Portrait of a Lady* by Alessandro Longhi; *Maria Adelaide of France* in Turkish costume, by Etienne Liotard; and Vittorio Alfieri and the *Countess of Albany* by Françoise Xavier Fabre.

At the end of the **west corridor** is exhibited a copy by Baccio Bandinelli of the Vatican group of the *Laocoön*. Also in this part of the corridor are the famous sculpted *Boar* (a copy of a Hellenistic original, and the model for the *Porcellino* in the Mercato Nuovo), a Roman statue of a *Nereid on a Sea-horse* (copy of a Hellenistic original), and, opposite, a standing veiled female statue (2C AD).

Café This has tables on the roof terrace of the Loggia della Signoria (**D**) from which there is a splendid view over Piazza della Signoria beyond the buildings of the city to the hills of Fiesole.

A long flight of stairs (see above), or a lift, descend from the west corridor to the **exit**. On the landing are Roman sarcophagi.

The Corridoio Vasariano

The *Corridoio Vasariano can normally be visited by previous appointment, ☎ 055 265 4321: in 2000 small groups were accompanied (see p 136) on a 2.5 hour tour starting from the Quartiere di Eleonora da Toledo in Palazzo Vecchio and finishing in the Boboli gardens. There are long-term plans to open it regularly to the public in order that visitors can pass directly from the Uffizi to the Pitti gallery, and to empty it of its paintings (which will be rehung on the first floor of the Uffizi).

The Corridoio Vasariano was built by Vasari in five months to celebrate the marriage of Francesco de' Medici and Joanna of Austria in 1565, and provides unique views of the city. Its purpose was to connect Palazzo Vecchio via the Uffizi and Ponte Vecchio with the new residence of the Medici dukes at Palazzo Pitti, in the form of a private covered passage-way nearly 1km long. It was particularly convenient in wet weather, and it was sometimes used as a nursery for the children of the grand-dukes. Elderly or infirm members of the family could be wheeled along it in basket chairs (since there were no steps). Paintings were first hung here in the 19C when the Savoy royalty put up their family portraits. In the late 19C the corridor was used as a deposit for the Uffizi. Since the early years of this century, the Uffizi's celebrated collection of self-portraits has been hung here.

Stairs lead down from a door in the west corridor of the Uffizi (see B on the plan) to two rooms which have been restored since they were severely damaged in the 1993 car bomb. They contain paintings by the school of Caravaggio including Gherardo delle Notti, Bartolomeo Manfredi and Artemisia Gentileschi. On a second flight of stairs are works by Borgognone.

To the right is the **entrance to the corridor** proper. Here, displayed by regional schools, are **17C works**: Guido Reni (*Susannah and the Elders*), Guercino (*Sleeping Endymion*), Domenico Fetti, Baciccio (*Portrait of Leopoldo de' Medici*); Mattia Preti, Salvator Rosa, Carlo Dolci, Sassoferrata, Giuseppe Maria Crespi, and Sustermans. There follow more 17C and 18C paintings by Vanvitelli, Sebastiano Ricci, Pompeo Batoni, Rosalba Carriera and others.

The corridor now reaches **Ponte Vecchio**. The *Collection of self-portraits begins on the bridge itself. It was started by Cardinal Leopoldo in the 17C. Having acquired the self-portraits of Guercino and Pietro da Cortona, he went on to collect some 80 portraits in his life time. The collection continued to be augmented in the following centuries up to the present day (only a selection is at present on display). The self-portrait of Vasari is hung opposite a charming large painting by Jacopo da Empoli, formerly in the chapel of the goldsmiths, showing *St Eligius*, their protector.

The self-portraits are arranged chronologically and include works by Agnolo Gaddi (with Taddeo and Gaddo Gaddi), Andrea del Sarto (two self-portraits, one in fresco on a tile), Baccio Bandinelli, Alessandro Allori, Beccafumi, Bronzino, Perino del Vaga, Santi di Tito, Cristofano Allori, Giovanni da San Giovanni (painted on a tile) and Cigoli. The self-portraits on the left wall include works by Jacopo Bassano, Titian, Niccolò Cassana, Rosalba Carriera, Domenico Parodi, Sofonisba Anguissola, Carlo Dolci and Correggio.

Beyond the centre of Ponte Vecchio. Right wall: Salimbeni, Federico and

Taddeo Zuccari, Lorenzo Bernini, Pietro da Cortona and Giuseppe Maria Crespi. Left wall: Agostino Carraccci, Francesco Albani, Guido Reni, Annibale Carracci, Salvator Rosa, Luca Giordano, Solimena, Pompeo Batoni and Andrea Pozzo.

On the **Oltrarno** (far side of the Arno) the corridor skirts the Torre di Mannelli and the display of self-portraits continues with 16C–18C foreign works by Pourbus, Rubens, Gerard Dou, Sustermans, Rembrandt, Van Dyck, Zoffany, Velasquez, Callot and Charles le Brun. British painters represented include Pieter Lely, Sir Geoffrey Kneller, James Northcote, George Romney, Sir Joshua Reynolds, John Opie and Jacob More.

The corridor now descends past a window overlooking the **interior of Santa Felicita**. Here are displayed miniature portraits including works by Nattier, Giovanna Garzoni, self-portraits by Pourbus and Lavinia Fontana, and works attributed to Holbein, Van Dyck and Samuel Cowper. Also here is a delightful series of miniature portraits of the Medici dynasty (from Bicci di Lorenzo to Cosimo I) by Bronzino and his *bottega*.

The last section of self-portraits has **19C and 20C works** (the Italians on the left wall and the foreign schools opposite). British and French artists represented include: Ingres, Delacroix, Corot, Jacques Louis David, Mengs, Vigèe Le Brun, Holman Hunt, Frederick Leighton, George Frederick Watts, Alma Tadema, John Everett Millais, Benjamin Constant, John Singer Sargent and Fantin-Latour, as well as the Russian painter Chagall. On the left wall: Andrea Appiani, Francesco Hayez, Stefano Ussi, Il Piccio, Domenico Morelli, Silvestro Lega, Giovanni Boldini, Giovanni Fattori, Giuseppe Pellizza da Volpedo, Armando Spadini, Galileo Chini, Elizabeth Chaplin, Giacomo Balla, Carlo Levi, Gino Severini and Renato Guttuso.

In the last section of the corridor are **17C and 18C family portraits** of members of the Medici and Lorraine dynasties, including some by Sebastiano Bombelli, Santi di Tito, Francesco Furini and Simon Vouet. The colossal head of *Zeus* is from a 4C or 3C BC original.

A door leads down to the exit through the Boboli gardens (see p 179).

Adjoining the side of the Loggia dei Lanzi, the ground floor of **Palazzo della Zecca**, with its well protected windows, is incorporated into the Uffizi building. The famous gold florins, first issued in 1252, were minted here; they became the standard gold coin in Europe. The **Sala delle Reali Poste** here, built by Mariano Falcini as a post office in 1866, is a fine hall with a huge skylight supported on a cast-iron framework. It is used for exhibitions. At the end of Via Lambertesca is the Porta delle Suppliche (removed for restoration) added after 1574 by Buontalenti and surmounted by a bust of Francesco I, the masterpiece of Giovanni Bandini.

Contini Bonacossi Collection

Since 1998, this collection has been housed in ten rooms in a wing of the second floor of the Uffizi building; the entrance is in Via Lambertesca (admission only by booking in advance, ☎ 055 265 4321, for a maximum of 20 people at a time).

It is a choice collection made by Alessandro Contini-Bonacossi (with the advice of Roberto Longhi) and contains Italian and Spanish paintings as well as 15C–17C majolica and furniture. Works by artists not already represented in the Uffizi were favoured. Contini-Bonacossi died intestate, and much of the collection was sold by the family after 1960, but they ceded this part of the collection to the

State in 1974. The paintings have frames typical of the 1920s. Some of the rooms have pretty 18C decorations.

In the corridor are Della Robbian coats of arms. In **Room 2** is a *Madonna and Child* by Duccio, a well-preserved altarpiece of *St John the Baptist* with stories from his life by Giovanni del Biondo and the *Madonna della Neve*, painted for the cathedral of Siena by Sassetta. **Room 3** contains two panels with *Scenes from the Life of St Nicholas* by Paolo Veneziano, a fresco from the castle of Trebbio showing the *Madonna and Child with Angels and Saints and Two Children of the Pazzi Family* by Andrea del Castagno, and two paintings of *St Jerome*, one by Giovanni Bellini and one by Cima da Conegliano. The *Supper at Emmaus* is by Vincenzo Catena. **Room 4** contains a portrait of the poet *Casio*, by Boltraffio and *Madonna and Child* by Defendente Ferrari. **Room 5** contains reliefs by Bambaia, a *Madonna Child with Saints* by Bramantino and *Saints Michael Archangel and Bernard* by Bernardino Zenale. **Room 6** has a portrait of *Count Suardo Crespi* by Tintoretto, a sculpture of the *Martyrdom of St Lawrence* by Gian Lorenzo Bernini and a portrait of *Count Giuseppe da Porto with his Son Adriano* by Paolo Veronese. On the other side of the corridor, **Rooms 7 and 8**, with pink and green 18C decorations, display a collection of ceramics. **Room 9** contains Spanish works (the attributions are uncertain): the *Water-carrier* by Diego Velazquez is a replica of a painting in the Wellington collection in London; the Bull-fighter is by Francisco de Goya, and the *Tears of St Peter* by El Greco. The last **Room 10** has ceiling panels with *Mythological Scenes* by Jacopo Tintoretto and a bronze bust of *Benedict XIII* by Pietro Bracci.

In Via della Ninna, incorporated into the Uffizi building, are some of the nave columns of the church of San Pier Scheraggio (see above). Here also can be seen the beginning of the Corridoio Vasariano (described above), forming a bridge between Palazzo Vecchio and the Uffizi.

7 • Galleria degli Uffizi to Palazzo Pitti

From the riverside façade of Palazzo degli Uffizi (**Map 1; 8**) there is a striking view of Palazzo Vecchio with its tower. The Corridoio Vasariano (1565), a covered way built by Vasari (see Ch. 6) to link Palazzo Vecchio and the Uffizi with the new residence of the Medici, Palazzo Pitti, can also be seen here. From the Uffizi building it crosses above the busy road and continues on a raised arcade towards Ponte Vecchio. On the bridge, its line of rectangular windows passes above the small picturesque shops which overhang the river. The fine old Palazzo Girolami (no. 6) with a pretty loggia and coat of arms stands on this very narrow part of the Lungarno.

Ponte Vecchio

The fame of Ponte Vecchio (**Map 1; 5,7**; open to pedestrians only), lined with quaint medieval-looking houses, saved it from damage in 1944 (although numerous ancient buildings at either end were blown up instead, in order to

Ponte Vecchio

render it impassable). Near the site of the Roman crossing (which was a little farther upstream), it was the only bridge over the Arno until 1218. The present
bridge of three arches was reconstructed after a flood in 1345, probably by
Taddeo Gaddi (also attributed to Neri di Fioravante). The bridge on this site has
been lined by shops since the 13C; an edict issued by the Grand-duke Ferdinando
I in 1593 established that the butchers' shops and grocery shops here should be
replaced by those of goldsmiths and silversmiths. The present jewellers' shops
have pretty fronts with wooden shutters and awnings, and overhang the river
supported on brackets. The excellent jewellers here maintain the skilled tradition
of Florentine goldsmiths whose work first became famous in the 15C. Many of
the greatest Renaissance artists trained as goldsmiths (including Ghiberti,
Brunelleschi and Donatello). The most famous Florentine goldsmith, Benvenuto
Cellini, is aptly recorded with a bust (1900) in the middle of the bridge.

Above the shops on the left can be seen the round windows of the Corridoio
Vasariano. From the centre there is a view of Ponte Santa Trìnita (see Ch. 17). On
the corner of a house is a sundial and worn inscription of 1345. The Corridoio
Vasariano leaves the bridge supported on elegant brackets in order not to disturb
the Torre dei Mannelli, the medieval angle tower which defended the bridge
(restored after the War).

On the other side of the river, across Borgo San Jacopo (described in Ch. 17) is
a fountain reconstructed here in 1958, with a bronze statue of Bacchus by
Giambologna and a Roman sarcophagus. Via Guicciardini continues towards
Piazza Pitti; on the left opens Piazza Santa Felicita with a granite column of 1381
marking the site of the first Christian cemetery in Florence.

Santa Felicita

Here, behind the Corridoio Vasariano, is Santa Felicita (**Map 1; 7**), probably the
oldest church in Florence after San Lorenzo. In the 2C, Syrian Greek merchants
came to settle here, on a site near the river and on a busy Roman consular road,
and they are thought to have introduced Christianity to the city. The early
Christian church, built at the end of the 4C or the beginning of the 5C, was ded-

icated to the Roman martyr, St Felicity (a tombstone dated 405 has been excavated here). A new church was built in the 11C and the present church was erected in 1736–39 by Ferdinando Ruggieri.

In the **portico** is the funerary monument (right) of Cardinal Luigi de' Rossi (d. 1518) by Giovanni Battista del Tasso, and (left) beneath the tomb-slab of Barduccio di Cherichino (d. 1416), the monument of the musician and painter Arcangela Paladini (d. 1622) by Antonio Novelli, with a portrait bust by Agostino Ubaldini.

Interior The fine interior by Ferdinando Ruggieri takes its inspiration from late 16C Florentine architecture.

The church is chiefly visited for the superb *paintings by **Pontormo** in the Cappella Capponi (first on the right), which were commissioned by Ludovico Capponi in 1525, after he purchased the chapel from the Barbadori. The remarkable altarpiece of the *Deposition* is in a magnificent contemporary frame attributed to Baccio d'Agnolo. The head of St Nicodemus on the right may be a self-portrait. The fresco of the *Annunciation* has been detached and restored. These are considered among the masterpieces of 16C Florentine painting. The tondi in the cupola of the Evangelists are attributed to Pontormo and Bronzino. The chapel was originally designed for the Barbadori by Brunelleschi (c 1420–25), but was altered in the 18C, when the cupola was lowered and some of its frescoes destroyed. The 15C stained-glass window by Giullaume de Marcillat has been restored but is to be replaced here by a copy.

Over the fourth altar on the right is a striking painting, the *Martyrdom of the Maccabei* brothers by Antonio Ciseri (1863). In the south transept, *Meeting of St Joachim and St Anne* by Michele di Ridolfo Ghirlandaio. The Choir Chapel was designed by Ludovico Cigoli in 1610–22. The high altarpiece of the *Adoration of the Shepherds*, traditionally attributed to Santi di Tito, is now thought to be the work of Francesco Brina. On the **north side**, the last chapel (beneath the organ) contains a wooden *Crucifix* by Andrea Ferrucci (da Fiesole) and the funerary monument of Giacomo Conti by Girolamo Ticciati. In the fourth chapel is Simone Pignone's, *St Louis Providing a Banquet for the Poor* (1682) and in the second chapel, Ignazio Hugford's *Tobias Visiting his Father*. The chapel opposite the Capponi chapel has a fresco of the *Miracle of Santa Maria della Neve* by Bernardino Poccetti, a vault fresco by Tommaso Gherardini and an altarpiece of the *Assumption of the Virgin* by Andrea del Minga.

The pretty **sacristy** off the right transept (unlocked on request), in the style of Brunelleschi, has a polyptych of the *Madonna and Child with Saints* by Taddeo Gaddi, in its original frame; a *Crucifix* attributed to Pacino di Bonaguida, two detached 14C frescoes of the *Nativity* and *Annunciation*, attributed to Niccolò di Pietro Gerini, and an Adoration of the Magi, attributed to Mariotto di Cristofano. The attractive polychrome terracotta half-figure of the *Madonna and Child* has been attributed to Luca della Robbia or his *bottega* since its restoration in 1980. A painting of *St Felicity and Her Seven Children* by Neri di Bicci has been removed indefinitely for restoration. The **chapter house** (sometimes unlocked on request) has a fresco of the *Crucifixion* signed and dated 1387–88 by Niccolò di Pietro Gerini. Another fresco by Gerini has been placed in the corridor near the chapter house.

At the end of the road (left) at no. 15 is **Palazzo Guicciardini** reconstructed in 1620–25 by Gherardo Silvani on the site of the residence of Luigi di Piero

Guicciardini, Gonfalonier of Justice, which was burnt down during a revolt against the government in 1378 by the *Ciompi* (cloth-workers). Francesco Guicciardini was born here in 1483. On his retirement from political life in 1530, he wrote his famous *History of Italy*. Part of the façade has remains of graffiti decoration. In the courtyard is a large stucco relief of **Hercules and Cacus** attributed to Antonio del Pollaiolo. Beyond can be seen the little garden created in the 17C but replanted in 1922. On the wall are numerous ancient reliefs. Casa Campiglio, nearby, where Machiavelli lived and died in 1527, has been destroyed. Guicciardini and Machiavelli, both great statesmen and writers, who had served different causes, became close friends at the end of their careers.

Beyond is Piazza Pitti (described on p 306) dominated by Palazzo Pitti, see below.

8 • Palazzo Pitti and the Boboli Gardens

History of Palazzo Pitti

Palazzo Pitti (**Map 6; 3**) was built by the merchant Luca Pitti as an effective demonstration of his wealth and power to his rivals the Medici. The majestic golden-coloured palace is built in huge, rough-hewn blocks of stone in different sizes. Its design is attributed to Brunelleschi although building began in c 1457, after his death. Luca Fancelli is known to have worked on the building, but it is generally considered that another architect, whose name is unknown, was also involved. The palace remained incomplete on the death of Luca Pitti in 1472; by then it consisted of the central seven bays with three doorways. Houses were demolished to create the piazza in front of the palace. The site, on the slope of a hillside, was chosen to make the palace even more imposing. Bartolomeo Ammannati took up work on the building c 1560 and converted the two side doors of the façade into elaborate ground-floor windows. These were then copied after 1616 by Giulio and Alfonso Parigi the Younger when they enlarged the façade to its present colossal dimensions (possibly following an original design). The two *rondos* (wings) were added later: the one on the right was built by Giuseppe Ruggieri after 1760, and the one on the left (known as the Rondo di Bacco) in the 19C (it incorporates a small theatre, now used for lectures).

In 1549, the palace was bought by Eleonora di Toledo, wife of Cosimo I. It became the official seat of the Medici dynasty of grand-dukes after Cosimo I moved here from Palazzo Vecchio (to which he connected the Pitti by means of the Corridoio Vasariano, see p 152). The various ruling families of Florence continued to occupy the palace, or part of it, until 1919 when Vittorio Emanuele III presented it to the state. Behind the palace are the superb Boboli gardens designed for Cosimo I.

The museums in Palazzo Pitti

The palace still contains the apartments used for four centuries by the grand-dukes and rulers of Florence and Tuscany, as well as the works of art acquired by them. It houses a number of important museums, including: the Galleria Palatina, with one of the finest collections of paintings in Italy, the Museo degli

Argenti, and the Galleria d'Arte Moderna. The state apartments used by the Medici and Lorraine grand-dukes, and later by the royal house of Savoy, have been beautifully restored to their appearance in 1911. The winter apartments on the top floor of the palace were opened in 1991, and other suites of rooms used in various seasons, and the attic floor, known as the 'Mezzanino degli Occhi' are to be restored. In the Meridiana wing of the palace is the Galleria del Costume, and one of the *rondo* is used to house a carriage museum.

- **Opening times** These vary for the different museums and the royal apartments, and are listed below:
  Galleria Palatina (S). 08.30–18.50; *fest.* 08.30–19.00; closed Mon (☎ 055 238 8611); Lire 12,000. See p 161.
  Appartamenti Reali (S). As for Galleria Palatina, but due to be closed for maintenance work in 2001.
  Galleria d'Arte Moderna (S). 08.30–13.50; closed on second and fourth Sunday, and first, third and fifth Monday of the month (☎ 055 238 8616); Lire 8000; see p 169.
  Galleria del Costume (S). As for Galleria d'Arte Moderna. See p 175.
  Museo degli Argenti (S). As for Galleria d'Arte Moderna (☎ 055 238 8709); Lire 4000; see p 176.
  Museo delle Porcellane (S). Weekdays 09.00–13.50; closed on second and fourth Sunday and first, third and fifth Monday of the month (☎ 055 238 8605); combined ticket with the Museo degli Argenti or Giardino di Boboli. See p 182.
  Museo delle Carrozze (S). Closed (☎ 055 238 8614). See p 179.
  Information and reservation service: ☎ 055 294 883 (Mon–Fri 08.30–18.30; Sat 08.30–12.30)

Tickets The ticket office for all the museums within the Palace is on the right side of the courtyard, left of the main staircase leading up to the Galleria Palatina and Museo d'Arte Moderna. Tickets for the Galleria Palatina include admission to the Appartamenti Reali and the Museo delle Carrozze (but this is at present closed). There is another ticket office, in an adjoining room, for the Galleria d'Arte Moderna (which includes admission to the Quartiere d'Inverno (Winter Apartments) shown only by appointment) and the Galleria del Costume. A separate ticket must be purchased here for the Museo degli Argenti. There is a **combined ticket** for all the museums and Boboli gardens valid for three consecutive days (Lire 20,000; or Lire 15,000 after 16.00). For admission to the **Boboli gardens** (separate ticket necessary, purchased at another ticket office in the courtyard), see below. (Admission to the gardens is included in the combined ticket for all the museums in Palazzo Pitti.)

Off the courtyard are a museum shop, café, cloakroom, toilets (there are more toilets, usually much less busy, in the Galleria d'Arte Moderna), and lifts for the Galleria Palatina (first floor) and the Museo d'Arte Moderna and Museo del Costume (second floor).

Museum plans The plan of the first floor with the Galleria Palatina and State Apartments is on p 160. The six main rooms of paintings are numbered 23–28. The Volterrano wing (numbered 4–11) is sometimes closed for certain periods of the year or if there is a shortage of custodians. The Appartamenti

Reali are numbered I–XV: the remaining rooms on the first floor (numbered XVI–XXI) are usually closed except for exhibitions.

The plan of the second floor with the Galleria d'Arte Moderna is on p 171. The rooms are numbered 1–30. The Winter Apartments (Quartiere d'Inverno), also on this floor, are numbered I–XV.

The courtyard

The central door in the façade leads through the atrium by Pasquale Poccianti (c 1850) into the splendid *courtyard (1560–70) by Ammannati, which serves as a garden façade to the palace. It is a masterpiece of Florentine Mannerist architecture, with bold rustication in three orders. Nocturnal spectacles were held here from the 16C to the 18C, and it is still sometimes used for concerts in summer. The lower fourth side is formed by a terrace with the Fontana del Carciofo (once crowned by an artichoke), beyond which extend the Boboli gardens (described on p 179).

The **Grotto of Moses**, beneath the terrace, was designed in 1635–42 around a porphyry statue of Moses (only the torso is antique). In the other four niches are 17C statues by Domenico Pieratti, Agostino Ubaldini and Antonio Novelli. The fountains (now dry) at the sides, decorated with reliefs of trees, are by Ludovico Salvetti. The pretty vault has paintings and stalactites. In the water are two swimming putti by Pompeo Ferrucci del Tadda. On either side of the entrance to the grotto are two Roman statues (copies of Hellenistic originals) above little fountains. At the end of the left colonnade is a restored Roman statue of *Hercules*, and, beneath, a charming 16C bas-relief commemorating a mule who worked particularly hard during the construction of the courtyard. At the end of the right colonnade is another Roman statue of *Hercules*. On the right side of the courtyard is the entrance to the **Cappella Palatina** (only open on special occasions) which dates from 1776. This has an interesting high altar, partly composed of pieces made for the altar in the Cappella dei Principi in San Lorenzo, an ivory **Crucifix** and **Mary Magdalen** attributed to Antonio Raggi, and painted decoration by Luigi Ademollo (1792).

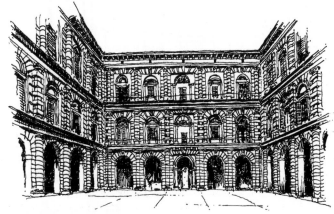

The courtyard of Palazzo Pitti

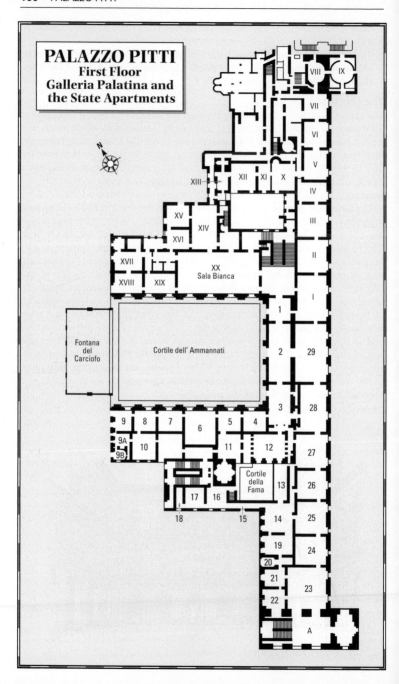

PALAZZO PITTI
First Floor
Galleria Palatina and
the State Apartments

Galleria Palatina

Off the courtyard is the staircase which leads up to the entrance to the celebrated Galleria di Palazzo Pitti or Galleria Palatina, a splendid collection of paintings acquired by the Medici and Lorraine grand-dukes, including numerous famous works by Raphael, Titian and Rubens. The gallery maintains the character of a private, princely collection of the 17C–18C. The aesthetic arrangement of the pictures which decorate the walls produces a remarkable effect of magnificence. The elaborately carved and gilded frames, many of them original, and especially representative of the Mannerist, Baroque and neo-classical styles, are particularly fine. Only some of the paintings (all of which are labelled) have been mentioned in the description below, and stars have been used sparingly.

History of the Palatina collection

The collection owes its origins to the 17C Medici grand-dukes, and in particular to Cardinal Leopoldo, brother of Ferdinando II, and to Cosimo III and his eldest son the Crown Prince Ferdinando (d. 1713), who added Flemish paintings, works of the Bolognese and Veneto schools, and altarpieces from Tuscan churches. Under the Lorraine grand-dukes, in 1771, the paintings were installed for the first time in the present rooms which had been decorated in the 1640s by Pietro da Cortona for Ferdinando II. The gallery was first opened regularly to the public in 1833, and in 1911 it was acquired by the state. Unfortunately, many of the paintings which formed the nucleus of the collection were removed to the Uffizi in the 20C (including Rembrandt's *Self-portrait* and Raphael's portrait of *Leo X*). The present arrangement of the pictures follows, as far as possible, the arrangement of 1833.

All the rooms are named as indicated in the description below; room numbers have been given to correspond with the plan on p 160. For admission, see p 158.

The **Grand Staircase** by Ammannati ascends past Antique sculpture and late 17C busts by Giuseppe Piamontini and (third landing) the *Genio mediceo*, a bronze statue attributed to the circle of Tribolo, to the entrance of the Galleria Palatina.

The Anticamera degli Staffieri (1) where tickets are shown, decorated in the 18C, contains sculptures by Pietro Francavilla (*Mercury*) and Baccio Bandinelli (*Bacchus* and a bronze bust of *Cosimo I*). From the window there is a splendid view of the courtyard and Boboli gardens (with the Forte di Belvedere on the skyline).

The Galleria delle Statue (2) is decorated with antique sculptures from the Villa Medici in Rome. Here are exhibited two seascapes by Van der Velde the Elder and the *Risen Christ*, an early work by Rubens.

The Sala del Castagnoli (3) is named after Giuseppe Castagnoli, the artist born in 1754 who decorated it. It contains a magnificent circular table in *pietre dure* made in Florence in 1837–50 with Apollo and the Muses (the bronze pedestal with the seasons is by Giovanni Duprè). This was the last important work in *pietre dure* made in the grand-ducal workshop of the Opificio delle Pietre Dure. Some of its best products (including table-tops and cabinets) are preserved in various rooms of Palazzo Pitti (in the Museo degli Argenti as well as the Galleria Palatina). Here is displayed a processional standard of *St Sebastian* by Sodoma.

The 'minor rooms'

Since the reopening of the Apartamenti Reali, the route around the Galleria Palatina has been changed. Visitors now pass through the 'minor' rooms—described next—before reaching the six reception rooms (see p 164) overlooking Piazza Pitti that contain the masterpieces of the collection.

From the Sala del Castagnoli, a door (sometimes closed) leads into a series of rooms called the Volterrano wing, which is not always open.

The Sala delle Allegorie (4) has a statue of the young *Michelangelo* by Emilio Zocchi (1861). The vault was frescoed in the 17C by Volterrano and other paintings by him here include (on the entrance wall) *The Parson's Jest*, showing a jovial group enjoying the pranks of the Pievano Arlotto, which is interesting as a picture of Florentine life of the time. There are also works by his master Giovanni da San Giovanni and his contemporaries Sustermans and Artemesia Gentileschi.

The Sala delle Belle Arti (5) has paintings by Cigoli and Carlo Dolci.

The Sala dell'Arca (11) is to the left of the Sala delle Belle Arti and has delightful frescoes of 1816 by Luigi Ademollo.

The early 17C oval **chapel** was built for Maria Maddalena d'Austria, wife of Cosimo II, and contains stuccoes and a high altarpiece by Battistello Caracciolo, and cupboards painted by Matteo Rosselli, Filippo Tarchiani, Fabrizio Boschi and Giovanni Bilivert.

The Corridoio delle Miniature is beyond the chapel and is used to display miniature paintings. The tiny Dutch paintings were acquired by Cosimo III on a trip to Holland in 1667; also here are paintings (1701–02) by Richard van Orley; a delightful collection of *paintings of fruit and vegetables by Giovanna Garzoni (1600–57) painted for Vittoria della Rovere; and works by Valerio Mariani (fl. 1606–18).

The Salone d'Ercole (6) is frescoed with scenes from the *Life of Hercules* by Pietro Benvenuti (1828). The huge Sèvres vase dates from the early 19C and there are two battle scenes by Borgognone.

The Sala dell'Aurora (7) contains paintings by Empoli, Lorenzo Lippi, Cristofano Allori, Jacopo Ligozzi and Jacopo Vignali.

The Sala di Berenice (8) contains works by Francesco Furini, Carlo Dolci, Orazio Riminaldi and Giovanni Bilivert.

The Sala di Psiche (9) has fine works by Salvator Rosa including: *The Wood of the Philosophers*, landscapes and seascapes, a battle scene and sketches on wood. The vestibule and bathroom (9A and 9B) of Empress Maria Luisa (the wife of Napoleon, who stayed here in the early 19C when the grand-duchy was conferred on Elisa Baciocchi, his sister) were designed in neo-classical style by Giuseppe Cacialli (c 1803).

The Sala della Fama (10) has Flemish works (some by Willem van Aelst).

From the Sala del Castagnoli (3; see above) is the entrance to a series of rooms decorated in the neo-classical style in the Napoleonic period when Elisa Baciocchi was in residence. They contain the smaller works in the collection.

Sala della Musica (12) This neo-classical room designed by Cacialli dates from 1811–21 and has frescoes by Luigi Ademollo, a gilt-bronze and malachite table by Pierre Philippe Thomire, and drum-shaped commodes.

The Galleria del Poccetti (13) received its name from the traditional attribution of the frescoes in the vault to Poccetti, although these are now thought to be by Matteo Rosselli and his pupils (c 1625). The beautiful table inlaid in *pietre dure* is attributed to Giovanni Battista Foggini (1716). The paintings on either side of the door are a portrait of the *Duke of Buckingham* by Rubens and a remarkable portrait in profile of *Francesco da Castiglione* by Pontormo (also attributed to Rosso Fiorentino). At the other end of the room, beside the far door is Rubens' portrait of the *Duchess of Buckingham*, and, above, a portrait of **Cromwell** by Peter Lely. On the other side of the door is hung a *Portrait of an Artist* by Niccolò Cassana. On the wall opposite the windows are landscapes by Gaspare Dughet (Poussin's brother-in-law) and *Hylas and the Nymphs*, the masterpiece of Francesco Furini.

The Sala di Prometeo (14) contains the earliest paintings in the Pitti including some good portraits and a number of fine tondi of the Madonna, the largest and most beautiful of which is the *tondo of the *Madonna and Child*, a charming composition with scenes from the life of the Virgin in the background. This is one of **Filippo Lippi**'s best works, and had a strong influence on his contemporaries. Above is a delightful painting of the *Young Bacchus* by Guido Reni (the fine frame dates from the end of the 17C). Also on this wall is a delicately painted *Epiphany* by an unknown painter of the 15C Umbrian school. On the left wall is a tondo of the *Holy Family*, by Luca Signorelli, in a lovely frame, and above it a tondo of the *Madonna and Child with Angels* by the school of Botticelli. Displayed one above the other are two interesting portraits: the damaged *Portrait of a Man*, in a typical Florentine head-dress, is by Botticelli, and the *Portrait of a Lady* in profile (called the *Bella Simonetta*) is now usually attributed to his *bottega*—the identity of both the sitter and the painter have been much debated. High up on the wall is another tondo by Cosimo Rosselli. The unusual *Portrait of a Woman* in profile in a white veil (once thought to be Caterina Sforza) is now attributed to Piero di Cosimo. Above is a tondo by Beccafumi. The *Eleven Thousand Martyrs* is by Pontormo. Above the fine painting of Mary Magdalen by Il Bachiacca is a tondo by Mariotto Albertinelli.

On the entrance wall is a *Portrait of a Man* by Francesco Salviati and, on the other side of the door, an unusual *Adoration of the Magi* by Pontormo. On the window wall: *Dance of Apollo with the Muses*, by Baldassarre Peruzzi (beneath is a table in scagliola with a copy of the painting) and *Madonna and Child with the Young St John*, attributed to Botticelli. Above the door into the Sala di Ulisse is another tondo by Francesco Botticini. In the centre of the room is a huge Sèvres vase made in 1844.

The Corridoio delle Colonne (15) A door (not always open) leads from the Sala di Prometeo into this room, which is hung with small Flemish paintings by Cornelis van Poelenburgh, Paul Brill, Frans Franken, Jan Breughel (*Orpheus*), David Rychaert (*Temptations of St Anthony*) and others.

The Sala della Giustizia (16) contains a superb *Portrait of a Man*, thought to be Vincenzo or Tommaso Mosti, which is one of **Titian**'s first portraits. He also probably painted the other *Portrait of a Gentleman* opposite the windows, and the *Redeemer*, another early work. There are other portraits by Veronese here and works by Bonifazio Veronese. If the curtain is open there is a good view of the tower of Palazzo Vecchio and the hill of Fiesole behind.

The Sala di Flora (17) contains (on the wall opposite the windows) a small

half-length figure of *Mary Magdalene* by Perugino, similar to his self-portraits.
The Sala dei Putti (18) has exquisite still-lifes by Rachele Ruysch, the *Girl with a Candle* by Godfried Schalken, and other 17C–18C Dutch works by Willem van Aelst and Ludolf Backhuysen. Also here is a fine small painting in mono-chrome of the *Three Graces* by Rubens, and a mythological scene in a landscape by Salvator Rosa.

Sala di Ulisse (19) This lies beyond the Sala di Prometeo (see above). Opposite the entrance there is a good *Portrait of a Man* in a hat by the 16C Florentine school and an *Ecce Homo* by Cigoli. Beyond the door and on the next wall are some fine portraits by Moroni. The beautiful small painting, once part of a *cassone* (dower chest), of the *Death of Lucrezia* is by Filippino Lippi (showing the influence of Botticelli). On the last wall is Raphael's *Madonna dell'Impannata* (so named from the window covered with cloth instead of glass in the background), a mature composition, perhaps with the collaboration of his workshop.

Sala dell'Educazione di Giove (21) This lies beyond the splendid Empire bathroom (20) by Cacialli. It contains one of the most famous Florentine works of the 17C, *Judith with the Head of Holofernes* by Cristofano Allori (with portraits of the artist, his mistress and her mother). On the opposite wall is another well-known painting, a *Sleeping Cupid*, by Caravaggio, painted in Malta in 1608 (in its beautiful original frame). Beyond the door is a small portrait of *Claude of Lorraine* by Jean Clouet. On the last wall the *Portrait of a Man* formerly attributed to Anthony van Dyck is now generally considered to be the work of Van Ravesteyn.

The *Sala della Stufa (22) contains beautiful frescoes by Pietro da Cortona showing the *Four Ages of the World*. This was his first work in Palazzo Pitti (1637) and the elaborate allegories include references to his patrons, the Grand-duke Ferdinando II and his wife Vittoria della Rovere (the oak tree symbolises the name Rovere and the lion refers to the *marzocco* (the heraldic lion) of Florence). This part of the palace was formerly a loggia and the vault fresco is by Matteo Rosselli (1622). Cortona's frescoes recreate the effect of an open terrace. The room was called *della stufa* (meaning stove) when heating was installed in this wing. The majolica pavement (*Triumph of Bacchus*, 1640) is by Benedetto Bocchi.

A door leads out to a **vestibule** (A) at the top of the *grand staircase* (open only in summer), a monumental work by Luigi del Moro (c 1895–97) which descends to the Boboli gardens. Here is displayed a fountain from the Medici Villa di Castello attributed to Francesco di Simone Ferrucci, and a 17C wooden model of Palazzo Pitti.

The main rooms

From here, visitors enter the six rooms on the *piano nobile* overlooking Piazza Pitti that house the masterpieces of the collection.

The Sala dell'Iliade (23) has a ceiling by Sabatelli (1819) which illustrates Homer's *Iliad*. Two large paintings of the *Assumption* by **Andrea del Sarto** are hung here: that on the right wall is one of his most important late works. The other large painting on the third wall, the *Pala di San Marco* is by Fra' Bartolomeo. Also on this wall are two full-length standing male portraits, both by **Titian**, one of them a portrait of *Philip II of Spain*. Above this is *Mary Magdalen*, by one of the few women artists represented in the gallery, Artemesia Gentileschi (she also painted the *Judith* on the adjoining wall). On the other side of the door, the small *Portrait of a Man* (thought to be a goldsmith) is by Ridolfo del Ghirlandaio and shows the influence of Raphael. He also painted the fine *Portrait of a Lady* on the next wall, hung beside Del Sarto's altarpiece, on the other side of which is another beautiful **Portrait of a Lady*, known as *La Gravida* as she is expecting a child, painted c 1506 by **Raphael**. Above is a *Portrait of a Man*, attributed to Joos van Cleve. On the window wall is an unexpected 16C portrait of *Elizabeth I of England* by an English artist. On the last wall is a small equestrian *Portrait of Philip IV of Spain* by Velazquez, and, on the other side of the door, *Portrait of Count Valdemar Christian of Denmark* by Justus Sustermans (who also painted *Prince Mattias de' Medici*, on the opposite wall). This Flemish painter (more correctly known as Suttermans) was appointed to the Medici court in 1619 and remained in its service until his death in 1681. Above is hung *Eleonora de' Medici* by Frans Pourbus the Younger, who was Sustermans' master. Above the door is the *Baptism of Christ* by Veronese. In the centre of the room is a fine early 19C marble group representing *Charity* by Lorenzo Bartolini. The 17C–18C gilded bronze decoration of the four vases displayed here is by Massimiliano Soldani.

The Baroque ceiling decorations

The *ceilings of the Sala di Saturno, Sala di Giove, Sala di Marte, Sala di Apollo and Sala di Venere were beautifully decorated in the 1640s by **Pietro da Cortona**, founder of the Roman Baroque school of painting, for Ferdinando II. The decoration in these five reception rooms, which includes fine gilded and white stuccoes by both Roman and Florentine craftsmen, illustrates the virtues of the young Medici prince and exalts the grand-ducal family by means of extravagant allegories (Ferdinando is represented by the figure of Hercules). The frescoes also celebrate Galileo and the discoveries he had made earlier in the century through numerous illustrations of the constellations and planets, after which the rooms are named. The decorative programme was designed by the librarian, Francesco Rondinelli, and had a great influence in the decoration of royal apartments all over Europe including Versailles.

The Sala di Saturno (24) The ceiling, completed by Pietro da Cortona's able pupil Ciro Ferri in 1665, is being restored and the masterpieces from this room are on temporary display elsewhere in the palace. The following description, however, documents the room as it normally appears with its famous masterpieces by **Raphael**. His **Madonna della Seggiola* (named after the chair), a beautifully composed tondo, is one of his most mature works (c 1514–15). It was purchased by the Medici shortly after the artist's death, and became one of the most popular paintings of the Madonna. The frame is by Giovanni Battista Foggini. On the opposite wall is Raphael's **Madonna del Granduca*—named after Grandduke Ferdinando III of Lorraine, who purchased it in 1800, while in exile. It is probably an early work (c 1504–05) and is painted in a very different style showing the influence of Leonardo. Also on this wall is Raphael's portrait of *Cardinal Bernardo Dovizi da Bibbiena*. On the last wall are four more works by Raphael: **Maddalena Doni*, in the pose of Leonardo's *Mona Lisa*, and her husband **Agnolo Doni*, both dating from 1505, with splendid landscapes in the background; the tiny **Vision of Ezekiel*; and a large altarpiece known as the

Madonna del Baldacchino, commissioned in 1507 by the Dei family for their chapel in Santo Spirito. It was left unfinished in 1508 and enlarged at the top by Niccolò Cassana after Prince Ferdinando purchased it in 1697.

Also in this room is a very fine *Deposition* painted in 1495 by Perugino; the *Head of a Man* by Annibale Carracci; a *Disputation on the Trinity* by Andrea del Sarto; and the *Martyrdom of St Agatha* by Sebastiano del Piombo.

The Sala di Giove (25) This was the throne-room of the Medici and contains Pietro da Cortona's most refined decoration in this suite of rooms. Beautifully restored in 1999, it shows the young prince Ferdinando in glory, surrounded by the virtues. By the far door is **Raphael**'s, **Portrait of a Lady* (*la Velata* or lady with a veil), one of his most beautiful paintings. The grace and dignity of the sitter pervade the work, rendered with a skill which anticipates the hand of Titian. It was purchased by Cosimo II de' Medici. On the other side of the door is the beautiful Venetian painting known as the **Three Ages of Man* (though in fact, it probably represents a concert); this has had various attributions, the most convincing of which seems to be **Giorgione**. On the wall opposite the window, the **Head of St Jerome*, an exquisite small work painted on paper, in an elaborate 19C frame, once attributed to Pollaiolo is now thought to be by Verrocchio. Above it is *Jacobina Vogekort* by the 16C Flemish school. The *Annunciation* is an early work by Andrea del Sarto. On the next wall is *Guidobaldo delle Rovere* in armour, by Bronzino, and the *Fates* by Francesco Salviati. The *Deposition* is Fra' Bartolomeo's last work and one of his best. During its restoration in 1983–88, the two figures of Saints Peter and Paul were revealed in the background: this proves that it is a fragment. Above it hangs a picture of *Nymphs and Satyrs* in a fine landscape by Rubens and next to the door, the **Young St John the Baptist* by Andrea del Sarto (1523), which is one of the best-known representations of the Baptist. The picture was owned by Cosimo I and formerly hung in the Tribuna of the Uffizi. On the other side of the door is the *Madonna in Adoration* by Perugino, and, at the top of the wall, the *Madonna 'of the House-martin'* a delightful work by Guercino. The marble statue in the centre of the room representing *Victory* is by Vincenzo Consani.

The Sala di Marte (26) The largest painting in the room is the **Consequences of War*, one of **Rubens**' most important works. It is an allegory showing Venus trying to prevent Mars going to war, while both figures are surrounded by its destructive and tragic consequences. It was painted in 1638 and sent by the artist to his friend and fellow countryman at the Medici court, Sustermans. Below are two beautiful small works by Andrea del Sarto with scenes from the **Life of St Joseph*. On the right hangs **Titian**'s superb portrait of **Cardinal Ippolito de' Medici*, in Hungarian costume. The Cardinal was the illegitimate son of the Duke of Nemours and Lorenzo the Magnificent's grandson, and was nominated Cardinal against his wishes when he was twelve years old by Clement VII. He commissioned this portrait from Titian to celebrate his return from Hungary where he had been successful in a battle against the Turks. On the other side is another splendid **Portrait of a Man* in fur robes, this one by Veronese ; the sitter was once identified as Daniele Barbaro. On the next wall, two paintings of the *Madonna and Child* by the Spanish painter Murillo, flank Rubens' delightful portrait group known as **The Four Philosophers* (from left to right: Rubens, his brother Filippo, Justus Lipsius and Jan van Wouwer). Rubens' brother and Van Wouwer were both pupils of the great Flemish humanist Lipsius, famous for his studies of Seneca, whose bust is shown in the painting. To the left of the door into the next room is Tintoretto's supposed portrait of *Luigi Cornaro*, and a fine official portrait of *Cardinal Guido Bentivoglio* by Anthony van Dyck.

The Sala di Apollo (27) To the right of the entrance door is one of **Titian**'s masterpieces, his *Portrait of a Gentleman*, probably dating from 1540–45 or perhaps much earlier. Recent research has suggested that the sitter might be Gian Luigi Fieschi from Genova. The painting was acquired by Crown Prince Ferdinand, son of Cosimo III, in 1698, but its provenance is unknown. It was restored (probably for the first time) in 1999. On the other side of the door is Titian's *Mary Magdalen*, another beautifully painted work, which was frequently copied. Also on this wall is Andrea del Sarto's *Deposition* (1523). Rosso Fiorentino's *Madonna Enthroned with Saints* has been removed from the wall opposite for restoration. It is a typical Florentine Mannerist work painted in 1522 for the church of Santo Spirito; when Crown Prince Ferdinand acquired it in 1691, he had it enlarged to fit its new frame. The *Portrait of Vittoria della Rovere* dressed as a Roman vestal is by Sustermans. On the next wall are hung: *Holy Family* by Andrea del Sarto, *Cleopatra* by Guido Reni and, beyond the door, *Isabella Clara Eugenia*, dressed in the habit of a nun by Rubens, and a double portrait of Charles I and Henrietta Maria by Anthony van Dyck.

The **Sala di Venere** (28), with the earliest ceiling (1641–42) by Pietro da Cortona, is named after the *Venus Italica* sculpted by Canova. This was presented by Napoleon in 1812, in exchange for the *Medici Venus* which he had stolen from the Tribuna in the Uffizi and transported to Paris. It is one of the masterpieces of neo-classical art in Florence. By the door is **Titian**'s *Portrait of a Lady* (*la bella*), commissioned by the Duke of Urbino in 1536, apparently an idealised portrait similar to the *Venus of Urbino* in the Uffizi gallery. This superb work came to Florence as part of the dowry of Vittoria della Rovere in 1631. Also on this wall is his exquisitely painted portrait of *Pietro Aretino*, one of his most forceful works. Aretino was disappointed with the painting and after a quarrel with the artist, he presented it to Cosimo I in 1545 (and it was the first of the eleven portraits by Titian here to be hung in Palazzo Pitti). Above is a large *Seascape* (one of a pair; the second picture is on the opposite wall), painted for Cardinal Gian Carlo de' Medici by Salvator Rosa. On the wall opposite the windows are two lovely landscapes by **Rubens**: *Return from the Hayfields*, with a delightful joyful scene, and its companion *Ulysses in the Phaeacian Isle*. On the last wall the portrait of *Pope Julius II* is a copy by Titian of Raphael's painting which survives in two versions (one in the National Gallery, London, and one in the Uffizi). The famous *Concert* is a superb painting of c 1510–12, the attribution of which has been much discussed. Some scholars believe it is by Titian but it appears that more than one hand was involved, and Giorgione may have been responsible for the figure on the left. The portrait of *Baccio Valori* is by Sebastiano del Piombo.

Appartamenti Reali

The other half of the *piano nobile* along the façade of the palace is occupied by the Appartamenti Reali, or royal apartments. These lavishly decorated rooms were used as state apartments from the 17C onwards by the Medici and Lorraine grand-dukes and later by the royal house of Savoy. They have been carefully restored (as far as possible) to their appearance in 1880–1911 when they were first occupied by the house of Savoy. The contents, which reflect the eclectic taste of the Savoy rulers, as well as the neo-Baroque period of the 19C Lorraine grand-dukes, includes splendid silk curtains, drapes, wall hangings and furnishings made in Florence and France during the last period of the Lorraine grand-dukes; sumptuous gilded chandeliers, neo-classical mirrors, candelabra, wall brackets and frames; very well-preserved early 19C carpets from Tournai; huge oriental vases; furniture decorated with *pietre dure*; and a number of interesting paintings and sculptures.

The Sala delle Nicchie (29) This neo-classical room was redesigned by Giuseppe Maria Terreni and Giuseppe Castagnoli in the late 18C. The original room by Ammannati (1561–62) had been built to house Cosimo I's collection of antique sculpture which was then transferred to the Uffizi: only six uncatalogued Roman statues remain here in the niches.

The Sala Verde (I) Green silk furnishings adorn this room, including drapes and wall hangings made by the Florentine firm of Francesco Frullini in 1854–55. The ceiling has monochrome frescoes by Giuseppe Castagnoli with a small painting of the *Allegory of Peace between Florence and Fiesole* by Luca Giordano at its centre. On the wall opposite the window are delightful portraits of the daughters of Louis XV by Jean Marc Nattier: Maria Enrichetta is portrayed as *Flora* and Maria Adelaide as *Diana*. On the end wall is a portrait of a *Knight of Malta*, generally considered to be the work of Caravaggio. In two corners of the room are marble busts by Giuseppe Piamontini. On the window wall is a very fine ebony cabinet made for Vittoria della Rovere in 1677, decorated with *pietre dure*.

The Sala del Trono (II) This has red damask curtains and wall hangings made in France in 1853–54, which are typical of the Napoleonic period. The Japanese vases date from the Edo period (c 1700), and the Chinese vases from the 19C. The carpet was made in Tournai in 1854, and the Italian chandelier and mirrors are of the same period.

The Salotto Celeste (III) The 18C ceiling in this room dates from the time of Pietro Leopoldo. The round table (1826) has a fine top in *pietre dure*, and the chandelier was made by Vittorio Crosten in 1697. The room also contains ten Medici portraits by Sustermans.

The Chapel (IV) was formerly the *alcova* (official bedroom) of Crown Prince Ferdinand (son of Cosimo III de' Medici). Here are portraits of *Cosimo I* and *Piero il Gottoso* by Cristofano dell'Altissimo and a sketch of a lady by Anthony van Dyck. The *Madonna and Child* by Carlo Dolci is in a rich frame of ebony and *pietre dure* (1697) probably designed by Giovanni Battista Foggini.

The Sala dei Pappagalli (V) This room has three doors and a large decorative wood-burning stove. By the entrance is a portrait of *Giulia Varano della Rovere*, Duchess of Urbino, by the *bottega* of Titian, and (by the stove) a small portrait, thought to be the work of Andrea del Sarto (perhaps depicting his wife), but also attributed to Pontormo. The small *Portrait of a Man*, also on this wall, is a work of the early 16C Veneto school. Volterrano painted the portrait of *Cardinal Giancarlo de' Medici*. The table, with a top in *pietre dure*, dates from 1790–1831. The bronze clock-case is by Pierre Philippe Thomire (c 1812).

The rooms straight ahead (not always open) form part of the Quartiere della Regina Margherita di Savoia.

The Salotto della Regina (**VI**) This is decorated with yellow silk made in France c 1805–10. The paintings date from the 19C, except for the delightful studio scene (based on Rubens' house in Anversa), painted in the 17C by Cornelis de Baellieur. Beside it is an ebony cabinet decorated with ivory, alabaster and gilded bronze, which was produced in the grand-ducal workshop by Giovanni Battista Foggini and others in 1704.

The Camera della Regina (**VII**) has a pretty bed decorated in 1885 and a prie-dieu in ebony and *pietre dure* made in 1687. The paintings include (window wall), *Deposition* by Lattanzio Gambara and (end wall) a small sketch for the ceiling of *Santa Cecilia in Rome* by Sebastiano Conca.

The Gabinetto Ovale (**VIII**) This charming room, along with the Gabinetto Rotondo, was created by Niccolò Gasparo Paoletti at the end of the Lorraine regency (1765) for the Grand-duchess Maria Luisa of Lorraine by Ignazio Pellegrini and Giuseppe Ruggieri in 1763–65. The stucco decoration of the vault is the work of Francesco Visetti (c 1765). The beautiful silk chinoiserie furnishings were made in Florence in 1780–83.

The Gabinetto Rotondo (**IX**) This circular room has stuccoes by Domenico Ruschi and painted decoration by Giuliano Traballesi. The furniture and mirrors around the walls date from the 18C and the stuffed chairs in the centre of the room from the 19C.

It is now necessary to return to the Sala dei Pappagalli and go right into the **Quartiere del Re Umberto I di Savoia**. The yellow **Camera del Re** (**X**), decorated at the end of the 18C, has another huge stove. In the centre is a fine table by Giuseppe Colzi (1822) in the Empire style. Off this room can be seen the Toilette del Re. The small **Studio del Re** (**XI**), with yellow silk furnishings dating from 1770, has a portrait of *Claudia de' Medici* by Sustermans. The last two rooms, the **Salone Rosso** (**XII**) and the **Anticamera del Re** (**XIII**) have 19C paintings and furniture.

From the corridor, when the curtains are open, there is a view of the camellia garden, in flower from late March to early April.

The apartments are usually left through the Sala di Bona (**XIV**), frescoed by Bernardino Poccetti (1608), and the 18C Sala Bianca (**XXI**), a magnificent ballroom designed by Gaspare Maria Paoletti.

The Appartamento degli Arazzi (**XV–XX**) These rooms were restored in 2000 and, as far as possible, furnished as they were in 1911. They have ceiling decorations by Bernardino Poccetti, Passignano, Ludovico Cigoli, and Cristofano Allori and a loggia (enclosed in the 19C) with earlier frescoes (1588) of charming domestic scenes by Alessandro Allori. Many of the precious tapestries here were made in the Gobelins factory (some to designs by Charles Le Brun); others were made in the Florentine workshops. The interesting furniture dates mostly from the early 18C–19C, and there are also clocks and a marble sculpture representing an allegory of Music by Vincenzo Consani.

Galleria d'Arte Moderna

On the floor above the Galleria Palatina is the Galleria d'Arte Moderna, opened here in 1924. The collection was formed around 1784 by the Lorraine grandduke Pietro Leopoldo when it was part of the Accademia di Belle Arti. Later acquisitions were made by the Savoy rulers and by the Comune of Florence, and since 1914 it has been administered jointly by the Comune and State, and the collection continues to be augmented. The works currently on show, arranged chronologically and by schools, cover the period from the mid-18C up to the First World War. Tuscan art of the 19C is particularly well represented, notably the Macchiaioli school which was active in Tuscany before 1864. These artists took their inspiration directly from nature, and their paintings are characterised by *macchie* or spots of colour. The most important Macchiaioli painters, who could be termed Tuscan Impressionists, are Giovanni Fattori, Silvestro Lega and Telemaco Signorini. Many of the rooms were decorated around 1825 for the Lorraine grand-dukes by Pasquale Poccianti. The works are beautifully displayed and the gallery extremely well kept.

For admission, see p 158.

Room 1 Neo-classicism On the entrance wall hangs *Hercules at the Cross-roads* by Pompeo Batoni (1742), which was purchased by Ferdinando III in 1818 for Palazzo Pitti. The charming seated statue of *Psyche*, by the window, is by Pietro Tenerani (1816–17). It was commissioned by Carlotta Lenzoni Medici who held a salon in Florence, attended by the famous literary figures of her day including Byron, Leopardi, Alfieri, Rossini and Manzoni. The charming view of the Boboli gardens beyond the Fontana del Carciofo in the courtyard takes in the amphitheatre and the steps rising to the fountain of *Neptune* and the colossal statue of *Abundance* at the top of the gardens. On the skyline can be seen the Forte di Belvedere. Also in this room are two large works by Gaspare Landi and two small landscapes by Philipp Hackert, a German artist who was court painter to Ferdinand IV of Naples.

Room 2 This room illustrates the influence the French had when they occupied Florence in the first decade of the 19C. The most famous artist who worked for the French court was **Antonio Canova** whose signed bust of the muse *Caliope* (1812) is displayed here. It is a very fine work which retains its original patina (numerous other neo-classical marble works were later polished). It is probably an idealised portrait of *Elisa Baciocchi*, Napoleon's sister whom he appointed grand-duchess of Tuscany in 1809; she is also shown here with her daughter in the Boboli gardens in a painting by Giuseppe Bezzuoli. The huge painting of *Napoleon* with his troops is by Pietro Benvenuti who Elisa appointed as director of the Accademia di Belle Arti. It was commissioned for Versailles but was returned to Florence when Benvenuti was sent to Paris after the Congress of Vienna in 1814, by the grand-duke Ferdinando III, to reclaim the Tuscan works of art which had been requisitioned by the French during their occupation of Tuscany. The fine portrait of the engraver *Antonio Santarelli* is by François-Xavier Fabre.

Room 3 Florence before Italian Unification The portraits here include one (on the left wall) of Maria Luisa Borbone, queen of Etruria (with two red roses in her hair) by François-Xavier Fabre. The sumptuous lapis lazuli centrepiece, decorated with mosaics and pearls, was made for Napoleon, and the huge Sèvres vase has a bronze mount by Pierre-Philippe Thomire.

Room 4 This room is dedicated to the Russian Demidoff family who lived in Florence. It includes the *model for the monument on the Lungarno commissioned from Lorenzo Bartolini by Anatolio and Paolo Demidoff to commemorate their father Nicola. The portrait here (in a very elaborate frame) of Anatolio's wife Matilde was painted in 1844 by Ary Scheffer (1795–1858).

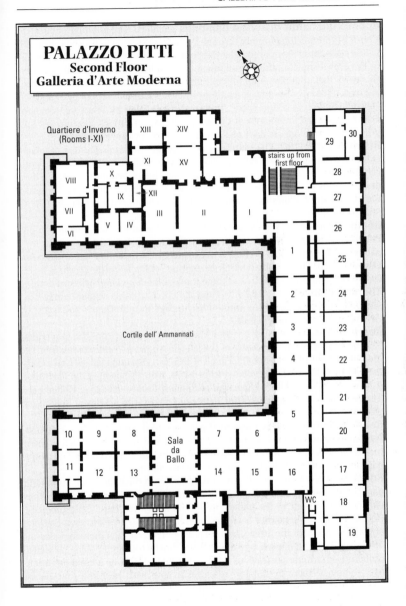

Room 5 Romantic historical paintings Included here is a huge painting of *Charles VIII Entering Florence* through Porta San Frediano by Giuseppe Bezzuoli (1829). Girolamo Savonarola, Pier Capponi and Niccolò Machiavelli are present in the crowd showing their disapproval. Derived from 17C historical canvases, this work had a fundamental influence on the 19C Tuscan school of historical painters. There is also a large painting by Amos Cassioli. Works by Francesco Hayez include a Venetian scene. The small *Deposition* by Francesco Coghetti (1848) is painted in the style of Caravaggio in patriotic tones of white, red and green. The two bronze statues of *Cain* and *Abel* are by Giovanni Duprè.

Room 6 Later 19C The paintings here include the exquisite tiny **Cloister* (1860) by Giuseppe Abbati which shows a new interest in light and volume, concerns which were to dominate the art of the Macchiaioli group of painters. There are also scenes of medieval Florence by Odoardo Borrani and Vincenzo Cabianca, four still-lifes by Giovacchino Toma, and a portrait of Linda Ussi by Stefano Ussi.

Room 7 This is the first of a suite of rooms known as the Quartiere Nuovo Palatino, with early 19C painted ceilings. It displays works by the famous portrait painter of the second half of the 19C **Antonio Ciseri** including one of *Giovanni Duprè* (1885). The striking portrait of another sculptor *Emilio Zocchi* is by his friend Raffaello Sorbi (1868), and there is self-portrait by *Luigi Mussini* here.

The Ballroom Begun c 1825 by Pasquale Poccianti, this displays **early 19C statues**, including two of the young *Bacchus* by Giovanni Duprè, and works by Aristodemo Costoli and Pio Fedi.

Room 8 The ceiling is by Niccola Montiand the room contains **portraits**. Amongst them, one in the centre of the left wall shows a **Noblewoman* from the Morrocchi family by Antonio Puccinelli (1855–60). Next to it is displayed a **Self-portrait* by Giovanni Fattori dating from 1854, who also painted the *Portrait of a Man* (c 1865) and the oval portrait of *Signora Biliotti* (1870) exhibited here. The portrait of *Giulia Tempestini Kennedy Lawrie* is by Giovanni Boldini (an early work).

Room 9 The ceiling is by Gaspero Martellini and the room displays **mid-19C landscapes** showing the influence of the Barbizon school of French painters including works by Serafino de Tivoli (a pastoral scene of two cows), and a large painting by Antonio Fontanesi entitled *After the Rain* (c 1861).

Room 10 This room overlooks the Amphitheatre in the Boboli gardens and the panels of its ceiling were painted by Luigi Catani. The **Cristiano Banti collection** which was left to the gallery in 1955 is displayed here. Cristiano Banti (1824–1904) was a painter from Tuscany; he was also a well-known collector and a great friend of the artist Giovanni Boldini. The collection here includes late 19C works by Banti himself, and a portrait of him by Giovanni Boldini, as well as numerous charming portraits of Banti's daughter *Alaide* as a child at various ages (many of them by Boldini, who was in love with her) and (by Michele Giordano) as a grown woman. The *Portrait of a Lady* in profile (to the right of the window) is by Francesco Saverio Altamura.

Room 11 This room is decorated with another ceiling by Catani. It contains the **Diego Martelli collection*, which was bequeathed to the Comune of Florence in 1897 with the intention of founding a modern art gallery. Diego Martelli (1839–96) was a collector interested in both the Macchiaioli painters and the French Impressionists. He gave hospitality to some of the best known

Macchiaioli painters including Fattori and Lega at his home in Castiglioncello on the Tuscan coast. On the window wall are two delightful *portraits of *Martelli* by Federico Zandomeneghi. His collection has some notable works by the Macchiaioli school who Martelli encouraged, and (on the far wall) two landscapes by Camille Pissarro, acquired when the Impressionists were out of fashion. Also on this wall are two more remarkable paintings by Federico Zandomeneghi—who lived in Paris and was clearly influenced by contemporary French painters—entitled *In Bed and *Honeymoon*. The rest of the collection consists of small works by protagonists of the Macchiaioli school including Giovanni Fattori, Silvestro Lega (the charming *Walk in the Garden*, on the wall opposite the window, and *Portrait of a Peasant Girl*), and Giuseppe Abbati who stayed with Martelli at Castiglioncello on the Tuscan coast. The bust of Garibaldi is by Ettore Ximenes.

Room 12 Above the fireplace is *Singing a 'stornello'* another masterpiece by **Silvestro Lega**, a 'conversation piece' showing a scene in a villa in the environs of Florence, pervaded with a delightfully evocative atmosphere. Beside it has been hung Adriano Cecioni's *Portrait of his Wife*: he is also represented in the room with a number of plaster sculptures. There are also historical and genre scenes here.

Room 13 This features a large historical canvas by **Giovanni Fattori** showing the desolate Italian camp after the *Battle of Magenta in 1859 when the French and Italians (the Piedmontese) beat the Austrian troops in the second War of Independence (beautifully restored in 1999). There are other military scenes here by Silvestro Lega, Vincenzo Cabianca, Telemaco Signorini, and Alessandro Lanfredini.

Room 14 The room contains **historical canvases** by Antonio Ciseri and Gabriele Castagnola. From the window can be seen the green dome of the synagogue and the top of the tower of Palazzo Vecchio.

Room 15 More historical works by Stefano Ussi are displayed here, including the large *Expulsion of the Duke of Athens* and a group of very small works by him.

Room 16 This room contains a bust of *Giuseppe Verdi* commissioned by him from the Neapolitan sculptor Vincenzo Gemito. Here are more battle scenes by Giovanni Fattori and Carlo Ademollo, and a stand made in the late 19C for the Crown of Italy.

Room 17 There is a fine view from this room which overlooks Piazza Pitti: straight ahead is the small dome and campanile of Santo Spirito with the domed San Frediano in Cestello beyond. To the left rises the church of the Carmine, and further left is the green hill of Bellosguardo, and the neo-Gothic tower in the garden of Palazzo Torrigiani, on the extreme left. To the right can be seen the top of the façade of Santa Maria Novella next to its campanile, and further right the dome of the Cappella dei Principi. On the extreme right is the Campanile and Duomo with the top of Orsanmichele in front. On the walls are displayed middle-class **portraits dating from the 1870s and 1880s**, including several by Vittorio Corcos (the one of the *Lady with a Dog and Umbrella* in particular shows the influence of elegant Parisian life). The statue of *Victor Hugo* is by Gaetano Trentanove.

Room 18 Entered from the right side of Room 17, this room has some very important works by the **Macchiaioli** painted in the last two decades of the 19C and purchased by the Comune of Florence. On the wall opposite the windows are three fine works by Giovanni Fattori: *Ritratto della figliastra*, a portrait by of the artist's step-daughter; and two late works, the dramatic *Staffato* showing a horse bolting and dragging its rider to death (his foot having been caught in the stirrup), and a solitary white horse (*Cavallo Bianco*), both of which express Fattori's sad last years when he was unjustly ostracised by his contemporaries. Next to them is displayed Telemaco Signorini's *Bagno penale di Portoferraio*, showing a prison scene. On the wall opposite the entrance are scenes of the Maremma area (in southwest Tuscany) by Fattori, and another famous work (in two versions) by him: the *Libecciata*, representing a windy day at the coast with a stormy sea behind a windblown tamarisk tree—an allegory of life devoid of human figures. In the table case is Fattori's well-known *Rotonda di Palmieri*, a charming beach scene at Livorno (1866), and other delightful small works by Signorini.

Room 19 This room displays the **Ambron collection** and contains more works by the Macchiaioli. Leone Ambron, who died in Florence in 1979, left his important private collection to the gallery. It consists mainly of Macchiaioli and post-Macchiaioli works. On the wall opposite the entrance Giovanni Fattori's small early portrait of *La cugina Argia* is displayed next to Telemaco Signorini's *Leith*, a grey street scene painted during a visit to Scotland in 1881. There are also numerous other works by Fattori, Signorini, Silvestro Lega and Antonio Mancini, as well as more sculptures by Adriano Cecioni.

Room 20 This opens off the left-hand side of Room 17. On the far wall are two charming paintings by **Telemaco Signorini** (*September in Settignano* and a hot August day in *Pietramala*) flanked by two Maremma scenes by Fattori. On the opposite wall are idyllic country scenes by Egisto Ferroni, typical of the paintings favoured by Florentine bourgeois society in the 1880s.

Room 21 continues the display of country scenes with works by Enrico Banti and Adolfo Tommasi.

Room 22 Hanging on the wall opposite the entrance are a *Cemetery Scene* in Constantinople by the important Neapolitan painter Domenico Morelli and a fine landscape (*On the Banks of the Olfanto*) by Giuseppe De Nittis.

Room 23 This features late 19C Tuscan works influenced by contemporary European painting. It includes a portrait of the frivolous *Bruna Pagliano*, dressed in black, by Edoardo Gelli, and works by European artists who came to live in Florence at the end of the 19C. The female nude is by Adolfo de Carolis, a painter much admired by the eccentric poet Gabriele D'Annunzio.

Room 24 This illustrates the beginning of the Divisionist and Symbolist movements in art in the first years of the 20C. There are some early works by Plinio Nomellini showing his experiments in Divisionism and Symbolism, and sculptures by Medardo Rosso.

Room 25 At present, the Emilio Gagliardini collection of Macchiaioli paintings is shown here. It includes works by Giovanni Fattori, Telemaco Signorini, Silvestro Lega and Giuseppe Abbati.

Room 26 contains portraits by Elisabeth Chaplin (1890–1982) who donated most of her works to the gallery in 1974.

Room 27 contains early 20C works by Armando Spadini (1883–1925) and Oscar Ghiglia (1876–1945). Spadini's work contains elements of Symbolism but he was also much influenced by Renoir.

Room 28 works influenced by European artists, including a *Self-portrait* by Lorenzo Viani and a scene of the *Carrara Marble Mines* (*La Mina*) by Giuseppe Viner (1876–1925).

Room 29 has works by Giovanni Costetti (1874–1949). Most of his paintings were left to the gallery by his widow.

Room 30 displays works acquired at an exhibition in Florence in 1922 by Galileo Chini, Francesco Franchetti and others.

The works dating from 1922–45, not at present on view, are to be exhibited in 13 rooms on the floor above, known as the **Mezzanino degli Occhi**, because it has round windows. Artists represented include Virgilio Guidi, Arturo Tosi, Mario Sironi, Guido Peyron, Giovanni Colacicchi, Felice Carena, Primo Conti, Felice Casorati, Ardengo Soffici, Filippo de Pisis, Carlo Carrà, Gino Severini, Giorgio de Chirico, Emanuele Cavalli and others.

The Quartiere d'Inverno

The Quartiere d'Inverno (I–XV) can be seen by appointment (☎ 055 294 883). These apartments were used by the Medici grand-dukes, but are named after their last occupants the Duchessa d'Aosta and Principe Luigi of the royal house of Savoy, who lived there until 1946. They are interesting for their 18C and 19C decorations and furniture.

The first three rooms (**I–III**) are usually open with the rest of the Galleria d'Arte Moderna for exhibitions, or to display important works from rooms temporarily closed. The **Anticamera** (**I**) has 19C tempera decoration on the walls and ceiling. The **Salone da Ballo** (**II**) was designed in 1815–30 by Pasquale Poccianti and has neo-classical stuccoes by Luigi Catani. The **Sala da Pranzo** (**III**; formerly called the Sala della Music) was designed c 1795 by Niccolò Gaspare Paoletti with painted decoration by Giuseppe Maria Terreni.

The remaining rooms are only open by appointment. The walls of the **Salotto Giallo** (**IV**) and the **Salotto Rosso** (**V**) were covered in silk in 1907. Stairs lead up to the **Appartamento del Principe Luigi** (not always shown). These four rooms were occupied by Cardinal Leopoldo dei Medici in 1658–75, but they are named after Luigi, eldest son of Umberto I who lived here before he became Vittorio Emanuele III. They have attractive wall paper dating from c 1870 and 18C and 19C furniture. The **Studio** (**VI**) has neo-classical decorations by Terreni, a fireplace with Ginori tiles (1791–1832), and paintings by Giovanni Cobianchi.

The ceiling of the **Toilette** (**VII**) dates from 1821. The **Camera da Letto** (**VIII**) has furniture by Giuseppe Colzi and a bed dating from c 1820. The painting of the *Rest on the Flight into Egypt* is by Giovanni Domenico Gabbiani. Beyond the **Guardaroba** (**IX**) is the **Loggia** (**X**) which has a display of objects in *pietre dure* by Enrico Bosi. The **Camera da letto di SM il Re** (**XI**) has blue furnishings, and the **Bathroom** (**XII**) has 18C stuccoes on the ceiling. The green **Studio** (**XIII**) contains a fine cabinet in *pietre dure* by Enrico Bosi, acquired by Vittorio Emanuele II in 1861 and two 19C clocks.

From the red **Salotto Rosso** (**XIV**) can be seen the **Salotto Cinese** (**XV**) with furniture in the Chinese style. Interesting paintings hang here by Giuseppe Maria Terreni showing celebrations in the Cascine held in honour of grand-duke Ferdinando III in 1791; by Antonio Cioci showing traditional Florentine festivals; and portraits of members of the Bourbon family by Antonio Raphael Mengs.

Galleria del Costume

The Galleria del Costume (for opening times see p 158) was founded in 1983 on the ground floor of the **Palazzina della Meridiana**. It is the only museum of the history of fashion in Italy.

This wing of Palazzo Pitti, which faces the Boboli gardens, was begun for the

Lorraine grand-dukes in 1776 by Niccolò Gasparo Paoletti and was finished in 1832 by Pasquale Poccianti. The decoration of the rooms dates mostly from the 1860s. It is reached directly by a corridor and stairs from the Museo d'Arte Moderna. This delightful collection is made up largely from private donations—which continue all the time—and illustrates the history of costume from the 18C to the mid-20C. The beautiful displays of clothes are changed about every two years and frequent exhibitions are held. There are also some clothes dating from the 16C, including those worn by Eleonora di Toledo, wife of Cosimo I de' Medici and her son Don Garzia. The precious 18C collection includes some rare men's apparel. The Umberto Tirelli (1928–90) collection of costumes used in theatrical and cinemagraphic productions has been donated to the museum. Other donations include those of the Sicilian noblewoman Donna Franca Florio, and (in 2000) the Italian fashion designer Gianfranco Ferrè. The present display illustrates fashion in Italy between the two World Wars. Decorating the rooms are contemporary paintings and sculpture from the Galleria d'Arte Moderna.

Museo degli Argenti

The Museo degli Argenti is arranged in the summer apartments of the grand-dukes, some of which were used as state rooms. They now contain the eclectic collection formed by the Medici and Lorraine grand-dukes of precious objects in silver, ivory, amber and *pietre dure*, including antique pieces, jewellery, and some exotic curiosities. The silver was first exhibited here in the middle of the 19C (hence the name of the museum) and in the 20C all that remained of the grand-ducal treasury (formerly kept in the Uffizi) was collected here and opened to the public.

For **opening times and tickets**, see p 158. The **entrance** is from the left side of the courtyard.

Ground floor

The Sala di Luca Pitti This is named after the first owner of the palace Luca Pitti, who is commemorated here in a delightful polychrome terracotta bust made in the 15C. The series of terracotta busts (acquired in 2000) of the seven Medici grand-dukes from Alessandro to Gian Gastone are by the workshop of Giovanni Battista Foggini (they are on pretty early-18C stands). The two Medici portraits are by Sustermans, and their genealogical tree dates from 1669. The two serpentine marble vases were decorated in gilded bronze by Massimiliano Soldani Benzi.

The Sala di Giovanni da San Giovanni Exuberant and colourful **frescoes by **Giovanni da San Giovanni** completely cover the walls and ceiling of this room. They were begun after the marriage of Ferdinando II and Vittoria della Rovere in 1634 (an allegory of which is represented on the ceiling). They illustrate the apotheosis of the Medici family illustrated through the life of Lorenzo il Magnifico. The sequence begins at the far end of the entrance wall which has two scenes symbolising the *Destruction of Culture* including the *Muses fleeing from Mount Parnassus*. The particularly successful third scene (around the entrance door) shows the *Muses and Poets Finding Refuge in Tuscany* (represented by an allegorical female figure). The two scenes on the adjacent short wall by San Giovanni's pupil Cecco Bravo show *Lorenzo il Magnifico Receiving the Muses* and *Prudence Instructing Lorenzo* (as a consequence *Peace*, represented by a woman on the lower part of the wall, takes off her armour, while high above *War*, in the form of the chariot of Mars gallops away). The scenes on the window wall are by Ottavio Vannini: the central one shows *Lorenzo Seated in the Sculpture Garden of San Marco* while the young Michelangelo presents him with his sculpture of the head of a faun. On the last wall, two scenes by Francesco Furini show *Lorenzo at his Villa of Careggi Surrounded by Members of the Platonic Academy* and an elaborate *Allegory of his Death*. On the painted pilasters are *trompe l'œil* decorations imitating bas-reliefs of classical myths and the seasons.

The Sala Buia (left) The central case in this room displays the magnificent *collection of 16 *pietre dure* vases** which belonged to Lorenzo il Magnifico, and which bear his monogram 'LA V.R.MED'. Although it is very difficult to date many of them and their provenance is usually unknown, they include late Imperial Roman works, as well as Byzantine and medieval Venetian works. Others come from Persia and Egypt. The collection was begun by Piero il Gottoso and enlarged by Lorenzo. Many of the vases were formerly used as reliquaries and were mounted in silver-gilt in the 15C (some by Giusto da Firenze) or later in the grand-ducal workshops. Lorenzo il Magnifico's death mask and portrait by Luigi Fiammingo are also displayed here.

Four more cases display exquisite smaller works, including Roman cups and dishes in *pietre dure*, and some Byzantine works (most of them with later mounts). Also exhibited here are late-15C church vestments made for the Medici, and precious liturgical objects (13C–15C).

The Grotticina This lies beyond the Sala Buia and contains a small fountain and a frescoed ceiling with birds by Florentine artists (1623–34), and a lovely pavement in *pietre dure* and soft stone. The exquisitely carved limewood relief by Grinling Gibbons was presented to Cosimo III in 1682 by Charles II. The table in *pietre dure* was made in Prague in the early 17C. There is an exhibition of of 17C and 18C frames, including four by the Dutch craftsman Vittorio Crosten (who also carved the base of the table).

Cappella This lies to the right of the Sala di Giovanni da San Giovanni and was decorated by local craftsmen in 1623–34.

Beyond are three reception rooms decorated with delightful *trompe l'œil* *frescoes by the Bolognese painters **Angelo Michele Colonna** and **Agostino Mitelli** (1635–41), who worked as partners for over 20 years. The frescoes—which are in exceptionally good condition—cover the wall surfaces with architectural perspectives, animated by the occasional human figure. The first room was a public audience chamber and has an elaborate cabinet made in Augsburg and brought to Florence in 1628, and a 17C prie-dieu in ebony and *pietre dure*. In the next room are five tables in *pietre dure* (16C–17C) and the partial reconstruction of the unfinished *ciborium designed for the altar for the Cappella dei Principi (see p 224). Commissioned by Don Giovanni de' Medici, it was designed by Matteo Nigetti: the eight rock crystal columns are by Buontalenti and the statuettes in *pietre dure* by Orazio Mocchi.

The last room contains a cabinet designed by Giovanni Battista Foggini in 1709, given by Cosimo III to his daughter, the Electress Palatine; a table with an antique Roman porphyry top and a 16C base; and two tables decorated with agate tops made in the 17C. On the window wall is a table designed by Giorgio Vasari and made by Dionigi Nigetti which belonged to Cosimo I.

The rooms towards the Boboli gardens were the living quarters of the grand-dukes. It is here, and on the mezzanine floor, that their eclectic collection of personal keepsakes is displayed—these include gifts presented by other ruling families and *objets d'art* made specially for them.

Camera da letto del Granduca Gian Gastone This contains three splendid gilded wood display cabinets displaying 16C–17C amber and ivories. On an 18C table there is an amber centrepiece in the form of a fountain dating from c 1610. The framed terracotta models of the *Four Seasons* are by Soldani Benzi.

The room to the right displays exquisitely made vessels in rock crystal and *pietre dure* including, in the case to the right of the entrance, a lapis lazuli vase (1583) designed by Buontalenti with a gold mount by Jacques Bylivelt, a rock-crystal vase in the form of a bird (with a gold enamelled mount, c 1589), and a lapis lazuli shell, with the handle in enamelled gold in the form of a snake. The next case contains a goblet in rock crystal, with an intricately decorated enamelled gold lid, which is thought to have been made for Henry II of France. Displayed on its own is a reliquary casket in rock crystal and gilded silver by Valerio Belli dated 1532. In the centre of the room is a splendid antique marble table with Cufic inscriptions.

The rooms to the left contain an important collection of 17C ivories, many of them made for Cardinal Leopoldo by the German artists Balthasar Stockamer, Balthasar Permoser, and Christoph Daniel Schenck. Particularly remarkable pieces from a technical point of view are the long-haired dog lying down, given to Maria Maddalena d'Austria by Cosimo II, the horse in a spherical cage, the series of turned vases (1618–31) and an elaborate composition of *Curtius* riding his horse into the abyss.

Mezzanine floor

A pretty little staircase leads up to the mezzanine floor where the grand-ducal collection of jewellery has always been kept.

In the room at the top of the stairs on the right, a central display case contains a relief of Cosimo I and his family in *pietre dure* by Giovanni Antonio de' Rossi (1557–62; it used to contain a medallion with the personification of Florence); an oval in *pietre dure* of the equestrian statue of Cosimo I and Piazza Signoria by Bernardo Gaffurri (1598); a Roman head of Hercules; and seven bas-reliefs in gold set on precious stones made for the Studiolo of Francesco I by Giambologna. Also exhibited here are a chessboard in *pietre dure*, made in 1619 to a design by Jacopo Ligozzi, cameos, miniature vases and busts in *pietre dure*, and Cosimo I's seal.

The adjoining room has a magnificent display of the **jewellery collection of the last of the Medici, the electress Anna Maria; including numerous charming pieces made with huge baroque pearls, rings with cameos and intaglio, and an ex-voto in precious stones of Cosimo II in prayer made in the grand-ducal workshops in 1617–24.

The rooms at the top of the stairs on the left contain gold and silversmiths' work from the Treasury of Ferdinando III brought to Florence in 1814 (mainly from Salzburg), including elaborate nautilus shells, a double chalice made from an ostrich egg mounted in silver gilt (c 1370–80) and two ornamental cups made from buffalo horns with silver-gilt mounts (14C). The series of silver-gilt dishes from Salzburg were made by Paul Hübner, c 1590.

Off the early 17C painted **loggia** with four 17C Mexican vases, is access to the tiny **tesoretto** (not always open). This has a frescoed barrel vault and a charming display of miniature vases and objects in *pietre dure* made in the 16C.

The frescoed room beyond the loggia, which overlooks the courtyard, contains exotic and rare objects from all over the world. These include an Islamic powder horn, nautilus shells, 17C shell figurines, and a mitre with scenes of the Passion depicted in gold thread and birds' feathers (Mexican, c 1545).

The last four rooms have a display of 18C Chinese porcelain; Japanese porcelain and lacquer work; 18C and 19C watches, silverware and jewellery; and plaster casts of the silver plates belonging to the last Medici grand-dukes which were melted down in 1799, and 18C church silver. A step leads up to a corridor with more casts and then on the left is another corridor (sometimes closed) with wax and paper objects, and more church silver.

Museo delle Carrozze

The Museo delle Carrozze is in the south *rondò* of Palazzo Pitti, though it is currently closed. It contains seven carriages and two sedan chairs dating from the period of the Lorraine grand-dukes and the royal house of Savoy, including the gilded silver carriage of Ferdinando II made in 1818, and decorated by Antonio Marini. There are other berlins (carriages), decorated with charming paintings, and a coupé of 1730.

Giardino di Boboli

On the hillside behind Palazzo Pitti lie the magnificent Boboli Gardens, among the most beautiful and best-preserved in Italy. Laid out for Cosimo I on the slope of the hill stretching up from behind Palazzo Pitti to Forte di Belvedere, they were designed by Tribolo and continued after his death in 1550 by Davide Fortini, Giorgio Vasari and Bartolommeo Ammannati. After 1574, Francesco I employed Bernardo Buontalenti to direct the works. The gardens were extended downhill to the west in the early 17C, between the 14C walls and Via Romana as far as Porta Romana, by Giulio and Alfonso Parigi. They were opened to the public for the first time in 1766. The origin of the name Boboli is unknown, but may be derived from the name of the former proprietors of the hillside (Borbolini).

• **Opening times** Daily 09.00–dusk, but closed on first and last Monday of month (☎ 055 265 1838); Lire 4000.

There are four **entrances** (with ticket offices): one from the courtyard of Palazzo Pitti, one at Porta Romana (**Map 6; 5**; see also the plan of the Boboli gardens), one at the Annalena gate on Via Romana (**Map 6; 3**), and at the top of the hill which leads into Forte di Belvedere (however, this is at present closed because of work on the Forte di Belvedere). There is another exit through the archway in the left wing of Palazzo Pitti. The Grotticina di Madama and the Grotta Grande (when restoration work is finished) can be visited by appointment (☎ 055 265 1838).

This is the biggest park in the centre of Florence and the gardens are beautifully maintained. They are always cool even on the hottest days in summer. Laid out on two main axes, the gardens are divided into two distinct areas: the lower gardens around the Viottolone and the Isolotto, which are the most attractive, tend to be visited mostly by Florentines with their children, while tourist groups often only visit the upper part of the gardens. A nature trail was laid out in 1994 for

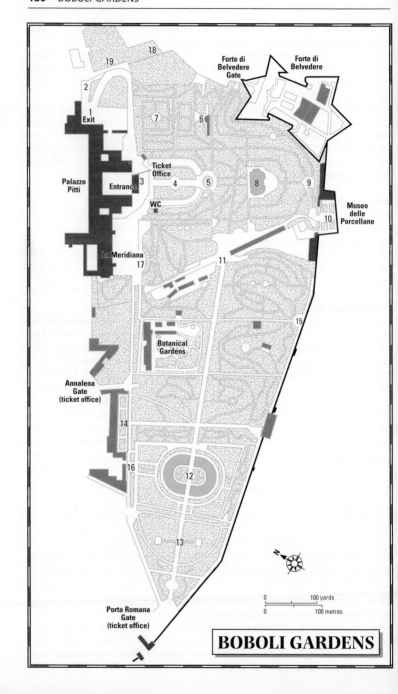

BOBOLI GARDENS

bird-watchers. However, since admission charges were introduced in 1992, the Boboli gardens are no longer classified as a public park and therefore, sadly, picnics are no longer allowed there.

The plants are predominantly evergreen, and a special feature of the gardens has always been the **tall double hedges** (5m–8m high) formed by a variety of shrubs and bushes in different shades of green—such as laurel, laurustinus, viburnum, box, myrtle and prunus—below a higher hedge of ilex. About half the area of the gardens is covered with ilex woods: these thickets were used up to 1772 for netting small birds. The first deciduous trees were planted in 1812. The botanical sections of the gardens, introduced by the Medici, where mulberries, potatoes and pineapples were once grown, no longer survive. However, there is a splendid collection of citrus fruits (including a rare type of orange) and flowers, cultivated in pots (although many of these were severely damaged in the great freeze of 1985). Despite the introduction of entrance tickets, the Boboli gardens still attract some one million visitors a year, and there are still some residents living in the garden houses, and even one or two cars, all of which present great problems to conservation.

There are plans to restore the complicated 17C hydraulic system created by Buontalenti and the Parigi to irrigate the gardens and feed the fountains: at present only two fountains work. There are pebble mosaics in some areas of the gardens, and there used to be hidden jets of water to surprise visitors. The appearance of the gardens was drastically altered in 1833 by Leopoldo II when he inserted the long carriage road which crosses the gardens from west to east.

About 170 **statues** decorate the walks, a typical feature of many Renaissance gardens derived from ancient Roman villas. Many of them are restored Roman works, but some of them still remain unidentified; some came to Florence in the 18C from the Medici collection in Rome, and others in the 18C and early 19C from the Villa di Pratolino outside Florence. Two worn statues in the gardens were recognised as works by Cellini only just before the last War (they are now in the Bargello museum). Other statues were added in the 16C and 17C by Giambologna, Valerio Cioli, Giovanni Battista Caccini, Cosimo Salvestrini, Domenico Pieratti, Romolo Ferrucci del Tadda and others. Since 1984, some of the statues have been restored *in situ*; others have been removed for restoration and may not be returned to the gardens (unless they can be safeguarded against deterioration). For conservation reasons, casts of some of the marble statues have replaced the originals, though it has not yet been decided whether casts in synthetic materials or copies in marble or stone will be made in future of the restored works. Restored statues which cannot be returned to the open air are eventually to be exhibited in a museum here.

The **entrance** at the back of the courtyard of Palazzo Pitti emerges on the terrace behind the palace, overlooking the courtyard and the splendid Baroque **Fontana del Carciofo** (3), by Francesco Susini (1641), named after the bronze artichoke on top, which has been lost. It has 12 little statues of cupids on the basin. It replaced a fine 16C fountain by Ammannati (now reassembled in the Bargello). There is a magnificent view of the Duomo and Campanile behind Orsanmichele from the terrace.

The **Amphitheatre** (4) was laid out as a garden (probably with ilexes and olive trees) by Ammannati in 1599, in imitation of a Roman circus. The open-air theatre was constructed in 1630–35 by Giulio and Alfonso Parigi for the spectacles held here by the Medici. These elaborate theatrical performances were designed to exalt the prestige of the Medici and offer the public entertainment on a grand scale—sometimes there were elephants or horses combined with fantastic scenery and dramatic lighting. The most stunning event was the festivities for the marriage of Cosimo, son of Ferdinand II, to Margaret Louise of Orléans in 1661.

The **obelisk** of Rameses II, taken from Heliopolis by the Romans in 30 BC, found its way to the Villa Medici in Rome in the 17C. In 1789, it was brought from Rome and set up here by Niccolò Gasparo Paoletti. The huge granite basin, from the Baths of Caracalla, was installed in 1840 by Pasquale Poccianti. The restored statues in the niches include some Classical works (restored in later centuries), notably the young athlete in the fifth niche on the right side, as well as 16C and 17C works.

A series of terraces rise above the amphitheatre. On the first terrace are three Roman statues (**5**), standing on funerary altars, including a fine Ceres and there are hedged walks with pretty vistas on either side. On the upper level is a large fishpond with the **Neptune Fountain** (**8**) by Stoldo Lorenzi (1571). It was surrounded by terraces in the 17C and planted with plane trees in the Napoleonic era. The Forte di Belvedere can be seen above on the hill top.

A short detour to the left leads through romantic winding alleys overshadowed by ilexes and a cypress grove, to the rococo **Kaffehaus** (**6**), built for Pietro Leopoldo in 1775 by Zanobi del Rosso (the café is open all year except November and December). It is decorated with charming frescoes by Giuseppe del Moro, Giuliano Traballesi and Pasquale Micheli. In the garden in front, which has a good view of Florence and Fiesole, there is a cast of the **Ganymede Fountain** (**7**). The 16C original is attributed to Stoldo Lorenzi. Behind the Kaffehaus there is a gate (a secondary entrance to the gardens, temporarily closed) which leads up to the Forte di Belvedere (see p 309).

From the Neptune Fountain steps continue to the top of the garden and a colossal statue of *Abundance* (**9**), in a niche of bay and ilex. Begun by Giambologna as a portrait of Giovanna d'Austria, wife of Francesco I, it was originally intended for a column in Piazza San Marco. Instead it was finished by Pietro Tacca, who transformed it into an allegory of Abundance. It was placed here in 1636 by order of Giovanna's daughter, Maria de' Medici. From here the view embraces the whole city, beyond the Pitti and the tower of Santo Spirito.

A short double flight of steps to the right, designed in 1792, continues to the **Giardino del Cavaliere** (**10**), a delightful secluded walled garden with box hedges laid out at the time of Cosimo III on a bastion constructed by Michelangelo in 1529. The fountain has a putto attributed to Pierino da Vinci or Stoldo Lorenzi (originally there were three bronze monkeys attributed to Pietro Tacca, though these have not been returned since their restoration). The view from the terrace is one of the most charming in Florence, embracing the rural outskirts of the city. On the extreme left is the bastion of Forte di Belvedere, then, behind a group of cypresses, San Miniato with its tower. The fields and olive groves are dotted with beautiful old villas. To the right is the residential area of Bobolino beside a splendid stretch of the city walls.

Museo delle Porcellane

The Museo delle Porcellane was opened in 1973. It is housed in the 17C Casino del Cavaliere in the Boboli gardens. The Casino may have been used by Cardinal Leopoldo for meetings of the Accademia del Cimento, an experimental scientific academy founded by the Cardinal in 1659. It was rebuilt in the 18C for the Lorraine grand-dukes by Zanobi del Rosso. For **admission**, see p 158.

The Museo delle Porcellance contains a well displayed collection of 18C–19C Italian, German and French porcelain from the Medici and Lorraine grand-ducal collections. The last Medici grand-duke, Gian Gastone, whose wife was from Saxony, had a special interest in porcelain which was much in vogue in the early 18C. Room 1 displays 18C French porcelain (Tournai, Chantilly, Vincennes, Sèvres, including the delicate *alzata da ostriche*, used for serving oysters). In the centre, beneath a Venetian chandelier, are two Sèvres dinner services which belonged to Elisa Baciocchi (grand-duchess of Tuscany), and a plaque with a portrait of her brother Napoleon in Sèvres porcelain, after Françoise Gérard (1809–10). Examples from the Doccia Ginori factory include works made in 1736 for the Lorraine family, and a 19C service with views of Florence. In the second room are works in biscuit ware made in Vienna, and in the last room Chinoiserie ware from Meissen.

At the foot of the double stairs, another flight of steps leads down between two fine Roman seated statues of the *Muses* in white marble (being restored) to the **Prato dell'Uccelare**, with a grove of cedars of Lebanon (view), at the end of a range of garden houses.

To the left, the magnificent long *Viottolone** (11) descends steeply through the second part of the gardens laid out on an east–west axis which extends as far as Porta Romana. This majestic cypress avenue was planted in 1612 by Giulio Parigi, but some of the trees have recently been attacked by disease. It is lined with statues, many of them restored Roman works from the Villa Medici in Rome (and others carved in the 16C and 17C); some of these have been removed for restoration. The 17C arboured walks beneath trellises over which ilex branches are trained, and little gardens to the right and left, with delightful vistas, are amongst the most beautiful spots in the gardens. The paths are laid out between box hedges and laurel avenues; these were originally symmetrically designed around three labyrinths, destroyed in 1833 when the curving paths were introduced.

Originally there were two fine Roman statues known as *Gladiators* at the top of the avenue: one has been removed, the other, with a beard, was freely restored by Romolo Ferrucci del Tadda. On the right is a little garden where citrus fruit trees are cultivated. On either side of the avenue are two more Roman statues, one of a divinity (restored c 1610–20) and one of a Roman matron with a veil. They were given to Cosimo I on a visit to Rome in 1560. At the first crossing are four statues of the *Four Seasons—Spring* and *Winter* by Giovanni Battista Caccini (c 1608; replaced by copies), and *Summer* and *Autumn* by Pietro Francavilla. A path to the left ends at a colossal bust of *Jupiter* (15) by Giambologna or his school. An unusual path, lined with a water 'staircase' composed of late 16C fountains with grotesque heads, follows a stretch of the 13C city walls.

On the other side of the Viottolone an ilex tunnel dating from the 17C leads to remains of the **Botanical Gardens**, known as the *Giardino degli Ananas* when pineapples were cultivated there. The Sicilian botanist Filippo Parlatore was director of the gardens between 1842 and 1872, and he designed the circular pools for aquatic plants. The larger of the two unheated greenhouses (to be restored) was designed by Giuseppe Cacialli. Ammannati's statues for a fountain in Palazzo Vecchio were kept here up until 1920, when they were removed to the courtyard of the Bargello. The garden was abandoned after 1966 though restoration has been under way since 1989.

At the next crossing, lower down the Viottolone and beyond two more restored Roman statues, are three more statues (restored Roman works). The main avenue continues downhill past a 16C statue to end at a short 19C avenue of plane trees which runs across it at right-angles (the orangery described below can be seen at the right end). Of the four statues here, two are restored Roman works: *Aesculapius* has an antique torso and a head restored by Gian Simone Cioli in the early 17C. The statue of *Venus*, usually considered an allegory of Secrecy, also has an antique torso (it was restored by Giovanni Francesco Susini). The statue of *Andromeda* dates from the 17C. Beyond, in niches in the hedges, are two groups of statues depicting folk games; the one on the left is by Orazio Mochi and Romolo Ferrucci del Tadda (17C), and the one on the right was added c 1770 by Giovanni Battista Capezzuoli.

The **Isolotto** (12), or *Vasca dell'Isola*, was laid out by Giulio Parigi in 1612. The island recalls the design of the so-called Naval Theatre, Hadrian's retreat at his villa near Tivoli. A circular moat with fine sculptural decorations surrounds an island and the huge **'Fountain of Oceanus** designed by Tribolo for Cosimo II. Three statues of the rivers *Nile, Ganges* and *Euphrates* surround the central figure of *Neptune*, which is a copy (c 1910) by Raffaello Romanelli of the original by Giambologna, which now in the Bargello museum. These stand above a huge granite basin quarried by Tribolo in Elba—the design included another large basin, but it cracked during transportation. Some 200 terracotta pots, some still with the Medici crest, filled with citrus fruit trees are put out here in the rose garden from the end of April for the summer, and the island is usually open at this time.

Four marble statues of cupids (one of which has been removed) by Domenico Pieratti, Cosimo Salvestrini and Giovanni Francesco Susini (with Giovanni Battista Pieratti) were placed to the north and south of the island in 1623–24.

The Isolotto in the Boboli Gardens

On the other two sides, by the gates with capricorns (the emblems of Cosimo II) on the gate posts, are grotesque harpies by the school of Giambologna to a design by Giulio Parigi (these are copies of the originals, made in marble by Innocenzo Spinazzi in 1776). In the water are *Perseus on Horseback*, restored by Giovanni Battista Pieratti, and *Andromeda*, also attributed to Pieratti. A high ilex hedge surrounds the water with niches cut into it which contain delightful restored 17C statues in *pietra serena* (some of them in very poor condition and propped up by scaffolding) of peasants and hunters by Giovanni Battista and Domenico Pieratti. Other statues include *Two Men Fighting*, a *Hunter with Two Dogs* and a *Moorish Hunter* (removed and restored) by Giovan Simone and Valerio Cioli, Bartolomeo Rossi and Francesco Generini. The dogs are by Romolo Ferrucci del Tadda.

Beyond two small 17C obelisks made in Carrara marble is the **Hemicycle** (13), an English-style green surrounded by plane trees, which provides a cool playground for children in summer. The two Roman columns in Egyptian granite surmounted by neo-classical vases were purchased from Lord Cowper by Pietro Leopoldo. On the central path are a statue of *Vulcan* by Chiarissimo Fancelli, and a 16C seated female statue. Some of the colossal busts in the laurel hedge which surrounds the lawn are Roman (including the fine *Head of Zeus*, although the bust is modern). The path continues past (right) a Roman restored statue of *Bacchus* and (left) a female statue known as *Flora* (in need of restoration). This has the body of an ancient Roman statue of *Venus* (derived from a Hellenistic original) but the head and arms were added by Giambattista Caccini. The statuary group of peasants is an 18C copy by Giovanni Battista Capezzuoli of a 17C work; the three grotesque figures in *pietra serena* dancing in silly attitudes, opposite, once thought to be by Romolo Ferrucci del Tadda have recently been attributed to Tribolo or Caccini (they have been restored). Beyond two more 17C and 18C statues, at the end of the garden, on top of a Roman sarcophagus of the 3C AD is a marble fountain (recently restored) of a peasant with a barrel by Giovanni Fancelli, bought here in 1773 from the Villa di Pratolino.

At the **Porta Romana** gate (with an exit from the gardens through the walls), is a statue of *Perseus* by Vincenzo Danti. The very fine Roman sarcophagus, with the *Labours of Hercules* (2C AD), has been removed for conservation reasons. Both the sarcophagus and statue were made for the Villa of Pratolino and moved here in the 18C.

A path leads back through the Boboli gardens following the left wall along Via Romana. Beyond a statue of a peasant at work by Valerio and Simone Cioli is the **Fontana della Vedemmia** (16; 1599–1608), also by the Cioli (showing a grape harvest), beside two terracotta dogs by Romolo Ferrucci del Tadda.

Entered through a fine gate dating from 1818 is the handsome **Orangery** (14), built by Zanobi del Rosso (1777–78) and painted in its original green and white colour. The pots of citrus fruit trees are kept here in winter. The 18C gardens in front are planted with antique roses and camellias and four Roman statues (restored by Innocenzo Spinazzi) adorn the walls. This was on the site of a small zoo for exotic animals. Near the **Annalena gate**, an entrance to the garden on Via Romana, is a small grotto with statues of *Adam* and *Eve* by Michele Naccherino. A path continues past more greenhouses to emerge beside the charming 18C Meridiana wing of Palazzo Pitti, which houses the Costume Museum (see above). The hillside was used probably since Roman times as a quarry for *pietra forte* and much of the palace was built out of the stone quarried here. It was covered over in the 18C, and is now surrounded by cedar trees. This is the setting for a huge Roman granite basin and a Roman statue of *Pegasus* (17), restored by Aristodemo Costoli in 1865. Wheels were installed beneath the statue and a metal track laid so that it could 'fly' during opera performances given here in the 1960s. The other statues are mostly restored Roman works.

The path continues past the Fontana del Carciofo (described above), below which on the extreme left can be seen a secret hanging-garden; this is the **Giardino delle Camelie** which is open for three weeks in late March and early April when the camellias are in flower (Tues, Thurs and Sat; 10.00–12.00; for information, contact the Amici dei Musei, ☎ 055 286 465).

In the 17C, this was a small private water-garden with two grottoes, one in the form of an arch, beside an exit from the apartment of Prince Mattias, brother of the grand-duke Ferdinando II. Camellias, first introduced into Italy around 1780, were planted here in the early 19C, and all 42 different species were replanted in the 1990s, although the taller ones survive from the first garden.

On the other side of the Fontana del Carciofo, a wide gravel carriage-way descends past two pine trees (right) at the entrance to a narrow path lined with box hedges which leads through a pretty little garden of parterres with peonies and roses (planted with dwarf fruit trees in the time of Cosimo I) to the **Grotticina di Madama** (18; recently restored, admission by appointment). This was the first grotto to be built in the gardens, which later became famous for them. It was commissioned by Eleonora di Toledo in 1553–55 and is the work of Davide Fortini and Marco del Tasso. The sculptures are by Baccio Bandinelli and Giovanni Fancelli. It contains stalactites and bizarre goats. The frescoes are attributed to Bachiacca, and the fine terracotta pavement was designed by Santi Buglioni. The gravel road continues to wind down past a rose-garden and a colossal seated figure (19) by Baccio Bandinelli. Representing *God the Father*, this was made for the high altar of the Duomo, but was moved in 1824 to Boboli, where it has been known ever since as *Jupiter*. The ancient square bell-tower of Santa Felicita is visible nearby. The beginning of the carriage-way is flanked by two colossal porphyry and marble Roman statues (2C AD; recently restored) of *Dacian Prisoners* (brought here from the Villa Medici in Rome), with bas-reliefs of the late 3C on their pedestals.

On the right is a cast of the so-called *Fontana del Bacco* (1), really an amusing statue of Pietro Barbino, the pot-bellied dwarf of Cosimo I, seated on a turtle, by Valerio Cioli (1560). Here can be seen the last stretch of the Corridoio Vasariano from the Uffizi (see Ch. 6) with remains of graffiti decoration.

A path lined with magnolia trees planted in the 19C descends to the ***Grotta Grande** (2). This is currently closed for restoration and admission will be by appointment when it reopens. Begun in 1557 by Vasari, the upper part was finished by Ammannati and Buontalenti (1583–93). The two statues of *Apollo* (or David) and *Ceres* (or Cleopatra) in the niches on the façade (probably by Vasari) are by Baccio Bandinelli, and the decoration above was added by Giovanni del Tadda. The original paving with pebble mosaic in front of the entrance was discovered in 2000. The walls of the first chamber are covered with fantastic figures carved in the limestone by Piero di Tommaso Mati (on a design by Buontalenti). In the four corners are casts of Michelangelo's unfinished *Slaves* (the originals, placed here in 1585, were removed to the Accademia in 1908). The charmingly painted vault is by Bernardino Poccetti. Beyond is an erotic group of *Paris Abducting Helen* by Vincenzo de' Rossi. The innermost grotto contains a beautiful statue of *Venus Emerging From her Bath* (c 1570) by Giambologna, and more pretty murals by Poccetti.

The exit is through an arch in the left wing of Palazzo Pitti, which leads out into Piazza Pitti.

9 • Galleria dell'Accademia and Santissima Annunziata

Galleria dell'Accademia

From Piazza San Marco (see p 206) the straight Via Ricasoli (**Map 4; 5**) leads towards the Duomo (with a view of the Campanile). Beyond the Accademia di Belle Arti (see Ch. 10) is the entrance at no. 58 to the Galleria dell' Accademia (**Map 6; 6**), a museum famous for its works by Michelangelo, but also containing a good collection of Florentine paintings from all periods.

• **Opening times** 08.30–18.50; *fest*. 08.30–19.00; closed Mon; summer: Thurs, Fri and Sat also 20.30–23.30 (☎ 055 238 8609); Lire 12,000 (S).
The gallery can be very crowded with tour groups and there is often a long queue outside the entrance: it is therefore always best to book a visit (☎ 055 294 883; Lire 2000 booking charge). The least crowded time of day is always late afternoon. The works are all well labelled in English.

History of the Gallery

The gallery was founded in 1784 with a group of paintings given to the Accademia di Belle Arti (see p 206) by Grand-duke Pietro Leopoldo I for study purposes. Paintings from suppressed convents and churches were transferred here after 1786 and 1810. Some of these were subsequently moved to the Uffizi. In 1873, a huge tribune was constructed to exhibit Michelangelo's *David*, when it was decided to remove it from its original location in Piazza della Signoria. In 1882, a museum was inaugurated here dedicated to Michelangelo, consisting exclusively of casts of his sculptures, with the *David*, the only original, as centrepiece. In 1909 most of these casts were replaced by five originals by Michelangelo (his four *Slaves* and *St Matthew*), and the last casts were removed in 1938 to the Gipsoteca at Porta Romana. The 19C Salone was opened in 1985 and the upper floor in 1998.

Ground floor

The Galleria Beyond the ticket office and a room of paintings (described below), the Galleria displays five **sculptures** by **Michelangelo**. The four *Slaves* or *Prisoners* (variously dated 1521–23 or around 1530) were begun for the tomb of Pope Julius II in St Peter's, Rome, which was never finished—other sculptures which were to form part of it can now be seen in San Pietro in Vincoli, Rome. The *Slaves* were presented to the Medici in 1564 by Michelangelo's nephew, Leonardo. In 1585, they were placed in the Grotta del Buontalenti in the Boboli gardens (see Ch. 8), and they were bought here in 1909. In the centre of the right side is the *St Matthew* (1504–08; recently restored), one of the twelve apostles commissioned from the sculptor by the Opera del Duomo for the cathedral, and the only one he ever began. It was left abandoned in the courtyard of the Opera del Duomo until 1831, and moved here in 1909. These five sculptures are magnificent examples of Michelangelo's unfinished works, some of them barely blocked out, the famous *non-finito*, much discussed by scholars. They evoke Michelangelo's unique concept expressed in his poetry, that the sculpture already exists within the block of stone, and it is the sculptor's job merely to take away what is superfluous. The way in which Michelangelo confronted his task, as Cellini noted, was to begin from a frontal viewpoint, as if carving a high relief, and thus the statue gradually emerged from the marble.

By the entrance is a bronze bust of *Michelangelo* by Daniele da Volterra. The *Pietà* bought from Santa Rosalia in Palestrina in 1939 is an undocumented work, and is no longer considered to be by Michelangelo.

The tribune This was specially built in 1882 by Emilio de Fabris to exhibit the *David* by Michelangelo (1501–04) when it was removed from Piazza della Signoria (see Ch. 4).

Michelangelo's David

This is perhaps the most famous single work of art in Western civilisation, and has become something of a cult image, all too familiar through endless reproductions, although it is not the work by which Michelangelo is best judged. It was commissioned by the city of Florence to stand outside Palazzo Vecchio where its huge scale fits its setting. Here it seems out of place in its cold, heroic niche. The colossal block of marble, some 5m high, quarried in 1464 for the Opera del Duomo, had been left abandoned in the cathedral workshop. The marble was offered to several other artists, including Andrea Sansovino and Leonardo da Vinci, before it was finally assigned to Michelangelo. The figure of *David*, uncharacteristic of Michelangelo's works, stands in a classical pose suited to the shallow block of marble. The hero, a young colossus, is shown in the moment before his victory over Goliath. A celebration of the nude, the statue established Michelangelo as the foremost sculptor of his time, at the age of 29. The second toe of the left foot was broken by a vandal in 1991 but has been restored.

On the walls of the tribune are hung paintings by Michelangelo's Florentine contemporaries. On the right, Bronzino's *Deposition*; Pontormo's *Venus and Cupid* (on a cartoon by Michelangelo); Michele di Ridolfo del Ghirlandaio's two oval portraits; and works by Alessandro Allori and Francesco Granacci. In the hall to the left are works by Alessandro Allori (*Annunciation*), Santi di Tito (*Deposition*), Carlo Portelli and Stefano Pieri.

At the end of the hall to the left of the *David* is a huge light room. This was formerly the ward of the hospital of San Matteo which was founded in the 14C; a small detached monochrome fresco by Pontormo of the interior of the hospital is displayed here. It is now filled with a splendid display of *plaster models by Lorenzo Bartolini (1777–1850), arranged more or less as they were in his studio in Borgo San Frediano in Florence. They include the original models for his most important works, including public monuments (the allegorical figures from the Demidoff monument on Lungarno Serristori are in the centre of the room), as well as numerous tombs and portrait busts. There are also some other 19C sculptures and paintings by members of the Accademia di Belle Arti (see p 206), including casts by Luigi Pampaloni, and paintings by Luigi Mussini and Antonio Puccinelli.

Off the hall to the left of the *David* are three rooms which display the earliest Florentine paintings (13C–14C) in the gallery.

The Sala del Duecento e del Primo Trecento Dedicated to works dating from the 13C and early 14C, this room contains a *Crucifix* by a Florentine painter close to Cimabue; a *Tree of the Cross* (restored) by Pacino di Buonaguida; and *Mary Magdalen with Stories from her Life* by an unknown artist now known as the Maestro della Maddalena after this work.

The Sala degli Orcagna This room is dedicated to the Orcagna family. It includes a *Pentecost* from the high altar of Santi Apostoli by Andrea Orcagna, who also painted the *Madonna Enthroned with Saints*. There are also works by his brothers Jacopo di Cione, including *Coronation of the Virgin*, and Nardo di Cione (*Trinity and Two Saints*).

The Sala dei Giotteschi This room contains works by followers of Giotto. It has panels with *Scenes from the Life of Christ and from the life of St Francis* from a reliquary cupboard in the sacristy of Santa Croce by Taddeo Gaddi, and a *Crucifix* by Bernardo Daddi.

It is now necessary to return to the Galleria with Michelangelo's *Slaves* (see above), from which four more rooms of Florentine paintings dating from the 15C and 16C can be entered. The first three **Sale del Quattrocento fiorentino** contain 15C paintings.

Room 1 The first room has an altarpiece painted on both sides with the *Resurrection* and *Marriage of St Catherine* by Mariotto di Cristofano, and *Scenes from the Life of Christ* and the Madonna, also by him. The panel known as the *Cassone Adimari*, showing a busy wedding scene with elegant guests in period dress in front of the Baptistery, is by Lo Scheggia (1440–45), Masaccio's brother. The *Scenes from Monastic Life* (or *The Thebaids*) is now thought to be by Paolo Uccello. The *Nativity* which comes from the Villa Medici di Castello is by an unknown artist known after this work as the Master of the Castello Nativity. *Saint Barbara and Saints* is by Cosimo Rosselli and the *Annunciation* is an early work by Filippino Lippi, a copy of a painting by his father, Fra' Filippo Lippi. The 'Master of the Johnson Nativity' collaborated with Filippino in this work, and is thought to have painted the beautiful kneeling angel.

Room 2 The second small room is dominated by a large altarpiece of *Saints Stephen, James and Peter* (the figure of St Stephen is particularly striking), a work formerly attributed to Sebastiano Mainardi but now thought to be by his master Domenico Ghirlandaio. The *Pietà* is a very fine work thought to be by Jacopo del Sellaio.

Room 3 The third room displays the *Madonna and Child with the Young St

John and Two Angels, a beautiful early work by Botticelli, who probably also painted the enchanting small **Virgin of the Sea* (which has a seascape in the background). The *Madonna and Child with Saints* from the Castello di Trebbio is attributed to Botticelli, with the intervention of his *bottega*. Also here are: *St John the Baptist and St Mary Magdalen* by Filippino Lippi; *Resurrection* probably the best work of Raffaellino del Garbo; and *Adoration of the Child* by Lorenzo di Credi.

The Sala del Colosso In the centre of this large room, the **plaster model for the *Rape of the Sabine* (in the Loggia dei Lanzi) by Giambologna (1582) is displayed. Also on display here are some of the musical instruments from the Medici and Lorraine collections which will soon be exhibited in a special museum (see below). The paintings here date from the first two decades of the 16C. The **Descent from the Cross* was painted for the high altar of Santissima Annunziata. Filippino Lippi carried out only the upper part before his death in 1504, and the painting was completed by Perugino, who also painted the *Assumption and Saints* (signed and dated 1500), and (with the help of Gerino da Pistoia) *Christ on the Cross with the Madonna and Saint Jerome*. The panels of *Santa Monica* and her son *St Augustine* are by Francesco Botticini. The two prophets *Isaiah* and *Job* are by Fra' Bartolomeo. Ridolfo del Ghirlandaio painted the two *Scenes of St Zenobius*, which include remarkable contemporary portraits among the crowds as well as views of Florence. The *Annunciation* is by Mariotto Albertinelli, and the damaged fresco fragment of *Pietà* is by Andrea del Sarto.

It is now necessary to return to the rooms of the earliest paintings (see above), off the hall to the left of the *David* and take the covered way in the garden that leads to the exit and the stairs up to the first floor.

First floor

Four rooms on the first floor contain a fine collection of Florentine paintings dating from the end of the 14C and early 15C including numerous polyptychs.

Room 1 This room is named after **Giovanni da Milano**, since it displays his splendid **Pietà* (1365). Giovanni was one of the most interesting painters to succeed Giotto. Also here are other late 14C works, most of them by unknown painters.

Room 2 This contains many more **late 14C paintings** including: *Christ as Man of Sorrows with Symbols of the Passion* by Niccolò di Pietro Gerini; a polyptych of the *Madonna Enthroned with Saints* by Mariotto di Nardo; *Coronation of the Virgin* by Lorenzo di Niccolò; a polyptych in a splendid frame with an *Annunciation* in the central panel, and *St John the Evangelist Enthroned*, both by Giovanni del Biondo; a *Coronation of the Virgin* by Giovanni del Ponte (called Giovanni di Marco); and *St John the Baptist* and *St Francis* and a triptych of the *Coronation of the Virgin*, both by Rossello di Jacopo Franchi. There are also works by Spinello Aretino and Lorenzo di Bicci.

In addition to the paintings, there is an exquisitely embroidered **altar frontal* from Santa Maria Novella made by Florentine craftsmen and signed and dated 1336 by Jacopo Cambi. In the centre is the *Coronation of the Virgin between Angels and Saints* and on the border are scenes from the *Life of the Virgin* and numerous birds.

Room 3 Here are nine beautiful works by Lorenzo Monaco: **Prayer in the*

Garden, an early work painted around 1400 for the convent of Santa Maria degli Angioli where Lorenzo was a monk; *Man of Sorrows with Symbols of the Passion*; a polyptych of the *Madonna and Child Enthroned with Saints*, the *Redeemer* and *Annunciation* (1410); three small paintings (in rococo frames) of the *Madonna, St John the Evangelist* and the *Crucifixion*; a triptych of the *Annunciation* and *Saints*, painted for the Badia Fiorentina c 1418, and a painted *Cross*. A reassembled triptych has a central panel of the *Madonna with Saints and Angels* also by Monaco, and side panels attributed to an unidentified artist known as the Master of the Sherman Predella. Also here are two works by Agnolo Gaddi, including a *Madonna of Humility*, as well as a painted *Cross* by Bartolomeo di Fruosino (1411). The wall cases contain a display of 16C–18C Russian icons which entered the Lorraine grand-ducal collections in 1771–78.

Room 4 This displays works in the **International Gothic** style, including *St Francis Receiving the Stigmata* and a *Miracle of St Nicholas of Bari* by Giovanni Toscani, an *Annunciation* by the Master of the Madonna Straus, and a *Madonna and Child with Saints John the Baptist and Nicholas and Angels* by Gherardo Starnina.

Museum of musical instruments

The *Museum of musical instruments, which belongs to the Conservatorio (see below), is to be opened in another part of the building in 2001. This remarkable collection, begun by the last of the Medici and the Lorraine grand-dukes, is one of the most interesting in Italy. It includes the Viola Medicea built by Antonio Stradivari in 1690; violins and cellos by Stradivari, Guarneri, Amati and Ruggeri; a harpsichord by Bartolomeo Cristofori; and autograph compositions by important composers.

Florence has held a special place in the history of music since the change of style between Iacopo Peri's musical drama *Dafne*, performed in Palazzo Corsi in 1597, and his *Euridice* composed in 1600 to honour the marriage in Florence of Maria de' Medici to Henri IV of France, which is generally held to mark the beginning of opera. The pianoforte was invented in Florence in 1711 by Bartolomeo Cristofori (1655–1731). The composer Jean-Baptiste Lully (1632–87) was born in the city.

At the crossing of Via Ricasoli with Via degli Alfani is a small piazza with the entrance to the **Conservatorio Luigi Cherubini (Map 3; 6)**, the conservatory of music named after the greatest Florentine composer Luigi Cherubini (1760–1842) who spent most of his career in Paris.

Via degli Alfani continues left (the green dome of the synagogue is visible at the end) past the entrance (no. 78) to the Museum of the Opificio delle Pietra Dura (**Map 4; 5**).

Museum of the Opificio delle Pietre Dure

The Opificio was founded in 1588 by the Medici Grand-duke Ferdinando I, to produce mosaics in hard or semi-precious stones. Francesco I had invented the idea of making mosaics out of *pietre dure*, in imitation of classical works in marble intarsia. This refined craft, perfected in Florence (also known as *mosaico fiorentino*), is remarkable for its durability. Exquisite pieces were made in the workshops (which moved here from the Uffizi in 1798) to decorate such objects as cabinets and table-tops. Many of the best examples are preserved in Palazzo Pitti. The grand-dukes were fond of using them as gifts, often to foreign rulers. The most characteristic products are decorated with flowers, fruit and birds, against a black background. The museum, founded here at the end of the 19C, was reopened in 1995. Its newly arranged galleries provide a superb account of the workshop's history.

The headquarters of the Opificio delle Pietre Dure is also housed in this building. Since 1975, the Institute has been the seat of a state restoration and conservation laboratory dedicated to the restoration of stone, marble, bronze, terracotta and *pietre dure*. A state restoration school was set up here in 1978, and there is also a restoration archive and library. Another branch of the restoration laboratory, largely concerned with paintings and frescoes, operates in the Fortezza da Basso (see p 328).

• **Opening times** Daily 09.00–14.00 except *fest.* (☎ 055 265 111); Lire 4000 (S). The objects are all clearly labelled.

Piles of *pietre dure* left over from the deposits amassed by the grand-dukes can be seen in the courtyard. **Room 1** displays Roman fragments in porphyry as well as sculptures dating from the 16C by Francesco Ferrucci del Tadda, in which he reused ancient pieces of porphyry. There is also a tabernacle in ebony and *pietre dure* dating from the early 17C, and a portrait of Cosimo I by Francesco Ferrucci del Tadda.

In **Room 2** are works made for the Cappella dei Principi in San Lorenzo, an ambitious project begun by Ferdinando I which, if completed, would have been one of the most remarkable decorative schemes ever produced. These include 17C–19C panels executed for the altar, which was never completed, and panels intended for the decoration of the chapel walls which were begun some ten years before building commenced. On the window wall, cabinets display panels decorated with naturalistic designs in the 17C and 18C. Between the windows are numerous designs by Jacopo Ligozzi and Giuseppe Zocchi which were used by the workshop.

Room 4, at the foot of the stairs, displays 17C works made for the Medici, including some by Giovan Battista Foggini and Giuseppe Antonio Torricelli. The stairs (with *pietre dure* risers) lead up to a mezzanine floor with the 18C and 19C work benches and instruments once used by the craftsmen. Numerous catalogued samples of semi-precious stones are in wall cases. The 18C painted designs by Antonio Cioci, with shells and compositions with antique or porcelain vases, were used for the exquisite tables in *pietre dure* now in Palazzo Pitti.

On the ground floor, **Room 6** illustrates the period of the Lorraine grand-dukes, when neo-classical and more sober designs were used. **Room 7** has 18C examples (right wall) of scagliola works, many of them from Carpi in Emilia. Imitating marble and *pietre dure*, this material made from selenite was incised with a metal point. On the left wall are 17C paintings on stone. Two 19C tables, decorated with musical instruments to designs by Niccolò Betti, are particularly fine. **Room 8** contains sculptures in marble and *pietre dure* made after the Unification, and another table designed by Betti (with a gilded wood base of 1861). **Rooms 9 and 10**, the last two rooms, contain a splendid series of table tops made in the workshop from 1864–85 decorated with floral designs. The later ones, with magnolias, convolvulus and roses in Art Nouveau style, were designed by Edouard Marchionni, who was in charge of the Opificio 1873–1923. The monumental vase in the last room, also designed by him, was never finished.

Via degli Alfani continues across Via dei Servi (see below). On the right is the so-called **Rotonda di Santa Maria degli Angeli** (Map 4; 5). This octagonal building was begun by Brunelleschi in 1434 as a memorial to the soldier Filippo degli Scolari (d. 1424), and left unfinished in 1437. Modelled on the Temple of Minerva Medica in Rome, it was one of the first centralised buildings of the Renaissance. After a period of use as a church, then completed as a lecture-hall in 1959, it is now inappropriately used as a language laboratory for the University. In the square behind is the Faculty of Letters.

The entrance to the former church of **Santa Maria degli Angeli** is at no. 39 (the seat of the Amici dei Musei di Firenze). The church was remodelled in 1676 and is now used for lectures. The unusual interior with a barrel vault has frescoes by Alessandro Gherardini and stuccoes by Vittorio Barbieri and Alessandro Lombardi. In the former refectory is a fresco of the *Last Supper* (1543) by Ridolfo del Ghirlandaio. The cloister on the right of the church has graffiti decoration and lunettes by Bernardino Poccetti and Donato Mascagni, and busts attributed to Caccini and Francavilla. Off the cloister is a little chapel (1599) with a fresco in the dome by Poccetti who probably also painted the altarpiece, a detached fresco fragment of the *Pietà* (14C), and sculptured medallions attributed to Caccini and Francavilla.

At 48 Via Alfani, **Palazzo Giugni** is a characteristic work by Ammannati (1571) with a fine courtyard and small garden (with a grotto by Lorenzo Migliorini). The interesting garden façade, with a loggia, bears a copy of the family coat of arms (the original can be seen in the courtyard). The international **Lyceum Club** for ladies has occupied rooms on the first floor of the palace since 1953, and it maintains a tradition of high-quality concerts, exhibitions and lectures to which the public are welcomed. Founded in 1908 by Miss Constance Smedley, the first exhibition of the Impressionists in Italy was held here in 1910. The well-kept rooms are delightfully furnished and include a library, and a 17C galleria which preserves its decorations intact, including paintings by Alessandro Gherardini.

Via dei Servi

Via dei Servi (Map 4; 5), on the line of an ancient thoroughfare leading north from the city, is documented as early as the 12C as far as the Porta di Balla (see below). It was extended beyond the city gate in the 13C, and used by Brunelleschi in his Renaissance design of Piazza Santissima Annunziata to provide a magnificent view of the cupola of the Duomo. It is now lined by a number of handsome 16C palaces. Going towards the Duomo, on the right, nos 15 and 17 were restored in 1959 as government offices. The pretty fountain at no. 17 can be seen from the road. No. 15, **Palazzo Niccolini**, was designed by Baccio d'Agnolo in 1548–50. Its beautiful façade is typical of Florentine palaces of this period. The small courtyard has graffiti decoration, and in the garden beyond is an elaborate double loggia, probably by Giovanni Antonio Dosio. Opposite, **Palazzo Sforza Alimeni** (no. 12), c 1510–20, has two attractive ground-floor windows; the coat of arms on the corner has been replaced by a modern copy. The house across Via del Castellaccio is on the site of Benedetto da Maiano's studio, where he worked in 1480–98.

The next crossing, the Canto di Balla, is on the site of the old Porta di Balla, a postern gate in the 12C walls. Here there is a worn coat of arms by Baccio da Montelupo on the corner of **Palazzo dei Pucci**, one of the largest palaces in Florence, named after one of the oldest families in the city, who still live here. The central part of the long façade (which stretches as far as Via Ricasoli) dates from the 16C, and is in part attributed to Ammannati; the wings on either side are 17C extensions.

In the piazza is the church of **San Michele Visdomini** (Map 1; 2,4; also known as San Michelino). It is of ancient foundation and is known to have been enlarged by the Visdomini family in the 11C. It was demolished in 1363 in order to make way for the east end of the Duomo, and reconstructed on this site a few years later. Inside, on the right side are: Empoli's *Nativity* and Pontormo's **Holy Family* (commissioned in 1518 by Francesco Pucci); on the left side: Poppi's *Madonna and Saints*; Passignano's *Preaching of St John the Baptist* and Poppi, Immaculate Conception. Left transept, Poppi's *Resurrection*. The 18C vault fresco in the crossing showing the *Fall of Satan* is by Niccolò Lapi. In the chapel to the right of the high altar are interesting frescoes and sinopie, found in 1966 and attributed to Spinello Aretino. In the chapel to the left of the high altar is the 14C wood *Crucifix* 'de Bianchi' and more fresco and sinopia fragments.

Opposite the church is **Palazzo Incontri** (reconstructed in 1676) owned by Piero il Gottoso (son of Cosimo il Vecchio) in 1469. Via de' Pucci leads to Via Ricasoli, and on the corner is the **Tabernacolo delle Cinque Lampade** (of the five lamps), with a fresco (right) by Cosimo Rosselli. Via Ricasoli is named after Baron Ricasoli (1809–80), mayor of Florence. He lived at no. 9 which has a courtyard of the late 16C. The last palace on the left in Via dei Servi is Palazzo Grifoni Budini Gattai. It is thought to have been begun in 1557 by Ammannati for the Grifoni, probably to a design by Giuliano di Baccio d'Agnolo, then finished by Buontalenti and Giambologna. It has two ornate brick façades (one on the piazza) with decorative friezes and a delightful garden.

Piazza Santissima Annunziata

Piazza Santissima Annunziata (**Map 4; 5**) was designed by Brunelleschi. Surrounded on three sides by porticoes, it is the most beautiful square in Florence. On the right is the Spedale degli Innocenti; in front is the church of the Annunziata and the convent of the Servite order, with remains of five Gothic windows and to the left, the colonnade (modelled on the earlier one opposite), by Antonio da Sangallo and Baccio d'Agnolo (1516–25).

In the middle of the square is an equestrian statue of the Grand-duke Ferdinando I, by Giambologna; it was his last work and was cast by Tacca in 1608, who also designed the base. The two small symmetrical bronze fountains with bizarre monsters and marine decorations are delightful Mannerist works also by Tacca (with the help of his pupils Bartolomeo Salvini and Francesco Maria Bandini). Fairs with market stalls are held in the piazza on the festival of the Annunziata (25 March), 7 September (and the weekend before), and 8 December.

Spedale degli Innocenti

The Spedale degli Innocenti (**Map 4; 5**; its correct name is Ospedale degli Innocenti), was opened in 1445 as a foundling hospital, the first institution of its kind in Europe. It operated as an orphanage up until 2000 and is still an Institute dedicated to the education and care of children, and it is also used by UNICEF.

The Arte della Seta (silk makers guild) commissioned Brunelleschi (who, as a goldsmith, was a member of the Guild) to begin work on the building in 1419.

History of the Spedale degli Innocenti

Vincenzo Borghini, prior here from 1552–80, was an outstanding figure in 16C Florence—friend of Vasari's and counsellor to Duke Cosimo on artistic and literary matters. In the 16C, the Institute was able to care for some 2000 babies, and by the 19C this figure had increased to 3000. The first school of obstetrics in Italy was founded here, and pioneering studies into nutrition and vaccination were carried out in the hospital (cows and goats were kept in the garden). Some of the 2000 precious volumes dating from the 16C–19C which formed part of the library of the Società Filoiatrica Fiorentina, a learned society of doctors founded by Giuseppe Bertini in 1812 for the study of medicine, are preserved here, including some rare medical tracts, as well as models used for study purposes and surgical instruments.

Exterior

The *colonnade (1419–26) of nine arches is one of the first masterpieces of Renaissance architecture by Brunelleschi, inspired by classical antiquity as well as local Romanesque buildings. The last bays on the right and left were added in the 19C. In the spandrels are delightful *medallions, perhaps the best-known work of Andrea della Robbia (1487), each with a baby in swaddling-clothes against a bright blue background (the two end ones on each side are excellent copies made in 1842–43). Beneath the portico at the left end is the *rota* (turning-box or wheel) constructed in 1660 to receive abandoned babies. Before that time, orphan babies used to be abandoned between the figures of Mary and Joseph in a terracotta crib by Matteo Civitali, which is still kept in the hospital. The *rota* was walled up in 1875. The fresco under the central vault of the colonnade is by Bernardino Poccetti (1610), that in the lunette above the door of the church is by Giovanni di Francesco (1459; very damaged).

Medallion by Andrea della Robbia on the Spedale degli Innocenti

The **church** (open in the early morning only) was remodelled in neo-classical style in 1786 by Bernardo Fallani. It contains an altarpiece of the **Annunciation** by Mariotto Albertinelli and Giovanni Antonio Sogliani.

Interior of the convent

The convent, which houses the **Museo dello Spedale degli Innocenti**, may be visited (opening times 08.30–14.00 except Wed; ☎ 055 249 1708; Lire 5000), as well as the oldest parts of the convent buildings, designed by Brunelleschi. The main **Chiostro degli Uomini** (reserved for the men who worked in the Institute,

1422–45) was decorated in 1596 with a clock-tower, and graffiti (drawn with lime) showing the emblems of the Arte della Seta and the other two hospital foundations (San Gallo and Santa Maria alla Scala), which were united here in the 15C. Over the side door into the church is a pretty lunette of the *Annunciation* by Andrea della Robbia.

A door on the right leads out of the far side of the courtyard to the oblong *Chiostro delle Donne** (1438), another beautiful work by Brunelleschi, with 24 slender Ionic columns beneath a low loggia. The charming perspective of the colonnades is reminiscent of the background which appears in some Renaissance paintings. This part of the convent was reserved for the women who worked in the Institute. There is now a collection of games and toys in rooms off the cloister which is open to children (who can borrow them, as in a lending library). Exhibitions are also held in this part of the convent. The **archives** are preserved intact including the first register of 1445. They are now housed in an 18C room with handsome 19C bookcases.

Pinacoteca On the left of the Chiostro delle Uomini, stairs lead up to a long gallery (formerly the day nursery) which has been arranged as a Pinacoteca. On the left of the ticket desk, paintings include: *Coronation of the Virgin*, the master piece of the Master of the Madonna Straus; *Annunciation Between Saints* by Giovanni del Biondo; a detached fresco of the *Madonna and Child* by Cenni di Francesco; and *Coronation of the Virgin* by Neri di Bicci. The *Madonna and Child with an Angel* is an interesting early work by Botticelli, copied from his master Filippo Lippi. The bust of Cione di Lapo Pollini dates from 1536.

Beyond the archway is a little room dominated by the splendid *Adoration of the Magi* by Domenico Ghirlandaio. The brightly coloured work includes a scene of the *Massacre of the Innocents* and two child Saints in the foreground. The predella is by Bartolomeo di Giovanni. The altarpiece was commissioned for the high altar of the convent church by the prior, Francesco Tesori (d. 1497), whose tomb-slab has been placed in the floor here. The *Madonna and Child* in glazed terracotta by Luca della Robbia (c 1445–50) is one of his most beautiful works. The painting of the *Madonna Enthroned* is by Piero di Cosimo.

On the right side of the ticket desk the paintings include a triptych of the *Madonna and Child with Saints* by Giovanni di Francesco Toscani (usually identified with the Maestro della Crocifissione Gregg); *Madonna Protecting the 'Innocenti'* attributed to Pontormo; and the *Madonna of the Innocenti* attributed to Jacopino del Conte. At the far end of the room are illuminated choir books and a case which displays a touching series of 'identification tags' left by destitute mothers with their abandoned babies in the 19C, in the hope that one day they would be able to be reunited with them.

Santissima Annunziata

The church of the Santissima Annunziata (**Map 4; 5**; opening times 07.30– 12.30, 16.00–18.30) was founded by the seven original Florentine members of the Servite Order in 1250, and rebuilt, along with the cloister, by Michelozzo and others in 1444–81. Housing a famous painting of the Annunciation— held to be miraculous—it was one of the most important sanctuaries dedicated to the Madonna in Europe. Of the portico, the central arch is ascribed to Antonio da Sangallo, the rest is by Giovanni Battista Caccini (1600). Above the

SANTA CROCE

A selection of the works of art

chapels

A. *Castellani Chapel* - **AGNOLO GADDI**
B. *Baroncelli Chapel* - **TADDEO GADDI**
C. *Rinuccini Chapel* - **GIOVANNI DA MILANO**
D. *Velluti Chapel* - **GIOVANNI DEL BIONDO**
E. *Riccardi Chapel* - **GIOVANNI DA SAN GIOVANNI**
F. *Peruzzi Chapel* - **GIOTTO**
G. *Bardi Chapel* - **GIOTTO**
H. *Maggiore Chapel* - **AGNOLO GADDI**
I. *Pulci Beraldi Chapel* - **BERNARDO DADDI**
K. *Bardi di Vernio Chapel* - **MASO DI BANCO**
L. *Niccolini Chapel* - **VOLTERRANO**
M. *Bardi di Vernio Chapel* - **DONATELLO**
N. *Machiavelli or Salviati Chapel*
   - SOFIA ZAMOYSKA - **LORENZO BARTOLINI**

funerary monuments, altars and museum

1. *Crucifixion* - **SANTI DI TITO**
2. MICHELANGELO BUONARROTI
3. *The "Madonna del latte"* - **ANTONIO ROSSELLINO**
4. *Ascent to the calvary* - **GIORGIO VASARI**
5. DANTE ALIGHIERI
6. VITTORIO ALFIERI - **ANTONIO CANOVA**
7. *Pulpit* - **BENEDETTO DA MAIANO**
8. NICCOLÒ MACHIAVELLI
9. *Annunciation* - **DONATELLO**
10. LEONARDO BRUNI - **BERNARDO ROSSELLINO**
11. GIOACCHINO ROSSINI
12. *Christ's entry into Jerusalem* - **CIGOLI**
13. UGO FOSCOLO
14. *Deposition* - **ALESSANDRO ALLORI**
15. LEON BATTISTA ALBERTI - **LORENZO BARTOLINI**
16. *Pentecost* - **GIORGIO VASARI**
17. CARLO MARSUPPINI - **DESIDERIO DA SETTIGNANO**
18. *Pietà* - **AGNOLO BRONZINO**
19. *The incredulity of St. Thomas* - **GIORGIO VASARI**
20. *Supper at Emmaus* - **SANTI DI TITO**
21. *Resurrection* - **SANTI DI TITO**
22. GALILEO GALILEI
23. *Crucifix* - **CIMABUE**
24. *Tree of the cross* - **TADDEO GADDI**
25. *Saint Lodovic* - **DONATELLO**
26. *Saint Francis and San Giovanni Battista*
    - **DOMENICO VENEZIANO**
27. *Saint Francis receiving the stigmata*
    - **ANDREA DELLA ROBBIA**
28. GASTONE DELLA TORRE
    - **TINO DI CAMAINO**

ENTRANCE	🔼 ●
EXIT	🔽 ●
TOILET	🚻 ●
BOOKSHOP	📖 ●
INFORMATION	*i* ●
DISABLED ENTRANCE	♿ ●
TICKET OFFICE	💼 ●

THE HISTORY

The Basilica of Santa Croce in Florence, which they began to build in 1294 according to the plans of Arnolfo di Cambio, is the largest Franciscan church in the world. It was constructed with funding from the population and the Florentine Republic and built above the foundations of a small church which some monks had erected outside the walls of the city in 1252, just a few years after the death of Saint Francis. The remains of the original building were not identified until 1966, when, in the aftermath of the great flood that submerged the city, part of the paving belonging to the present Basilica gave way. From its beginnings, the history of Santa Croce has been closely linked to the history of Florence itself. Since its foundation, it has been continually re-planned and re-designed throughout the course of those seven centuries without suffering significant interruptions, and therefore acquiring new symbolic connotations each time. From the original Franciscan church it evolved to become a religious "town hall" for the important families and corporations when Florence was ruled by the Medici family. From being a craftsmen's laboratory and work-shop - first Humanist and then Renaissance – it became a theological centre; and in the 19th Century, it saw a change from being a pantheon of the nation's glories to a place of reference for the political history of Italy before and after its unification.

In Florence, Santa Croce has always been a prestigious symbol and a gathering place for some of the greatest artists, theologians, religious figures, writers, humanists and politicians. It has similarly served the powerful families that throughout the centuries have determined, both for good and bad, the identity of Florence during the Late Mediaeval and Renaissance periods. Within its walls, it has hosted many famous people in the history of the church, such as Saint

Bonaventure, Saint Anthony of Padua, Saint Bernadino of Siena, Saint Ludovico d'Angiò and the bishop of Tolosa. It was also a resting and reception place for Pontiffs such as Sixtus IV, Eugene IV, Leo X and Clement XIV.

With its impressive gothic architecture, marvellous frescoes, altar pieces, precious stained-glass windows and numerous sculptures, the Basilica represents one of the most important pages in the history of Florentine art from the thirteenth century onwards.

Inside it houses works of art by Cimabue, Giotto, Filippo Brunelleschi, Donatello, Giorgio Vasari, Lorenzo Ghiberti, Orcagna, Taddeo and Agnolo Gaddi, Della Robbia, Giovanni da Milano, Bronzino, Michelozzo, Domenico Veneziano, Maso di Banco, Giuliano da Sangallo, Benedetto da Maiano, Canova and many others.

In particular, the presence of Giotto and his school of art makes Santa Croce an extraordinarily complete testimony of Fourteenth Century Florentine art.

The historical and political upheavals that have accompanied Santa Croce right up until today have always left a precise mark as much in the artistic-architectural works (such as the radical transformations imposed by Vasari around the middle of the sixteenth century; or the exuberant commitment during the nineteenth century to transforming Santa Croce into a huge mausoleum of Italian history), as in the testimonies guarded in its archives which hand down to us a daily reconstruction, through the course of the centuries, of a great project befitting its own creators, its own resources, its own objectives and difficulties.

Santa Croce has been defined as "the Pantheon of the nation's glories" because within its walls are the tombs of famous figures such as Nicolò Macchiavelli, Galileo Galilei, Michelangelo Buonarroti, Gioacchino Rossini, Giorgio Vasari, Lorenzo Ghiberti, Vittorio Alfieri and Ugo Foscolo.

The indisputable fascination that this place exerts, in an unequalled synthesis of art, spirituality and history, is confirmed by the influx of around one million visitors a year.

OPENING HOURS

MONDAY THROUGH SATURDAYS 9,30-17,30
(TICKET OFFICE CLOSES AT 17,00)

SUNDAYS AND HOLIDAYS 13,00 -17,30 hrs
(TICKET OFFICE CLOSES AT 17,00 hrs)

FREE ADMISSION

1. FOR RELIGIOUS SERVICES

2. CHILDREN UNDER 11 YEARS OF AGE

3. DISABLED AND THEIR ESCORTS

4. RESIDENTS OF FLORENCE

5. TOUR GUIDES

REDUCTIONS

1. FROM 11 TO 18 YEARS OF AGE

2. GROUPS OF OVER 15 PERSONS, SCHOOL
   GROUPS AND ACCOMPANYING ADULTS

OPERA DI SANTA CROCE

PIAZZA SANTA CROCE 16
50122 FIRENZE
TEL.: 055 24 66 105
FAX: 055 24 66 105
E-MAIL: INFO@OPERADISANTACROCE.IT

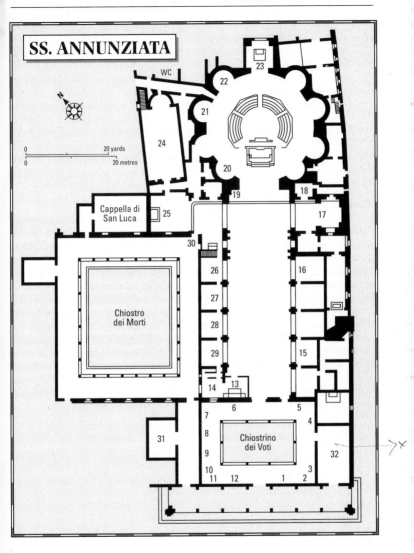

SS. ANNUNZIATA

WC

23
22
21
24
20
19
18
17

Cappella di
San Luca
25
30
26
16
27
Chiostro
dei Morti
28
29
15
14   13
6
5
7
8
4
31
Chiostrino
dei Voti
9
32
10
3
11   12
1
2

N

0   20 yards
0   20 metres

middle door is a lunette with an Annunciation in mosaic (very damaged) by
Davide Ghirlandaio.

The atrium

The atrium or Chiostrino dei Voti by Manetti (1447) is based on a design by
Michelozzo. The series of **Mannerist frescoes** on the walls are particularly
interesting since most of them were painted in the second decade of the 16C by
the leading artists of the time. They suffered from humidity and have been

Original site for Landor Pallainolo 1475

detached and restored before being returned here. Right to left: Rosso Fiorentino, *Assumption* (**1**), a very early work; Pontormo, *Visitation* (**2**); showing the influence of Andrea del Sarto); Franciabigio, *Marriage of the Virgin* (**3**)—the head of the Virgin was damaged by the painter himself in a fit of anger. Beyond, a marble bas-relief of the *Madonna and Child* by an unknown sculptor (sometimes attributed to Michelozzo); Andrea del Sarto, *Birth of the Virgin* (**4**) and the *Coming of the Magi* (**5**), which contains Andrea del Sarto's self-portrait in the right-hand corner. Two bronze stoups by Antonio Susini (1615) stand in front of the west door. The colours in the fresco of the *Nativity* (**6**) by Alesso Baldovinetti (1460–62) have faded because they were badly prepared by the artist. The landscape is particularly beautiful. Beyond the *Vocation and Investiture of San Filippo Benizzi* (**7**) by Cosimo Rosselli (1476) are more scenes of *San Filippo* (**8–12**), interesting (but damaged) works by Andrea del Sarto (1509–10).

The interior

The heavily decorated and dark interior has a rich ceiling by Pietro Giambelli (1664–69) on a design by Volterrano. The nave has stucco and painted decoration by Cosimo Ulivelli, Francesco Silvani, Pier Dandini and Tommaso Redi (c 1703). At the west end, the shrine of the Madonna (**13**), still highly venerated by Florentines, is bedecked with ex-votos, hanging lamps and candles. The huge *tabernacle* (almost hidden by the devotional images), commissioned by Piero il Gottoso (dei Medici), was designed by Michelozzo and executed by Pagno di Lapo Portigiani (1448–61) to protect the miraculous painting of the *Annunciation*. It has a bronze grille by Maso di Bartolomeo and an incongruous 17C canopy. The highly venerated painting of the *Annunciation* (also difficult to see) was traditionally thought to have been painted by a friar who was miraculously assisted by an angel. The adjoining chapel (**14**) was built as an oratory for the Medici (1453–63). It has five beautiful panels inlaid in *pietre dure* dating from 1671 with the *Symbols of the Virgin* (the rose, lily, moon, sun and star). Here, amidst ex-votos, is a small painting by Andrea del Sarto of the *Redeemer* (1515).

South side The first chapel contains an altarpiece of the *Madonna* by Empoli and vault frescoes by Matteo Rosselli. The second chapel (**15**) has a wooden *Crucifix* by Antonio da Sangallo (1483) and a neo-classical funerary monument to Luigi Tempi by Ulisse Cambi (1849). The third chapel, the Colloredo chapel, was designed by Matteo Nigetti in 1651. The frescoes in the cupola are by Volterrano. In the fifth chapel (**16**), there is a monument to Orlando de' Medici, a delicate work by Bernardo Rossellino (1456). In the transept chapel (**17**), built to a design by Ferdinando Fuga in 1768, the small painted processional *Cross* is attributed to Andrea del Castagno. In the next chapel (**18**), there is a *Dead Christ Supported by Nicodemus*, whose head is a self-portrait of the sculptor Bandinelli (he is buried here). On the back of the monument are two small reliefs with the portraits of Bandinelli and his wife. In the nave is a splendid *organ* (1509–21) by Domenico di Lorenzo da Lucca, and Matteo da Prato. It is the oldest in the city, and the second oldest in Italy, and the only organ by Domenico di Lorenzo to have survived virtually intact.

Tribune The large circular tribune at the east end of the church was begun by Michelozzo and completed in 1477 by Leon Battista Alberti, at the expense of Ludovico Gonzaga. It has a very unusual design: a rotonda preceded by a triumphal arch, derived from ancient Roman architecture. The huge fresco in the cupola shows the **Coronation of the Virgin** and is by Volterrano. The high altar, with a frontal by Giovanni Battista Foggini (1682), bears a silver ciborium by Antonio Merlini (1656) to a design by Alfonso Parigi. Behind (difficult to see) are the choir stalls and two lecterns of English workmanship (15C). On the left of the great arch, in the pavement beneath a statue of St Peter by Pier Francesco Silvani, is the burial place of Andrea del Sarto. The *tomb of Bishop Angelo Marzi Medici (**19**) is signed by Francesco da Sangallo (1546) and has an expressive effigy of the Bishop, charged with the fervour of the Counter-Reformation.

The entrance to the nine semicircular chapels which radiate from the sanctuary is on the left. In the chapel to the right (**20**) is Alessandro Allori's **Birth of Mary** and four paintings of the **Miracles of the Blessed Manetti** (one of the founders) by his son, Cristofano Allori. In the chapels to the left are: *Madonna and Saints* (**21**) by Perugino; **Resurrection** by Bronzino and a wooden statue of **St Roch** by Veit Stoss (**22**; removed). The east chapel (**23**) was reconstructed by Giambologna as his own tomb, and contains fine bronze reliefs and a bronze **Crucifix** by him, and statues by his pupils including Francavilla. The **Madonna and Child** is attributed to Bernardo Daddi. Behind the altar, above the sarcophagus of Giambologna and Pietro Tacca, is a **Pietà** by Ligozzi. The **sacristy** (**24**; usually locked), with a fine vault, was built by Pagno di Lapo from Michelozzo's design.

The chapel in the **north transept** (**25**) is also the work of Michelozzo (1445–47) and contains a terracotta statue of the **Baptist** by him. The walls were covered in 1746 by trompe l'œil frescoes. The **Deposition** (removed) was painted by Ferdinando Folchi (1855). A door here leads to the cloisters (see below).

North side The fourth chapel on the north side of the nave (**26**) contains an **Assumption** by Perugino; the third chapel (**27**), a **Crucifixion** by Giovanni Stradano. The **Last Judgement** by Alessandro Allori is a copy of various figures in Michelangelo's fresco in the Sistine Chapel. In the second chapel (**28**), there is a fresco of the *Holy Trinity with St Jerome* by Andrea del Castagno. The elaborate Cappella Feroni (**29**) is a fine Baroque work by Giovanni Battista Foggini (1692). Behind the altarpiece (shown on request) there is another fresco by Castagno showing *St Julian and the Saviour*.

The cloisters

The cloisters, known as the Chiostro dei Morti, because they contain memorial stones to the dead, are entered from the door in the north transept of the church (unlocked on request in the sacristy), or from outside the church by the door on the left of the portico. Over the door into the church (**30**) is Andrea del Sarto's *Madonna del Sacco* (which gets its name from the sack that St Joseph is leaning on), an original portrayal of the Rest on the Flight into Egypt and one of the artist's best works. The other colourful frescoed lunettes in the cloister are by Donato Mascagni, Bernardino Poccetti, Matteo Rosselli and Ventura Salimbeni. They illustrate the origins of the Servite order and are interesting documents of 17C Florence.

The **Cappella di San Luca** is also sometimes opened on request in the sacristy; it has belonged to the Accademia delle Arti del Disegno since 1565 and a special Mass for artists is held on St Luke's Day (18 October). In the vault below are buried Cellini, Pontormo, Franciabigio, Montorsoli, Bartolini, and many other artists. In the vestibule is a **Crucifix** attributed to Antonio da Sangallo and a 15C sinopia of the **Madonna Enthroned**. The chapel altarpiece of **St Luke**

Painting the Madonna is an interesting self-portrait by Vasari, a founder member of the Academy. North wall: a detached (and damaged) fresco by Pontormo of the *Madonna with Saints* (including St Lucy). South wall: a fresco of the *Trinity* by Alessandro Allori. On the west wall, Santi di Tito, *Allegory of Architecture*. The ceiling fresco of the Vision of St Bernard is by Luca Giordano. The clay statues which lean dramatically out of their niches are the work of various Academicians, including Montorsoli (who was also a member of the Servite Order). The small organ (1702) was made by Tommaso Fabbri da Faenza.

In the **refectory** (usually closed), there are sketches made in 1358 by Francesco Talenti and Giovanni di Lapo Ghini for the columns and capitals in the Duomo and a fresco by Santi di Tito.

The 17C **Sagrestia della Madonna** (31), also off the cloister, has an *Assumption* by Jacopo Vignali. The **Oratorio di San Sebastiano** (32; usually closed), entered from the portico (right of the atrium) has a vault fresco by Poccetti. The convent also owns a rich treasury (with works of art from the 13C–19C).

Museo Archeologico

Via della Colonna leads out of Piazza Santissima Annunziata beneath an archway and skirts Palazzo della Crocetta, with its garden. This palace was built for the Grand-duchess Maria Maddalena of Austria in 1620, probably by Giulio Parigi. It has been the home of the Museo Archeologico (**Map 4; 5**; entrance at no. 38) since 1879, which includes one of the most important collections of Etruscan antiquities in existence.

- **Opening times** Mon 14.00–19.00; Tues and Thurs 08.30–19.00; Wed, Fri, Sat and Sun 08.30–14.00; in summer also on Sat 21.00–24.00 (☎ 055 23575); Lire 8000 (S).

The museum has been in the process of rearranging its collection for decades, and most of the topographical section devoted to Etruscan sites in Tuscany is closed at present.

History of the museum

The Etruscan Museum was founded in 1870 and many of its most precious artefacts came from the Medici collections. The Etruscan Topographical Museum was inaugurated in 1897 by Luigi Adriano Milani. The Egyptian Museum was founded by Leopold II after the Egyptian expedition in 1828–29 organised by the Egyptologist Ippolito Rosellini and François Champollion, the French archaeologist and founder of modern Egyptology. In 1845, Leopold II also acquired the famous François vase (see p 204).

At the bottom of the stairs is a bust of *Ippolito Rosellini* and some heavy Egyptian sculptures, including limestone sarcophagi, a pink granite sarcophagus, and a small tabernacle from the Temple of Isis from an island in the Nile. At the top of the stairs is a painting by Giuseppe Angelelli of 1830 showing the *Franco-Tuscan expedition to Egypt*.

Egyptian Museum

The Egyptian Museum is housed on the first floor, and its entrance is at the top of the stairs on the left. The decoration of the rooms, in Egyptian style, was carried out in 1881–94. **Room I** displays works from the Prehistoric period to the Middle

Kingdom, including two fine polychrome statuettes (restored) of a maidservant preparing yeast for beer and a maidservant kneading dough (c 2480–2180 BC). There is also a granite statue of a Pharaoh from the period of the Middle Kingdom. **Room II** shows material of the XIIth Dynasty (19C BC), including funerary stelae and objects found in tombs. There are bas-reliefs, among them one with the plan of a tomb preceded by a courtyard (14C BC); one showing craftsmen at work (7C–6C BC); a polychrome relief for the tomb of Seti I, representing the goddess Ma'at and Hathor, and the Pharaoh (c 1292 BC); and a fragment showing scribes (c 1400 BC).

Rooms III has finds from 1780–1551 BC including *canopic* vases and a granite statue from Thebes. The portrait of a young woman from the Fayum necropolis dates from the Roman period (1–2C AD). The very rare Hittite *chariot made of wood and bone which was found in a Theban tomb dates from the 14C BC (it was probably used by the man with whom it was buried). **Rooms IV and V** are two parts of the same room which display material from the 18th and 19th dynasties (1552–1186 BC). In **Room IV** are reliefs from tombs and stele and in **Room V** are a small limestone pyramid dedicated to Nehi and a painted relief from the tomb of Sethos I at Thebes. **Room VI** displays more finds from Thebes (1552–1186 BC) including sarcophagi, vases, and stele. Around the walls are exhibited papyri of the 'Book of the Dead'. **Room VII** contains finds from Saqqara (1552–1186 BC). Funerary stele, statuettes, reliefs and *canopic* vases, *ushabtis* and scarabs. **Room VIII** preserves its delightful decorations in the Egyptian style and old-fashioned show-cases. It contains mummies and mummy-cases, *canopic* vases, basket work, furniture, objects of daily use and musical instruments. **Room XI** has finds from Saqqara (664–343 BC) including a huge limestone coffin and *canopic* jars. **Room XII** has a temporary exhibition of Rosellini's *The Monuments of Egypt and Nubia*, published 1832–44, and stelae, sculptures, glass and papyri dating from Greek and Roman Egypt (378 BC–6C AD). The last **Room XIII** contains finds from the city founded in Egypt in 130 AD by Hadrian and named after his favourite Antinuous. The remarkable Coptic fabrics (some of them kept in open drawers) include clothing.

The Etruscan, Greek and Roman collections

These sections of the museum are at present entered from Room XI of the Egyptian Museum.

The long gallery (**Room XIV**) contains three important monumental bronzes. The first of these is the *Chimera*, which was found outside Arezzo in 1553 and acquired by Cosimo I. This is a famous representation of the chimera, a mythical animal, with the body and head of a lion, the head of a goat on its back, and a serpent's tail (incorrectly restored in 1785). The myth relates that the chimera was killed by Bellerophon, and it is here shown wounded. It is an Etruscan ex-voto probably dating from the end of 5C or beginning of 4C BC and it was made in southern Etruria (Chiusi, Arezzo or the Val di Chiana). The second monumental bronze is the statue of *Minerva* (removed for restoration), which was found in 1541 in Arezzo and acquired by Cosimo I in 1552. In the 16C, the lower part of the statue was assembled in plaster, and in the 18C the right arm was wrongly restored. It is thought to be a Roman or Etruscan copy from an original by Praxiteles. The *Arringatore* is the last of these bronzes; it shows the orator Aule Meteli (son of Vel) and was found at Pila near Perugia and acquired by Cosimo I in 1566. It is a votive statue made in seven parts, dating from the late Republican era. In the old-fashioned showcases there is also a large collection of Etruscan and Roman small bronzes (poorly labelled).

The two rooms entered from the right of the gallery are devoted to Etruscan funerary sculpture. **Room X** has Etruscan urns with mythological subjects and scenes from the heroic cycles of the Greek world. In the centre, alabaster sarcophagus from Tarquinia (4C BC) with tempera paintings of a battle between the Greeks and Amazons. **Room XI** exhibits Etruscan urns, sarcophagi and statues. These include an urn in the form of an Etruscan house; an urn with banqueting and dancing scene; and a *sarcophagus lid in alabaster with an obese Etruscan, found in Chiusi and dated 300–250. Four important works from the Etruscan Topographical Museum (at present closed) are also displayed here: the famous *Mater Matuta* is a *canopic* vase in the form of a woman (a portrait of the deceased) on a throne holding a baby. Made out of volcanic tufa, it was found in 1846–47 and dates from c 440. The *tomb of the noblewoman Larthia Seianti** (wife of Sevnia) shows her reclining effigy adorned with jewels. Her name is incised on the border of the sarcophagus. It was found in 1877 and is dated 150 BC. The cinerary urn (no. 73577) with a man (the head is not original) and a woman (late 5C or early 4C) is the earliest known large polychrome alabaster urn. The other urn bears a realistic portrait of the dead with the goddess Vanth. It is made out of stone similar to volcanic tufa and dates from the beginning of the 4C BC.

At the end of the long gallery (see above) is **Room XV** which has a fine display of Etruscan inscribed mirrors in bronze, and (in the central case) Etruscan bronze armour. From here a door leads into the **Corridoio delle Gemme** (unlocked on request for a maximum of 10 people about every hour). This is a long covered passageway built in the 15C to connect the monastery to the church of Santissima Annunziata. It was restored in 1996 to exhibit the Medici and Lorraine grand-ducal *collection of precious stones, gems, cameos and jewellery**. They are beautifully arranged by subject matter, with classical pieces displayed beside those dating from the 15C–18C. They are labelled in Italian: AC, or *avanti Cristo*, means before Christ (BC), and DC, or *dopo Cristo*, means after Christ (AD). In the first case is a cameo restored in gold by Benvenuto Cellini, and a gem bearing the initials of Lorenzo il Magnifico. At the far end of the corridor a passageway leads to a balcony overlooking the inside the church of Santissima Annunziata. This was built for Maria Maddalena, the invalid daughter of the grand-duke Ferdinando I and Maria Cristina of Lorraine, so that she could be present when Mass was held in the church.

The modern pavilion Set on two floors, this encloses the Corridoio delle Gemme, and is now used for exhibitions on the ground floor. On the balcony, the most famous work in the collection, the *Idolino*, will be displayed after its restoration. This is a remarkable bronze statue of a young man, thought to have been used as a lamp stand at banquets. There is still uncertainty about its date and attribution: the torso appears to date from the 1C BC and the head is in the style of Polyclitus. It is now usually considered a Roman copy of a Greek original, but in the past it was identified as a Greek original of 450–430

BC. It was found at Pesaro in 1530 and donated to Francesco I Maria della Rovere, Duke of Urbino. It passed to the Medici when Ferdinando II married Vittoria della Rovere. The pedestal (c 1543–50) is attributed to Girolamo Lombardo.

The fine display of *jewellery comes mostly from 18C and 19C collections, much of it from that of the grand duke Pietro Leopoldo. The first case displays material acquired by the museum in the 1890s from the Passerini collection (including Hellenistic jewellery from Bettolle near Siena); the Pacini collection of eleven silver fibulae; and the Piccolomini collection of goldsmiths' work from Sinalunga (7C–6C BC). There is also material from the 8C–6C BC, from Pescia Romana, and a late Antique fibula from Volterra (7C AD). Nos 202–203 (a fibula and a pair of earrings) donated to the museum in 1911 are now recognised as fakes. The second case contains antique gold jewellery from the collection of Sir William Currie which he donated to the museum in 1863; this consists of Etruscan gold ornaments from Southern Etruria. In the third case is goldsmiths' work from Orbetello (early 3C BC), the Cinci collection from Volterra acquired in 1828. The fourth case has more material from Orbetello (4C–3C BC) and also acquired in the early 19C. At the far end is the Galluzzi collection from Volterra purchased in 1768 by Pietro Leopoldo, with jewellery dating from the 1C BC–6C AD.

It is likely that a splendid *silver amphora decorated with 132 concave medallions in bas-relief will also be displayed here. This amphora is thought to originate from Antioch, and to date from 380–390 AD, possibly the work of a Syrian silversmith. It was found in the sea off Baratti in 1968. The gilded silver situla from Chiusi dates from the end of the 7C BC, and shows orientalising influence; the *patera* is a work of the late 4C BC. The gold fibula from Populonia acquired in 1911 is now usually recognised as a fake. The silver presentation plate of Flavius Adraburius Aspar (5C AD) from Carthage (found in 1769 near Grosseto), and the back of a throne with silver and bronze intarsia dating from the 4C AD may also be displayed here.

There is also a collection of ancient Greek, Roman, medieval and modern Italian coins.

On the **second floor**, there is a splendid collection of Attic vases (see below), but just before the galleries displaying this, there is a room to the right that exhibits **Geometric Greek pottery** from Attica dating from the 8C BC.

The Attic vases

This outstanding *collection of Attic vases is displayed in 11 rooms on the second floor. All the exhibits are well labelled and they make an extremely interesting study of the development of black-figure and red-figure vases in the 6C and 5C BC. They are decorated with numerous representations of the Greek myths as well as scenes of everyday life. The nucleus of the collection goes back to the time of the Medici, but it was considerably augmented by finds from excavations in Tuscany ordered by the Lorraine grand-dukes and in particular in the early 19C. Some of the works come from the important collection of Augusto Campana.

Room I 7C and 6C BC vases from Corinth and Athens. Cases 1 and 2: black-figure vases by the Gorgon Painter or his circle. Case 3: black-figure kylixes. Cases 5 and 6: fine amphorae, some signed by Lydos.

François Vase

This unique work is displayed on its own. It is a huge and magnificent Attic crater—beautifully proportioned despite its vast dimensions—which bears the signatures of the potter Ergotimos and the painter Kleitias. One of the earliest black-figure Attic vases known, it was made in Athens c 570 BC. It was discovered by Alessandro François in an Etruscan tomb at Fonte Rotella, Chiusi, in 1844 and was restored in 1845—and twice more, in 1900–02 (after it had been broken) and in 1973. It was used for mixing wine with water at banquets. The decoration comprises six rows of more than 200 exquisite black-figure paintings of mythological scenes, identified by inscriptions.

The largest and widest band shows the arrival of the gods after the wedding of Peleus and Thetis. In the band below, we can see the pursuit of Troilos by Achilles, and the return of Hephaistos to Olympus. In the lowest band are six decorative groups of symbolic animals, while on the foot of the vase, there is an exquisite little frieze showing the battle between the pygmies and cranes. Around the rim of the crater is the Kalydonian boar hunt, and a dance of the youths and maidens liberated by the killing of the Minotaur by Theseus (who is shown playing the lyre, opposite Ariadne). In the band below, the chariot race at the funeral games of Patroklos is depicted, and the battle between Centaurs and Lapiths. On the handles are the winged figure of Artemis as queen of wild beasts, and Ajax carrying the dead body of Achilles (having been killed by Paris).

Room II Case I: an amphora with Theseus and the minotaur. Cases 2 and 3: kylixes, one with an octopus. Case 4: amphorae with scenes of Hercules; a hydria with a quadriga and warriors; and a restored kylix with two exquisite female figures. Case 5: examples of works in the mannerist style by the so-called Affecter, including an amphora (c 559 BC) with Zeus enthroned. Case 6: an amphora with a scene of Theseus killing the minotaur. Wall case: a hydria with a row of women bearing water from a fountain.

From here there is access to three rooms which have a temporary display of **Greek and Roman bronzes** belonging to the museum. Exhibited in the far room is a bronze torso of an athlete, found in the sea off Livorno, now thought to be a Greek original of c 480–470 BC. Owned by Cosimo I, it is the earliest known example of a Greek bronze statue cast with the lost-wax technique. The *horse's head* probably came from a Greek quadriga group of the 2C–1C BC. Owned by Lorenzo il Magnifico, it is thought that both Verrocchio and Donatello saw it in the garden of the Palazzo Medici-Riccardi (where it was used as a fountain) before they began work on their own equestrian statues. Small Renaissance bronzes after classical works are also exhibited here. In the second room, the display includes a bronze head of *Antinous*, which belonged to the Medici and has recently been identified as an original (it is the only bronze head of Antinous to survive); helmets in the form of masks found in a marble quarry at Serre di Rapolano; bronzes found on an island in the Arno near Signa; and four bronze portrait heads, only one of which, larger than life size, is probably an original late Roman work of 3C AD. The last room contains four bronze heads, known as the Philosophers of Melonia, which were found in the sea near Livorno in 1722. Long considered rare Roman replicas of Greek originals, they are now believed to date from the 17C. The Roman bronze model of the branch of a tree with a serpent emerging from the trunk (1C AD), found in the sea near the island of Gorgona in 1873, was used as a candelabrum for oil lamps.

Beyond is a **corridor** which displays sculptures, some Greek originals and some Roman copies of Greek works. The two fine **Archaic Greek kourai** were acquired by Luigi Adriano Milani in 1902. The date of the larger one, known as *Apollo*, is usually attributed to c 530 BC. The *Apollino* dates instead from 520–510 BC. The small head of an athlete is a Roman copy (or restoration) of a Greek original of 440 BC; the male torso is a 5C BC Roman copy; and the female head is a Greek work of 575–550 BC. Off the corridor are more rooms which continue the display of Attic vases.

Room IV Entered from the right side of the corridor. Case 1: an amphora with Apollo and Artemis seated beneath the palm of Delos. Case 4 begins the display of red-figure vases, the earliest of which date from 520–500 BC. A fragment of a kylix has two warriors advancing behind a shield. A kylix is displayed on its own in the centre of the room, in case 5. This is signed by the potter Kachrylion (510 BC) and has scenes from the legend of Theseus in which the hero overcomes brigands and monsters. In the centre is the figure of Eros flying over the sea.

Room V Case 1: works by the Berlin Painter including a *pelike* with two scenes of the legend of Theseus (an early work) and a large amphora (c 480 BC) with two Amazons. Also here is an exquisite fragment of a vase (a *skyphos*) by the Kleophrades Painter showing Iris with Centaurs. Case 3: a *stamnos* with a scene of a nude girl bathing, and a *pelike* with figures playing musical instruments. Case 4: small vases still in the earlier black-figure style.

Rooms VI–XI Case 1: kylixes with figures of young athletes. Case 2: kylixes with a banqueting scene, and scenes of Theseus. Case 3: works by Douris (c 480 BC) with interesting scenes of everyday life. Room VII Case 2: a crater by the Florence Painter (460–450 BC) with a fine scene of a battle with centaurs. Case 4: a *skyphos* by the Lewis Painter. Off the other side of the corridor is Room VIII. Here there are interesting examples of a new technique of vase painting, using a white ground: Case 1: a kylix by the Lyandros Painter, showing Aphrodite enthroned and a *lekythos*. Case 2: an *oinochoe* by the 'Florence Painter' with Selene, the moon-goddess, riding a horse. Room IX has works dated c 450–425 BC. Case 3: craters by the Dinos Painter. Room X Cases 1 and 2: two beautiful hydria by the Meidias Painter (420–400 BC), probably from Populonia. Case 4: examples of the last period (400–320 BC) in which Attic vases were produced. Room XI contains two vases restored in the 19C.

There are also study collections (including important sculptures) that are open to scholars. The Institute of Etruscan and Italic Studies with its extensive library is housed in the same building.

The **garden** was reopened in 2000 (admission by appointment; enquire at the ticket office). It was laid out in 1903 and includes reconstructions (using the original stones) of Etruscan tombs at Casale Marittimo, Vetulonia, Populonia and the Tomba Inghirami in Volterra. Plants include pines and cedars of Lebanon, and tubs of azaleas in late spring.

The Etruscan Topographical Museum

This museum housing a collection of finds from Etruria is currently closed. It will reopen in the palace next door, although this is not expected to happen for a number of years. The collection includes finds from Roselle, Val di Cecina, Pisa, Volterra, Cortona and Val di Chiana, as well as the contents of tombs at Vetulonia and Populonia.

10 • San Marco, Palazzo Medici-Riccardi and San Lorenzo

Piazza San Marco

Piazza San Marco (**Map 4; 5**) is one of the liveliest squares in the city and, with several cafés, is a meeting-place for students from the University and Academy of Art, both of which have their headquarters here. In the garden is a statue of general Manfredo Fanti by Pio Fedi (1873).

On one corner is the ***Loggia dell'Ospedale di San Matteo**, one of the oldest porticoes in Florence (1384). The seven arches may have inspired Brunelleschi's Loggia degli Innocenti (see p 195). This is now the seat of the **Accademia di Belle Arti**, an art school opened in 1784 by the Grand-duke Pietro Leopoldo, but formerly part of the Accademia delle Arti del Disegno, founded more than two centuries earlier (see p 316).

Over the three doors there are fine Della Robbian lunettes: those showing the *Madonna of the Cintola* and the *Resurrection* are by Andrea della Robbia. The Mannerist courtyard has unusual columns. A little frescoed chapel with the *Rest on the Flight into Egypt*, one of Giovanni di San Giovanni's best works, was moved here in 1788 by Pietro Leopoldo from the convent of the Crocetta. The charming scene shows the Madonna stepping off a mule onto a stool, while above a woman with a child holding a cat look down. It can sometimes be seen on request (entrance at no. 11 Via Cesare Battisti). The famous Gallery of the Accademia is in the adjoining building (entrance at 60 Via Ricasoli; see p 187).

Church of San Marco

The church of San Marco (**Map 4; 5**), founded in 1299, and rebuilt with the convent next door in 1442, assumed its present form in 1588 according to a design by Giambologna. The façade (recently cleaned) was designed by Agostino Nobili in 1778; he also executed the sculptures.

Interior (see the plan of the Museo di San Marco on p 208). On the west wall, there is a 14C fresco of the *Annunciation* (A), a version of the famous painting in Santissima Annunziata (see p 198), and above the door, a painted *Crucifix* dating from c 1360 in the style of Giotto.

South side: *Ecce Homo* (B), a devotional figure in wood by Jacopo Maria Foggini (1654). First altar, *St Thomas in Prayer Before the Crucifix* by Santi di Tito. Second altar (C), *Madonna and Six Saints* by Fra' Bartolomeo (1509) showing the influence of Raphael. Above the third altar (D), *Madonna in Prayer*, a remarkable 8C mosaic which had to be cut into two pieces for its journey from Constantinople. It is surrounded by frescoes of saints in imitation of mosaic, added in the 17C. The fourth altar was designed by Giambologna, who also made the statue of St Zanobius high above the arch. The altarpiece, by Matteo Rosselli dates from 1735, but incorporates a 15C painting in its centre.

The **tribune** was added in 1678 by Pier Francesco Silvani; the dome was frescoed by Alessandro Gherardini in 1717. The small painted Crucifix is by Fra' Angelico. A corridor—with a statue of the *Risen Christ* by Antonio Novelli flanked by bas-reliefs of the Passion (1640–41) by Francesco Conti—leads to the **Sacristy**. Designed by Michelozzo, this contains a black marble sarcophagus with the bronze figure of St Antoninus attributed to Giambologna. The **Chapel**

of the Holy Sacrament has statues by Domenico Pieratti and Lodovico Salvetti, and paintings by Santi di Tito (closed).

The **Chapel of St Antoninus (E)**. This contains the saint's body. It was designed by Giambologna and decorated by his contemporaries: in the vestibule are frescoes by Passignano; the altarpiece of the *Descent into Limbo* is by Alessandro Allori; to the right is the *Calling of St Matthew* by Battista Naldini; and to the left, the *Healing of the Leper* by Francesco Morandini. The bronze reliefs are by Giambologna and Francavilla.

On the **north side**, the third altarpiece (**F**) is by Cigoli. On the wall there are the tomb-slabs (**G**) of the great humanist scholar and Platonic philosopher Pico della Mirandola (1463–94), and of his friend, the poet Politian (Angelo Ambrogini, 1454–94). Fragments of 14C–15C frescoes have come to light on this wall, including a piece of a *Last Judgement* and scenes of kneeling warriors. The second altar has a *Marriage of St Catherine* by Antonio Domenico Gabbiani, and first altar, *St Vincent Ferrer* by Passignano. In a niche is a charming little crèche; the Child in terracotta is a 15C work. On the west wall, there is an interesting *Transfiguration* by Giovan Battista Paggi (1596).

Museo di San Marco

The Dominican convent of San Marco contains the Museo di San Marco (**Map 4; 3**), which is famous for its paintings and frescoes by the 'Blessed' Fra' Angelico, who was a friar there. Peaceful and beautifully maintained, this is one of the most delightful museums in Florence.

History of the convent and museum

Originally a medieval convent of the Silvestrine Order, it was transferred to the Dominicans of San Domenico di Fiesole by Cosimo il Vecchio who ordered Michelozzo to enlarge the buildings (1437–52). Cosimo founded a public library here, the first of its kind in Europe. The founding prior, the Dominican reformer Antonino Pierozzi (1389–1459), was made Archbishop of Florence in 1446, and was canonised in 1523 as St Antoninus. Another famous defender of Republican values, Girolamo Savonarola (1452–98; see p 125), a native of Ferrara, became prior in 1491. His dramatic preachings ended when he was burnt at the stake in Piazza della Signoria seven years later. The painter Fra' Bartolomeo was a friar here. The museum was founded at the convent in 1869 and in 1921 nearly all Fra Angelico's panel paintings were transferred here from other museums in Florence. In 1898, another museum was opened here to house architectural fragments saved during demolitions in the centre of Florence.

- **Opening times** 08.30–13.50; Sat and Sun 08.30–19.00; closed first, third and fifth Sunday and the second and fourth Monday of the month (☎ 055 2388608); Lire 8000 (S). There is disabled access.

Ground floor

Cloister of St Antoninus With its broad arches and delicate Ionic capitals, this attractive cloister was built by Michelozzo. A venerable cedar of Lebanon stands at its centre. The lunettes are decorated with early 17C frescoes showing scenes from the *Life of St Antoninus*, begun by Bernardino Poccetti and finished by Matteo Rosselli,

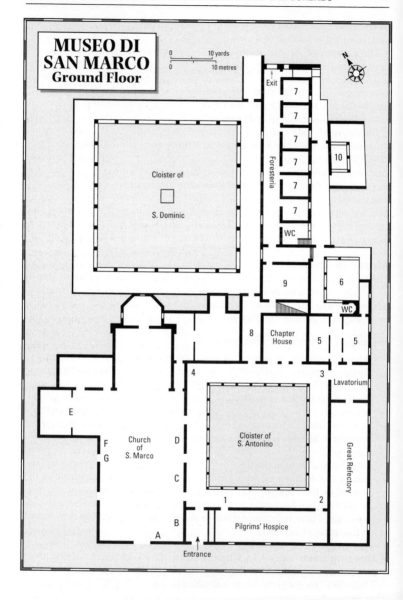

MUSEO DI SAN MARCO
Ground Floor

0 ——— 10 yards
0 ——— 10 metres

Exit

Cloister of
S. Dominic

Foresteria

7
7
7
7
7
7

WC

10

9

6

WC

8

Chapter
House

5

5

4

3

Lavatorium

E

Church
of
S. Marco

D

C

F
G

Cloister of
S. Antonino

Great Refectory

1

2

B

A

Pilgrims' Hospice

Entrance

Ludovico Buti, Alessandro Tiarini, Lorenzo Cerrini and Fabrizio Boschi. In the corners are frescoes by Fra' Angelico: *St Thomas Aquinas* (**1**), which is very worn; *Christ as a Pilgrim Welcomed by Two Dominicans* (**2**); *Pietà* (**3**), which has been restored; **St Dominic at the Foot of the Cross* and a lunette of St *Peter Martyr* (**4**).
Pilgrims' Hospice Doors lead off the cloister into the Pilgrims' Hospice,

Refectory and Chapter House. The Hospice was built by Michelozzo. Its walls are now hung with superb paintings by **Fra' Angelico**, collected here from churches and convents in Florence and its environs. Some are large altarpieces, while others are tiny works, exquisitely painted as if they were miniatures for illuminated manuscripts. All repay the closest examination and exude a joyous spirit, with superb colouring and decoration in gold leaf, and numerous delightful botanical details. Most date from the 1430s and are very well preserved. The *Deposition*, one of Angelico's most beautiful paintings, was commissioned by Palla Strozzi for the church of Santa Trìnita, c 1435–40. The earlier cusps are the work of Lorenzo Monaco. The *Last Judgement* (1431), from Santa Maria degli Angeli, is painted with extraordinary skill and numerous charming details, including the dance of the blessed with angels in Paradise which is separated from the vivid scenes of the dammed in Hell by a stark representation of the empty tombs of the dead. The 35 beautifully painted small panels which served as cupboard doors in Santissima Annunziata illustrate scenes the *Life of Christ*. Three scenes from the same series are displayed on their own—the *Marriage at Cana*, the *Baptism of Christ* and the *Transfiguration*—and are thought to be by Alesso Baldovinetti. The *Madonna della Stella* is a charming little reliquary tabernacle from Santa Maria Novella. Beyond is another *Deposition* painted for the Compagnia del Tempio (the lower part was damaged when the Arno flooded in 1966).

At the end of the room is the large *Tabernacle of the Linaiuoli*, with the *Madonna Enthroned with Saints*, commissioned by the flax-workers guild for their headquarters in 1433 (and now in rather poor condition). The beautiful marble frame was designed by Ghiberti. On the last wall, there are three more altarpieces of the *Madonna and Child with Saints*: one painted for Bosco ai Frati which is a late work (c 1450); one for the high altar of the church of San Marco (c 1438–40; in poor condition), with two scenes from the predella of *Saints Cosmas and Damian* (one showing a leg transplant) displayed on either side; and the last one painted for the convent of the Annalena (which preserves most of its predella). There are also two more exquisite small *reliquary tabernacles* from Santa Maria Novella, one with the *Coronation of the Virgin*, and the other, even more beautiful, with a bright gold ground showing the *Annunciation* and *Adoration of the Magi*.

In the **lavatorium** is a detached fresco of the *Last Judgement* by Fra Bartolomeo and Mariotto Albertinelli (very ruined, but restored), two frescoed tondi by Fra Bartolomeo, and a seated *Madonna and Child* in polychrome terracotta attributed to Luca della Robbia (recently removed from the Oratory of San Tommaso d'Aquino). On the end wall of the **Great Refectory** is a fresco of *St Dominic and his Brethren fed by Angels* by Giovanni Antonio Sogliani (1536). Here have been hung 16C and 17C paintings by Sogliani, Fra' Paolino, Jacopo Vignali, Lorenzo Lippi, and Jacopo Ligozzi.

Room 5 A door leads from the lavatorium into this room which contains fine works by Fra' Bartolomeo, including a *portrait* of *Savonarola* in profile (Savonarola's preachings had convinced Bartolomeo to take the Dominican habit in 1500). He also painted the large *Madonna with St Anne and Other Saints* in monochrome, commissioned by Pier Soderini for the Sala del Maggior Consiglio (council room) of the Republican government in Palazzo Vecchio, but never finished since the Medici returned in 1512 and Fra Bartolomeo died in 1517. However, when the Republican government was restored in 1529, it was installed in the room for a few years. Also here are frescoed heads of *Saints*, detached from the convent of the Maddalena, a painting of **St Vincent Ferrer** from the church of San Marco, and facsimiles of some of Fra' Bartolomeo's drawings. The room on the left has 15C paintings and frescoes including a processional standard with a *Crucifix and St Antoninus* by Baldovinetti (in a beautiful 15C frame, but in very bad condition), and, above a door, a very damaged detached lunette of the *Madonna and Child* by Paolo Uccello. In summer there is access from the corridor here to a little cloister (**6**), see below.

Off the cloister of St Antoninus is the **chapter house**. A large fresco covers one wall of this, showing the **Crucifixion and Saints* by Fra' Angelico and assistants (1441–42). The figure of Mary Magdalene supporting the grieving Madonna is particularly striking. The convent bell, with a frieze of putti, was commissioned by Cosimo il Vecchio and is now attributed to Donatello and Michelozzo. It was rung in defence of Savonarola until he was arrested in the convent and imprisoned in Palazzo Vecchio before being burnt at the stake. After his death, it was seized and taken to San Miniato al Monte, but was returned here in 1501 by order of Julius II (it was carefully restored in 1999).

To the left a door opens onto a corridor (**8**) with a painting of the *Crucifixion* by Lorenzo Lippi (c 1647). To the left, at the foot of the stairs up to the dormitory, is the **small refectory** (**9**) with a charming *Last Supper* frescoed by Domenico Ghirlandaio and his workshop. This is one of four frescoes of the Last Supper painted by Ghirlandaio in Florence between 1476 and 1480. On the walls are Della Robbian terracottas.

Beyond is the Museo di Firenze Antica (described below) and the new exit.

First floor

The dormitory This consists of 44 small monastic cells beneath a huge wooden roof, each with its own vault and adorned with an intimate fresco by Fra' Angelico and his assistants. It is still uncertain how many of the frescoes are by the hand of the master alone, and how many are by artists (whose names are unknown) employed in his studio. Others are attributed to Zanobi Strozzi and Benozzo Gozzoli. The old wooden shutters and doors have been preserved, and the cells retain their intimate atmosphere. At the head of the staircase is Fra' Angelico's **Annunciation*, justly one of his most famous works.

Fra' Angelico's paintings in the cells are as follows (beginning in the left corridor; see the plan on p 208): (**1**) **Noli me tangere*; (**3**) **Annunciation* (with a particularly beautiful angel); (**5**) *Nativity* (perhaps with the help of an assistant); (**6**) **Transfiguration*; (**7**) *Mocking of Christ in the Presence of the Madonna and St Dominic* (perhaps with the help of an assistant); (**8**) *Marys at the Sepulchre*; (**9**) **Coronation of the Virgin*; (**10**) *Presentation in the Temple*; (**11**) *Madonna and Child with Saints* (probably by an assistant).

In the next corridor, the cells have frescoes of **Christ on the Cross** by followers of Fra' Angelico. Important medieval fresco fragments (c 1290–1310), thought to depict the founder of the Silvestrine convent, **Silvestro Gozzolini and St Anthony Abbot**, can be seen beneath the floor in cell **17**. These are among the earliest frescoes known in Florence. In cell **15** Savonarola's cloak is displayed: it has been carefully preserved over the centuries by a series of (documented) proprietors. The pieces missing were cut out as relics of the great churchman. Also here is a small polychrome wooden *Crucifix* attributed to Benedetto da Maiano which used to be in Savonarola's cell.

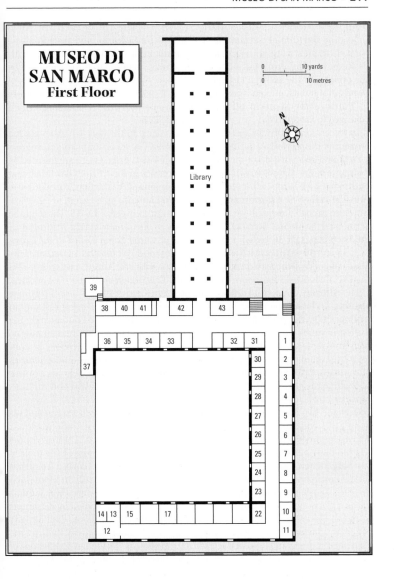

MUSEO DI
SAN MARCO
First Floor

0   10 yards
0   10 metres

Library

39
38 40 41   42   43

36 35 34 33   32 31   1
37   30   2
                            29   3
                            28   4
                            27   5
                            26   6
                            25   7
                            24   8
                            23   9
14 | 13 15   17   22   10
12   11

At the end of the corridor are the three little rooms (**12–14**) occupied by
Savonarola when he was prior in 1482–87, and 1490–98. Above the door is an
oval detached fresco of the *Glory of St Catherine* by Alessandro Gherardini
(1701). In the former chapel (**12**) is a monument to Savonarola, with a bronze
bust and marble relief, by Giovanni Duprè (1873). Also here are detached frescoes by Fra' Bartolomeo, his supporter and fellow friar, and a portrait of him

(with the attributes of St Peter Martyr, c 1497). A late 15C or early 16C panel shows the *Burning of Savonarola in Piazza della Signoria*, and there is also a book of his preachings and sermons. In the adjoining cell (**13**), arranged as a little study, is a 19C desk, and a chair traditionally supposed to have been used by the prelate. In the last cell (**14**) are some more Savonarola relics, fragments of Dominican habits, and another late 15C painting of the *Burning of Savonarola in Piazza della Signoria* attributed to Cosimo Rosselli. A standard which belonged to Savonarola is to be displayed in cell **16**.

In the entrance corridor, cell **22** has a glass panel in the floor which shows the remains of the previous convent here with two late 14C fresco fragments of a monk, a *Pietà* and geometric decoration, discovered in 1991. Cells **23–29** are frescoed by assistants of Fra' Angelico, while on the wall outside in the corridor is a **Madonna Enthroned with Saints*, attributed to the master himself. In the third corridor is cell (**31**), the **cell of St Antoninus**, with *Christ in Limbo* by an assistant of Angelico, who also probably painted the scenes in the next four cells (**32–35**) showing the *Sermon on the Mount*, *Arrest of Christ*, *Agony in the Garden* and the *Institution of the Eucharist*. Cell **36** has an unusual scene of *Christ Being Nailed to the Cross*. Cells **38** and **39** were occupied as a retreat by Cosimo il Vecchio; the *Adoration of the Magi* painted by Benozzo Gozzoli in collaboration with Fra' Angelico was restored in the 19C. Cells **40–43** have worn frescoes of the *Crucifixion* by Angelico's workshop.

The **library*, a light and delicate hall by Michelozzo (1441), is one of the most pleasing architectural works of the Florentine Renaissance. During restoration work in 2000 the original emerald green colour of the frescoed intonaco on the walls and vaults was discovered under four layers of plaster (and this can now be seen in several places). It is known that the colour green was symbolic of contemplation and repose and was used on the walls of other Renaissance libraries and studies. Before this discovery art historians had praised the clear lines of this hall where the grey *pietra serena* stands out against the white walls and vaults as representing a typical Renaissance interior.

Over the two doors are frescoes (1671) of the Blessed Alberto Magno and his pupil St Thomas Aquinas, attributed to Jacopo Chiavistelli or Carlo Molinari. Above the two blocked doors on the left wall are small paintings of the two saints teaching attributed to Fra Angelico and a collaborator. At the end of the room is the **Sala Greca**, added in 1457, which preserves its painted ceiling from that time. The cupboards, dating from 1741, now contain vases made in Montelupo in 1570 for the pharmacy of San Marco. The library of San Marco was famous for its collection of Greek and Roman authors and was augmented by donations from the Florentine Humanists. However, dispersion of the books had already begun by the beginning of the 16C and in 1571 many of them went to the Biblioteca Laurenziana (and in the 19C to the Biblioteca Nazionale). Exhibitions of some of them, together with illuminated choirbooks and psalters (mostly 15C–16C), and a missal illuminated by Fra' Angelico as a young man are held here.

Ground floor
Museo di Firenze Antica From the small refectory (see above) at the bottom of the stairs there is access to the Museo di Firenze Antica, arranged in the cells of the **foresteria** (**7**). These were guest-quarters of the convent and some of them have a lunette over the door by Fra' Bartolomeo. The material salvaged from the demolition of the Mercato Vecchio and part of the Ghetto at the end of

the 19C (the central part of this area of the city is now occupied by Piazza della Repubblica; see p 119) was collected here. This includes numerous architectural fragments dating from the Medieval and early Renaissance periods. The arrangement of 1904 has been preserved but the rooms have been restored. From the windows can be seen the **Cloister of St Dominic** (not open to the public since it is still used by the Dominican friars), also by Michelozzo (1437–43), with frescoes of the *Life of St Dominic* (1697–1701) by Cosimo Ulivelli, who completed the east and north walks. Alessandro Gherardini continued the west walk, but only the lunette survives by him. The last walk is by his pupils, including Niccolò Lapi. In the centre of the cloisters, with palm trees and box, is a statue of St Dominic by Alessandro Baratta (1700).

One of the rooms displays the pavement tomb of Luigi Tornabuoni (1515), with its fine marble effigy in relief and another, with a 15C painted wooden ceiling, contains 14C–16C fragments of painted wall decoration and a wooden model of the church of San Giuseppe by Baccio d'Agnolo. Material from the Sepolcreto di San Pancrazio has been arranged in the **Chiostrino dei Silvestrini** (10), usually only open in summer. There is another charming little cloister, known as the **Chiostro delle Spese** (6). The exit at the end of the corridor is through a charming little garden.

At No. 4 Via La Pira is the entrance to the **Giardino dei Semplici** (Map 4; 3). This is on the site of a botanical garden laid out in 1545–46 by Tribolo for Cosimo I and is the third oldest botanical garden in the world. Opening times Mon–Fri 09.00–13.00; closed Sat and Sun; Lire 6000 (reduction for children between 6 and 14 years, and free for over 65s); ☎ 055 2757402.

The garden contains medicinal plants, Tuscan flora, azaleas, irises, water plants, coniferous trees, yews and cork trees. In the greenhouses (the two largest of which date from the end of the 19C) are tropical plants, palms, ferns, orchids and citrus fruits.

The entrance to the Natural History study collections of the University is also located at no. 4 via La Pira. These moved here from Via Romana at the end of the 19C. The **Botanical Museum**, founded in 1842, is the most important in Italy, with some four million specimens, the Central Italian Herbarium, the Andrea Cesalpino Herbarium (1563), one of the oldest in the world, and the Philip Barker Webb Herbarium (1854), which contains plants collected by Charles Darwin on his first voyage in The Beagle. It has been closed since 1996 (☎ 055 275 7462).

The **Museum of Minerals** includes samples of minerals and rocks from Elba, the Medici collection of worked stones, and a huge Brazilian topaz weighing 151kg (the second largest in the world). Opening times Mon–Fri 09.00–13.00, second Sun of month 09.30–12.30 (☎ 055 275 7537).

The **Geological and Palaeontological Museum**, the largest and most important in Italy, includes interesting material from the grand-ducal collections: vertebrates, skeletons of mammals from the Lower Pleistocene period in Tuscany, a gallery of invertebrates and plants, and a research section. Opening times 09.00–13.00 except Mon and Sun (☎ 055 275 7536); Lire 6000. The museum was moved from Palazzo Pitti to the Specola in 1775, and has been here since 1925.

On the other side of Via La Pira (26 Via Micheli) is the church of **Holy Trinity**, owned by the Waldensian Community since 1967. (Originating in the south of France c 1170, the Waldensians were condemned by the Lateran Council in 1184 and fled to northern Italy, especially around Turin.) An Anglican church, built by Domenico Giraldi was founded here in 1846. The present neo-Gothic building, with stained glass windows, was designed in 1892 by the English architect George Frederick Bodley. The choir screen and wooden stalls, designed by Bodley, were made in Florence by the workshop of Mariano Coppedè in 1902.

Via La Pira leads back towards Piazza San Marco at the corner of which are the administrative offices of the University of Florence. At nos 10–12 Via Cesare Battisti is the **Istituto Geografico Militare**, with a remarkable cartographic library (opening times Mon–Fri 09.00–12.00) with works up to 1862 and an archive (maps from 1863–1963). The later material is kept in another building near the Fortezza da Basso (see p 329).

On the west side of Piazza San Marco is the **Casina di Livia** built by Pietro Leopolo in 1775 for his mistress Livia Raimondi. It is now used as an officers' club, and the lower hall has frescoes by the school of Giuseppe del Moro. A plaque on the garden wall beside five tall cypresses records the site of the **Giardino di San Marco**. Vasari described this garden which contained Cosimo il Vecchio's and Lorenzo il Magnifico's collections of antique sculpture, and where Lorenzo's great friend Bertoldo di Giovanni worked in bronze and restored antique sculpture, as well as instructing young sculptors. It is known that the painter Francesco Granacci took the young Michelangelo to see the school.

Via Cavour (**Map 4**; **3**) runs north of Piazza San Marco. On the left is the Casino Mediceo, built for Francesco I by Buontalenti (1568–74), and used by him as a studio for his scientific studies. It is now occupied by law courts.

Chiostro dello Scalzo

At no. 69, beyond, is the *Chiostro dello Scalzo (**Map 4**; **3**). Opening times Mon, Thurs and Sat 08.30–14.00 (☎ 055 2388604); Lire 4000 (S). It is a charming little early 16C cloister, with very fine *frescoes** in monochrome by **Andrea del Sarto** (1510–26). They depict the Life of St John the Baptist, but the scenes were not painted in the narrative order of the story, and two of them were painted by Franciabigio when Del Sarto left for France—though he returned to complete the cycle. They were restored in 1963–68, and again in 1990. Above the scenes, Andrea del Sarto also painted the decorative friezes.

To the right of the door are: *Faith* (c 1523); *Angel Announcing the Birth of the Baptist to St Zacharias* (1523); *Visitation* (1524); *Naming of the Baptist* (1526); *Blessing of the Young St John Before Leaving for the Desert* (by Franciabigio, 1518–19); *Meeting of Christ with the Young St John* (Franciabigio, 1518–19). The scenes on the end wall are almost totally ruined, they are *Baptism of Christ* (c 1507–08) and the *Preaching of the Baptist* (1515); *Baptism of the Multitude* (1517); *Capture of the Baptist* (1517); *Dance of Salome* (1521); *Beheading of the Baptist* (1523). On the entrance wall is the *Banquet of Herod* (1523). The terracotta bust of *St Antoninus* dates from the early 16C.

From Piazza San Marco, Via Cavour leads in the other direction south towards the Duomo. On the right is the **Biblioteca Marucelliana** (**Map 3**; **6**), a library founded by Francesco di Alessandro Marucelli (1625–1703) and opened to the public in 1752 in the present building built by Alessandro Dori (the reading room retains its 18C bookcases, and the holdings now number over 300,000 volumes). It is particularly rich in works on Florence. On the other side of the road are two palaces (nos 22 and 4) by Gherardo Silvani. Opposite Palazzo Medici-Riccardi (see below), on the bend, is Palazzo del Cardinale Panciatichi, by Antonio Ferri (1696).

Set back from the road, at the beginning of Via de' Martelli is the little church of **San Giovannino degli Scolopi** (Map 1; 2), begun by Ammannati in 1579. The fourth chapel on the right was built in 1692–1712 for the Grand-duke Cosimo III. The altarpiece of the *Preaching of St Francis Xavier* is the best work of Francesco Curradi. The vault fresco is by Pier Dandini and the stucco angels by Girolamo Ticciati. The first chapel on the left has *Angels*, *Jacob's Dream* and the *Fall of Lucifer*, by Jacopo Ligozzi. The second chapel on the left was designed by Ammannati as his burial place (1592); the altarpiece is by Alessandro Allori. The confessionals date from the late 17C.

From Piazza San Marco (see above), Via degli Arazzieri (the site of the Florentine tapestry factory) leads into Via XXVII Aprile. Here on the left is the former convent of **Sant'Apollonia** (Map 3; 4), founded in 1339 and enlarged in 1445. Opening times 08.30–13.50; closed first, third and fifth Sunday and second and fourth Monday of the month (☎ 055 238 8607); (S).

The vestibule contains works by Neri di Bicci and Paolo Schiavo, Andrea del Castagno's master. In the **Refectory** is a *Last Supper*, the masterpiece of **Andrea del Castagno** (c 1450; restored), set in an unusual painted marble loggia. This is one of the most beautiful frescoes of the Last Supper in Florence, and the particularly peaceful setting is usually little disturbed by visitors. The equally fine frescoes of the *Crucifixion, Deposition* and *Resurrection* above are also by him (very damaged, but recently restored). The sinopia is displayed on the opposite wall. Among other frescoes by Castagno displayed here are lunettes with the *Crucifixion Between the Madonna and Saints* and a *Pietà with Two Angels*. The sinopia is from his fresco of St Jerome in Santissima Annunziata.

The detached fresco fragments on the end wall with panels of painted marble are all that remains of the important frescoes of stories from the *Life of the Virgin* in Sant'Egidio by Domenico Veneziano, Piero della Francesca, Andrea del Castagno and Alesso Baldovinetti. The cycle was destroyed in the 17C and these fragments were found in 1950. The large wooden *Crucifix* is by Raffaello da Montelupo.

Via San Gallo (Map 3; 4, 6) leads towards Piazza della Libertà. To the right is the church of **Gesù Pellegrino**, also known as the Oratorio dei Pretoni (usually closed). This was rebuilt in 1588 by Giovanni Antonio Dosio and has a fresco cycle (1590) and three altarpieces by Giovanni Balducci (Il Cosci). In the nave is the tomb-slab of the Pievano Arlotto (1400–84), rector of the church, with an inscription which in translation reads: 'This tomb was ordered by the Pievano Arlotto for himself and for whoever wishes to enter it.'

To the right is the Loggia dei Tessitori, part of the weavers' guild-house (c 1500; the columns have been poorly restored). On the left, on the corner of Via delle Ruote, is a tabernacle with a fresco by Andrea Bonaiuti, restored in 1991.

At no. 66 is the church of **San Giovannino dei Cavalieri** (Map 3; 4; usually closed), preceded by an unusual vestibule, with original cupboards. In the tribune, surrounded by worn frescoes by Alessandro Gherardini (1703), is a large *Crucifixion* by Lorenzo Monaco. At the end of the right aisle is an *Annunciation*, a painting by the Master of the Castello Nativity. On the right wall is a worn fresco of *St Michael Archangel* by Francesco Granacci. In the left aisle is a *Nativity* by Bicci di Lorenzo, and a *Coronation of the Virgin* by his son, Neri di Bicci. On the west wall is the *Birth of the Baptist* by Santi di Tito and the *Beheading of the Baptist* by Pier Dandini. The two altars in the nave are attributed to Giovanni Tedesco.

The **Palazzo Pandolfini** lies beyond at no. 74. It was built as a villa on the outskirts of the town for Bishop Giannozzo Pandolfini and is still owned by the Pandolfini family. It was designed by Raphael and is the most important architectural work by him to survive; it was executed by Giovanni Francesco and Aristotile da Sangallo (1516–20). The handsome classical inscription records Giannozzo Pandolfini. When the portone is open the pretty garden façade can be seen. It has a terrace on the first floor, and a big garden (redesigned in the 19C).

Farther on, at no. 110, is the church of **Sant'Agata** (used by the military hospital and rarely open), with a façade designed by Allori in 1592, who also painted the high altarpiece of the *Marriage at Cana* (in a handsome frame). The church also contains frescoes by Giovanni Bizzelli, and paintings attributed to Lorenzo di Credi, Lorenzo Lippi and Neri di Bicci.

Via San Gallo leads south from Via XXVII Aprile. On the left (no. 10) is *Palazzo Castelli* (Marucelli), built by Gherardo Silvani c 1630. It is now used by the University and is one of the best palaces of its period in the city. The elaborate doorway is flanked by two grotesque satyrs sculpted by Raffaello Curradi. The coat of arms above was set up by its later owner Emanuele Fenzi (1784–1875), a banker who financed the Florence–Livorno railway.

Across Via Guelfa, **Via de' Ginori** (Map 3; 6) continues, lined with a number of fine palaces on the right. no. 15, **Palazzo Taddei** was built by Baccio d'Agnolo for the merchant Taddei who commissioned the tondo from Michelangelo which now bears his name and is owned by the Royal Academy, London. Raphael, while staying here as a friend of the family in 1505, saw and copied the tondo (the plaque is on the wrong house). The tabernacle in Via Taddei has a *Crucifixion* by Giovanni Antonio Sogliani. **Palazzo Ginori** (no. 11; Map 3; 6) is also attributed to Baccio d'Agnolo (c 1516–20). **Palazzo Montauto** (no. 9) has remains of 15C graffiti and two ground-floor windows attributed to Ammannati. Diotisalvi Neroni lived at Palazzo Neroni (no. 7; with pronounced rustication) before his exile as an enemy of the Medici in 1466. Neroni was a leading figure in Florentine politics in the turbulent period following Cosimo il Vecchio's death in 1464. Together with other noble Florentines, he tried to exclude Cosimo's son Piero from holding office but failed when a popular assembly called for his banishment. This was a significant moment in the consolidation of the (hereditary) power of the Medici.

On the left (no. 14) is the entrance to the **Biblioteca Riccardiana** founded by Riccardo Riccardi and opened to the public in 1718. It is a fine example of a private library, with a delightful reading room frescoed by Luca Giordano. The original bookshelves contain illuminated manuscripts and incunabula. The library forms part of the 17C extension of Palazzo Medici-Riccardi which stands on the corner of Piazza San Lorenzo. Opening times weekdays 08.00–14.00; closed Easter week and the last half of August.

Palazzo Medici-Riccardi

Palazzo Medici-Riccardi (**Map 1; 2**; entrance at no. 3 Via Cavour) was built for Cosimo il Vecchio by Michelozzo after 1444 as a town mansion (on Via Larga, renamed Via Cavour in the 19C). It was the residence of the Medici family until 1540 when Cosimo I moved into Palazzo Vecchio. Its rusticated façade served as a model for other famous Florentine palaces, including those built by the Strozzi and Pitti. Charles VIII of France stayed here in 1494 and the Emperor Charles V in 1536. It was bought by the Riccardi in 1659 and before the end of the century was extended towards Via de' Ginori; the façade on Via Cavour was lengthened by seven bays. It is now the seat of the Prefect, the provincial representative of the central government, and of the Province of Florence, although there are plans to remove these offices and open the whole palace to the public as a museum dedicated to the Medici family. At present, the only part open to the public is the courtyard and the famous little chapel (the Cappella dei Magi) frescoed by Benozzo Gozzoli and the galleria frescoed by Luca Giordano.

• **Opening times** the chapel and gallery are open 09.00–19.00 except Wed. Lire 8000. To book a visit, ☎ 055 276 0340.

The Medici

The Medici family held power in Florence from 1434 for nearly 300 years, with only two brief Republican interludes in the early 16C. They had accrued a fortune through banking and became great patrons of the arts. Cosimo il Vecchio, perhaps the wealthiest man in Europe, was decreed 'pater Patriae' on his death, and his famous grandson Lorenzo il Magnifico was a highly cultivated figure of the Renaissance as well as a respected statesman. During the 16C, the importance of the family was further strengthened when two members became popes (Leo X and Clement VII). Later in the century, the power of the Medici dynasty as hereditary rulers was formalised during Cosimo I's long term of office, when he became first duke, and then grand-duke of Tuscany.

Cortile d'Onore The dignified main courtyard of the Palazzo Medici-Riccardi is usually known as the Cortile d'Onore. It has composite colonnades dating from the 15C and twelve tondi in relief (copies of ancient sculptures inspired by antique gems in the Medici collections) and the Medici arms. These were carried out c 1450 by Donatello's circle (usually ascribed to Bertoldo) and are united by graffiti festoons by Maso di Bartolomeo. When the Medici lived here, Donatello's statue of *Judith and Holofernes* was in the garden and his bronze *David* adorned the courtyard until 1495. After 1715, Francesco Riccardi arranged the courtyard as a museum of ancient sculpture, setting up numerous reliefs and inscriptions inside decorative frames. The statue of *Orpheus and Cerberus*, under the arch towards the garden, is by Baccio Bandinelli (on a fine base by Benedetto da Rovezzano). In the pretty second court are more statues, some of them Roman works, and pots of lemon trees.

Chapel The main staircase off the Cortile d'Onore leads up to the dark little *chapel (only 15 people are admitted at one time), the only unaltered part of Michelozzo's work. It is one of the oldest chapels in Florence to have survived in a private palace. It has a lovely carved wood ceiling and a splendid inlaid floor in red porphyry and green serpentine marble. The finely carved wooden choir stalls are on a design by Giuliano da Sangallo. The walls are entirely covered with decorative *frescoes that are Benozzo Gozzoli's masterpiece.

Benozzo Gozzoli's fresco cycle

Gozzoli's sumptuous fresco cycle in the chapel of the Palazzo Medici-Riccardi shows the *Procession of the Magi to Bethlehem* (begun in 1459 and finished before 1463). It is one of the most pleasing, even if not one of the most important, fresco cycles of the Renaissance. It was probably commissioned by Cosimo il Vecchio, but it is known that his son Piero di Cosimo (il Gottoso) also took an active interest in the work. The procession was probably intended partly as an evocation of the festival held by the Compagnia dei Magi of San Marco at Epiphany in which the Medici usually took part. The decorative cavalcade is shown in a charming landscape with hunting scenes, which seem to be inspired by Flemish tapestries. Some members of the Medici family are depicted wearing their emblem of the three ostrich feathers, but discussion continues about the identification of the various figures, some of which are vivid portrait studies.

The frescoes were designed around an altarpiece (commissioned c 1444–56) of the *Adoration of the Child* by Filippo Lippi which was already on the altar of the chapel.

The procession is seen approaching along the distant hills on the **right wall**. The two men mounted on the extreme left are usually identified as Sigismondo Pandolfo Malatesta and Galeazzo Maria Sforza. In the crowd behind (just above their heads) the two boys in red hats may have been intended to portray Lorenzo and Giuliano, sons of Piero il Gottoso, then around ten and six years old. Above them, the man looking out of the fresco is a self-portrait of Benozzo with his signature in gold lettering on his red beret. In front, the man in a red beret on a mule is often taken as a portrait of Cosimo il Vecchio; the man just in front of him, dressed in green and gold brocade, on a grey horse with the Medici emblems on its bridle, may be his son, Piero il Gottoso. The man on foot beside the horses' heads could be Piero's brother Carlo or Giovanni. The young King on this wall, on a splendid grey charger, is usually considered to be an idealised portrait of Lorenzo il Magnifico.

On the **wall opposite the altar**, the three girls on horseback with the Medici feathers in their hair may be Piero il Gottoso's daughters. The second King is dressed in splendid Oriental dress, with green and gold brocade. On the last wall, the older grey-bearded King on a grey mule was cut in two when the wall was moved to accommodate the staircase in the 17C. In front of him the huntsman in blue with a cheetah sitting on his horse is sometimes taken to be an idealised portrait of Giuliano, son of Piero il Gottoso. The head of the man just in front of his horse, with a blue and white turban, may be a second self-portrait by Benozzo. The procession, with camels and horses, winds on uphill towards Bethlehem.

On the walls on either side of the **altar** are beautiful landscapes with angels, recalling those of the painter's master, Fra' Angelico. The altarpiece of the *Adoration of the Child* is a copy by the *bottega* of Filippo Lippi (late 15C; usually attributed to pseudo Pier Francesco Fiorentino) of the original altarpiece by Filippo Lippi which was here until 1494 when it was taken to Palazzo Vecchio, and after 1814 found its way to Berlin. The copy was put here in 1929.

Another door off the courtyard opens onto another flight of stairs (or a lift) up to the first floor. Beyond a vestibule with a beautiful painting of the *Madonna and Child* by Filippo Lippi (with the sketch of a head on the back) is the *gallery, an elaborate Baroque loggia (1670–88) covered by a fresco of the *Apotheosis of the Second Medici Dynasty* by Luca Giordano (1683). The stucco decoration was designed by Giovanni Battista Foggini. The four painted mirrors are by Antonio Domenico Gabbiani, Bartolomeo Bimbi and Pandolfo Reschi.

Exhibitions are held in other rooms of the palace.

Piazza San Lorenzo

The back of Palazzo Medici-Riccardi stands on the corner of Piazza San Lorenzo (**Map 1; 2**), filled with a busy **street market** open all day (except Sunday and Monday in winter); the stalls, also in Via dell'Ariento (see below), have leather-goods, clothing, straw and jewellery for sale (usually good value). The seated statue of *Giovanni delle Bande Nere* is by Baccio Bandinelli (1540). The long façade (14C–15C) of Palazzo della Stufa (no. 4) overlooks the piazza.

Opposite the façade of San Lorenzo, at no. 6 Piazza San Lorenzo, is the Osservatorio Ximeniano. It contains a museum (founded in 1888) with instruments used by Ximenes and his successors, a telescope built in 1861, and maps of Tuscany drawn by Giovanni Inghirami in 1830, as well as two important libraries. A meteorological observatory was installed in 1813, and since 1889 it has been an important seismological institute.

The building is part of the convent of San Giovannino, built for the Jesuits by Ammannati in the mid-16C. An astronomical observatory was founded here in 1756 by the Jesuit Leonardo Ximenes.

San Lorenzo

The church of San Lorenzo (**Map 1; 1**; opening times 10.00–12.00, 15.30–17.30; *fest.* 15.30–17.30; ☎ 055 216 634), was intimately connected with the Medici after they commissioned Brunelleschi to rebuild it in 1425–46. It is the burial place of all the principal members of the family from Cosimo il Vecchio to Cosimo III. A basilica on this site, outside the walls, was consecrated by St Ambrose of Milan in 393, and is thought to be the earliest church in Florence. As the church of St Zenobius, the most famous Bishop of Florence, this served as cathedral of the city before the bishop's seat was transferred, probably in the late 7C, to Santa Reparata (on the site of the present cathedral). On 14 July 1564, a solemn memorial service was held here in honour of the 'divine' Michelangelo, organised by the Accademia del Disegno.

Exterior

The church rises above the market stalls with its large dome of the Chapel of the Princes and the smaller cupola of the New Sacristy (the gilded bronze ball on the lantern was designed by Michelangelo and was made by Giovanni di Baldassare

San Lorenzo

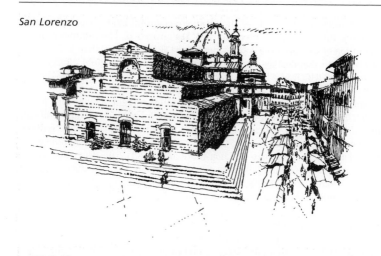

c 1526). The campanile dates from 1740. The **west front** remains in rough-hewn brick as it was in 1480. Leo X held a competition for a façade, and the participants included Raphael, Giuliano and Antonio da Sangallo, Iacopo Sansovino and Baccio d'Agnolo, but in 1516 Michelangelo was given the commission. He spent much time designing a grandiose façade (his model survives in the Casa Buonarroti, see p 275), but only the interior façade was ever built.

Interior
The grey cruciform interior, built with *pietra serena*, with pulvins above the Corinthian columns in *pietra forte*, is one of the earliest and most harmonious architectural works of the Renaissance. It was completed to Brunelleschi's design by Antonio Ciacheri Manetti (1447–60) and Pagno di Lapo Portigiani (1463). The fine wood ceiling has been restored. On the inner façade, above the west door, and supported by two columns in *pietra serena*, is a little balcony built by Michelangelo (1530) for Clement VII, for the exhibition of the Holy Relics (kept in a treasury behind the three doors).

South aisle In the second chapel (**1**) is Rosso Fiorentino's **Marriage of the Virgin* (1523) and the Gothic tomb-slab of the organist Francesco Landini (1398). At the end of this aisle is a *tabernacle (**2**) by Desiderio da Settignano, of extremely fine workmanship (perhaps intended for the high altar of the church).
Nave In the nave are two bronze ***pulpits** (**3** and **4**) raised on Ionic marble columns (c 1560) and made up of sculptured panels by Donatello (c 1460). These were his last works and they were finished by his pupils Bertoldo and Bartolomeo Bellano. The exquisitely carved panels (unfortunately very difficult to see), which may have been intended for the former high altar of the church, have a border of classical motifs around the top. Many of the scenes are crowded and grim and present a unique iconography. The pulpit on the north side (**3**) shows the *Agony in the Garden*, *St John the Evangelist* and the *Flagellation* (these last two both 17C imitations in wood); *Christ Before Pilate* and *Christ Before Caiaphas*; the *Crucifixion* and *Lamentation over the Dead Christ*; and the *Entombment*. The pulpit on the south side (**4**) shows the *Marys at the*

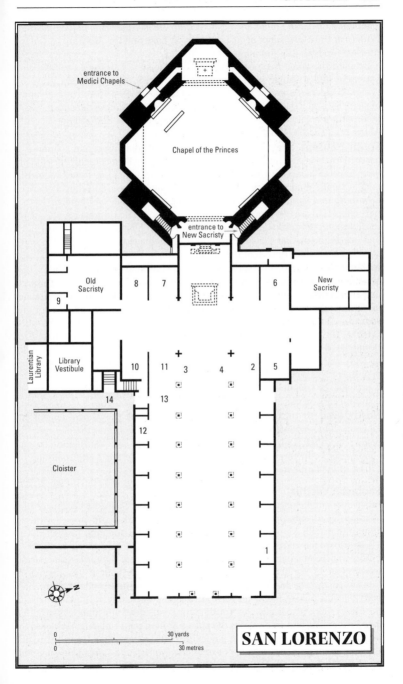

entrance to
Medici Chapels

Chapel of the Princes

entrance to
New Sacristy

Old Sacristy

New Sacristy

9

8   7

6

Laurentian Library

Library Vestibule

10   11   3   4   2   5

14

13

12

Cloister

1

0   30 yards
0   30 metres

SAN LORENZO

Sepulchre; *Christ in Limbo*; the *Resurrection*; *Christ Appearing to the Apostles*; *Pentecost*; the *Martyrdom of St Lawrence*, *St Luke* and the *Mocking of Christ* (the last two both 17C imitations in wood).

Beneath the dome frescoed by Vincenzo Meucci (1742), three grilles in the pavement and a simple inscription with the Medici arms mark the grave of Cosimo Il Vecchio, named by the Signoria Pater Patriae (d. 1464). The high altar in *pietra dura* on a design by Gaspare Maria Paoletti was consecrated in 1787; it incorporates a panel of the *Fall of Manna* designed by Bernardino Poccetti. Above is a *Crucifix* by Baccio da Montelupo.

South transept The architecture here, with splendid Corinthian columns, is particularly beautiful and was certainly carried out by Brunelleschi himself. The first chapel (**5**) contains a Roman sarcophagus, a detached 14C fresco fragment, and a *Crucifix* made of cork by Antonio del Pollaiolo. In the end chapel, there is a *Nativity and Saints* attributed to the school of Domenico Ghirlandaio. In the next chapel (**6**) are two funerary monuments by Leopoldo Costoli (1871), one to the goldsmith Bernardo Cennini, who printed the first book in Florence in 1471, and one to the painter Pietro Benvenuti. In the chapel to the right of the high altar is a charming triptych of the *Annunciation* by Puccio di Simone.

North transept In the first chapel (**7**) is a charming mid-14C statue of the *Madonna and Child* in polychrome wood, and two late 15C paintings. The second chapel (**8**) contains a good painting by the school of Domenico Ghirlandaio of *Saints Anthony Abbot, Leonard and Julian*, a funerary monument by Giovanni Duprè (1864), and a silver reliquary sarcophagus of St Cesonius (1621). The last chapel in the north transept (**10**) contains a monument to Donatello (d. 1466; buried in the vault below) erected in neo-Renaissance style in 1896 (by Dario Guidotti and Raffaello Romanelli). The marble sarcophagus opposite of Niccolò and Fioretta Martelli (c 1464) in the form of a wicker basket is probably by Donatello. The painting of the **Annunciation* is one of the most beautiful early works of Filippo Lippi.

North aisle In this aisle, there is a huge fresco of the *Martyrdom of St Lawrence* (**11**) by Bronzino. The cantoria above the door into the cloister (see below) is after Donatello. The organ was built by Vantaggini-Tronci (1502–1773). In the last chapel in this aisle (**12**): there is a 20C painting of *Christ in the Carpenter's Workshop* by Pietro Annigoni.

Sagrestia Vecchia

Inlaid doors in the north transept provide access to the *Sagrestia Vecchia or Old Sacristy (1422–28). Opening times opened by volunteers of the Amici dei Musei Fiorentini usually Mon, Wed, Fri and Sat 10.00–11.45; Tues and Thurs 16.00–17.45; closed in August and in winter.

This was the first part of the church to be rebuilt. One of the earliest and purest monuments of the Renaissance by Brunelleschi, it was built at the expense of Giovanni di Bicci de' Medici. The vault is particularly beautiful and the chapel has been painstakingly restored. The decorative details are mainly by Donatello: above the frieze of cherubs' heads, the ***tondi** in the pendentives and lunettes depict the four *Evangelists* and scenes from the *Life of St John the Evangelist*. Modelled in terracotta and plaster, they are remarkable for their composition. Over the two little doors are large reliefs of *Saints Cosmas and Damian* and *Saints Lawrence and Stephen*. The former relief may have been designed by Michelozzo.

The remarkable dark blue frescoes in the small dome over the altar depicts the zodiacal sky as it was on 6 July 1439 (the date of the successful conclusion of the Council of Florence between the Greek and Roman Catholic churches). The *bronze doors have figures of the *Apostles* and *Martyrs* in animated discussion (usually considered the work of Donatello but now also attributed by some scholars to Michelozzo). The terracotta *bust of *St Lawrence* (or St Leonard) has been attributed to Donatello or Desiderio da Settignano. The raised seats and presses are decorated with exquisite inlay, restored in 1998. In the centre is the sarcophagus of Giovanni di Bicci de' Medici (d. 1429) and Piccarda Bueri, the parents of Cosimo il Vecchio, by Buggiano (c 1433). Set into the wall is the magnificent porphyry and bronze *sarcophagus of Giovanni and Piero de' Medici* the sons of Cosimo il Vecchio. This was commissioned from Verrocchio in 1472 by Lorenzo il Magnifico and his brother Giuliano. In the little chapel (**9**) is an exquisitely carved *lavabo* with fantastic creatures, commissioned by Piero de' Medici c 1467, by an unknown master (variously attributed to Verrocchio, Antonio Rossellino, Desiderio da Settignano, and Donatello).

The **cloister** was designed by Manetti (1457–62), and is entered from the north aisle (**13**) or from the left of the façade. It has graceful arcades with Ionic capitals and an orange tree is planted at its centre. From the cloister there is an entrance (kept closed; but sometimes open for exhibitions) to the **crypt** of San Lorenzo and the vaults with the simple classical tomb of Cosimo il Vecchio by Verrocchio. Nearby is the tomb of Ferdinando III, surrounded by commemorative inscriptions to the other Lorraine grand-dukes arranged here in 1874 by Emilio De Fabris. Donatello is also buried here.

Biblioteca Laurenziana

A staircase (**14**), near a statue of the historian Paolo Giovio, by Francesco da Sangallo (1560), ascends to the Biblioteca Laurenziana (or Laurentian Library; **Map 1; 1**). Opening times 09.00–13.00 except *fest.* (☎ 055 210 760). Exhibitions of the libraries' holdings are usually held here about twice a year.

It was begun by Michelangelo c 1524 at the order of Clement VII (Giulio de' Medici) to house the collection of manuscripts made by Cosimo il Vecchio and Lorenzo il Magnifico. It is a remarkable monument of Mannerist architecture.

The solemn *vestibule, filled with an elaborate freestanding staircase, was constructed by Vasari and Ammannati from Michelangelo's design in 1559–71. This remarkable work has been interpreted by scholars in numerous ways, but whatever their conclusions, it clearly shows Michelangelo's sculptural conception of architecture.

The peaceful *reading room, a long hall, provides an unexpected contrast. Here the angle at which the architectural decoration can be seen has been carefully calculated, and the carved desks, also by Michelangelo, form an intricate part of the design. It is interesting to note that the heavily decorated vestibule is invisible from the aisle (only a blank wall is framed in the doorway). The very fine wood ceiling and beautiful terracotta floor are by Tribolo.

Exhibitions from the collection are held every year in the adjoining rooms (the circular tribune was added in 1841). The collection is famous above all for its Greek and Latin manuscripts; it has been augmented over the centuries and now includes 11,000 manuscripts and 4000 incunabula. The oldest codex is a famous 5C Virgil. Other works owned by the library include: Syrian gospels of the 6C; the oldest manuscript of Justinian's *Pandects* (6C–7C); the Codex Amiatinus (from Monte Amiata) written in the monastery of Jarrow in England in the 8C; a choir book illuminated by Lorenzo Monaco and Attavante; a Book of Hours which belonged to Lorenzo il Magnifico; the *Città di Vita* of Matteo Palmieri, with illuminations in the style of Pollaiolo and Botticelli; a *Treatise on Architecture* with manuscript notes by Leonardo da Vinci; the manuscript of Cellini's autobiography; and a parchment of the Union of Greek and Roman churches recording the abortive effort of the Council of Florence in 1439.

Cappelle Medicee

The Cappelle Medicee (**Map 1; 1**), or Medici Chapels, are approached from outside the east end of San Lorenzo, where a statue by Raffaello Salimbeni of the *Electress Palatine*—the last descendent of the Medici family who settled her inheritance on the city of Florence—was placed behind a railing in 1995. The entrance to the chapels is in Piazza Madonna degli Aldobrandini. Opening times 08.30–16.30; closed second and fourth Sunday of month and first, third and fifth Monday of month (☎ 055 282 984); Lire 11,000 (S).

The **crypt** of the Cappella dei Principi was designed by Buontalenti and contains the tomb slabs of numerous members of the Medici family. A selection of the most precious objects from the church treasury are exhibited here: reliquaries by Massimiliano Soldani Benzi, including that of San Casimiro, and two early 15C Venetian reliquaries. The mitre, made in Rome in the 16C and decorated with numerous Baroque pearls, was donated to the basilica by Leo X, and the pastoral stave with St Laurence is also a 16C Roman work.

Cappella dei Principi A staircase leads up from the crypt to the Cappella dei Principi, the opulent, if gloomy, mausoleum of the Medici grand-dukes, begun by Matteo Nigetti (1604) on a plan by Don Giovanni de' Medici, illegitimate son of Cosimo I. It is a high octagon, 28m in diameter, entirely lined with dark-coloured marbles and semi-precious stones, a *tour de force* of craftsmanship in *pietre dure*. The lowest part of the walls are adorned with particularly fine mosaic coats of arms (1589–1609), belonging to the 16 towns which were bishoprics of Tuscany. Between them are 32 inlaid vases in red and green jasper (early 17C). In the sarcophagi around the walls, from right to left, are buried Ferdinando II, Cosimo II, Ferdinando I, Cosimo I, Francesco I and Cosimo III. The second and third sarcophagi are surmounted by colossal statues in gilded bronze, by Pietro and Ferdinando Tacca (1626–42). Work continued until 1836 when the decoration on the drum of the cupola was completed (but not to the original design, which envisaged a covering in *pietre dure*). The vault frescoes were painted at this time by Pietro Benvenuti. The pavement was executed in 1882–1962.

The **altar** is a model in wood hastily set up in 1938 which bears *pietre dure* panels of various dates, including the *Supper at Emmaus* (1853–61) and four fine panels with liturgical emblems against a deep blue ground (1821–53). Behind the altar are two treasuries at present closed to the public (the most important works are now exhibited in the crypt, see above).

Sagrestia Nuova A passage to the left leads past two trophies attributed to Silvio Cosini, intended to decorate a tomb in the Sagrestia Nuova. The so-called Sagrestia Nuova, or New Sacristy, may have been begun by Giuliano da Sangallo

Michelangelo's Day *on the tomb of Giuliano, Duke of Nemours, in the Sagrestia Nuova, San Lorenzo*

c 1491. Work was continued by Michelangelo in 1520–24 and 1530–33, but was left unfinished when he finally left Florence for Rome in 1534 in anger at the political climate in the city. It balances Brunelleschi's Old Sacristy (see above) and drew inspiration from it, but was used from its inception as a funerary chapel for the Medici family. It is built in dark *pietra serena* and white marble in a severe and idiosyncratic style. It produces a strange, cold atmosphere, in part due to the diffusion of light exclusively from above, and the odd perspective devices on the upper parts of the walls. Vasari is known to have worked on the chapel in 1550–56.

Michelangelo executed only two of the famous ****Medici tombs**, out of the three or more originally projected. The sculptures were carefully cleaned in 1988–91. To the left of the entrance is that of **Lorenzo, Duke of Urbino** (1492–1519), grandson of Lorenzo il Magnifico. The statue of the Duke shows him seated, absorbed in meditation, and on the sarcophagus below are the reclining figures of *Dawn* and *Dusk*. Opposite is the tomb of **Giuliano, Duke of Nemours** (1479–1516), the third son of Lorenzo il Magnifico. Both these comparatively insignificant members of the Medici family are shown through idealised portraits; only their tombs ensured their fame. Beneath are the figures of *Day* and *Night*, the last, with the symbols of darkness (the moon, the owl, and a mask), is considered to be among the finest of all Michelangelo's sculptures.

The entrance wall was intended to contain an architectural monument to Lorenzo il Magnifico and his brother Giuliano; the only part carried out by Michelangelo is the ***Madonna and Child**. It is his last statue of a Madonna and one of his most beautiful. The figures on either side are *St Cosmas* and *St Damian*, the medical saints who were the patrons of the Medici, and are by Montorsoli and Raffaello da Montelupo. Lorenzo il Magnifico's coffin was transferred here from the Old Sacristy in 1559.

The austere altar bears two candelabra designed by Michelangelo (the one on the left, with the more delicate carving, is the work of Silvio Cosini and that on the right

Night, *companion figure to* Day *on the tomb of Giuliano, Duke of Nemours, in the Sagrestia Nuova, San Lorenzo*

was made in 1741). On the walls behind the altar are architectural graffiti, some of them attributed to Michelangelo, and others to his pupils, including Tribolo. The door to the left of the altar gives access to a little room where ***charcoal drawings** of great interest were discovered on the walls in 1975. Small groups of visitors are usually shown the room every 30–60 minutes or so (by appointment at the ticket office, 09.00–12.00). The drawings have aroused much discussion among art historians, most of whom recognise them as works by Michelangelo. It is thought that he hid here for a time under the protection of his friend, the prior of San Lorenzo, after the return of the Medici in 1530. Michelangelo had supported the Republican government and when the Medici returned the Florentine governors issued an order calling for his execution. Michelangelo went into hiding until later in the year when the Medici pope Clement VII requested that he be treated with clemency. The drawings clearly refer to works by Michelangelo, such as his statue of Giuliano in the adjoining chapel. The large figure study for a Resurrection of Christ on the entrance wall is particularly remarkable.

At no. 4 in Piazza Madonna, **Palazzo Mannelli-Riccardi** has a painted façade of the mid-16C (very ruined) and a bust of Ferdinando I by Giovanni dell'Opera. Off Via de' Conti, which leads out of the piazza, is Via Zanetti (**Map 1; 1,3**). Here, at no. 8, is the modest façade of **Palazzo Martelli**, with a tabernacle on the exterior which contains a *Madonna and Child with St John* attributed to Mino da Fiesole. The palace was left by the last member of the Martelli family to the Curia Vescovile in 1986 on condition that it was preserved as a gallery, and it has since been acquired by the state, together with the Martelli coat of arms by Donatello which is now kept in the Bargello Museum (see p 254). There are plans to open the palace to the public in the future, perhaps as a museum illustrating the history of the Florentine noble families.

A house was acquired here by the Martelli family in 1520. Up until the mid-15C, they were one of the richest merchant families in Florence and close friends of the Medici. Roberto Martelli (1408–64) was an important patron of

Donatello. Alterations were carried out to the house in 1668, and again in 1737 by Bernardino Ciurini. After 1819, the interior was decorated in neo-classical style. It retains the atmosphere of a discreet patrician family house, and contains one of the most important private collections left in Florence formed by Marco di Francesco Martelli in the 1640s (and augmented by the Roman collection of Abbot Domenico Martelli who died in 1735). It includes two good works by Beccafumi, a tondo by Piero di Cosimo (dated 1510, acquired by the Martelli in 1648) and a painting by Salvator Rosa. The main room and chapel have frescoes by Vincenzo Meucci (1738–39), and on the ground floor is a room decorated by Niccolò Contestabile (1759–1824).

The animated **Via dell'Ariento** leads away from San Lorenzo. It is lined with numerous market stalls (see above), and passes the huge **Mercato Centrale**, or Mercato di San Lorenzo (**Map 3; 6**). This is the principal food market in the town and is well worth a visit (opening times Mon–Sat, 07.00–13.00; also 16.30–19.30 on Saturday except in July and Aug). The magnificent cast-iron building by Giuseppe Mengoni (1874) was restored in 1980 when a mezzanine floor was constructed for the sale of fruit and vegetables, and a car park opened in the basement. The market produce is good value.

Via Sant' Antonino is another crowded street with popular food shops. On the corner of Via Faenza is an 18C tabernacle which encloses a 14C *Madonna and Child* attributed to the school of Taddeo Gaddi or to Michele di Maso Michelozzo. Another tabernacle in Via Sant'Antonino (on the corner of Piazza Unità Italiana) contains an enamelled terracotta *Madonna and Child* by Andrea della Robbia. In Via Panicale are more market stalls selling cheap clothes (locally known as 'Shanghai'). Via Chiara was Cellini's birthplace. Via dell'Ariento ends in **Via Nazionale**, a busy street. Here, above a fountain, there is a huge tabernacle by Giovanni della Robbia (1522). At the station end, at no. 15 Largo Alinari is the headquarters of **Fratelli Alinari**, founded in 1852 and famous for its black and white photography, particularly its documentation of Italy's art and architecture. The photo archive is open to the public Mon–Fri 09.00–13.00. A small museum illustrates the history of the firm.

In Via Faenza (**Map 3; 5,6**), just to the left, by a tabernacle with a fresco of the *Madonna and Child with Saints* by Giovanni di San Giovanni (1615), is the entrance (no. 42) to the **Cenacolo di Fuligno** named after the ex-convent of Sant'Onofrio (or Fuligno). Opening times 09.00–12.00 or when the custodian is available; ring any bell; ☎ 055 286 982 (S).

A convent was founded here in the early 14C, and part of the present building dates from 1420. After its suppression in the 19C, a beautiful *fresco of the *Last Supper* was discovered in the refectory. At first attributed to Raphael (whose bust was set up here at that time), it was later thought to be by the hand of Perugino. Recent studies have suggested that Perugino designed the work while he was in Florence in the last decade of the 15C but that it was executed by a member of his *bottega*, perhaps Giovan Maria di Bartolomeo, called Rocco Zoppo. It is in very good condition. In the background is a lovely landscape with the *Agony in the Garden*.

On the next corner (left), the poet Lamartine, then a diplomatic secretary, lived in 1826–29. In **Via Guelfa** (**Map 3; 3,6**), which also crosses Via Nazionale, is the church of **San Barnaba**. It preserves a 14C portal with a Della Robbian lunette. The pretty interior (only open on Sunday) was remodelled in 1700 and there is a Baroque organ above the nuns' choir. On the left wall a painting of the *Madonna and Saints* by Pier Francesco Toschi has been removed. The fragment of a fresco of Saints enthroned is attributed to Spinello Aretino. Nearby is a big edifice (which has been undergoing restoration for years) built by Bartolomeo Silvestri on the site of the **Convent of Sant'Orsola** as a tobacco manufactory in 1810. At no. 39 Via Panicale, there is a fresco in a niche by the circle of Botticelli (restored in 1995).

At the northwest end of Via Guelfa, then on the outskirts of the city, Luca della Robbia and his nephew Andrea had their house and kiln (after 1446): the kiln was used by the Della Robbian workshop up until the mid-16C.

Opposite the end of Via Montanelli is the Istituto Sant'Agnese (no. 79), an old people's home run by the Compagnia del Bigallo (see p 117), with a pretty little Baroque chapel (early 18C; frescoes by the school of Sagrestani).

11 • Santa Maria Novella and Ognissanti

Santa Maria Novella

Santa Maria Novella (**Map 3; 5**; opening times 07.00–11.30, 15.30–18.00) is the most important Gothic church in Tuscany. The first church (the foundations of which have been found), called Santa Maria delle Vigne, was built in 1094 on the site of a chapel (probably 9C). The Dominicans were given the property in 1221, and building was begun in 1246 at the east end of the present church. The Dominican friars Sisto and Ristoro are thought to have been the architects of the impressive

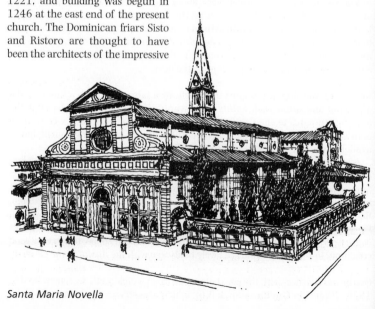

Santa Maria Novella

nave, begun in 1279. The church was completed under the direction of Fra' Jacopo Talenti in the mid-14C, when the great Dominican preacher Jacopo Passavanti was Prior. Nine Dominican monks still live in the convent.

The façade

The lower part of the distinctive marble façade is typically Tuscan Romanesque in style and is attributed to Fra' Jacopo Talenti. The upper portion (1456–70) is by Leon Battista Alberti, who Giovanni di Paolo Rucellai commissioned to complete the façade. Its classical lines are in perfect harmony with the earlier work. He also added the main portal (executed by Giovanni di Bertino). Exquisite inlaid friezes bear the emblems of the Rucellai (a billowing ship's sail) and of the Medici (a ring with ostrich feathers); in 1461 Giovanni Rucellai's son Bernardo married Nannina, daughter of Piero de' Medici. Below the tympanum, an inscription in handsome classical lettering records the name of the benefactor and the date 1470. Alberti's use of scrolls to connect the nave roof with the lower aisle roofs was an innovation which was frequently copied in church façades of later centuries. The two astronomical instruments (a quadrant with eight sundials and an equinoctial armilla) were made by Egnazio Danti in 1572–75.

To the right of the façade is a long line of Gothic arcaded recesses, the *avelli* or family-vaults of Florentine nobles. These extend around the old cemetery, with its cypresses, on the right side of the church. The painter Domenico Ghirlandaio (d. 1494) was buried here (4th *avello*). The **campanile**, also attributed to Fra' Jacopo Talenti, was grafted onto an ancient watch tower.

Interior

The spacious nave has remarkably bold stone vaulting, its arches given prominence by bands of dark grey *pietra serena*. Frescoes of **Saints** dating from the 14C have been exposed on the intrados of the arches. The composite pillars between nave and aisles have classical capitals. The bays decrease in width as they approach the three fine stained glass lancet windows at the east end. The interior was altered by Vasari in 1565, when the rood-screen (which formerly divided the church at the steps in the fourth bay) and the friars' choir were demolished, and side altars were set up in the nave (replaced by the present neo-Gothic ones in the 19C).

Although the church has recently been carefully restored with the *intonaco* of the walls returned to its original appearance and a new illumination system installed, the most important chapels (including the Cappella Rucellai, the Cappella di Filippo Strozzi, the main east chapel, and the Cappella Strozzi) are cordoned off and so difficult to examine in detail. For admission to visit the interiors, ☎ 055 286 086.

West wall Here there is a fresco (**1**) by the Florentine school (late 14C). The stained glass in the rose window is thought to have been designed by Andrea di Bonaiuto (c 1365). Over the west door is a frescoed lunette of the **Nativity** attributed as an early work to Botticelli (the artist's famous **Adoration of the Magi**, now in the Uffizi, was commissioned by a money dealer called della Lama for a small altar here). On the left of the door (**2**), **Annunciation**, by Santi di Tito.

South aisle First altar (**3**), **Martyrdom of St Lawrence** by Girolamo Macchietti. The monument (**4**) to the Blessed Villana delle Botti (d. 1361) by Bernardo Rossellino (1451), has two pretty angels. Second altar (**5**) **Nativity** by Giovanni Battista Naldini. The 16C monument (**6**) to Giovanni da Salerno, founder of the convent, by Vincenzo Danti, is an imitation of Rossellino's monument. The next two altarpieces (**7** and **8**) are also by Naldini. To the right of a *Deposition* is a monument (**9**) to Ruggero Minerbetti (d. 1210), by Silvio Cosini (c 1528) with bizarre Mannerist trophies. Beyond a highly venerated 20C statue of the Madonna of the Rosary with St Dominic, the fifth altar (**10**) has a painting of St Vincent Ferrer by Jacopo del Meglio.

In the 15C Cappella della Pura, or Purità (**A**; sometimes closed), the 14C fresco of the *Madonna and Child with St Catherine and a Donor*, was detached from an *avello* (tomb) outside the church. The wooden *Crucifix* over the other altar is by Baccio da Montelupo. On the sixth altar (**11**) is the *Miracle of St Raymond* by Jacopo Ligozzi.

South transept There are three Gothic tombs (**12**) here. The highest one (moved here by Vasari) is that of Bishop Aliotti (d. 1336), once attributed to Tino da Camaino, the one on the left is of Fra' Aldovrando Cavalcanti (d. 1279), and below it is the tomb of Joseph, Patriarch of Constantinople, with a contemporary fresco of him. The patriarch, who was in Florence to attend the Council of Florence in 1439, died in the convent in the following year.

The simple, classical sarcophagus tomb of Paolo Rucellai precedes the **Cappella Rucellai** (**B**), which housed Duccio's famous *Madonna* in the 18C (removed to the Uffizi in 1948). It now contains a marble *statue of the *Madonna and Child* signed by Nino Pisano, and the bronze tomb-slab of the Dominican general Lionardo Dati by Lorenzo Ghiberti (1425; removed from the nave in front of the high altar). The walls have traces of 14C frescoes: those flanking the closed Gothic window are attributed to the circle of the St Cecilia Master (c 1305–10). The large painting of the *Martyrdom of St Catherine* is an interesting work by Giuliano Bugiardini. On the wall outside the chapel is a tomb-slab with the effigy of Corrado della Penna, Bishop of Fiesole (d. 1313).

The **Cappella dei Bardi** (**C**) was formerly used by the Laudesi brotherhood, which was founded c 1245 by St Peter Martyr. They commissioned the so-called *Rucellai Madonna* from Duccio for this chapel (later moved to the Cappella Rucellai, see above) in 1285. The bas-relief of *Riccardo di Ricco Bardi Kneeling Before St Gregory* dates from the year after his death in 1334 when his heirs took possession of the chapel. Frescoes of the late 14C partially cover earlier fresco fragments. The damaged lunettes above (with the *Madonna Enthroned*) of c 1285 have recently been attributed to Cimabue. The altarpiece of the *Madonna of the Rosary* is by Vasari.

The ***Cappella di Filippo Strozzi** (**D**) is decorated with splendid exuberant ***frescoes** by **Filippino Lippi**. The Gothic chapel was acquired in 1486 by the great Florentine banker Filippo Strozzi who built Palazzo Strozzi (see p 243) and was agent for the Medici in Naples. He commissioned the frescoes from Filippino as soon as he had finished work on the Brancacci chapel in the church of the Carmine (see p 298), and the contract for the work survives (and makes copious mention of the necessity to add lapis lazuli to the surface of the fresco after it had dried, *a secco*). The artist interrupted the work when he was called to Rome to fresco the Carafa chapel in Santa Maria sopra Minerva, and only finished it after his return to Florence in 1502. Full of allusions to Antiquity and including grotesques, they are quite different from other Florentine fresco cycles of this period. They show that Filippino was a superb draftsman (the preparatory drawings for the frescoes survive in the Uffizi). The chapel was beautifully restored in 1997–2000. On the right wall is the *Crucifixion of St Philip the Apostle*, and his

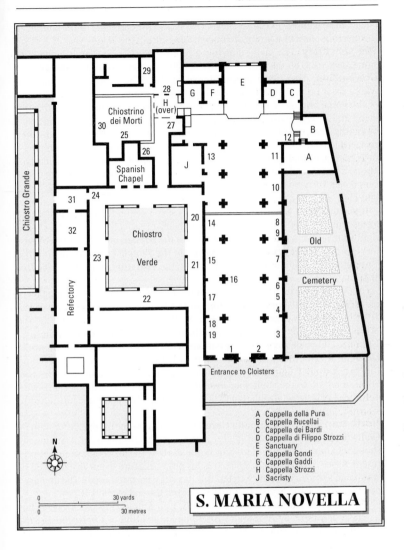

A Cappella della Pura
B Cappella Rucellai
C Cappella dei Bardi
D Cappella di Filippo Strozzi
E Sanctuary
F Cappella Gondi
G Cappella Gaddi
H Cappella Strozzi
J Sacristy

S. MARIA NOVELLA

Miracle Before the Temple of Mars (on the extreme right is a portrait of Filippino's black servant). On the left wall is the *Martyrdom of St John the Evangelist* and the *Raising of Drusiana*. In the vault, *Adam*, *Noah*, *Abraham* and *Jacob*. Filippino also designed the beautiful stained glass window and the splendid classical *trompe l'œil* frescoes in grisaille on the altar wall. Strozzi ordered that his *tomb, exquisitely carved by Benedetto da Maiano, should be given pride of place on the altar wall itself (although an altar was subsequently placed in front of it). The four *Patriarchs* in the vault were the first part of the chapel to be painted. In the *Decameron*, Boccaccio uses this part of the church as the meeting-place of a group of young people during the Plague year of 1348.

The sanctuary The main altar has a bronze *Crucifix* by Giambologna. The sanctuary (E) is decorated with delightful *frescoes by **Domenico Ghirlandaio**. They were commissioned in 1485 by Giovanni Tornabuoni, whose sister Lucrezia married Piero il Gottoso. Giovanni was for years manager of the Rome branch of the Medici bank. The frescoes are Ghirlandaio's masterpiece, and he was assisted by his brother Davide, his brother-in-law, Sebastiano Mainardi, and his pupils, including perhaps the young Michelangelo. They replaced a fresco cycle by Orcagna (fragments of which, with heads of *Prophets*, have been detached from the vault), and follow a similar iconographical design. Many of the figures are portraits of the artist's contemporaries, including members of the Tornabuoni family, and the whole cycle mirrors Florentine life in the late 15C.

Unfortunately it is normally no longer possible to enter the chapel and so the frescoes are very difficult to see in detail (to book a visit, 📱 055 286 086). On the right wall are scenes from the *Life of St John the Baptist*, including (lower register) the *Angel Appearing to St Zacharias in the Temple* (with portraits of the Tornabuoni and famous humanist scholars), the *Visitation*, and (above) *Birth of St John*.

On the left wall, there are scenes from the *Life of the Virgin*, including (lower register) the *Expulsion of St Joachim from the Temple* (with members of the Tornabuoni family, and, in the group on the right, the self-portraits of the artists), and the *Birth of the Virgin* (with portraits of the Tornabuoni ladies).

On the end wall, there is a *Coronation of the Virgin*, *Miracle of St Dominic*, *Death of St Peter Martyr*, *Annunciation*, *St John the Baptist in the Desert*, and the two kneeling figures of the donors, Giovanni Tornabuoni and his wife Francesca Pitti. In the vault, four *Evangelists* are shown. The stained glass windows (c 1491) were also designed by Ghirlandaio. The stalls are attributed to Baccio d'Agnolo.

North transept The **Cappella Gondi** (F) has handsome marble decoration by Giuliano da Sangallo. There is also a *Crucifix* by Brunelleschi, traditionally thought to have been carved to show Donatello how the Redeemer should be represented (see Santa Croce, p 269). It is his only sculpture to survive in wood (it was made to include a loin cloth but this has since been removed). The damaged vault frescoes of the *Evangelists* may date from the end of the 13C.

The **Cappella Gaddi** (G) designed by Giovanni Antonio Dosio (1575–77) has a cupola decorated by Alessandro Allori, and a painting of *Christ Raising the Daughter of Jairus* by Bronzino. The two bas-reliefs on the walls are by Giovanni Bandini.

At the end of the transept the *Cappella Strozzi* (H) is a remarkably well-preserved example of a mid-14C Tuscan chapel. It contains celebrated *frescoes (c 1357) by **Nardo di Cione**; they are his most famous work and are carefully designed to cover the entire chapel. They represent (in the vault), *St Thomas Aquinas* and the *Virtues*; on the end wall, the *Last Judgement*; on the left wall, *Paradise*, a huge crowded composition; and on the right wall, *Inferno*, a pictorial commentary on Dante's Inferno. The splendid frescoed decoration is completed on the intrados of the entrance arch with a frieze of *Saints*. The stained-glass window was designed by Nardo di Cione and his brother Andrea di Cione

(Orcagna), who painted the fine *altarpiece of the **Redeemer Giving the Keys to St Peter and the Book of Wisdom to St Thomas Aquinas** (1357), remarkable for its unusual iconography. On the outside wall of the chapel, at the base of the campanile (closed, but containing very old frescoes) is a ruined fresco of the **Coronation of the Virgin**, traditionally attributed to Buffalmacco.

The Sacristy The Sacristy (J) has a fine cross-vault by Fra' Jacopo Talenti (c 1350). The stained glass windows date from 1386 and are thought to have been designed by Niccolò Gerini. On the left of the door is a lavabo in terracotta with a charming landscape—the first documented work by Giovanni della Robbia (1498); the upper part may be by Andrea della Robbia. A *Crucifix* that is an early work by Giotto used to be hung above the entrance; it was removed for restoration in 1987 and is expected to be rehung in the nave of the church when it returns. The huge cupboard on the opposite wall was designed by Buontalenti (1593). On the walls are paintings of the **Conversion of St Paul** by Jacopo Ligozzi; **Baptism of Christ** by Giovanni Stradano; **St Vincent Ferrer** by Pietro Dandini; and **Crucifixion** by Vasari.

North aisle Notable paintings in this part of the church include: on the sixth altar (**13**), **Saints** by Alessandro Allori and on the fourth altar (**14**), **Resurrection and Saints** by Vasari. **Masaccio**'s famous fresco of the *Trinity* (**15**) is at present covered for restoration. It shows the **Virgin and St John the Evangelist with Donors**, above a skeleton on a sarcophagus. It is one of the earliest works to use accurately the system of linear perspective developed by Brunelleschi; indeed, it may be that the architect himself intervened in the design of the shadowy niche. The prefect composition gives it an almost metaphysical quality. The fresco was commissioned by the Lenzi family (shown as the donors) for their altar here. To the left is a painting of **St Lucy** with a donor by Davide Ghirlandaio. The gilded pulpit (**16**) from which Caccini denounced Galileo's astronomical theories, was designed by Brunelleschi and executed by his adopted son Buggiano. On the second altar (**17**) is Alessandro Allori's **Christ at the Well**; and to the left an **Annunciation**, in the manner of Bicci di Lorenzo. The monument (**18**) to Antonio Strozzi (1524) is by Andrea Ferrucci, with a **Madonna** by his pupil, Silvio Cosini. The first altar (**19**) has a **Resurrection of Lazarus** by Santi di Tito.

Museo di Santa Maria Novella

To the left of the church is the entrance to the Museo di Santa Maria Novella, arranged in the Convent of Santa Maria Novella which was one of the richest and largest in Florence. Opening times 09.00–14.00; closed Fri (☎ 055 282 187); Lire 5000 (C).

The cloisters remain an oasis of calm in this busy part of the city. Eugenius IV transferred the Papal court here in 1434–43 during sessions of the Council of Florence (1439) which attempted to heal the Eastern schism. Foundations of the church of 1094 have been found during excavations.

Chiostro Verde

The Romanesque *Chiostro Verde (c 1330–50) takes its name from the green colour of its famous decoration (in the vaults are roundels of Dominican saints). The damaged *frescoes by **Paolo Uccello** and assistants (including Dello Delli) are painted in *terraverde*. They illustrate stories from Genesis (the biblical references are given below each scene), and the cycle begins at the far end of the **east**

(entrance) walk beside the door into the church. The numerous frescoes with animals are particularly charming. The following scenes are usually considered to be by Paolo Uccello himself (perhaps with the help of Dello Delli): the *Creation of Adam and the Animals*, the *Creation and Temptation of Eve* (c 1425; 20), and the *Flood, and the Recession of the Flood* (with Noah's ark), and the *Sacrifice and Drunkenness of Noah* (c 1446; 21). Although much damaged, they are most remarkable for their figure studies and perspective effects; the later works are among the most mysterious and disturbing paintings of the Florentine Renaissance.

The frescoes in the **south walk** (**22**) are attributed to a Florentine painter of the first half of the 15C. In the **west walk** (**23**) the first fresco is attributed to Dello Delli, and the others to another Florentine painter of the first half of the 15C. Over the door into the Refectory (see below) is a detached fresco of *Christ on the Cross with Saints Dominic and Thomas Aquinas* attributed to Stefano Fiorentino (mid-14C). At the beginning of the north walk (**24**) is a fresco attributed to Bernardino Poccetti (c 1592), and a lunette of the *Madonna and Child*, a Sienese work of c 1330, possibly by Lippo Memmi.

At the centre of this peaceful cloister stand four cypresses around a raised well, and there is a good view of the side of the church, the exterior of the sacristy with its stained glass windows, and of the campanile.

Cappellone degli Spagnuoli

Off the cloister opens the Cappellone degli Spagnuoli, or Spanish Chapel. It received its name in the 16C when it was assigned by Duchess Eleonora di Toledo to the Spanish members of her retinue. It was originally the chapter house, built by Jacopo Talenti in the mid-14C with a splendid cross-vault and two fine Gothic windows. The walls and vault are entirely covered with colourful *frescoes* by **Andrea di Bonaiuto** (sometimes called Andrea da Firenze) and assistants (c 1365), the most important work by this otherwise little-known artist who was influenced by the Sienese school of painting. Restoration of the frescoes was begun in 1991 and has been completed except for the altar wall.

The pictorial decoration, on a monumental scale, is carefully designed to fit the wall space. In the vault are the *Resurrection*, the *Ascension*, and the *Pentecost*. The *Navicella* is particularly beautiful and thought to have been painted before the other scenes by a master close to Giotto. On the altar wall are the *Via Dolorosa*, *Crucifixion*, and *Descent into Limbo*. On the right wall are various scenes illustrating the *Mission*, *Works* and *Triumph of the Dominican Order*. In front of the elaborate church, the artist's vision of the completed Duomo, is the *Church Militant with the Pope and Emperor and Church Dignitaries*. In the foreground (right), behind a group of kneeling pilgrims, are the presumed portraits of Cimabue, Giotto, Boccaccio, Petrarch and Dante. The scene on the bottom right shows *St Dominic Sending Forth the Hounds of the Lord* (*Domini canes*), with St Peter Martyr and St Thomas Aquinas. Above, four seated figures symbolising the *Vices* are surrounded by representations of dancing *Virtues*. A *Dominican Friar Taking Confession* shows the way to salvation, and those absolved are sent on towards the Gate of Paradise guarded by St Peter. On the other side of the gate, the Blessed look up towards *Christ in Judgement* surrounded by angels.

The opposite wall shows the *Triumph of Catholic Doctrine* personified by St

Thomas Aquinas, who is shown enthroned beneath the winged Virtues. On his right and left are Doctors of the Church. In the Gothic choir stalls below are 14 female figures symbolising the Arts and Sciences, with, at their feet, historical personages representing these virtues. On the entrance wall is the *Life of St Peter Martyr* (damaged). The polyptych by Bernardo Daddi painted for the chapter house in 1344 has been removed for restoration. The apse chapel was decorated in 1592 with vault frescoes by Bernardino Poccetti and an altarpiece of *St Jacob* by Alessandro Allori.

From the cloister, there is a passage (**31**), which displays the sinopie of the frescoes of *Paradise* by Nardo di Cione that are in the Cappella Strozzi (inside the church). The passage leads towards the imposing **Chiostro Grande** (no admission as it is part of a police barracks), which can be seen through a glass door. The frescoes were carried out in the early 1580s by Poccetti, with the help of Bernardino Monaldi and Cosimo Gheri, and are the first example in Florence of religious painting inspired by the Counter Reformation.

On the left of the passage is the entrance to the **Cappella degli Ubriachi** (**32**). This chapel was built by Francesco Jacopo Talenti (1365–66) and it preserves the tomb-slab of the Ubriachi family and traces of wall decoration showing their emblem. Here also are displayed detached frescoes of *Prophets* by Andrea Orcagna and his school, from the vault of the main chapel in the church, and the sinopie of the first frescoes by Paolo Uccello from the east walk of the Chiostro Verde. In the showcases, there are charming reliquary busts (Sienese school, late 14C), and a frontal made for the high altar of the church, beautifully embroidered with scenes from the life of the Virgin (Florentine, c 1460–66).

The large **refectory** has superb cross-vaulting in three bays also by Talenti. On the entrance wall there is a large fresco of the *Manna in the Desert* by Alessandro Allori which surrounds a good fresco attributed to a follower of Agnolo Gaddi, contemporary with the building, and probably part of a larger composition which covered the entire wall. It shows the *Madonna Enthroned Between St Thomas Aquinas, St Dominic St John the Baptist and St Peter Martyr* (the tiny figure of the Prior of the convent, Fra' Jacopo Passavanti, is shown at the feet of St Dominic). On the left wall there is a *Last Supper* by Alessandro Allori (1583). The showcases display 16C and 17C reliquaries, church silver and vestments belonging to the convent.

Other parts of the convent have been closed for restoration for some years: they include the oldest part, the **Chiostrino dei Morti** (**25**; c 1270), and chapels (**26, 27** and **28**) with mid-14C frescoes. In another chapel (**29**) is displayed a colossal statue of St John of Salerno by Girolamo Ticciati. A tabernacle (**30**) in the cloister contains a terracotta by the workshop of Giovanni della Robbia.

Additional parts of the convent off the Chiostro Grande only open on special occasions include the remarkable vaulted dormitory (now used as a refectory) and (upstairs) the **Cappella dei Papi** built in 1515 for Leo X, with frescoes of the *Veronica* and of putti on the barrel vault by Pontormo, and a *Coronation of the Virgin* by Ridolfo del Ghirlandaio.

Piazza Santa Maria Novella, with its irregular shape, was created by the Dominicans at the end of the 13C. The two obelisks were set up in 1608 (resting on bronze tortoises by Giambologna) as turning posts in the course of the annual chariot race (Palio dei Cocchi) which was first held here in 1563. The **Loggia di San Paolo** was erected on the south-west side of the square in 1489–96 (restored in 1999). It is a free copy of Brunelleschi's Loggia degli Innocenti, with polychrome terracotta roundels of Franciscan saints by Andrea della Robbia, who also produced the beautiful *lunette beneath the arcade (right) of the *Meeting of St Francis and St Dominic*.

The tabernacle on the corner of Via della Scala contains a fresco by Francesco d'Antonio. In the house on the corner here Henry James began writing *Roderick Hudson* in 1874. Henry Wordsworth Longfellow stayed in the hotel here.

In Via della Scala (no. 16) is the **Farmacia di Santa Maria** Novella (opening times 09.00–13.00, 15.30–19.30 except Saturday afternoon and Monday morning). The pharmacy attached to the convent of Santa Maria Novella had become important as a chemist's shop by the mid-16C, and it is still famous as such in Florence, producing its own perfumes and soap. The present shop is in the ex-14C chapel of San Niccolò decorated in a delightful neo-Gothic style in 1848 by Enrico Romoli. It has Art Nouveau lamps and frescoes representing the four continents by Paolino Sarti. The other rooms are shown on request: one overlooking the former physic garden has late 18C furnishings, pharmacy jars (including Montelupo ware), and a carved Medici coat of arms with a painted portrait of St Peter Martyr by Matteo Rosselli. The charming old chemist's shop, overlooking the Great Cloister of Santa Maria Novella (see above), has 17C vases including *albarelli* (pharmacy jars) and mortars. The sacristy of San Niccolò has frescoes of the *Passion* thought to be by Mariotto di Nardo.

Off the east side of Piazza Santa Maria Novella, the winding Via delle Belle Donne leads shortly to a crossroads in the middle of which stands the **Croce del Trebbio** (from the Latin, *trivium*, because it is at the meeting of three streets), a granite column reconsecrated in 1338 with a Gothic capital bearing symbols of the Evangelists. Above this, protected by a quaint little wooden roof, is a Cross of the Pisan school protected by a wooden tabernacle. It is traditionally thought to commemorate a massacre of heretics which took place here in 1244.

Via de' Fossi leads towards the Arno. It takes its name from the ditch outside the city walls built here in 1173–75, and contains a number of well-known antique shops. The church of Ognissanti may be reached from here either by Via de' Fossi and then Borgo Ognissanti, or by Via Palazzuolo (right) and then (left) Via del Porcellana. On the corner between Via del Porcellana and Via Palazzuolo a stone tabernacle encloses a 14C fresco of the *Madonna and Child Enthroned with Saints Anthony Abbot and John the Evangelist*.

In Via Palazzuolo stands the church of **San Paolino** (Map 3; 7) which was founded in the 10C and has a bare façade. Opening times 09.00–11.30, 16.00–17.00, or 16.30–17.30 in summer.

The **interior** was rebuilt in 1669 by Giovanni Battista Balatri, and is interesting for its 17C–18C paintings.

On the south side, the first chapel contains two Albizzi funerary monuments attributed to the *bottega* of Giovanni Battista Foggini, which incorporate two skeletons. In the second chapel, there is an *Annunciation* by a follower of Giovanni Antonio Sogliani and two paintings by (left) Francesco di Antonio Ciseri (1891) and (right) Volterrano. The south transept has a polychrome marble altar and an altarpiece of the *Death of St Joseph* by Giovanni Domenico Ferretti. On either side of this are the *Marriage of the Virgin* by Vincenzo Meucci and the *Rest on the Flight* by Ignazio Hugford. In the Sanctuary is the *Ecstasy of St Paul* by Francesco Curradi.

On the north side, the north transept has a marble altar by Girolamo Ticciati, and another altarpiece by Francesco Curradi. In the first chapel (left wall) is *Christ in the Garden* by Tommaso Gherardini and (right wall), the *Adoration of the Magi* by Giovanni Domenico Ferretti. The pretty 18C confessionals have tondi painted by Ottaviano Dandini.

At 17 Via Palazzuolo is the **Oratorio di San Francesco dei Vanchetoni** (now owned by the Comune and usually closed, but the custodian lives next door and sometimes shows it on request). It is often used for concerts. It was built in 1602 by Giovanni Nigetti, with a vestibule and façade by Matteo Nigetti (1620). The ceiling frescoes are by Pietro Liberi, Volterrano, Cecco Bravo and others (possibly including Giovanni da San Giovanni and Lorenzo Lippi). The chapel behind the altar contains a 16C *Crucifix*, and the charming sacristy has inlaid cupboards.

In the wide Borgo Ognissanti stands the church of **San Giovanni di Dio** (open for services), built by Carlo Marcellini (1702–13) next to the ex-hospital of San Giovanni di Dio, founded in 1380 by the Vespucci family. It was enlarged in 1702–13 by Carlo Marcellini incorporating the Vespucci house on this site, including the birthplace of Amerigo (see below). The hospital here was closed in 1982. In the fine atrium (1735) are sculptures by Girolamo Ticciati. In 1770, Mozart stayed at no. 8—then the Albergo Aquila Nera—when he came to give a concert at Poggio Imperiale. At no. 26, there is an Art Nouveau house designed by Giovanni Michelazzi (c 1911).

The church of Ognissanti

The church of Ognissanti (**Map 3; 7**; opening times 07.45–12.00, 17.00–18.30; *fest.* 8.45–13.00, 17.00–19.30) was founded in 1256 by the Umiliati, a Benedictine Order particularly skilled in manufacturing wool. This area of the city became one of the main centres of the woollen cloth industry, on which medieval Florence based her economy. Mills on the Arno were used for washing, fulling, and dying the cloth. Since 1561, the church has been owned by the Franciscans; it was rebuilt in the 17C. The original *pietra serena* **façade** by Matteo Nigetti (1637) was rebuilt in travertine in 1872 (and cleaned in 2000). Above the portal is a glazed terracotta lunette of the Coronation of the Virgin ascribed to Benedetto Buglioni. The **campanile** dates from 1258.

Interior

The *trompe l'œil* ceiling frescoes are by Giuseppe Benucci and Giuseppe Romei (1770). The fine large pavement tomb of Antonio di Vitale de' Medici (d. 1656) bears the Medici arms in marble intarsia.

South side First altar, *Ascension* by Lodovico Buti; second altar, frescoes of the **Pietà** and the **Madonna della Misericordia**, early works by Domenico Ghirlandaio. The Madonna is shown protecting the Vespucci family (Amerigo is supposed to be the young boy whose head appears between the Madonna and the man in the dark cloak). The family tombstone (1471) is in the pavement left of the altar. The Vespucci, who lived in Borgo Ognissanti, were merchants involved in the manufacture of silk. As supporters of the Medici they held political office in the 15C. Amerigo (1451–1512), a Medici agent in Seville, gave his name to America having made two voyages in 1499 and 1501–02 following the route charted by his Italian contemporary Columbus.

Third altar, *Madonna and Saints* by Santi di Tito. Between the third and fourth altars is a fresco of **St Augustine in his Study*, a splendid work by Botticelli. This, together with its pendent opposite by Ghirlandaio of *St Jerome*, was painted in 1480 for the choir of the church. They were moved here when the church was altered in 1564. **Fourth altar**, *St Francis Receiving the Stigmata* by Nicodemo Ferrucci. The fine pulpit is attributed to Battista Lorenzi; the bas-reliefs have been attributed to a pupil of Benedetto da Rovezzano. The **fifth altarpiece** is by Vincenzo Dandini.

South transept The frescoes in the Baroque chapels in the south transept date from c 1717–22. First altar (on the right), *San Diego Healing the Sick* by Jacopo Ligozzi. The adjacent chapel was decorated in 1727: it has pretty stuccoes, a dome frescoed by Matteo Bonechi, and two frescoes on the side walls by Vincenzo Meucci. The round tombstone in the pavement marks the burial place of Sandro Filipepi (Botticelli), whose family lived in the parish. In the chapel at the end of the transept, there are ceiling frescoes by Gian Domenico Ferretti, and an altarpiece by Vincenzo Dandini (1667). On the side walls are two late 16C paintings, interesting as portraits of contemporary Florentines in period costume. In the next chapel, which has a dome frescoed by Ranieri del Pace, there are two paintings by Matteo Rosselli (the *Martyrdom of St Andrew* is particularly good). The handsome pavement tomb of Lorenzo Lenzi (d. 1442), with a coat of arms bearing a bronze relief of the head of a bull, has been attributed to Lorenzo Ghiberti. The altarpiece is by Giuseppe Pinzani. In the second chapel to the right of the high altar are frescoes by a little-known artist called Giovanni Cinqui (1667–1743), and in the first chapel right of the high altar, an altarpiece by Pier Dandini.

Choir chapel This is decorated with precious marbles and has frescoes in the dome by Giovanni da San Giovanni (1616–17). The beautiful high altar (1593–1605), probably by Jacopo Ligozzi, has a frontal in polychrome marble intarsia and mother-of-pearl of exquisite workmanship, and three mosaic panels in *commesso fiorentino*, with a tabernacle above in *pietre dure*. The bronze figure of Christ on a wooden Cross was commissioned from Bartolomeo Cennini in 1669. It is flanked by two marble angels by Andrea Ferrucci.

North transept In the first chapel left of the high altar, there are paintings by Pier Dandini. In the second chapel is exhibited the habit worn by St Francis in 1224 when he received the stigmata at La Verna. It was given by the saint to Count Alberto Barbolani when he stayed with him in the castle of Montauto in the same year, and in 1503 the relic was captured by the Florentines in a war against Arezzo. Formerly beneath the high altar, it was put here in 1985. The 14C reliquary casket in which it was kept is also displayed here. On the wall is a *Crucifix* by a sculptor of the school of Veit Stoss (c 1437–1533).

The sacristy is now usually visited from the cloisters (see below). Steps lead up to the chapel at the end of the transept, which has a small portable organ by Giovanni Francesco Cacioli of Lucca and Tronci of Pistoia (1741). Beneath the steps is a niche, the arch of which has sculptures dating from 1375. The sculpture of the *Dead Christ* dates from the 17C.

North side Above the fifth altar (with a 14C Crucifix) is an organ by Onofrio Zeffirini (1565). Between the fourth and the third altars is Domenico Ghirlandaio's fresco of *St Jerome in his study*, a pendant to Botticelli's fresco opposite (see above). On the third altar, the painting of the *Assumption* has recently been attributed to Pier Francesco Foschi (the angels above are by Santi di Tito). Above the font is a fresco of the *Trinity*, with the *Coronation of the Virgin* above, by Ridolfo del Ghirlandaio. On the first altar, there is an *Annunciation* by Bartolomeo Traballesi.

Cenacolo di Ognissanti

On the left of the church, beneath a fine polychrome terracotta Della Robbian coat of arms of Alessandro de' Medici, is the entrance (no. 42) to the **Convent**, occupied by Franciscan friars of the Osservanza since 1561 (opening times Mon, Tues and Sat 09.00–12.00). In the vestibule are early 17C frescoes of the *Life of Mary* by Ulisse Ciocchi. The 15C **cloister**, with reused Ionic capitals, in the style of Michelozzo, was altered in the 16C. It incorporates octagonal pilasters which support part of the Gothic church. The 13C campanile can also be seen here.

The frescoes illustrating the *Life of St Francis* were executed in 1599/1600–24 under the direction of Jacopo Ligozzi. Sir Joshua Reynolds came here in 1752 to copy the frescoes. The cycle begins on the left of the entrance in the **south walk**. Jacopo Ligozzi: the *Birth of St Francis*; the *Saint Giving his Cloak to a Poor Man*; the *Saint Comforting a Leper in a Wood*; the *Saint Before the Crucifix of San Damiano*, the *Saint Renouncing his Worldly Goods in Front of his Father*; and the *Saint Attacked by Brigands* (in a wood after a fall of snow) beside a scene of the *Saint with his First Followers*. The last lunette in this walk shows Innocent III giving his approval of the Order.

The scenes in the **west walk**, also by Ligozzi, begin with the *Meeting of St Francis and St Dominic* and *St Francis Appearing Before his Companions in a Chariot of Fire* and end with the lunette showing the *Saint Before the Sultan*.

The first five lunettes in the **north walk** are by Giovanni da San Giovanni (the first shows the *Expulsion of the Demons from Arezzo*). The sixth lunette is by Galeazzo Ghidoni, the seventh by Filippo Tarchiani, and the last in this walk, showing the *Meeting of St Francis with St Dominic in San Giovanni in Laterano*, is another work by Ligozzi.

The first lunette in the **east walk** is also by Ligozzi and shows *St Francis Receiving the Stigmata*—though it is in very poor condition. The other lunettes in this walk are by Nicodemo Ferrucci, ending with the *Death of St Francis*, and *St Dominic and St Francis* on either side of a door.

The pretty vaulted **refectory**, with its lavabos and pulpit in *pietra serena*, contains a *Last Supper* by **Domenico Ghirlandaio** (1480), the most beautiful of his several frescoes of this subject in Florence. The delightful background includes plants and birds which are Christian symbols. Its sinopia is displayed on another wall. The fresco of the *Annunciation* dates from 1369.

On request, the custodian shows the **sacristy** which has decorative wall-paintings of the early 14C. The *Crucifixion*, with its sinopia, is attributed to Taddeo Gaddi or his circle, and the *Resurrection* and fragment of the *Ascension* have been attributed to Pietro Nelli. The large painted *Crucifix*, for long attributed to a close follower of Giotto, sometimes identified as Stefano Fiorentino, is now thought by most scholars to be by the master himself. A small museum (closed indefinitely), on the other side of the cloister, has a charming 15C *Madonna and Child* in polychrome terracotta by Nanni di Bartolo, as well as choir books, altar frontals, church silver and reliquaries.

Piazza Ognissanti, with two luxury hotels, opens onto the Arno. On the right is Palazzo Lenzi, built c 1470. The graffiti were repainted when the palace was restored in 1885. It is now occupied by the French Consul and French Institute, founded in Florence by Julien Luchaire for the University of Grenoble in 1907–08. Across the Arno, the domed church of San Frediano in Cestello and the green hill of Bellosguardo are prominent.

12 • Santa Trìnita, Palazzo Strozzi and Palazzo Rucellai

This chapter describes the Gothic church of Santa Trìnita and the Baroque church of San Gaetano at either end of the fashionable Via Tornabuoni, as well as the very fine 15C–16C palaces in this street, including Palazzo Strozzi. In Via della Vigna Nuova, which runs into Via Tornabuoni, is the Renaissance Palazzo Rucellai.

Ponte Santa Trìnita (see Ch. 17) crosses the Arno at the beginning of **Via Tornabuoni (Map 1; 5)**. This is the most elegant street in Florence, famous for its fashionable shops which include Ferragamo and Gucci. At the beginning on the right stands the splendid battlemented ***Palazzo Spini-Feroni (Map 1; 5)**, one of the best-preserved and largest private medieval palaces in the city. It was built for Geri degli Spini in 1289, possibly by Lapo Tedesco, master of Arnolfo di Cambio and was restored in the 19C. The palace was bought by the Comune in 1846 and was the seat of the town council in 1860–70. The palace contains a private chapel frescoed by Bernardino Poccetti in 1609–12.

In 1938, it was purchased by Salvatore Ferragamo, a shoe designer who set up his famous shoe manufactory here. The shop is still on the ground floor, and on the second floor is the **Museo Salvatore Ferragamo**, a private museum opened in 1995 to illustrate the history of the firm (opening times Mon–Fri 09.00–13.00, 14.00–18.00; closed in Aug; prior appointment is advisable for visits ☎ 055 336 0456, 🖹 055 336 0475). It contains a collection of some 10,000 shoes made out of the most diverse materials; these are beautifully exhibited in rotation every two years in four rooms, taking a particular theme or period. Temporary exhibitions are also held in the basement. Ferragamo, who was born in a poor family in southern Italy in 1898, emigrated to America in 1914 and set up a shoe shop in Hollywood. He returned to Italy in 1927 and became world famous for his skill as a fashion shoe designer (his clients included Greta Garbo, Audrey Hepburn and Marilyn Monroe) before his death in 1960.

Santa Trìnita

Opposite is the church of Santa Trìnita (**Map 6; 1**; closed 12.00–16.00). The Latin pronunciation of its name betrays its ancient foundation. A church of the Vallombrosan Order existed on this site at least by 1077. Probably rebuilt in 1250–60, its present Gothic form dates from the end of the 14C and is attributed to Neri di Fioravante. The **façade** was added by Buontalenti in 1593–94. The relief of the *Trinity* is by Giovanni Caccini, who also carved the statue of St Alexius in the niche. The campanile (1396–97) can just be seen behind to the left.

Interior

The fine interior has the austerity characteristic of Cistercian churches. On the entrance wall, the interior façade of the Romanesque building survives. The church is unusually dark (best light in morning); each chapel has a light: the switches are inconspicuously placed to the left. High up on the outside arches of many of the chapels are remains of 14C–15C frescoes; the most interesting are those by Giovanni del Ponte outside the choir chapels.

South aisle **First chapel**, highly venerated wooden *Crucifix* (probably 14C) and detached fresco and sinopia of the 14C; **second chapel**, altarpiece of the *Preaching of St John the Baptist* by Francesco Curradi; **third chapel**, altarpiece of the *Madonna Enthroned with Four Saints*, by Neri di Bicci (removed). On the walls, detached fresco and sinopia by Spinello Aretino (considerably ruined) found beneath a fresco by Lorenzo Monaco in the adjoining chapel. The **fourth chapel** has damaged but beautiful *frescoes (including the entrance arch) by Lorenzo Monaco (1422). The *altarpiece of the *Annunciation*, with a lovely predella (beautifully restored in 1998) is also by him. **Fifth chapel**, *Pietà*, fresco attributed to Giovanni Toscani, and a handsome altar by Benedetto da Rovezzano, part of a monument to St John Gualberto, founder of the Vallombrosan Order (damaged in the siege of Florence, 1530). The painting of *Christ Resurrected and Saints* is by Maso di San Friano. In the side entrance porch are six worn Gothic tombs. The organ by Onofrio Zefferini (1571) was reconstructed in 1763 by the Tronci brothers.

The **sacristy** (opened on request) was formerly a Strozzi chapel, begun by Onofrio and completed by his son Pala Strozzi who was known for his learning as well as his wealth and died in exile as an opponent of the Medici. Onofrio's tomb here has been variously attributed to Piero di Niccolò Lamberti, Michelozzo, and, most recently, to Lorenzo Ghiberti. The painted decoration on the arch is by Gentile da Fabriano, who also painted his famous *Adoration of the Magi* (now in the Uffizi) for this chapel. The detached frescoes of the 14C include a *Pietà* and *Noli me tangere*.

Choir chapels The *Sassetti Chapel* has *frescoes by **Domenico Ghirlandaio** (coin-operated light in chapel) of the *Life of St Francis*. These were commissioned in 1483 by Francesco Sassetti, a merchant, manager of the Medici bank, and typical figure of Renaissance Florence. The scene in the lunette above the altar (*St Francis Receiving the Rule of the Order from Pope Honorius*) takes place in Piazza della Signoria and those present include: (in the foreground, right) Lorenzo il Magnifico with Sassetti and his son, and, to his right, Antonio Pucci. On the stairs are Agnolo Poliziano with Lorenzo il Magnifico's sons, Piero, Giovanni and Giuliano. In the *Miracle of the Boy Brought Back to Life* (beneath) is Piazza Santa Trìnita (with the Romanesque façade of the church and the old Ponte Santa Trìnita). The altarpiece shows the *Adoration of the Shepherds*

(1485) and is also by Ghirlandaio. It is flanked by the kneeling figures of the donors, Francesco Sassetti and Nera Corsi, his wife. Their tombs, with black porphyry sarcophagi, are attributed to Giuliano da Sangallo. The decoration of the chapel includes numerous references to classical antiquity (the Sibyl announcing the coming of Christ to Augustus on the outside arch; the four Sibyls on the vault; the Roman sarcophagus used as a manger in the *Adoration of the Shepherds*; and the carved details on the tombs).

In the chapel to the right of the main altar, the *Crucifix* (repainted in the 17C) is traditionally said to be the one which bowed approvingly to St John Gualberto in San Miniato when he pardoned his brother's assassin (it was probably, instead, the one now in the first south chapel). The painting of the *Madonna dello Spasimo* is by Bernardo di Stefano Rosselli.

In the **sanctuary,** there is a 15C classical altar above which is a triptych with the *Trinity and Saints* by Mariotto di Nardo (1424). The fine figures in the vault of *David*, *Abraham*, *Noah* and *Moses* are almost all that remains of the fresco decoration of the sanctuary by Alesso Baldovinetti. The first chapel left of the altar was redecorated in 1635. The bronze altar frontal of the *Martyrdom of St Lawrence* is by Tiziano Aspetti, and, on the left wall, *St Peter Receiving the Keys*, is by Empoli. The two lunette frescoes are by Giovanni di San Giovanni. In the second chapel left of the altar is the *tomb of Benozzo Federighi*, Bishop of Fiesole (d. 1450), by Luca della Robbia (1454–57). This was made for San Pancrazio and was moved here in 1896. The beautiful marble effigy is surrounded by an exquisite frame of enamelled terracotta mosaic on a gold ground. On the walls are detached fresco fragments by Giovanni del Ponte. The little chapel in the north transept, decorated by Passignano (1574), contains a reliquary of St John Gualberto.

North aisle **Fifth chapel**, *Mary Magdalen*, a fine wooden statue by Desiderio da Settignano, finished by Benedetto da Maiano. The fresco of a *Bishop Saint* in the niche here has recently been restored and attributed to Alesso Baldovinetti. **Fourth chapel**, detached fresco of *St John Gualberto* surrounded by Vallombrosian saints, by Neri di Bicci, and (on the outside arch) fresco of *St John Gualberto Pardoning his Brother's Assassin* by Bicci di Lorenzo. The painting of the *Annunciation* (1475) is by Neri di Bicci. **Third chapel**, altarpiece of the *Coronation of the Virgin* by Bicci di Lorenzo (1430). Also here are 14C frescoes and an *Annunciation* by Neri di Bicci. The tomb of Giuliano Davanzati (1444, attributed to Bernardo Rossellino) was adapted from an early Christian sarcophagus with a relief of the *Good Shepherd*. **Second chapel**, *Annunciation* and *St Jerome*, good works by Ridolfo del Ghirlandaio. The vault of the **first chapel** (1603) was painted by Bernardino Poccetti. It contains two statues by Giovanni Caccini, and an altarpiece of the *Annunciation* by Empoli.

The 11C **crypt** survives from the earlier church. It is approached from the nave (coin-operated light). The head of the Saviour in painted terracotta is attributed to Pietro Torrigiano (c 1519).

In the little **Piazza Santa Trìnita** stands the **Column of Justice**, a granite monolith from the Baths of Caracalla in Rome, presented by Pius IV to Cosimo I in 1560, and set up here in 1563 to commemorate his victory at Montemurlo in 1537. The porphyry figure of Justice, by Tadda (1581), has a bronze cloak added subsequently. The three narrow medieval streets leading out of the east side of the piazza are described in Ch. 21. Opposite the impressive curving façade of Palazzo Spini-Feroni is Palazzo Buondelmonti (no. 2) with a façade of c 1530 attributed to Baccio d'Agnolo.

Across Via delle Terme is **Palazzo Bartolini-Salimbeni** (no. 1), perhaps the best work of Baccio d'Agnolo (1520–23). Various types of stone were used in the fine façade, and the unusual courtyard has good graffiti decoration, and a delightful loggia on the first floor. The Hôtel du Nord was opened here in 1839, and the American writers Ralph Waldo Emerson, James Russell Lowell and Herman Melville all stayed here.

Beyond Via Porta Rossa (with a good view of Palazzo Davanzati, see p 317) Via Tornabuoni continues, lined with handsome mansions. On the left Palazzo Minerbetti (no. 3) dates from the 14C–15C. Palazzo Strozzi del Poeta (no. 5) was reconstructed by Gherardo Silvani in 1626. The Palazzo del Circolo dell'Unione (no. 7) may have been designed by Vasari. The pretty doorway is surmounted by a bust of Francesco I by Giambologna. On the right, a shop has replaced Doney's, a famous café, once frequented by foreigners in Florence, including Edmond and Jules Goncourt in the mid-19C, and, in this century, 'Ouida', D.H. Lawrence, Norman Douglas and the Sitwells.

Palazzo Strozzi

The huge Palazzo Strozzi (**Map 1; 3**) is the last and grandest of the magnificent Renaissance palaces in Florence, built for Filippo Strozzi (d. 1491). It is a typical 15C town-mansion—half-fortress, half-palace—with all three storeys of equal emphasis, constructed with large rough blocks of stone but left unfinished. The most complete side faces Piazza Strozzi. It is thought that Strozzi himself took an active part in the design of the building but it is not known who drew up the project. It was begun in 1489 and Cronaca is known to have been involved at a certain stage: he was responsible for the great projecting cornice, suggested by ancient classical examples, which was left half-finished when money ran out after the death of Filippo Strozzi. Cronaca also built the courtyard (finished in 1503). Giuliano da Sangallo executed a model (now in the Bagello museum), but he is no longer thought to have been involved in the building. The wrought-iron torch-holders and fantastic lanterns were designed by Benedetto da Maiano and executed by Caparra. The palace was recently bought by the state and the Comune will use it for exhibitions.

Vieusseux Library

The palace is also the seat of various learned institutes, including the Gabinetto Scientifico Letterario G.P. Vieusseux, with an excellent lending library. Opening times Mon–Fri 09.00–13.00, 15.00–18.00; Sat 09.00–13.00; the library is also open to non-residents.

It has some 300,000 volumes, half of which are in Italian. Dating mostly from the 19C and 20C, they cover literature, history, the arts and sciences, travel and biography. Sadly, 90 per cent of the library's holdings were severely damaged in the Arno flood in 1966. Lectures are given from time to time in the Sala Ferri which has attractive bookcases made in 1679 by Antonio Ferri for the hospital of Santa Maria Nuova and moved here in 1952.

The scientific and literary association was founded nearby in Palazzo Buondelmonti, on Via Tornabuoni, in 1819 by the Swiss scholar Gian Pietro

Vieusseux. It ran a circulating library with reading rooms and was directed by a member of the Vieusseux family throughout the 19C as a commercial enterprise. It stayed open every day until 23.00, membership was available to all on various terms (from a daily subscription to an annual one), and both reading rooms (where foreign periodicals were also available), and conversation rooms (where chess and other board games could be played) were provided, as well as a café. In 1873, the library moved to Palazzo Feroni, and soon after it became the property of the Comune; in 1921, it was moved again to Palagio di Parte Guelfa. Since 1940, it has been housed in Palazzo Strozzi.

The library has always been important in the intellectual life of the city, especially during the Risorgimento period, as a meeting place for foreigners, Florentines and Italians. It became famous throughout Italy and was frequented by all the well-known intellectuals of the day when they visited Florence, including Stendhal (1824), Alphonse de Lamartine (1825), Alessandro Manzoni (1827), James Fenimore Cooper (1828), Hector Berlioz (1831), Eugène Viollet-Le Duc (1837), Franz Liszt (1838), Robert Browning (1839), John Ruskin (1840), William Makepeace Thackeray (1845), Walter Savage Landor (1861), Dostoyevsky (1862), Carlo Lorenzini (Collodi; 1865), Tolstoy (1872), W.D. Howells (1882), John Singer Sargent (1883), Bernard Berenson (1889), Mark Twain (1893), Emile Zola (1894), Andrè Gide (1895) and Gabriele d'Annunzio (1899). In the early years of this century, it was visited by Arnold Bennett (1910), Rudyard Kipling (1912), Mario Praz (1915), Enrico Caruso (1918), Aldous Huxley (1921), Iris Origo (1924) and D.H. Lawrence (1926).

In Piazza Strozzi, Palazzo dello Strozzino, also built for the Strozzi, has a façade by Michelozzo, completed by Giuliano da Maiano. The language school of the British Institute (see p 292) has its headquarters here.

The crossroads in Via Tornabuoni with Via Strozzi Via della Vigna Nuova and Via della Spada, marks the centre of the Roman colony, and subsequently the west gate of the Roman city (see the plan on pp 90–91). The palace, fitting the awkward site between Via della Vigna Nuova and Via della Spada, was the home from 1614 of Sir Robert Dudley (1574–1649), Duke of Northumberland, who, on leaving England, became a naval engineer and took charge of the Arsenal in Livorno for Cosimo II and Ferdinando II (plaque placed in Via della Vigna Nuova in the 19C by his biographer John Temple Leader). In the corner house (left) George Eliot stayed while gathering material for Romola.

Via della Vigna Nuova, on the site of a huge orchard, leads past the narrow old Via dell'Inferno (left) to a little opening in front of **Palazzo Rucellai (Map 3; 7)**. This was the town house of Giovanni Rucellai (1403–81), one of the most respected intellectual figures of Renaissance Florence (author of the *Zibaldone*, his memoirs), as well as one of the wealthiest businessmen in Europe. It was almost certainly designed for him by Leon Battista Alberti and executed by Bernardo Rossellino (c 1446–51). Its dignified **façade** with incised decoration is in striking contrast to the heavy rustication of other Florentine palaces of the period. The three storeys, with classical pilasters and capitals of the three orders, are divided by delicately carved friezes bearing the Rucellai and Medici emblems. The five bays of the front were later increased on the right to seven bays. The design of the façade had a lasting influence on Italian architecture. This palace is not open to the public.

The **Loggia dei Rucellai** has three arches also attributed to Alberti and a graffiti frieze.

Via della Vigna Nuova continues to the Arno; Via dei Palchetti skirts Palazzo Rucellai (right) and Via de' Federighi (view left of the garden of Palazzo Niccolini above a high wall) continues into Piazza San Pancrazio. Here is the former church of **San Pancrazio** (**Map 3; 7**), one of the oldest in the city, founded before 1000. Deconsecrated in 1809, it was later used as a tobacco factory, and as a military store. The beautiful classical *porch is by Alberti. It has been converted into the **Museo Marino Marini** which exhibits works left to the city by the sculptor Marino Marini (1901–80). Exhibitions are held in the 15C crypt. Opening times 10.00–17.00; closed Tues and

Palazzo Rucellai

the whole of Aug; *fest.* 10.00–13.00 (☎ 055 219 432); Lire 8000. Exhibitions of modern art are held in the crypt.

In Via della Spada (no. 18) is the entrance (usually open only on Sat at 17.30, but closed July–Sept) to the remarkable **Cappella di San Sepolcro**, built in 1467 by Alberti for Giovanni Rucellai. In the middle of the lovely barrel-vaulted chapel, there is a perfectly preserved *model by Alberti in inlaid marble with exquisite carving of the Sanctuary of the Holy Sepulchre in Jerusalem. There is also a much-blackened *Resurrection* attributed to Giovanni di Piamonte. Via della Spada, a local shopping street, returns to Via Tornabuoni (view of Palazzo Strozzi).

At 19 Via Tornabuoni, Palazzo Larderel (**Map 1; 3,5**), attributed to Giovanni Antonio Dosio (begun 1580), is a model of High Renaissance architecture. Opposite is Palazzo Corsi (the headquarters of a bank since 1924) which was built in the mid-15C for the Tornabuoni by Michelozzo; it was reconstructed in 1862, though its original courtyard is preserved. On the corner of Via Corsi is a loggia designed by Cigoli in 1608. Inside are two fresco cycles by Agostino Ciampelli.

San Gaetano

Beyond, preceded by a wide flight of steps, is San Gaetano (correctly called Santi Michele e Gaetano) which is the most important 17C church in Florence (**Map 1; 3**; opening times 09.00–12.00, 15.30–18.00). The fine façade (1648–83) was designed by Pier Francesco Silvani. There was a Romanesque church on this site, mentioned in 1055.

Interior

The dark grey interior (best light in the morning) in *pietra serena* was built in 1604–49 by Matteo Nigetti (possibly influenced by a design of Bernardo Buontalenti) and (after 1630) by Gherardo Silvani. The sombre decoration in various precious marbles and dark wood survives almost totally intact and nearly all the frescoes and altarpieces were painted in the 1630s and 1640s (unless otherwise indicated below). The colossal white marble statues (with bas-reliefs below) of the *Apostles* and *Evangelists* (1640–90) are by Giovanni Battista Foggini (Saints Peter and Paul on the triumphal arch), Antonio Novelli and others. Splendid hangings in silk, gold thread and velvet from Lyons were made in Florence in 1728–50 to adorn the church on festivals; they still survive and are sometimes displayed.

South side First chapel, *Madonna* in glazed terracotta by Andrea della Robbia (1465–70) and two paintings and vault frescoes by Ottaviano Vannini. Second chapel, two paintings by Jacopo Vignali and vault frescoes by Angelo Michele Colonna. Third chapel, Altarpiece of *Saints* by Matteo Rosselli and vault frescoes by Sigismondo Coccapanni. South transept, *Adoration of the Magi* by Ottaviano Vannini. Chapel to the right of the high altar, Matteo Rosselli, *Nativity* and *Visitation*, and vault frescoes, and *Annunciation* by Fabrizio Boschi.

Choir chapel The dome (being restored) was frescoed by Filippo Maria Galletti in the late 17C. The bronze *Crucifix* on the east wall is by Giovanni Francesco Susini and is his most important work (1634–35).

North transept In the chapel to the left of the high altar are the *Finding of the True Cross* by Matteo Rosselli, two paintings on the side walls by Giovanni Bilivert, and vault frescoes by Jacopo Vignali. The *Exaltation of the Cross* on the end wall of the transept is by Giovanni Bilivert.

North side Third chapel, *Death of St Andrea Avellina*, signed and dated by Ignazio Hugford (1738), and (on the right wall) a 15C *Madonna Surrounded by Angels* painted by Francesco Boschi. On the opposite wall, *Presentation in the Temple* by his brother Alfonso. The vault frescoes of the *Coronation of the Virgin* surrounded by putti and the three lunettes of angels (very difficult to see) are by Lorenzo Lippi. **Second chapel**, Pietro da Cortona, *Martyrdom of St Lawrence* (c 1653); on the right wall, *Madonna Appearing to St Francis* by Jacopo da Empoli, and on the left wall, *St Lawrence Giving to the Poor*, by Matteo Rosselli. The vault frescoes are by Angelo Michele Colonna. **First chapel**, altarpiece of *St Michael Archangel* by Jacopo Vignali, and vault frescoes by Filippo Maria Galletti (late 17C).

The **Antinori Chapel** (open on request) on the left side of the church, was built in 1635–37. It contains a *Crucifix* and *Saints* by the school of Filippo Lippi (in poor condition), three curious bas-reliefs from the Romanesque church, a monument to Alessandro Antinori (d. 1557), with a good bust, and a painting of the *Martyrdom of St Andrew* by Ottaviano Vannini.

Palazzo Antinori in Piazza Antinori has been owned by the Antinori since 1506 and is one of the most beautiful smaller Renaissance palaces in Florence. Built in 1461–69, with a splendid courtyard, it is attributed to Giuliano da Maiano.

Santa Maria Maggiore

Via degli Agli and Via Vecchietti (left) lead to the church of Santa Maria Maggiore (**Map 1; 3**; opening times 07.00–12.00, 15.30–17.30), which has a rough exterior in *pietra forte*. It is of ancient foundation (first mentioned in 1021), and was rebuilt in its present Gothic Cistercian form at the end of the 13C. At the corner of the façade is the Romanesque campanile.

In the dark **interior** on the pilasters and on the west wall are 13C–14C frescoes, some by Mariotto di Nardo. The inner façade was designed by Cigoli, who also painted the altarpiece to the right of the door. On the south side are two 17C altarpieces: the first by Matteo Rosselli, and the second by Onorio Marinari. The third south altar has a large terracotta high relief dating from 1897 (by Francesco Collina) flanked by two late 17C statues. The middle altarpiece on the north side of *Santa Rita* is by Primo Conti (1949), and the third altarpiece of *St Francis Receiving the Stigmata* is by Pier Dandini (flanked by two statues by Giovanni Battista Caccini). In the chapel to the left of the choir is the *Madonna Enthroned* (removed for restoration since 1989, and replaced by a photograph), a Byzantine relief in painted wood, attributed to Coppo di Marcovaldo. To the right is a column which survives from the tomb of Brunello Latini (d. 1294), Dante's teacher, and to the left, the tomb (1272) of Bruno Beccuti with an effigy attributed to Tino da Camaino. The detached fresco of the *Crucifix* is by Giovanni di Francesco. The two frescoes (in very poor condition) in the sanctuary, which has a neo-Gothic stained glass window (1901), are attributed to a contemporary of Spinello Aretino.

13 • Museo Nazionale del Bargello

The massive crenellated Palazzo del Bargello (**Map 1; 6**) dominates Piazza San Firenze. Built in 1255 as the Palazzo del Popolo, it is the oldest seat of government that survives in the city.

History of the palace

The Bargello was begun, according to Vasari, to a design by a certain Lapo, the master of Arnolfo di Cambio. Building continued until 1330–50. The ancient tower is 57m high. Well restored in 1857–65, the building, constructed in *pietra forte*, still preserves its 14C appearance.

At first it was the seat of the *Capitano del Popolo*, who, during his one-year term of office, held supreme authority in the government of the city. From the end of the 13C until 1502, the palace was the official residence of the *Podestà*, the governing magistrate of the city, who was traditionally a foreigner. In the 16C, the building became known as the Bargello, when the police headquarters were moved here and prisons were installed (in use until 1858–59). In 1786, when the Grand-duke Pietro Leopoldo abolished the death sentence, instruments of torture were burnt in the courtyard. On the exterior of the building (corner of Via dell'Acqua and Via Ghibellina) a neo-Gothic tabernacle (1859) protects a fresco by Fabrizio Boschi (1588). This commemorates the feast day of St Bonaventura when the prison was opened to various confraternities of the city and charitable companies, who were allowed to visit the prisoners and bring them food and clothing.

Museo Nazionale del Bargello

The palace now contains the Museo Nazionale del Bargello, one of the most important museums in the city, and the best place to get a thorough understanding of the Florentine Renaissance. It is famous for its superb collection of Florentine Renaissance sculpture, including numerous works by Donatello and the Della Robbia family. Florentine sculpture from the 16C is also well represented, with pieces by Michelangelo, Cellini and Giambologna, among others, and an exquisite collection of small Mannerist bronzes. The building also houses a notable collection of decorative arts. The entrance is in Via del Proconsolo.

- **Opening times** 08.30–13.50; closed first, third and fifth Sunday and second and fourth Monday of month; ☎ 055 238 8606; Lire 8000 (S). The rooms of sculpture are arranged mostly by period and school. Room numbers refer to the numbers on the plans in the text. On some days, some rooms on the second floor of the museum are closed due to a lack of custodians, these rooms include the Medagliere Mediceo and the Sala delle Armi (enquire at the ticket office). The museum is hardly ever over-crowded and it is rare to find a queue at the ticket office. The exhibits are beautifully arranged and the museum is very well kept.

The museum came into being in 1859 when the collection of sculpture and applied arts formerly in the Uffizi was transferred here, and it was first opened to the public in 1865. In 1888, the important Carrand Collection was left to the museum, and later acquisitions included the Ressmann collection of armour and Franchetti collection of fabrics.

Ground floor

Room 1 This fine hall contains 16C sculpture by Michelangelo and his Florentine contemporaries. The four superb works by Michelangelo represent different stages in the great sculptor's highly successful career. The *Bacchus Drunk* is his first important sculpture and shows the influence of Classical works. It was made on his first visit to Rome c 1497 for the banker Jacopo Galli, who kept it in his garden for over 50 years. Galli was an important patron for Michelangelo when he was in Rome, and he also commissioned his famous *Pietà* now in

Palazzo del Bargello

the Vatican. The **Bacchus Drunk** was later purchased by the Medici and brought to Florence. The tondo of the ***Madonna and Child with the Infant St John** was made for Bartolommeo Pitti c 1503–05. It is a charming work, and a fine example of the sculptor's *schiacciato* (very low relief) technique. The bust of ***Brutus** is a much later work (probably dating from the 1540s), derived from Imperial Roman portrait busts, and is the only bust Michelangelo ever sculpted. It was made after the murder of Duke Alessandro de' Medici by his cousin Lorenzino, and is an exaltation of Republicanism. It was made for Michelangelo's friend Cardinal Niccolò Ridolfi. It was left unfinished, and Michelangelo's pupil Tiberio Calcagni added the drapery. The small figure called ***Apollo** who is apparently extracting an arrow from his back, is another beautiful unfinished work by Michelangelo with a *contrapposto* (serpentine) pose. Also known as **David**, according to Vasari, it was carved for Baccio Valori (a Medici supporter who governed Florence in 1530), and later formed part of the Medici collection. It was then moved to the Boboli gardens and later to the Uffizi corridor, where it was displayed with the antique sculpture collection.

Also in this part of the room are works which show Michelangelo's influence on other artists, such as Giovanni Francesco Rustici and Andrea and Jacopo Sansovino. They include a tondo and a terracotta group of horsemen engaged in battle (after Leonardo da Vinci) by Rustici, a terracotta **Madonna and Child** by Andrea Sansovino, and a statue of ***Bacchus** by his pupil Jacopo Sansovino, which takes its inspiration from Michelangelo's statue close by. The statuettes, models and replicas (in cases against the wall) by followers of Michelangelo include works by Pietro Francavilla, Tribolo, Giambologna (a model for his giant **Appennino** at Pratolino, see p 362), Bartolommeo Ammannati and Vincenzo Danti. The marble figure of **Leda** by Ammannati (c 1540–50) is one of the best works inspired by a famous painting by Michelangelo commissioned by Alfonso d'Este and later destroyed. The allegory of ***Fiesole** by Tribolo, in the delicate stone known as *pietra serena*, was one of a series of statues (the others now lost) representing allegories of the cities and mountains of Tuscany, made for the garden of the Medici Villa di Castello.

The marble bust of **Cosimo I** is a fine work by Baccio Bandinelli who also carved the two colossal statues of **Adam and Eve**, which were not considered suitable for the Duomo. His pupil Vincenzo de' Rossi carved the ***Dying Adonis** and the framed clay bas-reliefs of the **Passion of Christ**. The two statues by Ammannati were intended for the Nari tomb in Santissima Annunziata (1540), but because of the opposition of Bandinelli they were never set up there.

There follow a group of *works by **Benvenuto Cellini** who was one of the greatest sculptors of the age, with a style all his own, less influenced than his contemporaries by the art of Michelangelo. His works often have echoes of Hellenistic sculpture. The **Narcissus**, carved from a worn block of grey Greek marble with two holes (hence the position of the arms), was damaged in Cellini's studio during a flood of the Arno. There are charming naturalistic details on the pedestal showing classical influence. Together with the **Apollo and Hyacinth**, also displayed here, it was given to Francesco I who sent them to the park of Pratolino. They later found their way to the Boboli gardens, and the two statues were only re-identified and brought under cover just before the Second World War. The figure of **Apollo** was never finished as the marble (which had been supplied by Cellini's rival Baccio Bandinelli) was defective. The **Ganymede** consists of

MUSEO NAZIONALE DEL BARGELLO

Second Floor

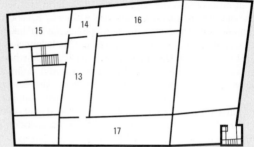

First Floor

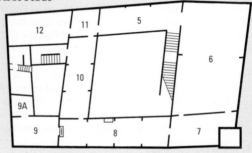

Ground Floor

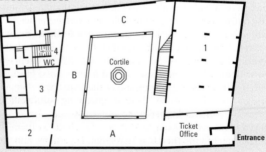

an antique marble torso, to which Cellini added the beautiful head and arms, the eagle and the naturalistic details on the base. We know that Cosimo I kept this piece in his bedroom, together with the statue of *Bacchus* by Andrea Sansovino (see above) and another statue of *Bacchus* by Baccio Bandinelli (now in Palazzo Pitti). The splendid bronzes exhibited here include a scale model of Cellini's famous statue of *Perseus* (in the Loggia della Signoria, see p 124), and the relief (*Perseus Releasing Andromeda*) and statuettes (*Danae and Perseus, Mercury, Minerva* and *Jove*) displayed on the original pedestal of this statue (which has been replaced *in situ* by a copy). A small wax model for the *Perseus* is also preserved here. This great statue was Cellini's last public commission and took him nine years to complete: afterwards Bandinelli was favoured by the grand-dukes and Cellini retired to write his *Autobiography*, which is one of the most important literary works of its time.

Vincenzo Danti's statue representing *Honour Overcoming Deceit* (his first work in marble, which was placed in the Boboli gardens in 1775) is exhibited near Giambologna's colossal *Virtue Repressing Vice* (or Florence victorious over Pisa). The bronze *Mercury* is Giambologna's most successful and influential statue: it seems almost on the point of flying away. It was a fountain in front of the garden façade of the Villa Medici in Rome and was brought from there to Florence by the Lorraine grand-dukes. The cupboard door made for Cosimo I, and the relief of *Moses and the Serpent* are both bronzes by Vincenzo Danti. The colossal bust of *Cosimo I* was Cellini's first work cast in bronze (1545–48). His talent as a goldsmith can be seen in the delicate carved details of the armour. The portrait bust of *Michelangelo* is by Daniele da Volterra.

Courtyard

The Gothic *courtyard, the finest part of the palace, is adorned with a large number of coats of arms of the former Podestà. Under the colonnade (**A**): Benedetto da Maiano, large high relief of the *Coronation of Ferdinand of Aragon*, with six boy musicians and a seated statue of *Alfonso of Aragon* attributed to Francesco Laurana. The statue of *St Luke the Evangelist* by Niccolò di Pietro Lamberti was formerly in a niche of Orsanmichele, and the *St John the Baptist* has recently been attributed to the 17C sculptor Domenico Pieratti. The cannon, cast by Cosimo Cenni in 1620, shows the planet Jupiter with its four satellites discovered by Galileo in 1610. The extraordinary lamp on the wall dates from the 16C.

Under the next colonnade (**B**) are six fine statues (including *Juno*) by Ammannati (1556–63) from an *allegorical fountain which was intended for the south end of the Salone dei Cinquecento in Palazzo Vecchio (see p 129). Instead it was first set up for eight years in the Villa di Pratolino, and then, in 1588, moved to the terrace above the courtyard of Palazzo Pitti (where it is now replaced by the Fontana del Carciofo). The statues were then dispersed in the Boboli gardens and were only finally reassembled here in the 1970s. The *Fisherboy* (1877) is by the Neapolitan sculptor Vincenzo Gemito.

Under the last colonnade (**C**) is Giambologna's colossal statue of *Oceanus* from the Boboli gardens and the *Cannon of St Paul*, a wonderful piece of casting by Cenni (1638) which was commissioned by Grand-duke Ferdinando II for Livorno Castle.

Off the courtyard is the **Sala del Trecento** (2) with 14C sculpture, including colossal statues of the *Madonna and Child* and *Saints Peter and Paul* from the Porta Romana, by Paolo di Giovanni, a pedestal with three *Acolytes* by Arnolfo di Cambio, and a high relief of the *Madonna and Child* by Tino da Camaino. The room next door (3) is used for exhibitions.

First floor

This may be reached by the open stairway in the courtyard (or the internal staircase, 4). The **loggia** (5) provides a charming setting for *works by the Flemish-born **Giambologna**, perhaps the greatest Mannerist sculptor who worked in Florence, who had a wide influence on his contemporaries. The life-like group of bronze *Birds* was made for the grotto at Villa di Castello, and is a masterpiece of casting. The turkey, 'fluffed up' in anger is particularly fine (turkeys were first introduced from America into Italy in the 16C). The peacock and cockerel are probably by an assistant. The female statue in marble, by the master's hand, represents Architecture. The Stemma of the Amico della Torre on the wall near the door into the Salone del Consiglio Generale is probably an early work by Luca della Robbia

The Salone del Consiglio Generale (6) This is a splendid Gothic hall, vaulted by Neri di Fioravante and Benci di Cione in 1345. The neo-Gothic painted decorations were carried out in 1857–65. Works by Donatello and his contemporaries have been displayed here since 1887.

Donatello

Donatello (c 1386–1466) was the most important sculptor of the Quattrocento and of fundamental importance to the development of Renaissance art; indeed, he is often considered the greatest sculptor of all time. He was born in Florence around 1386 of humble parentage (his father was a wool-carder who had taken part in the famous Ciompi revolt) and he probably had little idea how to read and write. Donatello first worked as assistant to Lorenzo Ghiberti, the bronze sculptor, and as a young man visited Rome with his friend Brunelleschi to study antique sculpture. He worked almost exclusively throughout his exceptionally long life (he died in his eighties) in Florence, except for an important period in Padua. He produced superb sculptures in all mediums, whether bronze, marble or terracotta. Cosimo il Vecchio recognised his exceptional talent and protected him and ordered that he be buried beside him in the Medici vaults below San Lorenzo (the great ruler died just two years before the sculptor). The attribution of many undocumented works to Donatello remains a great art historical issue up to this day. In this room can be seen some of his most famous works in bronze, marble, terracotta and *pietra serena* (the attribution of some of them is still under discussion). Other splendid works by him can be seen in Florence in San Lorenzo, the Museo dell'Opera del Duomo, Palazzo Vecchio, Santa Croce and the Baptistery.

In the **middle of the room** is Donatello's *Marzocco*, the Florentine heraldic lion, in *pietra serena*. On the end wall is the reconstructed tabernacle from Orsanmichele which contains *St George*, as the young Champion of Christendom, made for the guild of armourers c 1416. By endowing this remarkably well-composed statue with a sense of movement, Donatello's work represents a new departure from traditional Gothic sculpture where the static figure was confined to its niche. The bas-relief of *St George and the Dragon* is a remarkable work in low relief, using the new *schiacciato* technique and showing a fresh interest in linear perspective and pictorial space.

Other works by Donatello include (left) his bronze *David with the Head of Goliath*. One of the earliest and most beautiful free-standing male statues of the Renaissance, it was probably made between 1430 and 1440 for the courtyard of the Medici palace. After their expulsion from Florence, it was moved in 1495 to Palazzo della Signoria. The other *David*, in marble (in the centre between the windows), is an early work by Donatello. It was commissioned by the Opera del Duomo, but placed in Palazzo della Signoria in 1416. The two statues of *St John the Baptist* are of uncertain attribution: the one of him as an older man is ascribed to the school of Donatello (Michelozzo?), and the *Young St John* (from the Casa Martelli) is attributed to Desiderio da Settignano.

Also in the centre of the room are two fine busts of a *Young Woman* and a *Boy*, fine works by Desiderio da Settignano, and a *bust in coloured terracotta (c 1430), full of character, traditionally thought to be a portrait of **Niccolò da Uzzano**, and now usually considered to be by Donatello. The humorous bronze putto known as *Atys-Amorino*, also by Donatello, represents a mythological subject of uncertain significance and dates from 1430–40. The statuette of a cupid in bronze is by Bonacolsi.

Arranged around the **walls** (from the entrance door) are a wooden statue of *St Bernard* by Vecchietta and a lunette from Via dell' Agnolo with the *Madonna and Two Angels* attributed to Andrea della Robbia. The bronze statuette of a *Dancing Putto*, beyond, shows the influence of Donatello. Then come two very important works: trial reliefs by Ghiberti and Brunelleschi for the second bronze doors of the Baptistery.

Competition reliefs for the Baptistery doors

The Bargello contains the two *trial reliefs of the *Sacrifice of Isaac* executed by Lorenzo Ghiberti and Brunelleschi in competition for the second bronze doors of the Baptistery (see p 102). In 1403, Ghiberti was given the commission, a decision reached by a narrow majority, though it reflected approval for his new conception of art. It is wonderful that the reliefs by Ghiberti and Brunelleschi have survived from this famous contest, which was the first of its kind and which is usually regarded as the point at which Renaissance art was born. The subject chosen presented each contestant with a series of difficulties. These included fitting the narrative into an awkward space (the quatrefoil frames copied from the first set of doors by Andrea Pisano) and the need to depict both the nude figure of Isaac as well as the clothed figures of Abraham and his servants, and also animals and the rural setting of the event. Although the greater skill of Ghiberti is hardly perceptible, his victory meant that he would later go on to carve the superb east door, considered one of the greatest masterpieces of sculpture ever produced in Western art, leaving Brunelleschi free to concentrate his energies on the construction of the huge dome of the cathedral.

The *reliquary urn (1428), beneath, is also by Ghiberti. The fine works by Giovanni di Bertoldo, Donatello's pupil, include a *Battle* scene (a relief based on a Roman sarcophagus at Pisa), an unfinished statuette of *Apollo* (or Orpheus), and, on the end wall, reliefs of the *Pietà*, *Triumph of Bacchus* and the *Crucifixion*.

The *Bust of a Youth* with a medallion at his neck is usually attributed to Desiderio da Settignano (or possibly Bertoldo). One of the fine painted marriage-chests below, which shows the procession of San Giovanni (with a view of the Baptistery), is by Giovanni Toscani (c 1428–29). The gilded relief of the *Crucifixion* is now attributed to Donatello, and the profile relief of the *Young St John* is by Desiderio da Settignano.

On the next wall can be seen a bronze head of a *Sea God* attributed to Donatello, and (above) the Martelli coat of arms, almost certainly by Donatello (acquired by the state in 1998; repainted in the 19C). The exquisite marble relief of the *Madonna and Child with Angels* in a *pietra serena* tabernacle is a master-piece by Agostino di Duccio, who was born in Florence but worked mostly in other regions of Italy. The *Madonna and Child* (from Palazzo Panciatichi) is a beautiful work in very low relief by Desiderio da Settignano. The other two reliefs—of the same subject—one in marble and one in terracotta are by Michelozzo, the architect and sculptor who worked with Donatello on some pro-jects. There follow a number of charming glazed enamelled Madonnas by **Luca della Robbia**. He invented a special technique of enamelled terracotta sculpture which was a jealously guarded secret of his workshop for most of the 15C and was handed down through three generations of his family. Luca was also a highly skilled marble sculptor (his masterpiece is the Cantoria in the Museo dell'Opera del Duomo, see p 115). His colourful, luminous half-length Madonna reliefs became popular for private devotion. He is recognised as one of the most important early Renaissance sculptors and was clearly influenced by classical art. The *Madonna and Child* in a rose-garden is by Luca; the tondo of the *Madonna and Child with Two Angels* is thought to be an early work by his nephew Andrea. Below, there is a bronze *Effigy of Mariano Sozzino*, which for a long time was attributed to Vecchietta, but is now thought to be the work of Francesco di Giorgio Martini. The fine wooden model of Palazzo Strozzi is by Giuliano da Sangallo. The *Bust of a Lady*, probably a female saint, is attributed to Luca della Robbia or his nephew Andrea.

On the last wall, there are two marble *reliefs of the *Deliverance* and *Crucifixion of St Peter* made for an altar in the Duomo and left unfinished in 1439 by Luca della Robbia, who also made the *Madonna of the Apple* (c 1460), which was owned by the Medici. The *Madonna and Child* from Santa Maria Nuova, in its original gilt wooden tabernacle, is attributed to the Della Robbia workshop. Another fine *Madonna and Child* is by Michelozzo, who also made the statue of the *Young St John* (from the Casa dell'Opera di San Giovanni) exhibited beside the door.

The next three rooms (7–9) are dedicated to the **decorative arts** and display the *Carrand collection (well labelled). This includes pieces from all over Europe, dating from earliest times up until the 17C, which were assembled by Louis Carrand, a wealthy Lyons art-collector who bequeathed his collection to the museum in 1888.

In the **Sala della Torre** (7) is a fine *collection of **Islamic art** including 15C armour, 16C and 17C brocade, damascened dishes, works in brass and ivory, a case of ceramics (including Persian tiles), and carpets.

The Salone del Podestà (8) Amongst the many exquisite works here are: a painting of a *Money-changer and his Wife* by Marinus van Reymerswale (1540); Limoges enamels; 11C–12C ivories; French and Italian cutlery (15C–16C); European clocks; ecclesiastical ornaments, many of them enamelled, including reliquary caskets, pastoral staves, processional crosses and ewers; 15C–16C metalwork from France; a 15C Venetian astrolabe in gilt bronze; a painted diptych of the *Annunciation* and the *Presentation in the Temple* (with monochrome figures on the reverse), a 15C Flemish work attributed to the Maestro della Legenda di Santa Caterina, a close follower of Rogier van der Weyden; a tondo of the *Judgment of Paris* by a Florentine painter c 1420; a chimneypiece of 1478; and Venetian and Bohemian glass (16C–17C). At the end of the room, flat cases contain a beautiful collection of jewellery and goldsmiths' work from the Roman period to the 17C. The tiny Flemish and Italian paintings displayed together here include three fragments by Agnolo Gaddi, a *Madonna and Child* by Dirk Bouts, and a *Coronation of the Virgin* and *Noli me tangere* by the Master of the St George Codex.

The Cappella del Podestà (9) This chapel dates from the early 14C. The damaged frescoes (restored) were attributed to Giotto when they were discovered in 1841, but it is now thought likely that he began them in the year of his death (1337). On the altar wall, the scene of *Paradise* includes a portrait of Dante as a young man (in the group to the right, dressed in maroon). Also on this wall there is a frescoed roundel of the *Madonna and Child* by Bastiano Mainardi (1490). The triptych of the *Madonna and Saints* is by Giovanni di Francesco (mid-15C). The lectern decorated with intarsia is from San Miniato and is dated 1498. The stalls are of the same period. In the small adjoining room (9A) cases contain two paxes decorated with niello by Maso Finiguerra and Matteo di Giovanni Dei, and a bronze dove by Luca della Robbia which comes from his tabernacle in Peretola. Also here are goldsmiths' work, chalices, processional crosses and reliquaries.

Room 10 A fine collection of *ivories from the Etruscan period onwards is displayed here. In the first flat case: Persian, Arabic, German and Sicilian ivories, and Carolingian reliefs (9C); in the other flat case: valve of a diptych which belonged to the Roman Consul Basilio (6C); part of a Byzantine diptych with the Empress Arianna (8C); an early Christian diptych (5C) showing Adam in earthly Paradise and scenes from the life of St Peter in Malta. The case on the entrance wall contains a fragment of an Anglo-Saxon coffer (8C) in whale-bone (the rest is in the British Museum). In another central case: Byzantine coffer; French pastoral staves (11C–14C), and a 12C liturgical flabellum. The chessboard with intarsia ornament and bas-reliefs is a 15C Burgundian work.

Displayed around the walls are wooden sculptures including a *Madonna of the Misericordia* (Umbrian, late 14C) and an unusual seated polychrome wooden statue (sometimes interpreted as a *Madonna Annunciate* or a *Sibyl*) by Mariano d'Angelo Romanelli (c 1390), and a painted and gilded 14C statue of a *Bishop Saint*. The painting of the *Coronation of the Virgin* is by the 14C Florentine school (formerly attributed to Giottino).

Room 11 This room displays the collection of furniture recently donated to the museum 1983 by the Florentine antiquarian Giovanni Bruzzichelli. Also exhibited here are: Jacopo Sansovino, *Madonna and Child*, a large relief in *papier mâché*, and a collection of Venetian glass.

Room 12 The **Sala delle Maioliche** contains part of the Medici collection of Italian majolica (mostly 15C and 16C) including works from the Deruta, Montelupo, Faenza and Urbino potteries, and part of a service which belonged to Guidobaldo II della Rovere, Duke of Urbino. The beautiful *garland, on the end wall, with the Bartolini-Salimbeni and Medici emblems is by Giovanni della Robbia.

Second floor

This is reached from Room 10 (see above).

Room 13 Set at the top of the stairs, this room contains colourful and elaborate enamelled terracottas, many of them by **Giovanni della Robbia**, son of Andrea, who used more colours than his father and uncle Luca. These include a fine tondo of the *Madonna and Child and Young St John*, partly unglazed. The large relief in white terracotta (*Noli me tangere*) is by Francesco Rustici (perhaps with the collaboration of Giovanni della Robbia). Works by Benedetto Buglioni include a polychrome terracotta statue of the *Madonna and Child* and a relief of the *Noli me tangere*. The four-figure group of the *Lamentation*, an unglazed terracotta work by Andrea della Robbia, was acquired in 1998.

In the cases are displayed a superb collection of bronze plaquettes and medals arranged by artists and school from the early 15C to the 18C. Most of them were collected by the Medici grand-dukes, but some come from the Carrand collection. Italian masters represented include Antico (Pier Jacopo Alari-Bonacolsi), Valerio Belli, Caradosso, Cellini, Filarete, Giambologna, Leone Leoni, Moderno, Riccio (Andrea Briosco) and Giovanni Francesco Rustici. There are also examples from France and Germany.

Room 14 This contains beautiful works in enamelled terracotta by **Andrea della Robbia**, nephew of Luca, who produced the famous tondi which decorate the Spedale degli Innocenti in Florence (see p 195). His charming *Bust of a Boy* is in the centre of the room, and around the walls are tabernacles including the *Madonna of the Cushion* and *Madonna of the Stonemasons* (1475). The *Portrait of a Lady* (a circular high relief) is now usually attributed to Andrea's uncle, Luca.

Room 15 Here there is a superb display of Renaissance portrait busts and some very fine works by **Verrocchio**. In the centre is Verrocchio's bronze *David* made for the Medici, and then acquired by the Signoria in 1476. It owes much to Donatello's earlier statue of the same subject in the Salone on the floor below. Also in the centre is a wooden *Crucifix*, recently found in the Oratory of San Francesco Poverino in Piazza Santissima Annunziata and attributed to Verrocchio since its restoration. To the right of the door are charming marble works by **Mino da Fiesole**: busts of Cosimo il Vecchio's two sons, *Giovanni* and *Piero il Gottoso* (1453; the first dated portrait bust of the Renaissance) on either side of a portrait of *Rinaldo della Luna*. The two reliefs of the *Madonna* above are also by him.

The works exhibited along the window wall include: *Pietro Mellini*, signed and dated 1474 by Benedetto da Maiano, a remarkable portrait of this rich Florentine merchant as an old man; 15C bust of *Giuliano di Piero de' Medici*, murdered in the Pazzi conspiracy, of unknown attribution; a profile relief of *Federico da Montefeltro* and *Francesco Sforza*, attributed to Gian Francesco Romano; and an exquisite little tabernacle by Desiderio da Settignano. On the end wall, the works by Antonio Rossellino include a bust of *Francesco Sassetti* (the general manager of the Medici bank who commissioned the Sassetti chapel in Santa Trìnita); a painted relief of the *Madonna* in a tabernacle; a marble tondo of the *Nativity*; busts of a *Young Boy* and of the *Young St John the Baptist*; and the portrait bust of *Matteo Palmieri*, Renaissance statesman and scholar (1468). This was on the façade of his Florentine palace until the 19C, which accounts for its weathered surface.

On the wall opposite the windows can be seen: *Young Cavalier* by Antonio del Pollaiolo, a bust thought to be a portrait of a member of the Medici family (in terracotta); and works by **Verrocchio**, including a portrait bust of *Piero di Lorenzo de' Medici* (in terracotta; sometimes attributed to Piero del Pollaiolo); *Resurrection*, a polychrome relief; a bas-relief in terracotta of the *Madonna and Child* from Santa Maria Nuova; and a *Bust of a Lady Holding Flowers*. Formerly part of the Medici collection, this is one of the loveliest of all Renaissance portrait busts, and was once attributed to Verrocchio's pupil Leonardo da Vinci. There follow another marble portrait *Bust of a Man* by Antonio del Pollaiolo, the *Death of Francesca Tornabuoni-Pitti*, a tomb relief by Verrocchio, and two reliefs (*Faith* and the *Portrait of a Lady* in profile) by Matteo Civitali. The remarkable marble bust of *Battista Sforza*, duchess of Urbino, is by Francesco Laurana, a Dalmatian artist who worked at the Court of Urbino.

Rooms 18 and 19 These rooms contain beautiful displays of the **Medagliere Mediceo**, a huge collection of Italian medals started by Lorenzo il Magnifico. Room 18: Case A, L'Antico (Jacopo Alari Bonacolsi), two circular reliefs with the *Labours of Hercules*; Case I, *medals by Pisanello, the 15C Ferrarese school and Matteo de' Pasti. In the centre of the room is Bernini's *bust of his mistress *Costanza Bonarelli*; on the wall, a silver *Penitent Magdalen* by Giuseppe Piamontini (acquired in 1998), and a small model in terracotta for a fountain in Pistoia. The chronological display of medals continues in the next room (**19**), which has an allegorical female statue in the centre by Domenico Poggini. Beyond the marble bust of *Virginia Pucci Ridolfi*, also by Poggini, **Cases II and III** have medals including works by Francesco di Giorgio Martini, Sperandio and Niccolò di Francesco Spinelli. On the wall above, there is a 1C Roman relief (reworked in the 17C) of *Ganymede*. On the end wall can be seen Jacopo Sansovino's *Christ in Glory*, a bas-relief in a tabernacle. **Case IV**, medals by Francesco da Sangallo and Domenico Poggini. **Cases V and VI**, medals by Gasparo Mola and 16C Roman artists. On the walls, three late-15C reliefs of allegorical triumphs. **Case VII**, medals by Leone Leoni. **Wall case B** has a series of wax reliefs by Giovanni Antonio Santarelli (1758–1826). **Case IX**, medals by Massimiliano Soldani Benzi. The bust of *Cardinal Paolo Emilio Zacchia Rondanini* is by Alessandro Algardi. **Cases XI–XII**, Baroque and neo-classical medals. On the walls, two high reliefs of *St Teresa* and *St Joseph* by Massimiliano Soldani Benzi. **Case XIII** has 16C–18C foreign medals.

Salone del Camino (16) This is entered from room 14 and contains a superb display of *small Renaissance bronzes*, the most important collection in Italy. The fashion of collecting small bronzes was begun by Lorenzo il Magnifico following a Roman tradition. The statuettes, which include animals, bizarre figures and candelabra, were often copies of Antique works, or small replicas of Renaissance statues. In the wall cases on the right, there are splendid bronzes by Giambologna including several statuettes of *Venus*, *Animals*, *Architecture* and *Hercules and the Caledonian Boar*; as well as Benvenuto Cellini's relief of a *Dog*. There are works by Danese Catteneo (including *Fortune*), Tribolo and a fine group of statuettes by Baccio Bandinelli. The splendid *chimneypiece is the work of Benedetto da Rovezzano, and the firedogs are by Niccolò Roccatagliata. The

Ganymede is attributed to Cellini or Tribolo.

The wall cases on the opposite wall contain: an *Anatomical Figure*, a famous work made in wax by Lodovico Cigoli (1598–1600) and fused in bronze by Giovanni Battista Foggini after 1678. Beyond are charming animals by 15C and 16C artists from the Veneto and Padua; fantastical works by Il Riccio; and works by Giovanni Battista Foggini and Pietro da Barga. On the entrance wall, there are works by Pier Jacopo Alari and copies from Antique statues. The *Frightened Man* or *Pugilist* is a very unusual work attributed by most scholars to Donatello (c 1435–40).

The central cases contain copies from works by Giambologna, as well as the dwarf *Morgante Riding a Monster* by Giambologna and Vincenzo della Nera; works by Giovanni Francesco Susini; a *Satyr* by Massimiliano Soldani Benzi; and 16C–18C bronzes from the Veneto. In the centre of the room, there is a *Hercules and Anteneas* by Antonio del Pollaiolo, a beautiful small bronze group—he also made a painting of this subject, which is now in the Uffizi.

From Room 13, a door leads into the **Sala delle Armi** (17) with a magnificent display of *arms and armour* from the Medici, Carrand and Ressmann collections. It includes saddles decorated with gold, silver and ivory, a shield by Gaspar Mola (17C), and numerous sporting guns, dress armour and oriental arms. There is also a fine bust in marble by Francesco da Sangallo, which is an idealised portrait of *Giovanni delle Bande Nere*. The bronze bust of *Ferdinando I* is by Pietro Tacca.

14 • The Badia Fiorentina and the Museo Nazionale di Antropologia

In **Piazza San Firenze** (Map 1; 6), where seven streets converge, there is a miscellany of buildings. Opposite the corner of Palazzo Vecchio stands Palazzo Gondi (no. 2), a beautiful palace built c 1489 by Giuliano da Sangallo with a pretty little courtyard (now occupied by a florist). It was completed (and the façade on Via de' Gondi added) with great care by Giuseppe Poggi in 1872–84.

The square is dominated by **San Firenze**, a huge Baroque building, now occupied by the law courts designed by Francesco Zanobi del Rosso (1772–75). It is flanked by two church façades designed by Ferdinando Ruggieri (1715). The church of **San Filippo Neri** (left), by Gherardo and Pier Francesco Silvani (1633–48) has an unusually tall interior, decorated in 1712–14 (the ceiling was painted by Giovanni Camillo Sagrestani).

The Badia Fiorentina

At the end of the piazza, the slender tower of the Badia rises opposite the Bargello (see Ch. 13). At the beginning of Via del Proconsolo (left) is a portal by Benedetto da Rovezzano (1495), with a *Madonna* in enamelled terracotta by Benedetto Buglioni. This leads into the courtyard of the Badia Fiorentina (**Map 1; 6**), the church of a Benedictine abbey founded in 978. This entrance is currently closed, and the church is approached through the side door in Via Dante Alighieri (at present open only on Mon 15.00–16.00).

History of the Badia Fiorentina

Willa, the widow of Uberto, Margrave of Tuscany, founded the abbey in his memory, richly endowing it with property. Their son, Count Ugo, a benefactor of the abbey, is buried in the church. One of the first hospitals in the city was established here in 1031. The tolling of the bell, mentioned by Dante (*Paradiso*, XV, 97–98), regulated life in the medieval city. At one time, the *Consiglio del Popolo* met here. The church was rebuilt on a Latin cross plan in 1284–1310, probably by Arnolfo di Cambio. This building was radically altered in 1627–31 when Matteo Segaloni reconstructed the interior. The church is now used by a monastic institution known as the Communion of Jerusalem, founded in Paris in 1975.

The **vestibule**, with a Corinthian portico, is by Benedetto da Rovezzano. From here there is a good view of the graceful **campanile**, the bottom portion of which is Romanesque (1307) and the top Gothic (after 1330)—though it has been totally covered for restoration for a number of years.

The 17C **interior** preserves fragments of frescoes from the old church on the west wall. The carved wooden ceiling by Felice Gamberai dates from 1629. On the left, there is Filippino Lippi's *Madonna Appearing to St Bernard* (c 1485), a large panel of great charm. On the right, the tomb of Giannozzo Pandolfini, from the workshop of the Rossellino brothers, and a sculpted altarpiece of the *Madonna and Saints* (1464–69) by Mino da Fiesole. In the right transept stands the tomb of Bernardo Giugni, a Florentine statesman (1396–1466), with a good effigy and statue of *Justice*, also by Mino. A Baroque chapel here has vault frescoes by Vincenzo Meucci and an altarpiece by Onorio Marinari (1663). Above is a fine organ (1558; well restored) by Onofrio Zeffirini with paintings by Francesco Furini and Baccio del Bianco.

In the chapel to the left of the presbytery is the *Way to Calvary* by Giovanni Battista Naldini. In the left transept is a *monument to Ugo (d. 1001), Margrave of Tuscany, son of the foundress of the church, an exquisite work by Mino da Fiesole (1469–81). Above is a good painting of the *Assumption* and two *Saints* by Vasari. In the chapel are displayed four damaged frescoes detached from a wall of the church. They illustrate the *Passion of Christ* (including the suicide of Judas) and are attributed to Nardo di Cione. The two 19C statuettes are by Amalia Duprè.

In the choir, interesting but very damaged fragments of 14C frescoes showing the *Life of the Virgin* (by Giotto and his *bottega*) were detached in 1959 with their sinopia. These have been restored but have not been returned here.

On the right of the choir (with stalls of 1501), a door opens onto a flight of stairs which lead to the upper loggia of the **Chiostro degli Aranci**, a peaceful cloister where orange trees were once cultivated (open at the same time as the church). It was built in 1432–38 to designs by Bernardo Rossellino. The interesting and well-preserved *fresco cycle illustrates scenes from the *Life of St Benedict* (restored in 1973, when the sinopie were also detached). The frescoes are by an unknown master (usually called the Master of the Chiostro degli Aranci), working in the decade after the death of Masaccio. They have been attributed to Giovanni di Consalvo, a Portuguese artist and follower of Fra' Angelico. In a lunette in the north walk is an early fresco by Bronzino.

In Via del Proconsolo, next to the church, a palace was demolished in 1994 and excavations on the site (which has been left abandoned) revealed remains of a Roman fuller's workshop of the 1C AD and the foundations of a tower in the Roman walls of 30–15 BC, the shape of which can be seen in the roadway nearby. At no. 10 rises the handsome **Palazzo Pazzi-Quaratesi** (no admission) attributed to Giuliano da Maiano (1458–69). The Pazzi coat of arms (removed from the exterior) is displayed in the vestibule which leads to a pretty courtyard (with good capitals). The Pazzi, one of the oldest Florentine families, who made their fortune as bankers, organised a notorious conspiracy against the Medici in 1478 (see p 92) when Giuliano, brother of Lorenzo il Magnifico, was killed by Francesco de' Pazzi. Francesco, who was wounded, hid here before being seized by the mob and hung from a window of Palazzo Vecchio.

Museo Nazionale di Antropologia ed Etnologia

Across Borgo degli Albizi, a street lined with fine palaces described in Ch. 21, is Palazzo Nonfinito, begun in 1593 by Buontalenti. The great courtyard is attributed to Cigoli. The building was continued by Vincenzo Scamozzi and others, but was left unfinished, hence its name. It now houses the Museo Nazionale di Antropologia ed Etnologia (**Map 1; 4**). This was founded in 1869 by Paolo Mantegazza, and was the first museum of its kind in Europe. Opening times daily except Tues, 09.00–13.00 (☎ 055 239 6449); Lire 6000.

This is the most important ethnological and anthropological museum in Italy. Its collection is displayed in some 35 rooms, in charming old-fashioned showcases, although it is not very well labelled. It covers: Africa (notably Ethiopia, Eritrea, Somalia and Libya); North Pakistan (a rare *collection of material relating to the Kafiri assembled in 1955–60 by Paolo Graziosi); South America (including mummies from Peru, collected in 1883) and Mexico; Asia (Melanesia, the islands of Sumatra—including the Modigliani collection c 1880—Tibet and Japan, with the Fosco Maraini collection of Ainu material); and artefacts from the Pacific Ocean probably acquired by Captain Cook on his last voyage in 1776–79.

Museo di Firenze com'era

Via del Proconsolo emerges in Piazza del Duomo (see Ch. 2); to the right Via dell'Oriuolo leads to the ex-Convento delle Oblate (no. 24) which houses the Museo di Firenze com'era (**Map 4; 7**), a small (rather disappointing) museum with maps, paintings and prints of the city. Opening times 09.00–14.00 except Thursday, Lire 5000, ☎ 055 261 6545 (C).

In the room to the right are a 19C copy in tempera of the *Pianta della Catena*, an engraving of 1470 (now in Berlin), and the first topographical plan of Florence drawn by Stefano Bonsignori in 1584 for the Grand-duke Francesco I. It makes use of an ideal perspective from an elevated viewpoint, and the city is represented using extremely accurate planimetric measurements. The charming series of lunettes of the Medici villas by the Flemish painter, Giusto Utens (1599) are from the Villa di Artimino. The cartographical collection includes works by Valerio Spada (1650), F.B. Werner (1705), and Federigo Fantozzi (1843 and 1866). There are views of Florence by Thomas Patch and Giuseppe Maria Terreni, and engravings by Telemaco Signorini of the Mercato Vecchio in 1874 before its demolition. The fine series of engravings (1754), with views of the city and villas in the environs, are by Giuseppe Zocchi, and there are lithographs by A. Durand (1863). The elevations and sections of the Duomo, Baptistery and Campanile published by Sgrilli in 1755, were drawn by Giovanni Battista Nelli (1661–1725) who made the first measured survey of these buildings for the Opera del Duomo. The famous *Fiera of Impruneta* was engraved by Jacopo Callot in 1620. In the hall to the left of the entrance are prehistoric and Roman finds from excavations in the city and a model of the Roman town. There are plans to move the Collezione Alberto Della Ragione of modern art here (see p 125).

On the opposite side of Via dell'Oriuolo, in the 18C Palazzo Bastogi (no. 33), is the **Archivio Storico del Comune di Firenze**, the historic archives of the Comune of Florence established by Pietro Leopoldo in 1781 (the documents, now computerised, cover the period up until 1960). The main hall has neo-classical stuccoes and painted decoration.

Via Folco Portinari leads north from Via dell'Oriuolo to **Santa Maria Nuova** (**Map 4; 7**), a hospital founded in 1286 by Folco Portinari, believed to be the father of Dante's Beatrice, and still one of the main hospitals of Florence. The unusual portico (1574–1612) is by Bernardo Buontalenti. Beneath it is the church of **Sant' Egidio** (c 1420) with a cast of a terracotta by Dello Delli (1424) in the lunette. In the interior are remains of the Portinari tomb, and an altarpiece (*Madonna and Child with Saints*) by Felice Ficherelli (1654–57). The splendid high altar with a ciborium in *pietre dure* dates from 1666. To the left is a small marble tabernacle by Bernardo Rossellino (1450); the bronze door by Lorenzo Ghiberti is replaced here by a copy.

A door to the right of the church (usually kept closed; admission through the hospital buildings) leads into a cloister, the oldest part of the hospital, with a *Pietà* by Giovanni della Robbia. To the left of the church, in another old courtyard, is the tomb-slab of Monna Tessa, the servant of Portinari who persuaded him to found the hospital, and a small tabernacle with a fresco of *Charity* by Giovanni di San Giovanni. The incongruous neo-classical pavilion is a monument to the benefactor Count Galli Tassi.

In the offices of the Presidenza, above (sometimes opened on certain days of the year or by appointment), are the original lunette by Delli (see above) and a *Madonna and Child* by Andrea della Robbia. The Salone di Martino V contains detached frescoes of Martin V consecrating the church, by Bicci di Lorenzo (with its sinopia), and the same pope confirming its privileges, by Andrea di Giusto (repainted); the *Resurrection* is attributed to Pietro Gerini.

At no. 1 Via Bufalini, a plaque marks the site of Ghiberti's workshop, where the Baptistery doors were cast. In Via Sant'Egidio (no. 21) is the entrance to the **Museo Fiorentino di Preistoria** (**Map 4; 7**), a museum of prehistory founded in 1946. Opening times 09.30–12.30 except Sun (☎ 055 295 159); Lire 6000.

Exhibited in three large rooms, the material is well labelled and arranged chronologically and geographically. The lower hall is dedicated to Italy, and includes a human skull of the Palaeolithic era found at Olmo near Arezzo in 1865; the upper hall displays material from Europe, Africa and Asia, including an interesting collection from the Graziosi expedition to the Sahara.

In Via della Pergola is the house (no. 59) where Cellini cast his *Perseus* (see Ch. 4), and where he died in 1571. At no. 8 is the **Oratorio di San Tommaso**

d'Aquino (usually closed) built in 1567 on a design by Santi di Tito who also painted the high altarpiece with the ***Crucifix*** and ***St Thomas***. The **Teatro della Pergola** (Map 4; 7), on the site of a wooden theatre erected in 1656 by Ferdinando Tacca (famous for the comedies performed here), dates in its present form from the 19C. When Gordon Craig, actor and stage designer and son of Ellen Terry, was director here in 1906, *Rosmersholm* was produced starring the great actress Eleonora Duse.

15 • Santa Croce and Casa Buonarroti

Santa Croce is in the centre of a distinctive district of the city, with numerous narrow old streets of small houses above artisans' workshops. In medieval Florence, the area was a centre of the wool industry. The church of Santa Croce is one of the most important in the city, particularly interesting for its 14C frescoes by Giotto and his followers. The Pazzi chapel is one of Brunelleschi's masterpieces. The Casa Buonarroti, nearby, is a delightful small museum with works by Michelangelo.

Piazza Santa Croce (Map 7; 1), one of the most attractive and spacious squares in the city, has been used since the 14C for tournaments, festivals and public spectacles, and the traditional football game celebrating St John's Day (24 June) has been held here for many centuries. One side of the piazza is lined with houses whose projecting upper storeys rest on brackets; these are known as *sporti* and

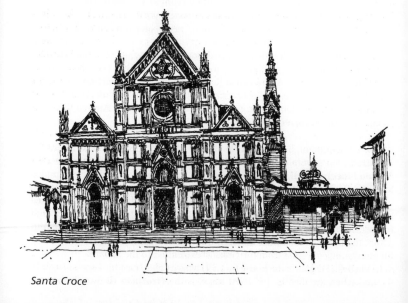

Santa Croce

were a familiar architectural feature of the medieval city. The wooden brackets were replaced in the 15C and 16C by stone supports.

Palazzo dell'Antella (no. 2) was built by Giulio Parigi and its polychrome façade is supposed to have been painted in three weeks in 1619 by Giovanni di San Giovanni, Passignano, Matteo Rosselli, Ottavio Vannini, and others. The unusual palace at the end of the square facing the church is **Palazzo Cocchi** (Serristori), built above a 14C house c 1470–80, probably by Giuliano da Sangallo. The huge statue of Dante, beside the church, is by Enrico Pazzi (1865). At no. 12 is the **Museo del Rinascimento**, a private museum of waxworks opened in 1999 illustrating the history of Florence through tableaux representing the most important figures in its history. It is well labelled in English (opening times daily 10.00–19.00; ☎ 055 263 8732; Lire 12,000).

Santa Croce

Santa Croce (**Map 7; 1**) is the Franciscan church of Florence (opening times, in summer 08.00 or 9.30–17.30 or 18.30; in winter 08.00–12.30, 15.00–17.30; Sun 15.00–17.30). It was rebuilt in 1294, possibly by Arnolfo di Cambio. The nave was still unfinished in 1375 and it was not consecrated until 1442. Remains of an earlier 13C church were found beneath the nave in 1967.

The campanile was added in 1842 by Gaetano Baccani. The bare stone front was covered with a neo-Gothic **façade** in 1857–63 by Niccolò Matas; it was paid for by an English benefactor, Francis Sloane. It is a *tour de force* of local craftsmanship. The lunette above the main door of the *Triumph of the Cross* is by Giovanni Duprè. Along the left flank of the church a picturesque 14C arcade survives and at 5 Via S. Giuseppe there is access to the exterior of the Gothic apse.

Interior

The huge wide interior has an open timber roof. The vista is closed by the polygonal sanctuary and the 14C stained glass in the east windows. The Gothic church was rearranged by Vasari in 1560 when the choir and rood-screen were demolished and the side altars added, with tabernacles by Francesco da Sangallo. Fragments of frescoes by Orcagna which formerly decorated the nave have been uncovered, and some are exhibited in the museum (see below). In the pavement are numerous fine tomb-slabs. For 500 years, it has been the custom to bury or erect monuments to notable citizens of Florence in this church; it is the burial place of Ghiberti, Michelangelo, Machiavelli and Galileo.

Along the **west wall**, a round window has a stained glass *Deposition* which has been attributed to Lorenzo Ghiberti since its restoration in 2000. Monuments here commemorate the 19C patriots Gino Capponi and Giovanni Battista Niccolini (by Pio Fedi).

South aisle On the first pillar, (**1**) *Madonna del Latte* is a charming relief by Antonio Rossellino (1478), above the tomb of Francesco Nori, who was killed in the Pazzi conspiracy (see p 92). The **tomb of Michelangelo** (**2**) was designed by Vasari and includes a bust by Battista Lorenzi. Battisti also sculpted the allegorical figure of *Painting* which is flanked by *Sculpture* by Valerio Cioli and *Architecture* by Giovanni dell'Opera. The fresco of the *Pietà* is by Giovan Battista Naldini. Michelangelo died in Rome in 1564 but his body was transported to Florence for an elaborate funeral service in San Lorenzo before his

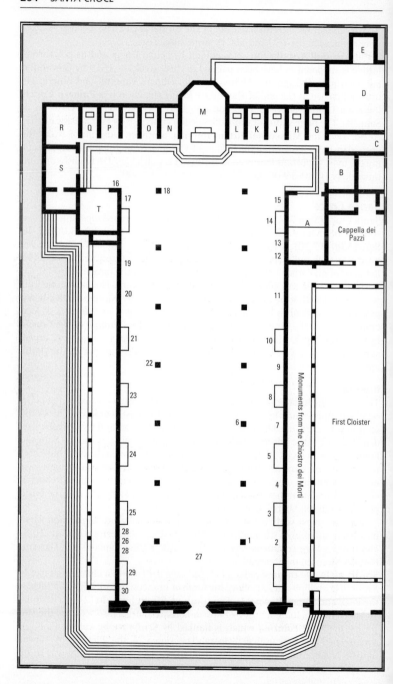

E

D

M

R Q P O N   L K J H G

C

S

B

16

T 17

18

15

14   A

13

12

19

Cappella dei Pazzi

20

11

21

10

22   9

8

23

6   7

24   5

4

25   3

28
26   2
28

29

30   27

1

Monuments from the Chiostro dei Morti

First Cloister

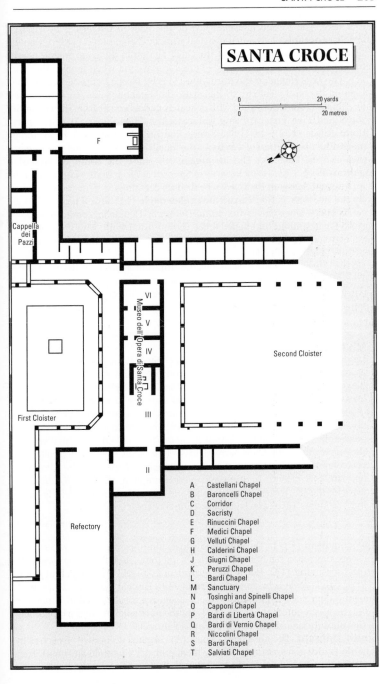

SANTA CROCE

0 _____ 20 yards
0 _____ 20 metres

F

Cappella dei Pazzi

First Cloister

Second Cloister

Museo dell'Opera di Santa Croce

VI
V
IV
III
II

Refectory

A	Castellani Chapel
B	Baroncelli Chapel
C	Corridor
D	Sacristy
E	Rinuccini Chapel
F	Medici Chapel
G	Velluti Chapel
H	Calderini Chapel
J	Giugni Chapel
K	Peruzzi Chapel
L	Bardi Chapel
M	Sanctuary
N	Tosinghi and Spinelli Chapel
O	Capponi Chapel
P	Bardi di Libertà Chapel
Q	Bardi di Vernio Chapel
R	Niccolini Chapel
S	Bardi Chapel
T	Salviati Chapel

burial here. The second altarpiece (**3**) of the *Way to Calvary* is by Vasari. **Dante's cenotaph** (**4**) is a neo-classical work by Stefano Ricci (1829). Dante, exiled in 1302 as an opponent of the Guelf faction in the government, never returned to his native city, and was buried in Ravenna when he died there in 1321. The *Ecce Homo* on the third altar (**5**) is by Jacopo Coppi di Meglio. The *pulpit on the nave pillar (**6**), by Benedetto da Maiano (1472–76), is a beauti-fully composed work decorated with delicately carved scenes from the *Life of St Francis* and *Five Virtues* (being restored). The *monument (**7**) to the poet Vittorio Alfieri (1749–1803) is a very fine neo-classical work by Antonio Canova. The *Flagellation of Christ* on the fourth altar (**8**) is a good painting by Alessandro del Barbiere. The monument (**9**) above the **tomb of Niccolò Machiavelli** (d. 1527) is by Innocenzo Spinazzi (1787). On the fifth altar (**10**) is an unusual *Agony in the Garden* by Andrea del Minga.

By the side door is the *Cavalcanti tabernacle (**11**) with a beautiful high relief in gilded limestone of the *Annunciation* by Donatello, commissioned by Niccolò Cavalcanti for his chapel. It is a very unusual work, with a remarkable bond between the figures of Mary and the Angel Gabriel. The terracotta putti above are also by Donatello.

On the other side of the door, stands the *tomb of Leonardo Bruni (**12**) by Bernardo Rossellino (c 1446–47), one of the most harmonious and influential sepulchral monuments of the Renaissance. The architectural setting takes its inspiration from Brunelleschi.

Leonardo Bruni

Leonardo Bruni, who died in 1444, was an eminent Florentine humanist and a Greek scholar who translated Aristotle and Plato into Latin. He was also an historian who wrote a history 'in praise of the City of Florence' and who wrote lives of Petrarch and Dante. He was papal secretary in 1405–15 and then Chancellor of the Republic in 1427, and was greatly admired by his contem-poraries for his diplomatic ability and skill in public speaking. He was given an official public funeral in the church of Santa Croce and on his tomb there is shown crowned with a laurel wreath in a serene effigy. The touching epitaph was composed by Carlo Marsuppini, his successor as Chancellor, who is buried opposite (see below). In translation, the epitaph reads: 'After Leonardo departed this life, history is in mourning and eloquence is dumb, and it is said that the Muses, Greek and Latin alike, cannot restrain their tears.'

The monument (**13**) to the composer Gioacchino Rossini (1792–1868) is by Giuseppe Cassioli, a sad imitation of the Bruni tomb, and placed too close to it. On the sixth altar (**14**), *Entry into Jerusalem* by Cigoli. The sepulchral statue (**15**) of Ugo Foscolo is by Antonio Berti (1939). Foscolo (1778–1827), a well-known Italian poet, whose most famous poem is *I Sepolcri*, died in London in 1814; he was re-interred here in 1871. On the nave pillar, there is a monument to Giovanni Antonio degli Alberti by Emilio Santarelli (1836).

South transept The Castellani Chapel (**A**) contains decorative *frescoes by **Agnolo Gaddi** and assistants (among them probably Gherardo Starnina). They depict (right) the histories of *St Nicholas of Bari* and *St John the Baptist*, and (left) *St Anthony Abbot* and *St John the Evangelist*. On each wall is a white ter-racotta statue of a saint by the Della Robbia. The altar relief of the *Marys at the Sepulchre* is by a follower of Nicola Pisano. Behind is a tabernacle by Mino da Fiesole and a painted *Crucifix* (1380) attributed to Niccolò di Pietro Gerini (per-haps with the help of Pietro Nelli. Among the monuments here is one by Emilio Santarelli to the Countess of Albany, who married Charles Stuart the Young Pretender (d. 1824; see p 280), and later Vittorio Alfieri.

The **Baroncelli Chapel** (B) has stained glass and *frescoes by **Taddeo Gaddi** (father of Agnolo) who worked with Giotto for many years and was his most faith-ful pupil. These are considered among his best works, executed in 1332–38, and reveal his talent as an innovator within the Giottesque school (they include one of the earliest known night scenes in fresco painting). On either side of the entrance arch are *Prophets* and the tomb (right) of a member of the Baroncelli family (1327) with a *Madonna and Child* in the lunette, also by Gaddi. The two stat-uettes of the *Annunciation* are attributed to Giovanni di Balduccio. The fresco cycle in the chapel illustrates the *Life of the Virgin*. The altarpiece of the *Coronation of the Virgin* (restored) is by Giotto, perhaps with the intervention of his workshop (including possibly Taddeo Gaddi). On the back wall can be seen (right), *Madonna of the Girdle*, a large 15C fresco by Bastiano Mainardi and a 16C statue of the *Madonna and Child*, a good work by Vincenzo Danti.

A portal by Michelozzo, with an inlaid door attributed to Giovanni di Michele, leads into a **corridor** (C) also by Michelozzo. Here there is a large *Deposition* by Alessandro Allori (1560) and a monument to Lorenzo Bartolini, who sculpted a number of monuments in the church (d. 1850), by his pupil, Pasquale Romanelli. On the left another carved and inlaid door gives access to the ***Sacristy** (D) with frescoes of the *Crucifixion* by Taddeo Gaddi the *Way to Calvary*, attributed to Spinello Aretino and the *Resurrection* by Niccolò di Pietro Gerini. The fine inlaid cupboards, by Giovanni di Michele, contain antiphonals. The bust of the *Redeemer* is by Giovanni della Robbia. The **Rinuccini Chapel** (E) is closed by a Gothic grille (1371). It is entirely covered with *frescoes by **Giovanni da Milano** representing scenes from the *Life of the Virgin* and *St Mary Magdalen* (c 1365). Giovanni da Milano was a Lombard artist who worked in Florence, and was one of the best and most sophisticated followers of Giotto. Over the altar is a polyptych by Giovanni del Biondo (1372).

Remains of an old courtyard can be seen from an adjoining room, where some frescoes painted by Gaetano Bianchi during his restoration of the Giotto frescoes in the Bardi chapel (see below) are preserved. The **Medici Chapel** (F), also by Michelozzo (1434), is entered through a door by Giovanni di Michele. It contains a *Madonna with Saints* by Paolo Schiavo and *St John the Baptist* by Spinello Aretino. The terracotta *altarpiece of the *Madonna and Child with Angels* is by Andrea della Robbia (c 1480; the saints were probably added by an assistant).

The chapels at the east end of the church The **Velluti Chapel** (G) has damaged frescoes of *St Michael Archangel* by a follower of Cimabue (possibly Jacopo del Casentino). The polyptych on the altar is by Giovanni del Biondo. The *Calderini Chapel* (H), by Gherardo Silvani (c 1620), has a painted vault by Giovanni di San Giovanni, and an altarpiece by Giovanni Biliverti (the *Finding of the True Cross*, 1621). The **Giugni Chapel** (J) contains the tomb of Charlotte Bonaparte (d. 1839) by Lorenzo Bartolini.

Giotto's frescoes in Santa Croce

Giotto di Bondone (1266/7–1337) was born in the Mugello just north of Florence. A pupil of Cimabue and friend of Dante, his painting had a new monumentality and sense of volume which had never been achieved in medieval painting. His remarkable figures are given an intensely human significance, which the art historian Bernard Berenson defined as 'tactile values'. Giotto carried out his most famous fresco cycle in the Cappella degli Scrovegni in Padua in 1303–05 (the only cycle to survive intact). In Florence, he was appointed *capomaestro* of the cathedral works and is also famous as the architect of the campanile (1334). Paintings by him which are still in Florence can be seen at the Uffizi, Museo Horne and Museo Diocesano dell'Arte Sacra, and in the churches of Santa Maria Novella, Ognissanti, and San Felice there are painted Crucifixes by his hand.

However, it is in the Peruzzi and Bardi chapels in Santa Croce that his greatest Florentine works survive. These frescoes probably date from the 1320s and were commissioned by the Peruzzi and Bardi, two of the richest merchant families in the city, and had a fundamental influence on Florentine painting. The Giottesque school continued to flourish in the city throughout the 14C. Michelangelo was later to make careful studies of these frescoes. When they were rediscovered in 1841–52, the lower scenes in the Bardi chapel had been irreparably damaged by funerary monuments. They were restored by Gaetano Bianchi and others and the missing parts repainted, but in another restoration in 1957–61 the repainting was removed.

Giotto's ***Peruzzi Chapel** (K) mural paintings, not true frescoes, are damaged and in extremely poor condition. They were painted in his maturity, probably after his return to Florence from Padua. The architectural settings contain references to classical antiquity. In the archivolt, there are eight heads of *Prophets*; in the vault, symbols of the *Evangelists*; on the right wall, scenes from the life of *St John the Evangelist* (*Vision at Patmos*, *Raising of Drusiana*, *Ascent into Heaven*); and on the left wall, scenes from the *Life of St John the Baptist* (*Zaccharias and the Angel*, *Birth of St John*, *Herod's Feast*). A drawing by Michelangelo survives (now in the Louvre) of the two male figures on the left in the *Ascension of St John the Evangelist*. The altarpiece of the *Madonna and Saints* is by Taddeo Gaddi.

The ***Bardi Chapel** (L) frescoes by Giotto were certainly designed by him, although it is possible that some were executed by his pupils. They illustrate scenes from the *Life of St Francis*. Giotto received commissions for other Franciscan fresco cycles in Rimini and Padua, both now lost, but his most famous works on this subject are in the upper church of San Francesco in Assisi. On the entrance arch here is the *Saint Receiving the Stigmata*; in the vault, *Poverty*, *Chastity*, *Obedience* and the *Triumph of St Francis*. On the end wall, *Franciscan Saints*, including *St Catherine*. Left wall: the *Saint Stripping off his Garments*; the *Saint Appearing to St Anthony at Arles*; and the *Death of St Francis*. Right wall: the *Saint Giving the Rule of the Order*; the *Saint Being Tried by Fire Before the Sultan* (a particularly fine work); and the *Saint Appearing to Brother Augustine and Bishop Guido of Assisi*. On the altar, *St Francis and Scenes from his Life* by a Florentine artist of the 13C.

The polygonal vaulted **sanctuary** (M) is frescoed by Agnolo Gaddi (c 1380), and has fine stained glass lancet windows also designed by him. Frescoes in the vault show *Christ*, the *Evangelists*, and *St Francis*, and (on the walls) the *Legend of the Cross*. Over the altar is a large polyptych made up in 1869 from panels by various hands when it was given its neo-Gothic frame (probably designed by Nicola Matas). The central *Madonna and Saints* is by Niccolò Gerini and Lorenzo di Niccolò, and the four seated *Fathers of the Church* are by Giovanni del Biondo. The central panel of the predella is a very fine work by Lorenzo Monaco. Above hangs a fine *Crucifix* by the Master of Figline.

The **Tosinghi and Spinelli Chapel** (N) has an *Assumption of the Virgin* above the entrance arch, also attributed to the Master of Figline. The **Capponi Chapel** (O) contains sculptures including a *Pietà* by the Florentine sculptor Libero Andreotti (1926). The next chapel was decorated in 1828–36 by Giuseppe and Francesco Sabatelli. The **Bardi di Libertà Chapel** (P) contains an altarpiece by Giovanni della Robbia and frescoes of the *Life of St Lawrence* and the *Life of St Stephen* by Bernardo Daddi.

The **Bardi di Vernio Chapel** (Q) has colourful *frescoes by **Maso di Banco**, perhaps the most original follower of Giotto, showing the *Life of St Sylvester* and the *Emperor Constantine* (after 1367; restored in 1998). The first Gothic tomb contains a fresco, also attributed to Maso di Banco, of the kneeling figure of *Bettino de' Bardi* with Christ in the sky above receiving his soul into heaven (c 1367); in the second niche, the *Deposition*, is attributed to Taddeo Gaddi. The stained glass is also by Maso (only the two lower figures are modern replacements). The altarpiece by Giovanni del Biondo was removed for restoration many years ago.

North transept The **Niccolini Chapel** (R) was designed by Giovanni Antonio Dosio c 1580, using a profusion of rare marbles. The dome has good frescoes by Volterrano (1652–64). The statues are by Pietro Francavilla and the paintings by Alessandro Allori. The second **Bardi Chapel** (S) contains a wooden *Crucifix* by **Donatello**, though it is not seen to its best advantage here; Vasari recounts how Brunelleschi complained that it showed a mere 'peasant on the Cross' (see p 231). In the **Salviati Chapel** (T) is the *tomb of **Sofia Zamoyska Czartoryska** (d. 1837), with a beautiful Romantic effigy by Lorenzo Bartolini. Here also is the pavement tomb of the philosopher Giovanni Gentile killed in Florence by anti-fascists in 1944. Outside the chapel (16) is a monument by Odoardo Fantacchiotti to the composer Luigi Cherubini (d. 1842; born at 22 Via Fiesolana not far north of the church).

North aisle This contains a monument (17) to the engraver Raffaello Morgheni (d. 1833), by Fantacchiotti. On the nave pillar (18), is a 19C monument to the architect and theorist Leon Battista Alberti (d. 1472), by Lorenzo Bartolini. On the right of the side door, *monument to Carlo Marsuppini* (19), the humanist scholar and Chancellor of the Republic (d. 1453), by Desiderio da Settignano. It takes its inspiration from the Bruni monument opposite (see above) and incorporates some exquisite carving. The fine classical sarcophagus may possibly be the work of Verrocchio. The organ above the door is by Nofri da Cortona (1579; restored).

Beyond the door is a monument (20) to Vittorio Fossombroni (d. 1844) by Lorenzo Bartolini. The *Ascension* on the fifth altar (21) is by Giovanni Stradano.

The painting of the *Deposition* is by Bronzino. In the pavement between the fifth and fourth altar (**22**), there is a handsome tomb-slab with niello decoration and the emblem of an eagle which marks the burial place of Lorenzo Ghiberti and his son Vittorio. On the fourth altar (**23**) is Vasari's *Incredulity of St Thomas*. On either side are neo-classical funerary monuments by Innocenzo Spinazzi. The tomb of Eugenio Barsanti (1821–64) is also here. With Felice Matteucci, Barsanti invented the internal combustion engine in 1854. He was born in Pietrasanta and taught in Florence at the Osservatorio Ximeniano, and the first model of the engine was constructed near Porta al Prato in 1856. The next two altarpieces, the *Supper at Emmaus* (**24**) and the *Resurrection* (**25**), are good works by Santi di Tito. Between them is a 19C funerary monument by Stefano Ricci.

The **monument to Galileo Galilei** (**26**) (1564–1642), the great scientist who spent the latter part of his life in Florence, was set up in 1737 on a design by Giulio Foggini when his remains were allowed to be given Christian burial (see Ch. 17). Giovanni Battista Foggini carved the bust and the statues are by Girolamo Ticciati (*Geometry*, on the right), and Vincenzo Foggini (*Astronomy*, on the left). In the pavement in the centre of the nave, in front of the west door (**27**) is the tomb-slab with a relief of his ancestor and namesake Galileo Galilei, a well-known physician in 15C Florence. The remains of frescoes on the wall (**28**) have been attributed to Mariotto di Nardo. The *Deposition* on the first altar (**29**) is by Giovanni Battista Naldini. On the wall (**30**) are remains of 15C frescoes of three saints.

Museo dell'Opera di Santa Croce

On the right of the church is the entrance to the conventual buildings and the Museo dell'Opera di Santa Croce (**Map 7; 1**). Opening times 10.00–18.00 or 19.00 except Wed (☎ 055 244 619); Lire 8000.

The **first cloister** dates from the 14C. Beneath the arcade, along the bare Gothic flank of the church, is a gallery with a remarkable series of 19C monuments (including works by Aristodemo Costoli and Ulisse Cambi) from the Romantic Chiostro dei Morti (demolished in 1869). Beneath the colonnade beside the entrance to the cloister (right) is a memorial to Florence Nightingale, named after the city where she was born. On the green lawn is a group of cypresses with acanthus plants (and two incongruous statues: the seated figure of *God the Father* by Baccio, made for the choir of the Duomo and moved here in 1842, which now serves as a war memorial, and the statue of a *Warrior*, donated to the city by Henry Moore).

Cappella dei Pazzi

The neo-Gothic campanile rises behind the charming dome and lantern of the Cappella dei Pazzi, one of the most famous works by Brunelleschi. It was commissioned as a chapter house by Andrea de' Pazzi in 1429 or 1430. Most of the work was carried out by Brunelleschi from 1442 until his death in 1446, but it was not finished until the 1470s.

The portico may have been designed by Giuliano da Maiano. The terracotta frieze of cherubs' heads is attributed to the Della Robbia workshop. In the centre of the barrel vault is a shallow cupola lined with delightful polychrome enamelled terracottas by Luca della Robbia, with a garland of fruit surrounding the

Pazzi arms. Over the door is a medallion with *St Andrew*, also by Luca (c 1461). The carved wooden door is by the brothers Da Maiano.

The serene *interior is one of the masterpieces of the early Renaissance. Delicately carved *pietra serena* is used to articulate the architectural features against a plain white ground. The illumination in the chapel is increased by little oculi in the rib-vaulted dome. The 12 *roundels in enamelled terracotta of the seated *Apostles* (c 1442–52) are by Luca della Robbia. In the pendentives of the cupola are four polychrome roundels of the *Evangelists*, thought to have been added c 1460. These may have been designed by Donatello and glazed by the Della Robbia (although some scholars attribute them to Brunelleschi). In the sanctuary are decorations by the school of Donatello and a stained glass window attributed to Alesso Baldovinetti.

On the left of the chapel, nearly 6m up, is a plaque marking the water level of the Arno in the 1966 flood. There is a room with an exhibition of wood cuts by Pietro Parigi (1892–92), and, beyond, a small courtyard between the Pazzi chapel, the corridor outside the sacristy with windows by Michelozzo, and the exterior of the Baroncelli chapel of the church.

The *second cloister is reached through a doorway by Michelozzo. This is another beautiful work by Brunelleschi, finished in 1453 after his death. It is one of the most peaceful spots in the city.

The museum

Off the first cloister is the entrance to the Museo dell'Opera di Santa Croce (see the plan on pp 264–265).

The refectory This is a fine Gothic hall with large windows. Cimabue's great *Crucifix* is displayed here, now carefully restored after it was almost completely destroyed in the 1966 Arno flood. The end wall of the refectory is decorated with a huge *fresco by **Taddeo Gaddi** (detached in one piece and restored) of the *Last Supper* below the *Tree of the Cross* and four scenes showing *St Louis of Toulouse*, *St Francis*, *St Benedict* and *Mary Magdalen Annointing the Feet of Christ in the House of Simon the Pharisee*. On the two long walls (below roundels of saints) are detached fragments of a large fresco by Orcagna showing the *Triumph of Death* and *Inferno* which used to decorate the nave of the church before Vasari's side altars were set up.

The detached 14C fresco (attributed to Giovanni del Biondo) includes one of the earliest views of the city (including the Baptistery and Duomo). In a reconstructed tabernacle (a cast) is Donatello's colossal gilded bronze *St Louis of Toulouse*, commissioned by the Parte Guelfa for a niche in Orsanmichele (but replaced there by the *Incredulity of St Thomas* by Verrocchio). On the entrance wall, there are two detached frescoes by Andrea di Giusto of *Christ Carrying the Cross* and the *Crucifixion*. Above the door into the next room is Maso di Banco's *Coronation of the Virgin* and, to the right, Domenico Veneziano's *Saint John the Baptist and Saint Francis*.

Room II This gallery contains stained glass fragments, including a tondo of a prophet and two martyred saints, formerly part of a large window at the end of the south aisle of the church, which have been attributed to Giotto since 1985. The large fresco of *St Francis Distributing Bread to Friars* is by Jacopo Ligozzi. Also here are two smaller detached frescoes, one of the *Madonna and Child* by the 15C Florentine school, attributed by some scholars to Paolo Uccello (and by others to a 14C artist), and the other an unusual scene showing the young *Madonna Sewing*, a charming work attributed to the Master of the Bambino Vispo.

Room III Formerly the Cappella dei Cerchi, this contains traces of late 13C painted decorations. Enamelled terracottas by Andrea della Robbia and his workshop, and frescoes by Niccolò di Pietro Gerini are on display here. The silver reliquary bust of the blessed Umiliana de' Cerchi is a Florentine work of c 1380. The painted 14C Crucifix is by Filippo Benivieni. In the corridor is a fine fresco from the 15C tomb of a cardinal.

Room IV The three large sketches exhibited here were detached from the walls of the Cappella dei Pazzi during restoration work in 1966. These interesting studies include a colossal head of *St John the Baptist* and an architectural study, which have been attributed by some scholars to Donatello; and another colossal head (with a halo) attributed to Desiderio da Settignano. Also here are 14C–15C detached frescoes, including a fragment of the Virgin attributed to Giotto, and a sinopia of the *Madonna Enthroned* by the Master of the Straus Madonna.

Room V This room contains sculptural fragments including the reconstructed tomb of Gastone della Torre by Tino da Camaino (1318/19); a relief of *St Martin Dividing his Cloak with a Beggar* in *pietra serena*, from a demolished rood-screen chapel in the church (15C); and a *Madonna Annunciate* by Tino da Camaino.

Room VI This room is used as a book shop. It contains 17C works including ceiling paintings of two angels by Matteo Rosselli and the sinopia of the fresco by Ligozzi in Room II.

To the right of the monastic buildings of Santa Croce is the modern extension of the **Biblioteca Nazionale** (Map 7; 3), the older buildings of which extend to the entrance on Piazza dei Cavalleggeri. The main building was erected in 1911–35 by Cesare Bazzani. The National Library was formed from a collection bequeathed by Antonio Magliabechi (d. 1714), the librarian of the Palatina and Laurenziana libraries, and was first opened to the public in 1747. The Biblioteca Palatina-Medicea (1711) and the library of Ferdinando III (1861), together with several monastic collections, were later additions. It includes an important collection of material relating to Dante and Galileo. It became a copyright library for books published in Italy in 1870. In 1966, nearly a third of the library's holdings was damaged when the Arno flooded and a restoration centre here is still at work salvaging and conserving the books.

Corso dei Tintori takes it name from the dyers' workshops which are documented here as early as 1313. Nearby is **Borgo Santa Croce**, a handsome street in which Palazzo Spinelli (no. 10), built in 1460–70, has good graffiti decoration on the façade and in the courtyard. No. 8, the Casa Morra (no admission), belonged to Vasari and contains frescoes by him. Palazzo Antinori-Corsini (no. 6) has a beautiful courtyard dating from the end of the 15C.

On the left side of Santa Croce is Largo Bargellini which leads into Via di San Giuseppe, where, in the house next to the church, the Trollope family lived in 1843–45. The little church of **Santa Maria della Croce al Tempio** (deconsecrated and usually closed), contained frescoes attributed to Bicci di Lorenzo. These have been detached for restoration.

Beyond is the church of **San Giuseppe** (Santa Maria del Giglio; opening times 17.00–19.00; Wednesday also 09.30–12.00), built in 1519 to a design by

Baccio d'Agnolo. The portal dates from 1852 (thought to be based on a design by Michelangelo). The oratory with pretty graffiti decoration and the elegant campanile (designed by Baccio d'Agnolo) both date from 1934.

The handsome **interior** has pretty frescoes in the centre of the vault and in the choir by Sigismondo Betti (1754), with architectural perspectives by Pietro Anderlini. The fine organ, with its original mechanism, is by the workshop of the Agati of Pistoia (1764). On the **south side**, the first chapel has a 16C lunette (left side) and an unusual funerary monument by Odoardo Fantacchiotti (1854). The second chapel was decorated in 1705 with a cupola frescoed by Atanasio Bimbacci. The damaged triptych attributed to Taddeo Gaddi and the 14C carved wooden *Crucifix* both belonged to the Compagnia di Santa Maria della Croce al Tempio. The third chapel has frescoes by Luigi Ademollo (1840), and on the altar is a *Nativity*, an early work by Santi di Tito. Above the high altar, inlaid with a floral decoration in *pietre dure* in 1930, is a painted Crucifix of the early 15C Florentine school. The 17C stalls and 16C paintings in octagonal frames complete the decoration of the choir. On the **north side**, the third chapel (left wall) contains an *Annunciation* attributed to the Maestro di Serumidio; the second chapel, an early 16C copy of the fresco of the *Madonna del Giglio* (formerly in the tabernacle outside the church) and a painted *Crucifix* attributed to Lorenzo Monaco. The first chapel (left wall) has *San Francesco di Paola Healing a Sick Man* by Santi di Tito, and, on the altar, a polychrome wooden *Crucifix* of the 17C and two figures in stucco of the 18C. Two paintings by Cigoli and Giovanni Antonio Sogliani are being restored.

Across Via delle Casine is the huge **Pia Casa di Montedomini**, a hospice for the elderly, the buildings of which extend as far as the Viali. This is on the site of a 15C hospital, later used by two Franciscan convents of closed orders (Montedomini and Monticelli). The buildings were redesigned in the early 19C by Giuseppe del Rosso as a hospice and it became a Pia Casa di Lavoro, or workhouse, and was further enlarged in 1860. It incorporates a church (entered from Via dei Malcontenti) consecrated in 1573 with a vault painted by Agostino Veracini in the 18C. A wing of the hospice, used from 1894 to 1938 as a military hospital, has painted decorations by Galileo Chini.

In Via delle Conce, where the old tanneries have recently been restored and converted into flats, a tabernacle in *pietra serena* (1704) on the corner of Via dei Conciatori contains a copy made c 1920 of an early 16C painting of the Madonna and Child from the church of San Giuseppe. Beyond, at 30 Via Ghibellina is **Palazzo Vivarelli Colonna**, acquired by the Comune in 1979 and now the seat of the Assessorato alla Cultura (the city's cultural department). The interior is interesting for its early 19C frescoes by Angiolo Angiolini and Francesco Nenci. The little walled garden (restored in 1999), which is sometimes open to the public, was laid out in the early 18C with an elaborate Baroque wall fountain in the form of a grotto with shells added in the 19C and a painted background. On the top of the walls are terracotta eagles, vases and putti. The central fountain, decorated with an eagle and serpent, is surrounded by Renaissance parterres, with beds marked out in *pietra serena*, a bed of camellias, tubs of lemon trees and a magnolia and a pine tree as well as ilexes.

Opposite the side of Santa Croce (see above) Via delle Pinzochere leads past a fine palace (no. 3) to Via Ghibellina.

Casa Buonarroti

At No 70 Via Ghibellina is the Casa Buonarroti (**Map 7; 1**), a delightful little museum dedicated to Michelangelo. Three houses on this site were purchased in 1508 by Michelangelo. He left the property to his only descendant, his nephew Leonardo, who joined the houses together following a plan already drawn up by Michelangelo. In turn, his son, called Michelangelo, an art collector and man of letters, made part of the house into a gallery in 1612 as a memorial to his great-uncle. The last member of this branch of the Buonarroti family founded the present museum in 1858, and it is still run by a foundation. In the charming little rooms of the house are displayed three of Michelangelo's sculptures and some of his drawings. There is also a small but eclectic collection of works of art made by Michelangelo's descendants. On the façade is a 19C bust of Michelangelo by Clemente Papi.

• **Opening times** 09.30–13.30 except Tues (☎ 055 241 752); Lire 12,000.

Ground floor

On the right is the **Archaeological Room** which displays a collection of Etruscan and Roman works formed by Michelangelo Buonarroti the Younger (1568–1647), and continued by the archaeologist Filippo Buonarroti (1661–1733). The two archaic stelae from Fiesole in *pietra serena*, one showing a seated satyr playing a lyre (late 6C BC; found in 1720), and the other with a warrior (also 6C BC), are among the best preserved Etruscan stelae of this period. The five Etruscan urns include two polychrome terracotta urns from Chiusi (2C BC) with battle scenes, and a fragment of an alabaster urn representing Ulysses and the Sirens. The Roman pieces include sculptural fragments, two statues of magistrates (1C AD), found in Florence in 1627 and restored for Michelangelo Buonarroti the Younger by Antonio Novelli and Bastiano Pettirossi; 1C AD cinerary urns, vases, small bronzes, terracotta reliefs and lamps.

The next room contains **paintings and sculptures based on works by Michelangelo**, many by unknown 16C artists. The small *Crucifixion* was copied by Marcello Venusti from a drawing made by Michelangelo for his close friend Vittoria Colonna (1490–1547), a remarkable Renaissance figure and poet. The *Anima danata* was painted by a Tuscan artist. The statue of *Venus* and two cupids is attributed to Vincenzo Danti. Alessandro Allori made the copy of *Christ* from the *Last Judgement* in the Sistine Chapel in 1559. The tiny copy of the entire fresco is by a follower of Giulio Clovio (c 1570).

The next room displays the **Buonarroti collection** made by Michelangelo Buonarroti the Younger in the 16C–17C. Works by the *bottega* of Andrea della Robbia include a statuette of *Abundance* by Fra' Matteo della Robbia. The charming portrait of *Three Young Men* from the Buonarroti family is by Gregorio Pagani. The **Love Scene* (perhaps *Cornelia and Pompey*) is a 16C Venetian copy of a lost work by Titian. Also here are three 17C portraits of old men; two small works by Cristofano Allori; and 16C majolica from Pesaro, Urbino, Faenza and Cafaggiolo.

In the **courtyard,** there is a statue made up from a classical head and a medieval draped toga, a little Roman relief with two goats (1C AD), and an ancient Ionic capital used as a model by Giuliano da Sangallo in the cloister of Santa Maria Maddalena dei Pazzi. The rooms on the other side of the courtyard are used for exhibitions on themes related to Michelangelo. One of them has a ceiling fresco of the *Dream of Jacob* by Jacopo Vignali (1621) and an unfinished 16C statue of a *Slave*, which was attributed to Michelangelo in 1965 by the former director of the museum.

First floor

In the vestibule are 16C–19C **portraits of Michelangelo** based on a prototype (c 1535) by Jacopino del Conte (also displayed here). The sword is thought to have belonged to Buonarroto Buonarroti, Captain of the Guelf party in 1392.

The room to the left contains two small sculptures **by Michelangelo**: the *Madonna of the Steps*, a marble bas-relief, is his earliest known work, carved at the age of 15 or 16. The low *schiacciato* relief shows the influence of Donatello. In the 17C, it was owned by the Medici who then returned it to the Buonarroti family. It was a work intended for private devotion, possibly part of a triptych. The relief showing a *Battle scene* is also one of his earliest works, carved just before the death of Lorenzo il Magnifico in 1492, and then worked on a few years later, but left unfinished. This is his only early work documented by his biographers Vasari and Condivi, and it demonstrated Michelangelo's prodigious skill as a sculptor. Modelled on ancient sarcophagi, it represents a mythological battle between Greeks and centaurs. It shows the influence of Bertoldo di Giovanni who carved a very fine bronze battle relief (now in the Bargello), based on a Roman sarcophagus in Pisa.

Another room (left) contains the wooden model by Pietro Urbano for the façade of San Lorenzo designed by Michelangelo for Leo X in 1516 but never carried out. The colossal *torso* by Michelangelo, a model in clay and wood for a river god, was intended for the New Sacristy in San Lorenzo. It was presented by Ammannati to the Accademia del Disegno in 1583.

In the room in front of the stairs are displayed (in rotation) five or six *drawings* by Michelangelo owned by the museum.

Beyond are four **rooms decorated for Michelangelo Buonarroti the Younger** c 1613–37 as a celebration of his famous great-uncle and his family. The first room, the **Galleria**, painted in 1613–35, illustrates *Michelangelo's Life and Apotheosis*, with paintings by Giovanni Biliverti, Jacopo da Empoli, Artemisia Gentileschi, Francesco Furini, Giovanni di San Giovanni, Passignano and Matteo Rosselli. On the wall opposite the statue of *Michelangelo* by Antonio Novelli is a copy of the cartoon of the so-called *Epiphany* by Michelangelo's pupil, Ascanio Condivi. In the niches on either side, statues representing the Active and Contemplative Life by Domenico Pieratti.

The **Stanza della Notte e del Di'**, begun in 1624, is dedicated to the Buonarroti family, and off it is the tiny little study of Michelangelo the Younger. The *predella* with scenes from the *Life of St Nicholas of Bari* is by Giovanni di Francesco, and the marble *Cupid* was begun by Valerio Cioli and finished by Andrea Ferrucci. The portrait of *Michelangelo in a Turban* is attributed to Giuliano Bugiardini, and the painting of *Michelangelo the Younger* is by Cristofano Allori. The bronze head of Michelangelo is by Daniele da Volterra. The **Camera degli Angeli** was used as a chapel. It has a pretty ceiling with frescoes by Michelangelo Cinganelli and frescoes of *Florentine Saints* on the walls by Jacopo Vignali. The bust of *Michelangelo the Younger* is the masterpiece of Giuliano Finelli, Bernini's pupil. Also here is a 16C bronze copy of the *Madonna of the Steps*.

The **library** was decorated in 1633–37 with a delightful frieze of illustrious

Tuscans by Cecco Bravo, with the help of Domenico Pugliani and Matteo Rosselli. Roman fragments in marble and terracotta are displayed here. In case 410, there is a beautiful terracotta head of a child attributed to the school of Verrocchio or Antonio Rossellino. In the **Stanzina dell'Apollo**, an alcove, are displayed Roman sculptures, including a statuette of *Apollo*, and the right arm and hand from a good Roman copy of the *Discobolos of Myron*.

The room to the right of the stairs displays **bozzetti* in wax, terracotta, wood and plaster attributed to Michelangelo and his circle. In the centre, the *Two Wrestlers* in terracotta is recognised as by the hand of Michelangelo (c 1530). The wood *Crucifix* and *River god* in wax are also attributed to him. The two terracottas of a *female nude* and a *male torso* may be by him, while the terracotta *Madonna and Child* is attributed to Vincenzo Danti.

Another room has two paintings of the *Noli me tangere* derived from a lost cartoon by Michelangelo, one attributed to Pontormo, and the other by Battista Franco. Beyond the **Stanza dei Paesaggi** decorated with early 18C frescoes, is a room dedicated to the **cult of Michelangelo** in the 19C, with a 19C marble sculpture of the young *Michelangelo at Work* by Cesare Zocchi. Documentation relating to the celebrations in Florence in 1875 for the fourth centenary of Michelangelo's birth include designs for graffiti decoration which was to have been added to the façade of the Casa Buonarroti. Beyond a narrow corridor, a few steps lead down to a little room with plaster casts of works by Michelangelo, a large eagle, once thought to be a Roman work, and a wooden model for the 'carriage' built to transport the statue of the *David* from Piazza della Signoria to the Accademia in 1873. From here stairs continue down to the courtyard and exit.

On the second floor, there is an important library (open to scholars) with material relating to Michelangelo.

16 • Sant'Ambrogio and Santa Maria Maddalena dei Pazzi

This chapter covers the market area around the interesting little church of Sant' Ambrogio, and the church of Santa Maria Maddalena dei Pazzi, which has a fresco by Perugino and a beautiful 15C cloister.

Sant'Ambrogio

The church of Sant'Ambrogio (**Map 7; 2**) was rebuilt in the late 13C. The façade is 19C and the interior has pretty Renaissance side altars, and an open timber roof. The church was badly damaged when the Arno flooded in 1966.

Interior

The tribune, with its side chapels, was designed in 1716 by Giovanni Battista Foggini.

On the **south side** you will find a fresco of the *Deposition* by the school of

Niccolò Gerini (its sinopia is displayed nearby). In the pavement beside the first altar is the tomb-slab of Cronaca (d. 1508), the architect of a number of fine palaces in the city, and behind the second altar, a *Madonna Enthroned with St John the Baptist and St Bartholomew*, a beautiful fresco attributed to the school of Orcagna. On the third altar is a late 15C *Crucifixion*. Above the fourth altar is an interesting fragment of a mural drawing of *St Onuphrius*, attributed to the Master of Figline (14C). At the end of this wall there is a painting of the *Madonna with Two Saints and a Donor* attributed to Giovanni di Bartolomeo Cristiani.

In the **sanctuary** there are frescoes by Luigi Ademollo. In the chapel to the right of the sanctuary is a *Triptych* (recently restored) attributed to Bicci di Lorenzo or Lorenzo di Bicci. The chapel to the left of sanctuary (the **Cappella del Miracolo**) contains an exquisite *tabernacle by Mino da Fiesole (1481), who is buried here (tomb-slab in the pavement at the entrance to the chapel, 1484). The tabernacle contains a miraculous chalice and a large *fresco by Cosimo Rosselli that shows a procession with the chalice in front of the church. It includes portraits of many of the artist's contemporaries as well as his self-portrait (to the left). The sinopia is displayed on the wall nearby. Tradition relates how, in 1230, Uguccione the parish priest found blood instead of wine in the chalice while celebrating Mass.

On the **north side**, the fourth altar has a painting of *Saints* and the *Annunciation* by Raffaellino del Garbo (attributed). In the pavement are the tomb-slabs of Verrocchio (d. 1488) and Francesco Granacci (1544). The third altar has Cosimo Rosselli's *Madonna in Glory with Saints*. Between the third and second altars, a wooden statuette of *St Sebastian* by Leonardo del Tasso stands in a graceful niche with a tiny painted roundel of the *Annunciation*, attributed to the workshop of Filippino Lippi. The second altar has Andrea Boscoli's *Visitation*. The first altar has a fresco of the *Martyrdom of St Sebastian*, with unusual iconography, attributed to Agnolo Gaddi. On the wall is Alesso Baldovinetti's *Angels and Saints Surrounding a Nativity* by his pupil Graffione.

High up on the corner of Via de' Macci, there is an enamelled terracotta tabernacle with the statuette of *St Ambrose* by Giovanni della Robbia (c 1525). Off Via de' Macci is the **Mercato di Sant' Ambrogio** (Map 7; 2), open Monday–Saturday mornings. It is housed in a cast-iron building dating from 1873 and is the biggest produce market in Florence after the central market at San Lorenzo. Fruit and vegetables, some grown locally, are sold from stalls outside, and on the two short sides of the building there is a daily market (clothes, household linen and hardware), which is generally good value.

From Piazza Sant'Ambrogio, Via Pietrapiana leads to **Piazza dei Ciompi** (**Map 7; 1**), named after the famous revolt of Florentine clothworkers in 1378. The graceful Loggia del Pesce, designed in 1568 by Vasari for the sale of fish, was reconstructed here after the demolition of the Mercato Vecchio (see Ch. 3). It looks somewhat incongruous in these humble surroundings. In the square is the Mercatino, a junk and antique market where bargains can sometimes be found.

A damaged inscription on a house here records the home of Lorenzo Ghiberti. Cimabue lived in Borgo Allegri, which was given this name, according to Vasari, after Cimabue's painting of the Madonna left his studio in a joyous procession down the street. There is a small public garden in this street, opened and maintained by old age pensioners who live in the district. In Via Pietrapiana, there is a tabernacle with a fine relief of the **Madonna and Child** attributed to Donatello. Opposite is a large, incongruous building built as a post office by Giovanni Michelucci in 1959–67.

From Piazza Sant'Ambrogio, Via dei Pilastri leads towards Borgo Pinti passing (right) Via Farini with the huge **Synagogue** (**Map 4; 8**), an elaborate building in the Spanish-Moresco style with a tall green dome (opening times daily, except Saturday, 11.00–13.00; 14.00–17.00; 15 June–15 September, 09.30–17.30). It was built in 1874–82 by Marco Treves, Mariano Falcini and Vincenzo Michele. The Jews are first mentioned as a community in Florence in the 15C when they were called by the Republican government to operate in the city as money-lenders. In 1571, they were confined to a ghetto (in the area of the present Piazza della Repubblica, see Ch. 3) by Cosimo I and this was not opened until 1848. The ghetto was demolished at the end of the 19C.

A small **museum** was opened on the upper floor of the synagogue in 1981. Opening times Sun–Thurs 10.00–13.00, 14.00–17.00; Fri 10.00–13.00; closed Sat; ☎ 2346 654. The display is well labelled and includes ceremonial objects, silver and vestments, dating from the 17C–18C. In the garden is a Jewish School.

At one end of Via Farini can be seen the large **Piazza d'Azeglio**, planted with plane trees and reminiscent of a London square. At the other end, Via dei Pilastri continues to **Borgo Pinti** (**Map 4; 7**), a long narrow old street leading out of the city. On the corner is the church of **Santa Maria dei Candeli** (usually closed) redesigned by Giovanni Battista Foggini in 1704, with a ceiling fresco by Niccolò Lapi. On the corner of Via Alfani is the tabernacle of Monteloro with a fresco attributed to Puccio di Simone. At the beginning of Borgo Pinti (left) are two 17C palaces, Palazzo Caccini (no. 33) and Palazzo Roffia (no. 13). Palazzo Caccini, now Geddes da Filicaia, was famous for its garden in the 17C. The portico has neo-classical frescoes.

Santa Maria Maddalena dei Pazzi

To the right, on Borgo Pinti just before no. 58, is the entrance to the Convent of Santa Maria Maddalena dei Pazzi (**Map 4; 7**). It is named after a Florentine Carmelite nun (1566–1607) who was canonised in 1669, during the Counter-Reformation. A Cistercian convent, founded here in 1321, was taken over by the Carmelites from 1628 until 1888, and fathers of the Assumption of the Augustinian order (founded in Nimes in 1850) have been here since 1926 (the church serves the French community of Florence).

The church is entered through a *quadriporticus* or ***cloister** by Giuliano da Sangallo (1492) which has beautiful large Ionic capitals supporting a low architrave. The new bronze panels intended for the door of the church are by Marcello Tommasi. On the right of the entrance portico is the domed **Cappella del Giglio** (or Cappella dei Neri; for admission ask at the convent), built c 1505, which is beautifully frescoed by Bernardino Poccetti and assistants (1598–1600). The altarpiece of the **Martyrdom of Saints Nereus and Achilleus** is by Passignano.

If the church is closed ring at the convent at no. 58. Although the door is kept closed it is usually unlocked. The chapter house is only open 09.00–11.50, 17.00–17.20, 18.10–18.50; on Sat 09.00–11.50, 17.00–18.20; on *fest.* 09.00–10.45, 17.00–18.50. Although state-owned, a donation is requested for the lighting.

The **church** was begun in 1257 and the side chapels were added in 1488–1526, with pretty carved arches in *pietra serena* by Piero di Giovanni della Bella and his *bottega*. The *trompe l'œil* ceiling painting is by Jacopo Chiavistelli and Marco Antonio Molinari (1677), and the paintings in the nave are by Cosimo Ulivelli (c 1700).

On the south side, the first chapel contains the **Martyrdom of St Romulus** (1557), a fine work signed and dated by Carlo Portelli. The second chapel was decorated in 1778; on the altar is a wooden processional statue of the **Madonna and Child**. In the third chapel there is a **Coronation of the Virgin** by Matteo Rosselli in a fine frame of c 1490. The fourth chapel has a **Madonna and Child with Saints** by Domenico Puligo (1526; with a good frame by Baccio d'Agnolo). The fifth chapel has a stained glass window of St Francis (c 1500), and the sixth chapel early 19C frescoes by Luigi Catani and a small **Crucifix** attributed to Bernardo Buontalenti.

The well-lit **main chapel**, with colourful marbles, is one of the most important and complete examples of Florentine Baroque church decoration. It was designed in 1675 in honour of Santa Maria Maddalena by Ciro Ferri, who painted the high altarpiece, and by Pier Francesco Silvani. On the side walls are two paintings by Luca Giordano. The statues are by (left) Antonio Montauti (c 1690) and (right) Innocenzo Spinazzi (1781). The cupola was frescoed in 1701 by Piero Dandini.

On the north side of the church, the fine Renaissance organ (restored in 1719) has a cantoria attributed to Giuliano da Sangallo. In the fifth chapel, there is a **Martyrdom of St James** by Giovanni Bizzelli (1601); in the fourth chapel, in a pretty frame, **St Ignatius and St Roch** by Raffaellino del Garbo, flanking a wood statue of **St Sebastian**. The third chapel has stained glass designed by Domenico del Ghirlandaio and an altarpiece of the **Agony in the Garden** by Santi di Tito, signed and dated 1591. The second chapel contains a **Coronation of the Virgin** by Cosimo Rosselli in another fine frame.

The **chapter house** is now entered from the crypt since the second cloister was cut in two when Via della Colonna was built. It contains one of Perugino's masterpieces: his beautiful and well-preserved fresco of the *Crucifixion and Saints* (1493–96). Also here is **Christ on the Cross and St Bernard**, a detached fresco with its sinopia, by his workshop.

Borgo Pinti continues across Via della Colonna, in which the Museo Archeologico (see p 200) stands. On the right (no. 68) is **Palazzo Panciatichi Ximenes**, which became the home of the Sangallo brothers in about 1490. It was bought by Sebastiano di Tommaso Ximenes in 1603, and he employed Gherardo Silvani to restructure it (the façade dates from this time). Modifications in c 1720 include the atrium, a handsome double stair, and interior courtyard with three statues (the one of **Hercules and the Lion** is attributed to Giovanni Baratta). Beyond the closed loggia is a pretty garden with some fine trees. The Borgo next crosses Via Giusti.

In Via Giuseppe Giusti (left) is the **German Institute** (no. 44), which has an excellent art history library. No. 43 is a bizarre little house built as a studio by Federico Zuccari, the Roman painter, in 1579. It is connected by a garden to a larger house built by Andrea del Sarto in 1520 on his return from France, where he died ten years later (plaque on no. 22 Via Gino Capponi). This was also owned by Zuccari, and in 1988 was acquired by the German Institute. The large tabernacle at no. 27 contains a *Resurrection of Christ* by Alessandro Fei.

Via Gino Capponi, beyond, honours Gino Capponi (1792–1876), the statesman-historian whose grandiose home, **Palazzo Capponi** (no. 26) was built in 1698–1713 by Carlo Fontana. The huge palace has a fine garden. The poet Giuseppe Giusti died here suddenly in 1850. Palazzo di San Clemente (no. 15), on the corner of Via Micheli, is an interesting building by Gherardo Silvani. In the entrance hall is the British royal coat of arms. The palace was bought by Charles Stuart, the Young Pretender in 1777.

Charles Stuart, the Young Pretender

Bonnie Prince Charlie was born in 1720 in Rome. After his defeat by the English at Culloden in 1746, he spent some years in France where he assumed the title of Charles III of Great Britain. He retired to Florence where he also stayed at the Palazzo Corsini and Palazzo Guadagni. In 1772 he married Louisa, Countess of Albany (see p 282), though the marriage was a disaster and she fled from here in 1780 to the nearby Convento delle Bianchette, before marrying the dramatist Vittorio Alfieri. The young Pretender spent the last three years of his life in Rome where he died in 1788. He was buried in the Vatican grottoes, and has a monument in St Peter's by Canova.

At the other end of Via Capponi (just out of Piazza Santissima Annunziata) is the **Cloister of the former Compagnia della Santissima Annunziata** (or di San Pierino). This is at no. 4 (ring for admission at the Società Dante Alighieri). Above the entrance, there is a lunette in glazed terracotta; this shows the *Annunciation* with two members of the confraternity in white hooded robes and is the work of Santi Buglioni. The delightful little cloister has frescoes (c 1585–90) by Bernardino Poccetti, Andrea Boscoli, Cosimo Gheri, Bernardino Monaldi and Giovanni Balducci. The lunettes, representing the *Martyrdom of the Apostles*, are separated by monochrome figures of the *Christian Virtues*, and, above the doors, the *Resurrection* and *Pietà* (explained by a diagram *in situ*). In the vestibule beyond, there are two damaged frescoes of *Christ at the Column* and the *Crown of Thorns*, also by Poccetti, and a small triptych in glazed terracotta by Giovanni della Robbia. The ex-Oratorio has more frescoed lunettes by Poccetti (very damaged).

At the end of Borgo Pinti is the garden of Palazzo Salviati (no. 76), which was once famous but is usually closed and of slight interest. Opposite stands **Palazzo della Gherardesca** (no. 99), with an attractive 19C garden in the English Romantic tradition. It has fine magnolias, limes and ilexes. The small neo-classical temple was designed by Giuseppe Cacialli in 1842. The palace, built by Giuliano da Sangallo for Bartolomeo Scala in the 15C (with interesting bas-reliefs in the courtyard), was enlarged in the 18C by Antonio Ferri. Borgo Pinti ends at Piazza Donatello (described on p 333).

17 • The Arno between Ponte alla Carraia and Ponte alle Grazie

This chapter follows the right and left banks of the Arno between the four bridges in the centre of the city, all of them built for the first time by the 13C (the other bridges, up and down stream, were added after 1836). The roads along the Arno (recorded as early as the 13C) are known as the Lungarni (singular, Lungarno). Lined with handsome palaces and some elegant shops, they provide magnificent views of the city on the river.

Ponte alla Carraia (Map 6; 1) was the second bridge to be built over the Arno after Ponte Vecchio. Constructed in wood on stone piles in 1218–20, it was known as Ponte Nuovo. It was reconstructed after floods in 1269 and 1333; the 14C bridge may have been designed by Giotto. In 1559 it was repaired by Ammannati and then enlarged in 1867; it was replaced by a new bridge (a copy of the original) after it was blown up in 1944. From the foot of the bridge, there is a view looking southeast of the campanile of Santo Spirito, with the Forte di Belvedere and the bell-tower of San Miniato on the skyline.

At the north end, in the busy Piazza Goldoni, there is a statue of the playwright Carlo Goldoni (by Ulisse Cambi, 1873) and Palazzo Ricasoli (no. 2, with several coats of arms) built c 1475. A road leads to the church of Ognissanti (described in Ch. 11). **Lungarno Vespucci**, opened in the 19C, leads away from the centre of the city towards the park of the Cascine past two modern bridges which can also be seen downstream, Ponte Vespucci and Ponte della Vittoria. Also downstream on the left bank is the church of San Frediano in Cestello.

Palazzo Corsini

Lungarno Corsini leads past the huge Palazzo Corsini (**Map 6; 1**) built from 1656 to c 1737 in a grandiose Roman Baroque style. The palace has been used as the seat of the antiques fair known as the Biennale dell'Antiquariato since 1997, and exhibitions are also now held here. The architects included Alfonso Parigi the Younger and Ferdinando Tacca, and (after 1685) Antonio Ferri (perhaps to a design of Pier Francesco Silvani). The façade is crowned by statues and has a terrace overlooking the river.

The palace contains the **Galleria Corsini**, the most important private art collection in Florence (admission by appointment only at 11 Via del Parione, ☎ 055 218 994).

In the left wing is an ingenious spiral staircase by Pier Francesco Silvani. The monumental staircase in the other wing by Antonio Ferri leads up to the *piano nobile* and the splendid Salone del Trono designed by Ferri with statues and busts and two huge wood chandeliers made for the room. The fresco of the *Apotheosis of the Corsini Family* is by Antonio Domenico Gabbiani.

The collection, formed in the 17C by Marchese Bartolommeo Corsini and his son Filippo, is arranged in six rooms frescoed in 1692–1700 by Alessandro Gherardini and Antonio Domenico Gabbiani, with stucco decoration by the Passardi and Rinaldo Botti. The paintings are representative of the 17C Florentine school and are displayed in magnificent frames. They include: Carlo Maratta's, *Portrait of Filippo di Bartolomeo Corsini*; Luca Giordano's *bozzetto* for the vault fresco in the Cappella Corsini in the Carmine; Carlo Dolci's *Poetry*; a tondo of the *Madonna* by Luca Signorelli and his *bottega*; *Apollo and the Muses* by Giovanni Santi, Timoteo Viti and others, painted for the Ducal palace at Urbino; Sustermans' portrait of *Geri della Rena*; Giovanni Bellini's *Crucifix*; Pier Francesco Toschi's *Portrait of a Man*; Pontormo's *Madonna and Child with the Young St John*; a tondo of the *Madonna and Angels* by Botticelli (or his *bottega*); five *Allegorical Figures*, thought to be early works by Filippino Lippi; Ridolfo del Ghirlandaio's *Portrait of a Man*; Sustermans' portrait of his friend *Pietro Fevre*, who was tapestry-maker to the Medici (Sustermans' first portrait painted in Florence); four scenes of the *Passion of Christ* by Domenico Fetti; cartoon of Raphael's *Portrait of Julius II*; Lodovico Cigoli's *Head of Christ*; works by Giacinto Gimignani; Hyacinthe Rigaud, portrait of *Neri Corsini*. The marble bust of the Corsini pope *Clement XII* is by Bouchardon. The porcelain *Deposition* was made in the Doccia factory c 1752 to a design by Massimiliano Soldani Benzi.

Farther along the Lungarno is (no. 4) Palazzo Gianfigliazzi (1459; reconstructed). A plaque commemorates Alessandro Manzoni , who stayed in a hotel here in 1827. Next door, the **British Consulate** now occupies Palazzo Masetti (Castelbarco) where Louisa, Countess of Albany, widow of Prince Charles Edward Stuart, the Young Pretender (see p 280), lived from 1793 until her death in 1824. Her salon was frequented by Chateaubriand, Shelley, Byron, Foscolo and Von Platen. The dramatist Alfieri, her second husband, died here in 1803. The Countess was later joined here by Xavier Fabre, the French painter. She is buried in Santa Croce.

The next bridge is **Ponte Santa Trìnita (Map 6; 1)**, first built in 1252 and rebuilt several times after flood damage. The present bridge is an exact replica of the one that was begun by Ammannati in 1567 and destroyed in 1944. It was financed by public subscription from a committee presided over by Bernard Berenson and built under the careful direction of Riccardo Gizdulich and Emilio Brizzi in 1955–57. Ammannati's Ponte Santa Trìnita was the finest of all the bridges across the Arno. It was commissioned by Cosimo I and it is probable that Ammannati submitted his project to Michelangelo for approval. The high flat arches, known as catenaries (from *catena*, chain), which span the river recreate the unique curve of a chain suspended from two terminal points. They are perfectly proportioned and provide a magnificent view of the city. The statues of the *Four Seasons* were set up on the parapet for the marriage of Cosimo II; *Spring* (left), is the best work of Pietro Francavilla (1593).

At the beginning of Via Tornabuoni (Ch. 12; **Map 1; 5**) stands Palazzo Spini-Feroni. **Lungarno Acciaioli** continues with a good view of Ponte Vecchio. In a group of old houses overhanging the opposite bank of the river, there is the little tower

Spring, one of the statues on Ponte Santa Trìnita

and river gate belonging to the church of San Jacopo sopr'Arno. The Lungarno becomes narrower and an old lane (signposted) leads to the ancient church of Santi Apostoli (described on p 319). The modern buildings on both banks of the river here replace the medieval houses which were blown up in 1944 in order to render Ponte Vecchio impassable.

Ponte Vecchio is the most famous bridge across the Arno and is described in Ch. 7. At the foot of the bridge is the busy Por Santa Maria, at the bend of which can be seen the lantern of the Duomo above the top of Orsanmichele. Lungarno Archibusieri continues parallel to the raised Corridoio Vasariano (beneath which are market stalls) and narrows to follow the façade of the Uffizi; from the little terrace on the river there is a view of Palazzo Vecchio, framed by the Uffizi.

Museo di Storia della Scienza

In Piazza dei Giudici (with a view of the tower of Palazzo Vecchio) stands Palazzo Castellani, a fine medieval palace owned in the 14C by an important Florentine family whose wealth was based on the cloth trade. It now contains the Museo di Storia della Scienza (**Map 1; 8**), with its well displayed collection of scientific instruments.

• **Opening times** 09.30–17.00, except Tues 09.30–13; closed Sundays except for the second Sunday of the month, 10.00–13.00; summer: 09.30– 17.00 except Tues and Sat 09.30–13.00; closed Sun (☎ 055 239 8876); Lire 12,000.

Since the days of the Medici dynasty Florence has held an extremely important place not only in the arts but also in the history of science. A large part of this collection was owned by the Medici grand-dukes, and the Museum of Physics and Natural Sciences, directed by Felice Fontana and opened in 1775 by the Grand-duke Pietro Leopoldo of Lorraine, was moved here in 1929. A brief guide (also in English) is given to visitors and excellent handlists with more detailed information (also available in English) can be borrowed from the custodians on each floor. The museum is beautifully kept and extremely well run. Some of the models in Rooms IV, VI and VII are demonstrated for groups of visitors by the custodians. There is a lift for the use of the elderly and disabled.

On the **ground floor** is the Library of the Istituto di Storia della Scienza; this has some 80,000 volumes, including many which belonged to the Medici and Lorraine grand-dukes.

First floor

Room I Mathematical instruments in Florence. In the centre of the room there is an Arab globe showing the constellations (c 1080). Two cases display instruments for measuring the heavens, including 10C–16C astrolabes, quadrants and sundials, and 16C–18C Night and Day clocks. In another case are displayed compasses (mostly 17C) including a pair from the 16C traditionally thought to have been used by Michelangelo. The last case contains cases for mathematical instruments.

Room II Foreign mathematical instruments. Many of these were brought back from Germany by Prince Mattias, brother of Ferdinando II in 1635, and were made by Christoph Schissler and his son, including an astrolabe (1560) and a quadrant (1590). Another case contains surveying instruments including a quadrant of 1608 by Thobias Volckmer, and a compass made in 1572 by Christof Tressler. Three cases display the nautical instruments invented and used by Sir

Robert Dudley (1574–1649), Duke of Northumberland. He left England for Italy in 1605, became a naval engineer and administered the port of Livorno for Ferdinando II. Many of the astrolabes, quadrants and sextants were constructed by Charles Whitwell. In the last case are more astrolabes and a calculator invented by the diplomat Sir Samuel Morland in 1666.

Room III Tuscan instruments. These include compasses by Antonio Bianchini (1564), quadrants and a celestial globe by Mario Cartaro (1577), an armillary sphere attributed to Carlo Plato, and 17C mathematical instruments by the Lusvergs. The 16C astrolabe, traditionally associated with Galileo, is attributed to Egnazio Danti. In a wall case, quadrants by Giovanni Battista Giusti, instruments by Egnazio Danti, and a 'perpendiculum' designed by Antonio Santucci. In the last case are instruments made by the Della Volpaia and Stefano Buonsignori (Night and Day clocks, compasses, armillary spheres, astrolabes, sundials), and a pair of compasses used by Vincenzo Viviani, disciple of Galileo.

Room IV This room is devoted to the famous astronomer **Galileo Galilei**.

Galileo Galilei

Galileo (1564–1642) was born in Pisa, and lived and died in Florence. He perfected the telescope, and discovered the four satellites of Jupiter in 1610. He was appointed Professor of Mathematics at Pisa University by Cardinal Ferdinando de' Medici (later grand-duke), and then took up a chair at Padua University from 1592 to 1610, where he attracted pupils from all over Europe. He stayed in the Villa Medici (on the site of the Villa Demidoff at Pratolino) in 1605–06 as tutor to the future Cosimo II. In 1632, he published a defence of the Copernican theory of astronomy. He was condemned by the Inquisition in 1633 in Rome for his contention that the Earth was not at the centre of the Universe, but through the good offices of the Grand-duke Ferdinando II he avoided imprisonment and spent the latter part of his life in Florence, where he died in 1642. He bought a house for his son Vincenzio on Costa San Giorgio and lived, practically as a prisoner, at Villa il Gioiello in Pian de' Giullari (see p 351), under the protection of the grand-duke. Although almost blind and infirm, he wrote some of his most important tracts here and was visited by Evangelista Torricelli, Vincenzo Viviani, Thomas Hobbes and possibly also Milton. On his death he was not allowed a Christian burial inside Santa Croce: it was not until 1737 that his remains were permitted to be transferred there and a monument was set up to him in the church (see p 270). He was later honoured by Leopoldo II when he erected the tribuna in the museum known as La Specola (see p 305) in Galileo's memory in 1841. Eventually, in 1992, the Pope announced the rehabilitation of Galileo and cancelled the condemnation imposed on him in 1633.

On the middle shelf of the showcase in Room IV, there is the lens (in an ivory frame) Galileo used in to discover the four largest moons of Jupiter (cracked by the scientist himself before he presented it to Ferdinando II). The bones of Galileo's right middle finger, also on display here, were removed from his tomb when his remains were transferred to the church of Santa Croce. On the middle shelf are exhibited the Giovilabio, a brass instrument made from sketches by Galileo, and a pair of compasses used by him. On the bottom shelf are loadstones probably used by the scientist, one of which (of natural magnetic rock) was given by Galileo to Ferdinando II. The model of the pendulum clock designed by Galileo was made in 1877 by Eugenio Porcellotti. The models made in the 18C by order of the Grand-duke Pietro Leopoldo I of inventions by Galileo include a water pump and an instrument for measuring the acceleration of gravity.

Room V Telescopes. In the case to the left are two original telescopes made by Galileo, one covered in leather and one in paper. There are also telescopes by his pupil Evangelista Torricelli (1608–47). In the 1660s, Eustachio Divini (1620–85) and Giuseppe Campani were rivals in the production of lenses and telescopes, some of which are displayed here.

Room VI Instruments used in **optical experiments**. Magnifying glasses, lenses, 18C spectacles, models of the eye and 17C optical games.

Room VII This contains a superb display of *globes around the huge Ptolemaic armillary sphere (showing the movements of celestial bodies) built by Antonio Santucci in 1588. Along the left wall, celestial globes by Jansz Willem Blaeu; the 'Wheel of the Heavens' by Santucci; two showcases of armillary Ptolemaic spheres and a Copernican one. Standing in the far corner is an armillary sphere made of painted wood attributed to Vincenzo Viviani. In this part of the room, there are also four large globes by Vincenzo Coronelli, an 18C planetarium, a celestial globe by Adrianus Veen and Jodocus Hondius (1613), and two globes with covers by Mathaus Greuter. The maps include a copy of Fra Mauro's map of the world, and a map by Lopo Homen (1554).

Room VIII A fine collection of **microscopes**, including an early example, and 18C and 19C works based on designs by Galileo are displayed here.

Room IX This is devoted to the **Accademia del Cimento**, an experimental academy founded by Cardinal Leopoldo in 1657. Here are displayed a pedometer, probably made by Schissler, used to measure the shape of the Earth; a model of the hygrometer invented by Ferdinando II, and a quadrant by Carlo Rinaldini. The splendid display of glass made in Florence for the Academy includes elaborate thermometers.

Room X Meteorology. In the first case, there are barometers by Gian Domenico Tamburini, Daniel Quare and De Luc; 17C and 18C anemometers (to determine the direction of the wind); a barometer on a marble base by Felice Fontana; thermometers including some by Dollond and Fontana; hygrometers (including a large one hanging on the wall above by Viviani).

Room XI Astronomy in Florence in the 18C and 19C. On the left is a fine display of 18C telescopes. The large burning lens was made by Benedetto Bregans of Dresden and given by him to Cosimo III (used in the early 19C by Davy and Faraday to experiment with high temperature chemicals). Hanging on the wall is a large telescope made by Giovanni Battista Amici of Modena, and on a stand below another telescope by him. Also here is a telescope made by James Dollond and a repeating circle by Reichenbach.

Second floor

The **Lorraine scientific collections** are displayed on this floor, including numerous exhibits related to Pietro Leopoldo, Grand-duke in 1765–90. **Room XII** illustrates the origins of the **mechanical clock**, from the invention of the escapement device c 1330 to the first mechanical pendulum clock invented in 1640 by Galileo. A clock designed for Palazzo Vecchio in 1510 by Lorenzo della Volpaia was reconstructed in 1994: it shows the movement of the planets. Striking mechanisms are also displayed, as well as 17C spring-clocks, some signed by Filippo Treffler, and console clocks. **Room XIII** contains **18C and 19C mathematical instruments**: sextants, quadrants and odometers. **Room XIV** has a magnificent display of **magnetic and electrostatic instruments**. The development of the electric current and electromagnetism is illustrated with reference to Alessandro Volta (1745–1827) and Leopoldo Nobili (1784–1835). **Room XV** contains **pneumatic and hydrostatic instruments** for the study of the mechanics of fluids and gases.

Rooms XVI and XVII. These display instruments used in **mechanics** built for the Grand-duke Pietro Leopoldo in the Museum of Physics and Natural Sciences. **Room XVIII** contains the **surgical instruments** of Alessandro Brambilla (1728–1800) and wax and terracotta **anatomical models** made by Giuseppe Ferrini in Florence for use in obstetrics. **Room XIX** illustrates the historical development of **pharmacy**, including vases and mortars used in pharmaceutical laboratories. **Room XX** shows the origins of modern **chemistry** in Florence with exhibits relating to the 18C naturalists Felice Fontana and Giovanni Fabbroni. Here is preserved the desk used by Pietro Leopoldo for his chemical experiments. **Room XXI** contains **weights and measures**.

Lungarno Diaz continues past the heavy neo-classical colonnade of the Camera di Commercio and Piazza Mentana (with a monument to those who fell at Mentana in 1867). Just before the bridge is the garden of Palazzo Malenchini. Via de' Benci leads away from the Arno towards Santa Croce, lined with a number of fine palaces described on p 325.

Museo Horne

Palazzo Corsi, at no. 6, is an attractive small palace open to the public as the Museo Horne (**Map 7; 3**). It was formerly thought to be the work of Giuliano da Sangallo, but is now generally attributed to Cronaca (1495–1502).

• **Opening times** 09.00–13.00 except *fest*. (☎ 055 244 661); Lire 8000.

The English art historian and architect **Herbert Percy Horne** (1864–1916) presented the palace to the Italian nation, along with his interesting collection of 14C–16C paintings, sculpture and decorative arts (notably furniture and majolica). Horne first came to Florence in 1904 and purchased Palazzo Corsi in 1911. He carefully restored every detail (including the doors and shutters) to its late 15C appearance. He lived on the top floor for the last few months of his life. Many of the contents, charmingly displayed, were restored after damage in the 1966 flood. The works (unlabelled) are numbered on the wall (disregard the numbers on the works themselves) to correspond to a handlist lent to visitors.

The lovely courtyard has interesting capitals. On the ground floor is a copy of Horne's book on Botticelli, published in 1908, and a room of bronzes, medals, coins and majolica, as well as a stone bas-relief of the *Madonna and Child* by Jacopo Sansovino. Another room was opened here in 2000 to display a selection of the 929 very fine drawings collected by Horne from 1890 onwards. They include Renaissance as well as 16C and early 17C works by Raphael, Giulio Romano, Pietro Bernini, Pietro da Cortona, Guercino, Guido Reni, and Rubens.

First floor

Room I On the entrance wall, are: (**35**) Pseudo Pier Francesco Fiorentino, *Adoration of the Child*; (**36**) Correggio, *Adoration of the Shepherds*; (**39**) Jacopo del Sellaio, *St Jerome*; (**42**) Signorelli, *St Catherine of Siena*; (**38**) Dosso Dossi, *Allegory of Music* (c 1530); (**43**) Neroccio, *Madonna and Child with two Saints*. In the wall case: (**48**) Masaccio (attributed), *Story of St Julian* (a tiny work, unfortunately in very poor condition). On the table in the centre, *bozzetti* by Ammannati, Giambologna, and Gianfrancesco Rustici. On the long window wall; (**55**) Filippino Lippi, *Crucifix* (a late work, much faded, once used as a processional standard). On the end wall, above a *cassone* (**63**) in the style of Ammannati, (**61**) Pietro Lorenzetti, *Saints John Gualberto, Catherine of Alexandria and Margaret* (a fragment of a polyptych). The tondo of *St Jerome* is by Piero di Cosimo.

Opposite the windows: (**67**) Bernardo Daddi, *Madonna Enthroned* and *Crucifixion* (a diptych); (**69**) Benozzo Gozzoli, *Deposition*, a crowded composition left unfinished at the death of the painter (the colours have darkened with time); (**75**) Bartolomeo di Giovanni, *Mythological Scene*.

Room II (**83**), (**84**) and (**100**), paintings by Francesco Furini; (**85**) Luca Signorelli, *Redeemer*; (**86**) Domenico Beccafumi, *Mythological Scene*; (**87**) Marco d'Oggiono, *Redeemer*; (**88**) Jacopo del Casentino, *Madonna and Child*; (**91**) Giotto, *ˊSt Stephen*, the most precious piece in the collection and one of the most important paintings known by Giotto; (**98**) Neri di Bicci, *Madonna and Two Angels* (very ruined); (**102**) Il Boccati, *Madonna and Child*; (**104**) Carlo Dolci, *St Sebastian*. In the 17C cupboard from Emilia is a terracotta *bozzetto* of angels by Gian Lorenzo Bernini. On the table is a terracotta *bozzetto* of a male nude by Giambologna.

Room III (**111**) and (**116**), Niccolò di Tommaso, *Saint John the Evangelist* and *Saint Paul*; (**114**) frontal of a 15C *cassone* with a battle scene; (**113**) Lippo di Benivieni, *Madonna Enthroned with Saints*. In a cupboard, Lorenzo Monaco or his school, portable *Crucifix*. Over the fireplace, Desiderio da Settignano, Relief of the head of the *Young St John the Baptist* (replica of a work in the Bargello). (**127**) 13C Tuscan school, *Madonna and Child with a Donor*; (**128**) Beccafumi, tondo of the *ˊHoly Family*, with a beautiful contemporary frame. The statue of *St Paul* is by Vecchietta.

Second floor

Room IV (left) This room contains several fine pieces of 15C furniture, as well as the following works of art: (**155**) Ercole dei Roberti (attributed), *St Sebastian* (removed for restoration); (**158**) Bartolomeo della Gatta, *St Roch* (restored). In the wall case, (**168**) Filippo Lippi, *Pietà* (a pax); (**170**) Antonio Rossellino, *Madonna and Child*, a relief in polychrome terracotta; (**177**) Filippino Lippi, *Scene from the Story of Esther* (panel of a marriage chest); (above) (**182**) School of Sodoma, *Scene from the Battle of Anghiari* (of historical interest as a contemporary copy of Leonardo's lost fresco in Palazzo Vecchio); (**183**) Master of the Horne Triptych (14C Florentine), *Madonna and Saints*. In a case in the centre of the room: (**193**) Simone Martini (attributed), portable diptych of the *Madonna and Child* and *Pietà*.

Room V (**216**) Neri di Bicci, Archangel Raphael, Tobias and St Jerome; 209. Beccafumi (attributed), Drunkenness of Noah (in a tondo surrounded by putti). The old kitchen, also on this floor, has an interesting collection of cutlery and utensils.

Ponte alle Grazie (Map 7; **3**) was first built in 1237 and called Ponte Rubaconte. Its present name is taken from an oratory that was formerly on the bridge. Unfortunately, after its destruction in 1944, the bridge was redesigned and the present structure is of little distinction. The view from here takes in Lungarno delle Grazie with the Biblioteca Nazionale and the tall spire of Santa Croce; in the distance upstream can be seen the rural banks of the Arno; and across the river the tall Porta San Niccolò is conspicuous beyond the garden of Palazzo Demidoff (and above, on the skyline, stands San Miniato). At the south end of the bridge is Piazza dei Mozzi.

Lungarno Serristori leads away from the Oltrarno district past a palace at no. 25 where Rainer Maria Rilke stayed in 1898: 'At the Lungarno Serristori, not far from the Ponte alle Grazie, stands the house whose flat roof—both its closed-in part and its part wide-open to the sky—is mine' (*The Florence Diary*). It overlooks a small public garden with a pavilion and a monument to **Nicola Demidoff** (1773–1828), who made his fortune in Siberian mines, and moved to Florence from Paris in 1820. He took up residence here in Palazzo Serristori where he founded a school (the palace dates from 1515, but was given a river front in 1873). The monument was commissioned from Lorenzo Bartolini by Nicola's sons Paolo and Anatolio in 1830 and includes four allegorical figures of Art, Charity, Truth and Siberia. Some way farther on, at no. 5 on the Lungarno, is the **Casa-Museo Siviero** (opening times Sat 15.30–18.30 and Mon 09.30–12.30). This is the former residence of Rudolfo Siviero (1911–83) which he bequeathed to the Regione of Tuscany and it first opened to the public in 1992. Siviero was responsible for recovering works of art stolen from Italy during and after the War. The simple house contains his private collection with a miscellany of objects including a restored fragment of Roman mosaic (4C AD) and a painting of the *Nativity* attributed to the Master of the Johnson Nativity. The upper floor is to be opened with more works.

Museo Bardini

At 1 Piazza dei Mozzi (see above) stands the large Palazzo Bardini, built by the famous antiquarian and collector Stefano Bardini in 1883 to house his huge collection of works of art. He bequeathed these to the city in 1922 as the Museo Bardini (**Map 6; 4,6**). Closed for restoration in 2000 (C), ☎ 055 234 2427.

Bardini's eclectic collection includes architectural fragments, medieval and Renaissance sculpture, paintings, the decorative arts, furniture, ceramics, carpets, arms and armour and musical instruments. During the 19C, he supplied numerous museums all over the world with masterpieces from his collections, including the Isabella Stuart Gardner Museum in Boston, the Louvre, the National Gallery of Washington and the Hermitage. Many of the rooms were built specially to contain fine doorways, staircases and ceilings from demolished buildings. The rooms are crowded with a miscellany of works, all well labelled, and the museum is particularly well kept.

Ground floor

Room 1 is entered from the right of the vestibule and contains numerous medieval and Renaissance architectural fragments, including a carved 16C window from Sassari and sculptural reliefs attributed to Francesco di Simone Ferrucci. The bust of **St John the Baptist** dates from the early 16C (formerly attributed to Andrea Sansovino). Beyond is **Room 2** with interesting classical sculpture, including a sarcophagus with Medusa's head, used again in the Middle Ages.

Beyond **Room 6**, with a well-head and more architectural fragments, is the large **Room 7**. This was formerly a courtyard and is now covered by a coffered ceiling with glass inserted in the panels. It is used to display a remarkable statue of *Charity* ascribed to Tino da Camaino. The large Gothic aedicule behind the statue was made up by Bardini using various statuettes and reliefs (including two statuettes of angels in adoration by the Sienese school). The Romanesque architectural fragments here include capitals, pilasters and column-bearing lions. The little console in the form of a female head (on the right wall) has recently been attributed to Nicola Pisano. In the small adjacent **Room 8** is a well-head made from red Veronese marble and the tomb effigy of Riccardo Gattula (1417) by Paolo di Gualdo Cattaneo.

Room 9 (off the vestibule) is approached through a fine doorway. Inside there are two chimneypieces (one from the *bottega* of Desiderio da Settignano, and the other, with the Este coat of arms, a Lombard work). The putto was made for a fountain in the late 15C.

Stairs lead to **Room 10**, a large vaulted room built in the form of a crypt to display tomb slabs and wall-tombs. The wall-tomb in relief with the effigy of a bishop attended by an acolyte is ascribed to the circle of Arnolfo di Cambio. The relief of **St Jerome** from San Francesco della Vigna in Venice is by Giovanni Buora. The floor tomb-slabs include one of a friar from the circle of Donatello, and one (next to it) of Colomba Ghezzi della Casa, abbess of San Martino alla Scala, commissioned by her in 1540 from Francesco da Sangallo. An Antique sarcophagus bears a relief sculpted with the three faces of the *Trinity* attributed to Michelozzo. The altarpiece of the *Madonna and Child with Angels* in enamelled terracotta is thought to be an early work by Andrea della Robbia (or by his *bottega*).

First floor

A fine staircase leads up from Room 9. At the top of the stairs are displayed 14C wooden statues. Three rooms to the left display an interesting collection of arms and armour. In **Room 11**, there are 16C decorated swords, crossbows and weapons used by infantry. The case displays bronze helmets including one (**811**) that dates from the 6C BC, and a 14C painted crest in the form of a dragon's head. **Room 12** has 15C–17C halberds, pikes and spears, and 15C–16C painted shields, some with plaster reliefs, and a large pavise (shield) painted with the coat of arms of the Sienese Bonamici family, attributed to Taddeo Bartoli. In the cases, there are swords and rapiers—including a French sword of the early 15C—daggers, spurs and tournament weapons. Also here is a rare battle lantern such as those depicted in the frescoes in the Sala dei Cinquecento in Palazzo Vecchio. The cannon include a mortar possibly dating from the end of the 14C. In **Room 13** are displayed 16C Venetian shields and two cases of 16C–17C firearms.

Room 14, facing the stair-head, is entered through a marble doorway of 1548. Here are displayed two works sometimes attributed to Donatello: a charming high relief of the *Madonna and Child* in polychrome terracotta (recently attributed, as an early work, to Luca della Robbia), and the *Madonna dei Cordai*, a very unusual polychrome work in stucco, glass and mosaic. Two other reliefs of the *Madonna and Child* are by the circle of Verrocchio and a copy from a work by Benedetto da Maiano. A painted tondo fragment is attributed to Spinello Aretino.

Room 15 (right; beyond **Room 16**), is notable for its 17C carpets and portraits (including works by Francesco Salviati), and its furniture. The central cases contain bronze medals, plaques and statuettes. Also here are detached frescoes (from Palazzo Pucci) by Giovanni di San Giovanni, and two tondi by Volterrano.

Room 16 is a hall furnished like a sacristy, with a fine chimneypiece and ceiling. The paintings include a large *Crucifix* attributed to a follower of Bernardo Daddi; Michele Giambono's *St John the Baptist*; and a *Madonna and Child* thought to be by Giuliano Bugiardini. The sculpture in stucco and terracotta includes (left of the window) a relief of the *Nativity* and a damaged *Madonna and Child* both attributed to the circle of Donatello. On the sacristy cupboard are displayed more charming statuettes and high reliefs of the Madonna and Child dating from the early 15C (including one of the *Madonna and the Sleeping Child* by the *bottega* of Nanni di Bartolo), and a *Madonna in Adoration* dating from the end of the 15C. Above, in a Gothic tabernacle, is a 15C Venetian statue of St Peter.

Room 17 continues the collection of furniture, paintings and majolica. The 15C sculptural reliefs include two tondi in stucco of the *Madonna and Child*, one attributed to Michelozzo and one after Francesco di Simone Ferrucci, and a *Madonna and Child* by the *bottega* of Jacopo della Quercia. **Room 18** has 15C wooden statues including a *Madonna* and *St Catherine of Siena* by the circle of Domenico di Niccolò de' Cori. The *Virgin Annunciate* in terracotta, in the centre of the room, has for long been considered a Sienese work of the 15C. The damaged *Bust of a Woman* is now attributed to Tullio Lombardo, and the distinguished bust of *Gerolamo Andreasi* is considered to be the work of Gian Cristoforo Romano. The painting of **St Michael* is by Antonio Pollaiolo. **Room 19** displays old musical instruments (including a spinet made in Rome in 1577).

Upper floor

On the upper floor the **Galleria Corsi** (admission only with special permission) contains the large artistic bequests of Alice and Arnaldo Corsi (1939). Among the 15C–18C paintings on display here are: *Madonna and Child with St Anthony Abbott* attributed to Bartolo di Fredi; an early 15C polyptych with stories from the *Life of St Anthony Abbot*, an unusual work in a lovely frame; the *Madonna with Saints* by Francesco di Girolamo da Santacroce; two paintings of *Hagar and the Angel* by Lorenzo Lippi; the *Temptations of St Anthony* by Sebastiano Ricci; the *Serpent of Bronze* by Livio Mehus; and works by Johann Melchior Roos (1659–1731).

From Room 18, a small staircase descends to **Room 20**, with a wooden ceiling and a large *Crucifix*. Here also are fine inlaid stalls (15C); 15C–16C furniture; a 17C wooden model of Pisa Baptistery and three reliefs of the *Nativity* by the school of Donatello.

At the end of Piazza dei Mozzi, on Via de' Bardi, are the three 13C palaces that belonged to the Mozzi family; these were later owned by Ugo Bardini, son of Stefano, who was also an art collector, and were left to the state in 1965 (see p 307). Lungarno Torrigiani (**Map 6; 4**) follows the south bank of the Arno back towards Ponte Vecchio. Next to the 16C Palazzo Torrigiani is a small public garden with a Lutheran church (1899). Across the Arno can be seen the cupola of the Duomo with (right) the towers of the Badia and the Bargello, and (left) the Campanile and tower of Palazzo Vecchio. Beyond the garden of Palazzo Canigiani, the Lungarno merges with Via de' Bardi (see p 306) at a road fork. The old Costa dei Magnoli runs uphill beneath an arch of Palazzo Tempi to Costa San Giorgio (described on p 309), also reached by steps at the end of Vicolo del Canneto. Via de' Bardi continues to the foot of Ponte Vecchio, passing beneath the Corridoio Vasariano.

Via Guicciardini, which leads left to Piazza Pitti, and the bronze fountain on the corner are described on p 155. Here the houses front the Arno; **Borgo San Jacopo** (Map 6; 1), continues parallel to the river. The Borgo, an ancient road leading out of the city, is mentioned as early as 1182. By a modern hotel, a terrace opens onto the river opposite the campanile of Santi Apostoli, with a good view left and right of Ponte Santa Trìnita and Ponte Vecchio. Some restored medieval towers survive amongst the buildings here that were rebuilt after the Second World War. On the corner of the pretty Via Toscanella, Torre Marsili di Borgo (no. 17) is a fine towerhouse. Above the door is an *Annunciation* from the Della Robbia workshop and two angels (restored).

On the right of the road is the church of **San Jacopo sopr'Arno** (Map 6; 1), with an old portico of three arches, possibly dating from the 11C, transported here in 1529 from the demolished church of San Donato a Scopeto. Opening times Tues and Thurs 17.00–18.00; or ☎ 055 210 139. The church (which had a river gate) owned by the Comune is used by a cultural organisation for concerts and exhibitions. The Baroque interior dates from 1709 and contains painted decoration from this time, as well as Romanesque columns that were revealed in the 1960s. The vaults of the side aisles are decorated with oval mural paintings. In the first and second bays of the south aisle, there are mural paintings by Niccolò Lapi. The third bay has an altarpiece signed and dated 1731 by Antonio Puglieschi, and an unusual vault painting of the *Transition of St Joseph* by Ottaviano Dandini. The cupola over the sanctuary and the spandrels have mural paintings by Matteo Bonechi. The high altarpiece of the *Calling of St James* is a late 18C or early 19C copy of the original altarpiece by Pier Dandini flanked by two *Saints* in grisaille by Matteo Bonechi. In the north aisle, the third altarpiece is by Jacopo Vignali; the second altarpiece of the *Annunciation* is by Ignazio Hugford; and *God the Father with Angels* in the cupola above is by Ranieri del Pace. The first altarpiece of the *Martyrdom of St Lucy* is by the little-known painter Giovanni Casini (1708). In the dome above, the *Coronation of St Lucy* was frescoed by Matteo Bonechi.

The Borgo ends in the busy Piazza Frescobaldi with a pretty 17C corner fountain. Via Maggio, described on p 303, leads away from the river. The Arno is regained at the end of Ponte Santa Trìnita. The elaborate Palazzo Frescobaldi (right) was reconstructed in the 17C. Lungarno Guicciardini (**Map 6; 1**) provides a splendid view of the opposite bank of the river (with the imposing Palazzo Corsini) as far as the park of the Cascine. Beyond the red façade of Palazzo Capponi (no. 1; with a *salone* frescoed by Bernardino Poccetti in 1583) is Via dei Coverelli with a palace with restored graffiti. The famous garden (closed) of the yellow Palazzo Guicciardini (no. 7) includes a magnolia tree planted in 1787.

Palazzo Lanfredini (no. 9), by Baccio d'Agnolo, has bright graffiti decoration (restored). On the first floor are the Library and the office of the Director of the **British Institute of Florence** (Map 6; 1). A non-profit making independent institution, this was founded in 1917 by a group of Anglo Florentines—including Arthur Acton, Edward Hutton, G.M. Trevelyan, Lina Waterfield, Gaetano Salvemini and Aldo Sorani—and received a Royal Charter in 1923. Its role is to maintain a library of English books in the city, and to promote British culture in Italy and Italian culture to English-speaking visitors. The **Lending Library** (with about 50,000 volumes, the largest collection of English books in Italy) was named after its benefactor Harold Acton in 1989 (who, on his death in 1993, bequeathed the premises to the Institute). It can be used for a small fee and retains the atmosphere of a 19C general browsing library. The reading room has comfortable armchairs and English newspapers. The collection includes books on Italian art, history, music and numerous 19C novels (many of them obscure works). It has been augmented over the years by the donations of Anglo-American residents in Florence, including Sir Israel Gollancz, Mrs Waterfield, Lady Sybil Lubbock, J.A. Spranger, Violet Paget (Vernon Lee) and Edward Gordon Craig. Interesting public lectures are also held here (usually on Wednesdays at 18.00). The Institute runs a language school and courses in art history at no. 2 Piazza Strozzi (**Map 1; 3**).

Beyond the Presbyterian church (no. 19), and Ponte alla Carraia Lungarno Soderini (**Map 5; 2**) continues past a little pavilion-house, with a view of the huge church of San Frediano in Cestello and the Seminary. The diagonal stone dyke in the river, the Pescaia di Santa Rosa, was built at the same time as the water mills on the Arno.

In Piazza del Cestello is the rough-hewn façade of the church of San Frediano in Cestello (see p 300) and the **Granaio di Cosimo III** (grain store; 1695) designed by Giovanni Battista Foggini and now used as a barracks. From the piazza, there is a view across the river of Ognissanti and its bell-tower, with the campanile of Santa Maria Novella behind. Beyond the modern Ponte Vespucci is the wall of Porta San Frediano. and its bell-tower, with the campanile of Santa Maria Novella behind. Beyond the modern Ponte Vespucci is the wall of Porta San Frediano.

18 • The Oltrarno: Santo Spirito and Santa Maria del Carmine

The district known as the Oltrarno lies on the south bank of the Arno. Its two most important churches are Santo Spirito and Santa Maria del Carmine, and they provide a focus for life in this part of the city. Both churches, with their large convents, were founded in 1250 by the two mendicant Orders of the Augustinians and Carmelites.

Santo Spirito
From the south end of Ponte Santa Trìnita, Via di Santo Spirito and Via del Presto (left) lead to the church of Santo Spirito (**Map 6; 3**; opening times 10.00–12.00, 16.00–18.00 except Wednesday afternoon). Its modest 18C façade fronts a

pretty square. On the left is the rough stone wall of the convent's refectory and behind rises Baccio d'Agnolo's slender campanile (1503).

History of Santo Spirito

The Augustinian foundation dates from 1250 and the first church was begun in 1292. The convent became a centre of intellectual life in the city at the end of the 14C, and had an extremely important library. In 1428, Brunelleschi was commissioned to design a new church, the project for which he had completed by 1434–35. However, building was not begun until 1444, just two years before the great architect's death. Construction continued for most of the 15C, first under the direction of his collaborator Antonio Manetti, and then Giovanni da Gaiole, Giuliano Sandrini and Giovanni di Mariano. Salvi d'Andrea completed the cupola in 1481.

Interior

The *interior was designed by Brunelleschi but mostly executed after his death and modified in the late 15C. While it remains a superb creation of the Renaissance, remarkable for its harmonious proportions, its solemn colour, and the perspective of the colonnades and vaulted aisles, it also points the way forward to the more elaborate and less delicate 16C style of architecture. The plan is a Latin cross, with a dome over the crossing. The colonnade has 35 columns in *pietra forte* (including the four piers of the dome) with fine Corinthian capitals and imposts above. It continues around the transepts and east end to form an unbroken arcade. Around the walls there is a continuous line of 38 chapels formed by semicircular niches. The 15C wooden altar frontals are painted in imitation of precious materials, many of them by Bernardo di Stefano Rosselli. The beautiful paintings in the chapels are difficult to see on a dark day or late in the afternoon, although some coin-operated lights have been installed.

There is an elaborate **high altar** (1599–1607), with a *pietre dure* ciborium by Giovanni Battista Caccini, beneath a high baldacchino; but despite being a fine Baroque work in itself, the altar disturbs the overall harmony of the interior. It has eight statues of *Angels* by Caccini, Gherardo Silvani and perhaps also Ubaldini. It replaces a simpler altar designed by Brunelleschi. The handsome **interior façade** was designed by Salvi d'Andrea (1483–87). The stained glass oculus is from a cartoon by Perugino.

South aisle chapels First altar: (**1**) *Immaculate Conception* by Pier Francesco di Jacopo Foschi; (**2**) *Pietà*, a free copy of Michelangelo's famous sculpture in St Peter's, by Nanni di Baccio Bigio; (**3**) this prettily decorated niche contains a polychrome wooden sculpture of *St Nicholas of Tolentino* by Nanni Unghero (to a design by Jacopo Sansovino), and two *Angels* painted by Franciabigio; (**4**) *Christ Expelling the Money-changers from the Temple* by Giovanni Stradano; (**5**) the *Coronation of the Virgin and Saints* by Alessandro Gherardini. Beyond the side door, (**6**) the *Martyrdom of St Stephen*, a good work by Passignano; (**7**) *Tobias and the Archangel*, a large altarpiece in stucco and marble by Giovanni Baratta.

South transept chapels (**8**) *Crucifixion* attributed to Francesco Curradi or Pier Dandini; (**9**) *Transfiguration* by Pier Francesco di Jacopo Foschi; (**10**) *Madonna del Soccorso*, a 15C painting, recently attributed to the Master of the Johnson Nativity. The next polychrome marble altar (**11**) by Buontalenti encloses a 14C wooden *Crucifix* from the earlier church; (**12**) *Madonna and Child with the Young St

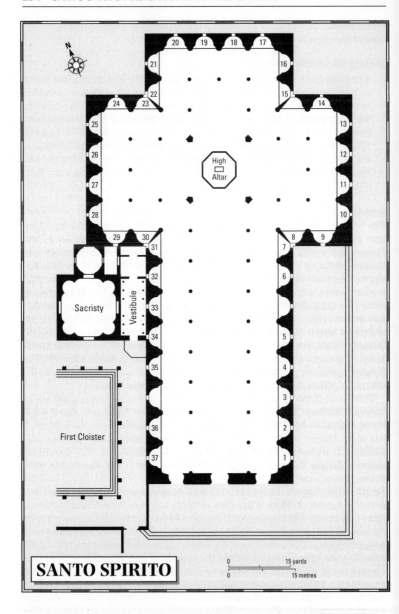

SANTO SPIRITO

High Altar

Sacristy

Vestibule

First Cloister

0 — 15 yards
0 — 15 metres

John, Saints and Donors—the donors are Tanai and Nanna (Capponi) dei Nerli—a painting which is one of the best and most mature works of Filippino Lippi, executed sometime after 1494. In the background is an extremely interesting early view of Florence, showing Tanai in a red cloak, taking leave of his family before setting out on a journey in front of Palazzo dei Nerli near Porta San Frediano. There are numerous classical elements in the altarpiece, and the 'dialogue' between the young St John and the Christ Child is an interesting detail which was to be developed by later painters such as Leonardo da Vinci. The splendid original frame was also designed by Filippino. On the next altar (**13**), in a prettily decorated niche, the original painting of the *Vision of St Bernard* by Perugino (now in Munich) has been replaced by a beautiful (and almost indistinguishable) copy by Felice Ficherelli; (**14**) the *Marriage of the Virgin*, the best work of Giovanni Camillo Sagrestani (1713). The sarcophagus of Neri Capponi by the *bottega* of Bernardo Rossellino (1458) is the only tomb that was allowed in the church.

Chapels at the east end (**15**) *Madonna and Saints*, a good painting in the style of Lorenzo di Credi by an unknown artist who was named after this work as the 'Maestro della Conversazione di Santo Spirito' (the frame is attributed to Baccio d'Agnolo); (**16**) polyptych of the *Madonna and Child with Saints* by Maso di Banco; (**17**) *Epiphany* by Aurelio Lomi. The next chapel (**18**) belonged to Luca Pitti from 1458. The altarpiece of *Martyred Saints* by Alessandro Allori (1574) incorporates a portrait of Cosimo I in the centre. The predella includes an interesting view of Palazzo Pitti before it was enlarged, with its owner Luca Pitti standing outside (in a red hat). The original 15C altar frontal with a painting of *St Luke* by Neri di Bicci survives. The Frescobaldi chapel (**19**) preserves its original little stained glass tondo and altar frontal. The beautiful **Christ and the Adulteress* by Alessandro Allori foreshadows the 17C; (**20**) *Mystical Communion of the Blessed Clara of Montefalco* by Jacopo Vignali; (**21**) *Annunciation* by Pietro del Donzello (late 15C Florentine school), showing the influence of the German and Flemish schools. The wall monument has a marble relief of *Anna Maria Frescobaldi* by Luigi Pampaloni (1844); (**22**) *Nativity* attributed to Pietro and Polito del Donzello (late 15C).

North transept chapels The painted altarpieces here, commissioned by various Florentine families for their chapels, have survived intact (**23**) *Madonna Enthroned Between Saints John the Evangelist and Bartholomew* attributed to the *bottega* of the Mazziere brothers (late 15C); (**24**) **St Monica and Augustinian Nuns*, traditionally attributed to Botticini, but now thought by many scholars to be the work of Verrocchio. It is a very unusual and beautifully composed painting with the striking dark habits of the nuns and circular designs. (**25**) *Madonna Enthroned between Saints* by Cosimo Rosselli. The Cappella Corbinelli (**26**) has a beautiful **altarpiece sculpted by Andrea Sansovino, with statues of *St Matthew* and *St James* above a carved predella with reliefs of scenes from their lives and a *Last Supper*. The altar frontal has a carved *Pietà*, and above the statues are two tondi of the *Annunciation*, and in the lunette above, the *Coronation of the Virgin*. The classical pilasters bear reliefs of the symbols of the Passion. After 1502, Sansovino completed the decoration of the chapel by adding the side panels in marble. This was the only chapel in the church in which a sculptured rather than painted altarpiece was allowed, since it was used for the Holy Sacrament. The balustrade dates from the 17C. (**27**) **Trinity with Saints Mary Magdalen and Catherine*, a good painting of the late 15C, attributed to the Mazziere brothers; (**28**) *Trinity*, also attributed to the Mazziere brothers. The Segni chapel (**29**) has a beautiful *Madonna Enthroned with Saints* by Raffaelino del Garbo (1505), the only one of four altarpieces commissioned from him for this church which has remained here. The altar frontal is attributed to the *bottega* of Donnino and Agnolo di Domenico del Mazziere; (**30**) *Way to Calvary*, copy by Michele Ghirlandaio of a painting by Ridolfo del Ghirlandaio, and a stained glass window showing the *Incredulity of St Thomas*.

North aisle chapels (**31**) *Madonna Enthroned and Saints* by the school of Fra' Bartolomeo. The marble bust (right) of **Tommaso Cavalcanti** is by Montorsoli. (**32**) Copy by Francesco Petrucci of the 'Pala Dei' by Rosso Fiorentino, which was commissioned by Prince Ferdinando in 1691 when he removed the original to Palazzo Pitti. The copy shows the original dimensions of the altarpiece (it was enlarged when it was hung in the Pitti).

(**33**) A door beneath the organ, leads into a grandiose *vestibule with 12 Corinthian columns supporting an elaborately coffered barrel vault, built in *pietra serena* by Cronaca in 1491 to a design by Giuliano da Sangallo. The decoration includes the Medici coat of arms and doves, and tondi with mythological scenes which are copies of the antique gems owned by Lorenzo il Magnifico. The adjoining *sacristy is an octagonal chamber inspired by the architectural works of Brunelleschi; it has Corinthian pilasters with delicately carved capitals designed by Giuliano da Sangallo (1489), and a lantern and dome executed on a model by Antonio del Pollaiolo and Salvi d'Andrea (1495). After its restoration in 2000, a *Crucifix attributed to Michelangelo in painted poplar wood, found in Santo Spirito in 1963, has been displayed here. It is known that the prior of the convent allowed Michelangelo to study anatomy here in the early 1490s. Documents also confirm that Michelangelo made a *Crucifix* for the Augustinians for the high altar of this church, which was thought to have been lost. Many scholars believe this is that Crucifix, but others attribute it to Taddeo Curradi (mid-16C). It shows the slight figure of Christ in an unusual *contrapposto* position, a design subsequently much copied. Off the vestibule is the 17C **first cloister** (no admission) by Alfonso and Giulio Parigi.

In the remaining chapels in the north aisle: (**34**) *Madonna with St Anne and Other Saints* attributed to Ridolfo del Ghirlandaio; (**35**) *St Thomas of Villanova* by Rutilio Manetti; (**36**) Copy by Taddeo Landini (1579) of a statue of the *Risen Christ* by Michelangelo in the church of the Minerva in Rome; (**37**) *Resurrection* by Pier Francesco di Jacopo Foschi.

The **second cloister** is a beautiful work by Bartolomeo Ammannati (c 1565). It is now part of a military barracks, but the cloister and chapel are usually open to the public on a few days every year. Off the cloister is the **Cappella Corsini** with the Gothic tombs of Tommaso Corsini (d. 1366) and Neri Corsini, Bishop of Fiesole (d. 1377) with a contemporary fresco of the *Resurrection* and two *Saints*. Also here (right wall) is a red porphyry monument with a bust of Bartolomeo Corsini (d. 1613) and two children, sculpted by Gherardo Silvani. Opposite is a monument to Lorenzo Corsini (Pope Clement XII) with a bust by Girolamo Ticciati (1731).

The refectory of Santo Spirito

To the left of the church, at no. 29, is the entrance to the refectory, the only part of the 14C convent to survive. Closed in 2000 (C), ☎ 055 287 043.

Above a fresco of the *Last Supper* (almost totally ruined) is a huge *Crucifixion (also damaged), both of them painted c 1360–65. They are attributed to Andrea Orcagna and his *bottega*, which probably included his brother Nardo di Cione. A partial restoration, after years of neglect, revealed one of the most dramatic scenes of the Crucifixion in 14C Florentine painting.

The **Fondazione Salvatore Romano** is also displayed here. Left to the city by the Neapolitan antiquarian Salvatore Romano in 1946, it consists of an interesting collection of sculpture (including many works from the Romanesque period). Beneath the fresco, two sea lions (**3**), Romanesque works from Campania, flank a polychrome high relief (**5**) of the *Madonna of the Misericordia* (15C Sienese school). Works against the far wall include: a *Madonna and Child* (**8**), large polychrome relief attributed to Jacopo della Quercia, and a fountain (**15**) attributed to Ammannati. On the end wall, the two damaged fragments of bas-reliefs showing two *Bishop Saints* (**21**) were found in Padua and are thought to be works by Donatello from the church of the Santo. The stone portal is signed by Natale di Ragusa (1471). In the centre of the room are: an *Angel* (**44**) and *Virtue* (**38**), both fine statuettes by Tino da Camaino; numerous 11C sculptural fragments and primitive stone reliefs; and a marble font (**45**) from Torcello (6C). The detached frescoes date from the 14C–15C.

Piazza Santo Spirito is one of the most attractive small squares in the city. It is planted with a few trees and is the setting for a little daily market. It is the centre of a distinctive district with numerous medieval houses and artisans' workshops. The most handsome house in the piazza is **Palazzo Guadagni** (no. 10), probably built by Cronaca c 1505. Its pleasing, well-proportioned façade with a top-floor loggia became the model for many 16C Florentine mansions. Borgo Tegolaio, which leads out of one corner of the piazza, is a medieval street which takes its name from the *tegola* kilns (a *tegola* is a roofing tile) which were once here. In Via delle Caldaie the wool-dyers had their workshops.

Via Sant'Agostino, a local shopping street, has public baths and the 17C church of San Carlo dei Barnabiti, the first seat of the Barnabites in Florence. (The Barnabites were founded in Milan in 1530 by St Antonio Zaccaria.) It was used as a gymnasium from 1890 up until a few years ago and is in urgent need of restoration (it is only occasionally open). An oratory here was enlarged on a design by Gherardo Silvani in the 17C, but its decoration dates from the mid-18C. The vault was frescoed in 1721 by Sigismondo Betti (the perspectives were added by Domenico Stagi in 1757), and the dome was frescoed by Giuseppe Zocchi in 1747. The façade (1756) incorporates a portal by Silvani.

Via Sant'Agostino contin-

Piazza Santo Spirito

ues across Via de' Serragli (see p 301) into Via Santa Monica. On the corner is a tabernacle with the *Madonna Enthroned and Saints* by Lorenzo di Bicci (1427).

The church of **Santa Monica** (usually closed) contains a circular fresco by Cosimo Ulivelli in the pretty vault. The 16C high altar encloses a *Deposition* by Giovanni Maria Butteri (1583). Above the nuns' choir is the organ and 17C panelling. In Via dell'Ardiglione (left) a plaque on a little house just beyond the arch across the road records the birthplace of Filippo Lippi in 1406.

Santa Maria del Carmine and the Brancacci Chapel

Via Santa Monica ends in **Piazza del Carmine**, a large square used as a car park. The rough stone façade of Santa Maria del Carmine (**Map 5; 2**) faces onto this. The church is famous for its frescoes by Masaccio in the small **Cappella Brancacci** at the end of the right transept which is now entered through the early 17C cloisters (entrance on the right of the façade at no. 14 in the piazza). Opening times 10.00–17.00 (*fest.* 13.00–17.00), except Tuesday; ☎ 055 238 2195. Only about 30 people are allowed into the chapel at a time.

Masaccio and the Brancacci Chapel

The frescoes illustrate the Life of St Peter and were commissioned by Felice Brancacci, a rich Florentine silk merchant and statesman, c 1424, from **Masolino** and **Masaccio**. The design of the whole fresco cycle may Masolino's. He probably worked on the frescoes in 1425 and again in 1427, together with his pupil Masaccio. Masaccio seems to have assumed full responsibility for the frescoes after Masolino departed for Rome in 1428. Later that year, Masaccio himself broke off work abruptly for an unknown reason, and left for Rome, where, by the end of the year, he died at the early age of 27. Brancacci was exiled from Florence in 1436 as an enemy of the Medici (he had married Palla Strozzi's daughter in 1431), and the cycle was only completed some 50 years later by **Filippino Lippi** (c 1480–85), who carefully integrated his style with that of Masaccio, possibly following an earlier design. In 1690, the chapel was saved from demolition through the efforts of the Accademia del Disegno and Vittoria della Rovere, mother of Cosimo III. In the 18C, the lunettes and vault of the chapel, probably frescoed by Masolino, were destroyed.

The frescoes by Masaccio were at once recognised as a masterpiece and profoundly influenced the Florentine Renaissance. All the major artists of the 15C came here to study the frescoes which combine a perfect application of the new rules of perspective with a remarkable use of *chiaroscuro*. 'Masaccio ... like Giotto a century earlier—himself the Giotto of an artistically more propitious world—was, as an artist, a great master of the significant, and, as a painter, endowed to the highest degree with a sense of tactile values, and with a skill in rendering them. In a career of but a few years he gave to Florentine painting the direction it pursued to the end.' (Bernard Berenson, *The Italian Painters of the Renaissance*.) The frescoes were beautifully restored in 1983–89, when it was found that an egg-based substance had been applied to the surface of the frescoes in the late 18C. As a result, mould had formed and obscured the colour. This was removed and the superb colouring and details of the landscapes can again be appreciated.

The frescoes

The **frescoes are arranged in two registers.

Upper row Right to left: on the **entrance arch**: Masolino, *Temptation of Adam and Eve*. **Right wall**: Masolino, *St Peter, Accompanied by St John, Brings Tabitha to Life* and *St Peter Heals a Lame Man* (with a charming view of Florence in the background). The figures on the left and some details in the background may be by the hand of Masaccio. **Right of the altar**: Masaccio, **St Peter Baptising*; **left of the altar**: Masolino, *St Peter Preaching*. On the **left wall**: Masaccio, **The Tribute Money*, perhaps the painter's masterpiece. Three episodes are depicted in the same scene: in the centre, Christ, surrounded by the Apostles, outside the gates of the city is asked by an official (with his back to us) to pay the tribute money owing to the city. Christ indicates a lake to St Peter, and (on the left) Peter is shown extracting the money from the mouth of a fish at the side of a lake. The scene on the right shows Peter handing over the tribute money to the official. The head of Christ has been attributed by some scholars to Masolino. On the **entrance arch**: Masaccio, **Expulsion from Paradise*, one of the most moving works of the Renaissance.

Lower row Right to left: on the entrance arch: Filippino Lippi, **Release of St Peter from Prison*. On the **right wall**: Filippino Lippi, *Saints Peter and Paul Before the Proconsul* and the *Crucifixion of St Peter*. On the **right of the altar**: Masaccio, *Saint Peter and Saint John Distributing Alms*; on the **left of the altar**: Masaccio, **St Peter, Followed by St John, Healing the Sick with his Shadow*. On the **left wall**: Masaccio, **St Peter Enthroned with Portraits of Friars*, his last work; the next half of this panel was begun by Masaccio and finished by Filippino. It shows *Saint Peter Bringing to Life the Emperor's Nephew* (the faces executed by Masaccio are more strongly illuminated; Filippino's figures are, in contrast, flatter and stand as if in shadow). On the **entrance arch**: Filippino Lippi, *St Peter in Prison Visited by St Paul* (on a design by Masaccio).

During restoration work, fragments of frescoes attributed to Masaccio—including two heads and part of the scene with *St Peter Healing the Sick with His Shadow*—were found behind the 18C altar (which has been removed). The altarpiece, the **Madonna del Carmine*, is attributed to Coppo di Marcovaldo.

The rooms off the cloister (closed since 1987) have extremely interesting frescoes detached from the cloister buildings by Alessandro Allori, Starnina, Filippo Lippi and Giovanni da Milano. In the second refectory, known as the **Sala Vanni** (open for concerts) is the *Supper in the House of the Pharisee* by Francesco Vanni, and detached frescoes attributed to Lippo Fiorentino.

The Carmelite convent was founded here in 1250 and the first church begun in 1268. This was almost completely ruined by fire in 1771 when the sacristy and the Cappella Brancacci and Cappella Corsini alone escaped destruction.

The huge wide interior of the church (opening times 09.00–12.00, 16.30–18.00) was rebuilt in an undistinguished late Baroque style in 1782. The *trompe l'œil* ceiling is by Domenico Stagi and Giuseppe Romei. In the **apse** there is a fine monument (difficult to see) to Piero Soderini (d. 1522) by Benedetto da Rovezzano. At the end of the left transept is the sumptuous ***Chapel of Sant'Andrea Corsini**, commissioned in 1675–83 by Bartolomeo and Neri Corsini from Pier Francesco Silvani in honour of their ancestor Andrea Corsini who died in 1374 and was canonised in 1629. It is one of the best Baroque works in Florence, with a ceiling by Luca Giordano (1682) and marble and silver reliefs by Giovanni

Battista Foggini. The Gothic **sacristy** (usually closed; with a 15C statuette of the *Madonna* over the door) contains a choir chapel frescoed with scenes from the life of St Cecilia by a master influenced by Bicci di Lorenzo, and a polyptych (entrance wall) attributed to Andrea da Firenze, and the *Martyrdom of an Apostle* by Lorenzo Lippi.

In Piazza Piattellina, just out of Piazza del Carmine (on the corner of Via del Leone), a fine tabernacle with a fresco of the *Madonna Enthroned with Saints* is attributed to the Master of San Martino a Mensola.

19 • The Oltrarno: Porta San Frediano to Porta San Niccolò

This chapter covers the Oltrarno except for Santo Spirito and Santa Maria del Carmine which are described in Ch. 18. It is a delightful district of the city, with numerous artisans' workshops and pretty streets.

Porta San Frediano (Map 5; 2), and the adjoining stretch of wall with crenellations which runs to the Torrino di Santa Rosa on the banks of the Arno, is the best-preserved part of the last circle of medieval walls built by the Comune in 1284–1333 (see the plan on pp 90–91). The gate, built in 1324 (perhaps by Andrea Pisano), with its high tower, protected the road to Pisa. It preserves interesting ironwork, and its huge wooden doors, decorated with nail heads, with their old locks. The city's emblem—an iris—is carved in stone high up on the tower. By the Torrino di Santa Rosa, a large 19C tabernacle protects a fresco of the *Pietà* (16C; very difficult to see).

At no. 4 Via Bartolini (Map 5; 2) is the **Antico Setificio Fiorentino**, a silk weaving factory which was moved here in 1786. Twelve artisans still use the 17C and 18C hand looms and late 19C machinery to produce exquisite silk fabrics which are hand-dyed and woven on traditional designs. Visitors are welcome to the showroom (opening times Mon–Fri 09.00–13.00, 14.00–17.00, ☎ 055 213 861) but the factory itself can only be visited once a year (usually on the last weekend in November).

Borgo San Frediano (Map 5; 2) gives its name to a district typical of this part of the city, with numerous artisans' houses and workshops. Among the local shops are a number of simple antique shops in the side streets. On the corner of Via San Giovanni is a tabernacle with the *Madonna and Child with Angels* (15C).

Farther on (left) is the bare stone exterior of the large church of **San Frediano in Cestello** (Map 5; 2), with its main entrance facing the Arno. The church was rebuilt in 1680–89 by Antonio Maria Ferri. Its fine dome is a conspicuous feature of this part of the city

Inside, all six side chapels have good frescoed decoration in the domes, spandrels and lunettes, carried out at the end of the 17C and the beginning of the 18C by Florentine painters, as well as stuccoes by Carlo Marcellini. On the **right side**, the first chapel has an altarpiece of *Santa Maria Maddalena dei Pazzi* by Giovanni Camillo Sagrestani and frescoes by Matteo Bonechi; the third chapel has an altarpiece and frescoes by Alessandro Gherardini. The *Virgin in Glory* *and Saints* in the right transept is by Francesco Curradi. The dome was frescoed by Antonio Domenico Gabbiani and the elaborate high altar also dates from the 18C. The *Crucifixion of Saint Lawrence* and the *Martyrdom of St Lawrence* in the left transept are by Jacopo del Sellaio. On the **left side**, the third chapel contains frescoes by Pier Dandini and a polychrome wooden statue of the *Madonna and Child* by the 14C Pisan-Florentine school; the second chapel has an altarpiece and frescoes by Antonio Franchi.

Next to the church is the huge Seminary; Piazza del Carmine opens off to the right, with the church of Santa Maria del Carmine (see p 298). The Borgo ends near the foot of Ponte alla Carraia.

Via de' Serragli (Map 6; 1), a long straight road, first laid out in the 13C, leads away from the Arno past a number of handsome 17C–18C palaces. Beyond the crossroads with Via Santa Monica (which leads right to Santa Maria del Carmine, see Ch. 18) and Via Sant'Agostino (which leads left to Santo Spirito, also described in Ch. 18), Via de' Serragli continues, now lined with simple, low medieval houses, through a local shopping area. It crosses Via della Chiesa, in which a house at no. 93 bears a plaque recording the death here of the writer Walter Savage Landor in 1864.

The **Albergo Popolare** opposite (no. 68) was built in 1930 as a hospice for the poor (and, with 125 beds, is still used to house those in need). The wing that occupies parts of the huge Carmelite convent attached to the church of Santa Maria del Carmine (see p 298) is no longer used as a hospice, and contains two splendid halls on the first floor. One has a beamed roof dating from the 14C and was once used by the monks as a dormitory, and the other, formerly the convent library (and used as a public dormitory in the 19C as the numbers on the walls and names of the benefactors show) has a panelled ceiling (1656) attributed to Ferdinando Tacca. These are awaiting restoration and reuse, but can sometimes be seen on certain days of the year. A reception room on the ground floor has recent frescoes by Luciano Guarnieri, pupil of Pietro Annigoni.

Further on, Via del Campuccio diverges right, skirting the garden wall of **Palazzo Torrigiani**. This is the biggest private garden in Florence (usually open a few days each year) created by Pietro Torrigiani (1773–1848). It has fine trees and sculpture by Pio Fedi (who had his studio in Via de' Serragli, see below), and encloses a stretch of town walls built by Cosimo I. The fantastic neo-Gothic tower was built by Gaetano Baccani in 1821 as an astronomical observatory. A corner of the garden can be seen from the nursery at 146 Via de' Serragli.

At 99 Via de' Serragli (corner of Via Santa Maria) is the **Studio of Pio Fedi**, a 19C sculptor and follower of Lorenzo Bartolini. Above the door, the tondo with supporting angels, is by Fedi. Lions rest on the top of the two high pilasters flanking the door. The building has recently been restored and is used as a printing works.

In Via Santa Maria, the little 19C **Goldoni theatre** (Map 5; 4) (420 seats) was reopened in 1998 (having been closed for over 21 years). It has a charming interior with a circular vestibule and horseshoe auditorium, decorated at the beginning of the 19C by Giuseppe del Rosso. On the Cinema Goldoni in Via de' Serragli is a plaque recording Gordon Craig's theatre workshop here in 1913.

On Via de' Serragli (corner of Via del Campuccio) is the small deconsecrated church of **Santa Elisabetta delle Convertite**. This was restored in 1996 and is now used as a hall for concerts and lectures. It was next to a convent founded in the 14C for destitute girls and converted prostitutes. The interior preserves a beautiful triumphal arch (1494) which shows the influence of Brunelleschi and a frescoed ceiling with the *Glory of St Mary Magdalen* by Alessandro Gherardini (1703). Frescoes have been discovered in the nuns' choir with *Stories of Martyrs*, almost certainly by Bernardino Poccetti.

At the other end of **Via del Campuccio** (see above) is Piazza Tasso (**Map 5; 4**) where, on fine days, old furniture (junk and 'antiques') is sometimes sold from lorries by dealers who drive up from the south of Italy. A car park was opened in 1997 between the 14C city walls and the garden wall of Palazzo Torrigiani which stretches as far as Porta Romana and makes a pleasant walk (see below). On the corner between Via del Leone and Via della Chiesa, a modern glass tabernacle protects a fresco of the *Madonna Enthroned with Angels*, which is a copy (made in 1958) of a painting by Giottino that was detached and removed in 1943.

Across the busy Viale Petrarca is **Via Giano della Bella** (**Map 5; 4**) where at nos 9 and 13 there stand two attractive, well preserved Art Nouveau villas. Opposite—on the site of a gravel pit filled with rubble in 1865 from the demolition of the Mercato Vecchio—is the Conventino a former Carmelite convent built in 1896 where 22 nuns lived until 1917. The cells around a little garden have been used as studios by artists and artisans since 1920. It was bought by the Comune in 1972 and saved from demolition in 1982 but its future is uncertain.

Off the other side of Piazza Tasso (entrance in Viale Ariosto; **Map 5; 2**) is the **Convent of San Francesco di Sales** (now a school), built in 1700 by Anton Maria Ferri. The church (usually closed) contains four monuments with busts of the Da Verrazzano family, 18C frescoes by Giovanni Antonio Pucci, and an altarpiece by Ignazio Hugford.

From Piazza Sauro at the south end of Ponte alla Carraia, **Via Santo Spirito** (**Map 6; 1**) continues parallel to the Arno. Here, on the right (no. 39), is the 17C **Palazzo Rinuccini** by Cigoli (enlarged by Ferdinando Ruggieri). Now used by a school of design, it incorporates a delightful little theatre on the first floor, designed by Girolamo Ticciati in the late 16C. The other Palazzo Rinuccini (no. 41) was built by Pier Francesco Silvani (with a coat of arms on the corner of Via de' Serragli by Giovanni Battista Foggini).

Palazzo Manetti (no. 23) has a 15C façade. This was the home of Sir Horace Mann in 1740–86 while serving as English envoy to the Tuscan court. His famous correspondence with Horace Walpole provides a remarkable picture of 18C Florence. In the early 19C, Lord and Lady Holland lived in the neighbouring Palazzo Feroni, with the painter George Frederick Watts as their guest.

Palazzo Frescobaldi (nos 5–13) has a very long façade with several interior courtyards and a little garden (occasionally open to the public) at the foot of the campanile and east end of Santo Spirito. Replanted at the end of the 19C, it has circular bay hedges, pots of azalias, and a Baroque grotto. From the little terrace, the dome of Santo Spirito can also be seen. One side of the palace is supported on *sporti* in Via dei Coverelli. Opposite is **Palazzo Guicciardini** (no. 14), and, on the corner of Via dei Coverelli, the restored graffiti decoration on the side of Palazzo Coverelli can be seen. Via Santo Spirito ends at a busy intersection of narrow streets near the foot of Ponte Santa Trìnita.

Via Maggio (Map 6; 1,3) leads out of Piazza dei Frescobaldi away from the Arno. Its name (from Maggiore) is a reminder of its origin as the principal and widest street of the Oltrarno. It was opened soon after Ponte Santa Trìnita was built in 1252, and it became a fashionable residential street after the grand-dukes moved to Palazzo Pitti in the 16C. It now has a number of antique shops.

On the left, Palazzo Ricasoli (no. 7), the largest palace on Via Maggio, dates from c 1520. The façade has numerous wrought-iron torch holders and flag staffs and a very fine courtyard. On the right is Palazzo Machiavelli (nos 16–18) which once belonged to a branch of Machiavelli's family. The palace was divided in two in the 19C (as the façade shows) but the interior is well preserved, having been bought in 1877–1905 by **St Mark's Anglican Church** (Map 6; 3).

The church, in part of the ground floor, is a Tractarian–Byzantine–Renaissance fantasy created by the Florentine resident John Roddam Stanhope Spencer in 1877–79. The pre-Raphaelite decoration, designed in detail by Spencer, survives virtually intact, including the bronze lamps, stencilled walls and fittings. A chalice incorporates the engagement ring of Holman Hunt's widow which she donated to the church in 1866 (Stanhope Spencer was a disciple of Holman Hunt), and the treasury and vestments have been carefully preserved. The large painting of *St Michael Archangel* by Giuseppe Catani Chiti, was commissioned by Sir Thomas Dick Lauder(d. 1919) who lived in Fiesole.

The church, founded by Anglo-Catholic zealots led by the Rev. Charles Tooth in the 1870s, is traditionally High Church, and the British residents managed to keep it open throughout the Second World War. There was another Anglican church in Florence up until 1967; this was the church of the Holy Trinity (see p 213), which had been founded in 1843 and came to be the established Low Church in Florence (the two congregations of St Mark's and Holy Trinity were fiercely independent of each other). The Anglican liturgy is still celebrated at Saint Mark's (with traditional Tractarian pomp and splendour) every Sunday morning at 10.30 (and there are services also at 09.00 on Sunday, 18.00 on Thursday, and 20.00 on Friday). The church and palace (the parson's residence) can usually be visited on request in the mornings (10.00–12.00). The church, together with Anglican churches all over Europe and North Africa, falls within the diocese of Gibraltar.

Palazzo di Bianca Cappello (no. 26) has good graffiti decoration attributed to Bernardino Poccetti (c 1579; restored in 1987). The house was built by Grand-duke Francesco I for the beautiful Venetian girl Bianca Cappello who was first his mistress and then his wife. Opposite, Palazzo Ridolfi (no. 13), built in the late 16C (attributed to Santi di Tito), stands next to Palazzo di Cosimo Ridolfi, a small palace built at the beginning of the 15C. The numerous narrow old streets on the left of the road lead to Piazza Pitti (see below). Farther on is **Palazzo Corsini Suarez** (or Commenda di Firenze; no. 42), named after Baldassare Suarez of Portugal who acquired the palace in 1590. It was built in the late 14C and reconstructed in the 16C, partly by Gherardo Silvani. It is now owned by the state and since 1979 has been the seat of the **Archivio Contemporaneo Alessandro Bonsanti**, a branch of the Vieusseux Library (see p 243). Here are conserved the papers of the artist and writer Alberto Savinio (1891–1952), the playwright Eduardo de Filippo (1900–84), and the writers Pier Paolo Pasolini (1922–75) and Vasco Pratolini (1913–91). It is also used as a restoration laboratory for books. In the Saletta dell'Alcova are tempera decorations attributed to Giovanni Camillo Sagrestani and it has a pretty courtyard.

Via Maggio ends in **Piazza San Felice**. A marble column, 12m high now stands here: it had first been set up in 1572 by Cosimo I, but had been removed to the Boboli gardens in 1838 by Leopoldo II; it was eventually returned here in 1992.

The palace at no. 8 was built in the 15C by the Ridolfi and acquired in 1619 by Count Camillo Guidi, secretary of state for the Medici. On the first floor is the **Casa Guidi**, a flat rented in 1847 by Robert and Elizabeth Barrett Browning after their secret marriage in 1846. Opening times Mon, Wed and Fri, 15.00–18.00 April–Nov (☎ 055 354 457); donations welcome. The apartment can be rented for short lets from the Landmark Trust, which is based in the UK (☎ 44 1628 825 925).

The Brownings in Florence

Robert and Elizabeth Barratt-Browning lived in the Casa Guidi until Elizabeth's death in 1861 (she is buried in the English Cemetery, see Ch. 22). The living room, dining room and study have been restored as far as possible to their simple appearance when the Brownings lived here. There is also a good library of works by and relating to the Brownings. The Brownings' son 'Pen', who was born here in 1849, purchased the house after their death in 1893. The apartment was sold to the Browning Institute in 1971, and since 1993 has been owned by Eton College and is leased to the Landmark Trust who helped restore and refurnish the rooms in 1995.

Both Robert and Elizabeth Barrett Browning wrote much of their most important poetry here, including Elizabeth's *Casa Guidi Windows* and *Aurora Leigh*, and Robert's *The Ring and the Book*. Robert's stay here also inspired him to write poems about the Florentine painters Fra Filippo Lippi and Andrea del Sarto, and the statue of Ferdinando I in Piazza Santissima Annunziata (*The Statue and the Bust*). The Brownings were visited by Walter Savage Landor, Anthony Trollope, Bulwer-Lytton, Nathaniel Hawthorne and 'Father Prout' (Francis Mahony), the Roman correspondent for Dickens' *Daily News*. Elizabeth took an active interest in the cause of Italian Independence from Austrian rule.

San Felice

San Felice (**Map 6; 3**) is a simple 14C church, altered in the mid-16C when it was taken over by the Dominicans. The Renaissance **façade** and the sanctuary are almost certainly by Michelozzo (1457). In the **interior**, the first half of the nave contains a closed gallery supported by eight columns and a pretty vault, added as a nuns' choir in the mid-16C. On the west wall are early 18C funerary monuments.

On the **south side**: the first altar has remains of a fresco of the *Pietà* attributed to Nicolò di Pietro Gerini (interesting for its iconography); the fifth altar has a *Pietà* terracotta group attributed to Cieco da Gambassi; the sixth altar has a *Madonna and Saints* by Ridolfo and Michele Ghirlandaio; the seventh altar has a lunette fresco of the *Virgin of the Sacred Girdle* (late 14C Florentine). Over the **high altar** is a large *Crucifix*, almost certainly by Giotto, which is in very good condition. In the chapel to the left of the presbytery is an altarpiece composed of paintings by different hands: in the centre the *Madonna and Child* is by Iacopo di Rossello Franchi, the two *Saints* are by Pier Francesco Foschi, and the *Pietà* is by the Maestro di Serumidio.

On the **north side**: the seventh altar has a fresco by Giovanni da San Giovanni (the angels are by Volterrano); the sixth altar has a triptych by Neri di Bicci beneath a frescoed lunette of the 14C; the first altar, a triptych by a follower of Botticelli (known as the Master of Apollo and Daphne). In the adjoining **convent** there is a *Last Supper* painted by Matteo Rosselli in 1614.

Via Romana (Map 5; 6), one of the most important thoroughfares of the Oltrarno, continues southwest towards Porta Romana.

Zoological Museum

At no. 17 (left) Palazzo Torrigiani was built in 1775 by Gaspare Maria Paoletti as a natural history museum. It is known as La Specola from the astronomical observatory founded here by Grand-duke Pietro Leopoldo. Here, in 1814, Sir Humphry Davy and Michael Faraday used Galileo's 'great burning glass' (see p 284) to explode the diamond. It is now the seat of the Natural Sciences schools of the University and (on the third floor) a **Zoological Museum** with a comprehensive natural history display. Opening times 09.00–13.00; closed Wed (☎ 055 228 8251); Lire 6000.

It is the largest zoological collection in Italy, including invertebrates, vertebrates, insects and shells. The remarkable and unique collection of anatomical models in wax, made in 1775–1814 by Clemente Susini, includes 'lo scorticato', a life-size model of a man (recently restored). There are also numerous anatomical wax models and compositions by Gaetano Zumbo (late 17C).

On the first floor is the **Tribuna di Galileo** designed by Giuseppe Martelli for Leopoldo II in 1841, in honour of Galileo. The elaborate decorations in marble and mosaic include a statue of *Galileo* by Aristodemo Costoli and brightly coloured neo-classical frescoes by Luigi Sabatelli. The busts are of pupils of Galileo. Formerly, the instruments and mementoes of Galileo now in the Museo della Storia della Scienza were displayed here; now cases protect two anatomical wax figures.

Further along Via Romana and nearly opposite the Annalena entrance gate to the Boboli gardens (see p 185) is the Giardino Corsi, a delightful little raised garden (only open a few days each year) laid out in 1801–10 by Giuseppe Manetti, with fine trees and a neo-classical loggia overlooking Via Romana. At no. 40 is **San Piero in Gattolino**, an attractive church whose unusual name is said to derive from its founder who was a ferryman over the Arno (*gattus* derived from *chiatta* meaning barge). It contains altarpieces by Alessandro Gherardini, Antonio Soderini (1722) and Bilivert. The oratory off the south side has pretty decorations with *quadratura* of 1770.

Via Romana ends at Piazza della Calza, named after the **Convitto della Calza**, here, with an attractive asymmetrical loggia. It was first built as a hospital in 1362, and later became a convent. It was restored in 2000 as a home for retired prelates, a hostel for visiting churchmen and pilgrim groups, and a conference centre (known as the 'Oltrarno Meeting Center', ☎ 055 222 287). In the refectory, there is a *Last Supper* by Franciabigio and on the walls pretty frames with frescoes by 18C Florentine artists including Tommaso Gherardini and Giuseppe

Zocchi. In another room, there is a polychrome stucco bas-relief, a 15C copy of Donatello's *Madonna de' Pazzi* and a 15C wooden *Crucifix*. From the piazza there is an entrance to a car park opened in 1997 between the city walls and the garden wall of Palazzo Torrigiani. A small gate in the **city walls** leads to steps up to the walkway along the top of the walls and into the Porta Romana guard-house over Via Romana.

Porta Romana (Map 5; 6) is a well-preserved gate built in 1328 to a design by Andrea Orcagna. On the inside face, the keystone of the arch is decorated with the iris of Florence, sculpted in marble in 1331 by Giovanni Pisano. In the lunette is a fresco by the Florentine school of the *Madonna and Child Enthroned with Saints* dating from the early 14C. Outside the gate is a busy intersection where Viale Machiavelli (see Ch. 20) and Viale del Poggio Imperiale (see p 351) terminate, and the road to Siena (Via Senese) begins. The incongruous colossal statue called *Dietro-fronte* ('back to front'; 1981–84), apparently a woman with a stone block on her head, is by Michelangelo Pistoletto. He gave it to the Comune and it was set up here in the 1980s, where it has remained, despite protests by local residents.

Just outside the gate (left) is an exit from the Boboli gardens (see Ch. 8). In the former royal stables, entered through another gateway and surrounded by a park, once part of the Boboli gardens (but now used as a car park), is the **Istituto d'Arte**, a state art school. It owns a famous Gipsoteca (admission by appointment at the art school), a museum of plaster-casts of numerous famous Antique and Renaissance sculptures, including many by Donatello and Michelangelo. They were mostly made at the end of the 19C and the beginning of the 20C by Giuseppe Lelli; his son left them to the Institute in 1922. The collection is arranged in a splendid hall. Nearby is the building known as Le Pagliere which serves as a deposit for restored sculptures from the Boboli gardens. There are buses from Porta Romana via Via Romana which return to the centre of the city.

Just out of Piazza San Felice is **Piazza Pitti**, with Palazzo Pitti, described in Ch. 8. The pretty row of houses facing the palace includes no. 16, the home of Paolo dal Pozzo Toscanelli (1397–1482), the famous scientist and greatest geographer of his time. Dostoyevsky wrote *The Idiot* while staying at no. 21 in 1868. Via Guicciardini (described in Ch. 7) leads past the church of Santa Felicita to Ponte Vecchio.

Via de' Bardi (Map 6; 4) begins here; it is named after the palaces along it where the Bardi lived. The Bardi were one of the richest mercantile families in medieval Florence, though they were bankrupt by 1340. Among the old houses at the end of Ponte Vecchio, which were destroyed in 1944, was the Casa Ambrogi, guest house of Horace Mann, where Gray and Walpole stayed in 1740.

Where the road forks with Lungarno Torrigiani the tall Porta San Niccolò is visible (see below). Via de' Bardi continues on a winding course past a series of noble town houses. On the left are three palaces in a row all owned by the Capponi family (with their gardens across the street): Palazzo Capponi delle Rovinate, Palazzo Larioni dei Bardi and Palazzo Canigiani. **Palazzo Capponi delle Rovinate** (no. 36) was built for the banker and learned ambassador Niccolò da Uzzano in the early 15C, and on his death went to his daughter's husband's family, the Capponi who have lived here ever since. It retains its handsome rough stone façade and its original studded wooden doors. The property originally extended as far as the Arno: the rear façade was built by Giuseppe Poggi after 1872 when he constructed the Lungarno Torrigiani. The Capponi family archives and private art collection survive here in rooms splendidly decorated in the 18C and 19C (admission by appointment). The remarkable Renaissance courtyard was altered in the 18C when copies of the busts were made. Niccolò's splendid terracotta bust was kept here until 1885 when it was moved to the Bargello (see p 253).

The family chapel has a *Madonna and Child* (1524–28; partially repainted) by Pontormo and a stained glass window by Guglielmo di Marcillat. The family paintings include works by Bilivert, Sustermans, Pontormo (*St Jerome*), and five seascapes and landscapes by Salvatore Rosa, and others attributed to Andrea da Brescianino, Cigoli, Michelangelo Cerquozzi, Santi di Tito, Bernardino Mei, Fra Bartolomeo and Francesco Furini. There is also a contemporary copy of a work by Andrea del Sarto. The sculpture includes a Roman porphyry lion (on the stairs) and a terracotta relief model of the *Stoning of St Stephen* probably by Ferdinando Tacca.

Next door is Palazzo Larioni dei Bardi (no. 30) which has a courtyard (in need of repair) begun by Michelozzo and perhaps completed by Benedetto da Maiano. The third palace, Palazzo Canigiani (no. 28) has a neo-classical façade. The famous English art historian John Pope Hennessy (1913–94) lived here at the end of his life. He was a great scholar of Florentine Renaissance sculpture and was made an honorary citizen of Florence.

At no. 24 is the little church of **Santa Lucia dei Magnoli** (open only for evensong). The glazed terracotta lunette over the door is by Benedetto Buglioni. Inside on the first altar on the left is *St Lucy* by Pietro Lorenzetti; and on the wall to the left are two panels of the *Annunciation* ascribed to Jacopo del Sellaio. The other altarpieces on the left side are by Jacopo da Empoli and Francesco Curradi. The high altarpiece of the *Madonna and Child with St Anne and Four Saints* is by the late 15C Florentine school. The choir, decorated in 1732 with a painting of the *Martyrdom of St Lucy* attributed to Pier Dandini, is partially hidden by the ugly organ. A photographic reproduction of the famous altarpiece painted for this church by Domenico Veneziano (now in the Uffizi; the predella was divided up between various museums) has been placed on the entrance wall.

Opposite the church, an attractive old road called the **Costa Scarpuccia** climbs up the hill between gardens to Costa San Giorgio. Via de' Bardi continues past Palazzo Nasi (Ulivieri Stiozzi Ridolfi), with a façade attributed to the son of Baccio d'Agnolo, to end in Piazza dei Mozzi. On the bend are the fine old **Palazzi dei Mozzi (Map 6; 6)** which were built in the 13C–14C and are among the most noble private houses of medieval Florence. The severe façades in *pietra forte* have arches on the ground floor. The Mozzi were one of the richest Florentine families in the 13C but, like the Bardi, they too lost most of their wealth in the 14C. Gregory X was their guest here in 1273 when he came to Florence to arrange a peace between the Guelfs and Ghibellines. The huge garden up to the walls was acquired by the Mozzi in the 16C. The building, garden and Villa Bardini were left indirectly to the state in 1965, together with a vast collection of decorative arts (including 16C and 17C furniture), and marble architectural fragments recovered during the demolition of the old centre of the city, by Ugo Bardini. There are long-term plans to open a museum here, which will probably be called the

Galleria di Palazzo Mozzi-Bardini and to make the garden public. The piazza opens out onto the Arno with, at no. 1, the Museo Bardini (described in Ch. 17), left to the Comune by Ugo's father Stefano.

Via di San Niccolò, another narrow street of medieval houses, continues beyond Piazza dei Mozzi. On the left, Palazzo Alemanni (no. 68) was built in the 14C and 15C and later reconstructed. It is decorated with a row of little demons, copies from Giambologna. At no. 24 is Il Bisonte, a well-known school of etching, lithography and manual press printing.

Beyond, at a bend in the road with local shops, is the church of **San Niccolò sopr'Arno** (or San Niccolò Oltrarno; **Map 7; 3**). Opening times 08.00–10.30, 17.30–19.00. This was founded in the 11C and rebuilt at the end of the 14C. In the tall **interior**, with an open timber roof, several interesting frescoes were found beneath the 16C altars during restoration work after the 1966 flood. On the west wall, there are detached frescoes of *St James the Apostle* (school of Neri di Bicci) and *St Anthony Abbot* (15C), and a 17C painting of **Abraham and Isaac**. On the **south side**, the first altar has the *Presentation of Christ in the Temple* by Giovanni Battista Naldini and the second altar has a wooden *Crucifix* by Michelozzo. In the chapel at the end of the south side, there is a fresco of **St Ansano*, attributed to Francesco d'Antonio, together with its sinopia. A door (not always open) leads into the **sacristy** which contains a **Madonna della Cintola*, a beautiful fresco of the late 15C Florentine school (attributed to Baldovinetti), within a *pietra serena* tabernacle by the *bottega* of Michelozzo. Beneath it is a 14C triptych attributed to the Master of San Niccolò. Also here are two small paintings of *St Michael* and *St Gabriel Archangel* by Il Poppi. The triptych of the **Madonna and Saints** is attributed to Bicci di Lorenzo.

In the chapels to the left and right of the high altar, there are a *St John the Baptist* by Empoli and a *Marriage of the Virgin* by Il Poppi. The precious **organ** by Dionisio Romani dates from 1581. The chapel on the **north side** contains an *Annunciation* by Alessandro Fei; the third altar has *Christ Bringing to Life the Widow's Son* by Il Poppi; and the second altar, the *Martyrdom of St Catherine* by Alessandro Allori.

At the end of Via San Miniato (right) can be seen Porta San Miniato (see p 310) in the walls. Via San Niccolò continues past simple houses with workshops on the ground floor, to the massive **Porta San Niccolò** (**Map 7; 3**), whose high tower remains intact. Built c 1340, it was restored in 1979. From here a ramp leads up the hill towards San Miniato (see p 310). A 9m-high monument to Galileo was set up here in 1997, to the surprise of many Florentines. It was donated to the city by the sculptor Giò Pomodoro.

20 • Forte di Belvedere and the Basilica of San Miniato

San Miniato can be reached directly from Stazione Santa Maria Novella and Porta Romana on bus no. 12 which follows Viale dei Colli (Viale Machiavelli and Viale Galileo) to a request stop at the foot of the steps up to the basilica (just before Piazzale Michelangelo). The church can also be reached on foot by the steps from Porta San Niccolò (**Map 7; 3**). However, if you have time, the following route on foot is highly recommended (bus 13 can then be taken back from Viale Galileo to Porta Romana and the Stazione Santa Maria Novella).

From the little piazza adjoining Piazza Santa Felicita (see p 155) the narrow **Costa San Giorgio** (**Map 6; 4**) winds up the hill towards Forte di Belvedere. At the junction with Costa Scarpuccia (a beautiful road which leads downhill to Via de' Bardi, see Ch. 19) is the church of **San Giorgio sulla Costa** (or Spirito Santo; **Map 6; 4**). The church has been undergoing restoration for many years and it is at present used by the Romanian Orthodox community of Florence (open only for a service at 10.30 on fest.).

The Baroque **interior** by Giovanni Battista Foggini (1705) is one of the best in Florence. The altarpieces are by Tommaso Redi, Jacopo Vignali and Passignano, and on the ceiling is the *Glory of St George* by Alessandro Gherardini. The high altar is also by Foggini. The church also contains a precious mechanical organ of c 1570 by Onofrio Zeffirini.

Farther up the street is the house (no. 19; with a portrait on the façade) purchased by Galileo for his son Vincenzio. To the left is the **Villa Bardini** (entrance at no. 8) with a huge park (**Map 6; 4**) which extends down the hillside to Palazzo dei Mozzi. A loggia was reconstructed here by Bardini, at the top of a long staircase; it has a magnificent view of Florence. The park, owned by the state, may one day be open to the public (see p 307).

The pretty Costa San Giorgio continues up between the high walls of rural villas to (left) **Porta San Giorgio** (**Map 6; 6**), which has a fresco by Bicci di Lorenzo and, on the outer face, the copy of a stone relief of St George (1284; original in Palazzo Vecchio). Dating from 1260, the Porta San Giorgio forms part of the walls built to protect the Oltrarno in 1258 (see plan on pp 90–91), and is the oldest gate to have survived in the city.

The entrance to **Forte di Belvedere** (**Map 6; 6**) is here. This is a huge fortress designed by Buontalenti (probably using plans drawn up by Don Giovanni de' Medici) in the shape of a six-pointed star. It was built by order of Ferdinando I in 1590, ostensibly for the defence of the city, but in reality to dominate the supposedly republican citizens. Although the ramparts are usually open as a public park (opening times 09.00–20.00; free admission), they are currently closed for restoration. When they reopen (probably not before 2003) there will be access through a gate into the Boboli gardens (see Ch. 8) again. The ramparts provide the best all-round *view of Florence. The handsome Palazzetto at the centre of the fortress has a loggia and two façades, one facing the city and the other facing south. The empty interior is only open for exhibitions.

Via di San Leonardo (**Map 6; 6**) begins here. It is one of the most beautiful and best-preserved roads on the outskirts of Florence (but beware of cars), lead-ing through countryside past villas and their gardens and between olive groves behind high walls. Some of the pretty incised decoration on the plaster of the walls survives. A short way along on the left the Villa Razzolini, now **Villa Spelman** (no. 13) is the seat of the Johns Hopkins University in Florence (The Charles S. Singleton Center for Italian Studies). The gate in front of the villa was designed by Cecil Pinsent. Beyond, preceded by a charming little garden with four cypresses, is the church of **San Leonardo in Arcetri** (Map 6; 6; open for ser-vices at 17.00 or 18.00 on Sat, and 08.00–11.00 on *fest.*; at other times ring at no. 25). This was founded in the 11C and contains a celebrated *pulpit of the early 13C, removed from the church of San Pier Scheraggio, with beautiful bas-reliefs. Over the high altar, there is a triptych of the *Madonna and Child with Saints* by Lorenzo di Niccolò and, on either side, *Madonna of the Sacred Girdle with Saints* and an *Annunciation with Angels and Saints* (decorating a taber-nacle), both by Neri di Bicci. The damaged painting of *Tobias and the Angel* is by the Master of San Miniato.

Via di San Leonardo continues past a house on the right (no. 64) where a plaque records Tchaikovsky's stay in 1878, to Viale Galileo (see below). The con-tinuation of Via di San Leonardo (and Arcetri and Pian de' Giullari) are described on p 351.

From Forte di Belvedere, **Via di Belvedere** (Map 6; 6), a picturesque country lane with olive trees, follows the straight line of the city walls. These were built in 1258, reinforced in 1299–1333, and again in the 16C. Even though greatly reduced in height, they are the best stretch of fortifications to survive in Florence. The road descends steeply with a fine view of the defensive towers and the tall Porta San Niccolò beyond. At the bottom is **Porta San Miniato**, a simple 14C arch in the wall. The doors, which were torn from their hinges in the Arno flood of 1966, were reinstalled here after restoration in 1996. A road leads straight uphill from the gate, and a short way up on the left begins the stepped Via di San Salvatore al Monte. Lined with cypresses, this ascends the hill past the wall of a little rose garden (open May and June), and an area reserved for the cats of the city. It ends at the busy Viale Galileo.

San Miniato al Monte

A monumental flight of steps leads up from Viale Galileo past a cemetery (1839) to San Miniato al Monte (**Map 7; 7,8**). Opening times in the winter 08.00–12.00, 14.30–18.00; in the summer 08.00–12.00, 14.00–19.00.

The finest of all Tuscan Romanesque basilicas, with a famous façade, San Miniato is one of the most beautiful churches in Italy. Together with the Baptistery and San Lorenzo, it was the most important church in 11C Florence. Its position on a green hill above the city is incomparable. The stunning *view from the terrace takes in the walls climbing the hillside to Forte di Belvedere on the left. Looking across the Arno, Palazzo Vecchio, the small dome of the Cappella dei Principi, the white roof of the Baptistery, the Campanile and the towers of the Badia Fiorentina and the Bargello, with the Duomo behind, are all visible. On the right, just above the trees can be seen the west end of Santa Croce and its campanile. In the distance, the Villa della Petraia with its tower is promi-nent at the foot of Monte Morello.

San Miniato al Monte

History of San Miniato al Monte

The deacon Minias was a member of the early Christian community from the East who settled in Florence. A legend even suggested he was an Oriental prince, the son of the King of Armenia. He is thought to have been martyred c 250 during the persecutions of the Emperor Decius and buried on this hillside. The present church, built in 1013 by Bishop Hildebrand, is on the site of a shrine protecting the tomb of St Minias. The Benedictine Cluniac monastery, founded here at the same time by the Emperor Henry II, was one of the first important religious houses in Tuscany. In the 17C, it was used as a hospital and later as a poor house. In 1924, 17 Olivetan Benedictine monks returned here and they still live in the monastery and look after the church which has been extremely well restored over the years.

The ***façade**, begun c 1090, is built of white and dark-greenish marble in a geometrical design reminiscent of the Baptistery. Above the exquisite little window in the form of an aedicule is a 13C mosaic (remade in 1861) of ***Christ Between the Virgin and St Minias***, the warrior-martyr. In the tympanum, supported by two small figures in relief, the marble inlay repeats the motifs of the pavement inside. It is crowned by an eagle with outstretched wings standing on a bale of cloth, emblem of the *Arte di Calimala* (the cloth-importers guild) who looked after the fabric of the building.

Interior

The fine interior, built in 1018–63, survives practically in its original state. Its design is unique in Florentine church architecture with a raised choir above a large hall crypt. Many of the capitals of the columns come from Roman temples in the city. The pavement is composed of tomb-slabs, except for the centre of the nave which has seven superb ***marble intarsia panels** (1207), designed like a

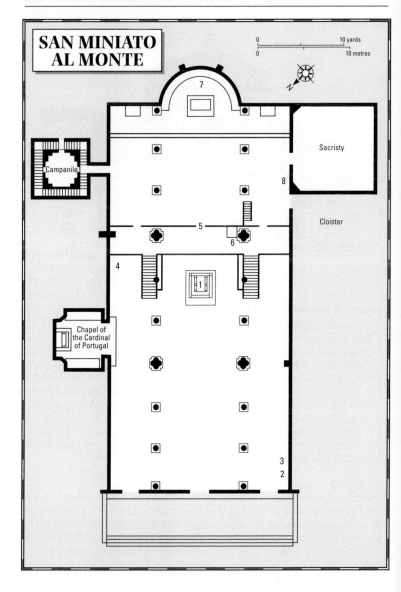

SAN MINIATO AL MONTE

0   10 yards
0   10 metres

Campanile

Sacristy

Cloister

Chapel of
the Cardinal
of Portugal

carpet, with signs of the Zodiac and animal motifs. The decoration on the inside of the upper part of the nave walls, in imitation of the façade, was carried out at the end of the last century, when the open timber roof, with polychrome decoration, was also restored.

At the end of the nave is the *Cappella del Crocifisso (1), an exquisite tabernacle commissioned by Piero il Gottoso from Michelozzo in 1448. It is superbly carved and ingeniously designed to fit its setting that was built some 400 years earlier. It was made to house the venerated *Crucifix* which is said to have bowed approvingly to St John Gualberto when he pardoned his brother's assassin (later removed to Santa Trinita, see p 242); the painted panels of the doors of the cupboard which protected the miraculous *Crucifix* are by Agnolo Gaddi (1394–96). The enamelled terracotta roof and ceiling are the work of Luca della Robbia. The inlaid coloured marble frieze bears the emblem of Piero de' Medici (whose arms also appear on the back of the tabernacle). The copper eagles on the roof are by Maso di Bartolomeo.

On the outer stone walls of the aisles are a number of frescoes. In the **south aisle**: (2) *Madonna Enthroned with Six Saints* by Paolo Schiavo, (1436) and a huge figure of *St Christopher* (3) dating from the 14C or earlier. Most of the other frescoes on this wall are by 15C artists. In the **north aisle** are two detached frescoes (a *Madonna and Child with Saints* and a *Crucifixion with Seven Saints*) by Mariotto di Nardo. Between them is a fine painted *Crucifix*, probably dating from 1260–70. By the steps up to the choir is a fresco (4) of the *Virgin Annunciate* and a fragment of a *Nativity* scene (late 13C).

Built onto the north wall of the church is the *Chapel of the Cardinal of Portugal**, the funerary chapel of Cardinal Jacopo di Lusitania who died in Florence at the age of 25. It was begun by Antonio Manetti, Brunelleschi's pupil, in 1460 (and finished, after his death in the same year, probably under the direction of Antonio Rossellino). It incorporates some of the best workmanship of the Florentine Renaissance and has been carefully restored. The exquisitely carved *tomb of the Cardinal is by Antonio Rossellino (1461–66). The ceiling has five *medallions (1461) by Luca della Robbia. These represent the *Cardinal Virtues* and the *Holy Ghost*, against a background of tiles decorated with classical cubes in yellow, green and purple, and are among the masterpieces of Luca's enamelled terracotta work. The altarpiece of *Three Saints* by Antonio and Piero del Pollaiolo (1466–67) has been replaced by a copy (original in the Uffizi). The frescoed decoration of this wall, including two angels, is by the same artists. Above the marble bishop's throne on the west wall is a painting on the *Annunciation by Alesso Baldovinetti (1466–73), who also frescoed the *Evangelists and Fathers of the Church* in the lunettes beside the windows, and in the spandrels.

Steps lead up to the raised **choir** which has a beautiful marble *transenna (5) dating from 1207, and *pulpit (6), also faced with marble. The lectern is supported by an eagle above a carved figure standing on a lion's head. The low columns in the choir have huge antique capitals. The apse (7; light at the top of the stairs on the right) has a beautiful inlaid blind arcade with six small Roman columns between opaque windows. The large apse mosaic representing *Christ Between the Virgin and St Minias with Symbols of the Evangelists* (1297) was first restored in 1491 by Alesso Baldovinetti. The *Crucifix* behind the simple Renaissance altar is attributed to the Della Robbia. The carved and inlaid stalls by Giovanni di Domenico da Gaiole and Francesco di Domenico (Il Monciatto) date from 1466–70. To the right of the apse is an altarpiece by Jacopo del Casentino showing *St Minias and Scenes from His Life*.

The **sacristy** (1387) lies to the south of the apse. It is covered with frescoes by Spinello Aretino; in the vault are the *Evangelists* and in the lunettes the *Life of St Benedict*, one of Spinello's best works (restored in 1840). There is also a polychrome bust of *St Minias* (wearing a crown) attributed to Nanni di Bartolo, two

Della Robbia statuettes, and stalls like those in the choir. In the lunette above the little door is a *Pietà* recently attributed to Giovanni di Piamonte (1470–72). Just outside the sacristy, on the walls of the **choir** (**8**) there are some very early frescoes of *Saints* (13C).

The 11C **crypt** beneath the choir has beautiful slender columns, many of them with antique capitals. The original 11C altar contains the relics of St Minias. The small vaults are decorated with frescoes of *Saints* and *Prophets* against a blue ground by Taddeo Gaddi that have been beautifully restored.

On the **west wall** of the church, there is the simple tomb of the poet Giuseppe Giusti (1800–50) and a monument to the Tuscan artist Giuseppe Bezzuoli (1784–1855) by Emilio Santarelli (returned here in 2000 after it had been removed to the cemetery of the Porte Sante in 1964).

The fine **cloister** of the Benedictine monastery (admission only by special permission), on the right side of the church, was begun c 1425. On the upper loggia, damaged fragments of frescoes in terraverde were detached in 1970 revealing the sinopie: the frescoes were returned here after restoration in 1976. Although extremely damaged, they are recognised as some of the most interesting works known by Paolo Uccello, illustrating scenes from monastic legends with remarkable perspectives and a beautiful figure of a woman. The sinopie are preserved in a room off the cloister. One of the frescoes dates from the 16C, and is signed by Bernardo Buontalenti. On the lower walk is a fragment of a sinopia attributed to Andrea del Castagno.

On the right of the façade is the crenellated **Bishop's Palace**, with attractive twin windows. This dates from 1295, when it was used as a summer residence by the bishops of Florence from the 14C to 16C. In later centuries, it was used as a barracks and hospital, and was restored in the 20C.

The massive stone **campanile** replaced one that collapsed in 1499; it was begun after 1523 from a design by Baccio d'Agnolo, but was never finished. During the siege of Florence (1530) Michelangelo mounted two cannon here, and protected the bell-tower from hostile artillery by a screen of mattresses.

The **fortezza** originated in a hastily improvised defence-work planned by Michelangelo during the months preceding the siege. In 1553, Cosimo I converted it into a real fortress with the help of Francesco da Sangallo, Tribolo and others. The walls now enclose a large monumental **cemetery**, called the Porte Sante(entrance on the left side of the church), laid out in 1854 by Nicolò Matas, and finished by Mariano Falcini in 1864. Surrounded by cypresses it has numerous neo-Gothic chapels and well-carved tombs. Collodi (Carlo Lorenzini), author of *Pinocchio* is buried here, as well as the writer Vasco Pratolini (1913–91), and the painter Pietro Annigoni. Near the entrance is the tomb of the sculptor Libero Andreotti (1875–1933) with a striking bronze of the *Resurrection*.

Near San Miniato, in a grove of cypresses on the side of the hill, is the church of **San Salvatore al Monte** (Map 7; **6**), a building of gracious simplicity by Cronaca, which Michelangelo called his *bella villanella* (his pretty country maid). The **interior**, which now has a rather gloomy abandoned feel about it, has an open timber roof. On the west wall is a bust of *Marcello Adriani* (d. 1521) by Andrea Ferrucci. On the north side are small 16C stained glass windows: the one over the south side door is attributed to Perugino. In the second north chapel is a large glazed terracotta group of the *Deposition* attributed to Santi Buglioni. Over the north door is another painted terracotta *Deposition* group attributed to Giovanni della Robbia or an assistant. In the sanctuary are two early 15C paintings, one of the *Pietà* attributed to Neri di Bicci, and the other of the *Madonna Enthroned* by Giovanni dal Ponte.

Steps lead down behind the Palazzina del Caffè (now a restaurant), built in 1873 by Giuseppe Poggi, to **Piazzale Michelangelo** (**Map 7; 5**), a celebrated viewpoint built c 1875, usually crowded with coaches and tourists. A balustrade surrounds the huge terrace from which there is a remarkable panorama of the city, its surrounding hills and beyond—on a clear day, one can see as far as the plain of Pistoia and the peaks of the Apennines. On the extreme left, are the olive fields on the hillside below Forte di Belvedere (on the skyline), and the city walls descending to Porta San Niccolò. The view down the Arno takes in Ponte Vecchio. On the other side of the river, Palazzo Vecchio can be seen, as well as the top of Orsanmichele, the dome of the Chapel of the Princes (San Lorenzo), the Campanile and cupola of the Duomo, with the stone towers of the Badia and Bargello in front. Nearer at hand is the huge church of Santa Croce and the green dome of the synagogue. Straight ahead is the hill of Fiesole.

The monument to Michelangelo (1875) on the terrace consists of bronze reproductions of some of his famous marble statues in the city. A delightful **Iris Garden** below the terrace is open in May (entrance on the right of the balustrade). On the hillside are some 2500 varieties of iris; a red iris on a white ground is the symbol of Florence. An international competition has been held here annually since 1957.

Viale dei Colli (**Map 7; 6**) is the name given to the sequence of three roads—Viale Michelangelo, Viale Galileo and Viale Machiavelli)—which form a fine roadway 6km long, laid out by Giuseppe Poggi in 1865–70. It is one of the most panoramic drives near Florence, following a winding course from Piazza Ferrucci (**Map 7; 4**) via Piazzale Michelangelo and the steps below San Miniato, to Porta Romana. The Viale is followed by bus 12 and 13 (see above).

Beyond San Miniato, off Viale Galileo, Via dei Giramontino leads up to Torre del Gallo, Arcetri and Pian de' Giullari (described on p 352). Viale Machiavelli, from Piazzale Galileo (**Map 6; 7**) to Porta Romana is particularly attractive, and passes pretty public gardens.

Off Viale Michelangelo, near Ponte San Niccolò (**Map 7; 4**), Via Marsuppini leads into Via Benedetto Fortini. The church of **Santa Maria a Ricorboli**, at the beginning of Via Fortini, contains in a chapel in the north aisle a very late, damaged *Madonna and Child* by Giotto. At no. 30 is **Villa il Tasso** where Roberto Longhi, the art historian, lived from 1939 to 1970. This is now the seat of the Fondazione Longhi. Longhi's interesting collection of paintings, which includes works by Caravaggio and Guido Reni, is preserved here but is not open to the public (open to scholars by prior arrangement).

Via Benedetto Fortini, an attractive old road, continues uphill past the public park of Villa Rusciano. Via Santa Margherita a Montici soon diverges right with a superb view of Florence. It continues all the way to the church of Santa Margherita a Montici (see p 353).

21 • Medieval Florence

This chapter follows an itinerary through many of the oldest streets in the city north of the Arno (the Oltrarno is described in Ch. 19). Important monuments are indicated but described in full in other routes; the objective here is to describe as many as possible of the medieval palaces and towers that survive in the city. Towers were first built in the 12C by wealthy Florentines next to their houses, as refuges in times of trouble, as well as status symbols. The towers had to be lowered after 1250 by order of the regime of the *primo popolo*. Later in the 14C, many of them were adapted as houses. The medieval streets often lie on the courses of their Roman predecessors. Destruction of much of the old city took place at the end of the 19C, when Piazza della Repubblica and its surrounding thoroughfares were laid out, and during the Second World War when the old towers and houses in Via Por Santa Maria and at either end of Ponte Vecchio were destroyed.

Orsanmichele (Map 1; 4), one of the most significant medieval monuments in the city (described in Ch. 3) stands next to the **Palazzo dell'Arte della Lana**, built in 1308 by the Guild of Wool Merchants, but arbitrarily restored in 1905. The *Arte della Lana* represented the most important Florentine industry which was responsible for the city's economic growth in the 13C (it has been estimated that a third of the population was employed in the woollen cloth industry in the 13C–14C). Among the *stemme* on the building is that of the guild, the Agnus Dei. At the base of the tower is the little oratory of **Santa Maria della Tromba** (late 14C), one of the largest of the many tabernacles in the city. It was moved here from the nearby Mercato Vecchio, the commercial centre of the city until the 19C, which was destroyed to make way for Piazza della Repubblica. Behind the neo-Gothic grille is a painting of the *Madonna Enthroned*, by Jacopo del Casentino and, in the lunette, the *Coronation of the Virgin* by Niccolò di Pietro Gerini. On Via Calimala is the 13C Torre Compiobbesi. In a shop here, there are remains of frescoes, including a *Madonna and Child and Two Saints*. On the first floor (admission sometimes granted by the Società Dantesca) are 14C frescoes.

In Via Orsanmichele is Palazzo dell'Arte dei Beccai (no. 4), the headquarters of the Butchers' Guild until 1534; their *stemma* (a goat) can be seen high up on the façade. The palace (c 1415–20) is the seat of the **Accademia delle Arti del Disegno**, the first of all art academies, founded in 1563 by members of the Compagnia di San Luca which already existed by 1339. Admission to the interior is usually granted on written application. The founders included Vasari, Bronzino, Francesco di Giuliano da Sangallo, Ammannati, Vincenzo de' Rossi, and Montorsoli. Cosimo I and Michelangelo were elected the first Academicians. It houses some interesting works of art including a frescoed *Crucifix* removed from a tabernacle in Via dell'Osservatorio, near the Villa della Petraia (see p 357), and a painting of the *Madonna and Saints*, both by Pontormo; a bronze bust of Michelangelo by Daniele da Volterra; and a fresco of the *Madonna and Child with Saints* by Mariotto di Nardo.

Via dell'Arte della Lana crosses Via Lamberti. On the corner is the site of the first headquarters of the Medici bank, set up in 1397 by Giovanni di Bicci, father of Cosimo il Vecchio. At the next intersection, Via Porta Rossa (so-named since at least the beginning of the 13C) leads (right) past the **Mercato Nuovo** (Map 1; 5), the Florentine straw-market (open daily in summer; closed Monday and Sunday in winter). It has been the site of a market since the beginning of the 11C. The loggia was erected by Cosimo I in 1547–51, to a design by Giovanni Battista del Tasso, for the sale of silk and gold. It is now a market-place for cheap lace, straw work, leather goods and souvenirs (usually good value). It is known to Florentines as **Il Porcellino** after a popular statue of a boar on the far side of the loggia. This bronze boar was copied by Tacca from the antique statue in the Uffizi; the delightful base is a copy of the original by Tacca. Coins thrown into the fountain are given to charity. The medieval buildings in Via Por Santa Maria which leads to Ponte Vecchio (Ch. 7) were all destroyed in 1944.

Palazzo Davanzati

Via Porta Rossa continues to Palazzo Davanzati (**Map 1; 5**) now the **Museo della Casa Fiorentina Antica**, and the best surviving example of a medieval nobleman's house in Florence (despite numerous restorations). It has been **closed since 1995** for major structural repairs which are not expected to be completed for another few years. It is particularly interesting as an illustration of Florentine life in the Middle Ages. The palace was built in the mid-14C by the Davizzi family and became the property of Bernardo Davanzati, the successful merchant and scholar, in 1578. It remained in his family until the end of the 19C. In 1904, the palace was bought by the antiquarian and art dealer Elia Volpi who restored it and recreated,

Palazzo Davanzati

with the help of skilled artisans, the interior of a medieval Florentine house. The antiques from his private museum here were later sold to various museums all over the world (in a famous sale in 1916, much of the contents went to American buyers). It helped form the taste of foreigners in furnishing their houses in the early 20C, and the last successful sale of its contents was held in 1929. The Italian State purchased the house in 1951. Interesting graffiti and drawings referring to contemporary events (1441–1516) have been found on many of the walls.

The typical 14C **façade** consists of three storeys above large arches on the ground floor. The proportions have been altered by the loggia at the top which was added in the 16C and probably replaced battlements. The ironwork is interesting and includes brackets which carry diagonal poles across the windows. These were used to hang out the washing, suspend birdcages, or for the hangings which decorated the façade on special occasions. The huge Davanzati coat of arms dates from the 16C; it was brought from another family house close by.

The **interior** is of great interest for its architecture and contemporary wall-paintings, which are rare examples of a decorative form typical of 14C houses. It has been beautifully arranged with the furnishings typical of a Florentine house from the 15C–17C, including tapestries, lacework, ceramics, sculpture, paintings, decorative arts and domestic objects. Furniture from the 16C–17C is a special feature of the house. However, serious structural problems caused by modifications over the centuries have meant that the entire palace has had to be closed, except for the spacious vaulted **entrance hall** which runs the whole width of the building and was used as a loggia, for family ceremonies, and later as shops. Here a few of the contents are temporarily displayed including pieces of restored furniture, the painted wood cupboard (a Sienese work of the 16C) which stored the family weapons, a charming series of hand-warmers in the form of shoes (18C), a case of 15C bas-reliefs, the family tree of the Davanzati, painted in the 17C, detached 15C frescoes from the courtyard, and a terracotta *Madonna Annunciate* attributed to Antonio Rizzo or Nanni di Bartolo.

Next to Palazzo Davanzati is a smaller medieval house (no. 15), and opposite, in the piazza, the old Casa Torre Foresi. Farther along the street on the left, at no. 77 (red), is a tabernacle with a painting of the *Crucifix Between St Nicholas and a Dominican Saint*, attributed to Giovanni Battista Naldini. Just beyond it is the old Albergo Porta Rossa, with a projecting upper storey supported on stone *sporti* and wrought-iron lanterns. The palace was built by the Bartolini-Salimbeni in the early 16C (their heraldic emblems decorate the façade), and the hotel opened here in the mid-19C.

Return along Via Porta Rossa to Via Pellicceria, at the end of which (right) is a little piazza surrounded by an interesting group of old buildings. On the right is Palazzo Giandonati, dating from the 14C, with two arches on the ground floor. Next to it is the 15C Palazzo Canacci (no. 3) with grisaille decoration and a fine loggia (heavily restored at the beginning of this century). At the end is **Palazzo di Parte Guelfa** (Map 1; 5; sometimes open specially by the Assessorato alla Cultura of the Comune, Via Ghibellina 30, ☎ 055 262 5945). This was built as the official residence of the captains of the Guelf party in the 13C. The Parte Guelfa was a political and military organisation which supported the Pope and virtually controlled the government of the city from c 1267 until 1376. The famous feud between the Guelfs and Ghibellines (on the side of the Emperor) coloured much of the history of the city during the Middle Ages (see p 88).

The outside stair was modified by Vasari, who added the pretty little terrace. Beneath the crenellations is a row of *stemme* and a tall Gothic window. In the 15C, the palace was enlarged by Brunelleschi who built a fine hall (since restored).

On the third side of the square is the rough façade of the former church of **Santa Maria Sovraporta** (once used as a fire station, and now a library). The Cappella di San Bartolomeo here (1345–52) preserves interesting frescoes high up in the vault, including a fragment of a townscape attributed to the school of Maso di Banco (restored in 1996).

Vicolo della Seta leads down by the side of the church to the Mercato Nuovo (see above) and Via di Capaccio (right), where the Palazzo dell'Arte della Seta (no. 3) stands. This was established as the headquarters of the guild of the silk-cloth industry at the end of the 14C. It still bears its beautiful *stemma* encircled by cherubs, in the style of Donatello. Next to it, and entering Via delle Terme, is the handsome extension by Brunelleschi to Palazzo di Parte Guelfa (the little loggia on the corner was added by Vasari).

Via delle Terme (Map 1; 5), a pretty medieval street, takes its name from the Roman baths which were in this area. At the beginning (right), by Chiasso Manetti, is the Casa Torre Buondelmonte (Guidi) which faces the back of the medieval portion of Palazzo di Parte Guelfa (see above). On the corner of Chiasso di Misure is another interesting palace (no. 9) with a Renaissance courtyard and (no. 13 red) a medieval tower. Opposite is Palazzo Canacci (see above). Beyond Chiasso Cornino is a small house (no. 17), one storey high, above two wide arches.

The road follows the side of Palazzo Bartolini-Salimbeni (described on p 243), a reconstructed 14C building with stone benches on the pavement, before emerging in Piazza Santa Trinita. Palazzo Spini-Feroni stands here and is the largest private medieval palace in Florence (p 240).

Borgo Santi Apostoli (Map 1; 5), parallel to Via delle Terme and the Arno, leads back out of the square. This was a Roman road which led from outside the south gate of the city to the Cassia. It had received its present name at least by the beginning of the 13C. On the corner of Via delle Bombarde is Palazzo Altoviti with its tower (13C or 14C).

Santi Apostoli

In the attractive little Piazza del Limbo, below the level of the pavement, is the Romanesque stone **façade** of Santi Apostoli (Map 1; 5), one of the oldest churches in the city (mentioned as early as 1075). The handsome doorway (1512) is ascribed to Benedetto da Rovezzano. According to legend, the church was founded by Charlemagne in 786, but it is now thought to date from the 10C when it was built partly on the remains of a Roman building. It was restored in 1938. The east end and campanile, the upper part of which is attributed to Baccio d'Agnolo, can be seen from the piazza behind.

The basilican *interior (opening times 10.00–12.00, 15.00–17.00) probably dating from the 11C and has fine green marble columns and capitals (the first two are from Roman baths). In the north aisle, the first chapel contains the *sinopia of the fresco of the *Madonna and Child*, formerly on the façade, by Paolo Schiavo. In the fourth chapel, there is a *Nativity* by Maso di San Friano and *St Andrew*, and on the side walls, the *Archangel Raphael with Tobias*. At the end of the north aisle is the *tomb of Prior Oddo Altoviti, by Benedetto da Rovezzano (1507; with a classical sarcophagus), and the *tabernacle of the Sacrament (1512) by Andrea della Robbia (and assistants), with two beautiful sculpted panels below from the tomb of Donato Acciaioli (1333). The high altarpiece by the school of Orcagna, and all the altarpieces in the south aisle (by Vasari, Pomarancio and others), have been removed for restoration since the Arno flood of 1966.

In the piazza, Palazzo di Oddo Altoviti (no. 1) is the work of Benedetto da Rovezzano (c 1512; altered). On the other side of the church is **Palazzo Rosselli del Turco** with various inscriptions and a relief of the *Madonna* by Benedetto da Maiano. The main façade in the Borgo is by Baccio d'Agnolo (1517). The *portone* (main entrance) faces a charming little garden, created in 1534. Beyond the picturesque Chiasso Cornino is the **Palazzi Acciaioli** (no. 8; 14C) with a tower, bearing the emblem of the Certosa del Galluzzo, which was founded by Niccolò Acciaioli

(1340–65). Opposite is a building (no. 27 red) parts of which date from the 13C. At no. 19 (red) are the 13C remains of **Palazzo Usimbardi** (Acciaioli) whose main 16C façade on the Arno was destroyed in the Second World War. In the 19C, when it was the Grand Hotel Royal, Ruskin, Dickens, Swinburne, Longfellow and Henry James all stayed here. The original masonry of the Buondelmonti palaces next door has been destroyed except for a 14C rusticated ground floor and a few stone arches; no. 6 is the oldest residence of this Florentine family to have survived; the remainder of the street was badly damaged in the Second World War. On the corner of Via Por Santa Maria is the restored 13C Baldovinetti tower.

Across Por Santa Maria (see above) is a secluded little piazza around **Santo Stefano al Ponte** (Map 1; 5), another very old church, first built in 969, but severely damaged in 1993 when a car bomb (placed by the Mafia) exploded in Via Lambertesca. The handsome Romanesque decoration of the façade dates from 1233. The interior (restored and now used as a concert hall) was altered by Ferdinando Tacca in 1649. It contains altarpieces by Santi di Tito, Matteo Rosselli, and others, a painting by Jacopo di Cione, and a bronze altar frontal of the *Stoning of St Stephen* by Ferdinando Tacca. At the elaborate east end, the altar steps (removed from Santa Trìnita) are a remarkable Mannerist work by Buontalenti (1574). Beneath is a large crypt.

In the Canonry, to the right of the church, the **Museo Diocescano di Santo Stefano al Ponte** was opened in 1996 to display works of art removed here for safe-keeping from churches in the diocese, some of them now deconsecrated, but it is not open regularly (for information, ☎ 055 225 843.

The museum contains some interesting Tuscan works of art from the 14C–15C. In the chapel, there are two polychrome wooden statues of the *Annunciation* attributed to Francesco da Valdàmbrino. In the **Stanza degli Orafi**, there are works by Bicci di Lorenzo and a *Madonna* by the Master of the Madonna Straus and a *Coronation of the Virgin* by Giovanni del Biondo. Stairs lead up to a long **corridor** with a triptych by Lorenzo di Niccolò and a panel by the Master of Santa Verdiana. At the end of the corridor are two paintings of *St Peter*, one by the Master of the Horne Triptych and one by Jacopo di Cione. In a little niche are two *Crucifixes* (one attributed to Parri Spinelli, c 1415) and a marble statuette of the *Madonna and Child* by the *bottega* of Nino Pisano. In another niche is church silver and a reliquary bust by Paolo Laurentin (17C).

The **sacristy** contains the most important works. The *Madonna and Child* by Giotto (from the church of San Giorgio alla Costa, dated 1295–1300) has been heavily restored after damage in 1993. Also here are two *Madonnas* by Domenico Michelino; a bust of the *Blessed Davanzati* by Pietro Tacca; an *Annunciation*, a *Madonna* and a triptych by the Master of the Madonna Straus; an *Annunciation* by Bicci di Lorenzo; *St Julian* by Masolino (c 1420); and an exquisite predella with the *Adoration of the Magi* by Paolo Uccello (c 1437). The carved wooden group of the *Lamentation* is by the *bottega* of Orcagna (1360–65), and the reliquary bust of *San Cresci* by Bernardo Holzmann (on a design by Giovanni Battista Foggini). The church silver exhibited here includes processional crosses from the 9C–15C. Stairs lead up from the corridor, past a terracotta *Nativity* attributed to Benedetto Buglione, to a little room at the top which contains vestments and choir books.

An alley leads past the Casa dell'Orafo, a rambling edifice which is honeycombed with the workshops of numerous Florentine goldsmiths. To the left, the dark Volta dei Girolami is spanned by a series of low arches; at the end, Via del Georgofili leads left to Via Lambertesca (with a glimpse right of the Uffizi). Several guilds had their headquarters in this street. A car bomb exploded here in 1993, killing five people and severely damaging buildings in the street (as well as the Uffizi gallery). The medieval **Torre dei Pulci** was almost totally destroyed but it has been carefully reconstructed. The tower is the headquarters of the **Accademia dei Georgofili**, which was founded in 1753 by Ubaldo Montelatici as the first scientific institute in Europe for the study of agriculture. Most of its precious archives were salvaged after the 1993 explosion.

Chiasso dei Baroncelli, a narrow medieval lane on which stands the 14C Palazzo Benini Formichi, leads left to emerge in Piazza della Signoria, dominated by Palazzo Vecchio, begun in 1298 (described in Ch. 5). Via Calimaruzza, another road leading into the piazza (left) was the seat from the late 14C of the Arte di Calimala (the wholesale cloth importers). Their *stemma* (an eagle holding a bale of cloth in its talons) survives at no. 2a.

Via de' Calzaioli leads out of the north side of Piazza della Signoria and Via Condotta soon diverges right. On the corner of the old Vicolo dei Cerchi is the well-preserved Palazzo Cerchi (no. 52 red), dating from the 13C. Beyond, Via delle Farine (right) has a good view of Palazzo Vecchio with its tower. The shop windows in Via Condotta are framed by a series of medieval arches.

On the corner of **Via dei Cerchi**—a local shopping street, with pretty iron lamp brackets—is the medieval Palazzo Giugni (reconstructed). The street leads north to Via dei Cimatori (Canto alla Quarconia) on the corner of which is a tabernacle, lit by a wrought-iron lamp, with a fresco of the *Madonna and Child Appearing to St Philip Neri* by Alessandro Gherardini. Also here is the Torre Cerchi (1292–98), and on Via dei Tavolini stands Torre Greci (Galigai) of the 12C–13C. Via dei Cimatori (with a view left of Orsanmichele, and right of the towers of the Bargello and the Badia) continues right from Via dei Cerchi to Via dei Magazzini in which is the large convent building (with a fine court-yard) of the Badia (see Ch. 14) stands. It is now occupied by the law courts, the entrance to which is (left) in the little **Piazza San Martino**. The splendid 13C Torre della Castagna stands here; it is one of the best-preserved medieval tow-ers in the city and was the residence of the *Priori* in 1282, before they moved to Palazzo Vecchio.

The charming little oratory of **San Martino del Vescovo** or San Martino dei Buonomini (**Map 1; 4**; opening times 10.00–12.00, 15.00–17.00, except *fest.* and some Friday afternoons) is near the site of the 10C parish church of the Alighieri and Donati families. On the exterior there is a tabernacle showing *St Martin Distributing Alms* by Cosimo Ulivelli. The chapel was rebuilt in 1479 when it became the seat of the Compagnia dei Buonomini di San Martino, a charitable institution of 'good men' founded in 1442 by St Antoninus for Florentine citizens (often merchants) who had fallen into penury, sometimes for political reasons, and were too proud to beg for charity. It was administered by 12 men who each held the office of *Proposto* for one month of the year, and the char-ter stipulated that alms should be distributed as soon as they were collected. When their resources ran out, the Compagnia would light a candle (*lumicino*) over the doorway to alert the populace to their need for funds (a Florentine expression *essere al lumicino* survives to this day, indicating that someone is in dire straights). The 12 members of the confraternity, with their assistants, still meet in a hall behind the oratory every Friday afternoon to deliberate: they receive written requests for financial help and then decide how to distribute the donations they receive (visitors are kindly asked to make a contribution).

Inside, the lunettes are decorated with charming *frescoes by the workshop of Domenico Ghirlandaio (also attributed to Francesco d'Antonio del Chierico). They are of great interest for their portrayal of contemporary Florentine life. They illustrate the seven works of mercy carried out by the Buonomini: (over the entrance) the **Distribution of Clothing**, **Giving Food and Drink to the Hungry and Thirsty**, and (on the left wall): **Visiting the Sick**, **Visiting Prisoners** (the grey-haired official in a red cloak shows the influence of Filippino Lippi), **Giving Lodging to Travellers** and **Burying the Dead**. On the altar wall are two scenes from the Life of St Martin: the **Saint Martin Dividing his Cloak with a Poor Man**, and **Christ Appearing to the Saint Martin in a Dream Wearing his Cloak** (the angels show the influence of Botticelli). On the right wall are two scenes of the Buonomini at work: **Compiling an Inventory of Possessions Left to Them in a Will** and **Providing a Poor Girl with a Dowry in a Marriage Settlement**. Also here are two beautiful *paintings of the **Madonna**, one of them Byzantine (11C) and the other attributed Nicolò Soggi, but very close to the work of Perugino. On the altar is a bust of **St Antoninus** attributed to Verrocchio. Two terracotta **Angels** by the school of Verrocchio are kept in the meeting hall.

On the wall of a trattoria (no. 4) in the piazza, a terracotta roundel of Mariotto Albertinelli records the Florentine painter who opened a restaurant here. The so-called **Casa di Dante**—where the poet is said to have been born—is one of a group of 13C-style houses that were restored in 1911. It contains a museum on three floors with material (little of it original) relating to Dante. Opening times 10.00–16.00 or 18.00 except Tues; Sun 10.00–14.00 (☎ 055 219 416); Lire 5000.

Dante Alighieri

This area of Florence is associated with the greatest of all Italian poets: Dante Alighieri (1265–1231), who was born in the city, probably on the present Via Dante Alighieri. His famous *Divina Commedia* established Tuscan as the literary vernacular of Italy. His master was the Florentine poet Brunetto Latini, and he was a friend of Giotto. As a young man he fought in the huge battle of Campaldino in the Casentino (1289) on the winning (Guelf) side against the Ghibellines of Arezzo. He became one of the six priors of the city in 1300 but was exiled in 1302 for political reasons and never returned to Florence (he died in Ravenna in 1321). His love for Beatrice inspired much of his work: Boccaccio, his biographer, identified her as the daughter of Folco Portinari, although Dante married Gemma Donati.

Via Santa Margherita continues past the little church of **Santa Margherita de' Cerchi**, of 12C foundation, where Dante is supposed to have married Gemma Donati. The 14C porch bears the arms of the Cerchi, Adimari and Donati who lived in the parish. In the interior, there is a lovely altarpiece of the *Madonna Enthroned with Four Female Saints* by Neri di Bicci.

An archway leads out onto the **Corso** (Map 1; 4), a Roman road. The church (left) of **Santa Margherita in Santa Maria de' Ricci** (1508) is preceded by a portico by Gherardo Silvani (1611). The interior was reconstructed by Zanobi del Rosso in 1769, and contains paintings by Giovanni Camillo Sagrestani (1707). Nearly opposite is the 13C Torre dei Donati.

Some way along the Corso (left) are several 12C towers on the corner of Via Sant'Elisabetta. The ancient round Torre La Pagliazza in Piazza Sant'Elisabetta was used as a prison in the 13C–14C. It was over-restored in 1988 for use as a hotel. **Via Sant'Elisabetta** leads to Via delle Oche with the 14C Palazzo Visdomini (restored) and its tower. On the corner of Via dello Studio (right) and Via della Canonica is the 13C Palazzo Tedaldini. Via della Canonica is another pretty old street (see p 118). **Via dello Studio** slopes gently downhill to the Duomo (good view of the cupola) and back to the Corso. The ground floor arches betray the medieval origins of the street. A doorway here is surmounted by a pretty Della Robbian lunette.

On the corner of the Corso is **Palazzo Salviati** (now the head office of the Banca Toscana), built in 1470–80 by the Portinari family, famous bankers in the 15C. In 1546, the palace was bought and enlarged by Jacopo Salviati, nephew of Maria Salviati, wife of Giovanni delle Bande Nere and mother of Cosimo I. In the banking hall there is a 14C fresco of the *Madonna and Child*. Other parts of the palace may sometimes be seen on special request. The charming little interior courtyard which dates from 1577 is flanked by two barrel-vaulted loggie decorated with mythological subjects including the *Story of Ulysses* by Alessandro Allori (with the help of Giovanni Maria Butteri and others). Another room here has a vault with *grotteschi* and small scenes of the *Labours of Hercules*. The chapel was also decorated by Allori, and a *galleria* was added in 1783 with frescoes by Tommaso Gherardini.

The Corso continues east and ends at the Canto de' Pazzi, on the site of the east gate of the Roman city; across Via del Proconsolo **Borgo degli Albizi** (Map 4; 7) follows the line of the Roman Cassia. The Borgo is named after one of the wealthiest families in Florence in the 14C and 15C who owned numerous palaces in the street. It is one of the most handsome streets in the city. The magnificent palaces at its entrance, Palazzo Pazzi and Palazzo Nonfinito, are described in Chapter 14. Next to Palazzo Pazzi (right) is a palace with 15C rustication on the ground floor. Opposite, **Palazzo Vitali** (no. 28) is a beautiful building attributed to Bartolommeo Ammannati (late 16C), with a handsome coat of arms. Next to it, **Palazzo Matteucci Ramirez di Montalvo** (no. 26) is a severe work also by Ammannati (1568). The graffiti decoration is attributed to Bernardino Poccetti. The owner set up the arms of his friend Cosimo I on the façade. On the corner of Via de' Giraldi is a 14C tabernacle with the *Madonna Enthroned*.

Further on, by Volta dei Ciechi, there is a house (no. 22) with medieval fragments. This is next to the huge **Palazzo Altoviti** (or dei Visacci; no. 18), which dates from the early 15C. It was enlarged in the late 16C when the amusing marble portraits of celebrated Florentine citizens by Caccini were placed on the façade. Facing a piazzetta is a narrow 14C house (no. 14). Beyond is the grandiose **Palazzo degli Albizi** (no. 12), the principal residence of the Albizi, a famous Florentine family (see above). The 14C fabric survives on the left, and the nine bays on the right were reconstructed by Silvani in the 17C. Opposite, an attractive palace stands next to the larger **Palazzo degli Alessandri** (no. 15), the best-pre-served palace on the street. A worn cornice divides the two storeys of its fine 14C façade in *pietra forte*, rusticated on the lower part. Canova had his studio here. On the left, no. 10 has a bust of poet *Vincenzo Filicaia* (1642–1707), who was born here. On the right is a 16C house (no. 11) with a marble bust of *Cosimo II*. A medieval tower, which belonged to the Donati, rises from the top of this house.

The small **Piazza San Pier Maggiore** (Map 4; 7) is the centre of a local shop-ping area with its handful of colourful market stalls. The 17C portico by Nigetti is all that survives of the church which gave the square its name. The little Palazzo Corbizzi (no. 1) dates from the 13C. Next to a pretty house with a pro-jecting upper storey rises the splendid 13C **Torre Donati** (Cocchi). Just out of the piazzetta, beyond the Volta di San Piero, an archway with shops, is the 14C–15C Palazzo Albizi (enlarged in the 16C and restored).

Via Matteo Palmieri (**Map 7; 1**; with a worn terracotta relief of the *Madonna and Child* on the corner) crosses Via Pandolfini and Via Ghibellina. In Via Pandolfini (right) the palace at no. 14 was built for Baccio Valori who led the siege of Florence in 1530 and was hanged in Piazza della Signoria in 1537 by order of Cosimo I. In the other direction, at no. 5 (on the corner of Via Verdi) is the **Oratorio di San Niccolò al Ceppo** (open for concerts) which was built in 1561 for a confraternity founded in the 14C. In the vestibule are two oval paint-ings of *Saints* by Onorio Marinari (1695) and a *trompe l'œil* ceiling by Giovanni Domenico Ferretti (c 1735). The statue in stucco of the *Madonna and Child* is by Camillo Camillani (1572). The Oratory has 17C wooden benches and a frescoed ceiling by Ferretti, Pietro Anderlini, and Domenico and Francesco Papi. The altarpiece of the *Crucifixion* is by Francesco Curradi, and on the walls are two paintings of the *Visitation* and *St Nicholas with Two Members of the Confraternity* by Giovanni Antonio Sogliani (1517–21). A *Crucifixion with Saint Nicholas of Bari and Saint Francis* by Fra' Angelico has recently been returned here. Outside on the corner of the street (Canto alla Badessa) is a taber-nacle with a 16C fresco of the *Annunciation* by Giovanni Balducci.

On the corner of Via Ghibellina stands the 14C Palazzo Salviati Quaratesi. The ground floor provided room for stores and shops. The large tabernacle in Via Ghibellina protects a fresco of *Senator Girolamo Novelli Displaying Acts of Charity to Prisoners* by Giovanni di San Giovanni (c 1616). Beyond is the entrance to the huge **Teatro Verdi**, founded by Girolamo Pagliano and built by Telemaco Bonaiuti, which opened in 1854 and can seat 1500 spectators. The largest cin-ema screen in Italy was installed here after 1966. It is also used for theatre perfor-mances, and concerts (it is the seat of the Orchestra Regionale Toscana).

At no. 110 in Via Ghibellina is the grandiose **Palazzo Borghese**, with a neo-classical façade by Gaetano Baccani (1822). It was built in less than a year by Camillo Borghese, husband of Pauline Bonaparte (sister of Napoleon I), for a party to celebrate the marriage of Ferdinando III. The elaborate period rooms (now used by a club; admission sometimes granted) include the Galleria and Salone degli Specchi which are heavily decorated with chandeliers and gilded mir-rors. The towers of the Bargello and the Badia can be seen at the end of the street.

Via delle Stinche, named after a prison on this site since the early 14C, contin-ues across Via Ghibellina past **Palazzo da Cintoia** (Salviati), one of the most interesting medieval palaces to survive in the city. It dates from the 14C, and its façade in *pietra forte* has picturesque *sporti*. In Via della Vigna Vecchia is the 14C Palazzo Covoni (no. 9).

In the little piazza stands the church of **San Simone** (Map 7; 1; open for services only), founded in 1192–93. The fine doorway is in the style of Benedetto da Rovezzano. The sombre interior is by Gherardo Silvani (1630), with a carved 17C wooden ceiling. The fine painting of *St Peter Enthroned* (first altar on the right) was painted by the Master of Santa Cecilia in 1307. *Christ Showing his Wounds to St Bernard* (1623) by Jacopo Vignali hangs over the last altar on the south side. At the end of the north side, there is a charming Gothic tabernacle (1363) with a 15C *Bust of a Lady* surrounded by enamelled terracotta decoration by the Della Robbia.

Opposite is *Vivoli*, the best-known ice-cream shop in the city. Beyond Via della Burella (right) with another medieval house, the streets follow the shape of the Roman amphitheatre which was built here in the 2C–3C AD. It is estimated that it was big enough to hold about 15,000 spectators. Via dei Bentaccordi follows the curve across Via Anguillara (with a view left of the Pazzi Chapel in Santa Croce) and Borgo dei Greci into **Piazza Peruzzi**, named after the famous Florentine family of bankers who reached their greatest prosperity at the end of the 13C. The medieval buildings here include the reconstructed Palazzo Peruzzi (13C–14C).

An archway leads out into the busy **Via dei Benci** (Map 7; 1) with its old rusticated houses. The view to the left is closed by the tower of the Duomo of Fiesole; to the right, across the river, the green hills of the Oltrarno provide a background to the medieval buildings in Piazza dei Mozzi. At no. 20, **Palazzo Mellini Fossi** has a façade frescoed for Domenico Mellini in 1575 with delightful mythological scenes of *Perseus and Andromeda*. This was one of the first of many palaces in Florence to be decorated with frescoes on its façade but by the beginning of the twentieth century only traces of them survived: they were restored by the present owners in 1996. Well sited on the corner of Borgo Santa Croce is the splendid polygonal 13C Torre degli Alberti, with a 15C loggia below. The interesting palaces in the Borgo are described on p 272.

On Corso dei Tintori is Palazzo Alberti (late 14C or early 15C) with a good courtyard. The church of **San Jacopo tra i Fossi** (now the Evangelical church) has a fine 18C ceiling incorporating a painting by Alessandro Gherardini. Opposite the 15C Palazzo Corsi (no. 6; described, with the Museo Horne, in Ch. 17) are several handsome palaces. **Palazzo Bardi alle Grazie** (Serzelli; no. 5) is an early Renaissance palace attributed to Brunelleschi (c 1430) with a fine courtyard. Here the famous *Camerata fiorentina di Casa Bardi* introduced operatic melodrama in 1598. **Palazzo Malenchini** (no. 1) was reconstructed in the 19C on the site of a 14C palace, the residence of the Alberti, an influential merchant family who were exiled in 1387 for political reasons. The great architect Leon Battista Alberti (who had been born while the family were in exile in Genoa) died here in 1472, as a plaque on the building records.

On the other side of Via de' Benci, **Via dei Neri** (Map 6; 2), named after the confraternity who comforted criminals on their way from the Bargello to execution, leads back towards Palazzo Vecchio (which can be seen at the end of the street). At the beginning, on the right, Via delle Brache has medieval houses with *sporti*. On Via de' Rustici, Palazzo Rustici (Neri) dates from the end of the 14C. The road bends at its junction with Via Mosca following the shape of the Roman port. Here, at no. 23, is the 14C Palazzo Soldani.

A road (right) with plaques showing the water levels of the Arno in the floods of 1333 and 1966, leads to the church of **San Remigio** (Map 6; 2; opening times 09.00–11.00, 16.00–18.30 except Sun) founded in the 11C, with an exterior in *pietra forte*. The **interior** (restored), a fine Gothic hall, contains fresco fragments by the school of Giotto and worn roundels of *Saints* in the vaults (14C). The beautiful panel painting of the *Madonna and Child* in the chapel to the right of the sanctuary is by a follower of Cimabue known from this work as the Master of San Remigio. In the chapel to the left of the sanctuary is a remarkable painting of the *Immaculate Conception* by Empoli, which dates from 1591. In a room below the campanile (admission on request), there are monochrome frescoes with hunting scenes, and in the refectory of the former convent upstairs are more very worn monochrome frescoes of the *Last Supper* and *Passion* scenes.

Farther along Via dei Neri (corner of Via del Guanto) is the 14C Palazzo Fagni (no. 35) next to the Loggia del Grano (**Map 1; 6**), a market erected at the time of Cosimo II by Giulio Parigi and his son Alfonso. In the piazza here work has been under way for years to build a new exit from the Uffizi galleries. Via della Ninna emerges in Piazza della Signoria (Ch. 4).

22 • The Viali

Wide avenues (or *viali*) were laid out in 1865–69 by Giuseppe Poggi after he had demolished the last circle of walls built around the north part of the city in 1284–1333. The architect left some of the medieval gates as isolated monuments in the course of this ring-road, which is now busy with traffic. The following places are not worth visiting on foot, so you should use public transport:

- the park of the **Cascine**: bus B from Ponte Vecchio or one of the *lungarni* north of the river to Piazzale Vittorio Veneto; bus no. 12 from Piazza Santa Maria Novella; or bus no. 17C from Piazza Unità Italiana near the Stazione Santa Maria Novella to Piazzale Kennedy in the centre of the park. On Sundays a small electric bus traverses the park from Piazzale Vittorio Veneto;
- the **Museo Stibbert**: bus no. 4 from Piazza Unità Italiana to Via Vittorio Emanuele;
- the **Cenacolo di San Salvi**: bus no. 6 from Via Tornabuoni and Piazza San Marco to the San Salvi request stop in Via Lungo l'Affrico.

Le Cascine
The main entrance to the park of the Cascine (**Map 2; 5**) is near the foot of Ponte della Vittoria by an equestrian statue of Vittorio Emanuele II (removed from Piazza della Repubblica) by Emilio Zocchi. It is the largest public park in Florence (160 hectares), which, although only a few hundred metres wide, skirts the Arno for 3.5km, with fine woods. During the day it is used as a recreation ground

by Florentines, old and young, and huge public concerts and festivals are held here in summer. Not as well maintained as it might be, it is not enclosed and it is not advisable to visit the park at night. Discussions have been under way for many years about the need to restore the gardens, replant the woods, and eliminate all motor traffic. A big general market (excellent value) is held here on Tuesdays and the *Festa del Grillo* (see p 54) on Ascension Day.

History of the Cascine

The park has its origins in the lands of a dairy-farm (*cascina*) that were acquired by Duke Alessandro de' Medici; it was later enlarged by Cosimo I. It was used as a ducal chase in the 17C, and public spectacles and festivals were held here under the Grand-duke Pietro Leopoldo in the 18C. The grounds were planned as a huge park by Elisa Baciocchi Bonaparte and first opened regularly to the public c 1811. Orchards and vegetable gardens used to be cultivated on the fertile, well-watered land in the first part of the park, and, beyond the present Piazzale delle Cascine, there were woods where deer were hunted.

The park now contains various sports grounds and a swimming-pool. The trees include pines (introduced in the mid-19C), plane trees, limes, oak, ilex, cypress and yew. The pleasant area along the river has numerous poplars. On Viale degli Olmi is the **Narcissus fountain**, on which a plaque (1954) commemorates the composition of Shelley's *Ode to the West Wind* which was 'conceived and chiefly written' here in 1819. In the central Piazzale delle Cascine is the **Palazzina Reale** (the seat of the faculty of Agriculture of Florence University since 1914) which was built by Giuseppe Manetti in 1785. Nearby, since 1997, are the stables of 12 horses and carriages which serve as horse-cabs for tourists. In Piazzale Kennedy, near the footbridge which leads over the Arno, and the terminus of bus 17C, is a **Monument to George Washington** donated by the British and American residents in Florence in 1932. The Viale dell'Aeronautica continues past the buildings of **Scuola di Guerra Aerea** built in 1938 by Raffaello Fagnoni (with mural decorations inside by Giovanni Colacicchi) to the far end of the park where the **Monumento dell'Indiano**. This was designed by G.F. Fuller (1874) to commemorate Rajaram Chuttraputti, the Maharajah of Kolhapur who died in Florence in 1870 at the age of 20 and was cremated here at the confluence of the Arno and Mugnone rivers. From here the view is dominated by a suspension bridge built over the Arno in 1978.

Near Piazza Vittorio Veneto (in Corso Italia) is the **Teatro Comunale** (Map 2; 6), the most important concert hall in the city, with a seating capacity of 2100. The disappointing interior was rebuilt in 1961. Nearby, on **Lungarno Vespucci**, is the American Consulate in a building by Giuseppe Poggi (1860).

Porta al Prato (Map 2; 6) is an isolated gateway (1284) from the city walls. Here Il Prato leads right to **Palazzo Corsini sul Prato**, begun in 1591–94 by Buontalenti. It was acquired in 1621 by Filippo di Lorenzo Corsini who employed Gherardo Silvani to complete the palace and garden. Prince Charles Stuart stayed as a guest here in 1774–77. It is still the residence of the Corsini family and the fine **garden**, beautifully maintained, with interesting statuary and parterres can be seen on request Mon–Sat 09.00–13.00, 14.00–17.00

(entrance at no. 58 Via il Prato; ☎ 055 210 564; Lire 12,000).

At no. 9 Via Bernardo Rucellai is **St James's church** (Map 2; 6), the American Episcopal church (open for services, and admission on request in the morning). It is a neo-Gothic building (1911) with good stained glass by Italian craftsmen.

On the right (no. 85) is the 17C **Palazzo degli Orti Oricellari**, formerly Ginori-Venturi, now owned by a bank (**Map 2; 6**), which contains a fresco by Pietro da Cortona. The **Orti Oricellari** (open only on certain days of the year) were a famous Renaissance *selva* (forest). The colossal 17C statue of *Polyphemus* is by Antonio Novelli (it can be seen through the trees in winter from Via Bernardo Rucellai).

Nearby, in Via Santa Lucia, is the church of **Santa Lucia** with a façade dating from 1838 and a pleasant interior of 1720. In the sanctuary is a fine marble ciborium (15C–16C). Near the church is a tall 19C palace built in a neo-Gothic style by Ignazio Villa.

The Viale continues to an underpass beneath the railway; the handsome subsidiary entrance to the station for pedestrians was designed in 1990 by Gae Aulenti. **Santa Maria Novella Railway Station** (Map 3; 5) is a functional building dating from 1935 designed by a group of very gifted young Tuscan architects, including Giovanni Michelucci, Piero Berardi and Italo Gamberini. In the café inside there are two paintings by Ottone Rosai.

Fortezza da Basso

Viale Filippo Strozzi continues round the huge pentagonal Fortezza da Basso (**Map 3; 1,3**; admission only when exhibitions are in progress), a building which has always been something of a white elephant. It is a massive fortress designed by Antonio da Sangallo the Younger and is of the first importance in the history of military architecture. The exterior wall in brick and *pietra forte* is still intact.

The fortezza was erected by order of Alessandro de' Medici in 1534 to strengthen his position in the city as first Duke of Florence, and as a refuge in times of trouble. It became a symbol of Medici tyranny, and Alessandro was assassinated here by his cousin Lorenzino in 1537. It was very soon obsolete as the grand-dukes had little need to defend themselves. In later centuries, it was used as a prison, arsenal and barracks. After years of neglect and discussion about its future, many of the buildings were altered or destroyed when it became an exhibition centre in 1967. The area within the walls was brutally transformed when a huge prefabricated steel building covered with aluminium was built in 1978, and another (circular) one in 1987; yet another new pavilion is planned. Here the Mostra dell'Artigianato and the prestigious 'Pitti' fashion shows are held annually.

The entrance on Viale Strozzi is through the 16C keep designed by Sangallo which incorporates the medieval tower of Porta Faenza. A long 19C building has been used since 1966 as a restoration centre (with a scientific laboratory) for paintings, frescoes, and works of art in wood and paper, by the Opificio delle Pietre Dure (see p 191). An adjacent building was restored in 1999 as an extension to the centre, but other buildings are now derelict. Archaeological finds, including Roman material, have been made here. Public gardens have been laid out on the glacis.

Opposite the Fortezza, across Viale Filippo Strozzi, is **Palazzo dei Congressi**, an international conference centre opened in 1964 on the site of a Contini-Bonacossi villa. It is surrounded by a park created in 1871 by the French poet Alphonse Lamartine. Nearby at No. 10 is a splendid building which houses part of the archive of the **Istituto Geografico Militare** (see Ch. 10), principally maps made after 1963 (also on sale to the public).

A short way to the southeast of the Fortezza (reached by Via Ridolfi) is **Piazza dell'Indipendenza** (Map 3; 4), laid out in 1869 as the first of the 19C squares in Florence. Here there are statues of Bettino Ricasoli and Ubaldino Peruzzi, mayor of Florence in 1870. At the north corner stands the Villino Trollope, home of the Trollope family in 1848–66, where, on a visit to Florence in 1857, Anthony wrote *Doctor Thorne*. In 1887, Thomas Hardy stayed in a *pensione* here.

About 2km north of the Fortezza da Basso (for the bus to Via Vittorio Emanuele II, see above) is **Villa Fabbricotti** (no. 48 Via Vittorio Emanuele II), now the seat of the Università per gli Stranieri. The beautiful **park** (also entered from Via Federico Stibbert), with ilexes, cypresses, limes, elms, laurels and cedars of Lebanon, is open to the public (an area reserved for children is open in the afternoon). The villa was restored in 1864 and leased to the British Consul who arranged for Queen Victoria to stay here in 1894.

Museo Stibbert

Villa Fabbricotti adjoins the park of the Museo Stibbert, entered from Via Federico Stibbert (for the bus from the centre of Florence, see p 326).

• **Opening times** Mon, Tues and Wed 10.00–14.00; Fri, Sat and Sun 10.00–18.00; closed Thurs; tours begin every 30 minutes and last 1 hour (☎ 055 486 049); Lire 8000. The Japanese collection has been closed since 1988, but there are plans to open it for pre-booked visits while restoration of the upper floor proceeds. There is a little **café** on the ground floor with a few tables in the garden.

History of the Museo Stibbert

The museum was created by Frederick Stibbert (1838–1906) in his home here. He had an Italian mother, and was born in Florence. Having inherited a great fortune, he became a collector, traveller, artist and, in 1866, a Garibaldian hero. He bequeathed his museum to the British Government which then passed it on to the city of Florence. He built this huge, rambling villa (incorporating part of an earlier building) in 1878–1905 with Cesare Fortini as architect, and employed Gaetano Bianchi, Annibale Gatti and others to decorate the interior. One part of the house was designed by Stibbert as a museum, and the other part he used as his residence.

The **park** (opening times daily, 09.00–dusk, except Thurs), also created by Stibbert, is landscaped in Victorian style and planted with conifers. It is in urgent need of restoration. Near the house is a Gothic terrace with a Venetian well-head and Gothic architectural fragments. Further downhill, on a lake, is an Egyptian temple, perhaps designed by J.B. Papworth, guarded by lions and sphinxes. The orangery was designed by Giuseppe Poggi, and the terracotta statues were probably produced by the Cantagalli workshop.

The numerous period rooms in the museum were designed for Stibbert's collections; alterations made since his death in an attempt to rationalise the arrangement are being slowly eliminated and the rooms are being restored, where possible, to their original appearance. There are also long-term plans to move the museum's entrance to the centre of the building. The north wing is currently used for special exhibitions of the collections which are changed every year. The exterior of the building is covered with a miscellany of escutcheons, plaquettes, Della Robbian works, *stemme*, garlands, tabernacles and other decorative details.

The eclectic collection has a remarkably bizarre atmosphere with 57 rooms heavily decorated and crammed with an extraordinary variety of objects. Stibbert's particular interest and field of study was armour and costume, and his collection is famous for its armour (including a remarkable collection of Asiatic armour).

Ground floor

The present entrance leads into the rooms designed by Stibbert as a museum. The **Sala della Malachite** (2), arranged as it was in Stibbert's day, is named after the malachite fireplace and tables, including the splendid table in the centre of the room in the Empire style, made by Henri Auguste for the Demidoff family. On the mantlepiece are fine gilded candelabra. The tournament and battle armour displayed here was made c 1540–80. The tapestries include one made in Brussels c 1520 with the **Resurrection of Lazarus** and one designed by Giulio Romano illustrating the **Meeting between Hannibal and Scipio**. The two paintings of **Susanna and the Elders** and the **Daughters of Lot** are by Luca Giordano. One of the fine *cassone* frontals was painted by the *bottega* of Francesco di Giorgio Martini. The paintings, of most interest for the costume of their sitters, include a fully armed **St Michael** by Cosimo Rosselli.

The two small adjoining rooms (3 and 4), both with fine Murano chandeliers, are called the **Salottino Luigi XV**—with period rococo furnishings—and the **Salottino Olandese**, which displays Flemish and Dutch paintings. In the **Sala del Condottiere** (5), decorated by Gaetano Bianchi, is a fully armed 15C condottiere mounted on his steed, and a display of pole arms. There are also cases with Etruscan, Roman and Lombard armour, and one of the finest collections of spurs in existence.

In the **Salone dell'Armeria** (9), or Salone della Cavalcata, Stibbert's original arrangement has been restored. It is a great neo-Gothic hall built by Cesare Fortini and frescoed by Gaetano Bianchi with a cavalcade of fully armed horses and knights of the 16C, with six soldiers wearing 16C Oriental armour. 16C armour is displayed in front of the fireplace; the armour found in the tomb of Giovanni dalle Bande Nere is also exhibited here. There are also three large Brussels tapestries with the **Labours of Hercules** which date from c 1535–50, while above the entrance there is a life-size equestrian model of **St George** designed by Stibbert. From the balcony, Queen Victoria took pleasure in watching the building works. The **Sala del Cavaliere Francese** (11) is named after a mounted French cavalier (1650). The funerary monument from south Germany in polychrome wood dates from 1732.

At this point, the series of rooms that formed Stibbert's private home begins. The **Sala Inglese** (12) was formerly the billiard room. It has interesting Art

Nouveau decorations including delightful Copeland tiles and stained glass windows. The entrance door was decorated with Pre-Raphaelite paintings by Stibbert himself. The room contains English and German armour, and 18C and 19C arms. Beyond it the **Vecchio Studiolo** (13) has more arms. The **Sala della Porcellana** (14) has a fine collection of porcelain, some of it Oriental. **Room 15** continues the Oriental porcelain display and also contains gilded bronze objects. The **Salotto di Giulia** (16) has interesting furnishings. **Rooms 17** and **18** contain a display of firearms and 19C armour.

The **Galleria** (28), or corridor outside the ballroom, contains 17C cabinets, stained glass and small bronzes, as well as Stibbert family portraits. The **Salone da Ballo** (26), with a frieze painted by Annibale Gatti, has been restored to its original appearance, with French Empire-style furniture and portraits including one of Stibbert as an old man by Edoardo Gelli (on the entrance wall), and of Giulia Stibbert and her daughter by Cesare Mussini (1853). The charming little Art Nouveau **Fumoir** (27), or smoking room, was created in 1890 and entirely decorated with ceramics from the Ulisse Cantagalli workshop. Cantagalli, who married Margaret Todd, carried out a lot of work in Florence for the Anglican community, and his ceramics show the influence of William Morris and William de Morgan. The statue of *Sleep* is by Tito Sarrocchi.

The **Sala da Pranzo** (29) has also been restored to its original appearance as the family dining room. Beyond the Salotto di Giulia, the **Saletta Bianca** (30) has stucco decorations modelled on those at Fontainebleau. Hunting weapons are exhibited here and a collection of porcelain is temporarily housed in this room. The four cabinets are made out of ebony and tortoiseshell. The **Sala Rossa** (31) has interesting furniture, a Murano mirror and chandelier, and portraits. The painting of *Mary Magdalen* is a fine work by Alessandro Allori. Beyond the Sala della Porcellana is the **Sala delle Bandiere** (32), named after the Sienese flags used at the Palio which decorate the ceiling. This room displays the best paintings in the collection, including a *Madonna and Child* by the school of Botticelli, *Saints Catherine and Dominic* by Carlo Crivelli, a *Madonna and Child* and two *Saints* by the Master of Verucchio, and a *Portrait of a Man* in profile. Also here are three *cassoni* with gesso decoration and two painted *cassone* frontals. The **hall** (33) is situated at the former main entrance to the house. This contains a portrait of *Ferdinando and Anna Maria Ludovica Medici with Their Governess* by Justus Sustermans.

First floor

A staircase leads up to the first floor. **Room 34** has a *Madonna Enthroned* attributed to Jacopo di Cione and a *Madonna and Child* by Mariotto di Nardo, wooden sculptures, church silver and reliquaries. **Room 35**, which overlooks the great hall, is normally closed to visitors. **Room 36** was decorated with *stucchi* in 1880 and contains a *Crucifixion* by Pietro Lorenzetti and his *bottega*, and a fine collection of church vestments (late 15C–18C). The pretty **Salotto Luigi XVI** (37) has furnishings made in 1880 by Tassinari Chatel of Lyons (to be restored by the same firm). **Rooms 38–41** display part of the fine collection of costumes as well as portraits, which are again of principal interest for the dress of their sitters. **Room 38** has neoclassical frescoes by Luigi Ademollo, which already decorated this part of the house before Stibbert bought it. **Rooms 42–44** contain Tuscan furniture and a display of fans. The **gallery** (46) overlooking the Salone da Ballo will display 19C ballgowns.

Beyond Room 47 is the **Camera da Letto** (48), Stibbert's bedroom, which has been restored to its original appearance. The paintings, some by Stibbert, include an interesting view of the property before his alterations. There are also family photographs and Stibbert's full dress kilt. The **Camera dell'Impero** (49), Stibbert's mother's bedroom, was also frescoed by Luigi Ademollo and is furnished in the Empire style. The **Sala Impero** (50), the former Loggetta, has splendid period decorations and contains Napoleon Bonaparte's costume worn at his coronation as king of Italy in 1805. The delightful **Salotto Giallo** (51) has Venetian furnishings and paintings. Beyond Room 38 (see above), **Room 52** has a notable collection of fabrics, mostly Italian (15C–18C).

The staircase leads back down to the ground floor. Beyond the Sala della Cavalcata a spiral staircase leads up to three rooms decorated by Gaetano Bianchi in neo-Gothic style, called the **Sale Japanese** (55–57). These are closed for restoration (see above), but usually contain the best ***collection of Japanese armour** in Europe (particularly notable for the arms and armour of the Edo period), as well as an interesting collection of swords and saddles. At the foot of the spiral staircase are the last two rooms (7 and 6) which display the splendid ***collection of Oriental armour**, much of it Turkish and used for the first time by Sultan Selim I at the end of the 15C. Also displayed here are Persian and Indian arms and armour and costumes. The stucco decoration of **Room 6** is modelled on the Alhambra, and the floor tiles were made by the Cantagalli workshop.

Viale Lavagnini continues from the Fortezza da Basso towards Piazza della Libertà. In Via Leone X (left) is the **Russian church** (Map 3; 2) built with funds raised from the large Russian colony in Florence (including the Demidoff family) and consecrated in 1904. Throughout most of the 19C, Florence was a fashionable place to spend the winter for many aristocratic Russian families. The architects of the fine building came from Russia, and the pretty majolica decoration on the exterior was carried out by the Ulisse Cantagalli workshop. It is now a national monument owned by the Russian Orthodox community of Florence and open for services (sung mass) on the third Sunday of the month and on major church festivals.

Piazza della Libertà (Map 4; 1) is a handsome arcaded piazza where many streets converge, though it is also extremely busy with traffic. The stranded city gate of Porta San Gallo stands in the centre, along with a triumphal arch that was hurriedly erected in 1739 to commemorate the solemn entry into the city of the Grand-duke Francis of Lorraine, and his wife Maria Teresa, heir to the Imperial throne. The modern bronze statue is by Marcello Tommasi.

The **parterre** on the north side of the square was created as a park by the Lorraine grand-dukes on the site of the convent of San Gallo. An underground car park was opened here in 1994.

From the junction just north of the piazza at Ponte Rosso (**Map 4; 1**), which crosses the Mugnone, is the beginning of Via Bolognese (see p 361). Just to the left (entered from Via Vittorio Emanuele II) is the **Giardino dell'Orticoltura** (open daily), a horticultural garden created in 1859, but now greatly altered. The splendid greenhouse built by Giacomo Roster in 1880 was restored in 2000, and an annual flower show is held here in spring. The gardens are divided by the railway line; the entrance to the upper gardens is in Via Trento; these gardens have a crescent of pine trees, and a delightful fountain in the form of a huge snake-dragon (1990).

In **Piazza Savonarola** (Map 4; 4), near Piazza della Libertà, there is a statue of *Savonarola* by Enrico Pazzi. A handsome studio block here (no. 18), built in 1912, houses the **Galleria Carnielo** on the ground floor. It contains sculptures by Rinaldo Carnielo (1853–1910) left by him to the Comune, but at present closed (☎ 055 27305).

Cimitero degli Inglesi

Viale Giacomo Matteotti leads back towards the river. The Protestant cemetery, which has always been known as the *Cimitero degli Inglesi*, or English Cemetery, lies in the centre of **Piazza Donatello** (Map 4; 6), on a mound shaded by cypresses (opening times Mon 09.00–12.00, Tues–Fri 15.00–18.00; closed Sun; ring at the main gate). It was opened in 1828 and many distinguished British, Swiss, North American, Italian and Russian Protestants are buried here. The cemetery was closed in 1878 when the new Cimitero degli Allori on the Via Senese was opened, but in 1996 the Russian ballet dancer Evgenij Poljakov was buried here. The little gatehouse dates from 1860.

To the left of the central path Elizabeth Barrett Browning (1809–61) is buried. The tomb, raised on six little columns, was designed by Robert Browning and sculpted by Lord Leighton (finished by Luigi Giovannozzi). Behind it is the Pre-Raphaelite sarcophagus of Holman Hunt's wife Fanny, who died in Fiesole at the age of 33. Also buried here are Isa Blagden (1818–73; see p 354), Arthur Hugh Clough (1819–61), Walter Savage Landor (1775–1864), Frances Trollope (1780–1863; the mother of Anthony), the American preacher Theodore Parker of Lexington (1810–60), Robert Davidsohn (1853–1937), the German historian of Florence, and Gian Pietro Vieusseux (1779–1863), the Swiss bibliophile.

Viale Gramsci continues to **Piazza Beccaria** (Map 4; 8), with another old city gate. It is named after Cesare Beccaria (1735–94) famous for his denunciation of capital punishment and torture, and his far-sighted theories of crime prevention. Nearby, in Via Scipione Ammirato are two Art Nouveau houses, the **Villino Broggi-Caraceni** (no. 99) built in 1911, and the **Villino Ravazzini** (no. 101) dating from 1907–08. They are both by Giovanni Michelazzi with ceramic decoration by Galileo Chini, and the best examples of their period in Florence. On the south side of Piazza Beccaria, a huge new building by Italo Gamberini was opened in 1989 to house the **Archivio di Stato**. Founded in 1582, the archives date back to the 8C, and provide scholars with a wealth of information on the political and economic history of the city.

The *viali* end at the Arno by another defensive tower and near Ponte San Niccolò (**Map 7; 4**).

San Salvi

The conventual buildings of the Vallombrosan abbey of San Salvi are just north of the railway line, off Via Lungo l'Affrico (about 1.5km from Piazza Beccaria; for the bus from the centre of Florence, see p 326). The entrance to the buildings is at no. 16 Via San Salvi and inside there is a celebrated fresco of the *Last Supper* by Andrea del Sarto—known as the Cenacolo di San Salvi—and a small museum of 16C works. Opening times 08.30–13.50; closed Mon; ☎ 055 238 8603; (S).

The **long gallery**, with fine vaulting, is hung with some interesting large 16C altarpieces, all of them labelled, including works by Franciabigio (***Adoration of*** *the Shepherds*), Michele di Ridolfo del Ghirlandaio, Vasari, Il Poppi, Carlo Portelli, Empoli and Giovanni Battista Paggi. In the room at the end, there are beautifully carved *reliefs by Benedetto da Rovezzano from the tomb of St John Gualberto formerly in the nearby church of San Michele a San Salvi (and willfully damaged during the Imperial siege of 1530, when most of the heads were defaced). There is also a plaster cast made in 1887 of the famous tomb of Ilaria del Carretto Guinigi by Jacopo della Quercia in the cathedral of Lucca.

On the right are two more rooms, one with a lavabo by Benedetto da Rovezzano, and the other with a huge fireplace which served the convent kitchen. There are paintings by contemporaries or followers of Andrea del Sarto, including Giuliano Bugiardini (*Madonna and Child*), Franciabigio, Pontormo, Giovanni Antonio Sogliani, Maso di San Friano, Raffaellino del Garbo (*Annunciation* and the *Madonna Enthroned between Saints*).

Andrea del Sarto's Cenacolo di San Salvi

The Refectory contains Andrea del Sarto's celebrated *Cenacolo di San Salvi* (1511–27), a masterpiece of Florentine fresco which is remarkable for its colouring and dramatic movement. Each apostle is beautifully painted; Judas is shown seated on the right of Christ and St John on the left. The austerity of the setting is relieved by the charming detail of two servants observing the scene from a balcony above. This is perhaps the most famous fresco of the Last Supper in Italy, after that by Leonardo da Vinci in Milan. It is extremely well preserved as the Convent of San Salvi was a closed order and remained inaccessible until the early 19C. The tondi of *Saints* and the *Trinity* on the intrados were the first part of the fresco to be painted (the *grotteschi* are by del Sarto's collaborator Andrea di Cosimo Feltrini).

In addition to the Cenacolo di San Salvi, the Refectory contains two more works by Andrea del Sarto: a very ruined fresco of the *Annunciation* detached from the Sdrucciolo di Orsanmichele, and a *Noli me tangere* from the convent of San Gallo.

Close by is the 14C–16C church of **San Michele a San Salvi**, entered through a charming late 14C cloister (the small upper loggia was added in the 15C). At the entrance to the chapter house there is a relief of *St John Gualberto* and two Vallombrosan monks by Benedetto da Rovezzano. The church has ceiling frescoes by Vincenzo Meucci, and a chapel off the south transept (now used as a sacristy) with interesting remains of early 15C frescoes in terraverde and a statue of a female saint attributed to Andrea Orcagna. On the west wall are frescoes detached from a street tabernacle nearby.

Farther north, off the other side of Via Lungo l'Affrico, is the sports ground of **Campo di Marte** with the Stadio Comunale, a remarkable building (1932) by Pier Luigi Nervi, altered and enlarged for the World Cup games in 1990.

Environs of Florence

FIESOLE AND SAN DOMENICO

Fiesole is the best known place in the environs of Florence and is well worth a visit. There is a frequent bus service from Florence and the journey takes about 30 minutes. The little town sits on a hill with splendid views of the city—best from the approach road and from the highest part of the hill around the convent of San Francesco. It is also interesting for its Roman theatre, Etruscan walls, Duomo, and small museums, all sited close together off the main piazza. There are lovely walks in the vicinity including the beautiful old road up from the hamlet of San Domenico di Fiesole. For the very energetic, both places can also be reached from Florence on foot by a number of old country roads with charming views.

Information
Public transport

Bus no 7, which leaves every 20 minutes from Stazione Santa Maria Novella (east side) and Piazza San Marco, goes to Fiesole via the hamlet of San Domenico, with a journey time of about 30 minutes.

Information office

(APT and Comune), 3 Via Portigiani, ☎ 055 598 720.

Car parking

In Fiesole parking can be difficult. There are four free car parks in Piazza Mercato, in Via Giovanni Duprè (outside the fence which encloses the Roman Theatre), below the Roman Theatre in Via delle Mura Etrusche, and in Via Banchi near the sports stadium. The car parks in Piazza Mino and Piazza Garibaldi (very limited space) have an hourly tariff.

Hotels and restaurants

See pp 29 and 41.

Map

See pp 338–339.

Walks

Short walks in the vicinity of Fiesole are described in this chapter; for longer excursions, the Comune of Fiesole and the APT have published a booklet entitled *Itinerari Fiesolani*, with a map and description of itineraries that are marked with painted signs showing a strip of purple and bright blue. All of these, which take a minumum of 3 hours and a maximum of 8 hours, pass through beautiful countryside and are highly recommended to experienced walkers. For information contact the APT di Fiesole, ☎ 055 598 720, or the Comune di Fiesole, ☎ 055 599 478.

Private gardens

For information on the days when private gardens belonging to villas in and around Fiesole are opened by the Comune of Fiesole (usually in spring and autumn) ☎ 800 414 240 or ☎ 055 599 478. These usually include Villa le Balze, Villa al Bosco di Fontelucente, Villa di Maiano, Villa Medici, Villa Riposo dei Vescovi, Villa Il Roseto, Villa La Torraccia, Castello di Vincigliata, and Castel di Poggio, all described in this chapter.

The Festa di San Romolo

This festival is celebrated as a holiday in Fiesole on 6 July, with an evening market in the piazza, and a delightful display of fireworks at 22.30, some of them set off in front of the Comune, and others from the hillside above, and from the top of the campanile of the Duomo. The bus service is suspended between 20.00 and 24.00.

There are a number of picturesque, narrow, old roads up to San Domenico which provide delightful approaches on foot from the bottom of the hill (Viale Alessandro Volta and Viale Augusto Righi).

These include **Via Giovanni Boccaccio** which passes (no. 126) **Villa Palmieri**, the garden of which, with fine lemon tress grown in pots, was the scene of one of the episodes in Boccaccio's *Decameron* (see p 349).

Farther on (no. 115–121) is the 15C–16C **Villa Schifanoia**. The early 20C Renaissance style garden is occasionally opened by the Comune di Fiesole (see p 335). Since 1989 the villa has been used by the European University Institute.

Via delle Forbici passes the park (open daily 07.30–sunset except Monday; entrance at no. 12 Via Giovanni Aldini) of **Villa il Ventaglio** built in 1839–53 by Giuseppe Poggi and now the seat of the Università Internazionale dell'Arte. **Via di Barbacane** is another old road, beautifully preserved at its upper end.

Via Lungo l'Affrico, which skirts the garden of Villa Camerata, passes close to Villa Il Palmerino where the writer Vernon Lee (Violet Paget) lived from 1889 until her death in 1935.

Via Vecchia Fiesolana is a very attractive old road, best followed downhill from Fiesole to San Domenico.

The main road to Fiesole (followed by the bus) is Viale Alessandro Volta (**Map 4; 2**), which begins at Piazza delle Cure. Beyond Piazza Edison, Via di San Domenico ascends the hillside with a beautiful view of Fiesole and its villas. A double curve precedes San Domenico.

San Domenico di Fiesole

San Domenico di Fiesole (see Map on pp 338–39) is a little hamlet within the Comune of Fiesole, with several beautiful private villas. The **church of San Domenico** (opening times 08.30–12.00, 15.30–17.30) dates from 1406–35; the portico (1635) and campanile (1611–13) were added by Matteo Nigetti.

In the **interior**, the side chapels have Renaissance arches in *pietra serena* and some of the altarpieces have handsome Mannerist frames. The fine chancel was designed in 1603 by Giovanni Caccini. On the **south side**, the first chapel has a wooden *Crucifix* of the mid-14C and a painting of the *Crucifixion* attributed to Jacopo del Sellaio. In the second chapel, there is a *Baptism of Christ* by Lorenzo di Credi. On the high altar is a gilded wooden tabernacle of 1613 (Andrea Balatri).

On the north side, the third chapel contains an *Annunciation* by Jacopo da Empoli (1615) and a *Miracle of Saint Antoninus* by Francesco Conti. The *Crucifix* is attributed to the school of Antonio da Sangallo. In the second chapel, there is an *Epiphany* by Giovanni Antonio Sogliani (completed by Santi di Tito). In the first chapel is Fra' Angelico's, **Madonna with Angels and Saints* (c 1430; there is a light on the right). The architectural background was added by Lorenzo di Credi in 1501, when the frame was redesigned (the paintings of Saints are by a follower of Lorenzo Monaco). The panels of the predella are copies; the originals are in the National Gallery, London.

In the **Convent of San Domenico** Saint Antoninus (Antonino Pierozzi, 1389–1459) and Fra' Angelico (Guidi di Pietro or Fra' Giovanni da Fiesole, 1387–1455) first entered the religious order. They moved down to the convent of San Marco after 1437. There are only a few monks left in the convent now, and it is not always easy to gain access to the little **chapter house** (ring at no. 4, right of the church). This contains a beautiful fresco of the *Crucifixion* by Fra' Angelico (c 1430) and a detached fresco (with its sinopia) of the *Madonna and Child*, also attributed to him. In the orchard is the little **Cappella delle Beatitudine** (1588) with frescoes by Lodovico Buti.

The pretty Via delle Fontanelle leads away from Piazza San Domenico, passing (left) Villa Sparta where the Swiss painter Arnold Böcklin lived from 1894. The long avenue of cypresses leads to a garden designed by Cecil Pinsent. Some distance further on is **La Torraccia**, a large villa with a loggia where Walter Savage Landor lived from 1829 until 1835, now the seat of the Music School of Fiesole, founded in 1974 (with a high reputation). It has a fine park and a charming little Italianate **garden**, partly redesigned by Landor (sometimes specially opened, see p 335).

Badia Fiesolana

The Badia Fiesolana (see Map on p 338–39), in Via della Badia dei Roccettini, was the cathedral of Fiesole until 1028. In a lovely position, it was probably built on the site of the *martyrium* of Saint Romulus. Bishop Donato of Fiesole (d. c 876), thought to have been an Irishman, was elected to the bishop's see when he stopped here on his journey back from Rome. The church was rebuilt in the 15C under the direction of Cosimo il Vecchio who founded a library here with the help of Vespasiano da Bisticci. The **European University Institute** was established in the conventual buildings in 1976. The cloister dates from 1459 and a statue of *Plato* by Pompilio Ticciati has been placed under a pretty loggia of 1461.

The rough stone front of the **church** (opening times 09.00–17.00; Sat 09.00–12.00; ☎ 055 59155) incorporates the beautiful *façade of the smaller Romanesque church with inlaid marble decoration. The interesting plan of the small church, begun in 1456, is derived from Brunelleschi. The side chapels have handsome round arches in *pietra serena* by Francesco di Simone Ferrucci. Five steps precede the east end, which is also decorated with *pietra serena*, and has an elegant inscription to Piero de' Medici (Il Gottoso) and the date of 1466. The high altar is a fine work in *pietre dure* by Giovanni Battista di Jacopo Cennini (1612) on a design by Pietro Tacca. On the first altar on the left, there is an unusual painting of the *Pietà with Saints* by Francesco Botticini. In the left transept, there is a *Crucifixion* by Bernardino Campi.

From the charming terrace in front of the church, the view extends beyond cypresses and olives to Florence.

Across the road from the Badia, the beautiful old Via delle Palazzine winds past lovely villas to the church of Fontelucente; it provides a delightful alternative approach to Fiesole (via Via Giovanni Duprè).

From San Domenico the ascent to Fiesole may be made either by the main road Via Giuseppe Mantellini and Via Beato Angelico or (on foot) by the shorter and prettier old road (Via Vecchia Fiesolana, very narrow and steep; see below); both are lined with fine villas and beautiful trees and provide splendid views of Florence. A short way before the top of the hill at no. 15 (right) is the entrance to **Villa il Roseto**, the former home of the architect Giovanni Michelucci (1891–1991), and seat of the Fondazione Michelucci since 1982. There is a splendid view from the little terraced garden which is sometimes opened specially, see p 335.

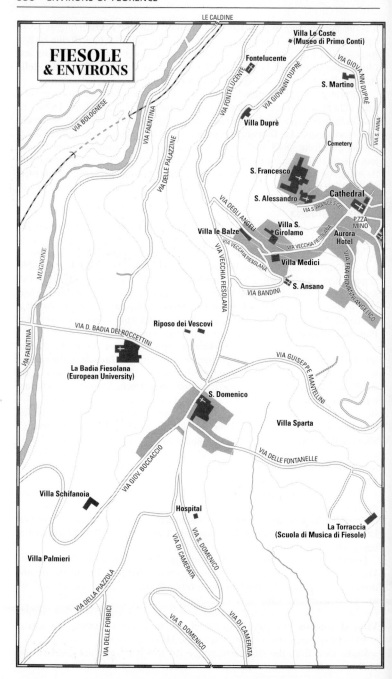

FIESOLE & ENVIRONS

LE CALDINE

VIA BOLOGNESE

VIA FAENTINA

VIA FONTELUCENTE

VIA DELLE PALAZZINE

VIA GIOVANNI DUPRÈ

VIA GIOVANNI DUPRÈ

VIA S. ANNA

Villa Le Coste
(Museo di Primo Conti)

Fontelucente

S. Martino

Villa Duprè

MUGNONE

VIA FAENTINA

Cemetery

S. Francesco

S. Alessandro

Cathedral

VIA S. FRANCESCO

VIA DEGLI ANGELI

Villa le Balze

Villa S. Girolamo

P.ZZA MINO

Aurora Hotel

VIA VECCHIA FIESOLANA

Villa Medici

VIA FRA GIOVANNI ANGELICO

S. Ansano

VIA BANDINI

VIA VECCHIA FIESOLANA

Riposo dei Vescovi

VIA D. BADIA DEI ROCCETTINI

La Badia Fiesolana
(European University)

VIA GIUSEPPE MANTELLINI

S. Domenico

Villa Sparta

VIA GIOV. BOCCACCIO

VIA DELLE FONTANELLE

Villa Schifanoia

Hospital

VIA S. DOMENICO

La Torraccia
(Scuola di Musica di Fiesole)

Villa Palmieri

VIA DI CAMERATA

VIA DELLA PIAZZOLA

VIA DELLE FORBICI

VIA S. DOMENICO

VIA DI CAMERATA

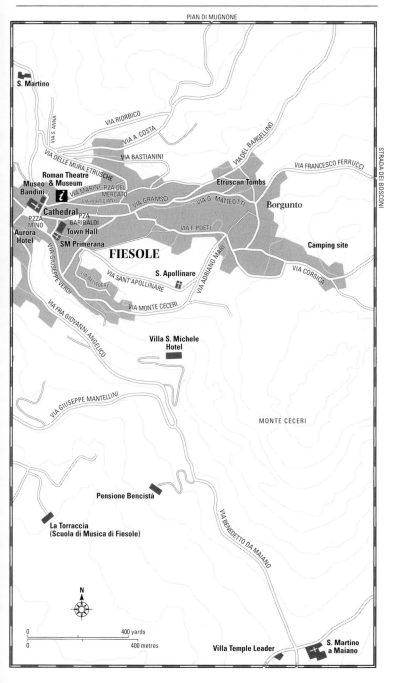

PIAN DI MUGNONE

S. Martino

VIA S. ANNA

VIA RIORBICO

VIA A. COSTA

VIA BASTIANINI

VIA DELLE MURA ETRUSCHE

Roman Theatre
Museo & Museum
Bandini

VIA MARINI PZA DEL
MERCATO
(VIA PORTIGIANI)

VIA GRAMSCI

Cathedral

P.ZA
MINO

P.ZA
GARIBALDI

Aurora
Hotel

Town Hall

SM Primerana

VIA GIUSEPPE VERDI

FIESOLE

VIA BELVEDERE

VIA SANT'APOLLINARE

S. Apollinare

VIA MONTE CECERI

VIA FRA GIOVANNI ANGELICO

Etruscan Tombs

VIA DEL BARGELLINO

VIA FRANCESCO FERRUCCI

STRADA DEI BOSCONI

VIA G. MATTEOTTI

Borgunto

VIA F. POETI

VIA ADRIANO MARI

Camping site

VIA CORSICA

Villa S. Michele
Hotel

VIA GIUSEPPE MANTELLINI

MONTE CECERI

Pensione Bencistà

VIA BENEDETTO DA MAIANO

La Torraccia
(Scuola di Musica di Fiesole)

N

0   400 yards
0   400 metres

Villa Temple Leader

S. Martino
a Maiano

On the other side of the road is the entrance to the **Villa Medici** (no. 2). This is privately owned, but willingly shown, usually on weekdays 09.00–15.00, and on Saturday 09.00–12.00, ☎ 055 239 8994, or specially opened, see p 335. The Villa Medici was built by Michelozzo in 1458–61 for Cosimo il Vecchio. It was a favourite retreat of Lorenzo il Magnifico, and Angelo Poliziano and Pico della Mirandola together with members of the Platonic Academy frequently met here. The villa was bought in 1862 by the painter and collector William Blundell Spence, and in 1911 by Lady Sybil Cutting (wife of the architect Geoffrey Scott) whose daughter Iris Origo (1902–88), the historian and biographer, made additions to the garden. The present villa dates from the 17C and 18C.

A broad ilex avenue descends to the villa and its beautiful *garden, one of the earliest of the Renaissance, built on several terraces on the steep hillside with a superb view of Florence. It is at its best after Easter. The upper terrace has two ancient paulownia trees, magnolias, geraniums, lemon trees in pots (brought out in the summer), tree peonies and a permanent hedge of oranges backed by a high ivy-covered wall. There is also an orangery and two grottoes behind which steps lead down to the lower terrace, which was laid out in 1915 by Geoffrey Scott and Cecil Pinsent. It has a box-edged geometric garden at either end and a circular fountain. There are more citrus trees here in pots, as well as magnolia and wisteria (also grown on the steps and on a low wall). A pergola is covered with a cream coloured double banksia rose. Lower down is the vegetable garden and lily house. Steps lead up past the villa to another small secluded garden with box hedges above Via Vecchia Fiesolana.

Fiesole

Fiesole (pronounced Fiésole) is a charming little village with a population of 15,000 inhabitants. It occupies a magnificent position on a thickly wooded hill overlooking the valleys of the Arno and the Mugnone (see Map on pp 338–39). It has always been a fashionable residential district, much favoured by foreigners in the 19C when its beautiful hillside was enhanced by fine villas surrounded by romantic gardens and stately cypress groves. An Etruscan city, its foundation precedes that of Florence by many centuries, and, with its own local government, it is still proudly independent of the larger city. It is crowded with Florentines and visitors in summer when its position (295m) makes it one of the coolest places in the neighbourhood of the city.

History of Fiesole

Excavations have proved that the hill was inhabited before the Bronze Age. The site of Faesulae, on a hilltop above a river valley, was typical of Etruscan settlements. Probably founded in the 6C BC or 5C BC from Arezzo, it became one of the chief cities of the Etruscan confederacy. It is first mentioned in 283 BC, when its inhabitants, in alliance with other Etruscans, were defeated by the Romans at Lake Vadimone. With the Roman occupation it became the most important town in Etruria, but the barbarian invasions led to its decline. In 854, the county of Fiesole was merged with that of Florence. After a decisive battle in 1125, in which only the cathedral and the bishop's palace escaped destruction, Florence finally gained control of Fiesole.

The bus terminates in **Piazza Mino da Fiesole**, the spacious main square of the town, named after the Renaissance sculptor (1429–84; born at Poppi in the Casentino) who made Fiesole his home. A market is held here on Saturdays.

The Cathedral (San Romolo)

The cathedral (open 07.00–12.00, 14.00 or 14.30–18.00 or 18.30) was founded in 1028, and enlarged in the 13C and 14C. It was over-restored in 1878–83. The tall bell-tower of 1213 (the crenellations were added later) is visible from Florence and the surrounding hills.

The bare stone **interior**, with a raised choir above a hall crypt, is similar in plan to San Miniato al Monte. The massive columns have fine capitals (some of them Roman). Above the west door, there is a garlanded niche containing a statue of Saint *Romulus*, Bishop of Fiesole, by Giovanni della Robbia (1521). The handsome high altar in grey-green and white marble dates from 1273. On the pillars on either side there are frescoes of *Saint Sebastian* (restored) and *Saint Benedict*, by the school of Perugino.

Stairs lead up to the **choir**, preceded by a 19C balustrade made by a local stonemason. On the right is the little **Cappella Salutati** with frescoes in the vault of the *Evangelists* by Cosimo Rosselli and two of Mino da Fiesole's best works: the *tomb of Bishop Leonardo Salutati* (1465) with a fine portrait bust, and an *altarpiece*. Over the high altar stands a splendid large *altarpiece* by Bicci di Lorenzo (c 1440), with the *Madonna and Child and Saints Alexander, Peter, Romulus and Donatus*. It was donated to the church by Bishop Benozzo Federighi just before his death in 1450. The apse is frescoed by Nicodemo Ferrucci (late 16C). In a chapel on the left is a marble altarpiece by Andrea Ferrucci (1493), brother of Nicodemo.

The **crypt** (coin-operated light) has four little columns with interesting primitive capitals. Behind the screen, surrounding the altar of Saint Romulus, are four marble columns with charming antique Ionic capitals. The vault was painted in the 15C in lapis lazuli with stars. In the apse is a marble reliquary urn. The lunettes (late 15C) are frescoed with *Stories of Saint Romulus*. Below the pavement can be seen Roman remains found during recent restoration work. The granite font is the work of Francesco del Tadda (1569). A small chapel contains an early 13C painting of the *Madonna and Child Enthroned* (the *Madonna del Soccorso*), based on Byzantine icons and restored in 1994.

The piazza slopes up to the old **Palazzo Pretorio**, now the town hall, which has a loggia decorated with the coats of arms of many *podestà*. Next to it stands the church of **Santa Maria Primerana**, rebuilt in the 16C–17C, with a quaint porch. The interior contains a 14C painted *Crucifix*, a bas-relief with the *Self-portrait* in profile of Francesco da Sangallo, and a *Crucifix with the Madonna and Saints* by Andrea della Robbia. The sanctuary contains a highly venerated early 13C painting of the *Madonna* in a Gothic tabernacle, and damaged frescoes by Niccolò di Pietro Gerini.

The equestrian monument (1906) in the piazza celebrates the meeting between Vittorio Emanuele II and Garibaldi at Teano in southern Italy in 1860, when the handshake between the King and the popular hero symbolised the unification of Italy. The lower end of the square is occupied by the seminary (1697) and the bishop's palace (1675).

Via San Francesco, a very steep paved lane, climbs up the hill. At no. 4 is the entrance to the **Cappella di San Jacopo** (opening times Sat, Sun and *fest.* 10.00–19.00; combined ticket with the Roman Theatre and Museo Bandini; Lire 10,000 or Lire 8000 for students and over 65s). Reopened in 2000, this was a 14C oratory attached to the bishop's palace. It houses an early 15C fresco of the *Coronation of the Virgin* attributed to Bicci di Lorenzo (the lunette of the apostle Saint *James the Greater* was painted by Antonio Marini in 1853). The chapel now houses a collection of goldsmiths' work from the diocese of Fiesole, including 13C and 14C processional Crosses, a 15C mitre decorated with enamels, a 16C crozier, and 17C and 18C church silver.

The lane continues up past (right) a public park (described below) and a terrace on the left planted with ilexes where there are two war memorials. From here there is a splendid **view* of Florence with the Duomo standing out in the middle.

Above, beside another viewpoint, is the church of **Sant' Alessandro** (open only twice a year for services, and closed at other times unless exhibitions are being held here). It was heavily restored in 1814 and again after 1957. Traditionally thought to be on the site of an Etruscan and Roman temple, it was probably founded in the 6C. The Romanesque church was altered in the 16C and 18C. The bare basilican **interior** is remarkable for its **cipollino marble columns* with Ionic capitals and bases from a Roman building. An oratory off the left aisle (light on right) contains an altarpiece of the *Assumption* by Gerino da Pistoia (showing the influence of Perugino) and 16C Mannerist frescoes of the *Life of the Virgin*.

Beyond (left) the church of Santa Cecilia at the top of the hill (345m), is the site of the Etruscan and later Roman acropolis, where the convent buildings of **San Francesco** (opening times 09.30–12.30, 15.00–18.00) now stand. The church dates from c 1330 and was restored in neo-Gothic style in 1905–07, with an attractive little rose window. The choir arch is attributed to Benedetto da Maiano. Over the high altar, there is a *Crucifixion and Saints* by Neri di Bicci. On the south side (first altar), the *Marriage of Saint Catherine* by Cenni di Francesco, surrounded by paintings of the early 19C. On the second altar, the *Immaculate Conception* by Piero di Cosimo. On the north side (first altar), there is an *Adoration of the Magi* by the school of Cosimo Rosselli, and (second altar), the *Annunciation* by Raffaellino del Garbo.

In the Franciscan friary, there are several charming little cloisters, some remains of the Etruscan walls, and a missionary **museum** of Eastern *objets d'art* with a remarkable miscellany of objects (mostly unlabelled). Opening times 09.30–12.30, 15.00–18.00; ☎ 055 59175. The museum contains a particularly interesting Egyptian collection (including a statuette thought to represent the wife of Rameses II) and works from China (including bronzes and Ming and Qing vases). The convent also owns a collection of 16C–17C ceramics including apothecary jars and tableware. From the piazza outside, a gate leads into a public park with an ilex wood, through which shady paths lead back downhill to the main square.

Roman Theatre and Museo Civico

From Piazza Mino, the street behind the apse of the cathedral leads to the entrance to the **Roman theatre and archaeological excavations, and the Museo Civico which contains the Costantini collection of Greek vases.

The Roman theatre at Fiesole

- **Opening times** 09.30–19.00; winter 09.30–17.00; closed Tuesday in winter (☎ 055 59477); Lire 10,000, with a discount (Lire 8000) for students and over 65s. Combined ticket includes entry to the Museo Bandini (see below) and the Cappella di San Jacopo (see above). There is a café in the grounds.

From the terrace above the theatre there is a good comprehensive view of the excavations in a plantation of olive trees, backed by the Mugnone valley and the dark cypresses of the hill of San Francesco. The excavations were begun in the 19C, and several of the edifices were arbitrarily restored in 1870–92.

The **Roman theatre**, built at the end of the 1C BC, was enlarged by Claudius and Septimius Severus. The *cavea*, which was partly dug out from the hillside (the sides are supported on vaults), is 34m across and held 3000 spectators. The seats on the right side are intact; the others have been restored with smaller blocks of stone. Plays and concerts are performed here during a festival held every summer (the Estate Fiesolana).

To the right of the theatre are the **Roman baths** (reconstructed in 1892), probably built in the 1C AD and enlarged by Hadrian. In front are three rectangular swimming baths. The chambers near the three arches (reconstructed) consist of the hypocausis, with circular ovens, where the water was heated, the calidarium with its hypocaust, and the tepidarium. In front of the arches is the palestra, and behind them the frigidarium. A small terrace here provides a fine view of a long stretch of **Etruscan walls** (4C–3C BC; reinforced in the Roman and medieval periods), with a gateway, which enclosed the city. On the other side of the theatre (to the northwest) is a **Roman temple** (1C BC), with its basement intact, and, on a lower level, remains of an **Etruscan temple** (4C or early 3C BC), both of them approached by steps. Nearby are copies of the two original altars from the temples (the larger one is Roman). In this area a Lombard necropolis (6C–7C AD) has also been excavated. There is a stretch of Roman road near the theatre.

Museo Civico

The museum was built in 1912–14 and the exterior is an idealised reconstruction of the Roman temple. Its collection was founded in 1878 and is now being re-evaluated in the light of new excavations. Under the portico, there is a fragment from the frieze of the Roman temple.

Ground floor The first five rooms contain a topographical collection from Fiesole and its territory. **Room I** has Etruscan-Roman finds and Bronze Age material. The well-preserved Stele Fiesolana (5C BC) shows a funerary banquet, and dancing and hunting scenes. **Room II** contains Etruscan urns in *pietra serena*; a cylindrical lead cinerary urn decorated with Roman reliefs; inscribed stelae in *pietra serena* (2C AD); small bronzes and Bucchero ware. **Rooms III** and **IV** contain artefacts found around the Roman theatre and temples, including terracotta antefixes; and a marble frieze from the theatre. The so-called bronze *She-wolf* (in fact the torso of a lioness) was found on the probable site of the Capitol of Faesulae.

Upper floor Two rooms on this floor display part of the *Antiquarium Costantini**, a splendid collection of Greek vases donated to Fiesole in 1985 by Alfiero Costantini. This includes Corinthian vases (7C BC) and models of animals (including deer, a hedgehog and a ram's head used for perfumes), and fine Attic black-figure amphorae, hydria, and craters (6C BC). The exquisite red-figure vases (late 6C BC) include a pelike with Theseus and the minotaur, and a stamnos signed by Hermonax (460–450 BC), a fine lekythos with the figure of Eros, attributed to the Pan Painter (480 BC), and an oinochoe with a female head. There is also a black-figure hydria with a banqueting scene, a two-handled cup in brown impasto, and Bucchero ware. The pottery from Daunia (Puglia) includes an unusually shaped pitcher (late 8C or early 7C BC), red-figure vases, a pair of large hydria (320–310 BC), and a red-figure amphora attributed to the Baltimore Painter, of the same date. The collection also includes Gnathian vases from Taranto, and black-glazed pottery.

The three other rooms on this floor contain the so-called **antiquarium**, made up of various collections donated to the museum, and a coin collection. Another room displays a torso of Dionysius, a Roman copy of the early Imperial period of a Greek original, and Roman marble heads.

Returning to the ground floor, from Room III there is access to a covered passageway which leads to another building. In the passageway is displayed a Lombard tomb found in Piazza Garibaldi in 1988. Outside can be seen part of a monumental entrance corridor dating from the 2C BC which was part of a large sacred enclosure, and a well. Stairs lead up to a room which displays finds made on the site (including fresco fragments dating from between the 1C BC and the 2C AD, ceramics and glass).

Museo Bandini

Via Portigiani leads downhill past the entrance to the Roman theatre, just to the left of which in Via Giovanni Duprè (no. 1) is the small Museo Bandini, a collection of 13C–15C Florentine paintings which belonged to Angelo Maria Bandini (born in Fiesole 1726), and which was left by him at his death in 1803 to the Diocese of Fiesole.

• **Opening times** 10.00–19.00; winter 10.00–17.00; closed Tuesday in winter (☎ 055 59477); Lire 10,000, with a discount (Lire 8000) for students and over 65s. Combined ticket includes entry to the Roman theatre and Museo Civico (see above) and the Cappella di San Jacopo (see above).

Bandini was the first librarian of the Biblioteca Marucelliana and later of the Biblioteca Laurenziana. The attractive little building that houses the collection was designed by Giuseppe Castellucci in 1913.

At the bottom of the stairs are two terracotta busts of *Apostles* attributed to Pietro Francavilla—the museum has eight more. The paintings are arranged chronologically in two rooms on the first floor.

Room 1 begins with a 13C Tuscan *Crucifix* attributed to Meliore and there is a case of Byzantine ivories including one with the *Archangel Gabriel* (11C–12C). Notable paintings include Bernardo Daddi's Saint *John the Evangelist* and Taddeo Gaddi's *Annunciation*; Nardo di Cione's *Madonna del Parto*; two (fragmentary) side panels of a tabernacle by Jacopo di Cione; and two panels with *Saints* from a polyptych by Giovanni di Bartolomeo Cristiani. On the end wall is Agnolo Gaddi's *Madonna Enthroned with Saints*; two panels from a polyptych by the Master of the Altar of San Niccolò; a *Madonna Enthroned with Saints* attributed to Jacopo da Firenze; a diptych by Jacopo di Mino del Pelicciaio; and four predella panels by the Master of the Ashmolean Predella.

Room 2 includes: Bicci di Lorenzo, Saint *Catherine*, *Baptism of Saint Augustine* and *Angels* (a fragment); Ventura di Moro, two panels with four *Saints*; Lorenzo Monaco, *Crucifixion*; Giovanni dal Ponte, two panels with four *Saints*; Giovanni del Biondo, *Coronation of the Virgin*; Master of the Johnson Nativity, *Deposition*; Neri di Bicci, painted *Cross*; Cosimo Rosselli and *bottega*, *Coronation of the Virgin*; 15C Florentine school, four panels from a *cassone* with four *Triumphs*; Neri di Bicci, *Madonna in Adoration*.

Lower down the hill, a road diverges left from Via Giovanni Duprè for the **cemetery**, where the sculptor Giovanni Duprè (1817–82) is buried. Against the hill of San Francesco is a large section of the **Etruscan walls**.

Another stretch of the walls can be seen by following Via Santa Maria from Piazza Mino. Via Sant' Apollinare or (right) Via Belvedere, with superb views, continue uphill to Via Adriano Mari which skirts the walls along the eastern limit of the Etruscan city. From here Via Montececeri (also with magnificent views) leads across to the extensive woods of **Montececeri**, once owned by Temple Leader, which was up to 1929 used as a quarry for *pietra serena*. The bare slopes and disused quarries were then planted with oak, conifers, cypresses and pines. There are some lovely paths here with views extending to Settignano and beyond. At the highest point (410m) a memorial stone records Leonardo da Vinci's flying experiments which he carried out here. A path leads to Maiano.

Walks near Fiesole

The walks described below follow many beautiful old roads. Even though most of them are very narrow, they are still used by cars, and you should take great care of the traffic. For other walks, see p 336.

The Via Vecchia Fiesolana

From Piazza Mino, the narrow Via Vecchia Fiesolana descends steeply between high walls, past the convent of **San Girolamo** (15C–17C), surrounded by a garden and fields. A broad ilex avenue ascends to the main entrance. On the left is the Villa Medici (since its main entrance is on Via Beato Angelico, it is described on p 340).

On the other side of the road is the inconspicuous entrance to **Villa le Balze** (no. 26), built in 1913 by Charles August Strong. The villa was left to Georgetown University, the oldest Jesuit college in America, in 1979. The beautiful **garden** (for admission, see p 335), designed in 1915 by Cecil Pinsent, runs along the side of the hill, in a sequence of garden 'rooms'. It is decorated with grottoes and ends in a little ilex wood, with meadows beyond.

The road continues downhill (or a path, Via degli Angeli, may be followed) below Villa Medici. After two sharp bends, there is a breathtaking *view of Florence from the road, here lined with venerable cypresses. Queen Victoria used to enjoy the view from a bench here.

At the intersection with Via Giovanni Duprè, Via Vecchia Fiesolana continues down to San Domenico (see above), passing several beautiful villas, including (no. 62) the **Riposo dei Vescovi** (privately owned, but sometimes opened specially, see p 335), which was the halting place in the 16C for the bishops of Fiesole on their way up the hill from their residence in Florence. Dutch and Swiss owners in the late 19C carried out alterations in an eclectic Jugendstil and neo-Gothic style, which were continued by the Dutch painter W.O.J. Nieuwenkamp (1874–1950) when he bought the house in 1926. The splendid Romantic **park** with numerous cypresses covers the hillside all the way down to Via delle Palazzine. Via Vecchia Fiesolana continues steeply downhill to San Domenico, passing a fountain on the left erected by Baccio Bandinelli in 1556 and restored with a neo-Gothic tabernacle in the 19C.

Via Giovanni Duprè leads right to a fork with Via Fontelucente, an even narrower old road which descends left to the church of **Fontelucente**, built over a spring, in a beautiful isolated spot above the Mugnone valley. The beautiful Via delle Palazzine leads from here to the Badia Fiesolana (see above). Via Duprè continues with a view across the valley towards Via Bolognese, where the hillside was disfigured by new houses in the 1950s. Villa Duprè (no. 19) was the home of the 19C sculptor Giovanni Duprè.

The road now climbs uphill to the 16C **Villa le Coste** (no. 18), where the painter Primo Conti (1900–88) lived. The **Museo di Primo Conti** was opened here in 1987, in the garden, and contains a representative collection of Conti's works, which was left to the Comune. Opening times 09.00–13.00, except *fest*. The painter is buried here in a chapel of 1702, decorated with episodes from the *Life of Saint Rosalia* attributed to Francesco Botti (recently restored). The road curves to the right round the hill, and from the hamlet of San Martino, with the campanile of the cathedral of Fiesole prominent ahead, it is a short way back past the Roman theatre to Piazza Mino.

Maiano

The pretty Via Benedetto da Maiano diverges from the main Florence road below Fiesole (see Map on pp 338–39). The bus can be taken downhill from Piazza Mino to the request stop here. It passes the entrance to the *Pensione Bencistà*, a hotel which has always been favoured by English visitors. It was formerly called Villa Goerike and was where the painter Arnold Böcklin (1827–1901) lived and died.

At a crossroads is the little group of houses called **Maiano**, the home of the brothers Benedetto and Guiliano da Maiano (1442–92 and 1432–90). The church of **San Martino a Maiano** (opening times Wed 16.00–19.30, Sat 15.30–17.30; *fest.* 09.00–13.00, or ring at no. 6) is of ancient foundation and was restored by John Temple Leader (see below). The choir is decorated with *pietra serena*. Above the west door, in its original frame, is a *Madonna and Child with Saint John and Two Saints* by Giovanni Battista Naldini. A farm (produce for sale) now occupies the Benedictine monastery. A road continues uphill for a few hundred metres past two *trattorie* and disused *pietra serena* quarries (now visited by rock climbers), with fine views. A marked path leads from the end of the road to Monte Ceceri.

Via del Salviatino runs from the crossroads down to Florence. It passes the gate of the **Villa di Maiano** (left) or Villa Temple Leader (now Corsini), with its tower. Privately owned, the villa is used for receptions and is sometimes shown by previous appointment (☎ 055 599 600, or ☎ 055 598 631, or opened specially (see p 335). It was restored in 1850–63 by Felice Francolini for John Temple Leader as his residence.

The road continues downhill with a view of Fiesole from a hairpin bend. It then skirts the garden wall with cypresses of **Villa il Salviatino** (entrance at no. 21), the 16C home of Alamanno Salviati, surrounded by a thick wood of ilexes.

Castel di Poggio and Vincigliata

East of Fiesole, beyond Borgunto (see Map on pp 338–339) the attractive Via di Vincigliata diverges right along a ridge round the north shoulder of Monte Ceceri through magnificent woods. Opposite a semicircle of cypresses is the entrance (at no. 2) to the **Villa al Bosco di Fontelucente** (now Peyron) or Villa di Bosco (privately owned, but sometimes shown by previous appointment, ☎ 055 59223, or specially opened, see p 335). The villa was acquired by the Peyron family in 1914 when the exterior was restored by the architect Ugo Giovannozzi. After it was severely damaged in the last War, the **garden** was redesigned and carefully replanted.

Just beyond the villa there is a superb view of Florence. The road climbs to a fork; on the left a road leads to Montebeni and Settignano; and to the right the road continues past the gate (right; no. 4) to **Castel di Poggio**. The park and interior are sometimes shown by appointment, ☎ 055 59174, or opened specially, see p 335.

Rebuilt in the late 15C by the degli Alessandri, one wing was added in 1820 when the garden was transformed into an interior courtyard. It was restored again in 1922 in neo-Gothic style. The *views in every direction are breathtaking, looking over unspoilt hillsides of woods and fields.

The road now descends, lined with magnificent cypresses planted by Temple Leader, to the **Castello di Vincigliata** (privately owned, but used for receptions and shown by appointment, ☎ 055 599 556, and sometimes opened specially, see p 335). The castle was built in 1031, but destroyed by Sir John Hawkwood in 1364. It was a complete ruin when John Temple Leader acquired it in 1855. He appointed a local architect Giuseppe Fancelli to rebuild the castle in neo-Gothic style, with the help of skilled stonemasons from Settignano and the painter Gaetano Bianchi.

PONTE A MENSOLA AND SETTIGNANO

Settignano is a pleasant little village on a hill, much less visited by tourists than Fiesole. It is reached in about half by hour by frequent buses from Florence. Above the village is one of the most famous Renaissance gardens of Tuscany, Villa Gamberaia (open regularly). The Settignano road passes through the hamlet of Ponte a Mensola, which is close to Villa i Tatti, once the home of the art historian Bernard Berenson. There are lovely country walks in the vicinity of Corbignano.

Getting there

Bus no. 10 leaves every 20 minutes from Stazione Santa Maria Novella and Piazza San Marco to Settignano via Ponte a Mensola, with a journey time of 30 minutes.

The main road for Settignano diverges left from Lungarno del Tempio near Ponte San Niccolò (Map 7; 4). The long, straight Via del Campofiore and its continuation, Via Lungo l'Affrico, run northeast, passing close to the former convent of San Salvi (see Ch. 22). Via Gabriele d'Annunzio, signposted for Settignano, diverges right. The road narrows at Coverciano, with a big sports centre and a football museum (Museo del Calcio).

Ponte a Mensola

The village of Ponte a Mensola lies at the foot of the hill of Settignano. In Via Poggio Gherardo is the park of the **Villa di Poggio Gherardo** (no admission), traditionally thought to be the setting for the earliest episodes in Boccaccio's *Decameron* (see p 349). In 1888, it was purchased by Janet and Henry Ross.

In a beautiful position above the village of Ponte a Mensola is **San Martino a Mensola** (open 16.30–18.00 and Sunday at 10.30; at other times ring at the priest's house under the portico on the right). This is a 9C Benedictine church, founded by St Andrew, who is thought to have been a Scotsman and archdeacon to the bishop of Fiesole, Donato, who in turn was probably from Ireland. It is preceded by a 17C loggia. The 15C campanile was damaged by lightning in 1867.

The graceful 15C interior replaced the Romanesque church (remains of which have been found beneath the nave). It was restored in 1857 by Giuseppe Fancelli and again in 1999. Over the altar in the south aisle is a painting of the *Madonna Enthroned with Saints Andrew and Sebastian*, dating from the early 16C. At the end of the aisle, is a triptych (altered) of the **Madonna Enthroned with Two Female Saints* by Taddeo Gaddi. The sanctuary is preceded by a beautifully carved arch in *pietra serena* with two pretty little tabernacles. On the high altar is a triptych of the *Madonna and Child with the Donor and Saints* (the donor is Amerigo Zati) by a follower of Orcagna (1391), known, from this painting, as the Master of San Martino a Mensola. At the end of the north aisle, there is an **Annunciation* by a follower of Fra' Angelico. In the pavement, a stone marks the burial place of St Andrew. Over the other altar in this aisle is an altarpiece of the **Madonna and Four Saints* by Neri di Bicci.

A **wooden casket* decorated with fine paintings, which formerly contained the body of St Andrew, and his wooden reliquary bust which dates from the end of the 14C are to be exhibited in the crypt.

Villa I Tatti

The little by-road leads from the church across a bridge over the Mensola to a group of houses by the garden entrance to Villa I Tatti (the main entrance is on Via Vincigliata which begins at Ponte a Mensola, and skirts the garden wall up to the house). The house and garden are not open to the public, but are shown to scholars with a letter of presentation, by previous appointment (in small groups usually on Tuesday and Wednesday afternoons).

The locality was known as 'Tatti' at least as early as the 15C. It was acquired by John Temple Leader in 1854, and by Bernard Berenson, the pioneer scholar of the Italian Renaissance, in 1905.

The villa contains Berenson's library and photographic library as well as his *collection of Italian paintings, which includes works by Domenico Veneziano, Sassetta, Michele Giambono, Cima da Conegliano, Luca Signorelli, Bergognone and Lorenzo Lotto, and a small but choice selection of Oriental works of art.

The lovely Italianate **garden** (admission as above) was laid out by Cecil Pinsent in 1911–15, in imitation of an early Renaissance garden. The terraces are planted with symmetrical parterres and descend the steep hillside surrounded by high hedges of cypresses. Beyond the garden, which is beautifully kept, is a small ilex wood.

From Via Vincigliata at the bottom of the hill, Via di Corbignano, a peaceful old country lane, leads past (right; no. 4) **Villa Boccaccio** (rebuilt), once owned by the father of Giovanni Boccaccio who probably spent his youth here.

Giovanni Boccaccio

Giovanni Boccaccio (1312–75) was born in Paris where his Florentine father had mercantile interests, but lived in Florence. His *Decameron* (1348–58) is a brilliant secular work which established him as the father of Italian prose, and which had a great influence on European literature (including Chaucer). The book is a collection of tales told by seven ladies and three gentlemen who decide to leave the centre of Florence in order to escape the Plague of 1348; they spend ten days in the garden of a villa in the surrounding hills recounting stories to each other. The Villa di Poggio Gherardo and the villa now known as Villa Palmieri are both thought to have been settings for some of the earliest episodes, and other places in the environs of Florence near Fiesole are associated with the book. Boccaccio acted as ambassador for Florence after 1350, and was a close friend of the famous poet and the first great humanist Petrarch (1304–74) and of Dante.

Above the charming little hamlet of **Corbignano** is the 16C **Oratorio del Vannella** (1719–21) recently restored (open for a service on the last Sunday of the month, otherwise ☎ 055 604 418). The fresco of the *Madonna and Child*, believed by Berenson to be an early work of Botticelli's, was for centuries venerated by the stonemasons and sculptors of Settignano. The road ends at the cemetery of Settignano (see below).

From Ponte a Mensola the main road continues up to Settignano, winding across the old road; both have fine views of the magnificent trees on the skyline of the surrounding hills. The main road passes the conspicuous neo-Gothic Mezzaratta by Alfonso Coppedè (1920) and (right) Villa Viviani where Mark Twain finished *Pudd'nhead Wilson* in 1892.

Settignano

Settignano (178m), a peaceful village on a pleasant hill, is little visited by tourists. It has narrow, picturesque lanes and many fine villas surrounded by luxurious gardens. Delightful country walks can be taken in the vicinity. It is known for its school of sculptors, the most famous of whom were Desiderio (1428–64) and the brothers Rossellino Antonio Gamberelli, (1427–79) and Bernardo Gamberelli (1409–64).

The bus terminates in the piazza. The church of **Santa Maria** stands here, built in 1518 and reconstructed at the end of the 18C. It contains a charming group of the *Madonna and Child with Two Angels* in white enamelled terracotta, attributed to the workshop of Andrea della Robbia. The 16C organ was reconstructed in 1908 and has been restored. The pulpit was designed by Bernardo Buontalenti. In the dome above the high altar is an *Assumption of the Virgin* by Pier Dandini. On the north side, the second altar has a painted terracotta statuette of *St Lucy* attributed to Michelozzo, surrounded by frescoes of 1593.

Outside in the piazza, there is a statue by Leopoldo Costoli of *Niccolò Tommaseo*, the patriotic writer who died here in 1874. In the lower Piazza Desiderio there is a superb view of Florence.

The numerous narrow lanes in and around Settignano, mostly with splendid views over unspoilt countryside, are well worth exploring on foot. From the right of the church, **Via Capponcina** leads downhill to Via dei Buonarroti-Simoni and **Villa Michelangelo** (no. 65; no admission), where Michelangelo spent his youth (a charcoal drawing of a triton or satyr, attributed to him, was found on the kitchen wall, and was detached and restored in 1979).

Further downhill, surrounded by a garden with cypresses and pine trees, is **Villa la Capponcina** (no. 32) where Gabriele d'Annunzio lived in 1898–1910 and wrote most of his best works.

The narrow main road of Settignano (Via San Romano) continues from the piazza and Via Rossellino soon diverges right to the **Villa Gamberaia** (no. 72). It has a famous *garden* considered one of the most representative of Tuscany, which is immaculately maintained and has remarkable topiary. It is privately owned, but open to the public (opening times 09.00–18.00, 09.00–19.00 in summer; ring the bell; ☎ 055 697 205; Lire 15,000). It was laid out in 1717 by Andrea Capponi. The famous parterre garden survives with cypress, yew and box hedges designed around a fountain (the beds were replaced by pools at the beginning of this century). From the terrace, there is a wonderful view beyond olive groves to Settignano on its ridge and the Duomo beyond. An ilex wood surrounds the garden as well as ancient cypresses and pine trees. There are two elaborate grottoes and a fine collection of azaleas.

POGGIO IMPERIALE AND PIAN DE' GIULLARI

The peaceful little hamlet of Pian de' Giullari, where Galileo spent the last years of his life, can be visited on a beautiful walk from the centre of Florence along Via di San Leonardo. In the vicinity are lovely country roads which pass impressive villas. The villa of Poggio Imperiale is not open regularly to visitors but can be seen by appointment.

Getting there
By bus

Bus no. 11 leaves Piazza San Marco and Via Serragli for **Poggio Imperiale**. Also bus no. 38 (infrequent service, but operates if pre-booked, ☎ 800 019 794) from Porta Romana via Poggio Imperiale (Largo Fermi) for **Pian de' Giullari**.

Poggio Imperiale

Outside Porta Romana (**Map 5; 6**), Viale del Poggio Imperiale (**Map 4; 8**)—a long, straight avenue of cypresses laid out in the 17C, lined with handsome villas and gardens—leads up to the huge villa of Poggio Imperiale. The neo-classical façade is by Pasquale Poccianti and Giuseppe Cacialli (1814–23). It contains 17C painted decorations by Matteo Rosselli and others, and 18C rooms. Admission readily granted by previous appointment.

After the villa was confiscated from the Salviati family by Cosimo I in 1565, it remained the property of the grand-dukes of Florence; it takes its name from the Grand-duchess Maria Maddalena, the widow of Cosimo II and the sister of the Habsburg emperor Ferdinand II. Mozart gave a concert here in 1770. Since 1865, it has been used as school.

To the left of the villa, in Largo Fermi, is the entrance to the **Observatory of Arcetri**, part of the Institute of Astronomy of the University.

Several narrow roads meet here, and there is a bus terminus (no. 38, see above). Via Suor Maria Celeste, named after Galileo's daughter (see below), is a lovely old road with fine views. To the right is Via Guglielmo Righini which winds up to join Via del Pian de' Giullari in front of the very high garden wall of **Villa Capponi** (no. 3). The villa was bought by Gino Capponi in 1572, and its beautiful *garden, divided into three parts, preserves its 16C character (privately owned and not open to the public; but admission sometimes granted to scholars by previous appointment). Via del Pian de' Giullari continues uphill to reach the junction with Via Torre del Gallo. Via del Pian de' Giullari continues right past the park of the **Torre del Gallo**, reconstructed in medieval style by Stefano Bardini in 1904–06.

In the picturesque little village of **Arcetri** or **Pian de' Giullari** stands **Villa il Gioiello** (no. 42), the house where the aged Galileo lived from 1631 until his death in 1642 (see p 284). The 16C house and farm, with a loggia overlooking its lovely gardens, are owned by the state (for admission ask at the Observatory). Beyond is the no. 38 bus terminus, from which several attractive roads can be explored on foot. On the right, Via San Matteo in Arcetri leads to the rebuilt convent where Galileo's illegimate daughter, Suor Maria Celeste, lived as a nun, before she died at the age of 33 in 1634. One hundred and twenty-four remarkable letters from her to Galileo survive. On the left, Via Pian dei Giullari (signposted for Santa

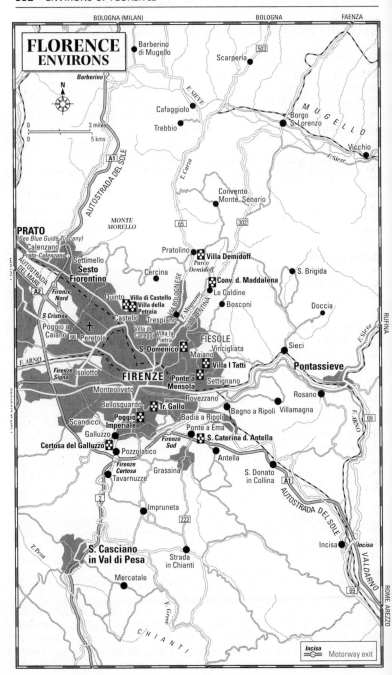

FLORENCE ENVIRONS

BOLOGNA (MILAN)

BOLOGNA

FAENZA

Barberino

N

0   3 miles
0   5 kms

A1

AUTOSTRADA DEL SOLE

Barberino di Mugello

Scarperia

503

Cafaggiolo

Trebbio

M U G E L L O

Borgo S. Lorenzo

Vicchio

F. Sieve

F. SIEVE

T. Carza

Convento Monte Senario

MONTE MORELLO

65

302

PRATO
(See Blue Guide Tuscany)

Calenzano
Prato-Calenzano

AUTOSTRADA DEL MARE

A2

Settimello

Sesto Fiorentino

Firenze Nord

S. Cristina

Poggio a Caiano

Peretola

66

Quinto

Villa di Castello
Villa della Petraia

Castello

Villa di Careggi

Villa la Pietra

Trespiano

VIA BOLOGNESE

T. Mugnone

VIA FAENTINA

Pratolino

Villa Demidoff
(Parco Demidoff)

Conv. d. Maddalena

Le Caldine

Bosconi

Cercina

S. Brigida

Doccia

F. Sieve

RUFINA

FIESOLE

Vincigliata

Sieci

S. Domenico

Maiano

Villa I Tatti

Pontassieve

F. ARNO

Firenze Signa

Isolotto

FIRENZE

Monteoliveto

Bellosguardo

Scandicci

Galluzzo

Certosa del Galluzzo

Poggio Imperiale

Tr. Gallo

Settignano

Ponte a Mensola

Rovezzano

Badia a Ripoli

Ponte a Ema

Firenze Sud

S. Caterina d. Antella

Pozzolatico

Firenze Certosa

Tavarnuzze

Grassina

Antella

Bagno a Ripoli

Villamagna

Rosano

RUFINA

F. Sieve

Rosano

69

F. ARNO

S. Donato in Collina

A1

AUTOSTRADA DEL SOLE

2

Impruneta

222

S. Casciano in Val di Pesa

Strada in Chianti

Incisa

Incisa

VALDARNO

69

T. Pesa

Mercatale

F. Greve

C H I A N T I

ROME, AREZZO

Incisa ⊨ Motorway exit

Margherita dei Montici) continues past **Villa Ravà** (no. 71), purchased by Francesco Guicciardini in 1527, who wrote his famous history of Italy here. Beyond several more villas the road continues through open countryside, leaving the locality of Pian de' Giullari, and climbs up to the church of **Santa Margherita a Montici** (opening times Sunday 10.00–12.30). This has a distinctive crenellated campanile and occupies a splendid position, with views of the two valleys of the Arno and Ema. The church contains two paintings by the Maestro di Santa Cecilia, one of which, *St Margaret and Scenes From her Life*, is thought to date from before 1300. Also in the sanctuary is a ciborium by Andrea Sansovino.

MONTEOLIVETO AND BELLOSGUARDO

Both Monteoliveto and Bellosguardo can be visited on foot from the Oltrarno. They are both lovely residential districts with some large villas where famous writers stayed in the 19C. There are superb views of Florence from the road up to Bellosguardo and delightful walks nearby.

Getting there
Bus no. 12 from Piazza Santa Maria Novella to Viale Raffaello Sanzio (for Monteoliveto) and Piazza Torquato Tasso (for Bellosguardo). Also bus no. 42 (nine times a day) for Bellosguardo (going on to Marignolle) from Porta Romana.

Monteoliveto
On the south bank of the Arno, near Ponte della Vittoria (**Map 2; 5**) is the thickly wooded hill of Monteoliveto.

It is reached via Viale Raffaello Sanzio and (right) Via di Monteoliveto (**Map 5; 1**). The church of **San Bartolomeo** was founded in 1334 by monks from the convent of Monteoliveto Maggiore in Tuscany, and rebuilt in the 15C; it has been restored several times since. For admission, ring at no. 72A, 09.00–13.00.

The west wall and triumphal arch have good frescoes by Bernardino Poccetti. On the second altar on the south side, there is an *Assumption of the Virgin* signed and dated 1592 by Domenico Passignano, below which is a little reliquary case with a charming 18C figure of the Virgin Mary as a baby. On the high altar, the *Entry of Christ into Jerusalem* is a copy by Il Poppi of an altarpiece by Santi di Tito. The domed sanctuary and triumphal arch are interesting works which show the influence of Leon Battista Alberti and Francesco da Sangallo. On the left wall, there is a fresco fragment (with its sinopia opposite) of the *Last Supper* by Sodoma. The first altarpiece on the north side is by Domenico Passignano and his follower Fabrizio Boschi, and the second altarpiece by Simone Pignone. Six 18C scagliola altar-frontals are to be reinstalled after restoration.

The road ends in front of an entrance to the **Villa Strozzi** (opening times daily 09.00–dusk). This has a beautiful wooded park with fine views of Bellosguardo and has been owned by the Comune of Florence since 1974. The gardens are now well kept, and the gravel paths have been lined with *pietra serena* curbs. The villa was restored in 1994 and is used by a school of design. There are two other entrances, one on Via Pisana (**Map 5; 1**), and one on Via Soffiano.

Bellosguardo

The adjoining hill, with cypresses and pine trees to the south, is aptly called Bellosguardo. Numerous illustrious visitors to Florence, including many writers in the 19C, stayed in the lovely villas here. It is approached from Piazza San Francesco di Paola (**Map 5; 3**).

In the piazza stands the church of **San Francesco di Paola** (open for services only). This was built by the Minims, the friars of San Francesco di Paola in 1593, and has early 18C decorations and a detached fresco of the *Madonna del Parto* by Taddeo Gaddi. To the right of the church is the gloomy Villa Pagani, with a tower built by Adolfo Coppedè in 1896.

Via di Bellosguardo climbs uphill to a little walled public garden behind a hedge, with a few pines and cypresses. Here is the Villa dello Strozzino, a fine Renaissance villa with a pretty loggia at one corner.

On the right, the narrow **Via Monteoliveto** leads to the ancient little church of San Vito (**Map 5; 3**; open for a service on *fest.* mornings) with a pretty porch. The interior was remodelled in 1662.

Via di Bellosguardo continues uphill with a superb view back of Florence, and, on the right beside a group of pine trees, is Villa Brichieri-Colombi (no. 20). This was owned by Miss Isa Blagden in 1849–73, and she was often visited here by the Brownings. Henry James wrote *The Aspern Papers* here in 1887. The old road narrows and a sharp turn left (Via Roti Michelozzi) ends at **Torre di Bellosguardo**, well restored as a hotel, with a delightful garden and magnificent views of Florence. Adjoining it (entrance from Piazza di Bellosguardo) is the **Villa dell'Ombrellino**, ostentatiously restored in 1988 as a trade centre and used for conferences and receptions. The villa was rented by Galileo in 1617–31 before moving to Arcetri. Violet Trefusis lived here until her death in 1973.

Piazza di Bellosguardo has a few trees and at no. 6 stands the Villa Belvedere di Saraceni by Baccio d'Agnolo with a courtyard (now in very poor condition). Via San Carlo leads downhill out of the piazza towards the conspicuous tower of Villa di Montauto where Nathaniel Hawthorne stayed in 1859. It provided the setting for the castle of Monte Beni in his novel *The Marble Faun* (1860).

From Piazza di Bellosguardo, Via Piana (beyond **Map 5; 5**) continues past more luxurious villas ending at Via di Santa Maria a Marignolle. The road to the left leads to **Villa la Colombaia** (**Map 5; 7**; no. 2), with a closed-in loggia, which is now a convent school. Florence Nightingale was born here in 1820. From here the lovely old Via delle Campora can be followed back down-hill to Porta Romana (**Map 5; 6**), with pretty views of Florence.

THE CERTOSA DEL GALLUZZO

This is a historic monastery which now has a remarkably peaceful atmosphere. It is interesting for its architecture as well as its frescoes by Pontormo. The Certosa del Galluzzo can be reached from the centre of Florence by bus in about 30 minutes.

Getting there
By bus

Bus no. 37 leaves Piazza Santa Maria Novella (every 20 minutes) and there is a request stop below the hill of the Certosa.

The Via Senese begins in the Porta Romana (**Map 5; 6**), described in Ch. 19; from here it climbs and then descends through Gelsomino to Galluzzo, passing (right) the thick cypresses of the **Cimitero Evangelico degli Allori**. Formerly, this was a cemetery only for Orthodox Greeks, but since 1878 it has been the Protestant cemetery of Florence. At Galluzzo, beside the Ema, a road just before the piazza diverges right and ascends behind the Certosa to **Villa i Collazzi**, a beautiful Mannerist villa built by Agostino Dino in 1560. The garden has fine trees, including cypresses, oaks and ilexes, and there is a parterre on a terrace below the villa.

Certosa del Galluzzo

Beyond the village of Galluzzo, immediately to the right of the road on the Colle di Montaguto, stands the Certosa del Galluzzo. The monks' cells, the church and the Gothic Palazzo degli Studi are on the edge of the hill. A road ascends to the car park. Opening times 09.00–11.30, 15.00–17.30 (winter 15.00–17.00); closed Mon (☎ 055 204 9226). Tours are conducted by monks about every half hour. There are usually very few people here and it is a remarkably peaceful place to visit.

The monastery was founded in 1342 by the Florentine Niccolò Acciaioli. In 1958, the Carthusians were replaced by Cistercians, their first reappearance in the area since their expulsion by the Grand-duke of Tuscany 176 years earlier. There are now only 7 monks here.

From the entrance, a long flight of steps ascends to the upper floor of the **Palazzo degli Studi** which was begun by Niccolò Acciaioli as a meeting place for young Florentines to study the liberal arts. Five frescoed *lunettes of the *Passion* cycle (severely damaged) by Pontormo (1522–25) are exhibited here—they are among his most important works and were detached from the Great Cloister. They were painted when he came to live in the monastery in order to escape the plague in Florence in 1522. Behind the *Crucifix*, which dates from 1350–60, are five oil paintings by Jacopo Chimenti, known as Empoli, which are excellent copies of Pontormo's lunettes showing their original appearance. Also here is a fresco by Empoli of the *Sermon on the Mount* detached from the top of the stairs, and another copy by him of a work by Pontormo, this time his *Supper at Emmaus*, now in the Uffizi. Other works belonging to the Certosa at present removed for restoration include: a tondo of the *Madonna and Child* by the school of Orcagna; *Saints Peter Martyr and George* by Raffaellino del Garbo; *Madonna Enthroned with Saints* by Ridolfo del Ghirlandaio; *Coronation of the Madonna with Saints* by Mariotto di Nardo; and a *Madonna* by Jacopo del Casentino.

An adjoining room displays 16C–17C works, including a series of paintings of the *Apostles* by Orazio Fidani (1653).

The spacious *courtyard dates from 1545. The 16C façade of the **church** is by Cosimo Fancelli. The interior is divided into two parts: the monk's choir has fine vaulting (covered in the 17C with frescoes by Orazio Fidani) and good 16C stalls. On the east wall is a fresco by Bernardino Poccetti (1591–92).

The visit continues through the extensive conventual buildings, entered through a door on the left wall of the church. Here the **colloquio**, reserved for conversation with visitors, has interesting 16C stained glass, and beyond is a charming little cloister reconstructed in the late 16C by Giovanni Fancelli. Off it is the **chapter house**, with the pavement tomb of Leonardo Buonafede, which has an expressive effigy by Francesco da Sangallo (1550), and a good fresco of the *Crucifixion* by Mariotto Albertinelli (1506). A door leads out into the secluded *great cloister* decorated with 66 tondi containing white majolica busts of Saints and Prophets, by Andrea and Giovanni della Robbia. In the centre is a well of 1521 and the monks' cemetery, still in use. One of the **monks' cells**, at the beginning of the right walk, may be visited; they each have three rooms, a loggia and a little garden. Most of the cells have a fresco over the door, and a little window through which their food was passed.

The church of **Santa Maria** was built in 1404–07 (the stained glass window is by Niccolò di Pietro Gerini) but remodelled in 1841. Beneath the lay brethren's choir is a chapel (closed at present) with the magnificent *tomb-slab of Cardinal Agnolo II Acciaioli*, now thought to be the work of Francesco da Sangallo. There are three more beautiful pavement tombs of the Acciaioli family and the Gothic monument to the founder, Niccolò Acciaioli (d. 1365).

THE MEDICI VILLAS AND SESTO FIORENTINO

The villas of Careggi, La Petraia and Castello on the outskirts of Florence were all Medici residences. The Villa di Careggi, although historically the most important, is now surrounded by hospital buildings, but has recently been opened to the public. The other two villas are very close to each other (10 minutes' walk) and are still surrounded by splendid well-kept gardens. The busy suburb of Sesto Fiorentino has an interesting Porcelain Museum.

Getting there
By bus

Bus no. 14C from Via de' Martelli or Stazione Santa Maria Novella (right side) to the Villa di Careggi (the penultimate request stop before the terminus). No. 28 from Stazione Santa Maria Novella (right side) for La Petraia (the second 'Castello' request stop), and for Villa di Castello (the last 'Castello' request stop), and Sesto Fiorentino (terminus). Although you should definitely take a bus to cross the uninteresting northern suburbs of Florence, you can take pretty country walks in the hills behind Careggi, La Petraia, and Castello.

The Medici Villa di Careggi

Careggi has given its name to the main hospital of Florence. At the top of the hill, beyond the buildings of the hospital at no. 17 Viale Pieraccini (request-stop), in a well-wooded park, is the Villa Medicea di Careggi. It is open 08.00–18.00; Sat 09.00–12.00; closed *fest*. (☎ 055 427 9755). This was one of the most important Medici villas, but only a few painted decorations from the early 17C survive and most of the rooms are still unfortunately used as administrative offices.

History of the villa

The 14C castellated farmhouse owned by Tommaso Lippi was acquired by Giovanni di Bicci de' Medici in 1417 for use as a suburban residence. His son Cosimo il Vecchio returned here after his exile in Venice in 1434, and employed Michelozzo to enlarge the villa and add a loggia. It became the literary and artistic centre of the Medicean court, and is traditionally taken as the meeting place of the famous Platonic Academy which saw the birth of the humanist movement of the Renaissance. Among its members, who met in the gardens here, were Marsilio Ficino, Angelo Poliziano, Pico della Mirandola, and Greek scholars, including Gemisthos Plethon and Argyropoulos, who came to Florence after the fall of Constantinople. Cosimo il Vecchio, Piero di Cosimo, and Lorenzo il Magnifico all died in the villa. It was burnt after the expulsion of the Medici at the end of the 15C, but renovated by Cosimo I who commissioned works from Pontormo (now lost) to decorate it. In the early 19C it was owned by Lord Holland, who sold it to Francis Sloane in 1848. He restored it and partly transformed the garden. It became a nurses' home in 1930, and is now used partly as administrative offices by the hospital of Careggi, and partly for meetings and lectures.

The **courtyard**, which incorporates parts of older buildings and has an ancient well, has composite capitals with acanthus leaves designed by Michelozzo. Off it, on the **ground floor**, is a room with early 17C frescoed lunettes by Michelangelo Cinganelli. In a garden loggia there is a fresco by George Frederic Watts of the *Murder of Pietro Leoni*, Lorenzo il Magnifico's doctor (who was thrown into the well in the courtyard accused of not saving Lorenzo's life) which was painted in 1844–45 while Watts was staying here as a guest of Lord Holland.

A 16C staircase leads up to the **first floor**. A little studio used by Carlo de' Medici in the early 17C has a vault fresco with grotteschi by Michelangelo Cinganelli. The delightful corner **loggia**, with columns on three sides, overlooking the garden, has a charming ceiling frescoed with birds and grotteschi.

Near the custodian's office on the ground floor is an interesting **underground cellar**, dating from the early 17C, with a barrel vault painted with a trellis and birds, a worn majolica floor, and a grotto decorated with shells.

Part of the **garden** survives, laid out c 1617 probably by Giulio Parigi, with laurel hedges and ilex groves. It was altered in the 19C and 20C when the palm trees, cedars, and sequoia were planted. The orangery dates from the mid 19C. Some paths with pebble mosaics survive, and there are plants in pots.

The Medici Villa della Petraia

Villa della Petraia standing on the site of a 14C castle of the Strozzi, was rebuilt in 1575 (preserving the tower of the castle) for the Grand-duke Ferdinando I by Buontalenti. In 1864–70 Vittorio Emanuele II lived here, and in 1919 it was presented to the State by Vittorio Emanuele III.

• Open 09.00–dusk; except second and third Mon of month; the villa closes 1 hour before dusk (☎ 055 451 208). Lire 4000 (cumulative ticket with the Villa di Castello gardens). (S). Refreshments are available.

The garden

The beautiful **lower garden** was designed in the late 16C for Ferdinando with symmetrical parterres on terraces descending from the moat in front of the villa which served as a fishpond as well as a cistern for irrigation (it is now full of gold-fish and carp). It was altered in the 19C under the influence of Victorian taste, but dwarf pear trees and persimmons have recently been replanted in this part of the garden, and the meadows of wild flowers (particularly beautiful in early spring) are left uncut as they were in the days of the Medici grand-dukes. The very fine hedges throughout the garden are planted with libernum, laurel, and box.

On the **upper terrace** of the garden, on either side of the villa, from which there is a fine view, pots of orange and lemon trees are put out around Eastertime (taken in in the winter). The beautiful **fountain** by Tribolo and Pierino da Vinci, with a bronze statue by Giambologna of *Fiorenza,* has been replaced by a very fine copy, and the original has been removed to the inside of the villa since its restoration. On the other side of the villa is a charming symmetrical **Giardino segreto**, or secret garden, recreated in 1991 as it would have been at the end of the 16C and in the 17C. This had rare plants such as asparagus, artichokes, tulips. The little garden is at its best from late February to April. A magnificent **park**, with ancient cypresses, extends behind the villa to the east. The park and gardens are beautifully maintained.

The villa

The villa is shown on request (ring the bell). The 16C **courtyard** was covered with a glass roof and given a Venetian floor and chandelier so that it could be used as a ballroom by Vittorio Emanuele II. The decorative *frescoes beneath the two side loggias, illustrating the history of the Medici family, are by Volterrano (1636–46); those on the other two walls have late 16C grotteschi by Cosimo Daddi. In two rooms off the courtyard are temporarily displayed the bronze group of *Antaeus and Hercules* by Ammannati (1558–59), removed from a fountain in the garden of Villa di Castello (see p 359), and four bronze putti from the same fountain. Another room displays two paintings by Crescenzio Onofrio and Alessandro Magnasco, and two sculptures of gladiators (also removed from the garden of Castello where they have been replaced by copies), one by Domenico Pieratti and the other an antique Roman work integrated by Pieratti.

On the other side of the courtyard is the splendid **Sala Rossa** hung with tapestries: four of them are 18C Flemish works from Parma and the other was made in Florence in the 17C. The huge 19C carpet has been restored in situ. There is a collection of clocks here and in the following rooms. In the **chapel** (1682–95), with frescoes attributed to Pier Dandini or Del Moro, is a painting of the *Madonna and Child* by Pier Francesco Fiorentino, and an altarpiece of the *Holy Family* by the school of Andrea del Sarto.

The private apartments on the **first floor** are decorated in neo-classical style. In the corridor is a remarkable long Chinese silk scroll painting of the Port of Canton (1765). In a room off the loggia is exhibited the original bronze statue of *Fiorenza* (Florence wringing the water of the Arno and Mugnone from her hair) by Giambologna, removed since its restoration in 1980 from the fountain in the garden. The **bedroom** of the 'Bella Rosina', wife of Vittorio Emanuele II, decorated in blue damask, has the best early 19C Piedmontese furniture. The **Salotto Giallo**, with yellow walls in the style known as *retour d'Egypte*, has French chairs, and a travelling desk made in Lucca, all in Empire style. In the **chapel** are frescoes by Cosimo Daddi and a copy of Raphael's *Madonna dell'Impannata*. The billiard room is a remarkable period piece, with chintz furniture, hung with 17C paintings by Francesco Curradi, Passignano, and two by Mattia Rosselli acquired by Cardinal Carlo de' Medici. There is a remarkable collection of late 19C or early 20C parlour games and mid 19C alabasters, including intricate globes.

In Via della Petraia is Villa 'Il Bel Riposo', with a castellated tower, where Carlo Lorenzini (Collodi) lived while writing *Pinocchio*. Opposite is **Villa Corsini**, rebuilt for Filippo Corsini in 1698–99 by Antonio Ferri, with an interesting Baroque façade. A plaque records the death here in 1649 of Sir Robert Dudley. The villa has been restored since its acquisition by the state, and is at present used as a store for works of art awaiting restoration. The villa and garden are sometimes open for exhibitions and concerts.

The Medici Villa di Castello

In front of Villa Corsini, Via di Castello leads in five minutes to the Villa di Castello.

- Admission to the gardens only, 09.00–dusk; closed second and third Monday of the month (☎ 055 454791). (S). Lire 4000. (Cumulative ticket with the Villa della Petraia.)

Although the fountains have been altered and some of the statues removed over the centuries, this is the Medici garden which perhaps best preserves its 16C appearance, and it was the model for all subsequent Italianate gardens. It is still of the greatest botanical interest, especially for its magnificent tubs of citrus trees.

History of the villa

The villa was acquired by Giovanni and Lorenzo di Pierfrancesco de' Medici, Lorenzo il Magnifico's younger cousins, in 1476. Here they hung Botticelli's famous *Birth of Venus*. Botticelli's *Primavera* and *Pallas and the Centaur* were also later brought here (and all the pictures remained in the house until 1761). The villa, inherited by Giovanni delle Bande Nere, was sacked during the siege of 1530, but restored for Giovanni's son, Cosimo I, by Bronzino and Pontormo. It was bought by the state since 1919, and drastically 'restored' and transformed in the early 1970s as the seat of a national research council and of the **Accademia della Crusca**, founded in 1582 for the study of the Italian language. The first edition of the institute's dictionary dates from 1612.

The garden

Cosimo I employed Tribolo in 1541 to lay out the garden. The **fountains** were laid out on a central axis intent on celebrating the establishment of the Medici family as absolute monarchs in Tuscany. This was altered in the 18C when the great marble *fountain by Tribolo (with the help of Pierino da Vinci) was moved to its central position: formerly it was the fountain closest to the villa, and the crowning bronze figures of *Hercules and Antaeus* by Ammannati (1559–60), represented the triumph of Hercules (or Cosimo) over Vice. Since its restoration this has been temporarily exhibited in the Villa della Petraia (see above), while the exquisitely carved base, some 6m high, has been carefully restored in one of the garden buildings here and a copy (the largest of its kind ever made in Italy) will be installed in situ.

The fountain which used to be in the centre of the gardens, which represented Florence as head of the grand-duchy, no longer exists, although the crowning figure of Fiorenza, is now in the Villa della Petraia. The third element, beneath the terrace, was the elaborate *grotto, also probably designed by Tribolo, full of exotic animals and encrusted with shell mosaics and stalactites, and lined with natural stone taken from real grottoes. The huge basin on the left has beautifully carved decorations thought to be by the hand of Tribolo himself. The grotto has been restored and survives in remarkably good condition. Giambologna's bronze birds, now in the Bargello, were removed from here. In the floor and round the walls are water spouts so that visitors (who were 'locked in' by a gate) could be surprised by a thorough drenching from their hosts.

From the **upper terrace**, backed by woods, there is a good view. Here, surrounded by an ilex wood, or *bosco*, inhabited by numerous birds, is a colossus representing *Appennino* rising out of a pool and feeling the cold, by Ammannati.

The garden is at its best from April to June, and when the magnificent collection of **citrus fruit trees**, in some 1000 terracotta tubs, are put out in the gardens for the summer around Eastertime. The citrus fruit trees make up one of the most important collections in the world of its kind, with over 100 varieties including some unique antique varieties. Some of the plants are 300 years old. Some citrus fruit trees are still grown outside at the top of the garden, and there is a fine collection of azelias. Inside the beds surrounded by low box hedges tulips, daffodills, and bluebells flower in March.

On the right is the charming little **giardino segreto** (opened on request, and its best in spring), created in the late 17C by Cosimo III, where an unusual variety of cream-coloured jasmine from India grows (in flower from July to October). The box hedges were replanted here ten years ago and some classical varieties of antique rose reintroduced. The lower area of this little garden has about 400 varieties of aromatic and medicinal herbs which were known to have been cultivated here in the 16C (including some 20 varieties of thyme and 20 of sage). The garden is beautifully maintained and the four gardeners take care not to use chemical fertilisers.

Sesto Fiorentino

The no. 28 bus route ends at Sesto Fiorentino, a small town (41,900 inhabitants). At the entrance on the left is **Villa Corsi Salviati**, where exhibitions are held, with a beautiful 17C and 18C garden.

Next to the Ginori porcelain factory, the **Museo della Porcellane di Doccia** (entrance at 31 Viale Pratese), in a fine modern building (by Piero Berardi, 1965), contains a large well displayed *collection of porcelain made in the famous Doccia factory founded by Marchese Carlo Ginori in 1735. Open Tues, Thurs & Sat 09.30–13.00, 15.30–18.30; closed August (☎ 055 420491). Lire 8000.

The museum includes some of the earliest porcelain painted by Carlo Wendelin Anreiter von Zirnfeld of Vienna, and the first models by Gaspero Bruschi and Massimiliano Soldani. The firm, known as Richard-Ginori since 1896, continues to flourish. Across the road, in a warehouse, Ginori seconds can be purchased.

VILLA LA PIETRA AND PRATOLINO

On the outskirts of Florence, on via Bolognese, is Villa La Pietra, the former residence of Harold Acton, famous for its private garden which is, however, at present closed for restoration. Further along the Via Bolognese is the huge park of the Villa Demidoff at Pratolino, only open on certain days of the week in certain months of the year.

Getting there
By bus

No. 25, which leaves the Stazione Santa Maria Novella (east side) and Piazza San Marco about every 25 minutes, goes as far as Pratolino, with a request stop for Villa la Pietra.

The Via Bolognese, which leaves Florence north of Piazza della Libertà (**Map 4; 1**) at Ponte Rosso, is the old Roman road to Bologna.

At the beginning of the road is the Giardino dell'Orticoltura, described in Ch. 22. Via Bolognese continues uphill out of the city past a number of villas, including **Villa la Pietra** (no. 120), surrounded by a park, and preceded by a long avenue of cypresses above pink China rose-bushes.

The garden is being restored, but is usually open to the public only by previous written appointment (☎ 055 474 448, 🖹 055 472 725)

The villa was built in the 1460s and remodelled by Cardinal Luigi Capponi in 1650. Carlo Fontana and Ferdinando Ruggieri redesigned it for the Capponi in 1705. It was bought in 1902 by Arthur Acton, and was the birthplace and residence of his son, the aesthete and historian Sir Harold Acton (1904–94), one of the most famous Anglo-Florentines of this century, who was made an honorary citizen of Florence in 1986. He bequeathed the villa to New York University and it is now used as a branch campus which takes undergraduate and graduate students, as well as a conference centre. It contains one of the most interesting private collections of works of art in Florence (formed by Arthur Acton) including a notable group of early Tuscan paintings.

The beautiful ***garden**, a successful imitation of a 16C Tuscan garden, was created in 1904 by Arthur Acton and was at its best around 1937. Many of the plants were replaced in 2000 in a ten year restoration project carried out by an English firm, and it is estimated that it will take at least two years before it begins to grow back. The master plan is based on archival material and is being implemented with the utmost care.

It is a green garden, on a very large scale, in which over 200 allegorical 17C statues, some by Orazio Marinali, are a special feature. The garden was designed to be viewed from the upper terrace and the house, and is laid out in 'rooms' on different levels. The planting is predominantly box, yew, cypress and ilex, with hedges of cypress and ilex, and low box edging with clipped bay trees. There is a green theatre and good topiary, and a *boschetto* of laurels. The very high terrace attached to the house has cascades of banksia rose and wisteria. The charming walled kitchen garden, or *pomaria*, is decorated with shell mosaic. This was part of the original Renaissance garden, and its pear trees and box and myrtle hedges have been replanted. The beds along the walls have viola and iris and yellow roses. Here orange and lemon trees are kept in pots, and two huge Portugal laurels grow in front of the orangery built in the 1650s. The huge estate has five boundary villas.

Villa Demidoff, Pratolino

Beyond Trespiano and Montorsoli the Via Bolognese follows the long ruined walls of the huge park of Villa Demidoff, the main entrance of which is at Pratolino (with an ample car park on the other side of the road). There is another entrance off the main road nearer Florence, with a car park inside the gate. Some 17–18 hectares of the splendid well-kept park belongs to the province and are open to the public.

• **Opening times** In March, *fest*. 10.00–18.00; April–Sept on Thurs, Fri, Sat and Sun 10.00–20.00; and in Oct, *fest*. 10.00–19.00 (☎ 055 409 427); Lire 5000; no dogs allowed.

The park is one of the most beautiful open spaces near the city, and its fields and woods make it a lovely place to picnic. There is a café-restaurant in one of the farm buildings. The park and garden buildings are being slowly restored.

In 1569, Buontalenti created a remarkable garden here for Francesco I de' Medici. This had many fountains, the most famous of which is Giambologna's colossal statue of *Appennino*, which is still one of the most extraordinary sights in Italy. The park was neglected in the 18C by the Lorraine grand-dukes; they ceased to maintain the fountains and let the aqueduct which fed them ruin the foundations of the villa, which was finally demolished in 1824. In 1872, the property was bought by Paolo Demidoff (1839–85; son of Nicola, a Russian emigré from St Petersburg; see p 288), who built a villa in the *paggeria* (service wing) of the former Medici villa. His descendents lived here until 1955. In the 1960s and 1970s numerous trees were felled and ugly conifers planted. In 1981, it was bought by the province, and since 1986 an artisans' school of builders has been installed in the old stable block and carries out numerous restorations here each year.

From the main entrance, an avenue descends to the main group of farm buildings. From here various paths are signposted. Behind the buildings is Giambologna's splendid colossal statue of **Appennino* (1579–80). The giant is pressing down the head of a monster (water used to gush out of its mouth).

From the farm buildings another path leads past a restored carriage-house (with a café-restaurant) and then winds down past a building constructed as an orangery by the Medici but transformed as a guest house by the Demidoff, to the **Grotta di Cupido**, by Buontalenti (1577). Nearby is the **Viale dei Zampilli**, a wide wooded avenue formerly decorated with fountains, which descends to a lake. Above it can be seen the reconstructed **Grotta del Mugnone**, also by Giambologna (1577). Another path leads up to the **Grande Voliera** (1580), restored by the Demidoff as a swimming pool in 1875. Steps lead up to the spacious green in front of the lovely russet-coloured **paggeria** of the Medici villa, the residence of the Demidoff. In front of the villa, there are three magnolia trees and the original feet and hands of the statue of *Appennino* (substituted in 1877). In a group of trees nearby, there is a well-preserved centrally planned **chapel** with a dome, designed by Buontalenti (1580), near which is the grave of Maria Demidoff who lived in the villa until her death in 1955. In the area of the park to the north are more statues and garden buildings, including a statue of *Jove* (which replaces the original by Baccio Bandinetti now in the Boboli gardens) and a neo-classical building designed by Luigi Cambrai-Digny in 1820 at the top of the park as a hunting lodge.

Glossary

Aedicule small opening framed by two columns and a pediment, originally used in classical architecture

Albarello (pl. *albarelli*) cylindrical shaped pharmacy jars, usually slightly waisted and produced by numerous potteries in Italy from the 15C to 18C.

Amorino (pl. *amorini*) a small cupid or putto

Amphora antique vase, usually of large dimensions, for oil and other liquids

Antefix an ornament at the eaves of the roof to hide the join between tiles

Antiphonal choir-book containing a collection of antiphons—verses sung in response by two choirs

Apse vaulted semicircular end wall of the chancel of a church or of a chapel

Archaic period in Greek civilisation preceding the classical era: from about 750 BC–480 BC

Architrave the lowest part of an entablature, the horizontal frame above a door

Arte (pl. *Arti*), Guild or Corporation

Attic topmost storey of a classical building, hiding the spring of the roof

Avello (pl. *avelli*) family burial vault

Badia, Abbazia Abbey

Baldacchino canopy supported by columns, usually over an altar

Basilica originally a Roman hall used for public administration; in Christian architecture an aisled church with a clerestory and apse and no transepts

Bas-relief sculpture in low relief

Biscuit (or *bisque*) fired but unglazed earthenware or pottery

Borgo a suburb; a street leading away from the centre of a town

Bottega the studio of an artist; the pupils who worked under his direction

Bozzetto (pl. *bozzetti*) sketch, often used to describe a small model for a piece of sculpture

Caldarium or Calidarium room for hot or vapour baths in a Roman bath

Campanile bell-tower, often detached from the building to which it belongs

Canopic jar (or vase), Ancient Egyptian urn used to preserve the internal organs such as the liver and lungs, and placed in the tomb beside the mummy

Cantoria (pl. cantorie) singing-gallery in a church

Cappella chapel

Capomaestro Director of Works or masterbuilder

Cartoon from *cartone*, meaning a large sheet of paper—a full-size preparatory drawing for a painting or fresco

Cassone a decorated chest, usually a dower chest

Cavea the part of a theatre or amphitheatre occupied by the rows of seats

Cenacolo a scene of the Last Supper (in the refectory of a convent)

Chasuble long, sleeveless outer garment worn by a priest when celebrating Mass

Chiaroscuro distribution of light and shade in a painting

Ciborium casket or tabernacle containing the Host

Cinquecento Italian term for the 'fifteen-hundreds' i.e. the 16C

Cipollino onion marble; greyish marble with streaks of white or green

Cippus (pl. *Cippae*) sepulchral monument in the form of an altar

Colloquio Parlour in an ecclesiatic building for conversation or visitors

Commesso fiorentino, Florentine mosaic, the art of working *pietre dure*, hard or semi-precious

Contrapposto a pose in which the body is twisted. First used in classical statuary, it is characteristic of Michelangelo's sculpture and works by the Mannerist school

Corbel a projecting block, usually of stone

Cornice topmost part of a temple entablature; any projecting ornamental moulding at the top of a building beneath the roof

Crater (or krater) a large, open bowl used for mixing wines, especially in ancient Greece

Crenellations battlements

Cupola dome

Diptych painting or ivory tablet in two sections

Duomo cathedral

Exedra semicircular recess

Ex-voto tablet or small painting expressing gratitude to a Saint

Flabellum a large ceremonial fan used in the Roman Catholic Church

Foresteria guest-wing

Fresco (in Italian, *affresco*), painting executed on wet plaster (*intonaco*). On the rough plaster (*arriccio*) beneath, the artist made a sketch (or *sinopia*) which was covered little by little as work on the fresco proceeded. Since the *intonaco* had to be wet during this work, it was applied each day only to that part of the wall on which the artist was sure that he could complete the fresco (these areas, which can now often be detected by restorers, are known as *giornate*). From the 16C onwards cartoons (*cartoni*) were used to help the artist with the over-all design: the *cartone* was transferred on to the *intonaco* either by pricking the outline with small holes over which a powder was dusted, or by means of a stylus which left an incised line on the wet plaster. In the 1960s and 1970s, many frescoes were detached from the walls on which they were executed and so the *sinopie* beneath were discovered (and sometimes also detached)

Frigidarium room for cold baths in a Roman bath

Gonfalone banner of a medieval guild or commune

Gonfaloniere chief magistrate or official of a medieval Italian Republic, the bearer of the Republic's *gonfalone*

Graffiti design on a wall made with an iron tool on a prepared surface, the design showing in white. Also used loosely to describe scratched designs or words on walls

Greek cross church plan based on a cross with arms of equal length

Grisaille painting in various tones of grey

Grotteschi (or grotesques) a style of painting or stucco decoration used by the ancient Romans and discovered in the 1490s in the Domus Aurea in Rome (then underground, hence its name, from 'grotto'). The delicate ornamental decoration, normally on a light background, is characterised by fantastical motifs with intricate patterns of volutes, festoons, garlands, and borders of twisted vegetation and flowers interspersed with small winged human or animal figures, birds, masques, griffins, and sphynxes. This type of decoration became very fashionable and was widely copied by late Renaissance artists

Hemicycle a semicircular structure, room, arena or wall

Hydria a large water jar

Hypocaust ancient Roman heating system in which hot air circulated under the floor and between double walls

Incunabula any book printed before 1500

Intarsia a decorative inlay made from wood, marble or metal

Intonaco plaster

Intrados underside or soffit of an arch

Kylix a shallow, two-handled drinking vessel used in ancient Greece

Kourai from the Greek word for young man (*kouros*) used to describe standing, nude male statues in the Greek Archaic style

Lantern a small circular or polygonal turret with windows all round, crowning a roof or a dome

Latin cross a cross with a long vertical arm, usually used to described the plan of a church

Lavabo (pl. *lavabi*) hand-basin usually outside a refectory or in a sacristy

Lavatorium the Latin name for a room with large hand-basins (*lavabi*) in stone or marble outside a convent refectory where the rites of purification were carried out before a meal

Lekythos an ancient Greek vase, tall and narrow-necked with one handle, used as a vessel for oil

Loggia covered gallery or balcony, usually preceding a larger building

Lunette semicircular space in a vault or ceiling, or above a door or window, often decorated with a painting or relief

Lungarno (pl. *Lungarni*), a road which follows the banks of the Arno

Macigno quartz, used as a building material in Florence

Maestà representation of the Madonna and Child enthroned in majesty

Majolica (or *Maiolica*) a type of earthenware glazed with bright metallic oxides that was originally imported to Italy from Majorca and was extensively made in Italy during the Renaissance

Mandorla an almond-shaped frame in a painting or sculpture

Medallion large medal; loosely, a circular ornament

Monochrome painting or drawing in one colour only

Monolith single stone (usually a column)

Mullion a vertical post or other upright in a window

Niello black substance (usually a compound of sulphur and silver) used in an engraved design, or an object so decorated

Oculus round window

Oinochoe an ancient Greek vase, the standard wine jug, with one handle and a round or trefoil mouth

Opera (del Duomo) the office in charge of the fabric of a building (i.e. the Cathedral)

Opus tessellatum mosaic formed entirely of square tesserae (pieces of marble, stone or glass)

Pala large altarpiece

Palazzo palace, any dignified and important building

Palestra a public place devoted to training athletes in ancient Greece or Rome

Patera a small circular ornamental dish, usually carved; a Greek or Roman dish for libations to the gods

Pax sacred object used by a priest for the blessing of peace and offered for the kiss of the faithful; usually circular,

engraved, enamelled, or painted in a rich gold or silver frame

Pelike an ancient Greek vase—a two-handled container for wine similar to an amphora but usually more capacious

Pendentive concave spandrel beneath a dome

Piano nobile main floor of a palace

Pietà representation of the Virgin mourning the dead Christ (sometimes with other figures)

Pietre dure hard or semi-precious stones, often used in the form of mosaics to decorate furniture such as cabinets and table-tops.

Pietra forte fine-grained limey sand-stone used as a building material in Florence, and often for the rustication of palace façades

Pietra serena fine-grained dark grey sandstone, easy to carve. Although generally not sufficiently resistant for the exterior of buildings, it was used to decorate many Renaissance interiors in Florence

Pilaster a shallow pier or rectangular column projecting only slightly from the wall

Pinnacle a small turret-like termination crowning spires, buttresses and roofs

Pluteus (pl. *plutei*), marble panel, usually decorated; a series of them used to form a parapet to precede the altar of a church

Podestà chief magistrate who ruled a medieval city with the help of a council and representatives from the corporations. He had to be someone who was not a Florentine, and was also a military leader

Polyptych painting or panel in more than three sections

Portone main entrance (large enough for carriages) to a palazzo or villa

Predella small painting or panel, usually in sections, attached below a large altarpiece, illustrating scenes of a story such as the Life of a Saint, or of the Virgin.

Presepio literally crib or manger. A group of statuary of which the central subject is the Infant Jesus in the manger

Pulvin cushion stone between the capital and the impost block

Putto (pl. *putti*) figure sculpted or painted, usually nude, of a child

Quadratura painted architectural perspectives

Quadriga a two-wheeled chariot drawn by four horses abreast

Quadriporticus rectangular court or atrium arcaded on all four sides, derived from the atriums in front of paleochristian basilicas

Quatrefoil four-lobed design

Quattrocento Italian term for the 'fourteen hundreds' i.e. the 15C

Rood-screen a screen below the Rood or Crucifix dividing the nave from the chancel of a church

Scagliola imitation marble or *pietre dure* made from selenite

Scarsella the rectangular recess of the tribune of the Florence Baptistery, first called by this name by the early 14C chronicler Giovanni Villani. Now also sometimes used for the rectangular sanctuary in a church

Schiacciato term used to describe very low relief in sculpture, where there is an emphasis on the delicate line rather than the depth of the panel (a technique perfected by Donatello)

Sinopia large sketch for a fresco made on the rough wall in a red earth pigment called sinopia (because it originally came from Sinope, a town on the Black Sea). When a fresco is detached for restoration, it is possible to see the sinopia beneath, which can also be separated from the wall

Skyphos an ancient Greek vase, a two-handled drinking cup

Spandrel surface between two arches in an arcade or the triangular space on either side of an arch

Sporti overhang, or projecting upper storey of a building, characteristic of medieval houses in Florence

Stamnos an ancient Greek vase, a large two-handled jar used as a container for wine

Stele (pl. *stelae*) upright stone bearing a monumental inscription

Stemma coat of arms or heraldic device

Stoup vessel for Holy Water, usually near the west door of a church

Stucco (pl. *stucchi*) plaster-work

Tempera a painting medium of powdered pigment bound together, in its simplest form, by a mixture of egg yolk and water

Tepidarium room for warm baths in a Roman bath

Term pedestal or terminal figure in human form, tapering towards the base

Terraverde green earth pigment, sometimes used in frescoes

Tessera small cube of marble, stone or glass used in mosaic work

Thermae originally simply Roman baths, later elaborate buildings fitted with libraries, assembly rooms, gymnasia and circuses

Tholos (Greek) a circular building

Tondo (pl. *tondi*) round painting or relief

Transenna open grille or screen, usually of marble, in an early Christian church

Tribune the apse of a Christian basilica that contains the bishop's throne or the throne itself

Triptych painting or tablet in three sections

Triton river god

Trompe l'œil literally, a deception of the eye; used to describe illusionist decoration and painted architectural perspective

Tympanum the area between the top of a doorway and the arch above it; also the triangular space enclosed by the mouldings of a pediment

Viale (pl. *viali*) wide avenue

Villa country house with its garden

Index to Italian Artists

This index lists painters, sculptors and architects mentioned in the Guide, with their dates. Only a few foreign artists who worked in the city are included.

N

R

S

Index

Palazzo di Bianca Cappello 303
Palazzo Borghese 324
Palazzo Buondelmonti 243
Palazzo Caccini 278
Palazzo Canacci 318
Palazzo Canigiani 307
Palazzo dei Canonici 119
Palazzo Capponi (Lungarno Guicciardini) 291
Palazzo Capponi (Via Gino Capponi) 280
Palazzo Capponi delle Rovinate 306
Palazzo del Cardinale Panciatichi 215
Palazzo Castellani 283
Palazzo Castelli (Marucelli) 216
Palazzo Cerchi 321
Palazzo da Cintoia (Salviati) 324
Palazzo del Circolo dell'Unione 243
Palazzo Cocchi 263
Palazzo dei Congressi 329
Palazzo Corbizzi 324
Palazzo Corsi 245, 286
Palazzo Corsini 281
Palazzo Corsini Suarez 303
Palazzo Corsini sul Prato 327
Palazzo di Cosimo Ridolfi 303
Palazzo Covoni 325
Palazzo della Crocetta 200
Palazzo Davanzati 317
Palazzo di Oddo Altoviti 319
Palazzo di Parte Guelfa 318
Palazzo di San Clemente 280
Palazzo Fagni 326
Palazzo Feroni 302
Palazzo Frescobaldi 291, 302
Palazzo della Gherardesca 280
Palazzo Giandonati 318
Palazzo Gianfigliazzi 282
Palazzo Ginori 216
Palazzo Girolami 154
Palazzo Giugni (Via Alfani) 193
Palazzo Giugni (Via dei Cerchi) 321
Palazzo Gondi 258
Palazzo Grifoni Budini Gattai 194
Palazzo Guadagni 297
Palazzo Guicciardini 156, 291, 302
Palazzo Incontri 194
Palazzo Lanfredini 291
Palazzo Larderel 245
Palazzo Larioni dei Bardi 307
Palazzo Lenzi 240
Palazzo Malenchini 325
Palazzo Manetti 302
Palazzo Mannelli-Riccardi 226
Palazzo Martelli 226
Palazzo Masetti (Castelbarco) 282
Palazzo Matteucci Ramirez di Montalvo 323
Palazzo Medici-Riccardi 217
Palazzo Mellini Fossi 325
Palazzina della Meridiana 175

Palazzo Minerbetti 243
Palazzo Montauto 216
Palazzi dei Mozzi 307
Palazzo Neroni 216
Palazzo Niccolini 193
Palazzo Nonfinito 260
Palazzo degli Orti Oricellari 328
Palazzo Panciatichi Ximenes 279
Palazzo Pandolfini 216
Palazzo Pazzi-Quaratesi 260
Palazzo Peruzzi 325
Palazzo Pitti 157
Palazzo dei Pucci 194
Palazzo Ricasoli 281, 303
Palazzo Ridolfi 303
Palazzo Rinuccini 302
Palazzo Roffia 278
Palazzo Rosselli del Turco 319
Palazzo Rucellai 244
Palazzo Rustici (Neri) 325
Palazzo Salviati 323
Palazzo Salviati Quaratesi 324
Palazzo Serristori 288
Palazzo Sforza Alimeni 193
Palazzo della Signoria 126
Palazzo Soldani 326
Palazzo Spinelli 272
Palazzo Spini-Feroni 240
Palazzo Strozzi 243
Palazzo Strozzi del Poeta 243
Palazzo Strozzi di Mantova 117
Palazzo dello Strozzino 244
Palazzo Strozzi-Niccolini 117
Palazzo della Stufa 219
Palazzo Taddei 216
Palazzo Tedaldini 323
Palazzo Torrigiani 291, 301, 305
Palazzo degli Uffizi 136
Palazzo Uguccioni 125
Palazzo Usimbardi (Acciaioli) 320
Palazzo Vecchio 126
Palazzo Visdomini 323
Palazzo Vitali 323
Palazzo Vivarelli Colonna 273
Palazzo della Zecca 153
Palmieri, Matteo 224, 257
Pandolfini, Giannozzo, Bishop 216
Parker, Theodore, of Lexington 333
Parlatore, Filippo 183
Parterre 332
Pasolini, Pier Paolo 303
Pazzi family 260, 270
Pensione Bencistà 346
Peri, Iacopo 191
Peruzzi, Ubaldino 329
Peyron family 347
Pian de' Giullari 351
Piazza d'Azeglio 278

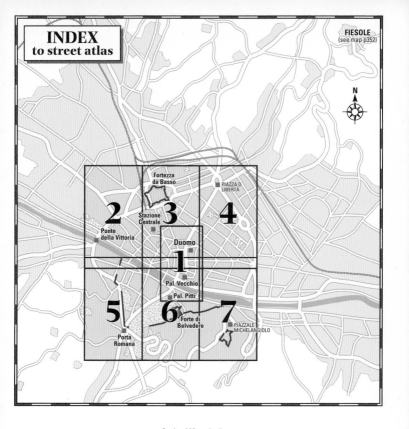

INDEX
to street atlas

FIESOLE
(see map p352)

N

2

Ponte
della Vittoria

**Fortezza
da Basso**

Stazione
Centrale

3

PIAZZA D.
LIBERTÀ

4

Duomo

1

Pal. Vecchio

Pal. Pitti

5

Porta
Romana

6

Forte di
Belvedere

7

PIAZZALE
MICHELANGIOLO

Scale of Maps 2 – 7

0   200 yards

0   200 metres

Scale of Florence Centre map 1

0   100 yards

0   100 metres

 Hotel

 Tourist information

Building of interest

Church

Other building

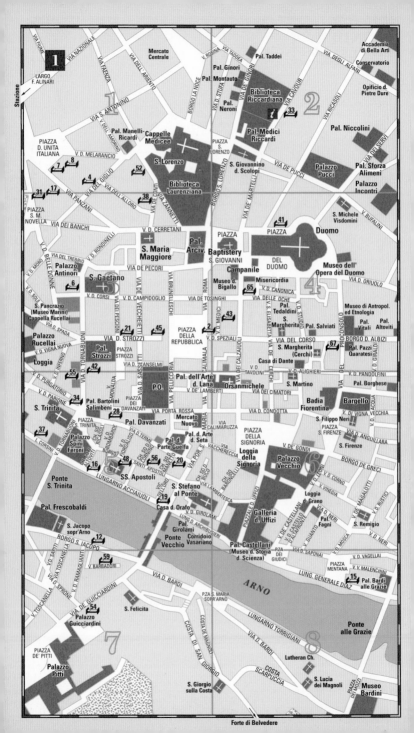

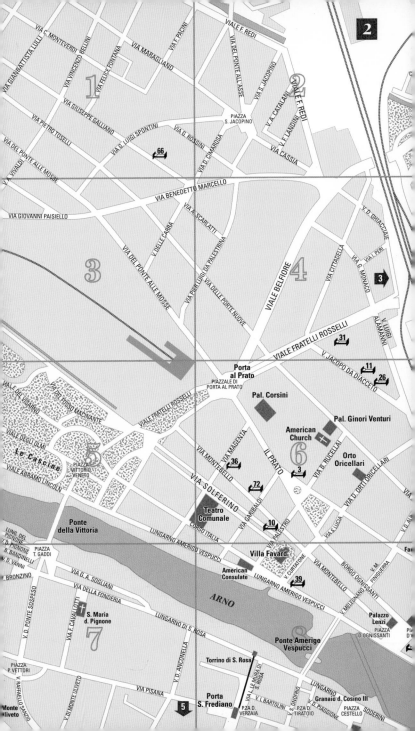

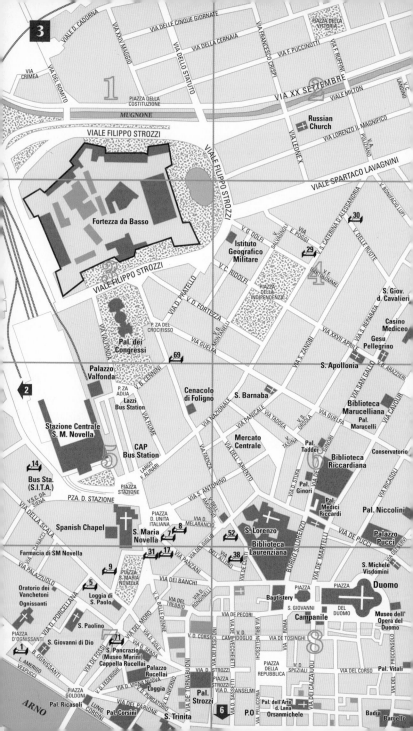

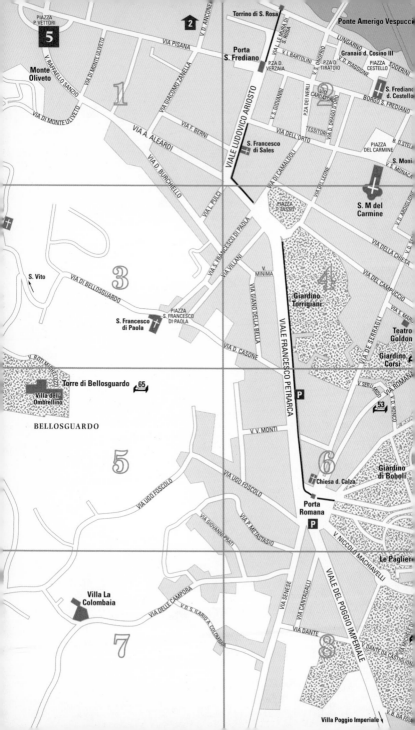

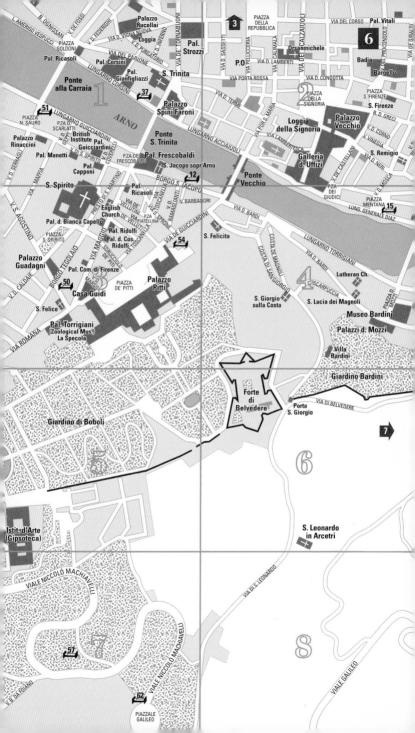

B. OGNISSANTI
L AMERIGO VESPUCCI
V. DE' FOSSI
PIAZZA GOLDONI
VIA D. FEDERIGHI
Palazzo Rucellai
V. D. VIGNA NUOVA
Loggia
V. DI PURGATORIO
VIA DEL PARIONE
V. D. TREBBIO
Pal. Strozzi
PIAZZA DELLA REPUBBLICA
3
VIA DEL CORSO
Pal. Vitali
VIA PORTA ROSSA
VIA DEI CALZAIUOLI
VIA CALIMALA
VIA D. LAMBERTI
Orsanmichele
6
V. D. PROCONSOLO
VIA DE GIRALDI
Badia
Pal. Ricasoli
Pal. Corsini
Pal. Gianfigliazzi
S. Trinita
P.O
VIA D. CONDOTTA
Bargello
VIA D. FERRON
VIA D. PURGATORIO
VIA D. TERME
PIAZZA S. FIRENZE
Ponte alla Carraia
1
ARNO
37
LUNGARNO CORSINI
Palazzo Spini Faroni
PIAZZA DELLA SIGNORIA
2
S. Firenze
B. D. GRECI
51
LUNGARNO GUICCIARDINI
PZA DI SCARLATTI
Ponte S. Trinita
LUNGARNO ACCIAIUOLI
VIA POR S. MARIA
Loggia della Signoria
Palazzo Vecchio
V. D. CORNO
PIAZZA N. SAURO
Palazzo Rinuccini
Pal. Manetti
Pal. Guicciardini
British Institute
Pal. Frescobaldi
S. Jacopo sopr'Arno
BORGO S. JACOPO
12
VIA LAMBERTESCA
Galleria d. Uffizi
V. VINEGIA
V. DE' CASTELLANI
S. Remigio
V. D. NERI
Pal. Capponi
V. DE' SERRAGLI
V. MAFFIA
S. Spirito
PRESTO DI S. MARTINO
V. DE' VELLUTINI
V. TOSCANELLA
V. DELLO SPRONE
V. RAMAGLIANTI
S. BARBAROLI
Ponte Vecchio
PZA DEI GIUDICI
PIAZZA MENTANA
15
LUNG. GENERALE DIAZ
V. D. MOSCA
English Church
Pal. d. Bianca Capello
Pal. Ridolfi
Pal. d. Cos Ridolfi
VIA DE GUICCIARDINI
VIA D. BARDI
S. Felicita
LUNGARNO TORRIGIANI
VIA D. BARDI
V. D. MOZZI
PIAZZA S. SPIRITO
V. S. AGOSTINO
BORGO TEGOLAIO
VIA MAGGIO
V. MAZZETTA
V. TOSCANELLA
SDRUCCIOLO DE PITTI
54
COSTA DI MAGNOLI
COSTA DI SAN GIORGIO
C. SCARPUCCIA
Lutheran Ch.
4
Palazzo Guadagni
Pal. Com. di Firenze
50
PIAZZA DE' PITTI
Palazzo Pitti
S. Giorgio sulla Costa
S. Lucia dei Magnoli
Museo Bardini
V. D. CALDAIE
Casa Guidi
Palazzi d. Mozzi
S. Felice
Villa Bardini
VIA ROMANA
Pal. Torrigiani (Zoological Mus) La Specola
Giardino Bardini
Forte di Belvedere
VIA DI BELVEDERE
Porta S. Giorgio
7
Giardino di Boboli
6
Istit. d'Arte (Gipsoteca)
S. Leonardo in Arcetri
VIALE NICCOLÒ MACHIAVELLI
VIA DI S. LEONARDO
8
7
57
VIALE NICCOLÒ MACHIAVELLI
V. B. DA FOIANO
62
PIAZZALE GALILEO
VIALE GALILEO

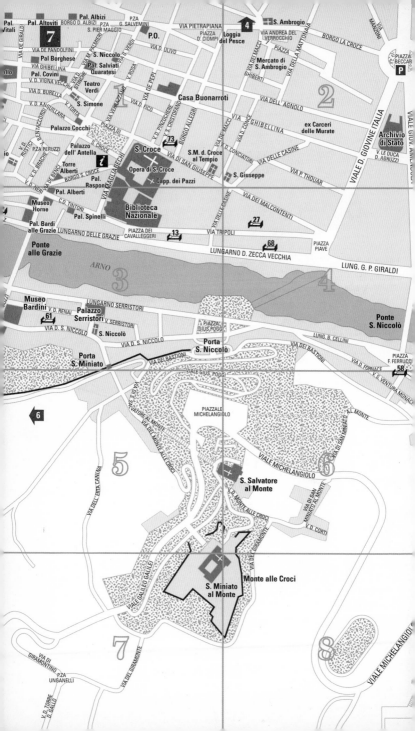